DATE DUE

NOV 4 1991		
MAY 27 1992		
NOV 30 1994		
NOV 26 1995		
JAN 2 1998		
NOV 9 1998		
DEC 20 1999		
NOV 1 2000		
JAN 2 2001		
603348 WEZ		
OCT 8 2001		
MAY 12 2009		

D1116812

DEMCO NO. 38-298

Marriage and Inequality in Chinese Society

This volume was sponsored by the Joint Committee on Chinese Studies of the American Council of Learned Societies and the Social Science Research Council, with funds provided by the Andrew W. Mellon Foundation.

Marriage and Inequality in Chinese Society

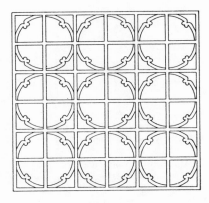

EDITED BY

Rubie S. Watson
Patricia Buckley Ebrey

UNIVERSITY OF CALIFORNIA PRESS

Berkeley   Los Angeles   Oxford

University of California Press
Berkeley and Los Angeles, California

University of California Press, Ltd.
Oxford, England

© 1991 by
The Regents of the University of California

Library of Congress Cataloging-in-Publication Data
Marriage and inequality in Chinese society/edited by Rubie S.
  Watson, Patricia Buckley Ebrey.
     p.   cm.—(Studies on China; 12)
  Includes bibliographical references.
  ISBN 0-520-06930-7 (alk. paper).—ISBN 0-520-07124-7 (pbk.: alk. paper)
    1. Marriage—China—History.   2. Marriage customs and rites—
China—History.   3. Sex role—China—History.   4. Equality—China—
History.   I. Watson, Rubie S. (Rubie Sharon), 1945–   .
II. Ebrey, Patricia Buckley, 1947–   .   III. Series.
HQ734.M3873   1991
306.81′0951—dc20   90-10839
                                                                CIP

Printed in the United States of America
     1   2   3   4   5   6   7   8   9

The paper used in this publication meets the minimum requirements of American National Standard for Information Sciences—Permanence of Paper for
Printed Library Materials, ANSI Z39.48-1984. ⊗™

STUDIES ON CHINA

A series of conference volumes sponsored by the Joint Committee on Chinese Studies of the American Council of Learned Studies and the Social Science Research Council.

CONTENTS

ILLUSTRATIONS

FIGURES

MAP

TABLES

PREFACE

In her autobiography, published in 1936, Hsieh Ping-ying described her parents as having traditional attitudes about marriage. They had betrothed her as an infant to the son of a prominent and well-to-do family. Both her father and mother considered the fulfillment of this agreement essential to their family's honor. Her mother took charge of preparing the dowry, using money and materials she had been saving for more than ten years. She supervised workmen who spent several months constructing and lacquering forty pieces of furniture. She had quilts and mosquito nets made. She called in tailors to make clothes for each season. When Ping-ying urged her mother not to have too many dresses made, as styles might change, her mother replied:

> To be a bride and not to have many dresses would be looked down upon by others. Many people have to sell their fields and their property to prepare a trousseau for their daughters. When your elder sister's husband's family married off their daughter they had thirty-two silk coverlets and twenty-eight woolen blankets, but I know that they had to sell their rice field to make a show. Although I like to do my best for my daughters, I do not hold that people should really dispose of their property handed down to them by their ancestors in order to be luxurious in the wedding ceremony. If the trousseau is not too modest, that is sufficient. (Hsieh Ping-ying, *Autobiography of a Chinese Girl*, trans. Tsui Chi [1943; reprint, London: Pandora, 1986], p. 169)

Ten days before the wedding was scheduled, Hsieh Ping-ying's dowry was delivered to the fiancé's home. But the wedding itself never took place because, after three attempts, Ping-ying ran away from her parents' house, where she had been confined under close watch.

This volume is a collaborative effort to explore the social and historical bases of the marriage system that Hsieh Ping-ying's parents took for granted. What logic led to betrothals in infancy? What social or economic realities required elaborate dowry preparations? What definitions of honor would lead parents to imprison a daughter rather than allow an engagement to be broken? To explore such questions, we organized the Conference on Marriage and Inequality in Chinese Society held in January 1988 at the Asilomar Conference Center, Pacific Grove, California. We asked a group of historians and social scientists to look beyond the descent paradigm, which has been so dominant in our thinking about Chinese kinship, to discern ways marriage was implicated in the formation of group identities, political and economic networks, mobility strategies, and differentiation by gender. We started with the proposition that marriage is inevitably linked to social and economic hierarchies and that it both structures and is structured by relations of inequality. On the assumption that the links between marriage and other social formations may have varied by class and changed over time, we invited participants with expertise in a wide range of time periods and social groups. As organizers of the conference and editors of the volume, our previous interests in marriage, kinship, and gender relations colored our original charge. We were fortunate to assemble a group of historians and social scientists who both complemented our interests and broadened our horizons.

Taken as a whole the chapters in this volume show that marriage was deeply involved in the exercise and manipulation of political power, in the creation and distribution of prestige, and in the structuring of gender relations. Despite our emphasis on discerning and analyzing change, we found continuities across time striking: from the classical period to the Revolution of 1949 there were similarities in exogamy rules, wedding rituals, and the treatment of women. Yet the authors also present evidence of change in monogamy, divorce, dowry, and symbolic uses of marriage that they relate to alterations in the composition of the elite and the commercialization of the economy. Those familiar with marriage systems elsewhere in Asia and Europe will recognize similarities in the ways honor and property came to be tied to marriage in China. Yet dowry in China, we argue, also had some unique characteristics. Confucian ideology—with its stress on patriliny over matrilateral and affinal ties—combined with legal restrictions on women's claims to property created a dowry complex distinct from the ones found in Europe and India.

The Conference on Marriage and Inequality in Chinese Society was sponsored by the Joint Committee on Chinese Studies of the American Council of Learned Societies and the Social Science Research Council, with funds provided by the Andrew W. Mellon Foundation. We are indebted to them for their support. We also acknowledge with gratitude the participation of scholars not represented in this volume: Beverly Bossler, Myron Cohen, Jerry Dennerline, Jack Goody, Dennis Grafflin, Diane Hughes, Cho-yun Hsu, Susan Naquin, Janice Stockard, Martin Whyte, and Arthur Wolf. The general arguments presented in the Introduction and Afterword, as well as the shape of individual chapters, owe much to their analyses and critiques during four days of intense discussion at Asilomar. We are also grateful to Stevan Harrell, who took time from a busy schedule to read the final manuscript with care and provide us with constructive criticism. The Asian Studies Program of the University of Pittsburgh and the Center for East Asian and Pacific Studies at the University of Illinois assisted in organizing the conference and in preparing the manuscript. We are pleased to acknowledge this help.

RSW
PBE

CHRONOLOGY OF CHINESE HISTORY

Classical period
  Chou dynasty, ca. 1000–256 B.C.
    Western Chou, ca. 1000–771 B.C.
    Eastern Chou, 770–256 B.C.
      Spring and Autumn period, 770–453 B.C.
      Warring States period, 453–256 B.C.
Imperial period, 221 B.C.–A.D. 1911

Major native Chinese dynasties	*Major non-Han dynasties*
Ch'in, 221–206 B.C.	
Former Han, 206 B.C.–A.D. 9	
Later Han, 25–220	
Southern dynasties, 317–589	Northern dynasties, 386–581
	Northern Wei (T'o-pa), 399–534
T'ang 617–907	
	Liao (Ch'i-tan), 916–1122
Sung, 960–1279	Chin (Jurchen), 1115–1234
	Yuan (Mongol), 1260–1368
Ming, 1368–1664	
	Ch'ing (Manchu), 1644–1911

Republic, 1911–1949
People's Republic, 1949–present

INTRODUCTION

Patricia Buckley Ebrey

Inequalities of many sorts characterized Chinese society. During the imperial period, the emperor outranked all of his subjects. Members of the imperial family and clan possessed titles, rank, privileges, and stipends that distinguished them from the rest of society. Government officials were set above commoners by their access to wealth and power and enormous social prestige. Crosscutting these political inequalities were social, economic, and geographic ones. Merchants and large landowners could dominate their communities through their control of resources; educated families of established reputations could expect deference based on their culture, history, manners, and style; residents of cities in economically developed areas had social, economic, and even political advantages over rural residents in the hinterlands. And throughout society, from the imperial court to the peasant household, men outranked women. In the twentieth century traditional political inequalities lost their legal force, and after 1949 most of the old sources of economic inequality, especially the private ownership of land, were eliminated. In addition, the state promoted greater legal equality of men and women in matters of marriage and property ownership. Yet in the second half of the twentieth century new sources of inequality emerged, such as class labels, party membership, and city residence.

The authors of this book examine the relation between marriage and these social, political, and economic inequalities. Inequality has not been a neglected topic in Chinese studies. The imperial institution, the civil service recruitment system, the distribution of landholding, and the ideology of class and gender differentiation have all been studied in detail. Little research has been devoted, however, to the mechanisms or processes through which inequalities were reproduced or transformed over time. Marriage also is not a neglected topic. Anthropological and sociological studies of China generally

1

include some discussion of marriage, and several studies analyze marriage practices and affinity in detail (e.g., Kulp 1925, Lang 1946, Hsu 1948, Gallin 1960, M. Wolf 1972, Ahern 1974, Cohen 1976, Freedman 1979, A. Wolf and Huang 1980, Watson 1981, Croll 1981). Yet little attention has been given to the ways marriage mediated inequality or inequalities structured marriage. In this volume we investigate these processes and mechanisms by focusing on how marriage relates to three forms of inequality: the political power of rulers; the social and economic differences among families; and the inequalities between men and women and among women. Because our goal is to discover the broad outlines of these processes, we examine marriage in a wide range of social settings from very early to very recent times.

MARRIAGE AND INEQUALITY

Before introducing the chapters in this volume, we must place our discussion in a broad theoretical and comparative framework. Whenever a marriage takes place, the standing of every party is somewhat different from what it had been. Almost invariably at least one person, the husband or wife, changes residence. In many cases control over wealth changes hands. In China, where most of the family estate was transmitted to patrilineal descendants, it was fairly common for some property to be diverted to daughters as dowries. Marriages regularly allocate privileges, claims, and obligations, usually in different ways for men and women. In the Chinese case, in a patrilocal marriage the husband gained sexual access to his wife and his patriline gained claims to her labor and the children she would bear. But the wife also gained privileges through marriage, such as the claim to maintenance on her husband's estate and a place of honor in ancestral rites. Marriages everywhere confer honor: individual men and women become recognized adults by marrying; at the same time families gain in standing by marrying their children respectably. In most societies weddings are great occasions for displaying status; sometimes more is spent on the ritual festivities than on the durable items that end up in the dowry as families perform the rites elaborately to confirm or enhance their status.

Viewed from the perspective of the individual family, every marriage provides a chance to gain or lose economically or socially. Marriages are thus occasions for thinking tactically, for balancing many considerations. A family head need not make similar matches for each daughter; in one case he may seek useful affines, in another emphasize the financial considerations, in a third think first of his daughter's welfare. Marriage choices can be compared to market choices, with the various decision makers weighing an assortment of factors, including the age and attractiveness of their children, the supply of potential spouses, other demands on their resources, and so on. In the Chinese context the flexibility of marriage decisions stands in contrast to inheritance and succession, where choices were few and preferences clear. Because property had to be divided among all sons, parents had little leeway to manipulate in favor of one heir or another.

Viewed from the larger society, however, the range of possibilities open for each match fades. Certain types of marriage systems structure the ways wealth, power, and status are distributed in the society from one family to another and from one generation to another and the ways rights, privileges, and honor are assigned differentially to men and women. Jack Goody has developed the most influential model of the structural consequences of systems of marriage exchange. In "Bridewealth and Dowry in Africa and Eurasia" (1973) Goody distinguishes between those societies that transmit property through daughters via dowry or inheritance (including to some degree most of the state-based societies of Eurasia) and those that do not (notably the bridewealth societies of Africa). He argues that societies with "diverging devolution" (the same types of property passing through both men and women whether through inheritance or dowry) are marked by monogamy, family control of daughters' marriages, emphasis on virginity, strong ties between affines, greater class distinctions, and stronger women's property rights (a set of characteristics I shall refer to here as the "dowry complex"). Goody shows many logical links between these characteristics. Where families send their daughters with dowries, Goody explains, they do not want misalliances and cannot risk letting daughters choose on the basis of attraction. When marriages require matching property, property stays disproportionately in the upper classes, and class inequalities are thereby strengthened. Families providing portions for a daughter want some guarantee that the property will be used to her benefit, especially if she is widowed (1973:17–47). In some societies (like China) daughters did not regularly receive family property but could be residual heirs, that is, allowed to transmit the family property through uxorilocal marriages when there were no sons; these, too, Goody classes as societies practicing diverging devolution (1976a:10–36). In *Production and Reproduction* (1976b) Goody adds a developmental dimension to this model, linking diverging devolution to the introduction of the animal-drawn plow and the greater economic surplus it allowed. Diverging devolution is thus also related to greater social and economic differentiation and the development of states. In this book he also analyzes concubinage and the inequality in the household created by an unbalanced marriage exchange (i.e., the purchase of concubines, who, unlike wives, do not bring dowries). In *The Development of Family and Marriage in Europe* (1983) Goody brings these conceptions to bear on the complex historical changes in Western history from the Roman Empire to early modern times, showing that marriage forms do not flow automatically from economic structures but are complexly tied to dominant institutions and ideologies. Goody's analyses, taken together, provide a new way to think about the linkage of gender and kinship. Goody's studies do not show women relegated to a domestic sphere defined by the biology of motherhood, while men operate in a public sphere shaped by the political economy and the forces of history. To the contrary, he describes a domestic domain shaped by productive processes and the transmission of property (see Collier and Yanagisako 1987:4–6).

Goody's work on marriage has been utilized by several China scholars (Parish and Whyte 1978; Ebrey 1981, 1986; Watson 1984; Holmgren 1985). His model provides an alternative to full reliance on the lineage model of Chinese kinship, which makes patrilineal kinship so central that transmission of property through women in uxorilocal marriage or via dowries appears to be a peripheral embellishment of little structural importance (cf. Freedman 1958; Baker 1979). Yet there are obstacles to wholesale acceptance of Goody's model: the relative weakness of women's legal claims to property in China; the fact that many, maybe even a majority, of marriages did not involve significant transfers from the bride's side; and the difficulty in characterizing China as either a dowry or a bridewealth society as both co-existed (e.g., McCreery 1976). Moreover, it is not clear that a model designed to explain the broadest differences between dissimilar societies can also provide insight into the narrower differences that China scholars seek to understand, such as why dowry was more prominent in India than in China, or why dowries were more substantial in some parts of China than in others. In some areas of north and central China, peasants are reported to have spent considerable sums on dowries (Fei 1939:44; Yang 1945:79, 110, 113; Gamble 1954:383; Cohen 1988). In the south, especially in areas with dominant lineages, dowries among the poor were often modest affairs, costing the woman's family significantly less than the amount they received in betrothal gifts (see Kulp 1925:173–75; Watson 1981). Do differences in kinship organization or agricultural methods explain these differences? Did women in areas with large dowries have higher status than those in areas without them?

Goody's theories do not place much weight on ritual and the display of status through marriage and have been criticized as being overly "econocentric" (see Comaroff 1980; Harrell and Dickey 1985). Other anthropologists have delved more deeply into the symbolic dimensions of marriage exchanges and the ways they establish and restructure the relations of all the parties concerned (wife-givers and wife-takers, but also husbands and wives, or husbands' families and daughters-in-law). The benefits that flow from a marriage are not all tangible or clearly specified. In the classic study of gift giving, the French sociologist Marcel Mauss argues that gifts create an imbalance between the giver and the receiver. The recipient is indebted to the giver until the gift is repaid, at which time the debt is canceled or, if the return gift exceeds the initial gift, a new state of imbalance is established (1966). Basing their analyses on Mauss's work, many anthropologists argue that the transfer of goods at marriage maintains economic and political differences by confirming them. Bourdieu, for instance, writes that marriage was "one of the mainstays of both the dynamic and the static elements of the entire social system" to the extent that it afforded the families he studied "one of the most important opportunities for monetary and also symbolic exchanges that asserted the family's position in the social hierarchy and thereby confirmed that hierarchy itself" (1976:124). Marriage, in effect, becomes part of the system of social reproduction in which status, rank, and class differences are passed on to the next generation. Marriage exchange, after all, involves not only the giving and receiving of land, money, and jewelry but also the offering of words, bows, and other "gifts" of respect. Sometimes the potential for expression of status is not equal in all forms of marriage. In China it is generally thought that only "major" marriages (patrilocal marriages of mature brides) could be used to full advantage in the display and celebration of high status (cf. Fei 1939:54–55; Freedman 1957:65).

Where marriages regularly join families of unequal rank, the relationship of marriage to inequality differs from the cases discussed above. Hypergamy (women marrying up) or hypogamy (women marrying down) creates patterns of social inequality based on prestige or rank, families confirming or enhancing their status by the partners they pick and often subsidizing families of higher rank by providing dowries (Leach 1954; Dumont 1957; Inden 1976; Parry 1979). These patterns sometimes create a visible pecking order, for the families to whom one sends daughters will never be the same ones from whom one receives brides. It has often been suggested that Chinese society tends toward hypergamy (see Ahern 1974; Freedman 1979), but the degree of status differences and the relative incidence of hypergamous marriages have never been adequately studied. A tendency toward hypergamy does seem plausible, however, given the asymmetry inherent in a patrilineal, patrilocal system. After marriage, a woman's status will largely be determined by the social and economic standing of the family she has joined, and so she will gain by marriage "up" into a prosperous family. By contrast, the welfare of the groom and his family is less affected by the family origins of the new daughter-in-law, so they have little to lose by taking a bride from a family of less wealth or social standing. Such brides had attractions; in fact, they were thought to be harder workers and more easily satisfied with their situations.[1]

In Goody's model, transmitting property through women is linked to strong social ties among affines. Indeed, in China and elsewhere marriages are often considered opportunities to make new allies. In the Chinese case, however, affines were not invariably considered useful; they could also prove burdensome or meddlesome. Within the Chinese repertoire of kinship practices, close or distant ties to affines were both well-established possibilities (see Gallin and Gallin 1985). For instance, in the dominant lineages of Kwangtung, the rich and the poor seem to have followed different strategies. The rich put great emphasis on strong ties to affines, gave handsome dowries, and married with families some distance away. The poor neither gave dowries nor made any efforts to maintain extensive ties to wives' or mothers' families (Watson 1981). In Taiwan, the value placed on affinity seems to have varied with the form of agriculture; where cooperation was needed for temporary agricultural labor or political assistance, affinal kinship tended to be strongest (Pasternak 1972:60–67).

From the work of European historians, we know that marriage also relates to inequality by means of succession and inheritance. In societies where only those born into fully legal marriages could succeed to thrones, fiefs, or estates, marriage was a crucial mechanism in the transmission of power. The authority to determine what constituted a legal marriage consequently became a source of contention between the church and civil authorities (e.g., Duby 1978). Thus, ritual and ideology need not merely highlight inequalities or obfuscate transactions: the power to define marriage can have great consequence for individuals' social status and inheritance. In the Chinese case, from early imperial times there were laws that defined a legal marriage (as opposed to common-law marriage or concubinage). Yet the legal status of a marriage did not determine the status of heirs, who could inherit at their father's will (Freedman 1979:118; Watson 1985:105–16). Ruling families are the exception to this generalization, for only one son could succeed to a throne or fief, and the status of their mothers' marriages was usually a key issue in deciding which of several sons succeeded, making the link between marriage and the status of offspring different from that in other families.

Placing the Chinese case in comparative perspective raises several key questions that the authors of this volume pursue. Did anything resembling a "dowry complex" develop in China? How significant were hypergamy or hypogamy? Did the symbolism and the tangible benefits of marriage exchanges reinforce or mask the inequalities between wife-givers and wife-takers and men and women? Did forms of marriage differ when succession to a fief or office was at stake?

COLLABORATION

Our current knowledge of Chinese marriage is based largely on observations made during the last century by social scientists. Given the many continuities in Chinese marriage practices, these studies provide considerable insight into earlier periods. Yet they are no substitute for historical research. We have as a consequence tried to remain open to the possibility that marriage institutions changed in some fundamental ways from early to modern times, as they did in the West. The historians writing here have had to decide how well the terms and concepts commonly used by anthropologists convey what they know of past societies. Although no set of terms is fully adequate, a common vocabulary aids communication among ourselves and with scholars of other societies. In this book we use key terms in the following ways:

wife. "Wife" seems a fully adequate translation of *ch'i* and any terms the Chinese considered a synonym for *ch'i* (such as *shih, shih-jen*) or a polite title for *ch'i* (such as *fu-jen*).

secondary wife. In the preimperial period aristocratic marriages often involved a principal wife bringing with her one or more younger women from her own or related lineages who could also serve as mates of her husband. These women, called *ying* in Chinese, are referred to here as secondary wives.

concubine. "Concubine" is used as a translation of *ch'ieh* and words used as alternatives for *ch'ieh*, such as *hou-shih* and *ts'e-shih*. We prefer it to "secondary wife" not merely to avoid confusion with the ancient practice described above but also because China from Han times on was legally monogamous—a man could have only one wife.

second wife. If a man remarried after the death or divorce of his first wife, his new wife is a second wife. From Han times on, she was usually called a *chi-shih*, or "successor wife" (or successor "room").

betrothal gifts/brideprice/bridewealth. Gifts (including money) presented by the groom's family to the bride's to seal the betrothal, no matter what their value, are referred to here by these terms, the choice depending on the context and the preferences of the authors. "Betrothal gifts" is a translation of the Chinese terms *na-ts'ai, p'in-ts'ai, p'in-li, li-chin, p'in-chin*, and other synonyms and as such avoids some of the difficulties of the common terms "brideprice" and "bridewealth." In contrast to the classic bridewealth systems of Africa, in China the money or goods received by the bride's family were often used to prepare her dowry.

dowry. We are labeling any material possession the bride brought with her into marriage, no matter how meager, her dowry. This could include clothes, jewelry, bedding, money, land, and so on. Chinese terms with much the same meaning are *chuang-lien, chia-chuang, tzu-sung, tzu-chuang*, and so on. Some authors here also use the term "trousseau" to refer to the part of a bride's dowry consisting of her clothes, jewelry, and cosmetics. Labeling something "dowry" is not meant to imply anything about the claims various parties had to its use or disposal, which are instead treated as subjects for research.

indirect dowry. When the bride's family used the betrothal gifts it received to prepare the dowry, the gifts from the man's family that eventually became dowry can be referred to as indirect dowry. This designation places emphasis on the final destination of the property, rather than the initial phase of the flow, and is useful in analyzing the transfer of property over time. It should be remembered, however, that "indirect dowry" is not a translation of a Chinese term, nor does it reflect the way Chinese conceptualized marriage gifts and payments.

Although we have agreed to use these terms in the ways described here, we have not fooled ourselves into thinking that such labeling solves all of our problems of classification and analysis. For instance, several of us have difficulty employing the vocabulary of dowry and indirect dowry, with the implication that these two are similar in that in either case the property ends up with the woman. In the Chinese case, lumping these two together may be useful for short-term perspectives (a woman with a substantial dowry may have status and power other women do not, whether the dowry came entirely from her parents or indirectly from her parents-in-law) but is inadequate for looking at the larger transfer of property over time. In China the notion of individual property rights was weak, circumscribed by the claims of potential heirs. The heirs to a woman's dowry were her sons and thus the patriline of her husband. Indirect dowry that originated from her husband's patriline would therefore end there also. This pattern is in marked contrast to the situation where a woman's parents detach part of their property and permanently transfer it to the patriline of her husband, giving her trusteeship during her lifetime. As this discussion makes clear, however, this distinction is relevant only to property that can be passed to heirs. Clothes, bedding, and even furniture would probably be worn out by the time the woman dies. A distinction between dowries in land or ones in movable goods would still not solve this problem because in a commercialized society like late imperial China cash could be used to buy land, and land could be sold to meet current expenses, such as funerals. Moreover, whether a wife's dowry served to enlarge the estate of her sons would depend not merely on the initial assortment of goods but also on how it was used and managed over the years.

IMPERIAL MARRIAGES

Rather than introduce the chapters of this volume chronologically, I will highlight some of the relationships among them by looking at marriage at three social levels: the imperial family and clan, the educated elite, and ordinary people. For the premodern period, there are more studies of the marriages of imperial families and clans than of any other segment of society. There have been studies of the families from which empresses and other consorts were selected, the kinds of families chosen to provide husbands for princesses, the methods used to keep empresses or their kin from gaining too much political power, and the needs of imperial families to exemplify ritually correct behavior in marriage practices and male-female differentiation (see de Crespigny 1975; Holmgren 1981, 1981–83, 1983, 1986; Wong 1979; Chung 1981; Soullière 1988). These studies place imperial marriage policies firmly within imperial politics; they deal both with the efforts of the throne to safeguard or enhance its political control and of other groups to use marriage to gain greater access to political power. From these studies we know that by marrying their daughter to an emperor or future emperor, a family could gain not merely prestige and wealth but also office. Years later its officials might have considerable influence in court affairs, especially if the daughter gave birth to the next ruler. Women were pivotal figures between the two families in imperial marriages and could sometimes make use of their position to gain exceptional power.

The theoretical literature on marriage discussed above offers new ways to approach imperial marriages. Is political power another resource that can be allocated through marriage, like wealth and prestige? Does the inevitable hypergamy and hypogamy of imperial marriages make them exceptional or only extreme? How did the public nature of imperial marriages affect the relations of the spouses or their families?

Three of the essays in this volume examine imperial marriages and the social, political, and gender inequalities they involved. In a path-breaking analysis, Jennifer Holmgren identifies the underlying structural logic of Han Chinese imperial marriages. Recurrent features can be explained, she argues, by the conjunction of the basic Chinese marriage system—monogamy, surname exogamy, women's continuing links to their natal families, and filial piety—on the one hand, with the unique requirements of succession to the throne by a single heir on the other. Because the emperors regularly forced collateral lines, even their brothers and adult younger sons, to leave the capital, the emperors' wives and mothers (empresses, empress dowagers, and grand empress dowagers) often played leading roles in decisions concerning succession and marriage, and their families could sometimes dominate the bureaucracy. Yet in many ways emperors' sisters had stronger positions than empresses, as they could come or go from the palace, were immune from punishment, could dominate their husbands, and could influence their brother the emperor even if he were a strong-minded adult. In tracing historical examples of these processes, Holmgren argues provocatively that changes in imperial marriage, such as the Ming practice of selecting imperial wives from nonelite families, were unrelated to changes in marriage practices in the larger society. Rather, she asserts that imperial marriage patterns are entirely explicable by reference to imperial politics and the underlying logic already described.

Holmgren contrasts these Han Chinese marriage patterns to those of several non-Han states whose native marriage systems allowed polygyny, the levirate, and marriage to distant agnates and generally fell more on the side of bridewealth than dowry societies. The imperial families of these states developed several different marriage systems, the T'o-pa of the Northern Wei denying any power to the mothers of emperors, the Ch'i-tan of the Liao marrying exclusively with one consort clan, and the Mongols of the Yuan marrying with the rulers of allied tribes, preventing their women from gaining control of the throne by allowing succession only to adult sons.

Holmgren's broad overview is complemented here by close studies of imperial marriages in two dynasties, one Han and one non-Han. John W. Chaffee examines the marriages of imperial clanswomen in the Sung dynasty, thus shifting the focus from control of the throne to the use of marriage as a means of connecting the civil elite to the large imperial clan with its thousands of members. He pays particular attention to the issue of hypogamy and the symbolic and political complexities of marriages in which the wife outranked her husband and his parents. His evidence shows clearly that even at a considerable distance from the throne, marriages involved a significant distribution of wealth and privileges. Imperial clanswomen had to be married into the elite not merely to help the throne forge ties to the political elite but also to avoid the dishonor of having its women marry too low. Given the size of the imperial clan, these marriages were decided not by the emperor but by a bureaucracy in which members of the official elite played leading roles.

In her study of the marriages of the Manchu rulers of the Ch'ing dynasty, Evelyn S. Rawski focuses on those closest to the throne, the sons and daughters of emperors and the emperor himself. The Ch'ing forbade intermarriage between the Manchu rulers and the civil elite of Han Chinese officials, thus using marriage to maintain the distinct identity of their special followers, the Chinese and Manchu bannermen. Whereas the Ch'ing adopted the traditional Han Chinese ritual code for wedding ceremonies, they did not adopt other, perhaps more fundamental, elements of Han marriage practices. In particular, Ch'ing empresses were not as powerful as their counterparts had been in Han Chinese dynasties because their sons were not the presumptive heirs. Rawski thus concurs with Holmgren that the differences in the marriage systems of different dynasties were closely related to differences in their succession practices.

Rawski makes the intriguing point that Manchu imperial marriages are difficult to classify as either monogamous or polygamous. As she sees it, a highly fluid set of social relations was made to appear sharply stratified by ritual and institutional distinctions not simply between the empress and consorts but also between each of the seven grades of consort. In reality, the mode of entry, social background, and privileges of these women, she argues, were not clearly distinguished, in contrast to Han commoner practice. Particularly significant was the emperor's right to promote his mother to empress dowager after he succeeded to the throne, leading to two empress dowagers in the senior generation (his father's empress and his mother).

These three chapters contribute not only to our understanding of imperial governance in China but also to our knowledge of Chinese marriage mythology. Stories about the marriages of emperors and princesses—along with the marriages of the rulers of preimperial states discussed in Thatcher's chapter—provided much of the stock of images used to think about marriage and affinal relations in Chinese society at large. The dangers of matrilateral or affinal interference were underlined to all by stories of emperors who had been reduced to puppets by powerful "outside" relatives. Indeed, the treachery and scheming of women were easily evoked by stories of the machinations of women close to the throne, from empress dowagers to slave girls.

ELITE MARRIAGES

Besides studies of imperial marriages, the existing literature on marriage in Chinese history includes detailed research on marriage connections among social and political elites. Studies of marriage from the late Han through the T'ang period have shown that the highest-ranking families marry as much as possible within their own ranks and use such marriages as markers of status. The state sporadically attempted to regulate these practices either by ruling that marriages must be confined to status equals or by attempting to prohibit exclusive practices that undermined the state's ability to control honor and prestige (Twitchett 1973; D. Johnson 1977b; Ebrey 1978; Wong 1979; Mather 1980).

After mid-T'ang, the state paid little attention to the marriage choices of political elites. The elite of the Sung dynasty and later are generally viewed as less closed than those of earlier periods, and historians have tended to look at their marriages as creating networks rather than closed circles. Robert Hymes has studied the marriages linking seventy-three elite families in Fu-chou, Kiangsi, in the Sung and Yuan (1986a; 1986b). He generally assumes that these marriages were motivated by political strategies. When officials' families had less need of ties to other official families, they used the occasion of their children's marriages to strengthen their links to local landowners and literati. Beverly Bossler has examined in similar detail the marriages of the national elite that resided in Kaifeng in the Northern Sung. Her findings raise doubts about the notion that marriages were politically motivated; she does not always find families following what has been thought to be the politically advantageous course or reaping the assumed benefits when they did (Bossler 1988). In a study of the Wu lineage of Hsiu-ning City, Hui-chou, during the Ming, Keith Hazelton found that lineage members had extensive marriage networks; about two-thirds of Wu wives came from nine different surnames, and no single surname accounted for more than 15 percent of the total (Hazelton 1986:158–60). By contrast, Hilary Beattie showed that the two most prominent lineages of T'ung-ch'eng in Ch'ing times intermarried for five generations, Yao women providing a majority of the wives of Chang men in several lines for two or three generations in a row (1979:104–5). Jerry Dennerline found a comparable situation in nineteenth-century Wu-hsi, with about a third of the marriages of one line of Ch'iens to Hua families. He shows that such patterns went back to the early Ming in some lines, while other lines, for various strategic reasons, had spread their marriages much more broadly (Dennerline 1986:181–86). The diverse patterns uncovered by these case studies demonstrate above all the flexibility of the ways marriage connections could be used by members of the elite in the late imperial period. Benefits were to be gained by alliances to powerful lineages in one's home area. But creating affinal links to as many families as possible also offered advantages, as did ignoring politics in some marriages and emphasizing instead property exchanges.

Three chapters in this volume complement these studies of elite marriages. Each focuses on a period of major social change and thus aids, in a preliminary way, our understanding of how changes in Chinese society were connected to shifts in marriage structures. Melvin Thatcher examines elite intermarriage patterns for an earlier period than attempted before, the part of the mid-Chou called the Spring and Autumn period. Besides describing basic marriage rules and practices, he examines the bilateral marriage relations among the ruling houses of the separate states of this period. According to his evidence, already in the Spring and Autumn period ritual and ideology were used to distinguish women by rank into wives and concubines of various grades, a distinction reiterated in other chapters. Moreover, marriages were already marked by property transactions. Although the main assets of the period (fiefs, offices, and land grants) could not be conveyed through marriage, grooms' families made gifts of cloth to brides' families, and brides might bring with them clothes, jewels, maids, or even bronze vessels. Men in the ruling elite could have more than one primary wife (unlike in later periods), and divorce was relatively easy and common. In this and other ways Thatcher's portrayal of the marriage system of this aristocratic society suggests parallels with some of the non-Han societies Holmgren describes. In these less bureaucratized societies marriage and kinship played larger roles in the structuring of political relations than they typically did in imperial China.

Thatcher's chapter can be usefully contrasted with mine, in which I link political strategies and property transfers. I argue that in the T'ang, when the aristocratic families depended on the inherited prestige of their family names, marriages with particular families could confer enormous honor and be worth the expenditure of large sums for betrothal gifts. In the Sung, when the prestige of old family status was much diminished and bureaucratic rank more highly valued, the elite often sent their daughters into marriage with large dowries, even of land. During this period many of the features of the dowry complex Goody has described as common in Eurasia were evident in China. Not only were there monogamy and parental control of marriages (well established at least by the Han), but also the landowning class transmitted significant amounts of property through daughters, and women's claims to dowry received some legal recognition. In exploring reasons for this trend toward larger transfers through dowry, I suggest that economic changes, such as freer transfer of land and commercialization, were preconditions. The political value of connections then served to push these trends further. Dowries made better bait than betrothal gifts because property was permanently transferred to the other line and affinal ties were stronger when both sides had lingering claims to property.

Susan Mann's chapter deals with another dimension of elite marriages: the connections writers saw between marriage and gender differentiation. Much of the existing research on marriage in Chinese history concerns the ideology of the ideal wife and the cult of widow chastity (see Swann 1932; O'Hara 1971; Ropp 1976; Holmgren 1981, 1985; Sung 1981; Waltner 1981; Elvin 1984; Mann 1985, 1987). It is by now well established that ideals of womanhood changed over time for reasons that varied from ethnic antagonisms to concerns for men's political loyalties and anxieties about status. Moreover, it can be shown that even constant ideals had different effects on behavior in different periods, depending on the incentives provided by property law, kinship groups, charitable ventures, and government honors. These studies show that we need to keep in mind how ideology and state power worked with the transfer of property in creating gender inequalities in China. In her chapter here, Mann brings the rhetoric on women's spheres into the discussion of elite marriage practices. She argues that the remarkable social mobility of the mid-Ch'ing period led to anxiety about the blurring of boundaries between people of different status, including the boundaries between wives and lower-status women. Literati writers of this period reexamined classical writings on marriage rituals and the proper roles of husbands and wives, emphasizing not wives' subordination but the ways they complemented their husbands by taking charge in their own spheres. Valorizing the role of wife, the literati placed much of the task of protecting family and class honor on wives and daughters.

Taken together, the three chapters on elite marriage show us three sides of marriage and also three points in time. The politics of alliance were never absent from elite marriages, but they were probably also never so well developed as they were among the ruling families of the Chou, where marriage had important links to succession by a single heir and where rulers needed alliances transcending their borders. Property, again, could never have been a trivial consideration in elite marriages, but the amounts involved seem to have become a particular concern in the T'ang-Sung period, and changes in the nature and direction of transfers were complexly associated with commercialization and increased competition for elite status. Nor was concern with the meaning of marriage new to the Ch'ing. Since the time when the ritual classics were written, writers had tried to deny or transcend the political and financial aspects of marriage and to reconcile the fact that marriages entailed not just unions of families but unions of men and women. Yet these efforts gained special urgency in the eighteenth century with the greater commercialization of society and the instability of social boundaries.

PROPERTY AND THE MARRIAGES OF ORDINARY PEOPLE

English-language studies of gender differentiation in premodern China have tended to concentrate on ideology, yet there is also a large literature, especially in Chinese and Japanese, on the history of marriage as a legal institution. Laws on family property, divorce, exogamy, incest, bigamy, adultery, and rape shaped the marriage practices of men and women in all social classes. Studies of marriage-related law are the basis for our characterization of traditional China as a society that practiced monogamy, concubinage, divorce, and adoption and followed a property regime that favored transmission through males (see Ch'ü 1965; McCreery 1976; Dull 1978; Tai 1978; Shiga 1978; Meijer 1981; Ng 1987; Ocko 1989). Since Engels's time, scholars have argued that the subordination of women was a result of their inferior property rights. Accordingly, scholars studying the legal and economic position of women in modern China have often drawn on these studies of traditional law, either as evidence of what China was like before modern reforms or as keys to understanding the traditional social forms that persisted into modern times.

Three chapters in this volume build on these prior studies of legal institutions to reconsider how women related to property. Focusing on the Hong Kong region in the early twentieth century, Rubie S. Watson analyzes the social and legal distinctions among wives, concubines, and maids. She argues that a crucial distinction between wives and concubines was the property transaction that marked their marriages, then goes on to examine the consequences that flow from these differences. In other words, she does not stop at the distribution of property, but looks at the consequences for the distribution of power, respect, and security within the domestic sphere. She stresses the importance of dowry in giving women the dignity of wives and the autonomy of property holders. Wives even had advantages over their husbands in one regard: they could have private property separate from the larger family property. Concubines not only lacked private funds but also usually lacked contact with their natal families and thus could not provide effective matrilateral relatives for their children. Maids were not permanent members of the household, but merely indentured servants until marriage or concubinage. Their lives were often harsh while in service, and when they left it was often to become a concubine in another household.

Although dowry seems indubitably to have enhanced a woman's prestige and autonomy, and the more dowry the better, the relation between women's status and money was not simply linear. Gail Hershatter's chapter on prostitution in early twentieth-century Shanghai shows that money, status, and autonomy were much more complexly related. The highest prices were paid for beautiful preadolescent girls who could be trained to serve the male elite. They lived in much greater comfort than lower-class prostitutes but were also watched more closely by their owners and faced much greater obstacles to getting out of prostitution because their owners would demand much higher redemption fees. Prostitution illustrates the extremes to which the commodification of women could go. Prostitutes had little control over their lives. Others sold or pawned them into prostitution; madames decided which clients they would accept; only with outside help did they have any chance to leave "the life." The existence of the market for prostitutes made it clear to all that there was a price for women. To a peasant family, a daughter was worth so much as a bride, so much as a maid, so much as a prostitute. Prostitution in China was treated as a legal contractual arrangement in which one owner of a woman sold or pawned her to another.

Jonathan K. Ocko explores in more depth the role of the state in defining and enforcing the links between property and women in his chapter in this volume. In the Ch'ing code, women's relation to property, unlike men's, was nearly always mediated by marriage. Whatever property a woman got from her natal family came as a marriage portion; whatever claims she had to the use of her husband's estate after his death depended on her staying there, not leaving her husband's family to marry someone else. In the twentieth century, new laws fundamentally altered the legal basis of gender differentiation, and Ocko examines the revisions of the law code aimed at improving women's property rights, especially the 1950 and 1980 marriage laws and the 1985 inheritance law. He shows that despite the persistence of long-held cultural notions now labeled "feudal," some real change is discernible, above all in the rights of widows to inherit from their husbands. In the Ch'ing widows were trustees for the heirs, but only if they did not remarry. In current law, admittedly not always enforced, widows own in their own right half of the community property of the marriage and inherit half of their husband's share; moreover, they are free to take this property into another marriage. Changes in behavior, Ocko shows, have lagged far behind changes in the law. Disjunctures between economic organization and legal strictures are probably partly to blame, as is the political instability of judicial institutions. In recent decades punishment of transgressions appears to have been sporadic.

The market aspects of marriage are viewed differently in William Lavely's chapter. Lavely examines how the marriage market served to alter women's economic circumstances (or, to put it another way, how economically desirable homes were distributed to young women through the mechanisms of a marriage market). He sees mate selection as largely explicable in market terms but does not see dowry and betrothal gifts as the most significant factors in decisions. Drawing on statistical evidence of the movements of women in a region of Szechwan in the 1970s, he infers that wife-givers were maximizing their daughters' comfort, not their own, and wife-takers were looking for better-educated brides from nearby areas, not simply ones that could be had for the least expense or who would bring the most goods (though they may have been expected to earn more income). As he stresses, comparing the process of mate selection to a market does not mean that people are bought and sold; it means that those making the decisions weigh all of the pros and cons of each possibility and try to maximize their advantage. His assumption that parents and their daughters can be seen as having a single interest in these transactions is, however, in direct conflict with Rubie Watson's argument that individual members of a household did not share the same interests or the same agenda.

These four chapters on marriage in the twentieth century bring us into intellectual engagement with the debates on the degree to which state power has been used to improve women's status in the twentieth century (see Croll 1981; Stacey 1983; K. Johnson 1983; Wolf 1985). They also provide insight into marriage in traditional times. They draw on the abundant documentation of the twentieth century, but the phenomena they analyze are not new to this period. Certainly the buying and selling of concubines and prostitutes were common features of Chinese society for many centuries (Ebrey 1986). Likewise, the more general commodification of women is not a new phenomenon, though scholars do not yet agree how far back to date its more extreme forms (see Ropp 1987; Gates 1989). Nor was the relationship between the law and behavior likely to have been any less complex in earlier times. Indeed, one would expect that the text of the law was if anything more clearly understood in contemporary times than in earlier ones. Even the geographic dimension of marriage inequality must have existed in earlier times, though without migration registers we may not be able to analyze it with any precision. Thus, these chapters can be read on two levels, as analyses of dimensions of marriage and inequality and as studies of twentieth-century conditions.

THE HISTORICAL DEVELOPMENT OF MARRIAGE IN CHINA

The research presented in this volume provides a preliminary basis for thinking about the historical development of marriage in China and how it fits into some of the larger comparative frameworks discussed at the beginning of this essay. At the conference we frequently marveled at the continuities in Chinese marriage practices. Wedding rituals, exogamy rules, and concubinage showed many similarities from the aristocrats of the classical Chou period well into modern times. From classical times on, marriages involved transfers of property through betrothal gifts and often also dowry. Even ideological writings about marriage continually asserted that marriage served both the family and society by allowing the perpetuation of the patrilineal descent line, creating alliances between families of different surnames, and differentiating the proper spheres of men and women. At the imperial level, empresses and their relatives continued to be seen as potential threats to concentration of power in the person of the emperor and his legitimate male heirs. In the twentieth century, despite radical social, political, and economic reorganization, conceptions of women as property have proved remarkably persistent.

Nevertheless, our research generally supports the proposition that increasing social and economic differentiation and state development in China were accompanied by tendencies toward the dowry complex. Chinese history is commonly divided into four periods—the ancient, early imperial, late imperial, and modern—based on changes in the state, elite, economy, and culture. The most visible changes in marriage institutions can also be roughly correlated with these broader historical transitions. In ancient times, as Thatcher shows, polygyny was allowed among the ruling elite, divorce was easy, and the key assets passed along the male line were not transmitted in marriages. Although Thatcher stresses the congruences he finds with Goody's model—such as marriages among social equals and strong ties between women and their natal families—I am more struck by what is missing. Later, in the Han, the centralized bureaucratic government was consolidated, hereditary aristocracy abolished, buying and selling of land made legally easy, and the small family established as the key kinship unit. In the new social and economic order, marriage became legally monogamous, divorce legally easy for men but socially difficult, succession less of an issue as there were fewer fiefs or offices to succeed to, and property, when inherited, was divided equally among all sons. Legal monogamy, in particular, was an important step toward the Eurasian dowry complex model. In late imperial times (Sung-Ch'ing), with a more commercialized economy and more competition for social status and political office, dowry itself was much more in evidence. Ideology, if anything, gave greater stress to the permanence of marriage, though not in the same way as in Europe (i.e., widow remarriage, not divorce, was the symbolically significant issue).

At least as important, historically, as these movements toward the dowry complex is the evidence that this complex did not develop fully. In no period was China a dowry society comparable, for instance, to India (cf. Tambiah 1973). In late imperial times, even prosperous families might pass very little property through their daughters. Nowhere did custom or law force families with sons to give daughters shares of property at all comparable to the sons'. Although the state took considerable interest in the orderly and equitable division of family property among sons, it did not mandate provision of dowries. After marriage, wives' dowries were given some protection from the members of the larger family into which the woman had married, but less from their husbands. As discussed in my chapter, orphaned daughters' claims to dowries were legally strengthened in Sung times, and widows' claims to retain their dowries even if they remarried were widely recognized, but the Ming witnessed a reversal of these gains, not undone until modern times. Moreover, one might note that at the imperial level some trends went against the direction of the dowry complex: as Holmgren notes, in Ming times the emperor's spouses came from unimportant families who could not maintain close ties to the throne.

By way of conclusion, I would like to explore in a tentative and speculative way some of the reasons why the dowry complex did not develop more fully in China. As best I can reconstruct from the limited research done so far, China's economy in some important respects favored the dowry complex, yet Confucian ideology and state-established legal institutions obstructed its full development.

The relationship of the state to the dowry complex was multifaceted; in many ways it can be seen as fostering it. State power underlay the system of private ownership of land and its relatively easy alienability and as a consequence the kind of class system based on highly unequal ownership of productive resources. It is under this sort of political economy that the features associated with the dowry complex have most frequently developed. Moreover, the state also facilitated advances in commercialization through maintenance of transportation networks, currency, and so on; commercialization, as I argue in chapter 3, facilitated using wealth to acquire useful social ties through the mechanism of dowered marriages. In the later imperial period the civil service recruitment system made it progressively more difficult for men to pass on their political rank to their sons, assuring that wealth, not office, would be the fundamental underpinning of long-term family status.

At the same time, the Confucian-educated elite and the legal institutions of the state erected obstacles to the transmission of property through women. Many Confucian scholars denied that women had rights or claims to property, their objections apparently based on fears of women gaining undue importance. To them, deviation from strict adherence to transmission of property along patrilineal lines could undermine the whole family system and thus implicitly erode the authority of senior males (e.g., Ebrey 1984a:231). On the issue of affines and matrilateral relatives, Confucian family ideology was relatively silent. Much was said about domestic family relations, including the relationships of husbands and wives, the social relationships of agnatic kinsmen, and the ceremonies to be performed for weddings and funerals, but little about how to treat wives' brothers or cousins through mothers. No standards were articulated for the choice of families for marriage partners except in the vaguest ways (spouses, for instance, should not be chosen on the basis of transient wealth or rank), nor was much said about how to interact with them after the wedding. The only widely discussed examples were the cautionary ones of the imperial family. Confucian ideology was reinforced by and reflected in the state's legal codes. The law required monogamy but otherwise contained nothing that would explicitly foster the dowry complex—not requiring daughters to be given dowries, or granting wives clear control over dowries in their possession, or granting wives' natal kin any say in disposition of her dowry after her death.

Were anyone's interests served by inhibiting the dowry complex? Consciously, writers opposed to women's control of property saw it as threatening to male authority, to hierarchy in general, and to the preservation of patrimonies. There may well be some truth to these perceptions, though patriliny and patriarchy were able to coexist with dowry and female inheritance in other parts of the world.[2] But limiting the transmission of property through women also discouraged full development of the organizational potential inherent in affinal ties. Thus, educated men who condemned women's control of property may have been acting in their interests as male family heads but not in their interests as members of a social and political elite that sought greater independence from the government. Connections, including affinal connections, provided ways to get around many obstacles to advancement and influence; as seen throughout this volume such ties were regularly used by elite men at the local, regional, and national level. The manipulation of marriage choices also served the interests of the elite because belonging to a relatively restricted circle of intermarrying families could serve as proof of elite status.

Following this line of thinking, it was the state, as an entity with interests in the efficiency, accountability, and predictability of the actions of its employees, that benefited from discouraging any further strengthening of matrilateral and affinal ties among the elite. If through its legal institutions the state had given more protection to dowries—assuring the return of the dowry if the wife died early without heirs or was divorced for a cause like barrenness—China might have evolved into a society with stronger bilateral tendencies and greater proclivities to organize along affinal lines. But emperors and their advisers saw nothing to gain from such a situation. Strong dynasties seem never to have encouraged the highest-ranking families to marry with each other either by providing incentives or by asserting the moral desirability of such matches. Emperors did not chide leading ministers for being too casual in the selection of their children's mates, or remind them that they had their honor to uphold, as European kings might their nobles.

This is probably because within the bureaucracy marriage connections were less visible and therefore more threatening to imperial control and bureaucratic rationality than patrilineal kinship ties. The government could easily suspect that two people from the same place with the same family name might be patrilineal relatives and take their likely bias into account. If men also sided with their sisters' husbands, wives' brothers, father's sister's sons, mother's sisters' and brothers' sons, and so on, too many surnames would be involved for anyone to keep track who did not know them closely. How much easier it is for the state if these affinal ties are weak.

The failure of the Chinese educated class and imperial state to encourage dowries, women's property rights, strong ties among affines, or intermarriage among elites did not prevent the "sprouts" of these developments, but it probably prevented these trends from going as far as they might have otherwise. In contrast to societies where the dowry complex was fostered by the ideologies of dominant institutions, China should be seen as a place where it was kept within limits by both ideology and state actions.

NOTES

1. In addition, the upper levels of society had to draw some of their wives from slightly lower social levels because they could not meet their full demands for women from within their own ranks. This demographic imbalance was largely the result of concubinage and upper-class men remarrying when widowed much more frequently than upper-class women did.

2. They do seem to have been more common, however, in cognatic societies. See Ortner 1981.

GLOSSARY

chi-shih　繼室　　　　　　*p'in-chin*　聘金
ch'i　妻　　　　　　　　　*p'in-li*　聘禮
chia-chuang　嫁妝　　　　*p'in-ts'ai*　聘財
ch'ieh　妾　　　　　　　　*shih*　室
chuang-lien　妝奩　　　　*shih-jen*　室人
fu-jen　夫人　　　　　　　*ts'e-shih*　側室
hou-shih　後室　　　　　　*tzu-chuang*　資妝
li-chin　禮金　　　　　　　*tzu-sung*　資送
na-ts'ai　納采　　　　　　*ying*　媵

REFERENCES

Ahern, Emily M. 1974. "Affines and the Rituals of Kinship." In *Religion and Ritual in Chinese Society*, ed. Arthur P. Wolf. Stanford: Stanford University Press.
Baker, Hugh H. D. 1979. *Chinese Family and Kinship*. London: Macmillan.

Beattie, Hilary J. 1979. *Land and Lineage in China: A Study of T'ung-ch'eng County, Anhwei, in the Ming and Ch'ing Dynasties*. Cambridge: Cambridge University Press.

Bossler, Beverly. 1988. "Northern Sung Elite Families in K'ai-feng." Manuscript.

Bourdieu, Pierre. 1976. "Marriage Strategies as Strategies of Social Reproduction." In *Family and Society: Selections from the Annales, Economies, Societies, Civilisations*, ed. Robert Forster and Orest Ranum. Baltimore: Johns Hopkins University Press.

Chaffee, John W. 1985. *The Thorny Gates of Learning: A Social History of Examinations*. Cambridge: Cambridge University Press.

Chang, K. C. 1983. *Art, Myth, and Ritual: The Path to Political Authority in Ancient China*. Cambridge: Harvard University Press.

Chen, Chung-min. 1985. "Dowry and Inheritance." In *The Chinese Family and Its Ritual Behavior*, ed. Hsieh Jih-chang and Chuang Ying-chang. Taipei: Academia Sinica, Institute of Ethnology.

Ch'ü, T'ung-tsu. 1965. *Law and Society in Traditional China*. Paris: Mouton.

Chung, Priscilla Ching. 1981. *Palace Women in the Northern Sung, 960–1126*. Monographies du T'oung Pao, no. 12. Leiden: E. J. Brill.

Cohen, Myron L. 1976. *House United, House Divided: The Chinese Family in Taiwan*. New York: Columbia University Press.

———. 1988. "Marriage Finance in Contemporary Hopei." Talk given at the Conference on Marriage and Inequality in Chinese Society.

Collier, Jane Fishburne, and Sylvia Junko Yanagisako. 1987. "Introduction." In *Gender and Kinship: Essays Toward a Unified Analysis*, ed. Jane Fishburne Collier and Sylvia Junko Yanagisako. Stanford: Stanford University Press.

Comaroff, J. L. 1980. "Introduction." In *The Meaning of Marriage Payments*, ed. J. L. Comaroff. New York: Academic Press.

Croll, Elisabeth. 1981. *The Politics of Marriage in Contemporary China*. Cambridge: Cambridge University Press.

de Crespigny, Rafe. 1975. "The Harem of Emperor Huan: A Study of Court Politics in Later Han." *Papers on Far Eastern History* 12:1–42.

Dennerline, Jerry. 1986. "Marriage, Adoption, and Charity in the Development of Lineages in Wu-hsi from Sung to Ch'ing." In *Kinship Organization in Late Imperial China, 1000–1940*, ed. Patricia Buckley Ebrey and James L. Watson. Berkeley and Los Angeles: University of California Press.

Duby, Georges. 1978. *Medieval Marriage: Two Models from Twelfth-Century France*. Baltimore: Johns Hopkins University Press.

Dull, Jack. 1978. "Marriage and Divorce in Han China: A Glimpse at 'Pre-Confucian' Society." In *Chinese Family Law and Social Change in Historical and Comparative Perspective*, ed. David C. Buxbaum. Seattle: University of Washington Press.

Dumont, Louis. 1957. *Hierarchy and Marriage Alliance in South Indian Kinship*. London: Royal Anthropological Institute.

Ebrey, Patricia Buckley. 1978. *The Aristocratic Families of Early Imperial China: A Case Study of the Po-ling Ts'ui Family*. Cambridge: Cambridge University Press.

———. 1981. "Women in the Kinship System of the Southern Song Upper Class." *Historical Reflections* 8:113–28.

———. 1984a. "Conceptions of the Family in the Sung Dynasty." *Journal of Asian Studies* 43:219–45.

———. 1984b. *Family and Property in Sung China: Yüan Ts'ai's Precepts for Social Life*. Princeton: Princeton University Press.

————. 1986. "Concubines in Sung China." *Journal of Family History* 11:1–24.

Elvin, Mark. 1984. "Female Virtue and the State in China." *Past and Present* 104:111–152.

Fei, Hsiao-t'ung. 1939. *Peasant Life in China*. New York: Dutton.

Freedman, Maurice. 1957. *Chinese Family and Marriage in Singapore*. London: Her Majesty's Stationery Office.

————. 1958. *Lineage Organization in Southeastern China*. London: Athlone Press.

————. 1979. *The Study of Chinese Society*, ed. G. William Skinner. Stanford: Stanford University Press.

Gallin, Bernard. 1960. "Matrilateral and Affinal Relationships of a Taiwanese Village." *American Anthropologist* 62:632–42.

Gallin, Bernard, and Rita S. Gallin. 1985. "Matrilateral and Affinal Relationships in Changing Chinese Society." In *The Chinese Family and Its Ritual Behavior*, ed. Hsieh Jih-chang and Chuang Ying-chang. Taipei: Academia Sinica, Institute of Ethnology.

Gamble, Sidney D. 1954. *Ting Hsien: A North China Rural Community*. Stanford: Stanford University Press.

Gates, Hill. 1989. "The Commoditization of Chinese Women." *Signs* 14:799–832.

Goody, Jack. 1973. "Bridewealth and Dowry in Africa and Eurasia." In *Bridewealth and Dowry*, by Jack Goody and S. J. Tambiah. Cambridge: Cambridge University Press.

————. 1976a. "Inheritance, Property and Women: Some Comparative Perspectives." In *Family and Inheritance: Rural Society in Western Europe 1200–1800*, ed. Jack Goody, Joan Thirsk, and E. P. Thompson. Cambridge: Cambridge University Press.

————. 1976b. *Production and Reproduction: A Comparative Study of the Domestic Domain*. Cambridge: Cambridge University Press.

————. 1983. *The Development of the Family and Marriage in Europe*. Cambridge: Cambridge University Press.

Harrell, Stevan, and Sara A. Dickey. 1985. "Dowry Systems in Complex Societies." *Ethnology* 24.2:105–20.

Hazelton, Keith. 1986. "Patrilines and the Development of Localized Lineages: The Wu of Hsiu-ning City, Hui-chou, to 1528." In *Kinship Organization in Late Imperial China, 1000–1940*, ed. Patricia Buckley Ebrey and James L. Watson. Berkeley and Los Angeles: University of California Press.

Holmgren, Jennifer. 1981. "Widow Chastity in the Northern Dynasties: The *Lieh-nü* Biographies in the *Wei-shu*." *Papers on Far Eastern History* 23:165–86.

————. 1981–83. "Women and Political Power in the Traditional T'o-pa Elite: A Preliminary Study of the Biographies of Empresses in the *Wei-shu*." *Monumenta Serica* 35:33–74.

————. 1983. "The Harem in Northern Wei Politics—398–498 A.D." *Journal of the Economic and Social History of the Orient* 26:71–90.

————. 1985. "The Economic Foundations of Virtue: Widow-Remarriage in Early and Modern China." *Australian Journal of Chinese Affairs* 13:1–27.

————. 1986. "Marriage, Kinship and Succession under the Ch'i-tan Rulers of the Liao Dynasty (907–1125)." *T'oung Pao* 72:44–91.

Hsu, Francis L. K. 1948; rev. ed., 1971. *Under the Ancestors' Shadow: Kinship, Personality, and Social Mobility in China*. Stanford: Stanford University Press.

Hymes, Robert P. 1986a. "Marriage, Descent Groups, and the Localist Strategy in Sung and Yuan Fu-chou." In *Kinship Organization in Late Imperial China, 1000–1940*, ed. Patricia Buckley Ebrey and James L. Watson. Berkeley and Los Angeles: University of California Press.

———. 1986b. *Statesmen and Gentlemen: The Elite of Fu-chou, Chiang-hsi, in Northern and Southern Sung*. Cambridge: Cambridge University Press.

Inden, Ronald. 1976. *Marriage and Rank in Bengali Culture*. Berkeley and Los Angeles: University of California Press.

Johnson, David G. 1977a. "The Last Years of a Great Clan: The Li Family of Chao chün in Late T'ang and Early Sung." *Harvard Journal of Asiatic Studies* 37:5–102.

———. 1977b. *The Medieval Chinese Oligarchy*. Boulder: Westview Press.

Johnson, Kay Ann. 1983. *Women, the Family and Peasant Revolution in China*. Chicago: University of Chicago Press.

Kulp, Daniel Harrison. 1925. *Country Life in South China: The Sociology of Familism*. New York: Teachers College Bureau of Publications.

Lang, Olga. 1946. *Chinese Family and Society*. New Haven: Yale University Press.

Leach, Edmund. 1954. *The Political Systems of Highland Burma*. London: Athlone Press.

McCreery, John L. 1976. "Women's Property Rights and Dowry in China and South Asia." *Ethnology* 15:163–74.

Mann, Susan. 1985. "Historical Change in Female Biography from Song to Qing Times: The Case of Early Qing Jiangnan (Jiangsu and Anhui Provinces)." *Transactions of the International Conference of Orientalists in Japan* 30:65–77.

———. 1987. "Women in the Kinship, Class, and Community Structures of Qing Dynasty China." *Journal of Asian Studies* 46:37–56.

Mather, Richard B. 1980. "Intermarriage as a Gauge of Family Status in the Southern Dynasties." Paper presented at the Conference on the Nature of State and Society in Medieval China.

Mauss, Marcel. 1925; reprint, 1966. *The Gift: Forms and Functions of Exchange in Archaic Societies*. New York: Norton.

Meijer, M. J. 1981. "The Price of a P'ai-lou." *T'oung Pao* 67:288–304.

Ng, Vivienne W. 1987. "Ideology and Sexuality: Rape Laws in Qing China." *Journal of Asian Studies* 46:57–70.

Ocko, Jonathan. 1990. "Family Disharmony as Seen in Ch'ing Legal Cases." In *Orthodoxy in Late Imperial China*, ed. Kwang-ching Liu. Berkeley and Los Angeles: University of California Press.

O'Hara, Albert Richard. 1971. *The Position of Women in Early China*. Taipei: Mei Ya.

Ortner, Sherry. 1981. "Gender and Sexuality in Hierarchical Societies: The Case of Polynesia and Some Comparative Implications." In *Sexual Meanings: The Cultural Construction of Gender and Sexuality*, ed. Sherry Ortner and Harriet Whitehead. Cambridge: Cambridge University Press.

Parry, Jonathan. 1979. *Caste and Kinship in Kangra*. London: Routledge & Kegan Paul.

Parish, William L., and Martin King Whyte. 1978. *Village and Family in Contemporary China*. Chicago: University of Chicago Press.

Pasternak, Burton. 1972. *Kinship and Community in Two Chinese Villages*. Stanford: Stanford University Press.

Ropp, Paul S. 1976. "The Seeds of Change: Reflections on the Condition of Women in Early and Mid Ch'ing." *Signs* 2:5–23.

———. 1987. "The Status of Women in Mid-Qing China: Evidence from Letters,

Law, and Literature." Paper presented at the Annual Meeting of the American Historical Association.

Shiga Shūzō. 1978. "Family Property and the Law of Inheritance in Traditional China." In *Chinese Family Law and Social Change in Historical and Comparative Perspective*, ed. David C. Buxbaum. Seattle: University of Washington Press.

Soullière, Ellen F. 1988. "The Imperial Marriages of the Ming Dynasty." *Papers on Far Eastern History* 37:15–42.

Stacey, Judith. 1983. *Patriarchy and Socialist Revolution in China*. Berkeley and Los Angeles: University of California Press.

Sung, Marina H. 1981. "The Chinese Lieh-nü Tradition." In *Women in China*, ed. Richard W. Guisso and Stanley Johannesen. Youngstown, N.Y.: Philo Press.

Swann, Nancy Lee. 1932. *Pan Chao: Foremost Woman Scholar of China*. New York: Century.

Tai, Yen-hui. 1978. "Divorce in Traditional Chinese Law." In *Chinese Family Law and Social Change in Historical and Comparative Perspective*, ed. David C. Buxbaum. Seattle: University of Washington Press.

Tambiah, S. J. 1973. "Dowry and Bridewealth, and the Property Rights of Women in South Asia." In *Bridewealth and Dowry*, by Jack Goody and S. J. Tambiah. Cambridge: Cambridge University Press.

Twitchett, Denis. 1973. "The Composition of the T'ang Ruling Class: New Evidence from Tunhuang." In *Perspectives on the T'ang*, ed. Arthur F. Wright and Denis Twitchett. New Haven: Yale University Press.

Waltner, Ann. 1981. "Widows and Remarriage in Ming and Early Qing China." In *Women in China*, ed. Richard W. Guisso and Stanley Johannesen. Youngstown, N.Y.: Philo Press.

Watson, Rubie S. 1981. "Class Differences and Affinal Relations in South China." *Man* 16:593–615.

———. 1984. "Women's Property in Republican China: Rights and Practice." *Republican China* 10.1a:1–12.

———. 1985. *Inequality among Brothers: Class and Kinship in South China*. Cambridge: Cambridge University Press.

Wolf, Arthur P., and Chieh-shan Huang. 1980. *Marriage and Adoption in China, 1845–1945*. Stanford: Stanford University Press.

Wolf, Margery, 1972. *Women and the Family in Rural Taiwan*. Stanford: Stanford University Press.

———. 1985. *Revolution Postponed: Women in Contemporary China*. Stanford: Stanford University Press.

Wong, Sun-ming. 1979. "Confucian Ideal and Reality: Transformation of the Institution of Marriage in T'ang China (A.D. 618–907)." Ph.D. diss., University of Washington.

Yang, Martin C. 1945. *A Chinese Village: Taitou, Shantung Province*. New York: Columbia University Press.

ONE

Marriages of the Ruling Elite in the Spring and Autumn Period

Melvin P. Thatcher

This chapter provides an overview and preliminary analysis of the marriage practices of the ruling elite in the aristocratic society of the Spring and Autumn period (770–453 B.C.).[1] Departing from previous Western-language investigations that frequently refer to classical ritual texts, such as the *I-li* and *Li-chi* (Granet 1920, 1930:152–60; Feng 1937:43–54), or draw on a narrow slice of historical data (Chang 1976:89–92, 1983:29–30), this is a study of references to marriage in the *Ch'un-ch'iu* and *Tso-chuan*, the most important primary sources for the Spring and Autumn period. It takes into account all 150 recorded marriages, but focuses on the 126 marriages that involve members of the ruling households,[2] namely, rulers, their sons, daughters, and grandsons. Analyzing these marriages has several purposes, the first of which is descriptive or classificatory. In this regard attention is given to the hierarchy of women in the ruler's household and to wedding rituals, marriage rules, and patterns of intermarriage. The second purpose of analyzing these marriages is to determine how aristocratic marriages were connected to the social and political systems of this period. The relation between marriage and inequality is very much at issue here; the evidence suggests that marriages were used above all to create and strengthen ties between social and political equals. The third purpose for analyzing these marriages is to provide a baseline for discussing continuities and disconti-nuities over the course of Chinese history.

The Chou dynasty (c. 1122–256 B.C.) is divided into the Western Chou (c. 1122–771) and Eastern Chou (770–256) eras. The former began with the successful conquest of the Shang dynasty by the Chou people from their western base. Having defeated the Shang, the kings of Chou established pockets of power in conquered territory by installing close kin and trusted lieutenants as their representatives and by recognizing the de facto power of

25

local chieftains who were willing to acknowledge Chou suzerainty. This policy allowed them to extend the sphere of their territorial control, although it ultimately led to their decline and fall as the outposts became embryonic states and the descendants of their founders established themselves as ruling lineages. With self-interest eventually prevailing over the demands of clan and affinal ties and political loyalty to the ruling house of Chou, the stage was set for epochal change as two of the Chou statelets joined with barbarian forces to depose King Yu (r. 781–71) in 771. In the aftermath of this event, a new Chou capital was established eastward in the Central Plain where the royal house could be given better protection from its internal and external enemies. The Eastern Chou era was inaugurated (Creel 1970; Hsu 1984).

The Eastern Chou was a time of great social and political changes that ultimately produced a unified Chinese empire. The first part of this era, the Spring and Autumn period, saw the emergence of a multistate system that covered most of the drainage areas of the Yellow, Yangtze, and Huai rivers and their major tributaries (Walker 1953; Liu Po-ch'i 1962). By the end of the first century of this period, the kings of Chou, no longer able to exercise effective military might, had lost political influence and real control over the various states. The institution of hegemon (*pa*) filled the power vacuum, and from 679, interstate relations were conducted through summitry and covenant making, with the most powerful state ruler holding sway as hegemon. In theory the functions of the hegemon were to respect the king of Chou, to repel barbarian invasions, and to protect the weaker states. An elaborate interstate protocol developed whereby the states, which are estimated to have initially numbered 124 or more (*CCTSP* 4:1a [1036, "Preface"]; Lü 1962:151–65), were ranked as first-rate (*ta-kuo*), second-rate (*tz'u-kuo*), and third-rate (*hsia-kuo*) (*TCCS* 26:4a [437, Ch'eng 3]). As we shall see below, this protocol was reinforced through marriage rituals. Competition among the more powerful states for the hegemonship resulted in the elimination of numerous weaker states, despite the precautions taken to ensure their survival. By the beginning of the Warring States period (453–222), only seven major states and fourteen minor ones remained viable (K. Yang 1980: 261–65). The rivalry among states was an important factor in marriages between ruling houses.

Early in the Spring and Autumn period the elite was defined by membership in a state's ruling house or appointment to a ranked office. The ruler presided over an administration staffed by officials of *ch'ing*, *tai-fu*, and *shih*, or equivalent ranks. Whereas minor offices were usually passed on, like occupations, from father to son, ranked offices, particularly those of *ch'ing* and *tai-fu* rank, were often filled through appointment by the ruler. In states that followed the Chou practice of awarding land grants to meritorious officials and military officers, politically effective lineages arose and competition was keen among them for the hereditary right to *ch'ing* (ministerial) status (*TCCS* 36:

17a–18a [625, Hsiang 25]). Control over the appointment process became the object of struggles between ruling houses and local lineages. When lineages were able to win control and establish the hereditary right to ranked offices, inter- and intralineage competition ensued for possession of that right. The way was thus prepared for major social and political changes (Thatcher 1977–78, 1985). These contests for power and status entered into marriage choices and created unstable conditions that were conducive to social mobility for individuals and groups alike.

Largely because of the dynamics of domestic politics, social mobility prevailed at the upper reaches of society during the Spring and Autumn period. The king of Chou sat at the apex of society, followed in descending order by members of ruling households (namely, the rulers of states and their brothers, sons, and grandsons), officials of *ch'ing*, *tai-fu*, and *shih* rank, and the bulk of the population, mainly commoners. In his discussion of social stratification and mobility, Hsu Cho-yun argues that in the earliest decades of the Spring and Autumn period the brothers and sons of rulers declined in importance as officials of the *ch'ing* and *tai-fu* ranks came to dominate the political scene, and that in the waning years of the period *shih* began to appear in significant roles, presaging their dominance in the subsequent Warring States period (Hsu 1965:24–37). There was, in fact, mobility both within states and across state boundaries. Ruling lineages lost their status when their states were extinguished by more powerful neighbors, but some lineage members might be appointed to relatively low-level positions in the new regime. Most were reduced, however, to commoner or lower status. As newly powerful lineages within particular states were able to usurp the rights of older, more established lineages to *ch'ing* status, it was possible for whole groups to climb the social ladder, while those whom they displaced became commoners. This particular mobility becomes evident during the late seventh century B.C. and is seen most clearly in the state of Chin (Thatcher 1977–78:153–59).

Individual social mobility was also possible and occurred under a variety of circumstances. In states that were not totally dominated by powerful lineages, officials rose or fell according to their performance. The number of political exiles seeking asylum made it necessary to formulate rules to accommodate them in their host states. Some refugees were able to significantly improve their political fortunes and, consequently, their social status. The growing importance of *shih* toward the end of the period, as noted by Hsu Cho-yun, stemmed from the need for specialized functionaries at higher levels and a resulting deemphasis on lineage membership and position. At the bottom of the social ladder, slaves were manumitted (*TCCS* 35:12a [603, Hsiang 23]). Social mobility influenced individuals' marriage choices.

The economy of the Spring and Autumn period was based on intensive agriculture. In theory all land belonged to the king of Chou, but in practice it was held by the rulers of states and aristocratic lineages. During much of the period, land could not be alienated or inherited by individuals. With the advent in the sixth century B.C. of iron implements, the ox-drawn plow, and taxation on land in various states, the seeds of land reform were sown and private ownership of land became possible. Nevertheless, lineage-held land remained the dominant form of landholding through the end of the period. In addition to agriculture, the local economies in the various states also included cottage industries that produced such products as iron, bronze, salt, lacquerware, and textiles. At the same time, commercial activity was growing with the establishment of marketplaces and appearance of merchants engaged in interstate transactions. Trade was conducted through barter, but toward the end of the period local currencies began to appear (Ch'i 1981:96–99; Liu et al. 1979:99–106; Tang 1982:6–64).

The Spring and Autumn kinship system was composed of patrilineal kin groups that can be classified as clans, lineages, and families.[3] Although patrilineages were distinguished by lineage names (*shih*), those that shared a clan name (*hsing*) regarded themselves as agnatic kinsmen (*KY* 10:7b [258, "Chin yü" 4]). A rule of clan exogamy was recognized, but it was frequently violated, as will be shown below. The patrilineage was the critical kin group in this aristocratic society. Patrilineages were segmentary, socially stratified organizations (Chang 1976:74–75). The generational depth of powerful Spring and Autumn lineages ranged from three to twenty generations (*CCTSP* 12a:1a–43a and 12b:1a–31b [1281–1318]).[4] The patrilineage was a corporate kin group, typically based on land held in common and on shared ancestral rites. Land was transmitted from generation to generation by males within the lineage. Movable property, however, could be owned and controlled by families, although there are no examples of its inheritance during this period. The rules of inheritance are therefore not clear. Succession to the headship of lineages and their segments was usually from father to son, but not necessarily to the eldest son, for all of a man's sons were eligible to become his successor. The patrilineage was the effective exogamous unit, and marriage choices were based on lineage or family considerations. Postmarital residence was usually patrilocal.[5]

Women held an inferior status in Eastern Chou society, evident in a postmarital naming system that suppressed the bride's given name, in the determination of a wife's rank and status by those of her husband, and in funerary practices whereby husbands, fathers, and sons were shown more respect than wives, mothers, and married daughters (Liu Te-han 1976:5–11). Chia Shih-heng argues that wives did not have the right to own private property, citing this as one cause for forced divorces in the Warring States period (1980:27). Although these generalizations pertain to the Eastern Chou as a whole, most are documentable in Spring and Autumn sources, particularly the points concerning discrimination in referential terms or naming, rank and status, and funerary practices. Gender inferiority is clearly manifest in the marriages I describe below.

THE HIERARCHY OF WOMEN IN RULERS' HOUSEHOLDS

The women of elite households during the Spring and Autumn period consisted of primary and secondary wives, concubines, and maids. All but maids served as socially approved sexual partners for their husband and/or master. This section focuses on these consorts. Particular attention is paid to polygyny; the recruitment of primary wives, secondary wives, and concubines; status changes and ranking of women within the houshold; and the implications of the mother's status for her children, especially sons.

In marked contrast to elite males of imperial China, men of the ruling elite of the Spring and Autumn period could have more than one primary wife at the same time (see table 1.1). A ruler's primary wife had the status of *fu-jen*. Because the ruler could have more than one primary wife, they were differentiated as principal primary wife (*yuan-fei*), second primary wife (*erh-fei*), and third primary wife (*hsia-fei*) (literally, "first mate," "second mate," and "third mate"). The basis of this distinction among wives is not altogether clear, but the order of acquisition, perhaps after a ruler had been installed, appears to be a determinant, for taking a principal primary wife was a top priority for new rulers.

That polygynous marriage was practiced by rulers of states is unequivocally clear in the following three examples. First, in 720 Chuang Chiang, the barren principal primary wife of Duke Chuang of Wei, took the son he sired by Tai Wei to be her own son. Tai Wei was the younger sister of the duke's second primary wife, Li Wei, whose own son had died prematurely (*TCCS* 3:9b–10b [53, Yin 3]). Second, after Duke Wen was installed as ruler of Chin in 636, primary wife Tu Ch'i yielded rank to Chi Wei (*TCCS* 19a:10a [315, Wen 6]). He had cohabited and fallen in love with Chi Wei after she was given to him as a female companion during his twelve-year exile among the Ti (*TCCS* 15:9a–b [251, Hsi 23]). He evidently sent for and married her after gaining the rulership of Chin.[6] Finally, when the king of Ch'u passed through Cheng in 638, he was entertained by Mi-shih and Chiang-shih, primary wives of its ruler (*TCCS* 15:5a–6a [249, Hsi 22]).

Some polygynous marriages may have been motivated by the desire to obtain progeny or increase the pool of potential heirs.[7] Rulers also apparently contracted polygynous marriages to extend affinal ties and the associated political alliances; for example, all primary wives of rulers came from different states (see table 1.1).

Concubines provided another source of polygynous primary wives, usually because a concubine had become a ruler's favorite, or he wanted to make her son his successor, or both (*TCCS* 12:14a–16a [203–4, Hsi 4], 37:10b–

TABLE 1.1   Rulers and Multiple Primary Wives by Marriage

Year B.C.[a]	Husband			Wives		
	State	Ruler	Reign	State	Clan Name	Name
722	Lu	Duke Hui	768–23	Sung	Tzu	Meng Tzu
720	Wei	Duke Chuang	757–34	Ch'i	Chiang	Chuang Chiang
720				Ch'en?	Wei	Li Wei
683–43	Ch'i	Duke Huan	685–43	Chou	Chi	Wang Chi
657–43				Ts'ai	Chi	Ts'ai Chi
643				Hsu	Ying	Hsu Ying
666	Chin	Duke Hsien	676–52	Chia	Chi	Chia Chi
666				Ta-jung	Chi	Hu Chi
666				Hsiao-jung	Yün	unknown
637–36	Chin	Duke Wen	636–28	Ti	Wei	Chi Wei
637				Ch'i	Chiang	Chiang-*shih*
636				Ch'in	Ying	Wen Ying
621				Tu	Ch'i	Tu Ch'i
638	Cheng	Duke Wen	659–28	Ch'u?	Mi	Mi-shih
				Ch'i?	Chiang	Chiang-*shih*
613	Chu	Duke Wen	d. 613	Ch'i	Chiang	Ch'i Chiang
613				Chin	Chi	Chin Chi
609	Lu	Duke Wen	626–09	?	Ying	Ching Ying
534	Ch'en	Duke Ai	569–38	Cheng	Chi	Cheng Chi
534				?	?	unknown
534				?	?	unknown

SOURCE: *Tso-chuan.*

NOTE: In the source, reference to a woman as *yüan-fei* implies other primary wives. Acquisition of primary wives by marriage is made explicit either in the text or through the use of verbs such as *ch'i* ("to [give as] wife"), *ch'ü* ("to take as wife"), and *kuei* ("to go to [the groom's home]") or implied by context.

This table does not include wives obtained through marriages that were contracted by a ducal son prior to his installation as ruler because such wives do not seem to have had the status of *fu-jen.*

[a] Year of mention in record.

12a [633–34, Hsiang 26], 60:19a–20b [1050, Ai 24]). Although promoting a concubine to the status of primary wife was done, it was not considered proper. The *Mencius* claims that in 651 this practice was made a punishable offense in an interstate covenant (*MTCS* 12b:1b [218]). When Duke Ai of Lu was going to install his favorite concubine as a primary wife in 471, he ordered the official in charge of ritual to offer the appropriate rite. The official asserted, however, that no such rite existed (*TCCS* 60:19a–b [1050, Ai 24]). Nevertheless, Duke Ai promoted her to primary wife because he intended to make her son his heir-apparent.

Secondary wives were acquired through a form of sororal polygyny (Granet 1920; Feng 46–51; Ruey 1958:14–15, 1959:249–51). Under the year 583 the *Tso-chuan* states: "Whenever the various rulers marry off their daughters, [ruling lineages] of the same clan name *ying* them. [Ruling lineages] of different clan names, however, do not" (*TCCS* 26:23a [447, Ch'eng 8]). On the first mention of this practice in the *Ch'un-ch'iu* in 675, the *Kung-yang Commentary* glosses: "What is *ying*? When a vassal lord took a bride from one state, then two states [each] sent a female to her accompanied by *chih* and *ti*. *Chih* means the daughter of her elder brother. *Ti* means her younger sister. The vassal lord in one betrothal [acquired] nine females. The vassal lord did not marry again" (*KYCS* 8:1b–2a [97, Chuang 18]). Tu Yü (A.D. 222–84) says that the principal bride and both *ying* were accompanied by a niece and a younger sister, so that the total number of females came to nine (*CCCS* 12: 23b [183, Ch'eng 8]).

In actuality the provision of *ying* was not exactly as outlined here. Ruling lineages of different clan names did not send secondary brides,[8] as in the example above of Ch'i, clan name Chiang, sending a secondary bride to Lu, clan name Chi (*CCCS* 26:28a [449, Ch'eng 10]). More than two states could supply females, as when Wei, Chin, and Ch'i sent secondary brides to Lu between 583 and 581 for Po Chi, who was wed to Duke Kung of Sung (*TCCS* 26:23a [447, Ch'eng 8], 25a [448, Ch'eng 9]; *CCCS* 26:28a [449, Ch'eng 10]). And contrary to the observation by the *Kung-yang Commentary*, the presence of secondary brides in the household did not prevent additional marriages by rulers of states.

As the *Tso-chuan* evidence covering the Spring and Autumn period shows (table 1.2), the principal brides of rulers and officials of the *ch'ing* and *tai-fu* ranks were accompanied into marriage by a niece or younger sister, or both. There are no examples, however, of related lineages sending females to accompany the principal bride of a *ch'ing* or *tai-fu*. Apparently, only rulers were entitled to marry nine females at one time.

All of the females who accompanied the principal bride into marriage became secondary wives (even though theirs were not "secondary marriages" temporally speaking because they were married at the same time as the principal bride [Ruey 1958:15]). If the principal bride proved infertile or her offspring suffered premature death, reproduction became the main task of the secondary wives, a practice that ensured that a potential heir issued from the lineage of the principal bride, or, in the case of brides of rulers, a related lineage. Another important function for a secondary wife was to assume the role, but not the status, of the primary wife in the event of her death. For example, in 550 when the wife of Tsang Hsuan-shu of Lu died, Tsang "continued her role with her niece [*chi shih i ch'i chih*]" (*TCCS* 35:18a [606, Hsiang 23]).[9] In the case of divorce or separation from the principal bride, the husband retained possession of his secondary brides (*TCCS* 58:26a–b [1018,

TABLE 1.2. Secondary Brides of Rulers and *Ch'ing* or *Tai-fu* Officials

Year B.C.[a]	Secondary Bride	Principal Bride	Married to	Son[b]
722	Sheng Tzu	Meng Tzu	Duke Hui of Lu	Y
720	Tai Wei	Li Wei	Duke Chuang of Wei	Y
675	(Lu girl)	(Wei girl)	Duke Hsuan? of Ch'en	
660	Shu Chiang	Ai Chiang	Duke Chuang of Lu	Y
620	Sheng Chi	Tai Chi	Kung-sun Ao of Lu	Y
583	(Wei girl)	Po Chi	Duke Kung of Sung	
582	(Chin girl)	Po Chi	Duke Kung of Sung	
581	(Ch'i girl)	Po Chi	Duke Kung of Sung	
554	Tsung-sheng Chi	Yen-i Chi	Duke Ling of Ch'i	Y
550	(Shou girl)	(Lu girl)	Tsang Hsuan-shu of Lu	Y
550	(Ch'i girl)	(Chin girl)	King Chu-fan of Wu	
484	(Sung girl)	(Sung girl)	Ta-shu Chi of Wei	

SOURCES: *Ch'un-ch'iu* and *Tso-chuan.*
NOTE: In the sources, secondary brides are revealed by the use of one or more of the following terms: *chi-shih, chih, ti,* or *ying.*
[a] Year of mention in record.
[b] "Y" indicates that the secondary bride bore a son.

Ai 11]), thus preserving the affinal relationships established or renewed by the marriage.

Secondary brides did not have to be sent to the groom at the time of marriage. If the niece or younger sister who was selected to accompany the bride was not old enough at the time of the wedding, she could be sent later. This was the case with Shu Chi of Lu, who was sent to Chi five years after her elder sister, Po Chi (aka Kung Chi), was married to its ruler in 721 (*TCCS* 2:30a [42, Yin 2]; *CCCS* 4:3b–4a [71, Yin 7—text and Tu commentary]). The secondary wives from Wei, Chin, and Ch'i for Po Chi were provided to Lu over a period of three years from 583 to 581 (see table 1.2).

Concubines made up the third category of consorts of the ruling elite. In the *Tso-chuan* there is evidence of the practice of concubinage by the rulers of nine states, certainly an incomplete record because most references to concubinage are incidental to discussions of succession struggles or other unusual circumstances. Concubinage was not limited to rulers, however; the *Tso-chuan* also refers to the concubines of high officials.

Females became concubines in a variety of ways. A fairly common practice was for rulers to send females of their lineage, or for fathers to send their daughters, into concubinage (*TCCS* 7:11a [123, Huan 11], 10:13a [177, Chuang 28], 15:12b–13a [253, Hsi 23], 19a:9b [315, Wen 6], 26:6a–b [619,

Hsiang 25]). Mothers may also have sent their daughters to become concubines (*TCCS* 15:6a [249, Hsi 22]). Females were probably sold into concubinage (*TCCS* 41:24a [707, Chao 1]). The *Tso-chuan* provides no examples, however, of the purchase of concubines. Under fortunate circumstances a maid could become a concubine (*TCCS* 37:10b–12a [633–34, Hsiang 36— text and Tu commentary]). Finally, some women voluntarily joined the harems of the powerful (*TCCS* 45:18b–19a [785–86, Chao 11]).

Rulers observed a truncated version of the marriage rites for some concubines, particularly those acquired from other powerful ruling lineages. When Duke P'ing of Chin secured Hsiao Chiang from Ch'i in 543, no reference is made to the betrothal request, but the rites of presenting betrothal gifts and fetching, escorting, and presenting the bride were performed. One can discern that Hsiao Chiang was not going to be a wife of Duke P'ing from the rank of the officer sent to fetch her and from that of the officer from Ch'i who escorted and presented the concubine to him (*TCCS* 43:3a–4a [719, Chao 2—text and commentaries]). Although some concubines may have been recruited in this fashion, most were acquired without any ceremony at all.

Duke Huan of Ch'i is reputed to have had many favored concubines. After noting that he had three barren wives, the *Tso-chuan* says that Duke Huan, "being fond of concubines, had many concubinal favorites. Six concubines were treated just like primary wives [*fu-jen*]." All six appear to have been from or related to the ruling lineages of their native states. Four had the clan name of Chi, one Ying, and one Tzu. Each bore at least one son, four of whom eventually became dukes of Ch'i (*TCCS* 14:18a–b [237, Hsi 17]).[10]

The masters of concubines looked after them like the personal property that they evidently were. Prior to 558 Duke Hsien of Wei had a music instructor flogged three hundred times because he had whipped one of the duke's favorite concubines, whom he had been assigned to teach the lute (*TCCS* 32:14a–b [560, Hsiang 14]). And before the battle of Fu-chih in 594 Wei Wu-tzu of Chin became ill and ordered his son, Wei K'o, to marry off a favorite concubine who was without child. Then, when he became seriously ill, he instructed that she be buried alive with his corpse (*TCCS* 24:12a [409, Hsuan 15]), something he would not have ordered for his wife. Evidently some masters felt their proprietary rights over concubines extended beyond this life.

Wives and concubines were formally ranked within the household. In the state of Chin, for example, we know that at least nine ranks existed among consorts of the ruler because Huai Ying (aka Chen Ying), the concubine of Duke Wen, was ranked ninth (*pan tsai chiu-jen*) (*TCCS* 19a:9b [315, Wen 6]). The consorts of Duke Mu of Cheng were evidently ranked, as the rank (*pan*) of Kuei Wei was inferior to (*ya*) that of Sung Tzu (*TCCS* 34:7a–b [587,

Hsiang 19]). Though the term *pan* does not appear in the *Tso-chuan* in reference to household women in other states, there is ample indirect evidence that they, too, were formally ranked.

The ranks of consorts were subject to change as the result of the addition of more primary wives or the promotion of sons. For example, among the women in the household of Duke Wen of Chin, Tu Ch'i yielded rank twice, once to Po Chi, who may have originally been a concubine and whose son was named heir-apparent, and again to Chi Wei, the captive girl mentioned earlier whom the Ti had given to Duke Wen during his exile among them. Tu Ch'i therefore ended up being ranked fourth (*pan tsai ssu*). According to Tu Yü's calculations, Tu Ch'i's original rank was second (*TCCS* 19a:9a–10A [315, Wen 6]). In 636 a daughter whom Duke Wen had wed to a loyal follower also yielded rank to another wife so that the latter's son could become her husband's heir (*TCCS* 15:16b–17a [254–55, Hsi 24]).

The distinctions among primary wives, secondary wives, and concubines were not simply matters of personal prestige. They also affected their children's status in the key event in the corporate life of state and lineage; namely, the selection of heirs and successors. The general rule was that the eldest son of the principal primary wife should be the first choice, then his full younger brothers in order of age, followed by half brothers by age. When Duke Hsiang of Lu died in 542, the son of Ching Kuei, a concubine from Hu, was selected to succeed him. But when this young man suddenly passed away, a half brother, the son of his mother's younger sister, was installed in his stead. Thereupon, an officer of Lu objected in vain saying:

> When the heir-apparent dies, if he has a younger full brother (*mu-ti*), then install him. If none, then install the eldest [half brother]. If their age is equal, then select the most worthy. If their sense of duty is equal, then divine [the selection]. This is the Way of antiquity. [Since the son of Ching Kuei] was not the legitimate heir (*shih-ssu*), why must the son of her younger sister [be installed]? (*TCCS* 10:14b–15a [685–86, Hsiang 31])

Thus, since Duke Hsiang's heir-apparent had not been the son of his principal primary wife, the substitute heir need not be determined on the basis of closeness to him.[11]

Overturning the order of birthright was seen to undermine social stability and moral order (see Holmgren, chapter 2 of this volume, for a discussion of succession in later periods). Alluding to the struggle of a former concubine to get her son installed as heir-apparent, in 660 an officer of Chin is said to have quoted an ancient admonition to the Duke of Chou: "Treating concubines equal to queens, allowing external favorites to share political authority [with the chief minister], making the son of a favorite concubine (*pi-tzu*) equal with the legitimate heir (*ti*), and letting major walled towns grow to match the capital, all of these give rise to chaos" (*TCCS* 11:14b [193, Min 2]). Concern about the ability of the son of a low-ranking woman to command the necessary respect is seen in Chao Tun's argument against installing Huai Ying's son as the ruler of Chin in 621: "Since she is lowly and her rank is ninth, what awe has her son?" (*TCCS* 19a:9a–10a [315, Wen 6]).[12]

MARRIAGE INSTITUTIONS

Among the ruling elite of the Spring and Autumn period, betrothals and weddings involved a series of rites. Although there is no complete record of the entire process on any one occasion, such rites include the following:

1. The tortoise shell and/or milfoil were consulted by the male and/or female side to divine the auspiciousness of initiating and/or continuing the betrothal and marriage process (*TCCS* 9:23b [163, Chuang 22], 14:8a–10b [232–33, Hsi 15], 36:2b–4a [617–18, Hsiang 25]).
2. Initial inquiry concerning the possibility of marriage would be initiated by either the male (*TCCS* 22:1b [367, Hsüan 5], 22:3a [377, Hsüan 6], 31:24b–25a [548, Hsiang 12], 43:11a (747, Chao 5]) or female side (4:6b [72, Yin 7]).
3. The marriage agreement was finalized either on the spot or at a later date (*TCCS* 4:6b [72, Yin 7], 31:24b–25a [548–49, Hsiang 12]).
4. The female side would respond to a request from the male side by offering a prospective bride for consideration (*TCCS* 43:11a [747, Chao 5]). (Requests for grooms from the female side, by contrast, were groom-specific.)
5. The groom's side had to make a formal petition for betrothal (*TCCS* 26:21b [446, Ch'eng 8], 51:6b–7a [887–88, Chao 25], 58:26b–27b [1018–19, Ai 11]).
6. The groom's side would then send betrothal gifts to the bride's family (*TCCS* 18:15b [304, Wen 2], 26:21b [446, Ch'eng 8], 41:14b–15a [702–3, Chao 1]).
7. Before fetching the bride, the groom reported to his key ancestors in their respective ancestral temples (*TCCS* 41:3a–b [697, Chao 1]).
8. The groom either sent a representative[13] or went himself[14] to fetch the bride from her home.
9. The bride was sent off by her parents (*CCCS* 6:3a [103, Huan 3—text and Tu commentary]; *TCCS* 4:6b [744, Chao 5]).[15]
10. A representative of the bride's family escorted the bride to the husband's home (*TCCS* 4:9b–10a [74, Yin 8], 6:4b–5a [104–5, Huan 3], 43:6b–13a [744–48, Chao 5]).

11. There the escort formally transferred the bride to her husband's family (*TCCS* 6:5a [104, Huan 3], *CCCS* 26:23b [447, Ch'eng 9], *TCCS* 26:25a [448, Ch'eng 9]).

12. In order for the marriage to be valid, the couple reported to the groom's ancestral temple before consummating their marriage (*TCCS* 4:9b–10a [74, Yin 8]).

13. After a trial period of about three months, the horse upon which the bride came was returned to her natal family, apparently as a sign that she was content to remain with her husband.

14. At some point after the marriage, the bride would also visit her parents to inquire about their welfare (*CCCS* 22:1a–b [376, Hsüan 5], *TCCS* 22:2a [376, Hsüan 5—text and commentaries]).[16]

The formal petition for betrothal (*p'in*) was critical in this series of rites for it established the woman's status as that of primary wife. Without it, she was held to be merely a concubine (*TCCS* 27:1b [456, Ch'eng 11—text and Tu commentary]). Rituals performed for marriages between members of ruling houses were designed to reflect and reinforce interstate protocol. For example, a ruler was expected to depute officers of *ch'ing* rank to present betrothal gifts to the bride's family and to fetch the bride. Likewise, the ruler who was father of the bride was expected to send a person of appropriate rank to escort his daughter to her husband's state as follows:

> When the daughter of a duke is married to [the ruler of] a state of equal rank, if she is an elder or younger sister [of the reigning duke], then a *shang-ch'ing* escorts her in order to show proper courtesy toward [her father] the former ruler. If she is the child of the duke, then a *hsia-ch'ing* escorts her. If the marriage is to the ruler of a greater state, even though she is the daughter of the duke, still a *shang-ch'ing* escorts her. If she is married to the Son of Heaven, then all those of *ch'ing* rank escort her. The duke does not himself escort her. If she is married to the ruler of a lesser state, then a *shang tai-fu* escorts her. (*TCCS*, 6:4b–5a [103–4, Huan 3])

Two types of prestations were associated with marriages among the ruling elite, namely, betrothal gifts and dowry. The former appear to have been presented by the groom's side to the family of the bride as part of the rite of initial inquiry and at the time of betrothal. Little is known about the goods that typically made up betrothal gifts. In 541 Kung-sun Hei of Cheng, who was seeking to claim his cousin's betrothed as his own, forced the woman's family to accept a fowl, perhaps to signal its favorable response to his overtures. When the woman's brother gave her the option of choosing between the two suitors, Kung-sun Hei came in the courtyard and "spread out his betrothal gifts" (*pu ch'i pi* [*pi* literally means "silk"]), while the woman looked on from her room (*TCCS* 41:14b–15a [702–3, Chao 1—text and Tu commentary]). In the event, the woman married her original fiancé, who for his presentation had come into the courtyard in full battle dress, shot an arrow to the left and another to the right, vaulted into his chariot, and departed. Betrothal gifts had important symbolic functions, for the continuation or termination of the marriage process depended upon their reception (Liu Te-han 1976:48). Because betrothal gifts were received by the bride's family, they appear to be akin to bridewealth; however, there is no evidence that they became part of a "circulating pool of resources" used to acquire wives for brothers of the bride (Goody 1973:5).

The practice of direct dowry, whereby property was given to the bride by her kinsmen (ibid., 17), is clearly evident in many Western and Eastern Chou bronze inscriptions, which record a father giving (*ying*) a bronze vessel to his daughter upon the occasion of her marriage.[17] From these inscriptions and the *Tso-chuan* a number of things can be learned about the outlays made by the bride's family in this period. Because of the political role of ruling-house marriages and the landholding system itself, land was not given as dowry. Bronze vessels, however, were gifts of considerable value. Servants were also sometimes given as dowry (*TCCS* 12:25b [205, Hsi 5]). The dowry provided by the bride's side could be very costly when a bride came from a ruling house. For example, the *Tso-chuan* reports that in 484 a high official in the state of Ch'en taxed grant lands (*feng-t'ien*) in order to marry off the daughter of the duke (*TCCS* 18:23a–b [1077, Ai 11]).

The Western Chou rule of clan exogamy (Wang n.d.: 453–54) continued to be voiced in the Spring and Autumn period. In *Tso-chuan* dialogues it is usually stated as "male and female distinguish clan names [*nan nü pien hsing*]," and it is mentioned only in contexts that make note of its violations (*TCCS* 15:11a–b [252, Hsi 23], 36:2b–4a [617–18, Hsiang 25], 38:25a–b [654, Hsiang 28], 41:24b [707, Chao 1]). Violation of this rule was thought to cause physiological problems for the perpetrators and any offspring that might be produced. For example, when Tzu-ch'an of Cheng was sent in 541 to the sickbed of Duke P'ing of Chin, who had four consorts with the same clan name as his own, he advised the duke to get rid of them:

> I have heard that wives and concubines do not reach to the same clan name [as the husband]. If they do, their offspring do not mature. When their physical attraction is first exhausted, indeed, then their relationship gives birth to trouble. Because of that the gentleman despises it. Therefore, the record says, "If when buying a concubine, you do not know her clan name, then divine [the purchase]." The ancients were wary about violating this rule. Male and female distinguishing clan names is a major regulation of ritual. (*TCCS* 41: 24a–b [707, Chao 1])[18]

In spite of perceptions that clan endogamy brought negative consequences, Chao I reports that the rule was violated more often during the Spring and Autumn period than in any other era in ancient Chinese history

TABLE 1.3   Violations of Clan Exogamy

Clan Name	Male	Female's Lineage	Female's Status[a]
Chi	Duke Hsien of Chin	Chia	W
		Ta Jung (Hu)	W
		Li Jung	C
Chi	Duke P'ing of Chin	Wei	W
		?	C
		?	C
		?	C
Chi	Duke Ting of Chin	Lu	W
Chi	Hsi Ch'ou of Chin	Kuan	W
Chi	Duke Chao of Lu	Wu	W
Chi	Shih Hsiao-shu of Lu	Kuan	W
Chi	Ta-shu Yi of Wei	Chin	W
Chi	(King of Wu)	Chin	W
Chiang	Ts'ui Chu of Ch'i	Tung-kuo	W
Chiang	Lu-p'u Kuei of Ch'i	Ch'ing	W
Mi	Wu Chü of Ch'u	Ch'u	W

SOURCE: *Tso-chuan.*
[a] W = wife; C = concubine.

(*KYTK* 31:646–47). The *Tso-chuan* records sixteen violations in the taking of wives and concubines (table 1.3). If secondary wives were factored into the above figures, the number of violations would be even higher.

Why was the rule of clan exogamy often ignored? In the fragmented polity and society of the period, clan ties had lost most of their relevance. In the pursuit of political alliances through intermarriage between ruling houses, political exigencies often outweighed exogamous considerations. In interstate relations clan ties provided no assurance of privileged treatment, as is evident in the complaint that when in 544 Duke P'ing of Chin fortified the capital of Chi, his mother's native state, he was assisting a state with a different clan name but had no pity for states bearing his own (*TCCS* 39:6b–7a [666–67, Hsiang 29]). At the individual level, self-interest overrode any concerns about endogamy. For example, in 545 Ch'ing She offered to marry a daughter to his retainer Lu-p'u Kuei, even though the Ch'ing and Lu-p'u lineages bore the same clan name of Chiang. A retainer of the prospective father-in-law criticized Lu-p'u Kuei for violating the rule on clan exogamy, but Lu-p'u countered that he had not taken the initiative in the match, and besides he stood to gain from it (*TCCS* 38:25a–b [645, Hsiang 28—text and Tu commentary]). By the Spring and Autumn period, the lineage had displaced the clan as the key kin group in the day-to-day affairs of state and society. In this environment, the rule of clan exogamy was ignored whenever it became inconvenient, while lineage exogamy was strictly observed. Ruling houses, for example, never took brides from or gave daughters to members of segments of their own lineage or to members of lineages that had split off from it.

Chang Kwang-chih has suggested the existence of positive marriage rules in Shang and Chou China in the following hypothesis:

> Within the framework of bilateral cross-cousin marriage, strong emphases were sometimes placed exclusively either on patrilateral (marrying father's sister's daughter [FZD] only) or the matrilateral (marrying the mother's brother's daughter [MBD] only)...the guiding principle of the shifting emphasis appears to be the political status of the intermarrying parties. Patrilateral cross-cousin marriages tended to take place between political equals, whereas matrilateral cross-cousin marriage tended to take place as a contributing factor to the delicate and dynamic balance of political power between lineages of unequal status. (1983:29)

While acknowledging that his own views on patrilateral cross-cousin marriage during the Shang are controversial, Chang argues for the existence of matrilateral cross-cousin marriage during the Eastern Chou, more particularly the Spring and Autumn period. His key points are, first, "intermarrying states referred to each other as 'maternal uncle and sororal nephew states' [Chang's translation of *chiu-sheng*], and this designation strongly suggests the probability that the relationship... was an ongoing one" (1983:29). Second, this term, "maternal uncle and sororal nephew states," applies to their respective states as states and not simply to particular rulers. Third, marriage exchanges tended not to be reciprocal, particularly from the perspective of lineage as opposed to clan. Fourth, there was a "difference in political status between the maternal uncle and sororal nephew states, and...the wife-receivers seem to have higher political and/or ritual status than the wife-givers" (Chang 1983:29–30). Anthropologists characterize this kind of marriage system as "asymmetrical" because women are always moving in one direction. Where prescriptive MBD marriage is practiced, it is found in stratified societies and results in perpetual marriage alliances between wife-givers and wife-receivers (Fox 1967:209–14).[19] My examination of *Ch'un-ch'iu* and *Tso-chuan* evidence does not bear out Chang's interpretation of marriage in the Spring and Autumn period.

For example, the most common usages of *chiu* ("father-in-law/mother's brother") and *sheng* ("sister's son/daughter's husband") imply sister exchange or reciprocal marriages (Granet 1930:156–60; Ch'en and Shyrock 1932:629–30; Feng 1937:43–46). Ruey Yih-fu notes a merging of consanguineous and affinal relatives in the uses of these terms, which he lists as

chiu: mother's brother, wife's father, husband's father
sheng: father's sister's son, mother's brother's son, wife's brother, sister's husband, daughter's husband, daughter's son

Ruey concurs that this phenomenon (i.e., the merging of consanguineous and affinal relatives in the usages of *chiu* and *sheng*) indicates, and might be caused by, "the practice of cross-cousin marriage and, to a certain extent, of sister exchange marriages among the noble class at least" (1958:8–9). Chang's "framework of bilateral cross-cousin marriage" is based on this interpretation of these terms (1983:29), but he seeks to break new ground by showing that emphasis was placed on unilateral MBD marriages. Ruey argues convincingly, however, that *chiu* or *sheng* are difficult to distinguish because intermarriage between kin groups continued for generations (1959:245–46). Although the meanings of *chiu* and *sheng* can be used as evidence of the possibility of reciprocal cross-cousin marriage, they do not support the argument for one-way, nonreciprocal marriage. Depending on one's point of reference, the other party could be either *chiu* or *sheng* because of past or present bilateral marriage links.

Chang's second point, that these terms could refer to relations between states and not simply to particular rulers, can be accepted. Ruey has shown this was clearly the case because subsequent generations continued to use the terminology brought into play by a marriage, even though they had not renewed the marriage relationship (1959:252–54). But this practice negates the notion that these terms suggest ongoing relationships, or perpetual marriage alliances, between intermarrying states.

Ample evidence shows that many lineages intermarried. Thirty-five percent of marriages (twenty–nine of eighty–three) by rulers fall in this category, which I label "bilateral" instead of "reciprocal" because in the Spring and Autumn period there is no evidence of the creation of mutual marriage rights to females and obligations to continue to intermarry. Chang's conclusion is based primarily on data for marriages between Lu and Ch'i. Table 1.4 takes into account the marriages of rulers and their sons and grandsons in all of

TABLE 1.4   Bilateral Marriage Links among Ruling Lineages

Husband		Wives	Husband		Wives
Ch'en	=	Wei (1)	Wei	=	Ch'en (1)
Ch'en	=	Ts'ai (1)	Ts'ai	=	Ch'en (1)
Chi	=	Lu (4)	Lu	=	Chi (1)
Ch'i	=	Chou (2)	Chou	=	Ch'i (1)
Ch'i	=	Lu (2)	Lu	=	Ch'i (7)
Chin	=	Ch'in (3)	Ch'in	=	Chin (1)
Lu	=	Sung (2)	Sung	=	Lu (1)
Sung	=	Wei (1)	Wei	=	Sung (1)

NOTE: This table does not include bilateral marriages between Lu and a non-ruling lineage, T'ang of Sung.

TABLE 1.5   Marriages by Social Status of Groom and Bride

		To Daughters Of		
Marriages By	Kings	Ruling Households	Ch'ing/ Tai-fu	No Details
Kings of Chou	—	5	—	1
Ruling households	3	77	4	18
Ch'ing/tai-fu	—	19	22	1

SOURCES: *Ch'un-ch'iu* and *Tso-chuan.*

the major states. It shows that the ruling lineages listed both gave and accepted each other's daughters in marriage (numbers in parentheses indicate number of recorded wives): not only did brides move in both directions, but there is also no evidence for marriage with FZDs[20] and very little for MBDs.[21]

Chang's assertion that wife-receivers tend to hold higher political or ritual status than wife-givers does not stand up. For example, when the marriages of the ruling houses of Ch'i, Chin, Lu, and Wei are considered, the record shows that in one-way relationships as wife-receivers *or* as wife-givers, the political strength of these states was usually equal to or greater than those of their ruling-house marriage partners.[22] When interstate protocol—in which ritual status may have tended to outweigh political strength—at the time of marriage is taken into account, most of the bilateral marriage ties between the states listed in table 1.4 were contracted between ruling houses of equal status (even Chi and Lu). Of course, according to ritual status, the royal house of Chou was superior to its marriage partners, but it both sent daughters to and received brides from these lower-ranking houses. These is no evidence of a preference for one-way MBD marriage exchanges in which the wife-receiver always held higher status than the wife-giver. Within the gradations of ruling houses, superiors were giving women to and receiving women from inferiors, and equals were exchanging women among themselves.

In the Spring and Autumn period, marriages among the ruling elite tended to be class endogamous. For example, male members of ruling households usually chose spouses from other ruling households. Such marriages were, indeed, quite common (see table 1.5). But as revealed in the discussion above, considerable intermarriage took place among ranks from the same class, indicating that marriage, in its social implications, was a means of perpetuating class solidarity.

Heterogamous marriages between social classes also occasionally occurred. In addition to being married to men from their class, some daughters of rulers were married up to the king of Chou (who, after all, had to take women from lower levels). A few *ch'ing* and *tai-fu* families married their daughters up to rulers, presumably as additional wives; one was pursued by the ruler of her state (*TCCS*, 10:22a [181, Chuang 28]) and the other, from a powerful ministerial lineage in a major state, was married to the ruler of a minor state (*TCCS* 48:22a [844, Chao 19]). Two marriages between sons of rulers and daughters of *ch'ing* and *tai-fu* involved sons who were not in line for the rulership.[23] Kings of Chou, who were without peer in the realm, married their daughters to rulers of select states (*TCCS*, 8:4a–b [137, Chuang 1]; 9:3b [153, Chuang 11]; 20:5b [349, Wen 16]; also *CCCS*, 9:1a [152, Chuang 1]). Even more common in the sources are unequal matches involving daughters of ruling households who married down. Eleven of sixteen such marriages, however, involved unusual circumstances;[24] so hypogamous marriages between ruling households and *ch'ing* and *tai-fu* lineages may not have been as common as these figures suggest (for marriages of imperial daughters in later periods, see Chaffee, chapter 4, and Rawski, chapter 5, in this volume).

If ruling-house marriages were not structured by patterns of accepting wives from lower-ranking ruling houses and giving them to higher ones or vice-versa, what did govern marriage choices? From my reading of the sources, these marriages, particularly when contracted by the ruler himself, were dictated by political considerations. From the points of view of both the groom's and the bride's side, they were political marriages. As a rule, they were not the product of perpetual marriage alliances that had to be renewed in every generation (cf. Goody 1973:35–36). When Lu experienced a famine in 666, its ruler was told that the way to obtain aid from neighboring states was to "secure the trust of the rulers, compound it through marriage, and enhance it through covenants" (*KY* 4:3a [111, Lu Yü *shang*]). Lü Hsiang of Chin echoed these remarks when he observed that the good relationship between deceased rulers Duke Hsien of Chin and Duke Mu of Ch'in had been extended by way of covenant and enhanced through marriage; namely, that of the daughter of Duke Hsien to Duke Mu in about 655 (*TCCS* 27: 11a–b [461, Ch'eng 13—text and Tu commentary]). The *Tso-chuan* states that marriage and the maintenance of good relations with affines were of the first order of importance in the affairs of a new ruler (*TCCS* 18:15b [304, Wen 21]). Rulers received brides from and gave daughters to other ruling houses to seal agreements, signal friendly intentions, extend recognition, and, most important, secure the support and protection of affines in the interstate, and sometimes domestic, struggle for power and survival. Despite the incompleteness of the marriage record in the *Ch'un-ch'iu* and *Tso-chuan*, it is evident that wives were received from and given to many different lineages (see table 1.6).

The major states of Ch'i and Chin and the less powerful states of Lu and Wei show a pattern of wide geographic dispersal of marriages. Chin provides a good example of how the geographic span of ruling-house marriages was influenced by interstate politics. Duke Hsien (r. 676–52), who ruled when

TABLE 1.6   Affinal Relations of Ruling Lineages

State	Received Wives From	Gave Wives To
Ch'en	Cheng, Chou, I-*shih*, Ts'ai, Wei	Cheng, Hsi, Ts'ai, Wei
Cheng	Ch'en, Chiang, Shen	Ch'en, Sung
Ch'i	Chi-*shih*, Chou, Hsu, Lu, Sung, Ts'ai, Yen	Chin, Chou, Chu, Lu, Wei
Ch'in	Chin	Chin, Ch'u
Chin	Chi, Ch'i, Chia, Ch'in, Hsiao Jung, Liang, Ta Jung, Ti, Tu, Wei	Ch'in, Chu, Ch'u, Lu, Wu
Chou	Ch'en, Chi, Ch'i, Ti	Ch'en, Sung
Ch'u	Cheng, Chin, Ch'in, Teng, Wei, Yuan	Ts'ai
Lu	Chi, Ch'i, Chu, Mou, Shen, Shou, Sung, Tang-*shih*, Wu	Chi, Chi, Ch'i, Sung, Tang-*shih*, Tseng, Yen
Sung	Cheng, Chou, Lu, Wei	Ch'i, Lu, Wei
Ts'ai	Ch'u	Ch'i
Wei	Ch'en, Ch'i, Sung, Tung-kuo-*shih*	Ch'en, Chin, Ch'u, Hsu, Sung

SOURCES: *Ch'u-ch'iu* and *Tso-chuan.*
NOTE: This table does not include (1) the marriage of King Wu of Ch'u to Hsi Wei, who was the wife of the ruler of Hsi and a woman from Ch'en, whom he took as wife after destroying the state of Hsi in 680; (2) marriages for which the state or the lineage name of the spouse is unknown; and (3) concubines who were elevated to the status of wife.

Chin was building its regional power base, received brides from the ruling houses of the weaker nearby states of Chia and the barbarian Ta Jung and Hsiao Jung, presumably to secure the peace and obtain their allegiance, and he gave a daughter to Ch'in (whom Chin was not strong enough to dominate) in order to firm up friendship with this rival power. Duke Wen (r. 636–28), who had received a "courtesy" bride from the ruling house of Ch'i while in exile as a ducal son, was installed as ruler of Chin through the intervention of Duke Mu of Ch'in. His first act as ruler was to take a daughter of the latter as principal wife. (Although Duke Mu had earlier received a half sister of Duke Wen as wife, this marriage should be interpreted in its political context rather than as an obligatory marital exchange.) Under the leadership of Duke Wen, Chin took the role of hegemon away from Ch'i, establishing itself as one of the most powerful states of the Spring and Autumn period. The rulers of Chin, now hegemons, established marriage ties with the rulers of more distant rival states. In 550 Chin sent a ruler's daughter to the state of Wu, a newcomer to power politics (*TCCS* 35:9b [602, Hsiang 23]). Duke P'ing received a bride from Ch'i in 539 (*TCCS* 42:8b–9b [721–22, Chao 2]). In 537 Duke P'ing gave a daughter to King Ling of Ch'u, the chief competitor of Chin, who had requested the match because

Ch'u perceived itself to be in a weaker military position (*TCCS* 43:11a [747, Chao 5]). As instruments of interstate politics, marriages followed shifting alliances among the competing states.

The ruling elite recognized both specific and diffuse obligations to affines and matrilateral kin. Mourning rites were observed for deaths of affines (*TCCS* 35:11a [603, Hsiang 23]; 45:6a [779, Chao 9]). One ruler aided in building or repairing defensive walls around the capital city of his mother's home state (*TCCS* 29:6b [666, Hsiang 29]). The marriage of the ruler of Yü to the daughter of the chief minister of Sung bore fruit in 523 when her brother persuaded the duke of Sung to send an army against the state of Chu because it had attacked Yü in the previous year (*TCCS* 48:17b–18a [842, Chao 18], 22a [844, Chao 19]). Duke Mu of Ch'in installed two of his wife's half brothers, Duke Hui and Duke Wen, as rulers of Chin (*TCCS* 13:13a–14a [220, Hsi 9]; 15:16a [254, Hsi 24]). A speech of Lü Hsiang, breaking relations with Ch'in in 579, enumerates many more instances of how Chin and Ch'in had helped each other in dealing with other states and settling succession problems since the time of Duke Hsien and Duke Mu (*TCCS* 27:11b–12a [461, Ch'eng 13]).[25]

Much of the responsibility for achieving the goals of a political alliance based on or reinforced by marriage fell to the woman who was transferred by the marriage. From the perspective of the ruling house that gave its daughter to another ruling house in marriage, the woman was to become its agent in her new home. In the short run she was to use her influence to look after the interests of the state ruled by her natal lineage and in the long run to produce a line of heirs who would be amenable to maintaining friendly and supportive relations with it (for later periods, see Holmgren, chapter 2 of this volume). These short- and long-term objectives must have accelerated the practice of sending a niece and a younger sister of the principal bride as secondary brides who were there to further buttress affinal and matrilateral relations as secondary wives and childbearers.

After a daughter married out as a primary wife, she would occasionally return to visit her parents. She visited her natal family to inquire about the welfare of her parents after her marriage (*TCCS* 10:10b [175, Chuang 27]), to present her new child (*CCCS* 12:16b [204, Hsi 5], and sometimes to request a bride for her son (*CCCS* 16:1a [262, Hsi 25]; 17:8a [286, Hsi 31]). She could also return home if rejected by her husband or his lineage (*TCCS* 10:10b [175, Chuang 27—text and Tu commentary]). Parents continued to be concerned about the welfare of daughters who married out. For example, in 613 Duke Wen of Lu asked Ch'i to return a daughter, who had been married to Duke Chao, because her son had been assassinated immediately upon assuming the rulership. Although he claimed he wanted to punish her, Duke Wen's real intent was to protect her (*TCCS* 19b:15a–b [335, Wen 14], 18a [336, Wen 14], 25a [340, Wen 15]).

For their part, married women retained a strong loyalty toward and acted as agents for their natal lineages. If forced to choose between her husband and father, the married daughter was expected to put her father first. This is revealed in the resolution of the dilemma faced by Yung Chi, the daughter of Chi Chung, who was the most powerful officer in Cheng in 594. When her husband was ordered to assassinate her father and she became aware of it, she went to her mother for advice and asked, "Which one is dearer, husband or father?" Her mother responded with a rhetorical question, "Any man can be a husband, [but] a father is simply unique. How can they be compared?" Satisfied, she tipped off her father, and he killed her husband to save his own life (*TCCS* 7:20a–b [127, Huan 15]; see also *TCCS* 38:27a–b [655, Hsiang 28]). Wives of rulers intervened in government affairs in behalf of their native states, as when the wife of Duke Mu of Ch'in secured the release of her captured half brother, Duke Hui of Chin, in 645 (*TCCS* 14:6a–7a [231–32, Hsi 15]) and the widowed wife of former Duke Wen talked his successor into freeing three captured generals from her home state of Ch'in in 627 (*TCCS* 17:15b–16a [290, Hsi 33]). Besides looking after the interests of their native state in circumstances such as these, married daughters continued to have an interest in events at home. Mu Chi, the wife of Duke Mu of Ch'in, for example, tried to influence internal affairs of her natal lineage, the ducal house of Chin, when her husband installed her half brother I-wu as ruler of Chin in 650 (*TCCS* 14:2b [229, Hsi 15]).

Despite the political importance of the affinal ties created by marriage, divorce was permitted. Marriages were sometimes terminated by one of the spouses for personal reasons (*TCCS* 2:30a [42, Yin 2]), but divorces could also be forced by kinsmen seeking to maintain harmony within the lineage or family (*TCCS* 19a:16a–b [318, Wen 7]), out of personal animosity (*TCCS* 27:1b–2a [456, Ch'eng 11]), or to obtain certain political objectives (*TCCS* 27:2a–b [456, Ch'eng 11]; 58:26a–b [1018, Ai 11]). Nonkinsmen could also force the termination of a marriage to promote their own interests. For example, in 558 the officers of Cheng set the stage for taking action against a leading member of the T'u lineage by sending the wife of one of his kinsmen back to her natal lineage in Chin, thereby breaking the claim of the T'u lineage to assistance from affines in a powerful state (*TCCS* 32:26b [566, Hsiang 15—text and Tu commentary]).

Just as the implications of marriage went beyond the bride and groom to the relations between their respective lineages and, in the case of ruling houses, their states, divorce was an equally far-reaching matter because it potentially involved these relationships. I say "potentially" because a wife could be divorced without severing the affinal tie established with her lineage if the proper procedure were followed. Two examples of this process involve the ruling houses of Chi and Lu. In 616 when Duke Huan of Chi appeared for the first time in the court of Lu, the *Tso-chuan* says Duke Wen acceded to his request to break off his relationship with Shu Chi while preserving marital relations with the ruling house of Lu (*ch'ing chueh Shu Chi erh wu chueh hun*). In the second month of the same year, she passed away (*TCCS* 19:5a–b [330, Wen 12]). When Duke Huan came to court in Lu again in 587, the *Tso-chuan* states that "it was for the purpose of returning Shu Chi [another Lu bride]" (*TCCS* 26:6b [438, Ch'eng 4]). Duke Ch'eng of Lu evidently agreed, for Shu Chi moved back the following year (*CCCS* 26:8a [439, Ch'eng 5]). After she died, possibly by committing suicide, in 583 (*TCCS* 26:23a [447, Ch'eng 8]), Duke Huan agreed to come and take her body back to Chi for proper burial, as if she were still his wife (*TCCS* 26:24b [447, Ch'eng 9]). Under ordinary circumstances a divorced woman was no longer regarded as kin (*TCCS* 8:3b [137, Chuang 1]) and thus not entitled to funeral rites or mourning by her former affines.

CONCLUSION

In this chapter I have focused on marriage in the ruling elite, especially the ruling households, of the Spring and Autumn period. Particular attention has been paid to the ways that marriage practices were related to the political and social organization of the period. I shall conclude with some observations on the marriage system and its continuities and discontinuities in later periods.

The political, social, economic, and marriage systems, as well as kinship terminology, of the Spring and Autumn period exhibit most of the characteristics that Jack Goody has associated with dowry systems in Eurasian society (1973, 1976). The polity in this period was complex, with large states and highly stratified local societies; the economy was based on intensive agriculture including the animal-drawn plough; in-marriage was practiced in the form of class endogamy; premarital sex was proscribed (Chia 1980:23); and kinship terminology distinguished siblings from cousins (for the latter, see *EYCS* 4:14a–19a [61–64]). The practice of polygyny, however, is an important exception to Goody's formulation. The coexistence and convergence of polygyny and dowry in the Spring and Autumn period are explicable with reference to the political and social context of the time in which politics, not economics, determined social status and marriage strategies. Polygyny was used as a diplomatic tool by the lineages of both bride and groom. Dowry helped to confirm the primary-wife status of the principal bride of rulers and heads of patrilineages and to secure her loyalty to her natal state and/or lineage.

In the Spring and Autumn period the patrilineage was the exogamous kin group. No positive or prescriptive marriage rule was followed. Although patrilateral or matrilateral cross-cousin marriages may have occurred, there is no evidence that they were frequent or preferred. Bilateral marriages were more common, but again there is no evidence that they were reciprocal between cross-cousins or based on perpetual marriage alliances. Mate selection had to be flexible in order to attain political objectives.

I would now like to highlight some continuities with marriage practices in later periods of Chinese history. Here it is useful to distinguish between continuities in marriage practices in general and those associated with the ruling elite. As to the former, significant continuity exists in the overall ritual sequence, which shows similarities from the rulers of the Spring and Autumn period to ordinary people of relatively recent times. Elite practices and their codification in ritual texts have served as guides to marriage since Han times (Dull 1978:34–51). Marriage prestations in the form of betrothal gifts from the groom's side and dowry from the bride's side have continued with varying degrees of emphasis. Concubinage continued unabated through most later periods, but usually as an adjunct of monogamy rather than polygyny. Also noteworthy is the continuing tie between women and their natal families. Continuities with later imperial marriage practices can be discerned in the ordering of women in harems into several ranks, in the preference for sons by a wife for heir-apparent or successor, and even in the promotion of the mother of a proposed heir to improve appearances (see the chapters by Holmgren and Rawski here).

Exogamy has been a general feature of marriage practices from the earliest times to the present. Subtle historical differences, however, should not be overlooked. Prior to the Eastern Chou era the rule of surname exogamy applied to those who shared the same *hsing*, or clan name. In the Spring and Autumn period the patrilineage was the exogamous unit; so those with the same *shih*, or lineage name, did not intermarry. By Han times *hsing* and *shih* had become synonymous, and the unit of exogamy had constricted further to include only those descended from more recent common ancestors; consequently, the rule of surname exogamy could be violated, but one could not marry within his or her natal *tsung* (Dull 1978:29–30; Liu Tseng-kuei 1980: 10–11). In later periods, however, the scope of exogamy was officially extended to all those with the same surname.

Another important shift in marriage practices took place after the Spring and Autumn period. Later emperors, particularly in Chinese regimes, married within their realm, unlike rulers during the Spring and Autumn period, which may explain the absence of powerful consort families in the management of state and lineage affairs at that time. By contrast, most dynastic regimes were constantly faced with problems created by powerful consort families and influential court women (see Holmgren's chapter).

The two most striking discontinuities with marriage practices in later periods are found in taking more than one wife at a time and in the principal bride's family and lineage sending secondary brides. In the multistate system of the Spring and Autumn period, general polygyny was used by rulers as a survival strategy to multiply political alliances and extend affinal relations, while sororal polygyny served the political interests of the bride's family, lineage, and state by increasing the likelihood of producing a successor to the bride's husband who would be amenable to maintaining friendly relations with his mother's family. These political exigencies did not exist in the imperial period. The power of affines presented more significant problems than hostile regimes on the outside. Taking additional wives would have compounded those problems.

Perhaps a more fundamental reason, however, for these discontinuities and the relative insignificance of dowry in the early imperial period (see chapter 3 by Ebrey) is the sweeping social and political changes that accelerated in the Warring States period and culminated in the formation of the empire. The upper echelons of the ruling elite were gradually swept away as powerful ministerial lineages rose to displace their ruling houses, and states were eliminated one by one in the process of unification. Officials of *shih* rank moved to the top of the official hierarchy, then major reforms, such as those instituted by Shang Yang in Ch'in (Li 1977:37–40), altered the system of ranks and fundamentally changed the status system, thereby depriving the old aristocracy of its prerogatives and enabling commoners to rise to high rank and status. By the time of the formation of the empire, the old aristocracy and its more extravagant ways had been swept away, and a new elite of commoner background was in place with its more modest customs and practices.

NOTES

1. All dates except those in citations are B.C. unless otherwise noted.

2. Two kinds of relationships not included here and in the discussion that follows are "cohabitation with consorts of one's father" (*cheng*) and "cohabitation with one's aunt" (*pao*). Some classify these relationships as forms of marriage (Li Hui 1954; Li Tsung-t'ung 1954, 2:154–60; Liu Te-han 1976:52–53). At the time they were generally regarded as aberrant and unacceptable types of behavior, however, even if some long-term relationships were established as a result of them. Two examples clearly show this to have been the case. First, prior to 660 when Chao Po of Wei refused to cohabit with the principal wife of his late father, the officers of Ch'i, her natal state, forced him to do so (*TCCS* 11:10a [191, Min 2]). And, second, the wife of Duke Mu of Ch'in became upset with her half brother, Duke Hui of Chin, because, among other things, he cohabited with Chia-chün, the concubine of their late father, whom she had entrusted to his care when Duke Mu installed him as ruler of Chin in 650 (*TCCS* 14: 2a–b [229, Hsi 15]).

Cohabitation was regarded as an illicit relationship rather than as another socially sanctioned form of marriage, a perception that is also evident in early lexicons. The *Fang-yen* defines *cheng* as *yin* (*FY* 12:7a), which means "to roam or wander" (*yu*) and is synonymous in local dialect with "to play" (*hsi*), "reckless, vagrant" (*tang*), and "to amuse oneself" (*hsi*) (*FY* 10:1a–b). The *Kuang-ya* defines both *cheng* and *pao* as *yin* and lumps them together with "illicit intercourse" (*t'ung*), "licentious" (*yao*), "frivolous" (*t'iao*), "excessive" (*yi*), and "vagrant" (*tang*) (*KYSC* 1a:135–36).

3. Here I follow Robin Fox, who defines lineage as a kin group in which descent from a common ancestor "can be demonstrated and is not simply assumed" and clans as "higher order units often consisting of several lineages in which common descent is assumed but cannot necessarily be demonstrated" (1976:49), and Jack Goody who classifies clans and lineages as unilineal descent groups, with clan being "the largest such unit, the members of which acknowledge common descent. . . but are unable to specify the exact ties" and lineages being more restricted units in which "specific genealogical ties are recognized" (1983:224).

4. The manner in which lineages split off from each other is clear from the historical record of the Western Chou and Spring and Autumn periods. Meritorious civil and military officials who were rewarded with hereditary land grants established their families there. They and their heirs were able to use the wealth generated from these grants to support their kinsmen and to attract followers and private soldiers. By the third generation the lineage and its new name (*shih*) were well established. When land grants were made to more than one person in a lineage, the result was often segmentation of the lineage and formation of ritually independent lineages through fission. (For more on the origins of lineages, see Sun 1931:4–17.)

5. The *Tso-chuan* gives only one possible example of uxorilocal marriage (see *TCCS* 7:20a–b (127, Huan 15]).

6. That they were not married earlier can be inferred from the following anecdote. When Ch'ung-erh, as he was then known, was about to leave for Ch'i, he tried to persuade Chi Wei to marry someone else if he did not return for her within twenty-five years. She allegedly refused, saying, "I am [already] twenty-five years old! If I [wait twenty-five more years] then marry, I will [have one foot in] the casket. I beg to wait for you" (*TCCS* 15:9b [251, Hsi 23]).

7. This probably was a factor in the marriages of Duke Chuang of Wei and Duke Hsien of Chin, whose first wives were infertile (for the latter, see *TCCS* 10:13a [177, Chuang 28]). If this was the motivation behind the marriages of Duke Huan of Ch'i, then his luck was extremely bad, for all three of his primary wives failed to bear children. Fortunately, the most favored concubines in his harem provided plenty of male progeny (*TCCS* 14:18a–b [237]).

8. In earlier versions of this chapter I referred to secondary brides as dowry brides because of the term *ying*. The *Erh-ya* defines *ying* as a verb "to send [something] to (*chiang sung*)" (*EYCS* 3:4a [38]). As a noun it refers to the thing or person sent. In Western and Eastern Chou bronze inscriptions that record the sending or giving of bronze vessels as dowry, *ying* is usually written with a cowry (*pei*) radical, connoting the sending of things (see n. 14 below). However, in the *Tso-chuan* it is used as a verb and written with the female (*nü*) radical, reflecting the practice of sending females as secondary spouses. When these females were provided from other families or lineages, they were sent to the family of the bride instead of directly to the groom. In effect, they were given to the bride and came into the marriage with her like the bronze vessel she received from her father as dowry. Nevertheless, they, too, became spouses of the groom, who retained possession of them in the case of divorce or separation from the principal bride (*TCCS* 12:25b [205, Hsi 5]). As Pat Ebrey has suggested in our discussions about this practice, however, it seems unlikely that parents who gave daughters

in this fashion would have regarded them as mere objects comparable to the kinds of things that usually made up dowry.

That parents did not view such daughters as things is clear in the refusal by one set of parents to replace a principal bride, who had died, because her younger sister was also married to the husband of the deceased and had borne a child by him (*TCCS* 19a: 16a [316, Wen 7]). There is at least one case, however, of the bride's family replacing a daughter who was married out as principal bride and had died prematurely despite the presence of a fertile secondary spouse from her family or lineage (*TCCS* 2:3b [29, Yin 1]). In this instance, the objective of the bride's family seems to have been to ensure that one of its daughters held the status of primary wife (*fu-jen*) in their son-in-law's household. I do not think that the bride's family was necessarily showing disregard for other daughters already in the household as secondary wives. I have therefore accepted Ebrey's point and chosen to refer to females who accompanied the principal bride and became secondary wives of her husband as secondary brides instead of dowry brides.

The term *ying* appears frequently in the *Shih-hun-li* chapter of the *I-li* in the sense of "handmaid" or "bridesmaid." Female servants were also part of the dowry of ruling elite brides in the Spring and Autumn period (*TCCS* 39: 23b [1036, Ai 15]), but the status of women in the household who entered as secondary brides was not the same as those who are identified as *ying* in this late source (refer to n. 15 below). By the time of the documentation of *shih*-class marriages in the *I-li*, the giving of daughters as secondary brides had ceased, and the only females who came into a marriage besides the bride were her maids.

9. The *Tso-chuan* states that prior to 722 when Meng Tzu, the principal wife of Duke Hui, died, her role was continued (*chi shih*) by Sheng Tzu. Tu Yü supposes that she may have been the niece or younger sister of Meng Tzu. He says that when the principal wife died, her place was taken by the next, or second, wife, who could not be referred to as the primary wife of a ruler (*fu-jen*); so she was called *chi-shi* (*TCCS* 2:3a [29, preface to Yin 1]). *Chi-shih* is commonly understood to mean "second wife"; but in both of the examples cited here, *chi* and *shih* function as verb + object, meaning literally "to continue, or succeed to, the [inner] chamber." The use of *chi-shih* as a compound noun in the sense of "second wife" is a later meaning derived from this usage. Chao I argues persuasively that there is no instance in the *Tso-chuan* where *chi-shih* has the meaning of "second wife," a usage that he says may not have become current until after the Han dynasty (*KYTK* 26:790–91). Nevertheless, the niece or younger sister who accompanied the bride into the household of her husband was eligible to become her de facto successor, even if only temporarily, as was the case with Sheng Tzu, who had to give way later to a new principal wife when the duke of Sung married his daughter Chung Tzu to Duke Hui (*TCCS* 2:3b [29, Yin 1]).

10. The *Kuo yü* has Duke Huan saying that his father Duke Hsiang "venerated only women, had nine wives (*fei*) and six special concubines (*pin*), and could array ordinary concubines numbering several hundred." While one commentator says that the nine *fei* refer to the women who came from three states as female dowry with his bride, Wei Chao argues that only the proper wife was called *fei* and that nieces and younger sisters were called ordinary concubines (*ch'ieh*) (*KY* 6:2a [159, "Ch'i yü"]). I think that the *Kuo yü* actually describes Duke Huan talking about himself. The nine *fei* are his three wives and the nieces and younger sisters who accompanied them, and the six *pin* are the concubines whom he favored like wives.

11. The frequency with which heirs-apparent were set aside by rulers of states, and heads of ministerial lineages as well, during the Spring and Autumn period suggests that from the perspective of the father all sons were prospective heirs regardless of the rank or status of their mothers. Nevertheless, as in the case of Duke Ai of Lu, installing as wife the concubine mother of the selected heir-apparent was somehow viewed as setting things right.

12. The succession problem that had arisen in Chin was precipitated by the fact that the legitimate heir of the deceased ruler Duke Hsiang was too young to succeed him. However, neither the fact that the heir-apparent of King P'ing of Ch'u, who died in 516, was still young or that his mother was not the king's principal wife stopped him from ascending the throne. The boy's mother had been requested from Ch'in to be wed to the original heir-apparent of King P'ing in 523, but upon the advice of the heir-apparent's disgruntled tutor the king had taken her for his own bride instead, and she became one of his primary wives (*TCCS* 48:21b–22a [844, Chao 19]). In this case an elder half brother of King P'ing turned down the opportunity to replace him as king, pointing out that since the boy's mother was from a powerful state and he had been appointed heir-apparent by the king, not to install him would bring enmity from affines and bad luck (*TCCS* 52:6a–b [902, Chao 26]).

13. *TCCS* 2:30a (42, Yin 2); *CCCS* 7:2b (118, Huan 8); *TCCS* 7:4b (119, Huan 8); *CCCS* 18:18s (305, Wen 4); *TCCS* 18:19b (306, Wen 4); *TCCS* 22:3b (377, Hsuan 6—text and Tu commentary); *CCCS* 32:23a (565, Hsiang 15); *TCCS* 32:23b–24a (565, Hsiang 15), 51:7a (888, Chao 25).

14. *TCCS* 4:9b (74, Yin 8); *CCCS* 10:3a (172, Chuang 24); *TCCS* 15:16b (254, Hsi 24), 22:2a (376, Hsüan 5), 45:8a (780, Chao 9—text and Tu commentary).

15. Yang Po-chün argues cogently that in the marriage process the term *sung* is used in two senses; namely, as it is defined in the *Shuo-wen*, "to send off," and also synonymously with *chih*, which is defined in the *Shuo-wen* as "to escort to the final destination" (4:1228 [Chao 5]). Both *sung* and *chih* are used in the two meanings suggested by Yang, and *chih* is used in the sense of "to present [the bride] to [her husband]" (see below).

16. The betrothal and marriage rituals outlined here generally conform to those described in the *Shih hun-li* ("*Shih* marriage rituals") chapter of the *I-li* (*ILCS* 4:1a–6:15b). This fact stands as evidence that the *I-li* description of marriage rituals is based on historical practices. One should point out, however, that the marriage rituals presented in this chapter of the *I-li* are for the *shih* class, probably of the Warring States period, and not the higher-level ruling houses and *ch'ing* and *tai-fu* classes of the Spring and Autumn period. The *shih* marriage rituals of the *I-li* appear to be scaled-down versions of the rituals of the ruling elite.

17. For some examples, see *YCCWCL* inscriptions 166, 561, 594, 813, 817, 818, 823, 824, 827, 830, 832, 931, 933, and 966; also Chia 1980:17–18.

18. For a psychological argument against clan endogamy, see (*KY* 10:8a–b [259–60, "Chin-yü 4]). This view appears about a century earlier as part of argumentation by Ssu-k'ung Chi-tzu to persuade Kung-tzu Ch'ung-erh of Chin to marry Huai Ying, who had been previously married to Tzu-lo (aka Duke Huai), the son of his half brother I-wu (aka Duke Hui). Duke Mu of Ch'in had given his daughter to Tzu-lo when the latter was sent to Ch'in as hostage, but she had elected to stay behind when he escaped and returned to Chin to succeed his father as ruler there. Ch'ung-erh was now in Ch'in preparing to usurp the ducal position from his nephew. Ssu-k'ung Chi-

tzu begins his argument by referring to the case of Huang-ti and Yen-ti, who had the same father but different mothers and surnames. He concludes it saying, "Now you and Tzu-lo are strangers. As to taking what he has abandoned in order to achieve [your] major objective, can it not be done?" (*KY* 10:8a–9a [259–60, "Chin yü" 4]).

In discussing this anecdote, Yang Hsi-mu claims Tzu-lo had been a slave in Ch'in and that Huai Ying had assumed his status by virtue of their marriage; so Ch'ung-erh did not want to marry her because of the difference in their statuses. Yang says that Ch'ung-erh and Tzu-lo were like strangers because they both intended to rule the state (1963a:1–5). Chao Lin, advocating the existence of a four-class marriage system in the Chou era, argues that they were strangers because Ch'ung-erh and I-wu were born of different mothers and, therefore, not of the same *hsing* and category (or kind). Thus, Ch'ung-erh need not view Tzu-lo as his brother's son. This being the case, he could marry Huai Ying (Chao n.d.: 72–79).

In my opinion, this anecdote demonstrates an aversion to leviratic marriage (Feng 1937:51–54). The idea that the status of Huai Ying was that of a slave does not agree with Duke Mu's professed love and concern for his daughter as the reason for presenting her to Ch'ung-erh. Ssu-k'ung Chi-tzu was trying to overcome Ch'ung-erh's aversion to marrying his nephew's wife by pointing out that *she* was of a different *hsing* and by appealing to his political estrangement from Tzu-lo in order to negate their agnatic relationship. There is no acceptable evidence from the Spring and Autumn period for the contention that the clan affiliation of children was determined by the mother. Although females were identified by their clan name (*hsing*) rather than their lineage name (*shih*), the clan name was passed on to them through the paternal line.

19. The stratified society of the Kachin of Burma, described and analyzed by E. R. Leach (1954), is held up as the classic example of this kind of system. There the prescriptive MBD marriage rule has resulted in the formation of marriage alliances involving three or more lineages in which no lineage can take wives from any other lineage to which it has given its own women as brides. The movement of women is unidirectional in a circular fashion, for example, from lineage A to lineage B to lineage C to lineage A. Leach states that among the Kachin, wife-givers tend to have higher political status than wife-receivers, and that the latter are vassals of the former. These relationships also structure the political relationship between villages, which are based on "exogamous patrilineages of small span," within a village cluster (1954:78–85). Fox maintains (1967) that in this kind of marriage system wife-receivers incur a debt to wife-givers that can never be repaid through the exchange of women. Although the debt can be canceled by the payment of bridewealth, if the wife-givers are politically or socially superior to wife-receivers, then the former will always be superior to the latter. When the connubium is confined to one social class, its effect is seen to be democratic because no single lineage can be absolutely superior on the basis of giving brides; however, when women marry down class, then it reinforces the social hierarchy (Fox 1967:209–14).

20. I have found, however, one example of a marriage between classificatory patrilateral cross-cousins. The mother of the wife of Chi P'ing-tzu of Lu was the daughter of the elder sister of Chi's father's half brother (*TCCS* 51:6a–7a [887–88, Chao 25—text and Tu commentary]).

21. Among the marriages between Ch'i and Lu, the marriage of Duke Chuang of Lu to Ai Chiang of Ch'i (*CCCS* 10:3a [172, Chuang 24]) provides the only possible example of marriage with MBD, if she is the daughter of Duke Hsi, who was the

brother of Wen Chiang, the wife of Duke Chuang. Of the seven rulers of Lu who married Ch'i women, only two were born of Ch'i women, namely, Duke Chuang and his son Duke Min, the latter being born of Shu Chiang, who was the younger sister of Ai Chiang, the principal bride of his father (*TCCS* 11:7b [190, Min 2]). Duke Hsiang, the great-great-grandson of Shu Chiang, is the last ruler of Lu shown marrying a woman from the ruling house of Ch'i. The clearest examples of MBD marriages are the return to Lu of Tang Po Chi to meet a wife for her son in 635 (*CCCS* 16:1a [262, Hsi 25]) and of Chi Po Chi to request a wife for her son in 629 (*CCCS* 17:8a [286, Hsi 31]).

22. The major state of Chin received a bride from its equal Ch'i and from its inferiors Chia, Ta Jung, and Hsiao Jung; it gave daughters to its equals Ch'u and Wu and its inferiors Lu (路) and Chu. The major state of Ch'i received brides from its inferiors Hsu, Sung, and Ts'ai; it gave daughters to its equal Chin and its inferiors Yen, Wei, and Chu. The state of Lu received a bride from Wu, which was its political superior but ritual inferior; it gave daughters to its inferiors Yen, Chi (紀), and Tseng. The state of Wei received a bride from its superior Ch'i; it gave daughters to its superiors Chin and Ch'u, its equal Cheng, and its inferior Hsü (許).

23. One of these marriages was initiated from the bride's side with the intent of making a good match with a son-in-law whose posterity were predicted to flourish (*TCCS* 9:23a [163, Chuang 22]), and the other was forced by the ruler's son, who was serving as chief minister, while he was in the bride's state on business (*TCCS* 41:3a–4a [697, Chao 1]). In Cheng two ducal grandsons, who held *tai-fu* rank, competed for the hand of the beautiful younger sister of an official (*TCCS* 41:14b–16a [702–3, Chao 1]).

24. Kao Ku of Ch'i extorted a bride from Duke Hsüan of Lu in 604 by having him detained in Ch'i (*TCCS* 21:1b–2b [376, Hsuan 5]). While in exile, Kung-tzu Ch'ung-erh took one of the two women originally given to him by his Ti hosts and married her to his loyal follower Chao Shuai (*TCCS* 15:9a–b [251, Hsi 23]). After gaining the rulership of Chin, he married his own daughter to Chao Shuai (*TCCS* 15:16b–17a [254–55, Hsi 24]). Thereafter, at least one grandson of Chao Shuai and another segment of the Chao lineage also married daughters of the ruling house of Chin (*TCCS* 26:8a [439, Ch'eng 4—Tu gloss on Chao Chi], 19b:7a [331, Wen 11]). In 552 Chi Wu-tzu, the chief official of Lu, married a paternal aunt of Duke Hsiang to an official from Chu who had defected to Lu with two towns under his control (*TCCS* 34:12a–b [589, Hsiang 21]; *CCTCC* 3:1056—[Yang commentary]). By treachery and deceit Ch'ü Wu (aka Shen-kung Wu-ch'en) of Ch'u was able to wed the much-married Hsia Chi, a daughter of the ruler of Cheng, in 589 (*TCCS* 25:19a–20b [428, Ch'eng 2]). Chi Mi, the younger sister of King Chao of Ch'u, was married to Chung Chien in 505 in order to preserve her purity, for he had carried her on his back when the king had fled to Yuan to escape the invading army from Wu in the previous year (*TCCS* 54:25a–b [925, Ting 4], 55:4a [959, Ting 5]). In 484 reference is made to two earlier marriages of officers of Wei to daughters of rulers' sons who had gone there in exile (*TCCS* 58:26a–27b [1018–19, Ai 18]). In 480 the exiled heir-apparent of the duke of Wei was able to return with the aid of his elder sister, the wife of K'ung Wen-tzu, an oppressive official who had just died (*TCCS* 59:23a–b [1036, Ai 15]).

25. This is not to say that affines were always dependable allies in external and domestic affairs, as Lu Hsiang's litany of complaints against Ch'in also shows (*TCCS* 27:12a–15b [461–63, Ch'eng 13]).

GLOSSARY

cheng 蒸, 烝
ch'i 妻
chi-shih 繼室
chi-shih i ch'i chih 繼室以其姪
chiang-sung 將送
ch'ieh 妾
chih (elder brother's daughter) 姪
chih (to escort to the final destination) 致
chih fu-jen 致夫人
ch'ing 卿
ch'ing chueh Shu Chi erh wu chueh hun 請絕叔姬而無絕婚
chiu 舅
chiu-sheng 舅甥
ch'ü 娶
erh-fei 二妃
fei 妃
feng-t'ien 封田
fu-jen 夫人
hsi (to amuse oneself) 嬉
hsi (to play) 戲
hsia-ch'ing 下卿
hsia-fei 下妃
hsia-guo 下國
hsing 姓
kuei 歸
mu-ti 母弟
nan nü pien hsing 男女辨姓
nü 女
pan 班
pan tsai chiu jen 班在九人
pan tsai ssu 班在四

pa 霸
pao 報
pei 貝
pi 幣
pi-tzu 嬖子
pin 嬪
p'in 聘
pu ch'i pi 布其幣
shang-ch'ing 上卿
shang-tai-fu 上大夫
sheng 甥
shih (officer) 士
shih (lineage name) 氏
shih-ssu 適嗣
sung 送
ta-kuo 大國
tai-fu 大夫
tang 錫
tang 惕
ti (younger sister) 娣
ti (legitimate heir) 敵
t'iao 窕
t'ung 通
tsung 宗
tz'u-kuo 次國
ya 亞
yao 嬈
yi 劮
yin 姪
ying 媵, 睦, 媻
yu 遊
yuan fei 元妃

REFERENCES

Primary Sources

CCSTP *Ch'un-ch'iu shih-tsu p'u* 春秋世族譜, comp. Ch'en Hou-yao 陳厚耀. In *Shao-wu Hsu-shih ts'ung-shu* 邵武徐氏叢書.

CCTCC *Ch'un-ch'iu Tso-chuan chu* 春秋左傳注, comp. Yang Po-chün 楊伯峻. Peking: Chung-hua shu-chü, 1981.

CCTK *Ching-chi tsuan-ku* 經籍纂詁. Taipei: Wen wen, 1967.

CCTSP *Ch'un-ch'iu ta-shih piao* 春秋大事表, comp. Ku Tung-kao 顧棟高. In *Huang-Ch'ing ching-chieh hsu-pien* 皇清經解續編, vol. 3.

EYCS   *Erh-ya chu-shu* 爾雅注疏. *SSCCS* edition.

FY   *Fang-yen* 方言, by Yang Hsiung 楊雄, with commentary by Kuo P'u 郭璞. Ssu-k'u ch'üan-shu chen-pen pieh-chi 四庫全書珍本別輯 edition. Taipei: Commercial Press, 1975.

ILCS   *I-li chu-shu* 儀禮注疏. *SSCCS* edition.

KY   *T'ien-sheng ming-tao pen kuo yü* 天聖明道本國語, commentary by Wei Chao 韋昭. Photolithic reprint edition. Taipei: I-wen, 1969.

KYCS   *Kung-yang chu-shu* 公羊注疏. *SSCCS* edition.

KYSC   *Hsin-shih piao-tien kuang-ya shu-cheng* 新式標點廣雅疏證, punctuated by Chan Hong-kam 陳雄根. Hong Kong: Chinese University Press, 1978.

KYTK   *Kai-yü ts'ung-k'ao* 陔餘叢考, by Chao Yi 趙翼. Shanghai: Commercial Press, 1957. Based on *Chan-i-t'ang* 湛貽堂 edition, 1790.

MTCS   *Meng-tzu chu-shu* 孟子注疏. *SSCCS* edition.

SSCCS   *Shih-san-ching chu-shu* 十三經注疏, comp. Juan Yuan 阮元. Photolithic reprint edition. Taipei: I-wen, 1973.

TCCS   *Tso-chuan chu-shu* 左傳注疏, comp. K'ung Ying-ta 孔穎達. *SSCCS* edition.

TCHC   *Tso-chuan hui-chien* 左傳會箋, comp. Takezoe Kōkō 竹添光鴻. Taiwan: n.p., n.d.

YCCWCL   *Yin-Chou chin-wen chi-lu* 殷周金文集錄, ed. Hsu Chung-shu 徐仲舒. Szechwan: Jen-min, 1984.

Secondary Works

Chang, K. C. 1976. *Early Chinese Civilizations: Anthropological Perspectives*. Cambridge: Harvard University Press.

———. 1983. *Art, Myth, and Ritual: The Path to Political Authority in Ancient China*. Cambridge: Harvard University Press.

Chao, Lin. N.d. *Marriage, Inheritance, and Lineage Organization in Shang-Chou China*. Taipei: I-chih.

Ch'en, T. S., and J. K. Shyrock. 1932. "Chinese Relationship Terms." *American Anthropologist* 34:623–69.

Ch'i Ssu-ho 齊思和. 1981. *Chung-kuo shih t'an-yen* 中國史探研 (Inquiries into Chinese history). Peking: Chung-hua shu-chü.

Chia Shih-heng 賈士蘅. 1980. "Yin-Chou fu-nü sheng-huo ti chi-ke mien" 殷周婦女生活的幾個面 (Some aspects of women's life during Yin and Chou dynasties). *Ta-lu tsa-chih* 60.5:7–39.

Creel, Herlee G. 1970. *The Origins of Statecraft in China*. Chicago: University of Chicago Press.

Dull, Jack. 1978. "Marriage and Divorce in Han China: A Glimpse at Pre-Confucian Society." In *Chinese Family Law and Social Change in Historical and Comparative Perspective*, ed. David C. Buxbaum. Seattle: University of Washington Press.

Feng, Han-yi. 1937. *The Chinese Kinship System*. Reprinted from *Harvard Journal of Asiatic Studies* 2:2 (July 1937). Taipei: Southern Materials Center, Inc.

Fox, Robin. 1967. *Kinship and Marriage*. Middlesex, Eng.: Penguin.

Goody, Jack. 1973. "Bridewealth and Dowry in Africa and Eurasia." In *Bridewealth and Dowry*, by Jack Goody and S. J. Tambiah. Cambridge: Cambridge University Press.

―――. 1976. *Production and Reproduction: A Comparative Study of the Domestic Domain.* Cambridge: Cambridge University Press.

―――. 1983. *The Development of the Family and Marriage in Europe.* Cambridge: Cambridge University Press.

Granet, Marcel. 1920. *La polygynie sororale et le sororat dans la Chine féodale.* Paris: Editions Ernest Leroux.

―――. 1930. *Chinese Civilization.* London: Routledge & Kegan Paul.

Hsu, Cho-yun. 1965. *Ancient China in Transition: An Analysis of Social Mobility, 722–222 B.C.* Stanford: Stanford University Press.

―――. 1984. *Hsi-Chou shih* 西周史 (A history of the Western Chou dynasty). Taipei: Lien-ching.

Leach, E. R. 1954. *Political Systems of Highland Burma: A Study of Kachin Social Structure.* London: G. Bell and Sons.

Li Hui 李卉. 1954. "Chung-kuo ku-tai ti shou-chi-hun" 中國古代的收繼婚 (Levirate marriage in ancient China). *Ta-lu tsa-chih* 9.4:17–20.

Li Tsung-t'ung 李宗侗. 1954. *Chung-kuo ku-tai she-hui-shih* 中國古代社會史 (Social history of ancient China). 2 vols. Taipei: Chung-hua wen-hua.

Li Hsueh-ch'in 李學勤. 1984. *Tung-Chou yü Ch'in-tai wen-ming* 東周與秦代文明 (The civilization of the Eastern Chou and Ch'in dynasties). Peking: Jen-min.

Li Yu-ning, ed. 1977. *Shang Yang's Reforms and State Control in China.* White Plains.

Liu Po-chi 劉伯驥. 1962. *Ch'un-ch'iu hui-meng cheng-chih* 春秋會盟政治 (Government by alliance during the Spring and Autumn period). Taipei: Chung-hua ts'ung-shu.

Liu Te-han 劉德漢. 1976. *Tung-Chou fu-nü sheng-huo* 東周婦女生活 (The life of women during the Eastern Chou). Taipei: Hsueh-sheng.

Liu Tseng-kuei 劉增貴. 1980. *Han-tai hun-yin chih-tu* 漢代婚姻制度 (The institution of marriage during the Han dynasty). Taipei: Hua-shih.

Liu Tse-hua 劉澤華 et al. 1979. *Chung-kuo ku-tai shih* 中國古代史 (A history of ancient China). Peking: Jen-min.

Lü Ssu-mien 呂思勉. 1941; reprint, 1962. *Hsien Ch'in shih* 先秦史 (A history of pre-Ch'in China). Hong Kong: T'ai-ping.

Ruey, Yih-fu. 1958. "The Similarity of the Ancient Chinese Kinship Terminology to the Omaha Type." *Bulletin of the Department of Archaeology and Anthropology* (Academia Sinica) 12:1–18.

―――芮逸夫. 1959. "Shih sheng-chiu chih kuo" 釋甥舅之國 ("Nephew and uncle" states: an interpretation). *Bulletin of the Institute of History and Philology* (Academia Sinica) 30.1:237–58.

Sun Yueh 孫曜. 1931; reprint, 1976. *Ch'un-ch'iu shih-tai ti shih-tsu* 春秋時代的世族 (Influential clans of the Spring and Autumn period). Ching-mei.

T'ang Ming-sui 湯明檖. 1982. *Chung-kuo ku-tai she-hui ching-chi shih* 中國古代社會經濟史 (Social and economic history of ancient China). Honan: Chung-chou.

Thatcher, Melvin P. 1977–78. "A Structural Comparison of the Central Governments of Ch'u, Ch'i, and Chin." *Monumenta Serica* 33:140–41.

―――. 1985. "Central Government of the State of Ch'in in the Spring and Autumn Period." *Journal of Oriental Studies* 23.1:29–53.

Walker, Richard Louis. 1953. *The Multi-state System of Ancient China*. Hamden, Conn.: Shoestring Press.

Wang Kuo-wei 王國維. 1973. *Kuan-t'ang chi-lin* 觀堂集林 (Collected writings of Kuan-t'ang). Reprint. Hong Kong: Chung-hua shu-chü.

Yang Hsi-mei 楊希牧. 1963a. "*Kuo-yü* Huang-ti erh-shih-wu tzu te hsing ch'uan-shuo ti fen-hsi shang p'ien" 國語黃帝二十五子得姓傳說的分析上篇 (A study of the legend of Huang-ti's descendants in the *Kuo-yü*). *Bulletin of the Institute of History and Philology* (Academia Sinica) 34.2:627–48.

———. 1963b. "Lun 'Chin-yü' Huang-ti ch'uan-shuo yü Ch'in Chin lien-yin ti ku-shih" 論晉語黃帝傳說與秦晉聯姻的故事 (On the legend of Huang-ti in the "Chin-yü" and stories of marriages of alliance between Ch'in and Chin). *Ta-lu tsa-chih* 26.6:1–6.

Yang K'uan 楊寬. 1980. *Chan-kuo shih* 戰國史 (History of the Warring States). 2d ed. Shanghai: Jen-min.

TWO

Imperial Marriage in the
Native Chinese and Non-Han State,
Han to Ming

Jennifer Holmgren

For about half its recorded history, China has been ruled either in part or wholly by peoples of non-Chinese (non-Han) origin. Indeed, in the last thousand years only two of six imperial families were of local or native Chinese background. The others came from the steppe/Manchurian area to the north of China proper (see the Chronology). One aspect of the cultural interaction during such periods of conquest has long fascinated both Chinese and Western scholars—namely, the influence of those northern cultures on Chinese attitudes toward women. It is often suggested, for example, that the high political profile of imperial wives and princesses during the early T'ang period (seventh–eighth centuries) was the result of the relatively high status of women in steppe society and their consequent involvement in court politics during the preceding conquest era. In a similar vein, the well-documented concern of the founder of the Ming dynasty to restrict the power of imperial wives in the fourteenth century has been seen as a reaction against the authority assumed by such women in the preceding Mongol-Yuan era. Although firmly entrenched in both the scholarly and the popular imagination, this hypothesis has never been seriously tested; it is based on accounts of curious lives and extraordinary events rather than on an examination of the principles behind continuity and change. This chapter seeks to redress that situation by looking at the structure underlying attitudes to imperial marriage and the political role of the emperor's wife in the native Chinese and non-Han state.

The first section of the chapter begins by establishing the principles behind events commonly encountered in the historical narrative of the native state from Han times through to the end of the Ming dynasty (206 B.C.–A.D. 1644). For our purposes, the most illustrative events include disputes between the emperor and the bureaucracy over the appointment of an empress;

accusations that imperial relatives were conspiring to usurp the throne; dethronements by dowager empresses; complaints about the conduct of imperial princesses; harem disputes leading to the murder of imperial wives and their offspring; and so forth. These "structural principles" are then used to evaluate the changes within and across individual native regimes. I shall show that some conditions previously thought to be unique to one particular period (and thus probably the result of foreign influence or externally derived ideas) are easily explained without reference to the non-Han state.

The second section of the chapter demonstrates the variety and political ingenuity of marriage systems designed by the leaders of the conquest dynasties. For reasons that shall become apparent, each non-Han regime is discussed separately. Three states, whose histories span both sides of the T'ang-Sung transition era—the T'o-pa state of Wei (A.D. 399–534), the Ch'i-tan (Khitan) Liao dynasty (A.D. 916–1122), and the Mongol empire (c. A.D. 1200–1368)—have been selected for investigation. The final section discusses how an analysis of the non-Han condition throws new light on the question of continuity and change in Chinese society and then summarizes the political status of different sets of imperial kin in each of the systems described

In this essay three main categories of the emperor's kin are distinguished—paternal, maternal, and sororal. The term "paternal kin" covers male and female relatives in the male line (e.g., the emperor's father's siblings, his father's brothers' offspring, his own siblings, his brother's offspring, etc.), while that of "maternal kin" (matrilateral kin) embraces relationships established through the mother (e.g., the emperor's mother's parents and her siblings and their offspring). The term "sororal relative" covers relationships established through the marriages of princesses (the emperor's paternal aunts [FZ], sisters, and daughters); i.e., it refers to the offspring of these women, their husbands, husbands' parents, and siblings (wife-taking families).

This chapter outlines the social and political inequalities between the different sets of women whose marriages provided the essential building blocks for political activity at court and highlights some unexpected features of the unequal relations between these women and the various males (including the emperor) with whom they were closely associated. Where non-Han states are concerned, the chapter also touches on the question of marriage and ethnic inequality. The theme of inequality between imperial clanswomen and their spouses is addressed more broadly by John W. Chaffee in his chapter on the Sung, while that of marriage and ethnic inequality is taken up again by Evelyn S. Rawski in her chapter on the Ch'ing.

THE NATIVE CHINESE STATE

In general, laws and regulations relating to marriage in the larger society also prevailed at the imperial level of the native Chinese state. Some were already in place in preimperial times (see Thatcher's chapter in this volume) and may be summarized as follows: (1) surname exogamy (*TL* 14:262–63; *SHT* 14:218–19; *ML* 6:16; Feng 1948:33–46); (2) serial monogamy with concubinage (*TL* 13:255; *SHT* 13:214; *TML* 13:275; Ch'ü 1972:46); (3) the wife as titular or legal mother to all offspring (Tjan 1949:260; Watson's chapter in this volume); (4) a ban on demoting wives to the rank of concubine and on elevating concubines to the status of wife (*SHT* 13:214–15; *ML* 6:9–10; *TML* 13:275–76; Ebrey 1986); and (5) a ban on cross-generational alliance (*TL* 14:263; *SHT* 14:218–19; *TML* 14:287; Ch'ü 1961:94–95). At the imperial level, the emphasis on monogamy meant that the title of empress went to the woman who had held the position of wife before her husband's accession to the throne. It also meant that there could be only one empress at any one time (Chung 1981:147) and that she was the titular mother of the next ruler whether or not she herself was his biological mother. The rule of surname exogamy meant that no matter how distant the relationship, members of the ruling family could not marry imperial clansmen but had to marry out and downward. Finally, although cousins of a different surname might marry (MBD/FZD), unions between heirs to the throne and their aunts (MZ/FZ) or nieces (FDD/MDD) were forbidden (see n. 3). These restrictions were but one of many conditions preventing individual families from gaining an exclusive permanent hold on marriage relations with the throne.[1]

There were other, more general customs and practices that conditioned marriage both in the larger society and at the imperial level. For example, married women continued ties to their natal kin (Ebrey 1981; the chapters by Thatcher and Watson in this volume); in the event of minority rule, widows managed their husbands'. estates on behalf of a successor (Ch'ü 1961:104; Shiga 1978:120; Holmgren 1985:7,16); and widows maintained rights in heir and spouse selection (Ch'ü 1961:30–31, 104; Waltner 1981:142; Ebrey 1984a:234–37). Widows also demanded total obedience from the father's sons (Ch'ü 1961:120–21; Ch'ü 1972:53). In its broader form, filial piety—obedience to parents, with the wife subordinate to the husband (see Mann's chapter in this volume)—underpinned the entire moral-political order from the highest levels of society down to the village.

Although members of the ruling family had to marry down in the native Chinese state, care was taken that alliances were contracted with families from the highest stratum of the elite. The intention was not so much to conform to any ideal of class endogamy but rather to control powerful interest groups. The usual pattern was for early supporters of the founder, often military leaders, to be given preference in marriage relations until such time as they had ceased to be actively involved in the critical functions of government. There was thus a strong pull toward repetitive intermarriage with the same set of families. But the marriage circle always remained open, tending to evolve according to shifts in the ruling elite.[2]

Where members of the ruling family were concerned, senior officials of the outer court (chosen, in theory, according to merit) acted as guardians of the moral-political order (see Fang 1952:106–7; 1965:384; Fitzgerald 1968:27–28; Chung 1981:47, 62–63). This is not to say that strong-minded rulers and those who controlled the throne, including senior bureaucrats, did not try to manipulate custom and law when it suited their purpose.[3] Indeed, as a group, senior officials often openly agreed to bend or break some rules in order to square conditions with other, more important considerations. They would not usually object, for example, to an emperor's wish to promote his favorite concubine to the rank of empress if that position were vacant and if the concubine were the mother of the eldest son (see Chung 1981:47, 49). As we shall see, the practical need to override the established rule that a concubine should not be elevated to the status of wife derived from the particular form of succession that operated at the imperial level.

Rather than partible inheritance among all sons regardless of the mothers' status—the normal and preferred option among the scholar-elite and peasantry (Schurmann 1955–56:511–12; Shiga 1978:135, 141–43)—only one person could succeed to the throne. That person was the eldest son born of the empress (Tao 1978:173–75; Chang 1966:5–6).[4] If she produced no son, the eldest, regardless of his mother's position, was usually selected as heir, with the empress/wife acting as titular mother (also discussed by Thatcher in this volume). The heir (and his eldest son) resided in the palace beside his parents. All other sons were given fiefs at some distance from the locus of power. Although well provided for, they spent their lives in political obscurity. Direct access even to the wealth of the fief was denied, centralized bureaucratic control over its management being absolute. In sum, a distinction was drawn between male offspring on the basis of seniority and the status of the mother, with inheritance portions for younger sons being limited to a share of the tax revenue. Such was the case in the mature systems of all major Chinese regimes.[5]

Because younger sons of the emperor were without political, military, or fiscal authority, the only kinship bonds that could be effectively used by the throne for political purposes were its ties to wife-givers and wife-takers. The marriages of women—both the bestowal of the ruler's aunts (FZ), sisters, and daughters on families outside the palace and the entry of women into the imperial harem—therefore took on unparalleled political importance, with the ruler's maternal relatives becoming at once his chief means of support and a most dangerous threat to his independence. The section below outlines the main features of the relations between the emperor, his mother, and his wife.

Whenever the throne was vacant or the emperor too young, ill, or feeble-minded to govern in his own right, the wife in the oldest surviving generation (empress, empress dowager, or grand empress dowager—hereafter referred to as the "widow" or "senior widow") acted as regent for state affairs (Chao 1937:155–58; Yang 1968:50–51; Bernard 1972:65–75). When the main line failed, the widow selected an heir from among her husband's collateral kin (de Crespigny 1975:5). She also had powers of spouse selection and de-thronement. Even when she was little more than a child, with de facto power in the hands of senior members of the bureaucracy who were her natal rela-tives (as happened in the case of the fifteen-year-old empress dowager, née Huo, of Former Han [Tao 1978:179]), the legal power of dethronement still lay with her (Wallacker 1987). In all this, the empire was treated as family property, the chief difference being that the widow worked in concert, not with her husband's collateral kin, but with senior members of the bureaucra-cy who were either unrelated to the throne or were its wifely or maternal kin.

Whereas the role of the widow accorded with basic Chinese principles of family management and the all-important code of filial piety and was con-siderably strengthened by the political restrictions imposed on male agnates, filial piety and the idea of a female regent were at odds with the concept of sovereign power of the emperor (see Ch'ü 1972:59). The compromise was an uneasy one, for it involved voluntary withdrawal by the widow, keeping her powers of heir selection and dethronement in reserve for times of emergency. In practice, the widow usually withdrew from court in the formal way de-manded by the bureaucracy but continued to maintain her hand in govern-ment affairs through (1) her psychological advantage as the emperor's mother or grandmother; (2) controlling the marriage process; and (3) plac-ing her male kin in key civilian and military posts. These strategies were first put into place in imperial times by the empress dowager, née Lü (d. 180 B.C.), of the Former Han (Ward-Czynska 1978:2–6) and from there became the standard means by which ambitious mothers, wives, and favorite con-cubines tried to perpetuate their influence. In these cases, MBD/FMBSD alliances for heirs to the throne (figure 2.1) aimed to avoid a clash with incoming women, while the placement of relatives in strategic administrative posts ensured control over information reaching the throne.

In the native Chinese state it was thus common to find relatives of the senior widow controlling communication between the emperor and the outer court. No consort family managed, however, to maintain its political domi-nance for more than two or, at the most, three generations of rule. One dif-ficulty lay in the legal restrictions imposed on intermarriage with close kin, and another in the role played by senior members of the bureaucracy as

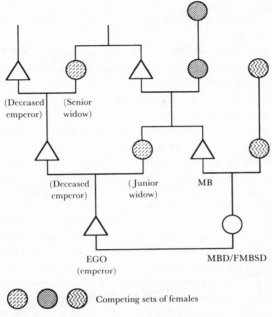

Fig. 2.1. Marriage with MBD/FMBSD in the Chinese state

guardians of the moral-political order, which led to their consequent interest and participation in the spouse-selection process (see Fitzgerald 1968:27–28; Chung 1981:62–63). Senior ministers jealously guarded their right to independent access to the throne and, through that, their right to join the imperial marriage circle. There were thus no customs or laws limiting the choice of wife to women from one particular family or group of families. This meant, however, that the system suffered from chronic tension between the throne, consort families, and the larger bureaucratic elite.

Another factor that prevented the development of a closed marriage circle lay in the custom whereby the wife could not control the marriage process until after the death of her husband.[6] Consequently, she often controlled only the marriage of a grandson and was thus constantly at odds with her son's wife chosen either by her husband or by his mother or grandmother. In this way, conflict between successive generations of imperial wives became a recurrent theme in the history of the native state. In the outer court, the conflict was represented by alliances between relatives and supporters of the ruler's grandmother and wife against the family of his mother.[7] From the emperor's point of view, his mother's family was useful in combatting either the combined influence of his grandmother and wife or that of the bureaucratic elite in general whenever it obstructed his purpose. Thus, when the emperor was in control, he often gave his mother's relatives the choice posts for high office.[8] In this way, the top echelons of the bureaucracy were rarely free from domination by consort kin, yet the position of any one family was highly unstable, with the death of an influential widow often heralding a violent shake-up of the administration.

Having lived long enough to reach the status of senior widow able to control the marriage of her grandson, a woman found that any alliance with her family arranged for the heir was marred by the incoming spouse, who came with a set of ready-made female relatives (namely, a mother and grand-mother) whose loyalties often lay with *their* natal kin. Thus, the senior widow always faced competition from relatives of incoming wives (see figure 2.1), and the throne might ally itself with any one of these families against that of the widow. But perhaps the most serious problem faced by imperial wives and their relatives lay in biology: the empress was often not the biological mother of the incoming ruler. Infertility and high infant mortality certainly were factors,[9] but the emperor's deliberate sexual avoidance of the empress also played a role (see de Crespigny 1975:29). The dislike felt by many an emperor for his wife is easily explained: the woman was imposed on him when he was little more than a child. His favorite, then, was usually a con-cubine or palace attendant, and these women, rather than the wife, tended to conceive heirs to the throne.[10] The emperor's dislike of his empress inten-sified when she was a close relative of an overly dominant senior widow. She was then seen to be an enemy or spy and indeed often acted as such (ibid., 8; Chung 1981:62, 75–76).

Such marriage dynamics explain many incidents related in the historical accounts of the Chinese court. They also explain the great variety of adoption and informal support strategies used by unrelated females in the harem and palace service sector—for example, the protection an empress or influential wet nurse gave to a young attendant, slave, or orphaned child. Here, the older woman hoped the young protegée might become the prince's favorite and keep rivals away from the throne. Such strategies were most effective when they cut across social barriers in the outer society and status hierar-chies within the palace. Only in this way could the older, more senior woman be fairly sure of maintaining her authority over the younger woman in the harem (see *PCS* 9:128; Fitzgerald 1968:18–20; Chung 1981:60; *MS* 113: 3514).

Like wives in the larger society, an empress could be divorced for barren-ness (see Tai 1978), and many a ruler tried to use this law to rid himself of his wife following the death of the senior widow (see Ward-Czynska 1978:14–17; Chung 1981:28, 47; *MS* 113:3513). Yet from the middle of the Former Han when wives came mostly from powerful lineages with secure footholds in the upper echelons of the administration (see Ward-Czynska 1978), members of the bureaucracy became increasingly adamant that the empress should not be cast aside simply to make way for a current favorite. In fact, T'ang and Sung law expressly forbad divorce on the ground of barrenness (Tai 1978:86–87). Against this, the bureaucracy had to weigh the cost of infighting between the biological concubine-mother and the titular mother (and regent) when both women survived into the next generation. Then, a clash of wills was inevitable. The Chinese solution to this problem was to prevent wherever possible the separation of the wife's political functions from her biological one of producing an heir to the throne. To this end, officials invariably agreed to elevate a favorite concubine who had produced the eldest son to the rank of empress if and when the current empress died or was divorced. The possibility of such promotions, however, encouraged rulers and favorite concubines, and sometimes mothers and maternal relatives, to engineer the death or disgrace of the empress, a problem also recorded for preimperial times (see Thatcher's chapter in this volume).

Given the frequency with which concubines' sons came to the throne (see n. 10), a ruler might well be surrounded by, not two, but up to four distinct sets of competing relatives centered around his biological and titular mothers (dowager empresses) and his biological and titular grandmothers (grand dowager empresses), some or all of which might be competing with the family of his wife (the empress). This competition, it should be noted, was important in preventing usurpation of the throne by consort families. Wang Mang (r. A.D. 9–23), whose case provides one of the few examples of successful usurpation, had to remove three other consort families from power before he could properly begin to engineer his coup d'état (Dubs 1955:44–49; Loewe 1974:286–306; Ward-Czynska 1978:41–47, 56–61). In contrast to Wang Mang, most imperial relatives confined themselves to the more realistic goal of domination. Even so, the lack of support from male agnates and the permanent tension among consort families, the throne, and members of the bureaucratic elite meant that fear of maternal kin was a major destabilizing factor in the history of the native state.

We have seen that an imperial wife held an unstable position in the early years of her career, when she relied in large part on the senior widow and members of the bureaucratic elite (including her own kin) for protection. With her husband's death, however, she might become head of the ruling house and on many occasions de facto ruler of the empire. Here, the widow not only assumed leadership of the ruling house but also (and quite logically) the de facto headship of her natal lineage (see Ch'ü 1972:58–59). Her influence was most widely felt when the emperor was her biological son or grandson and when he was young, weak-willed, or uninterested in government affairs. Thus, she invariably chose an infant or child rather than an adult when in a position to exercise her authority in choosing an heir (see *HHS* 10A:423). But the accession of a series of young and ineffectual rulers, as occurred during the Later Han (see Ch'ü 1972:215–16), did little for the morale of the administration because direct access to the throne was effectively blocked for all but the woman's family and supporters. For this reason, the death of an influential senior widow often heralded a violent fall in status for her family, sometimes bringing in its wake the death or disgrace of the empress and/or the wife of the heir-apparent.

In contrast to relatives of the emperor's mother and wife (wife-givers), the husbands and offspring of his sisters and daughters (sororal, or wife-taking, kin) were in a weak position when it came to succession politics. Sisters and sisters' sons were ineligible for the throne, and sororal kin were excluded from regency powers both by custom and by jealous wifely/maternal kin. In this way, however, the marriages of imperial sisters and daughters provided the throne with a way of establishing nonthreatening relations with influential members of the bureaucratic elite.[11]

As with incoming women, sororal ties were established by emphasizing customs and laws found in the wider society—property shares for daughters in the form of dowry (see Ch'ü 1972:273 n. 107, 283; Tai 1978:105–6; Ebrey 1981; Holmgren 1985) and educational and economic strategies centered on the mother (see Waltner 1981:144–52; Walton 1984:44–49). In addition, sororal ties benefited from the law of inheritance, that is, ranks and titles conferred on a woman without reference to her husband or son were to be treated as if granted to a man (*TL* 2:38; Johnson 1979:100–101). In the case of the princess, this condition was achieved by dispensing with the general law that made married women liable for punishments meted out to members of the husband's lineage (*TCTC* 76:2425). The princess's exemption from this law (see Ch'ü 1972:57; *HTS* 83:3647, 3650, 3653) meant that her status in no way depended on the position of her husband and his family. Rather, she retained her membership of the ruling line and was subject only to the throne (see Tang 1975:42; Wong 1979:136–37; *DMB* 1976.1:211). Because her status was conferred without reference to her husband, it could pass to her children. Thus, so long as they did not become wittingly involved in plots against the emperor, sororal cousins, nephews, and nieces were, like their mothers, exempt from severe punishment (see *SKC* 50:1198; 57:1340).

The material wealth a princess brought into marriage symbolized her condition. The lavish wedding gifts provided by the throne (see Chaffee's chapter in this volume) indicated the social and political superiority of her natal lineage over the husband and his family; the fief and its accompanying stipend (see Bielenstein 1967:21–22) symbolized that marriage had not altered her status. If the marriage lasted, most of the property eventually passed to the husband's family and out into the wider society through the woman's offspring, the fief title going to her eldest son in accordance with the general law (see Dull 1978: 63 n. 188; Tang 1975:100; Shiga 1978:118). As befitting their elevated status as honorary members of the imperial line, the woman's sons received imperial patronage in selection for high office. In this way, the sororal bond was transformed into an arm of the ruling line, reaching out into the wider community and establishing pockets of loyalty within other, potentially dangerous, lineages without the threat of domination or usurpation.[12]

Although the recipient lineage derived some comfort from the knowledge that at least one of its branches was insulated from political disaster, the throne benefited more from the arrangement because the princess could be counted on to put the imperial interest above that of her husband's family (see n. 12). For the woman's part, her exemption from severe punishment gave her a personal freedom denied to other members of the society, including her brothers. Unlike male agnates, who were perceived as a threat to the throne, the princess could remain in the capital at the center of power. Moreover, being female, she was not barred from the inner recesses of the palace as were the male officials of the outer court. Nor was she confined to the palace like an imperial mother or wife. In every respect, then, she was ideally placed to act as a power broker between the throne and families of the wider elite.

As a permanent member of the ruling line, the social status of the princess was higher than that of the imperial mother or wife. Indeed, her social position closely approximated that of the emperor himself. During the Southern Dynasties (A.D. 317–589), one woman used her exalted position to argue that, like her brother, the emperor, she too should have a harem. She was given thirty male "concubines" (Wong 1979:10). In short, although the princess never reached the political heights of an imperial mother or wife who acted as regent and de facto ruler of the state, and although her influence had no strong legal basis, her freedom of movement was considerable and her position solid. Because her status was not conditioned by ties beyond the throne, her influence depended on the accession of a strong ruler able to control his maternal relatives and to override any objections from the bureaucracy about her behavior. The tension between sisters and wives (princesses and empresses) at the imperial level was thus acute. Moreover, because all attention was directed toward a single male, competition among the princesses themselves was also intense—both among sisters and among different generations of female offspring (FFZ, FZ, and Z; see n. 15).

The princess's considerable status, which she passed to her children, meant that those children were eminently suitable as spouses for the next generation of imperial offspring. In fact, rulers often gave their children in marriage to sororal nephews and nieces. Although it was relatively easy, however, for a favorite sister to persuade her brother to give one of his many daughters in marriage to her son, her ultimate aim was to marry one of her daughters to the heir-apparent (FZD). Such a union would enable her to become de facto ruler of the state through her daughter, who would be in line

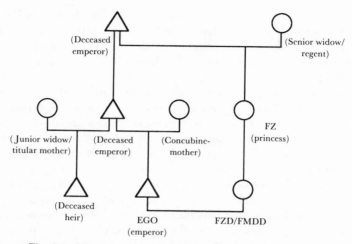

Fig. 2.2. Marriage with FZD/FMDD in the Chinese state

for the position of empress. Here, however, the princess faced fierce opposition from the ruler's grandmother, mother, and wife, as well as from other princesses with the same ambition. The senior widow, in conjunction with members of the outer court, controlled the marriage of the heir. So in practice a princess might achieve her ambition only (1) if she were the favorite sister of a strong-minded ruler whose mother and grandmother had passed away; (2) if she were the biological daughter of the senior widow; or (3) if an accident brought to the throne a younger half brother of the appointed heir—one who had previously married into her family (figure 2.2). Some women attempted to induce the latter condition by forming an alliance with an imperial concubine who had a son in order to bring about the disgrace and demotion of the appointed heir and his mother. But few women were able to bring such a complex strategy to fruition.[13] In practice, then, the empress in the native Chinese state was often a maternal cousin of the emperor (MBD or MBD/FMBSD), but she was rarely his paternal cousin (FZD).[14] In this way, sororal relatives (or wife-takers) tended to remain somewhat separate from wifely/maternal kin (or wife-givers), again helping to prevent the emergence of a truly aristocratic closed marriage circle. In short, the open-ended marriage system described in the chapter by Thatcher for the Spring and Autumn period continued on into late imperial times.

The political importance of the sororal bond for the throne meant that unmarried aunts (FZ), sisters, and daughters were always in short supply. Thus, those who were widowed (with or without children) usually remarried. If a recipient family fell from grace, the woman might well be summarily divorced and given to another lineage, young sons following her into the new alliance. Because a favorite sister was also well placed to obtain a divorce on grounds of incompatibility and because marital discord might itself bring political catastrophe to the lineage, it was not unusual for an imperial princess to become the de facto head of the husband's family, controlling its finances, organizing its marriages, and determining its political strategy. For this reason, some families tried to avoid a sororal relationship with the throne (see Ch'ü 1972:295–96; Wong 1979:206 n. 66). The problem was not confined, however, to imperial relationships: any family interested in furthering its economic, political, or social condition through the upward marriage of a son chanced subordination to the wife and her kin (on this point see Chaffee's chapter).

Although this inversion of the normal husband-wife relationship brought complaints (see *HHS* 62:2052–53; Wong 1979:95–96, 99; and below), and although praise might be heaped on the princess who refused to remarry after widowhood or forced divorce (see *Sui shu* 80:1798), greater exception was taken to women who flaunted their superior status before the husband's parents, thus violating the code of filial piety. In such cases, senior officials pressured the throne into trying to get the princess to moderate her behavior. As we have seen, however, the issue of filial piety posed an even greater problem for the emperor's personal relationships. Divorce was kept within reasonable bounds by the knowledge that a crucial political alliance was at stake and by the idea that the severing of an established bond between a man and his wife for political gain was objectionable to senior members of the bureaucracy because it undercut family harmony, the foundation stone of the moral-political order, and because they themselves were the potential victims of policies embracing arbitrary divorce (see Chaffee's chapter in this volume). In the main, then, an imperial princess was not summarily divorced unless her husband suffered a drastic punishment like exile or execution. At the same time, princesses, unlike other women, were not expected to undergo any hardship or punishment that might accrue to the husband's lineage, and a man who abused his princess-wife (whatever the provocation) could be sentenced to death (see Ch'ü 1972:58).

In summary, we can say that the political impotence of the emperor's male agnates, who were greatly distrusted by both the throne and the bureaucracy, heightened the political significance of the marriages of women and the position of the emperor's mother, wife, aunt (FZ), sister, and daughter. The mother, or senior widow, and her relatives provided support both against the ambitions of male collateral kin and against the larger bureaucratic elite when either attempted to obstruct the will of the throne. For this reason (and because the power of maternal kin was balanced only by sororal bonds established through the marriages of female offspring), the political authority of the imperial wife was greatly feared. Because attention was focused on a single male (the emperor or his heir), however, competition between different generations of imperial wives and between them and the ruler's sisters and daughters, as well as among sisters themselves, was fierce. Such rivalries helped to prevent the development of a monopoly by any one family, greatly reducing the threat of usurpation by maternal kin. Yet the marriage circle tended to follow shifts within the political elite, so that competition also destabilized government. The following discussion focuses on the development of this system and how the founders of some regimes addressed the problem posed by the power of maternal kin.

Historical Development and Evolution

Perhaps the nearest a native Chinese regime came to instituting an exclusive system of marriage exchange with one particular family was at the beginning of the Former Han, when the empress dowager, née Lü (d. 180 B.C.) arranged a series of strategic marriages in order to perpetuate control of the government by members of her family (Ward-Czynska 1978:2–5). With the struggle to oust the Lüs after her death, however, potential heirs to the throne who were connected with her family were killed. Moreover, the next emperor was chosen for the lowly status and meager numbers of his maternal and wifely kin (Ward-Czynska 1978:1–11; Tao 1978:178; Kamada 1962:80). The next few reigns saw a relatively free system of marriage that regarded the selection of a spouse as a purely private or family matter. No definitive marriage group emerged because little formal connection existed between consort families and the established elite. In this period, then, wifely and maternal kin were even more vulnerable to changes in fortune than in later times, when they had an independent foothold in the bureaucracy.

Emperor Wu (r. 140–87 B.C.) changed this marriage pattern. Coming to power through a palace intrigue manipulated by his paternal aunt (FZ), Emperor Wu began his reign under two warring consort factions (Ch'ü 1972:169). His first wife was his father's sister's daughter, chosen for him by his grandmother, the grand empress dowager, née Tou (FZD/FMDD; figure 2.3). He degraded his wife after the death of his grandmother, and replaced her with a singing girl introduced by one of his sisters (Ward-Czynska 1978:12–17; Loewe 1974:51). Then, after having lost his first heir through political intrigue, and with a very young son to succeed him, he tried to put an end to consort power by forcing the mother of that son to commit suicide. He chose three ministers of the outer court to act as regents after his death (Ward-Czynska 1978:20–25; Loewe 1974:35–70). But this strategy failed because the appointed regents, all of whom were connected by marriage, simply selected a relative (a child of six) to be wife and empress for the young ruler. This arrangement initiated a twenty-year period (87–66 B.C.) of complete subordination for both the bureaucracy and the throne to consort families (see Loewe 1974:73–81; Wallacker 1987:58–59). In the short term, then, Emperor Wu's strategy produced a return to conditions seen at the

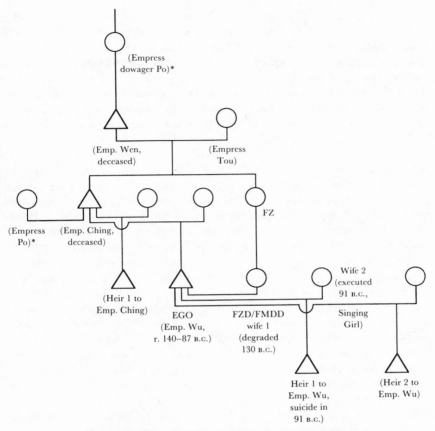

Fig. 2.3. Family ties of Emperor Wu of the Former Han

*Empress dowager Po and Empress Po were kinswomen.

beginning of the dynasty; that is, to domination of the government by a particular consort group. In the long term, the strategy instituted a system that drew wives from families of the political elite, with members of that elite deciding marriages in consultation with the senior widow (see Ch'ü 1972: 173–74, 210–29).

In Emperor Wu's time, the last vestiges of regional authority given to male paternal kin were stripped away (see Kamada 1962; Tao 1974). Some three centuries later, however, under the state of Wu (A.D. 222–80) in southeastern China, princes of the house were once again given regional military powers and made coregents and advisers to the throne (see Fang 1952; 1965). This condition continued on through Western Chin (A.D. 265–316) and the Southern dynasties (A.D. 317–589) into the early T'ang period (see Grafflin 1980:183–93; Tang 1975:50–54). For later Chinese the dramatic events of Western Chin (see Straughair 1973:2–5; Grafflin 1980:26–29, 94–95) reinforced two separate messages: first, that authority allotted to the ruler's male agnates would probably result in succession disputes that might well bring down the regime, and, second, that constant vigilance was needed against the ambitions of imperial wives, who—like the empress, née Chia, of Western Chin—might be tempted to depose the legitimate heir in favor of one of their own relatives (*CS* 31:965; *CS* 53:1459–62).

By comparing the history of Western Chin with that of other eras that gave male agnates a share of political power (see n. 5), we can see that influential male kin complicated the alliance patterns described above. An imperial wife could now appeal not only to her natal kin but also to individual princes of the house for support against other women or against the throne itself. Conversely, a princess was also able to support, or gain the support of, uncles and brothers whenever the throne appeared to be overly dominated by imperial wives. At such times, the political activities of female offspring were no longer masked by the machinations of the throne or maternal kin. As a consequence, the normal patterns of conflict between women not only spilled over into the outer court, disrupting the functions of government, but also set one prince against another, creating instability in the succession. Such disruptions were common in early and middle Former Han, Wu, and early T'ang and during the Western Chin when civil war erupted.

In the state of Wu, the roles played by princesses of the ruling house in succession problems (see Fang 1965) prefigure those of the early T'ang era (see Tang 1975). One can discern these same outlines in the history of early and middle Former Han (see Ward-Czynska 1978). In these periods, imperial princesses were not only divided among themselves and set in opposition to particular wives and heirs to the throne but also on occasion found themselves opposed to their own husbands. As members of the bureaucratic elite, the husbands of princesses sometimes sided with the heir or with another prince of the house to oppose female influence in general (that of mothers, wives, and sisters). Such alliances account in part for the high rate of divorce and widow-remarriage among imperial princesses in these periods. In early T'ang the underlying gender conflict between the all-male bureaucracy and females who provided the throne with its personal base of support was intensified by the presence of Empress Wu acting as de jure ruler of the state (A.D. 684–707).[15]

In sum, conditions in early T'ang represent one of several major realignments of the elite marriage system. The first of these shifts occurred during the Later Han when the throne, the bureaucracy, and even individual mothers and wives became subject to males of the consort family (see Young 1986 for details); the last was to occur during the Ming dynasty when the throne, mothers and wives, and their male relatives became subject to the bureaucracy, a development we shall discuss below.

It is commonly thought that with the establishment of the examination system in the T'ang-Sung era, late imperial China experienced a social and political mobility that put an end to the early aristocratic system of government and produced a concomitant shift away from class endogamy toward a marriage system in which rank could be exchanged for material wealth, scholastic repute, and so forth (see Ebrey's chapter, this volume). The status of emperor is said to have changed from that of "first among equals" (many of whom provided spouses for the imperial house) to autocrat (Sung) and, finally, to tyrant (Ming). The despotic tradition of the Mongol-Yuan era (c. A.D. 1200–1360) is believed to have influenced the development of tyranny during the Ming dynasty. In a recent study of imperial marriage strategy in the mid T'ang, Chang Pang-wei (1986) linked the idea of a shift away from class endogamy to a demonstrated decrease in the proportion of imperial wives and concubines coming from the upper ranks of the elite. But other scholars have begun to question the accuracy of the underlying hypothesis: they suggest that depictions of pre-T'ang society as particularly static and of Sung society as highly mobile may be exaggerated. They also challenge the idea of a Mongol tradition of despotism and the view of the late Ming ruler as tyrant.[16] The discussion below investigates some of these issues as they relate to imperial marriage under the Sung and Ming dynasties.

During Sung, certain founding families of the dynasty continued to provide spouses for, and to receive women from, the royal house long after their political fortunes had begun to wane.[17] This is one immediate explanation of Chang Pang-wei's data. By late Northern Sung these and other sororal kin were, furthermore, being specifically denied top-level posts in the central administration (SS 223:13579; SS 248:8777; HTCTC 153:4094; and Chaffee's chapter in this volume). In other words, royal spouses were no longer automatically chosen from the bureaucratic elite, and members of consort families were no longer given key administrative positions to the extent that they were able to enter and dominate the top ranks of the bureaucratic elite. The change had little to do with shifting attitudes toward marriage in the wider society. Rather, the initial impetus came from the throne and was an unintended side-effect of efforts to limit the power of the military. To this end, the first ruler of Sung came to an agreement with the founding generals of his regime that the latter would forgo real power in return for guaranteed social status through marriage ties with the royal house (Chung 1981:25). In fact, successful demilitarization of the political structure was a difficult and complex matter achieved through strategies that had nothing to do with marriage relations. Once demilitarization was under way, however, newly emerging bureaucratic groups saw the advantages of a policy that paired members of the ruling line with spouses from elite families on the decline.

The weakened relationship between political power at the top of the bureaucratic hierarchy and marriage relations with the throne also suited imperial wives. They could now dominate political affairs as dowagers and regents without hindrance from their male relatives or the emperor's sororal kin. For the consort families themselves, elevated social status coupled with political advantage at the lower levels of the hierarchy helped to sustain respectability at the local level (see Chung 1981:64–68, 79; Chaffee's chapter in this volume).

The growing disparity between the social and educational attributes of Sung princesses and their spouses heightened the former's haughtiness toward their husbands and in-laws—a phenomenon that hardened attitudes about the husband's superiority over his wife and the wife's subordination to her husband's parents. This development was independent but supportive of trends in the larger society. The declining status of imperial marriage partners in general led to discussion of the qualities required of an empress: here "pedigree," meaning membership in the founding elite and/or respectable middle-ranking military background, as well as individual social skills—education, intelligence, and reputation for ethical behavior (Chung 1981:24–25)—became the chief selection criteria.

If action against the power of consort families was particularly gentle in the Sung, this was not so in the Ming, the first native regime to maintain a deliberate policy of choosing imperial spouses from families with no bureaucratic connections (Soullière 1988). The strategy was not entirely new, however. It had been tried (with little success) as early as the first century B.C. by Emperor Hsuan (d. 49 B.C.) of the Former Han (see Ward-Czynska 1978:32–34, 40–41). But then the strategy had ignored the fundamental issue—the widow's role as final arbiter of the political process. The Ming addressed this issue by placing an additional ban on the delegation of imperial authority to harem women (Greiner 1979/80:6–7, 47; Soullière 1984:138; de Heer 1986:10). This too had been tried in earlier times—by the founder of Wei (A.D. 220–65), who had tried to dispense simultaneously with both the authority of the widow and support from close male agnates (*TCTC* 69:2206). Relying largely on sororal kin and a few select fraternal bonds to establish ties with the political elite of the former regime, the Wei throne had quickly fallen prey to usurpation by outsiders (see nn. 5, 8, and 12). The Ming dynasty did not suffer this fate, but a parallel nevertheless exists in the weakening position of the Ming throne vis-à-vis the bureaucracy in the absence of key matrilateral support.

Like the state of Wei, Ming governments found they still faced the problem of delegating authority during minority rule. Ironically, although no empress ever became regent (Soullière 1984:138), senior widows retained the authority to appoint a regent and to choose heirs and spouses just as they had in third-century Wei (see Fang 1965:165–66, 337, 352; de Heer 1986:25–27).

In practice, an imperial wife during the Ming dynasty played much the same role, albeit less prominently, as she had in the past.

Ming marriage strategy originated with the founder of the regime and reached maturity over the course of several reigns. Spouses were selected from low-ranking military families in the capital area on the basis of temperament and physical appearance (Soullière 1988:1, 20, 23–24, 30). Without a solid political base, families of the bureaucratic elite that supplied women for the imperial house could not supply more than one empress (ibid., 39). Consequently, this period witnessed a degree of upward and downward social mobility among imperial in-laws not seen in the native state since early Former Han. It would seem, then, that the phenomenon observed by Chang (1986) wherein imperial wives were increasingly drawn from the lower ranks of the elite and even from commoner families is best explained, not by changing attitudes in the wider society, but by the increasingly deliberate denial of power to consort families. The rationale and strategies underpinning this development during the Ming dynasty were firmly rooted in the Chinese tradition of pre-T'ang times.

Studies of Ming imperial marriage relations by Soullière (1984, 1987, 1988) support the current view that, far from being a despot, the Ming ruler had gradually been reduced to titular ruler and was made a virtual prisoner in his own palace. Without a powerful consort family as his ally, he was unable to assert his independence against the bureaucracy and sometimes sought to withdraw from the system entirely, forcing senior bureaucrats to turn to eunuchs and harem women for help in maintaining the link with the palace (Soullière 1984:132–34). In this period there was a swing away from educating imperial princesses in the virtues of wifely submission (as in the Sung) toward that of teaching their husbands and in-laws the art of being subordinate (see Soullière 1988:21). The development accorded with the new relationship between the bureaucratic elite and eunuch factions in the palace in cutting the emperor off from his traditional base of support. In short, the policy developed by the founder of the Ming to ensure the integrity of the throne against imperial wives and consort families was gradually appropriated by the bureaucratic elite so that all imperial women—mothers, sisters, and wives—now owed obedience, not to the husband or to male natal kin as in the past, but to the outer court.

In summary, power at the Chinese court oscillated between three officially sanctioned forces: the emperor, the senior widow, and members of the bureaucracy. Four other forces lay on the periphery (eunuchs, not dealt with here, and the emperor's paternal, sororal, and wifely/maternal kin). Any of these could be called into action by one of the major parties. Whether in Han times or Ming, however, the key to major shifts in the balance of power lay with close male relatives of the widow (wifely/maternal kin). When they were in a position to bridge the gap between the harem and the outer court by occupying senior positions in the bureaucracy, power tended to swing away from the throne and unrelated members of the bureaucratic elite toward the widow and her family. Conversely, the widow was at her weakest whenever her natal kin had no established foothold within the bureaucratic elite. When this happened—as in the Wei (Three Kingdoms) and the Ming—power initially resided with the throne but tended to gravitate quickly toward the bureaucratic elite. Caught between the other two forces, the throne attempted to play off the widow's party against the bureaucratic elite, or to invoke the aid of one of the lesser peripheral bodies named above.

Accounts of the relationship between the emperor and these other parties were mostly composed, or at least approved, by men whose families had well-established relationships with sectors of the bureaucracy mainly outside the imperial marriage system. Thus, any choice of words in these accounts suggesting despotism on the part of the emperor or usurpation of power by imperial wives, relatives, or eunuchs should be seen as a signal of a significant shift in power away from the bureaucratic elite. Conversely, literature on the Sung indicates the stable and equitable balance of power between the major parties. A similar absence for mid- to late Ming, however, would reflect the complacency of a dominant bureaucracy. In other words, the mature Sung and Ming dynasties were seen to have largely avoided not only the "faults" of the Later Han, when the bureaucracy (as well as the throne and individual wives) had been subject to the consort clan, but also the "problems" of Wu, Western Chin, and early T'ang in dealing with the emperor's paternal kin as well as the various evils of late T'ang, when eunuchs had been the dominant policymakers.

We have seen how shifts in the balance of power during the Sung and Ming dynasties were in fact brought on by one of the constants of early Chinese history—namely, the acknowledgment by all parties that the position of the senior widow was such that the emperor and the bureaucratic elite could best (or perhaps only) assert their power by breaking the bond between political service and intermarriage with the throne. In this respect, the institution and the development of a public examination system (T'ang-Sung) possibly helped to weaken that bond. Yet the examination system was only a coincidental factor, for, as we have seen, conditions under the Ming were quite unlike, and in no way contingent upon, developments in either the T'ang or Sung dynasties. Moreover, and most important, each of those developments, as well as those that took place during the Ming, fell within parameters of change (both structural and ideological) already set in place by the end of the third century A.D. In short, despite major social changes in the wider society (see Ebrey and others in this volume), structure and strategy at court remained much the same in the native Chinese state from Han through to the end of Ming.

THE NON-HAN STATE

In the non-Han culture of the steppe, marriage may be characterized as (1) a transaction in which considerable wealth (or its substitute, labor) passed from the family of the groom to that of the bride (i.e., the "brideprice"); (2) a polygynous arrangement whereby all wives, or a group of senior wives, had equal status; (3) cross-generational alliance; (4) separate residence for married sons; and (5) an exogamous system in which intermarriage with the paternal line was permitted after a given number of generations (five, seven, or nine) (see Krader 1963). Women were well integrated into the husband's family, so much so that they sometimes received a personal share of the husband's patrimony apart from that given to male offspring. This in turn meant that wives rarely left the husband's family to remarry. Should a widow be unable to survive on her share of the patrimony, that share would be amalgamated with that of another male in the family through the levirate— marriage to a brother, uncle, nephew, or son (by another woman) of the late husband. Polygamy, separate residence for adult sons, and the absence of a ban on cross-generational marriage alliance facilitated the movement of widows from one unit of the family to another (see Holmgren 1986b).

Leaders were selected primarily on the basis of maturity and competence, thus obviating the need for regents—male or female (Holmgren 1981–83b; Fletcher 1986; Holmgren 1986c, 1987). This meant that consort families participated in government only as heads of tribal subunits within the confederation, not as wifely, sororal, or maternal kin. Because marriage could not be used by one group to undermine the authority of another, it was able to develop as a diplomatic device, usually taking the form of a simultaneous exchange of women conducted across a range of leaderships. The condition contrasts with that of the Chinese state, which was hampered in foreign marriage diplomacy by its emphasis on lineal succession, monogamy, and the role of the wife and her relatives in supporting the throne during minority rule (Holmgren n.d.).

For China specialists, the absence of steppe customs in states of non-Han origin, or the presence of forms approximating those found in the native Chinese regime, is often seen as evidence of sinification. But similarities can be misleading. One cannot assume that they arise for the same reasons. For example, the Ch'i-tan (Khitan) abandoned the exchange of women with foreign states during the Liao period (A.D. 916–1122) because one particular group of outsiders had been given an exclusive permanent lien on marriage relations with the ruling house. In fact, the Chinese model was never completely adopted by any conquest regime. Rather, individual elements of the model were selected, modified, and integrated with the steppe tradition. In each case, the mix provided a well-integrated, workable system of control designed to meet specific political needs. At the same time, each approach was unique; that is, the amalgam of Chinese and steppe traditions was never exactly the same.

The variety and political ingenuity of systems developed by non-Han states are demonstrated below. Here it remains to point out some common characteristics. First, nearly all non-Han states actively discouraged or severely circumscribed marriage ties between the throne and the Chinese. Second, the circle of imperial marriage partners tended to remain relatively stable, and consequently the various sets of in-laws overlapped to a much greater extent than in the native Chinese regime; that is, the same groups continued to supply both wives and husbands for imperial offspring almost indefinitely. Third, in non-Han states there was a more carefully regulated, and thus much greater, correlation between political privilege and social status as seen through marriage relations with the royal house than in the Chinese state (on these points, see also Rawski's chapter in this volume). Even Northern Wei, the one great exception to these generalizations, moved toward this type of system in its later years.

All these characteristics grew out of the need to protect the non-Han minority's privileged place in government against encroachment by the Chinese. Finally, examination of the histories of these northern conquerors in predynastic and dynastic times reveals a link between the abrupt appearance of new forms and attitudes to marriage and a shift in power-sharing among males of the ruling lineage. The link is highlighted most forcefully in T'o-pa history, which saw two quite distinct shifts in attitudes to marriage and inheritance—the first occurring during the foundation era, the other at mid-point in the history of the imperial state. A similar, equally dramatic shift can also be observed in early Ch'i–tan and Mongol history (see Holmgren 1987). The sections below outline the main features of the marriage systems that developed in tandem with this new approach to power-sharing among male kin. As we shall see, the systems so devised had little in common with each other or with the model established by the native Chinese state.[18]

The T'o-pa Wei

Northern Wei (A.D. 399–534) developed a marriage system that emphasized the common interest between the throne and collateral branches of the ruling house in controlling the ambitions of outsiders, both Chinese and non-Han. That is, Wei marriage strategy protected the privileged place of paternal kin in selection for office by denying other interest groups access to power through marriage ties with the throne. Thus, in spirit and form Northern Wei policy resembles that of the Ming: imperial wives and concubines came from outside the ranks of the bureaucratic and military elite; there was active discrimination against the ruler's wifely and maternal kin in selection for high office; and there were few cross-ties between sororal and wifely kin; that is, daughters of princesses (FZD) and maternal cousins (MBD) were not taken into the imperial harem.

Wei strategy went much further, however, in that the T'o-pa attempted to separate the wife's biological function of producing an heir from her political role. First, mothers of eldest sons were never appointed to the rank of empress in their lifetimes and might well be made to commit suicide after the son was named as heir to the throne. Second, empresses were appointed only on an irregular basis and were invariably childless. They did not act as titular or foster mothers to eldest sons, and they all came from the ruling families of recently conquered states and thus had few if any relatives of influence in the outer court. They were thus purely symbolic figures representing the integration of their peoples into the T'o-pa empire. In short, the T'o-pa adopted the Chinese principle of primogeniture but rejected the idea of succession by a son of the empress. They thus dispensed with the most critical aspect of the Chinese system—the role of the senior widow as head of the ruling house and de facto head of state in times of political crisis. Under the T'o-pa such crises were to be addressed by senior officials of the outer court who were either unrelated to the throne or were princes of the blood or select sororal kin. In this system, imperial princesses were given in marriage either to leaders of refugee groups arriving in Wei from other states, or to members of a select line of a non-Han lineage (the Mu family). In the former case, the aim was to neutralize a potentially hostile group that had settled in the realm. In the latter instance, repeated bestowal of daughters upon sororal nephews (ZS) created a group of loyal kin who, being T'o-pa in all but name, could be chosen for office in the same way as princes of the blood, thus supplementing the latter's meager numbers. Care was taken, however, that these sororal bonds were never translated into wifely/maternal relationships.

Measures taken to control the ambitions of agnates centered not on supervising their marriages, but on bestowing equal rights in selection for office. Political rank and social standing within the ruling lineage therefore depended on loyalty and service to the throne as perceived by the emperor of the day. Thus, for princes of the house (the most privileged group in the empire), marriage was apolitical. And because brothers, nephews, and younger sons were free to choose wives without reference to the throne, many branches of the house intermarried with commoner, even slave, families— wives being chosen for reasons of love or physical beauty. It seems, then, that for the T'o-pa, the wife's social standing was of little consequence.

In summary, the early Wei ruler was not *primus inter pares* but a true autocrat who derived his chief support from, but nevertheless controlled in an absolute way, all members of the imperial lineage as well as senior bureaucrats of the outer court. In the early Wei system (400–490s) all paternal kin, males *and* females, were far more trusted than wives. Although the trust placed in sisters was in some cases extended to their husbands and sons, sisters' daughters did not marry back into the imperial line to become wives and mothers of emperors. Nor were the female offspring of distant male agnates permitted to marry back into the ruling line, as might have happened in the steppe tradition.

In the 480s the throne began to use the marriages of female offspring to gain access to the social network of the Chinese elite. The change in policy was geared to the better integration of wealthy provincial Chinese into state-controlled political and economic structures. In this way, the policy of marriage avoidance with the bureaucratic elite began to break down. Other strategies remained in place, however, in particular those relating to the political power of mothers and wives. A decade later, the narrow aim of protecting the government positions of paternal kin was widened to encompass all non-Han elites. To this end, the system of selection to office was overhauled so that political rank now depended on social status, with the latter being defined (for the non-Han) by ancestral service or degree of blood/marriage relation to the throne. The 490s thus saw a revival of the predynastic tradition whereby *all* lines of the ruling family were ranked according to seniority (birth). This revival was accompanied by a shift in attitude toward marriage for male offspring. That is, a controlled, elitist marriage strategy was developed during the 490s in an effort to establish a recognizable and "respectable" circle of families from which the ruling line and close paternal kin (males and females) could draw their spouses. From there, Wei moved rapidly toward the system seen under conquest regimes, namely, marriage exchange within a closed circle of mestizo and non-Han elites who dominated key administrative posts.

Such changes in the marriage system created instability in the top echelons of the bureaucracy as male agnates clashed with the throne over the issue of political privilege for relatives of the emperor's mother and wife. In addition, distant branches of the emperor's family suffered a decline in political status as they struggled to protect their place in government against incursions from the emperor's more privileged uncles and brothers and other non-Han elites who now had better access to power through wifely and maternal ties with the throne. In the search for ways to maintain their status, distant male kin turned to marriage alliance with the families of eunuchs and palace attendants. Here, long-term social security associated with membership of the imperial house was exchanged for informal, high-level (but often short-lived) political influence. Such cross-status alliances were no longer tolerated, however, for they were held to be subversive to the new political order.

The Ch'i-tan Liao

Whereas early Wei marriage strategy focused on protecting the throne and paternal kin from the ambitions of powerful outside interest groups, Liao (A.D. 916–1122) marriages were designed to minimize the dangers posed by the emperor's male agnates. The system grew out of the support given to the founder of the regime by his wife and her family against other tribal leaders and, more important, against the founder's uncles and brothers, who refused to relinquish their traditional leadership rights. In this system, princes of the blood who were only distantly or remotely related to the throne were more trusted than close male agnates. Accordingly, the latter were given mainly honorary titles and nonfunctional posts associated with the shell of the old political order. As reward for their support in helping to institute the new monarchical and centralized system of government, the family of the first empress (an outsider in relation to the old power structure) was given exclusive rights to marriage relations with the throne and a hereditary lien on key posts in the newly developing system of administration.

In the mature Liao marriage system, all branches of the imperial house (the Yeh-lü) as well as those of the consort clan (the Hsiao) were ranked according to degree of kinship with the founding emperor and empress. The highest-ranking branches of the ruling family (the emperor and his close relatives) married into those of the consort clan and vice-versa. In this way, the ruler was supported not only by his mother and her uncles and brothers (who doubled as senior officials of the outer court), as in the Chinese system, but also by his mother's female kin—her sisters and nieces—who doubled as consorts for his uncles (FB), brothers, and nephews (BS). Here, cross-generational alliance flourished, with members of the consort clan marrying down into younger generations of the imperial house, all of which increased the likelihood that the empress's sisters and nieces would be able to control their husbands and thus help to protect the ruling line from the threat of armed revolt or usurpation by close paternal kin (figure 2.4).

The Liao system, then, was almost a parody of that of the Chinese. Ranking within the harem was determined by the political status of the woman's male kin, and the status of her male kin was determined by social rank defined according to blood ties with the founding empress and current ruler. The correlation of social status, selection for office, and provision of spouses for the royal house was thus much higher than ever intended or seen under any Chinese regime. This is not to say that there was no political and social mobility. Indeed, the middle Liao period saw considerable upward mobility as the throne attempted to weaken the power of relatives of the first empress by broadening the base of the consort clan: here, the new rules of surname exogamy, repetitive marriage-exchange, and hereditary rights to office were circumvented by the simple device of surname adoption; that is, by using the steppe practice of fictive kinship to integrate outsiders into the political system. The same device was later taken up by the consort clan as a means of incorporating its followers into the system. It was only after the system was revamped in the latter part of the regime (1020s) that genuine blood ties with the founding unit were stressed.

Although most Liao rulers married maternal cousins (MBD), distinctions

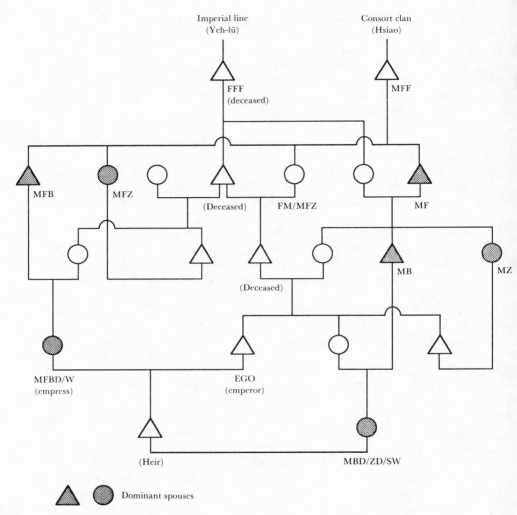

Fig. 2.4. Cross-generational marriage: Liao

such as MBD and FZD, relevant to the Chinese model, are less applicable because the system of exchange meant that a wife who was MBD might also be FZD. Cross-generational alliances complicated the situation. The eighth ruler, for example, married a woman who was his mother's paternal cousin (MFBD) and his father's maternal cousin (FMBD) (figure 2.5). Although Liao rulers could marry their maternal aunts (MZ) as well as daughters of the mother's or grandmother's brother (MBD or FMBD), they could not,

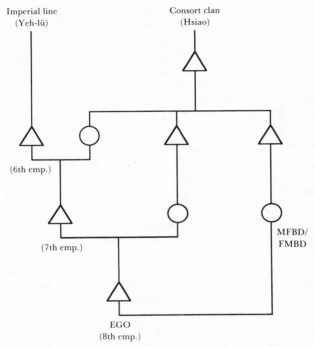

Fig. 2.5. Cross-generational marriage with MFBD/FMBD in late Liao

despite the high status of maternal aunts and cousins, take the female offspring of such women into the imperial harem (MZD). Liao practice here differed from China's because such offspring always carried the surname of the imperial house (Yeh-lü). This explains why power held by the empress's aunts and sisters did not pass to their offspring (although it did reappear in the following generation through the female line). For males of the consort clan, political status initially passed to both male and female offspring but from there was transmitted only through the male line. In short, all members of the consort clan, whatever their gender, tended to have more power than their spouses, including the emperor himself. Because the status of the empress dowager extended to her close relatives regardless of gender, the normal gender inequality between husband and wife was reversed, not for the emperor's sisters as in the Chinese model, but for those of the empress and empress dowager. The military authority assumed by these women in times of crisis (see Wittfogel and Feng 1949:200, 557) was a symptom of this condition.

In theory, the Liao system of marriage exchange should ultimately have incorporated the consort clan into the imperial house to such an extent that all divergent interests between it, the throne, and paternal kin would disappear. The system favored the consort clan, however, more than it did the throne. Even in early Liao, the emperor was in danger of being overshadowed by members of the consort clan. Action taken to redress this situation was short lived, ending in the fourth reign with the emperor's personal withdrawal from government in a manner similar to that seen in the late Ming. In the latter part of Liao, however, the authority of the throne was protected to some extent by factionalism within the consort clan as wives of one generation battled with those of the next, and as barren empresses struggled to hold their place in the system against fertile concubines. In effect, the various branches of the consort clan began to behave in the same manner as competing generations of wifely and maternal kin in the native Chinese state.

The Mongol Yuan

In predynastic times the Mongol leadership (early 1200s) developed a marriage system that achieved a near-perfect balance among all the parties discussed above. It continued on into the Yuan era (A.D. 1260–1368) with very little change other than a gradual drift in administrative, fiscal, and military power away from the periphery toward the center. This shift ultimately left secondary branches of the imperial house unable to defend the integrity of the throne against bureaucratic forces.

Distinctions were horizontal in the Mongol system rather than vertical. Paternal relatives and the leaders of subordinate tribes and allied states were invested with identical powers that, although located away from the center, were basically imitative of those held by the supreme ruler in the central domain. In this system, close paternal kin tended to be more trusted than remotely related male agnates. Accordingly, they were given a significant amount of autonomy on the outermost rim of the empire. Their role as regional overlords and the local autonomy granted to other tribal leaders together formed the linchpin of government. Power, then, was invested as much on the periphery of the realm as at the center.

Participation by princes and allied leaders in the selection of the supreme ruler and strict supervision of marriage and succession procedures within the various kingdoms and fiefs were some of the means the center used to control the strong centripetal forces within the realm. By early Yuan times, inheritance of territories held by collateral branches of the house was regulated so as to emphasize service to the center and to prevent control of the fief from falling into the hands of outsiders. Older sons were expected to earn their own kingdoms, and the fief went, not to the youngest son of the wife in the traditional manner (ultimogeniture), but to the youngest *adult* son who had no fief of his own at the time of his father's death or to a collateral male relative who held the territory in trust until the youngest son came of age. In

this way, families that married into the ruling lineage were unable to gain
control of the various princely domains. Marriage alliances were also carefully scrutinized by the center to prevent collusion between princes of the
house and allied tribal leaders also on the periphery.

The local autonomy granted to conquered and allied leaders was contingent upon their acceptance of a sister or daughter of the Mongol ruler
in marriage. This, combined with an enforced system of monogamy, lineal
succession (ultimogeniture), and female regencies within the allied state,
guaranteed effective control over the subject tribesmen by the central domain. In the final analysis, however, control rested on the demonstrated
military superiority of members of the ruling house. Herein lay one of the
chief weaknesses of the system: fragmentation could be prevented only by
continuous conquest and expansion or by instituting an overarching bureaucratic structure controlled by the center. The latter development in the
Yuan era (1270s) led to the emasculation of the male agnates' traditional
powers and domination of the throne by senior officials of the outer court who
were unrelated to the throne.

Traditional Mongol practice emphasized polygamy and the full integration of wives into the husband's family, so the position of the ruler's married
sisters and daughters as agents for the natal line was an anomaly. Thus, in
contrast to brideprice systems operating at other levels of Mongol society, the
imperial princess was furnished with a lavish dowry symbolic of her continuing membership of the ruling house. At the same time, remnants of the
traditional mentality wherein the husband regarded his wife (or wives) as an
integral, permanent part of the family worked to the advantage of the ruling
house in that the allied leadership did not see the woman's participation in
the affairs of the kingdom as a gross imposition. The continued existence of
traditional ideology is also seen in the center's use of the levirate: sisters and
daughters who failed to produce offspring able to inherit the kingdom simply
married the incoming heir—one of the late husband's uncles, brothers,
nephews, or sons by another woman. In this way, the center managed to
avoid problems of control arising from infertility, high infant mortality, and
sexual avoidance.

In theory, pacts with allied leaders were between equals. Each allied
group therefore had the right to exchange women with the ruling house in the
traditional manner. The pacts were structured, however, to benefit the central domain rather than the allied kingdom. On the one hand, real sisters and
daughters of Mongol rulers were sent out to become wives and mothers of the
rulers of allied states, but on the other, women selected as spouses for the
ruling house usually came from relatively powerless lines of the subject
leadership—branches that in many cases had only a remote blood connection with the real leaders of the kingdom. This was particularly so where the
Onggirat tribe was concerned, for it had a hereditary lien on the provision of

the senior wife who produced heirs for the supreme office. Thus, at the center, MBD alliances were as rare as those of FZD, and allied tribal leaders (sororal kin) had no chance of becoming wifely/maternal relatives of the emperor and were thus effectively barred from excessive interference in the affairs of the ruling house. All this helped to maintain an equitable balance of power between sororal and paternal kin stationed on the periphery of the realm.

Because the different sets of imperial relatives were confined to administrative duties associated with specific territories located beyond the center, the Mongol ruler, along with his mother and wife, worked in isolation with a group of advisers of non-Han, but largely non-Mongol, origin who were set quite apart from the marriage circle. In effect, then, the ruler's wife was cut off from her natal family both by physical distance and by sororal kin who controlled communication between the center and forces within the allied kingdom. As we have seen, identification of the empress with the interests of the throne and the bureaucracy free of reference to the aspirations of her natal kin had been a long-held dream of many Chinese. It was achieved by the Mongols primarily through the decentralized system of control, but the condition also accorded with traditional ideology that saw the wife as an integral part of the husband's family. In sum, the empress in the Mongol-Yuan dynasty was seen as an individual to be entrusted with power and authority in the same manner as an imperial sister or brother.

The alienation of brothers and sisters was prevented by their participation in the election of the supreme ruler. As in the Liao, all adult sons of the wife were potential heirs to the throne, with the final decision being made after the death of the ruler. The successor was chosen at an assembly of relatives who were major fief holders—princes of the house, the late ruler's paternal aunts (FZ), sisters, and daughters, their husbands and/or sons, and the late ruler's mother and wife. In the interim, either the youngest adult son by the wife, or the wife herself, acted as regent. Because only competent adults were eligible for the position of leader and adult males could assume regency powers, the opportunity for mothers and wives to assume the full powers of state fell well short of that provided by the Chinese system. As we have seen, in the Chinese state, male agnates were usually barred from holding regency powers, and the senior widow was able to govern in the name of an infant or child, retaining the power of dethronement. Neither that power nor heir selection was the sole prerogative of the Mongol wife; all such matters were decided through the family assembly.

This, then, was the system that prevailed in the early years of the Yuan dynasty. Expansion of the bureaucratic sector at the provincial and central levels in the dynastic era saw a gradual shift, however, in the balance of power away from the emperor at the center and the various kingdoms and fiefs on the periphery toward bureaucratic forces beyond the marriage circle.

In this shift, the power of the wife (the empress) moved away from her traditional place in the extended family of fief holders toward Chinese-style relations with members of the outer court. But, unlike conditions in most native
regimes, her working relationship with senior officials was not supported by
the presence of natal kin, and thus her position was far less secure than in the
native state. As we have seen, such conditions had existed in the early state
of Wei (A.D. 220–65), and a similar situation was to occur under the subsequent Ming regime, although in neither case did the system arise from influences or borrowings from the non-Han tradition.

CONCLUSION

We have seen that no non-Han regime was purely imitative of the native
Chinese state. Rather, imperial marriage policy under conquest dynasties
consisted of a judicious mix of elements taken from both the steppe and the
Chinese tradition. In each case that mix provided the leadership with an
integrated system of control geared to specific political demands. One demand common to all regimes was that the marriage system protect the privileged place in government of members of the non-Han community against
encroachment by the Chinese. To this end each state focused on excluding or
limiting in some way intermarriage with the Chinese and on emphasizing
a direct correlation between political privilege and social status, with the
latter being defined in part by consanguineous and marriage ties with the
ruling house.

Despite the common focus on excluding or limiting ties with the Chinese,
each dynasty developed a unique marriage system. The variety seen across
different regimes stemmed in part from the different approach to traditional
non-Han competitors, in particular the attitude toward the emperor's male
agnates: early Northern Wei practice saw imperial marriage as a means of
controlling outside groups for the benefit of all branches of the imperial
house; the Yuan focused on protecting the throne and *close* collateral kin; and
the Liao used marriage to control male agnates. The correlation between
forms and attitudes to marriage and the approach to power sharing among
males of the lineage in these states confirms the significance of a similar
phenomenon noticed in the Chinese case. There, we saw how imperial marriage practice was based on customs and laws found in the larger society,
with differences at the imperial level being determined in large part by the
difference between succession and the mode of inheriting family property. It
would seem, then, that whether in the non-Han or native Chinese regime,
forms and attitudes to imperial marriage were strongly influenced by the
relationship between the emperor and his uncles (FB), brothers, sons, and
nephews (BS). That influence was felt not only in the degree of power sharing between the throne and agnatic kin but also in the physical proximity of

those relatives to the throne, the latter being responsible for some of the differences seen in the strategies devised by Northern Wei, where agnates rotated between the center and the periphery, and in the Mongol system, where they were permanently stationed on the frontier.

Under the mature Chinese state the ruling line stood alone, isolated both physically and psychologically from its collateral branches. Consequently, regency powers were invested in outsiders—namely, the late emperor's widow, who acted as head of the imperial lineage and on occasion de facto ruler of the empire. When her natal relatives were members of the bureaucratic elite stationed in the capital, her power was extended, indeed often delegated, to them. In this way, maternal kin became the chief means of support for the throne against paternal uncles, brothers, cousins, and nephews and against the larger bureaucratic elite. Because of this, however, maternal relatives were also a most dangerous threat to the ruler's independence. Because the power of the widow and her family was balanced only by the presence of the wider bureaucratic elite and a set of sororal bonds created through the strategic marriages of female offspring, fear of the consort clan was a perennial destabilizing factor, with the history of the native state becoming one of shifts in the balance of power among the throne, the bureaucracy, and imperial wives and their families. Such shifts took place within as much as across individual dynasties. Within this scenario, the political activities of the imperial princess were often obscured, her influence becoming fully evident in the historical narrative only when male agnates were able to provide a viable alternative to a weak throne dominated by mothers, wives, and maternal kin. In other periods, the power of the princess was manifest mainly in the record of social problems arising from her superior social position vis-à-vis her husband and his family.

In late imperial times, the Sung, Yuan, and Ming dynasties all saw a shift in the balance of power toward members of the bureaucratic elite unrelated to the throne. The Ming condition was not contingent, however, on developments in either the Sung or the Yuan dynasties. Indeed, in each dynasty, marriage systems arose from unique internal developments, with developments in the Ming occurring well within the parameters of change established for the native state in early times. In short, when the processes of change are viewed from the Han dynasty through to the end of Ming, the T'ang-Sung transition era loses much of its apparent significance.

Both the Sung and the Ming regimes continued to be concerned about limiting the political influence of the imperial wife, and each developed a unique approach to traditional concerns about the status of the imperial princess vis-à-vis her husband. Conditions in the Sung dynasty permitted a more concerted effort toward complying with the status quo seen in the larger society; while Ming society endorsed earlier imperial practice, stressing the education of the husband to cope with his subordinate position. This latter approach grew out of the Ming's general emphasis on the subordination of consort families to the bureaucratic elite.

In sum, imperial marriage in the Chinese state was based on customs and laws found in the wider society, deviations and anomalies being explained in large part by the form of succession that prevailed at the imperial level. Once established, the system endured in basic form throughout the imperial era, from Han times through to the end of Ming, with very little reference to changing attitudes and practices in the larger society or to new modes of operation introduced by conquest regimes. Neither the history of early T'ang (when the historical narrative takes great account of the political activities of mothers, wives, and female offspring) nor that of early Ming (which saw a concerted effort to restrict the power of the imperial wife) deviates from the model established for the native state in pre-T'ang times.

If we were to take that model as a standard reference point in any comparative study of marriage relations, we could say that the Northern Wei and Liao dynasties represent two extremes in the spectrum of Chinese attitudes toward male agnates and maternal kin. As we have seen, Northern Wei history was dominated by excessive fear of outsiders working through the maternal bond. The practices of that era were therefore hedged around with numerous devices for keeping mothers and wives and their families from power. In contrast, the Liao system was characterized by fear of male agnates and thus placed an exaggerated trust in mothers and wives and their natal relatives. Such was that trust, the Liao state dispensed almost entirely with the checks and balances seen in the Chinese state: members of the consort clan were permitted to dominate the bureaucracy through an exclusive permanent lien on key offices; and the function of marriage for an imperial princess was solely biological—that of reproducing the consort clan. Here, then, as distinct from all other regimes, the imperial princess was subject to the authority of her husband. Liao was also the only dynasty to extend the status and power of the wife to all her relatives, both male and female. In this system, then, sisters of the mother were more trusted and given greater powers than imperial princes and princesses.

Both the Wei and Liao dynasties structured their marriage systems on the centralized bureaucratic state. Thus, those systems can be easily compared with each other and with that prevailing under the native regime. In contrast, imperial marriage under the Mongols evolved to fit a decentralized feudal mode of administration in which female offspring played a critical role in preserving the authority and independence of male agnates stationed on the periphery of the realm. In part because of decentralized control, the Yuan was one of the few regimes successful in breaking the link between authority delegated to the senior widow and the status and power of her family. In the Yuan, the position of the imperial wife was never dependent upon that of her family. Rather, she was entrusted with power in the same way as a sister or brother. Moreover, her authority did not challenge, and was not challenged by, the sister or brother. All three were integral, permanent members of the ruling house and thus social equals. Additionally, the sister and wife both had regency powers—the one on the periphery, the other at the center—and, like a brother, both participated in choosing the supreme ruler. This was not the case in the native Chinese regime, where the social status of the sister was higher than that of the wife and where her political influence was more solidly based, but where she was denied the chance to act as de facto ruler of the empire with authority in heir selection and dethronement.

In discussing the status of women among the ruling elite, it is therefore necessary to distinguish between different categories of females in the same generation (sisters and wives, wives and concubines, etc.). It is also necessary to distinguish between the attitude toward a political role for those different categories of women and the attitude toward their relatives and consort families in general. As we have seen, at least four regimes, two of Chinese origin and two of non-Han background (Northern Wei, Sung, Yuan, and Ming), managed to prevent domination of the throne by the emperor's maternal relatives. Only two states (Northern Wei and Ming), however, set out to achieve this by relieving the imperial wife of power: in Sung, the declining influence of maternal kin was a by-product of other concerns; while during the Yuan the authority of the wife remained intact even though her close kin were excluded from power.

Although both the Northern Wei and Ming dynasties, as well as the Yuan, succeeded in diminishing the influence of maternal kin, no regime was able to stop individual mothers and wives from amassing power. Even the Northern Wei, despite its brutal approach to this problem, was dominated on two separate occasions by female regents. And as we have seen, the Ming regime, like other Chinese dynasties before it, faced chronic problems of delegated authority during times of emergency and minority rule. Thus the wife continued to play much the same role as she had in Han, T'ang, and Sung times, albeit at a less prominent level. Ironically, the Liao regime, which gave greatest political privilege to maternal kin, saw only three influential dowagers—considerably fewer than under many Chinese regimes. In fact, neither Liao nor any other steppe or China-based non-Han regime offered the imperial wife greater legal authority and power than did the native Chinese state.

NOTES

1. As the Liao case illustrates (see Holmgren 1986a:55–57, 75–76, and figure 2.4), regular cross-generational alliance was essential to the development of an exclusive system of marriage exchange with a single lineage. See n. 3 below.

2. For brief comments on the evolution and decay of various marriage circles, see Grafflin 1980:155–56 and 1981:71; Wong 1979:134–36, 139; and n. 15 below.

3. Some laws were more easily broken than others. The ban on cross-generational alliance was, for example, broken more than once in early Chinese history by consort families for the purpose of political gain (see Ch'ü 1972:264 n. 63, 283–84; Ward-Czynska 1978:2–3; Dull 1978:32–33; Fang 1965:377, 384). In contrast, the rule of monogamy was rarely, if ever, violated.

4. For a case where fraternal succession nearly became an institution, see C. Chang 1966 on early Northern Sung.

5. The emperor's male agnates were given a share of political authority and acted as regents in the states of Wu (A.D. 222–80) and Western Chin (A.D. 265–316). The short-lived state of Wei (A.D. 220–65) gave distant collateral kin powers in government but carefully restricted close male agnates (see Fang 1952; 1965). In other regimes, male agnates held power only during the foundation era or early part of the dynasty. Former Han (see Kamada 1962; Tao 1974) and Ming (see Chan 1976) are the best documented cases.

6. These elements are illustrated in the life of Princess T'ai-p'ing of the T'ang dynasty. Her first marriage, undertaken in A.D. 681 when her father was alive, was to his sister's son. The second, undertaken in 690 during the reign of her mother, Empress Wu (see n. 14), was to a member of her mother's family (*HTS* 83:3650–52; *HTS* 206:5853).

7. For examples, see Ward-Czynska 1978:31–37, 43–48, 53–57; *CS* 31:950–66; *MS* 113:3513.

8. The lesson of the protective role of maternal kin vis-à-vis the larger bureaucratic elite was driven home to the Chinese after the usurpation of the Wei throne by the Ssu-ma family in A.D. 265. On Wei, see nn. 5, 11, 12, and the section on historical development in this chapter.

9. On infant mortality during the Former Han, see cases cited in Tao 1978:183; Ward-Czynska 1978:47. In the Northern Sung, the fourth ruler was the sixth and only surviving son of his father; and only five of the twelve sons of the sixth ruler survived infancy (Chung 1981:4–5, 50–51). On average about half the daughters born to each Northern Sung ruler also perished in infancy (*SS* 248:8771–90). Apart from natural deaths, there were those engineered for political purposes. Li (1970:272–74) argues that Later Han succession problems were largely the result of murder.

10. While only three out of the twelve adult rulers of the Former Han failed to produce a son, eight failed to have a son by the empress; i.e., eleven out of sixteen wives failed to produce an heir to the throne (see Tao 1978:180–83; Ward–Czynska 1978:63). Again, very few of the nine rulers of Northern Sung came to the throne as sons of appointed empresses (Chung 1981:2–3, 51). This pattern was repeated during the Ming with only one of ten rulers in the last two centuries of that regime coming to the throne as sons of the first empress. All this adds weight to the occasional direct reference to sexual avoidance.

11. In cases where sororal kin did threaten the throne, their power base was independent of, and indeed often existed in opposition to, their personal ties with the throne—see for example the case of the Ssu-ma family of Western Chin during the Three Kingdoms era (see nn. 8 and 12).

12. The loyalty felt to the throne even by female offspring of imperial princesses is

illustrated in the case of Lady Hsia-hou (d. A.D. 234), whose mother came from the royal family of the state of Wei (A.D. 220–65). Her support for the Wei house and the throne against the Ssu-ma family of her husband was so effective that the latter had to have her poisoned (*CS* 31:949).

13. Two women who were successful were a sister of Emperor Ching of the Former Han (see Ward-Czynska 1978:14–15; and figure 2.3), and a daughter of the founder of the state of Wu (see *SKC* 48:1151; *SKC* 50:1198–1200).

14. For two examples of FZD alliances, see *HS* 97A:3948; *HTS* 8:221; *HTS* 77:3504; *HTS* 83:3662; and figure 2.3.

15. The first marriage circle in T'ang times centered on the Chang-sun, Tou, and Yang families. In the third reign, this circle was replaced by that of the Wu, Wei, and Yang families groupe ' around the Empress Wu and later around her granddaughter, Princess An-lo. The latter was a daughter of Empress Wei, a daughter-in-law of the male head of the Wu family, and related by blood (through Empress Wu) to the Yangs. She was opposed by her aunt, Princess T'ai-p'ing, a daughter of Empress Wu. Princess T'ai-p'ing found support in a prince of the house and in a son from her first marriage (see n. 6). The tension between aunt and niece effectively ended the political dominance of the group and, consequently, its hold on marriage relations with the throne (see Fitzgerald 1968; Tang 1975).

16. See the discussion in Soullière (1984) on past and current views of the status of the Ming ruler; Endicott-West (1986) and Holmgren (1986b:146–51; and 1987) on traditional restraints imposed on Mongol leaders; Grafflin (1980, 1981) on political and social mobility in the early Southern Dynasties; Holmgren (1980, 1981a, 1983b) on mobility in the Northern Dynasties; and Hymes (1986), Hartwell (1982), and Walton (1984) on the Sung.

17. See, for example, the marriage of the youngest daughter of the sixth ruler of Northern Sung to a great-grandson of P'an Mei, a founding general (*SS* 248:8781). The declining status of these families was temporarily reversed during the Southern Sung transition in the 1120s, when the throne demanded support from all categories of imperial kin (*SS* 248:8777).

18. The following remarks about Northern Wei are based on Holmgren (1981–83b, 1983a, 1983c, 1984, and 1987) or drawn from an unpublished book-length manuscript, "*Marriage and Power in Imperial China.*" Comments on Liao are based on Holmgren (1986a and 1987) and Wittfogel and Feng (1949); those on Yuan drawn from Holmgren (1986b, 1987, and n.d.). For details about the Chin marriage system, see Sang (1969) and Sung (1982:145–48). On the Ch'ing, see Rawski's chapter in this volume.

REFERENCES

Primary Sources

CS   *Chin shu* 晉書, by Fang Hsuan-ling 房玄齡 et al. Peking: Chung-hua shu-chü, 1974.

HHS   *Hou Han shu* 後漢書, by Fan Yeh 范曄. Peking: Chung-hua shu-chü, 1973.

HS   *Han shu* 漢書, by Pan Ku 班固 et al. Peking: Chung-hua shu-chü, 1975.

HTCTC *Hsu tzu-chih t'ung-chien* 續資治通鑑, by Pi Yuan 畢沅 et al. Peking: Chung-hua shu-chü, 1979.

HTS   *Hsin T'ang shu* 新唐書, by Ou-yang Hsiu 歐陽修 and Sung Ch'i 宋祁. Peking: Chung-hua shu-chü, 1975.

ML   *Ming-lü chi-chieh fu-li* 明律集解附例. 1610; Taipei: Ch'eng-wen, 1970 facsimile of 1898 reprint.

MS   *Ming-shih* 明史, by Chang T'ing-yü 張廷玉 et al. Peking: Chung-hua shu-chü, 1984.

PCS   *Pei Ch'i shu* 北齊書, by Li Te-lin 李德林 and Li Po-yao 李百藥. Peking: Chung-hua shu-chü, 1972.

SHT   *Sung hsing t'ung* 宋刑統, by Tou I 竇儀. Peking: Chung-hua shu-chü, 1984.

SKC   *San-kuo chih* 三國志, by Ch'en Shou 陳壽. Peking: Chung-hua shu-chü, 1975.

SS   *Sung shih* 宋史, ed. T'o T'o 脫脫 et al. Peking: Chung-hua shu-chü, 1977.

Sui shu 隋書, by Wei Cheng 魏徵 et al. Peking: Chung-hua shu-chü, 1973.

TCTC   *Tzu-chih t'ung-chien* 資治通鑑, by Ssu-ma Kuang 司馬光. Hong Kong: Chung-hua shu-chü, 1971.

TML   *T'ang Ming lü ho-pien* 唐明律合編, ed. Hsueh Yun-sheng 薛允升. Kuo-hsueh chi-pen ts'ung-shu ed.

TL   *T'ang-lü shu-i* 唐律疏議, by Ch'ang-sun Wu-chi 長孫無忌 et al. Peking: Chung-hua shu-chü, 1983.

Secondary Works

Bernard, Elmar Maria. 1972. "Die Yuan-Hou und die Gesellschaftliche und Politische Stellung der Kaiserinnen gegen Ende der Ch'ien-Han-Periode" (Empress Yuan and the social and political position of empresses toward the end of Former Han). Ph.D. diss., Georg-August Universität zu Göttingen.

Bielenstein, Hans. 1967. "The Restoration of the Han Dynasty III." *Bulletin of the Museum of Far Eastern Antiquities* 39.2:5–198.

Chan, David B. 1976. *The Usurpation of the Prince of Yen, 1398–1402.* San Francisco: Chinese Materials Center.

Chang, Curtis Chung. 1966. "Inheritance Problems in the First Two Reigns of the Sung Dynasty." M.A. thesis, University of Chicago.

Chang Pang-wei 張邦煒. 1986. "Shih-lun Sung-tai 'hun-yin pu wen fa-yüeh'" 試论宋代"婚姻不问阀阅" (Examination of the Sung words "not considering family rank in marriage"). *Sung Liao Chin Yuan shih*, no. 2:21–36.

Chao Feng-chieh 趙鳳喈. 1937. *Chung-kuo fu-nü tsai fa-lü shang chih ti-wei* 中國婦女在法律上之地位 (Legal position of Chinese women). Shanghai: Commercial Press.

Chiba Hiroshi 千葉煦. 1974. "Sōdai no kōhi; Taiso, Taisō, Shinsō, Jinsō shichō" 宋代の后妃; 太祖, 太宗, 真宗, 仁宗四朝 (The imperial consorts of Emperors T'ai-tsu, T'ai-tsung, Chen-tsung, and Jen-tsung of Northern Sung). In *Sōdai shi ronsō* (Collection of essays on Sung history), special anniversary volume presented to Sadao Aoyama. Tokyo: Seishin shobo.

Ch'ü T'ung-tsu. 1961. *Law and Society in Traditional China.* Paris: Mouton.

————. 1972. *Han Social Structure*. Seattle: University of Washington Press.

Chung, Priscilla Ching. 1981. *Palace Women in the Northern Sung, 960–1126*. Leiden: E. J. Brill.

de Heer, P. H. 1986. *The Care-Taker Emperor: Aspects of the Imperial Institution in Fifteenth-Century China as Reflected in the Political History of the Reign of Chu Ch'i-yu*. Leiden: E. J. Brill.

de Crespigny, R. R. C. 1975. "The Harem of Emperor Huan: A Study of Court Politics in Later Han." *Papers on Far Eastern History* 12:1–42.

DMB (*Dictionary of Ming Biography, 1368–1664*). 1976. Ed. L. C. Goodrich and Fang Chao-ying. 2 vols. New York: Columbia University Press.

Dubs, Homer H. 1955. *The History of the Former Han Dynasty*. Baltimore: Waverly.

Dull, Jack L. 1978. "Marriage and Divorce in Han China: A Glimpse at 'Pre-Confucian' Society." In *Chinese Family Law and Social Change in Historical and Comparative Perspective*, ed. David C. Buxbaum. Seattle: University of Washington Press.

Ebrey, Patricia. 1981. "Women in the Kinship System of the Southern Song Upper Class." In *Women in China*, ed. Richard Guisso and Stanley Johannesen. Youngstown, N.Y.: Philo Press.

————. 1983. "Types of Lineages in Ch'ing China: A Re-examination of the Chang Lineage of T'ung-ch'eng." *Ch'ing-shih wen-t'i* 4.9:1–20.

————. 1984a. "Conceptions of the Family in the Sung Dynasty." *Journal of Asian Studies* 43. 2:219–45.

————. 1984b. *Family and Property in Sung China: Yüan Ts'ai's Precepts for Social Life*. Princeton: Princeton University Press.

————. 1986. "Concubines in Sung China." *Journal of Family History* 11.1:1–24.

Endicott-West, Elizabeth. 1986. "Imperial Governance in Yüan Times." *Harvard Journal of Asiatic Studies* 46.2:523–49.

Fang, Achilles. 1952. *The Chronicle of the Three Kingdoms*. Vol. 1. Cambridge: Harvard University Press.

————. 1965. *The Chronicle of the Three Kingdoms*. Vol. 2. Cambridge: Harvard University Press.

Feng, Han-i. 1948. *The Chinese Kinship System*. Cambridge: Harvard–Yenching Institute.

Fitzgerald, C. P. 1968. *The Empress Wu*. Melbourne, Canberra, and Sydney: F. W. Cheshire for the Australian National University.

Fletcher, Joseph. 1986. "The Mongols: Ecological and Social Perspectives." *Harvard Journal of Asiatic Studies* 46.1:11–30.

Grafflin, Dennis. 1980. "Social Order in the Early Southern Dynasties: The Formation of Eastern Chin." Ph.D. diss., Harvard University.

————. 1981. "The Great Family in Medieval South China." *Harvard Journal of Asiatic Studies* 41.1:63–74.

Greiner, Peter. 1979–80. "Die Frauen am Kaiserhof der Ming-Zeit" (Women at the Ming imperial court). *Monumenta Serica* 34:1–63.

Hartwell, Robert M. 1982. "Demographic, Political, and Social Transformations of China, 750–1550." *Harvard Journal of Asiatic Studies* 42:365–442.

Holmgren, J. 1980. "Lineage Falsification in the Northern Dynasties: Wei Shou's Ancestry." *Papers on Far Eastern History* 21:1–16.

————. 1981. "Widow Chastity in the Northern Dynasties: The *Lieh-nü* Biographies in the *Wei-shu*." *Papers on Far Eastern History* 23:165–86.

————. 1981–83a. "Social Mobility in the Northern Dynasties: A Case Study of the Feng of Northern Yen." *Monumenta Serica* 35:19–32.

————. 1981–83b. "Women and Political Power in the Traditional T'o-pa Elite: A Preliminary Study of the Biographies of Empresses in the *Wei-shu*." *Monumenta Serica* 35:33–73.

————. 1983a. "The Harem in Northern Wei Politics—398–498 A.D." *Journal of the Economic and Social History of the Orient* 26.1:71–96.

————. 1983b. "The Lu Clan of Tai Commandary and Their Contribution to the T'o-pan State of Northern Wei in the Fifth Century." *T'oung pao* 69.4–5:272–312.

————. 1983c. "*Wei-shu* Records on the Bestowal of Imperial Princesses during the Northern Wei Dynasty." *Papers on Far Eastern History* 27:21–97.

————. 1984. "The Making of an Elite: Local Politics and Social Relations in Northeastern China during the Fifth Century A.D." *Papers on Far Eastern History* 30:1–79.

————. 1985. "The Economic Foundations of Virtue: Widow-Remarriage in Early and Modern China." *Australian Journal of Chinese Affairs* 13:1–27.

————. 1986a. "Marriage, Kinship and Succession under the Ch'i-tan Rulers of the Liao Dynasty (907–1125)." *T'oung pao* 72:44–91.

————. 1986b. "Observations on Marriage and Inheritance Practices in Early Mongol and Yuan Society, with Particular Reference to the Levirate." *Journal of Asian History* 20.2:127–92.

————. 1986c. "Yeh-lü, Yao-lien and Ta-ho: Views of the Hereditary Prerogative in Early Khitan Leadership." *Papers on Far Eastern History* 34:37–81.

————. 1987. "Political Organization of Non-Han States in China: The Role of Imperial Princes in Wei, Liao and Yuan." *Journal of Oriental Studies* 25.1:1–48.

————. N.d. "A Question of Strength: Military Capability and Princess Bestowal in Imperial China's Foreign Relations (Han to Ch'ing)." *Monumenta Serica* (forthcoming).

Hymes, Robert P. 1986. *Statesmen and Gentlemen: The Elite of Fu-chou, Chiang-hsi, in Northern and Southern Sung*. Cambridge: Cambridge University Press.

Johnson, Wallace. 1979. *The T'ang Code*. Vol. 1, *General Principles*. Princeton: Princeton University Press.

Kamada, Shigeo, 1962. "Han Emperors' Policy of Oppressing Kingdoms." *Memoirs of the Research Department of the Toyo Bunko* 21:77–95.

Krader, Lawrence. 1963. *Social Organization of the Mongol-Turkic Pastoral Nomads*. Indiana University Publications, Uralic and Altaic Series, vol. 20. The Hague: Mouton.

Li Hsueh-ming (Lee Hok-ming) 李學銘. 1970. "Ts'ung Tung Han cheng-ch'üan shih-chih lun ch'i shih ti-shih hun-yin ssu-hsu yü wai-ch'i sheng-chiang chih kuan-hsi" 從東漢政權實質論其時帝室婚姻嗣續與外戚升降之關係 (The relationship between political power in Eastern [Later] Han and imperial marriage and succession and the mobility of distaff families). *Hsin-ya hsueh-pao* 9.2:225–82.

Loewe, Michael. 1974. *Crisis and Conflict in Han China*. London: George Allen & Unwin.

Sang Hsiu-yun 桑秀雲. 1969. "Chin-shih Wan-yen shih hun-chih chih shih-shih"

金室完顏氏婚制之試釋(A tentative study of the marriage system of the imperial Wan-yen clan during the Chin dynasty). *Bulletin of the Institute of History and Philology* (Academia Sinica) 39.1:255–88.

Schurmann, H. F. 1955–56. "Traditional Property Concepts in China." *Far Eastern Quarterly* 15:507–16.

Shiga, Shūzō. 1978. "Family Property and the Law of Inheritance in Traditional China." In *Chinese Family Law and Social Change in Historical and Comparative Perspective*, ed. David C. Buxbaum. Seattle: University of Washington Press.

Soullière, Ellen F. 1984. "Reflections on Chinese Despotism and the Power of the Inner Court." *Asian Profile* 12.2:130–45.

———. 1987. "Palace Women in the Ming Dynasty." Ph.D. diss., Princeton University.

———. 1988. "The Imperial Marriages of the Ming Dynasty." *Papers on Far Eastern History* 37:15–42.

Straughair, Anna. 1973. *Chang Hua: A Statesman-Poet of the Chin Dynasty*. Occasional Paper 15. Canberra: Australian National University, Faculty of Asian Studies.

Sung Te-chin 宋德金. 1982. "Chin-tai Nü-chen tsu su shu-lun"金代女真族俗述論 (Jurchen customs in the Chin). *Li-shih yen-chiu*, no. 3:145–59.

Tai Yen-hui. 1978. "Divorce in Traditional Chinese Law." In *Chinese Family Law and Social Change in Historical and Comparative Perspective*, ed. David C. Buxbaum. Seattle: University of Washington Press.

Tang, Karen Kai-ying. 1975. "Empress Wei, Consort Shang-kuan and the Political Conflicts in the Reign of Chung-tsung." M.A. thesis, University of British Columbia.

Tao Tien-yi. 1974. "Vassal Kings and Marquises of the Former Han Dynasty." *Bulletin of the Institute of History and Philology* (Academia Sinica) 46.1:155–72.

———. 1978. "The System of Imperial Succession during China's Former Han Dynasty (206 B.C.–9 A.D.)." *Papers on Far Eastern History* 18:171–91.

Tjan, Tjoe Som. 1949, 1952. Reprint, 1973. *Po Hu T'ung: The Comprehensive Discussions in the White Tiger Hall*. 2 vols. Westport, Conn.: Hyperion Press.

Wallacker, Benjamin E. 1987. "Dethronement and Due Process in Early Imperial China." *Journal of Asian History* 21.1:48–67.

Waltner, Ann Beth. 1981. "The Adoption of Children in Ming and Early Ch'ing China." Ph.D. diss., University of California, Berkeley.

Walton, Linda. 1984. "Kinship, Marriage and Status in Song China: A Study of the Lou Lineage of Ningbo, c. 1050–1250." *Journal of Asian History* 18.1:35–77.

Ward-Czynska, Bonnie V. 1978. "A Political History of the Imperial Distaff Relatives of the Former Han Dynasty." M.A. thesis, Columbia University.

Wittfogel, K. A., and Feng Chia-sheng. 1949. *History of Chinese Society. Liao*. Philadelphia: American Philosophical Society.

Wong Sun-ming. 1979. "Confucian Ideal and Reality: Transformation of the Institution of Marriage in T'ang China." Ph.D. diss., University of Washington.

Yang Lien-sheng. 1968. "Female Rulers in Imperial China." In *Studies of Governmental Institutions in Chinese History*, ed. John L. Bishop. Cambridge: Harvard University Press.

Young, Gregory C. 1986. "Court Politics in the Later Han: Officials and the Consort Clan, A.D. 132–44." *Papers on Far Eastern History* 34:1–36.

THREE

Shifts in Marriage Finance from the Sixth to the Thirteenth Century

Patricia Buckley Ebrey

People in the T'ang period [A.D. 618–907] celebrated the Ts'uis and Lus as top-rank families. Even when descendants of these families were poor and of low political rank, they were esteemed for their pedigree. Today people do not make much of family. If a girl of a noble family is poor and without resources, she may not be able to marry in her prime. Yet village rich families can marry into noble houses and get those who passed the examinations in the top group as their sons-in-law.

CHAO YEN-WEI, 1206 (*YLMC* 3:98)

A marriage in China, as in most places, normally involved some financial outlay by both the husband's and the wife's families and therefore some re-distribution of wealth. In the classical ritual prescriptions preserved in the *I-li* (Etiquette and Ritual), the husband's family would send a goose to the wife's family on several occasions, and midway between the first proposal and the wedding itself the groom's family sent more substantial gifts, given in the *I-li* as ten bolts of cloth and a pair of deer skins (Steele 1917 1:18–23). The bride's family was not obliged to present gifts to the groom's family, but the bride herself would be sent with clothes and personal items such as jewelry packed in cases, and could be supplied with female attendants who might serve as her maids or her husband's concubines (see also Thatcher's chapter here for exchanges between ruling families). In early texts these two types of outlays are generally treated as belonging to different realms. The gifts presented by the husband's family fell into the realm of ritual. Presenting and accepting these gifts was integral to the betrothal ceremony: one was not married ritually without some token transfer of objects from the groom's family to the bride's. The classic *Li chi* (Record of Ritual) asserts: "Without receipt of the betrothal gifts there is no contact and no affinity" (cf. Legge 1885 1:78). In later periods, at least, once betrothal gifts had been received, the girl's family could be prosecuted if they broke off the engagement (*TLSI* 13:119). By contrast, the validity of a marriage did not depend on the bride's bringing anything. Nor were the objects she brought termed gifts; they were simply her possessions. By the Han period (202 B.C.–A.D. 220) there is scattered evidence that how well a bride was equipped depended on how much her family wished to do for her, which in turn probably depended on how rich they were, how many sons they had, the importance they placed on the match, and probably sometimes the affection they felt for her. When either family was rich, they could make their outlays in style, giving generous gifts and supplying daughters with handsome dowries. A girl without brothers, as heiress, could receive the bulk of the family property as her dowry (see Yang 1933:17–19; Dull 1978:45–48).

In this chapter my concern is not with heiresses or routine marriage exchanges of modest size, but with marriage outlays that made a substantial economic difference to the two families. Demands for lavish betrothal gifts began to be heard among aristocratic families from the late fifth century on; a few centuries later demands for substantial dowries were made by the families of the Sung (960–1279) upper class. The motivations for these marriages were by no means simply economic; the marriages sealed with these transfers of property brought prestige and connections to affines. I therefore try to show how the tangible financial benefits and less tangible benefits of honor and connections worked together in these two periods. I also explain how the shift in the balance of marriage finance related to the changed political and economic environment of the ruling elite.

MARRIAGE FINANCE AMONG ARISTOCRATIC FAMILIES, SIXTH–NINTH CENTURIES

After the fall of the Han dynasty, Chinese society developed in distinctly aristocratic directions. By the late fourth century in the south and the late fifth century in the north, a relatively small number of families were preeminent in social and political life. Along with admiration for aristocratic pedigrees came an inflation in the value of the betrothal gifts the highest-ranking families could expect to receive when they sent out a daughter in marriage. In the south in about 490 Shen Yueh accused Wang Yuan of highly objectionable behavior. Wang had married his daughter to a man of much lower social status who had paid a "betrothal gift" (*p'in-li*) of fifty thousand cash. Wang made enough of a profit from this transaction to buy himself a concubine (*WH* 40:879–81; cf. Johnson 1977:9–11). A few decades later in his "Family Instructions," Yen Chih-t'ui (531–c. 591) complained that such transactions were all too common:

> In the present age, when marriages are arranged, some people sell their daughters for the betrothal gift or buy a wife by making a payment of silk. They compare the ancestry [of the two parties], calculate down to the smallest sum, demand much and offer little, exactly like bargaining in a market. As a result coarse sons-in-law may enter the family or arrogant daughters-in-law take over the house. (*YSCH* 1:64; cf. Teng 1968:20)

Note that Yen's complaint resembles Shen Yueh's: Those who had daughters profited, while those who needed wives would have to pay. Such conditions meant that girls from families with the most esteemed ancestry were marrying down. They seemed arrogant to their in-laws, while their husbands seemed coarse to their parents. Cross-culturally, marriage exchanges have often been compared to commercial transactions, so this does not necessarily mean that marriages were in some objective sense more like "sales" in this period (Comaroff 1980:40–41). What was probably new was the size of the betrothal gifts and weight assigned to ancestry, not the negotiation process itself.[1]

Yen Chih-t'ui implied that an eminent family could expect an even higher sum if they married their daughter into a family of lesser birth. Indeed, Yang Su (d. 606), perhaps the most powerful official of the early Sui (581–618), gave "extremely generous" betrothal gifts so that his son could marry the daughter of Ts'ui Piao, a Ch'ing-ho Ts'ui of eminent ancestry whose "family standing" (*men-ti*) he valued. Yang even put up with rude behavior on the part of Ts'ui Piao to bring the marriage about (*SuiS* 76:1733). Something of the size of an "extremely generous" betrothal gift can be imagined from the case of a Northern Ch'i (550–77) official who got into trouble because he embezzled 400,000 cash to pay for the betrothal gift for marriage to the daughter of a T'ai-yuan Wang (*PCS* 42:564). In this period, betrothal gifts could include fields and animals. One Northern Ch'i official known for his stinginess was accused of sending inferior items as parts of the betrothal gift when his son married a Fan-yang Lu girl. These items were lame mules, infertile fields, and secondhand brass vessels (*PCS* 43:573).

Further evidence of the size of betrothal gifts can be found in the sumptuary rules issued to regulate them. In the late fifth and sixth centuries, the various governments tried to fight persistent tendencies for prestige to become independent of the ranks and honors emanating from the court. For instance, governments in both the north and the south tried to control the publication of genealogical gazetteers that ranked families (see Johnson 1977b:33–43). When the ability to command large betrothal gifts became a sign of high status beyond the government's power to control, the Northern Ch'i government promulgated rules to make these gifts correspond to political rank. At each of the "six rites" (i.e., the steps in betrothal), everyone with rank (from the emperor down to rank-nine officials) could present a lamb, a pair of geese, and a *hu* each of wine, millet, rice, and flour. Commoners could present gifts half this large. For the betrothal gift, much more detailed specifications were given for five kinds of cloth and a variety of foodstuffs, varying in quantities according to official rank. For instance, the highest officials could give 140 pieces of plain silk (*chüan*), the lowest officials 34 (*SuiS* 9:179). Clearly by this time gifts of much greater monetary value than anything prescribed in the classics were commonly exchanged at weddings of aristocrats and other wealthy officials.

Even though substantial betrothal gifts received imperial approval as long as they were in line with official rank, negotiating their size was never deemed morally correct in the Confucian view of marriage. Wang T'ung (c. 584–617), a Confucian teacher, wrote: "Discussing wealth in arranging a marriage is the way of the barbarians," a saying frequently quoted by later writers (*CS* 1:11). He probably suspected that this practice—unattested in the classics—was the legacy of the non-Han rulers of the Northern dynasties (386–581). More likely, it reflects the growth of aristocracy.

In 632, after the founding of the T'ang dynasty (618–906), Emperor T'ai-tsung reiterated Yen Chih-t'ui's complaint about mercenary marriage arrangements. The emperor directed his remarks specifically against the leading families of the northeast (the Ts'uis, Lus, Lis, and Chengs), who were arrogant in their assumption of superior birth. He charged that "every time they marry out a daughter to another family they demand a large betrothal gift (*p'in-ts'ai*), taking quantity to be the important thing. They discuss numbers and settle an agreement, just like merchants in the market" (*CKCY* 7:226). Six years later T'ai-tsung chastised his own officials for their lack of self-respect, evident in their vying for marriage into these families out of "admiration for their ancestry (*tsu-tsung*)." Even when they presented valuable betrothal gifts, the officials' families accepted a position of inferiority vis-à-vis their affinal relatives and thus had to tolerate disrespectful behavior from their daughters-in-law (*CKCY* 7:227).

In 657 the next emperor, Kao-tsung, complained again about the snobbish exclusiveness underlying the leading families' marriage practices. He took several measures designed to curb them. First he prohibited marriage among eleven lines of seven old families of five surnames.[2] Limits were also set on how much wealth a family could receive in the form of betrothal gifts when marrying out a daughter. These limits were three hundred pieces of silk for families rank three or higher, two hundred for rank four and five, one hundred for rank six and seven, and fifty for anyone lower. (Because in this period silk was commonly used as a currency, the intention probably was that all the gifts given should not exceed these values, rather than that only silk should be used for the gifts.) Finally, he restricted the use of betrothal gifts: the bride's family was not to make a profit by marrying a daughter out but was to use all of the betrothal gifts to supply her dowry, and her husband's family was not to appropriate the dowry either (*THY* 83:1528–29). In other words, families could expend handsome sums only so long as they were seen as outfitting the bride; neither family could then be interpreted as seeking a profit or "selling" a bride.

As several scholars have shown, the highest level of the T'ang elite was very largely drawn from family lines well established in earlier dynasties (Twitchett 1973; Johnson 1977b; and Ebrey 1978). In this period, pedigree did not confer automatic access to office, yet a relatively small group of old families managed to do extraordinarily well in placing their sons in office through their traditions of education, success in examinations, use of "protection" privilege, reputation for correct behavior, and so on. Endogamous marriage practices were crucial in sustaining the concept of an aristocracy of "old families." In the case of the Po-ling Ts'uis, of ninety-two marriages during the T'ang, 52 percent were with others of the "seven old families," another 30 percent were with the other twenty-two old families identified by Liu Fang in the mid-eighth century as "aristocratic," and all but two of the others with the hundred-odd families listed in genealogical gazetteers of the most eminent families in the country (Ebrey 1978:94–96).

Among the T'ang elite, it was the larger "family," or patriline, of the marriage partners that mattered most (Johnson 1977b:59–60; Ebrey 1978: 94–100). That is, men could plausibly assert that it was more prestigious to marry a daughter of one of the "seven old families" than to marry the daughter of a current chief minister or even a princess. A minister in the late seventh century who had married an imperial princess is said to have lamented that he had neither gained the *chin-shih* degree nor married a daughter of one of the "five surnames" (*TYL* 4:140). In the eighth century a T'ai-yuan Wang woman who married a Po-ling Ts'ui (both among the "seven old families," or "five surnames") was praised for selecting spouses from the northeastern families rather than from the "powerful" for her offspring. She had married one son to her brother's daughter and the other to a Fan-yang Lu girl (Ebrey 1978:95, 183, 184). An early ninth-century emperor could complain that people paid attention only to pedigree and not to official rank in selecting marriage partners (*HTS* 172:5206). Even as late as the first half of the tenth century, a Lung-hsi Li was praised for not being arrogant like others in his "family," or the Ts'ui, Lu, and Cheng "families" with whom his family intermarried. Members of these families would only agree to marry a girl into another family after receiving "generous presents of gold and silk" (*CWTS* 93:1230).[3]

Exclusivity reaffirms prestige. By marrying their peers, households belonging to the highest levels of the aristocracy were confirming their status. Households of aristocratic descent that were not prospering financially or politically were making use of their best resource, pedigree, when they married peers or accepted large betrothal gifts to marry others. Families that were "buying in" by taking a bride of higher status than their own were making a long-term investment in the status of their grandchildren. This was possible because pedigree through mothers was considered in assessing family standing. A ninth-century epitaph noted that although the subject's immediate patrilineal ancestors had undistinguished careers, "their relatives through marriage were the top families in the northeast" (*CTW* 504:9b).

This concern for maternal pedigree may explain why the ambitious are portrayed as seeking, not aristocratic sons-in-law, but aristocratic daughters-in-law who would be the mothers of their grandchildren.

The affinal relations created by these aristocratic marriages were conceived in general terms. The statement that "our families have intermarried for generations" or "we have old marriage connections" was often used to evoke the notion of affinal relationship: the individual so addressed might not have any close current tie. For instance, Li Hua (fl. 740s), a Chao-chün Li, said he had called on a Po-ling Ts'ui, as their families were from "adjoining areas in the northern prefectures and had old marriage ties" (*CTW* 315:7a). The man he was calling on had never lived in the northeast himself, and the visit undoubtedly took place in one of the capitals, Ch'ang-an or Lo-yang. The marriage ties seem to have been just as distant.

In the T'ang, thus, betrothal gifts among the aristocratic families were of great monetary value and were linked to marital exclusivity and the preservation of a tiny super-elite. By marrying so disproportionately among themselves, the aristocrats showed that they believed their own claims to superiority and did not rate wealth or government title above pedigree or refinement. T'ang complaints about the size of the betrothal gifts of aristocrats almost always stressed the snobbishness involved. It was not that the old families willingly gave their daughters to whoever came up with the most money. Rather they were so reluctant to marry with anyone but their own kind that outsiders had to go to extraordinary lengths if they wished to penetrate their circle.

MARRIAGE FINANCE IN THE SUNG

By the Sung period (960–1279), the balance in marriage finance had changed so that wives' families, especially among the upper class, had larger net outlays than husbands' families. No survey of marriage institutions in Chinese history points out this fundamental change (see Ch'en 1936; Ch'ü 1965; Holmgren 1985; Lü 1935; Ma 1981; and T'ao 1966). Yet I am convinced it occurred because of evidence of six sorts: (1) complaints about mercenary marriages put more stress on men seeking large dowries; (2) people drew up detailed lists of dowries before concluding marriages; (3) the legal code was revised to protect a daughter's claims to a dowry if her father died before she was married; (4) biographies of women much more frequently mention their possession of substantial dowries; (5) discussions of family budgeting treat provision of daughters' dowries as a major family expense; and (6) the cost of dowry came to be recognized as a major problem even among ordinary people. Before reviewing this evidence, I should acknowledge that sources of all kinds survive in greater abundance for the Sung than the T'ang, making arguments based on the silence of T'ang sources weak.

Therefore, I give greatest weight to cases where the T'ang sources say some-thing, but what they say is different from what Sung sources say.

Complaints about Mercenary Marriages

I have already reviewed T'ang complaints about mercenary marriages. Wife-giving families snobbishly demanded large betrothal gifts. In the Sung there were just as many complaints about marriage being treated like a transac-tion, with bargaining and contracts (cf. Fang 1986). However, the issue was no longer simply the betrothal gift and its return as dowry, but the wife's family's contribution. The value of the dowry was often much larger than that of the betrothal gifts, so that the wife's family had made a major con-tribution to the new couple's economic foundations. Indeed, Sung dowries often included land.

One of the first signs of the escalation in the size of dowries is a reference to a tax imposed on them by one of the minor states in the tenth century, the Later Shu (934–65), which controlled the Szechwan area (*CP* 14:305). By the mid-eleventh century something of a dowry crisis appears to have emerged among the upper class.

Ts'ai Hsiang (1012–67), while prefect of Fu-chou (Fukien) in the 1050s, posted a notice pointing out that "the purpose of marriage is to produce heirs, not to acquire wealth." Instead of recognizing this truth, he charged, people ignored family status (*men-hu*) in choosing brides, their minds entirely on the dowry. Once the dowry was delivered to the groom's home, "they inspect the dowry cases, in the morning searching through one, in the even-ing another. The husband cruelly keeps making more and more demands on his wife. If he is not satisfied, it can spoil their love or even lead to divorce. This custom has persisted for so long that people accept it as normal" (*SWC* 108:1439). Note how Ts'ai would like to return to some vaguely conceived former system where men sought family status in brides, not just wealth.

Ssu-ma Kuang (1019–86) a few years later provided a similar depiction of the pressures created by demands for dowries:

> Nowadays it is the custom for covetous and vulgar people first to ask about the value of the dowry when selecting a bride and the amount of the betrothal gift when marrying a daughter. Some even draw up a contract saying "such goods, in such numbers, such goods, in such numbers," thereby treating their daugh-ters as an item in a sales transaction. There are also cases where people go back on their agreements after the wedding is over. These are the methods used by brokers dealing in male and female bondservants. How can such a transaction be called a gentleman-official (*shih-ta-fu*) marriage?

> When parents-in-law have been deceived, they will maltreat the daughter-in-law as a way to vent their fury. Fearing this, parents who love their daughter put together a generous dowry in the hope of pleasing her parents-in-law, not

realizing that such covetous, vulgar people are insatiable. When the dowry is depleted, what use will the bride be to these parents-in-law? They will then "pawn" her to get further payment from her family. Her family's wealth has a limit, but their demands will never stop. Therefore, families linked by marriage often end up enemies. (*SMSSI* 3:33)

Ssu-ma Kuang mentions both dowry and betrothal gifts as open to negotiation, but seems to see the greater problem with dowry (perhaps because betrothal gifts were returned as part of the dowry). Particularly troublesome was the problem of parents-in-law mistreating the bride if her dowry were smaller than they had been led to expect. Moreover, they might make new demands on her parents, which the latter felt obliged to meet because their daughter's welfare was at stake. The situation sounds more reminiscent of India in recent times than the world of Yen Chih-t'ui and T'ang T'ai-tsung. A century later this dowry crisis had still not abated, for Yuan Ts'ai (c. 1140–95) could argue that if a family did not begin planning for their daughter's dowry when she was very young, they would have to "sell land or buildings as temporary expedients, or callously watch [their] daughter's humiliation in front of others" (Ebrey 1984b:266).

Other Sung accusations about mercenary marriages inverted the complaints of Yen Chih-t'ui and T'ang T'ai-tsung in yet another way. It was not daughters with desirable ancestry going to the highest bidders, but men with good career potential. Ting Chih (c. 1060) wrote:

Your subject has heard that in recent years after a *chin-shih* passes the examination, he discusses wealth before taking a bride, in full violation of ritual and morality. Families of officials, depending on how wealthy they are, send go-betweens back and forth, sometimes almost begging. If anything is not quite to his liking [the new *chin-shih*] casts them aside and goes to another family. (*SWC* 61:852–53)

Apparently what these new *chin-shih* wanted were daughters of officials who would bring generous dowries. Similar comments were made by Chu Yü (c. 1075–1119):

In our dynasty the families of high-ranking men select their sons-in-law during the years of the metropolitan examinations, choosing from among the scholars who attend. They do not inquire into *yin* and *yang* or auspiciousness, nor into ancestry (*chia-shih*). This practice is called "seizing a son-in-law from under the lists." Strings of cash called "money for tying the one seized" are given to the prospective groom for his expenses in the capital. In recent years rich merchants, the vulgar, and those who have great savings also "seize a son-in-law from under the lists" when they arrange a marriage for a daughter. They make the "seizing money" generous in order to entice scholars to condescend to come. One son-in-law can cost over a thousand strings. When the wedding takes place, his family also demands "money all around" [a kind of tipping]. Often they calculate what is in the cases and sacks and want an agreement tied up like a legal document. (*PCKT* 1:16)

In this case dowry (the contents of the cases and sacks) is only a part of the transaction. The girl's family has also given money directly to the future son-in-law for his "expenses," apparently a kind of earnest given to the man himself.

The type of bidding for sons-in-law that Ting Chih and Chu Yü criticized is confirmed in Sung biographies. For instance, the biography of Feng Ching (1021–94) reports that when he passed the metropolitan examination in first place in 1049 he was still not married. Chang Yao-tso (987–1058), then powerful at court because a niece was the emperor's favorite consort, wanted Feng to marry his daughter; he gave him a gold belt and on another occasion brought out a list of her dowry. Feng refused the match, conceivably because he thought he could do better: he ended up marrying the daughter of Fu Pi (1004–83), a much more influential patron (*SS* 317:10338–39).[4] A similar case is mentioned in the epitaphs for Chiang Pao (1069–1117) and his wife. After Chiang received the *chin-shih* at twenty-five or twenty-six *sui*, the high official Tseng Pu (1035–1107) proposed marriage to his daughter by a concubine along with a gift of 300,000 cash. Chiang reportedly declined the gift but accepted the marriage proposal (*PSHC* 13:4a; 13b–14a).

Let me give one final quotation. Yuan Ts'ai, writing in 1178, referred to mercenary marriages in the context of the deceptions of matchmakers. As he noted, the classical complaint was that matchmakers fooled the girl's family by saying the boy was rich and the boy's family by saying the girl was beautiful. In his own time their chicanery focused on money matters: "Matchmakers deceive the girl's family by saying the boy does not seek a full complement of dowry presents and in fact will help in outfitting the bride. They deceive the boy's family by promising generous transfer of goods, and they make up a figure without any basis in fact" (Ebrey 1984b:223). Here the whole issue is dowry: the bride's family is told it can be small and come from indirect dowry; the boy's family is assured it will be large.

In comparing T'ang and Sung complaints about marriage payments, differences in the meaning assigned to these payments are striking. Snobbishness and exclusivity were regularly attributed to those who demanded large betrothal gifts in the T'ang, lack of self-respect to those who consented. In the Sung, social exclusivity was not associated with large dowries. Families insisting that a large dowry accompany daughters-in-law were not suspected of erecting status barriers to keep lowborn women out of their homes. Men who sought large dowries were accused of greed, not disdain for those below them. The ulterior motive of a family offering a handsome dowry was generally assumed to be a desire to attach to them a young man of promise, rather than more diffuse links to a famous family. Indeed, a concern with family pedigree was contrasted to a concern with dowries.[5]

Marriage Agreements

Ssu-ma Kuang's charge that people drew up contracts specifying betrothal gifts and dowries can easily be confirmed in other Sung sources, though most of the time the term "contract" (*ch'i-yueh*) was avoided. Sung marriage agreements were much more detailed than anything surviving from the T'ang.[6] The *Meng liang lu* (Record of Dreams of Glory), which describes the Southern Sung (1127–1279) capital of Hangchow, reported that an "agreement card" (*ting-t'ieh*) sent by the man's family would list the son's birth order in the family (first, second, or third son, and so on); the year, month, day, and hour of his birth; whether his parents were living, and, if not, who was presiding over the marriage; and, in the event that the marriage was uxorilocal, the wealth he would bring in "gold and silver, fields, productive property (*ts'ai-ch'an*), houses, rooms, hills, and gardens." The card that the girl's family returned would likewise give her seniority number and time of birth, then list what she was bringing, her "cases with jewelry, gold and silver, pearls and feathers, precious objects, items for use, and bedding, as well as the property accompanying her on her marriage, such as fields, houses, businesses, hills, or gardens" (*MLL* 20:304). In other words, dowry was specified in the first proposal, as was the man's "dowry" if he were to be an uxorilocal husband.

Sung guides to letter-writing often devoted several chapters to marriage correspondence. Like the *Meng liang lu*, these books show the dowry to be specified in the first proposal. In the next round of communications, lists of betrothal gifts were often attached to the "engagement letter" (*hun-shu*) sent by the groom's family.[7] The bride's family sent back comparable letters, including a list of the betrothal gifts they were refusing as well as a list of the objects in the trousseau (*CCCC* 489–90; *SLKC* ch'ien-chi 10:5a–b; *HLPY* 1; *HMTC* chia 5:2a–4b). One of these books explained the difference between the items of the dowry specified on these two occasions: the "agreement card" would list the "major numbers" of land and servants, while the "trousseau list" would give the "minor numbers" of the various items of cloth, jewelry, and other goods sent "to make up the room" (*HMTC* i 18:6b).[8]

A Sung agreement card and trousseau list survive for the marriage of the daughter of a prominent family in K'un-shan county (Kiangsu). Dated 1261, the agreement card divides her dowry into three items: five hundred *mou* of land, trousseau (*lien-chü*) of (or worth) eleven thousand strings of cash, and "marriage ties" (*ti-yin*) of (or worth) five thousand strings.[9] In the trousseau list, dated fourteen months later, there is a detailed breakdown of different types of cloth and miscellaneous objects (*STJC* 8:4a–5b).

Revision of the Law Code

A third sign of the increased weight given dowry in the Sung is revision of the laws for division of family property so that orphaned daughters were provided with dowries. Neither the T'ang nor the Sung government concerned itself with the decisions a father made about the property to assign his daughter as dowry, nor did they routinely interfere with the decisions of other family seniors in undivided families. But orphans posed special problems. Stories and anecdotes often refer to the plight of orphaned daughters without dowries, even daughters from official families. It was taken for granted that their lack of a dowry would make it impossible for them to be married into an otherwise appropriate family, and might even lead to them being sold as concubines (Ebrey 1986a:6). Probably because of the disastrous consequences of daughters left without dowries, Sung law provided them some protection from the greed of brothers, uncles, and other potential heirs when the family property was divided.[10]

Already in the T'ang, if brothers who were dividing the property included one not yet married, or if they had unmarried sisters (or aunts), marriage expenses were to be set aside before the group property was divided. Unmarried brothers were to be given the funds for a betrothal gift in addition to their share, and unmarried sisters were to get marriage funds half the size of their brothers' funds (*SHT* 12:12b). This law was probably intended to codify practice in the T'ang, when the man's family gave betrothal gifts that cost more than the net outlay of the bride's family. The code said nothing about the appropriate size of betrothal gifts, but because this provision came into play only when at least one of the brothers was already married, funds similar to those used for the married brother(s) would probably be considered fair.

Later the law was revised to match Sung custom more closely, for Southern Sung judges cited rules that gave unmarried daughters more substantial dowries. Three particular changes in the law are noteworthy. First, at division unmarried daughters were to be assigned a share, or portion, half that of a son's share (i.e., half the size of his share of the estate, not half the size of the allotment for his marriage expenses) (*CMC* 8:290–91; *HTHS* 193:7a, 14a). This would mean that in families where a boy and two girls survived, none yet married, the boy would get half the property and each girl a quarter. Second, an old T'ang rule was revised. When a house died out (*hu-chueh*) for lack of an established heir, the property had gone entirely to the unmarried daughters (or, in their absence, married daughters). This law was revised to reduce the amount going to married daughters (who already had dowries)[11] and was extended to cover cases where a man in an undivided family died leaving only daughters. The revised law stipulated that his daughters could succeed to his share of the property just as though the house had died out (e.g., *CMC* 8:280–82). Third, when an heir was set up posthumously, he would not be treated like a natural son or an adoptive son set up during the parents' lifetimes, whose presence would eliminate shares for married daughters and significantly reduce those for unmarried daughters (as seems to have been the case in the T'ang). Instead, the property would be divided, with one-fourth to the posthumous heir and three-fourths to the unmarried daughters (if there were also married daughters, he would get one-fifth, if only married daughters, he would receive a third [*CMC* 8:266–67; *HTHS* 193:11a]). (On all of these revisions, see Burns 1973:259–81.) These changes in the law seem clearly to reflect the much greater weight dowry had come to play in the transmission of property between mid-T'ang and mid-Sung. T'ang law left it up to the heirs to decide how to provide for their sisters, aunts, or nieces no matter what the circumstances. It made no difference if the heir was an adoptee or if the property was under the trusteeship of a widowed concubine who was not the mother of the daughters, or under the trusteeship of an uncle, and so on. Sung law saw unmarried girls' need for dowries to be great enough to warrant some legal protection from unscrupulous relatives.

When judges supervised the division of an estate, they did not always follow these rules as they were codified, but they usually made substantial provisions for dowries. For instance, in the *Ch'ing-ming chi*, there is an account of a man who died, leaving behind two daughters, the elder nine *sui*. A posthumous heir was appointed for him. Rather than giving a quarter to the heir and three-eighths to each daughter (as the statutes specified), the judge gave each one-third, with the daughters' property earmarked for their dowries (*CMC* 7:215). In a case decided by Hu Ying (*chin-shih* 1232), one of three brothers died before their property had been divided, leaving a single daughter (his wife was also dead). An earlier official had said the daughter should get one-third of what would normally go to her father, but Hu Ying revised this to half on the grounds that she had not been married when her father died and a girl should get half as much as a son, who would have received it all. Moreover, Hu Ying said that all of the private property of the girl's father's branch (such as her mother's dowry) was to go to her (*CMC* 8:280–82). In a case decided by Liu K'o-chuang (1187–1269), family property was first divided into two collateral lines. In one line, a brother got half and his two sisters each a quarter. In the other, a posthumous heir and two natural daughters each got a quarter, the remaining quarter to be used for the funeral expenses of the girls' father (*HTHS* 193:10a–17b).

One can also find cases where orphaned daughters received smaller shares. Judges took into account a variety of circumstances: fathers specifying a smaller share in the will, mothers remarrying and taking their daughters with them, or the presence of a step-mother or adopted brother (e.g., *CMC* 5:141–42, 7:230–32, 238–39). But the direction of the change in the law was undoubtedly to protect orphaned girls' claims to property for dowry.

References to Dowry in Epitaphs and Anecdotes

In T'ang epitaphs for women, references to their dowries are rare.[12] By contrast, they are fairly common in Sung epitaphs.[13] For instance, in the early eleventh century a woman from a rich official family married a man who passed the examinations at seventeen, the first in his family to have an official career that they knew of. According to her epitaph, she felt uncomfortable at having so much private property (*ssu-ts'ai*) when her husband's family was poor, and so contributed it all to the common pool (*KSC* 53:646). In the early twelfth century the daughter of an official married an orphan who had just passed the examinations. It happened that one of her husband's relatives had sold the hill with the ancestral graves on it to a temple. The husband was about to borrow money to try to redeem the hill when his wife stopped him and said: "The reason my parents sent me with property was to be of aid to your family. How could I use it while your family graves are not being preserved?" She emptied out her chests to redeem the hill and with the remainder bought more land and built a building on it for the protection of the graveyard (*NCCIK* 22:459). In a similar case recorded in another epitaph, some brothers were about to sell part of the family land to pay for their father's funeral. One of their wives insisted they should keep the ancestral property intact; she would give them what they needed from her dowry (*CWKWC* 91:14a). The epitaph for a woman who in 1160 married into a family with less than three *mu* of land reports that she told her husband that his land might be enough for the present but that they needed to increase it to plan for their descendants. Consequently, when a neighbor wanted to sell his land, she quickly sold the land she had brought as dowry in order to buy the neighbor's property and gave the deed to her father-in-law (*CCC* 12:254–55). Another epitaph records that a woman in the mid-twelfth century sold five *mu* of her dowry land to supply the money needed for her husband's brother to get a second wife after his first had died (*YSC* 14:263). Epitaphs might also praise a woman for her generosity in willing her dowry; one reported that a woman asked that her dowry be distributed to all the children and grandchildren in the family (*LCC* 28:14a).

These epitaphs were written by men who did not fully approve of wives' treating dowry as private property.[14] The women are portrayed as willingly using all or part of their dowries for larger family purposes, such as ancestral rites, funerals, or marriages of the husband's siblings, thus testifying to their commitment to the solidarity of the family. Indeed, these epitaphs may reasonably be used to infer that most women guarded their dowries with vigilance and never lost sight of the difference between their own property and the larger family's. Liu Tsai (1166–1239), for instance, noted that women by nature are tightfisted, thus making the woman he was writing about exceptional: she not only turned over all of her ample dowry and dowry fields to her husband, but she also never asked for an accounting of the income or expenses (*MTC* 34:18b).

Evidence of the Relative Cost of Dowry and Betrothal Gifts

Not only did dowries come to be substantial, but providing them also proved a more onerous burden than meeting a son's wedding expenses. Yuan Ts'ai mentioned three expenses for which families should plan long in advance: sons' educations, daughters' marriages, and parents' funerals. If a family took adequate steps—such as planting ten thousand pine trees at each daughter's birth—they would not need to worry that their daughters would "miss the best time" (Ebrey 1984b:266).

Numerical estimates of the relative costs of marriages are found in some rules for distributing income. The rules for the Fan lineage's charitable estate, formulated in 1050, specified that when a daughter was married out, thirty strings of cash were granted; twenty if it were her second marriage. When a son took a first wife twenty strings were supplied, but none for a second. These figures are on the order of the grants for funerals; the funerals of seniors were subsidized with twenty-five strings, of juniors fifteen, and of children, from two to ten strings depending on age (Twitchett 1960:9). Lü Tsu-ch'ien (1137–81), in rules he wrote up for an undivided family, specified that one hundred strings be given when a daughter was marrying and fifty when a son was marrying (*LTLWC* 10:243). A charitable venture set up in 1199 in Kwangtung for the dependents of officials who died there provided that five strings of cash be given to help in the marriage of daughters, but only three strings for the marriage of a son or a funeral (*SHY shih-huo* 60:1a–b).[15] Although each of these sets of rules stipulates different levels of funding, in each case parents of daughters were given 50 to 100 percent more than parents of sons.

Dowry in Lower Social Levels

Substantial dowries, in Sung times, were not confined to the families of officials. Memorialists sometimes complained that demands for excessively large dowries were making it impossible for girls to marry, or were forcing their families to sell land or borrow money to pay for them (e.g., *SHY hsing-fa* 2:154–55). One official even attributed female infanticide to the high cost of dowries (*CYIL* 117:1889). Hou K'o (1007–79), while magistrate of Hua-ch'eng (Szechwan), found that many girls grew old without marrying because "When people of Pa take wives they always demand property from the girl's family." His solution was to make up a schedule for dowries according to the wealth of the family and to set punishments for anyone who exceeded it. Within a year, we are told, every spinster had been married out (*ECC wen-chi* 4:504). Sun Chueh (1028–90) found a similar situation in Fu-chou (Fukien) and simply issued an order that dowries were not to exceed one hundred strings of cash, which promptly led to several hundred weddings (*SS* 344:10927). Chu Hsi (1130–1200) found that in southern Fukien girls were sent to Buddhist cloisters in part because their parents did not have the money for their marriage expenses (*CWKWC* 100:4a–5b). In these cases the clear implication is that dowry was a severe problem even among ordinary people. One Sung observer, commenting on the customs in the far south, noted that there poor girls of fourteen or fifteen worked to earn their own dowries so that their families would not have a single cash of expense (*CLP* 2:52). Clearly he expected his readers to understand the problem of providing dowries among the poor.

That dowries could be large among ordinary people is confirmed in cases in the *Ch'ing-ming chi*. Judges never registered surprise that families neither wealthy nor well educated would give land as part of daughters' dowries. Anecdotal evidence suggests that men from families with modest means could get larger dowries if they accepted a widow, a woman who had been a concubine or courtesan, or if they entered the woman's household as the uxorilocal husband of a girl or widow. For instance, a petty trader whose wife had died in an epidemic took as his second wife a former concubine with a dowry of three hundred strings (*ICC san-pu* 1807). Moreover, even modest dowries might be useful. In another anecdote, a dog butcher's wife brought a dowry worth several dozen strings of cash, which was used as business capital. At one point the husband sold a pair of silver hairpins from it to buy dogs to slaughter; later when he wanted to abandon the business on Buddhist grounds, his wife said that her trunks still had several bolts of cloth that they could use as capital for some new means of supporting themselves (*ICC pu* 3:1574–75).

If there were only one type of evidence indicating that the balance in marriage finance had shifted between T'ang and Sung, one might suspect that the change was historiographical rather than historical. References to substantial dowries could appear more often in Sung epitaphs because writers wished to give more concrete examples of women's virtues, for instance. The law could have been revised to take account of customary practices that had been in existence for many centuries. Differences in the types of marriages referred to as mercenary could be accidental, the result of the chance survival of certain texts and loss of others. Yet, taking all of this evidence together, the conclusion that a major shift had occurred in marriage finance seems inescapable.[16] Moreover, in Sung times dowries often included land or enough money to purchase land, something uncommon earlier.

For the rest of this paper I shall treat it as established that between the eighth and the eleventh centuries marriage finance among the elite shifted from one in which the groom's family bore the larger burden in laying the economic foundations of the marriage (through betrothal gifts used to prepare the dowry) to one in which the bride's family also made major contributions, equaling or outweighing the husband's family's. I shall now turn to examining the causes and consequences of this change in marriage finance.

SHIFTS IN MARRIAGE FINANCE AND THE T'ANG-SUNG TRANSITION

It is by now widely recognized that Chinese society underwent major transformations between the T'ang and the Sung dynasties. In standard textbook presentations, these transformations include the expansion of the economy, the growth of cities, a decline in state control over the distribution of land, the replacement of the aristocracy with an examination-based elite, the growth of autocracy, the decline of Buddhism, the rise of neo-Confucianism, the development of popular forms of culture, the shift in the center of Chinese culture to the south, the appearance of localized lineages, and so on. In this context it is not surprising that forms of marriage finance might also change. But what were the specific connections? Did certain changes in Chinese society lead to a decline in demands for expensive betrothal gifts? Did the same or other changes foster dowry escalation? Can other social or cultural changes be attributed to the increased importance of dowry?

Dowry escalation brought about not merely a change in the timing or direction of marriage payments, but a more major shift in the system of transmitting property toward "diverging devolution," to use Goody's (1973, 1976) term. Dowry involves transmission of property outside the patrilineal descent group through women whose sons and daughters bear their fathers' surnames. By contrast, betrothal gifts used by the bride's family to prepare the dowry (i.e., indirect dowry) normally ended up back under the control of patrilineal descendants. That is, for one generation these funds belonged to the wife who married in, but as long as she had a son, whatever was left would go to her offspring (if it had not already been absorbed into family property). In no period of traditional China did daughters inherit like sons, though they could be residual heirs when they had no brothers (see also McCreery 1976 and Chen 1985). In the Sung, therefore, when the cost of the dowry became substantial and exceeded the value of the betrothal gifts, families began regularly transmitting a portion of their wealth outside the boundaries of their patrilineal descendants.

Questions about the shift toward larger dowries and diverging devolution can be phrased at either the individual or the societal level. That is, one can ask why men in the transition period chose to send their daughters with valuable dowries when they could probably still have married them without such expenditures. One can also ask why property holders as a class would transmit some of their property through daughters to grandsons of other surnames. The best explanation would probably make sense at both of these levels.

In modern China, dowry has generally been more lavish among the rich than the poor, and so has been attributed to the status consciousness of the members of the wife-giving family who "do not wish to demean themselves before the other family" (Freedman 1979:258; see also Ahern 1974 and Watson 1981). Goody's (1976:99–114) comparative analysis also links diverging devolution to stratification, particularly the kind that comes in with plow-based agriculture. Linking dowry with status differentiation, however, provides no insight into the historical shift toward large dowries in China, as T'ang aristocratic society was if anything more concerned with status and prestige than the Sung elite. The T'ang case shows that the size of betrothal gifts (largely used for indirect dowry) could just as well serve as symbols of high status as direct dowry. Moreover, social and economic inequalities seem to have been just as well reproduced by this system of transmitting property.

The presence or absence of substantial dowry (that is, dowry in excess of the betrothal gifts) has also been linked to the need for affinal connections to people in distant localities (Watson 1981; Gallin and Gallin 1985). The logic here is that dowry makes marriage exchange unequal (the side that sent both the woman and the dowry clearly sent more), and as Mauss (1967) argued, unbalanced gifts keep relationships active. The possibility that affinal relations became more important in Sung times is discussed below.

A third explanation for the distribution of dowry payments stresses the role of commercialization (Harrell and Dickey 1985). Dowry is almost always displayed and its value readily interpreted by all concerned as a measure of the wealth of the bride's family. In more commercialized societies, determining status on the basis of wealth is common, as is competition for such status. Harrell and Dickey (1985) cite historical shifts where the introduction of dowry (generally in recent times) accompanied commercialization, sometimes spreading from town to country.

The kinds, timing, and value of marriage prestations also changed many times over the course of European history. Early imperial Roman families gave daughters dowries, the size of which slowly escalated. Then after about A.D. 200 the groom or his family started making premarital gifts to the bride (indirect dowry), which also followed an inflationary course, so that by the fifth century an emperor could denounce the avarice of parents with marriageable daughters. In the sixth century Justinian ruled that each family should make equal contributions. Herlihy associates these shifts with changes in the supply of potential mates caused by such things as female infanticide, the popularity of bachelorhood, changes in the age at marriage, and religions that promoted celibacy (1985:14–23; see also Saller 1984 and Dixon 1985 on the period to A.D. 200). In the Chinese case, it does not seem likely that changes in age at marriage or proportions marrying were large enough to affect the market for brides and grooms, so the Roman case is probably not a good model for comparison.

The Germanic peoples who invaded the Roman Empire in the fifth century made gifts from the husband to the bride (somewhat analogous to the indirect dowry of Chinese betrothal gifts), and these also seem to have followed an inflationary course. Gradually, the contributions of the wives' families also seem to have grown (Hughes 1978:265–69, 272–73). In the eleventh century, dowry from the wife's family had reemerged in Italy, southern France, and Spain "in the wake of peace, economic and demographic growth, and the establishment of public authority" as well as land shortage and a "crisis in status" (ibid., 1978:276, 288). By the fourteenth century, especially in northern Italy, dowries had become extremely burdensome to bride-giving families at all social levels. Hughes suggests that dowry inflation was related to its use as a mechanism for alliance in a "status-conscious yet mobile world" (ibid., 288). The parallels to the Chinese case shall be explored below.

Hughes also argues that this dotal regime reflects a revision of property rights that restrengthened patrilineal principles: husbands did not want to assign rights to their property to wives, but natal families were willing to do so to daughters, on the understanding that the daughters could make no further claims on them (ibid., 287–88). In the Chinese case, dowry escalation may have been linked to emphasis on patrilineal principles, but my guess is that cause and effect worked the other way around: men wished to reassert patrilineal principles in part because they objected to the transfer of property through women. Goody (1983:257–59) interprets this late medieval shift from indirect to direct dowry mostly as one of timing. That is, instead of inheriting property at their parents' deaths, daughters were receiving it when they wed. As mentioned above, the Chinese case cannot be interpreted this way, for inheritance was not normally bilateral.

For the Chinese case, I think that transformations in the economy laid the groundwork for the shift toward diverging devolution, but that the real growth in dowries occurred first and most crucially in the elite. Economic changes included commercialization and freer forms of land tenure. In mid-T'ang the government largely gave up attempting to control the private ownership of land or its transfer from one generation to the next. The use of money also began a steady climb, with the government issuing twenty times as much money per year in the mid-eleventh century as it had at its height in the T'ang. People at all social levels thus had new opportunities to use property (money, land, or the goods that could be bought with money) to offer dowries that would strengthen affinal relations. As part of their strategies for advancement, especially in the political sphere, men in the elite took to providing their daughters with substantial dowries. The prominence of the dowries of the elite brought the concept of dowry fully into the repertoire of Chinese kinship practices. The custom of channeling wealth through dowries would then have spread to lower levels largely through a trickle-down effect as people regularly attempted to raise their own status by copying the mores of those a step above them. From then on, although dowry became obligatory in the highest social level, it was optional at lower levels, and in Republican times at least was found among ordinary people in some parts of the country but not in others (Cohen 1976:164–91; Watson 1984; Chen 1985).

Because I think the escalation of dowry among the elite played a crucial role in its full admission to the repertoire of kinship practices and because there is so much more material on dowry among the elite, here I shall confine my analysis to the reasons elite men chose to send dowries with their daughters.

SOCIAL STRUCTURE AND DOWRY

Differences between T'ang and Sung social stratification are well known. The families that became established in the Northern Sung were rarely descendants of the leading T'ang families (even if some claimed such connections). Pedigree by itself was less of an asset in the Sung. The growing bureaucracy offered more opportunities for members of local elite families through the expanded examination system. The notion of an educated class of families whose members occasionally held office gained general recognition, displacing the T'ang notion of a super-elite of families whose members nearly all held office. Elite men were embedded in localized kinship groups, differing markedly from the dispersed kinship groups of the T'ang aristocratic families.[17]

The size of the educated class grew rapidly in Sung times, probably in large part because as the economy expanded, it could support more local landlords and wealthy merchants. As a consequence, the numbers of those competing for elite positions seem to have steadily outstripped the supply of valued places, at both the national and local levels. Thus the culture of the elite in Sung times was if anything more competitive than in T'ang. The basic rules of civil service recruitment were changed several times, and there was a persistent tendency for those with good connections to devise ways to favor people of their own kind (through "protection" privileges, "sponsorship," "facilitated," or "avoidance" examinations, and so on) (see Chaffee 1985:101–5; Umehara 1985:423–500; Chang Pang-wei 1986). Sung sources are full of complaints about the nepotism of those in high office. For instance, in 1041 Sun Mien charged that high officials would recommend or sponsor their affinal relatives (*ch'in-ch'i*) (*CP* 132:5a). In 1165 an official protested that the advantageous "avoidance" examinations were being taken not merely by agnatic relatives but by cousins through father's sister and mother's brother (both fifth-rank mourning relatives) (*SHY hsuan-chü* 16:13a–b). Even more common was the complaint that "cold, solitary" (*han-ku*) scholars had a hard time getting ahead. Men with high-ranking close agnatic relatives were not "cold" or "solitary," but neither were those with good affinal connections. At the same time, the dangers of nepotism were recognized and efforts made to contain them, especially by prohibiting specified relatives from serving under or examining each other (see Niida 1942:287–302 and Chang Pang-wei 1986). These efforts to curb nepotism also served to advertise the range and depth of kin who could be of use.

Does the inflation of dowries have anything to do with the political and social changes that led to this transformation of class structure in the Sung? Large betrothal gifts apparently disappeared with the social groups that practiced them. In the T'ang, there is no evidence that such gifts were common outside the circle of aristocratic families. But there is no reason that the disappearance of excessive betrothal gifts would have to lead to exaggerated dowries.

The tendency for dowry to escalate in the late Five Dynasties and Sung appears to be related to the ecological situation of the emerging elite. Officials and aspirants to office who needed connections in order to facilitate promotions through sponsorship, to gain allies in factional disputes, and so on had to build up networks. This could be done through nonkinship means, such as through the ties of teachers and students or officials and their subordinates. But kinship ties have advantages, for they can be extended much further, to brothers, sons, grandsons, and so on. The dislocations of the tenth century seem to have resulted in many men finding themselves cut off from both patrilineal and affinal kin. For instance, Shih Chieh (1005–45), in describing the history of his family, noted that the first ancestor to move to their current location 150 years earlier had found himself with neither brothers nor affinal kin (*TLSHS shih-wen*:251; see also Matsui 1968). In such cases it was easier to build up networks of affinal kin through marriages with families long settled in that place than to wait several generations for the family to grow into a sizable patrilineal descent group. This use of marriage to establish networks occurred at both the national and local levels. Robert Hartwell found that of 210 marriages involving the thirty-five most eminent "families" of the Northern Sung (960–1126), just over half (115) were to others in these families originally from other parts of the country (1982:423). Robert Hymes (1986) found that until the end of the Northern Sung when official families migrated to Fu-chou (Kiangsi), they quickly arranged marriages to the leading local families.

In the T'ang those with wealth could not change the key element in their social status except by fraud: their home prefecture (choronym) and family name were fixed. A family hoping to convert wealth into social status could perhaps facilitate ties to these prestigious families by offering betrothal gifts or dowries verging on bribes. But the marriages contracted could only be expected to change the general evaluation of the family's status very slowly, after at least a couple of generations. In the Sung, starting with very little of an established elite, family name per se meant little, so there was more to be gained by "buying" marriage connections.

Granting that there may have been more men eager to convert wealth into status in the early Sung, why did they use this wealth for dowries rather than betrothal gifts? Here I will argue that dowry offered three advantages over betrothal gifts: it made a better 'bribe"; it provided more flexibility for family strategies; and it made affinal ties stronger.

Dowry was a superior bait because betrothal gifts were supposed to be returned as dowry. By insisting on valuable betrothal gifts when marrying out a daughter, one may have guaranteed that she would have an adequate dowry, but one was not improving the financial health of one's own patriline. Dowry, by contrast, involved transfer from one patriline to another. Although the groom's father, who arranged the marriage, was not to have any control over the dowry, and even his son was supposed to gain his wife's consent on its use, it would eventually go to his son's sons and daughters (see *CMC* 5:140; *MCC* 33:31a–b, 33:34b–37a; Ebrey 1984b:101–20). Its final destination would not be trivial to a man worried about the eventual division of the family property among several sons. Mercantile families could use handsome dowries to marry their daughters into families of officials.[18] Epitaphs for the early Sung also show rich official families marrying their daughters to promising young men, giving them large dowries.[19] They did this in part to avoid marrying down or losing prestige, but also because even well-established families could benefit from connections to such men. And the groom also had much to gain. Ssu-ma Kuang criticized the practice of choosing brides on the basis of transient wealth and rank. "How could a man of spirit retain his pride if he got rich by using his wife's assets or gained high station by relying on her influence?" (*SMSSI* 3:29). Probably many young men would forgo some pride toward those ends.

My second argument is that dowry increased the options available in advancement strategies. Transmission of property along the patrilineal line through division among sons was inflexible: all brothers' shares were to be the same. Dowry allowed, to some extent at least, a differentiation among brothers inasmuch as dowries for each incoming bride were separately negotiated. Thus, a family with several sons and daughters could make different decisions for each one. Sometimes they could concentrate on affirming their prestige by arranging the best matches, ignoring how much dowry their sons' brides would bring and using up much of their disposable income for the daughters' dowries. Alternatively, they could worry about the future estates of their sons after division and try to soften the consequences by seeking sons-in-law who would take their daughters without large dowries or daughters-in-law for their sons who would come with good dowries. Another strategy might be to have one or more sons wait until he passed the examinations before arranging his marriage in the hope of securing a better dowry for him. Of course, dowry would never be the sole consideration in marriage negotiations; a well-connected father-in-law could be worth more than an ample dowry. Moreover, a family might consider it wiser to invest more in education and less in marriages.[20]

My third argument is that the obligations inherent in an affinal relationship could be strengthened by a large dowry. In an article published in 1981, I showed that the provision of dowry to daughters was associated with continuing obligations between the families of the bride and the groom (Ebrey 1981:124). The parents of the bride could expect more from their daughter, her husband, and her sons when they had married her out with a respectable dowry. The direct evidence I cited included Yuan Ts'ai's advice to families with ample property to give their daughters a share of it on the grounds that their sons might prove incapable and they might therefore have to depend on their daughters' families even for their funerals and ancestral sacrifices (Ebrey 1984b:224). I also pointed to strong ties between daughters and their natal families, ranging from daughters who took in their widowed mothers or arranged their parents' funerals or cared for their orphaned younger brothers, to parents or brothers who took responsibility for their widowed daughters or sisters.

One can easily posit (as Yuan Ts'ai did) that a woman who had received material assets from her parents had a greater obligation to aid them if they were ever in need than a woman who had not. One can also suppose that a widow with a dowry at her disposal (who either had no children or who was taking them with her) could more easily choose where she wished to live than one without much of a dowry. There is no obvious reason, however, for a family that had sent off a daughter with a substantial dowry to feel more obligated to take her back than one that had provided little if anything beyond recycling of the betrothal gifts. In these cases, the logic of unbalanced exchanges might be what kept these ties active. I also suspect that dowry strengthened affinal ties because it created lingering claims to common property. Just as brothers were bound to each other as coparceners of graveyards and ancestral halls even after division of the household, affinal relatives were linked through mutual interest in the disposition of the dowry and this kept their ties alive.[21]

Another way to bring out the relationship between dowry and continuing reciprocal obligations is to consider either end of the spectrum of marriage finance. Families who sold their daughter as a concubine provided no dowry but received large "betrothal gifts" of cash. It was generally understood that they were losing kinship rights over her, that they might never meet their grandchildren, that these grandchildren need not come to their funeral, and so on (Ebrey 1986a and Watson, this volume). At the other extreme were uxorilocal arrangements whereby families took in husbands for their daughters, generally expecting little or nothing in the way of betrothal gifts but

TABLE 3.1   Matrilateral and Affinal Relatives to Be Avoided by Officials

Woman Relative	Mourning Grade[a]	Relatives to Be Avoided
Mother	2a	her father, grandfather (FF), great-grandfather (FFF), father's brother, brother, cousin (FBS), nephew (BS and ZS), brother-in-law (ZH), and sister's daughter's husband
Wife	2b	same as mother[b]
Grandmother (FM)	2c	none
Uncle's wife (FBW)	2c	none
Daughter	2c	her husband, sons, husband's father and brother, daughter's husband
Aunt (FZ)	3	her husband
Sister	3	her husband and son
Son's wife	3	her father and brother
Nephew's wife (BSW)	3	none
Niece (BD)	3	none
Cousin (FBD)	4	none
Brother's wife	4	none
Granddaughter (SD)	4	her husband
Nephew's daughter (BSD)	5	none

SOURCE: *SHY chih-kuan* 63:4.

NOTE: For simplicity's sake, this table is limited to cases where the man might plausibly have lived sometime in a common household with the woman who provided the link.

[a] The mourning grades for female agnates are those they assumed upon marriage. These grades are based on *CL* 4:10b–15a.

[b] Not given in *SHY*, but probably a scribal error because in all the other lists, mother's and wife's natal relatives are given together (e.g., *CYTFSL* 8:101).

providing their daughter with a dowry of much or all of their property. Such sons-in-law had many obligations to their wives' families—to support them, bury them, and see to it that their sacrifices continued.

Among the elite, strong affinal ties could be used not merely for kinship purposes (care of widows and orphans) but also for political ones. As anecdotes attest, families of officials seem to have often thought they could recruit sons-in-law with better career prospects by offering better dowries. The goal of such efforts does not seem so much to have been prestige but connections: sons-in-law make good clients and political allies. This line of thinking is clearly reflected in Sung rules on nepotism. Table 3.1 lists affinal and matrilateral relatives under whom a man could not serve according to the nepotism rules of 1070. It is organized according to the woman who served as the kinship link between the two men.

As can easily be seen, the gradation in the scope of relatives to be avoided does not correspond to mourning grades. In Chinese kinship reckoning, a man is considered closely related to his father's brother and he mourns this uncle's wife at grade two. Yet his ties of obligation to this woman's natal family were not considered strong enough to make avoidance necessary in a bureaucratic setting. The same is true of the families of the wives of a man's brothers and nephews. Even in the case of the family into which his sister had married, only her husband and son had to be avoided, not, for instance, her husband's father or brother. A man was considered most likely to feel obligations to men in his mother's and wife's families, and then to a lesser extent, to those in the families of his daughter's husband and son's wife.

The logic here, I contend, is that of dowry and not of consanguinity. It is true that a man is related by blood to his mother's family, but he is also tied by blood to his father's mother's family, to his father's sister's family, and so on. Moreover, he is not related by blood to anyone in his wife's family. A fairly large number of people in the family that sent a girl and a dowry had to be avoided by her husband and sons, but other members of the family into which she married are generally not involved. (That is, one had to avoid serving in the same office with a first cousin of one's wife, but not with the brother or father of one's brother's wife.) The difference would seem to be that one received nothing from the dowry a brother's wife brought, but brothers, grandparents, and uncles of one's wife could all have been coparceners of the family that sent her dowry. Moreover, one was the foremost contributor to the dowry of a daughter, somewhat less to that of a sister and son's daughter, and much less to that of a brother's daughter, and so on.

Let me reorganize my argument to sort out the causal chain that includes the shift toward large dowries. I see the growth of the economy, increasing availability of money, and freer transfer of land as general preconditions for both the growth of the educated class and the greater transfer of wealth through dowry. I see the political situation of the tenth century as bringing to the fore people who had no pedigree but who had been able to build armies or staff bureaucracies through various personal connections. Whenever such connections are useful, affinal ties will gain importance. Dowry, I argue, was an especially good way for those with wealth to try to secure preferred affinal relations (because it made a better bait, allowed flexible family strategies, and strengthened the ties once they were arranged). Given the competitiveness with which Sung men pursued positions in the elite, it became difficult for families to gain a useful connection through a daughter without providing a dowry. In time, through market forces, it became nearly impossible to find any sort of suitable family for her. The civil service recruitment system was, meanwhile, evolving. The usefulness of affinal connections was continually confirmed and reproduced in this arena, both through the extension of privileges of facilitated entry into office to a wide range of kin and through provisions made to cut these privileges back. By the time nepotism rules were compiled in the mid-Sung, the transfer of dowry was clearly associated with the assumed flow of favors. There is no point in asking which came first: dowry as a means to transfer property; an elite that continually used affinal kinship to create and repair networks that would secure or advance one in local or national politics; or a civil service system that continuously struggled against and gave ground to the desire of those inside and outside the system to use personal connections for both entry and advancement. These three phenomena were systematically related to each other and each kept the others strong.

CONCLUSION

By way of conclusion, I would like to consider briefly the implications that my interpretation of the shifts in marriage finance from the T'ang to the Sung may have for some established ideas about marriage payments and social structure.

First I would like to consider Goody's (1976) suggestion that dowry is associated with exclusive marriage practices and tends to preserve economic inequalities, as dowered marriages are arranged predominantly among families with comparable wealth. From the Chinese case, one could argue that indirect dowry serves this purpose better than direct dowry. In the T'ang it was easy for the wealth of the aristocracy to stay within the aristocracy because a family's property seldom had to leave the patriline except for the journey of betrothal gifts to the homes of future brides where it was turned into dowries and then returned, to again become regular family property after a generation. If the families of the brides neither retained any of the gifts nor supplemented them (each of which happened some of the time), then all family property would eventually devolve to patrilineal descendants.

In the Sung substantial dowries regularly channeled property into other patrilines. At the same time, it is much harder to identify a circle that kept property within its own boundaries. The size of the educated class steadily expanded during the Sung, and new *chin-shih* seem to have been able to obtain dowries and therefore wealth from either rich families with no prior official connections or the families of officials. In the Chinese case, thus, betrothal gifts (bridewealth to be returned as indirect dowry) went along with a more constricted elite that passed down its standing and probably its wealth to its patrilineal descendants, and dowry was most visibly used by an expanding elite that was absorbing new families at both the local and national levels.

The second general issue I wish to raise concerns dowry and patrilineality. Bridewealth is much more common than dowry in African societies organized into segmentary patrilineages. Dowry is much more common in societies with bilateral inheritance and other bilateral tendencies (such as Europe). The civilizations of Asia fit between these two poles, dowry often coexisting with strong patrilineal kinship organization. Is there thus any generalizable relationship between marriage finance and forms of kinship organization? Will shifts in one have anything to do with shifts in the other?

In the Chinese case, new forms of localized patrilineages began to appear in several parts of the country in late Sung (Ebrey 1986b). These local lineages brought together agnatic relatives related through a common ancestor many generations back for joint ancestral rites. Groups of agnates frequently erected halls for these rites, set aside land to pay for them, and compiled genealogies. In many areas they became major forces in local politics. Chronologically, the shift toward substantial dowries was visible before such descent groups appeared. Could diverging devolution have somehow triggered the growth of lineages? Or could they both be manifestations of some larger change in Chinese kinship organization?

I would argue, from what evidence there is, that these began as independent developments, substantial dowries taking off first among the elite, localized lineages gaining strength among ordinary people, though in time each reached to all social levels and each shaped the other's development. Large dowries had a couple of hundred years to get well established before descent groups were significant, though later the form and distribution of dowries were shaped by a context that included descent groups. Descent groups in China developed in an environment in which the elite and often commoners transmitted some wealth through dowries.

The spread of dowry may even be thought to have had a small role in shaping the form descent groups took in China. I see a connection between the prevalence of substantial dowry and the call for a strengthening of patrilineal principles. Some Sung neo-Confucians recognized that the shift toward transmitting property through daughters was a threat to China's traditional patrilineal, patriarchal family system. Their call for a "revival of the descent line system (*tsung*)" was motivated in part by their objections to the strength of affinal relations and their fears concerning the breakup of patrimonies. This descent line rhetoric, in turn, helped to shape the way Chinese descent groups and lineages were eventually conceived (Ebrey 1984a; 1986b).

Descent line rhetoric and the growth of descent groups can also be given some credit for curbing the trend toward dowry. In Yuan (1215–1368) and Ming (1368–1644) times legal restrictions were placed on married women's control of their dowries, in particular their right to take them with them if they were widowed or divorced (*YTC hu-pu, hun-yin*:816–17; Tai 1978:105). As Jennifer Holmgren argues, these restrictions probably had much to do with problems relating to Mongol family practices, such as the levirate (1986). Yet the political success of Ch'eng-Chu neo-Confucianism also facilitated this revision of the law. Descent groups, where they existed, may also have limited the incentive for large dowries among ordinary people by providing them with an adequate set of social connections. In recent times, dowry among ordinary farmers seems to have been larger in areas without strong lineages. Where there were strong lineages, the rich gave dowries, but not the ordinary poor farmer.

By ending this essay with a discussion of how the escalation of dowries was curbed, I wish to underline the dynamic nature of the changes I have described here. The growth of dowries can be seen as an effect of economic and political changes, but it also had effects of its own. It generated not only compatible institutions (such as legal elaborations) and symbols (associations with prestige) but also opposing forces (in rhetoric, law, and descent groups). These conflicting effects also interacted through time in complex ways, obscuring simple functional relations in the flux of social life.

NOTES

1. Yen Chih-t'ui had spent his youth in the south but was taken to the north in 554; in his "Family Instructions," he frequently mentioned differences in the customs of north and south. That he mentioned no such difference in regard to bargaining about betrothal gifts may mean this custom was common in both areas.

2. These were specified lines of the Po-ling and Ch'ing-ho Ts'ui, the Chao-chün and Lung-hsi Li, the Fan-yang Lu, the Ying-yang Cheng, and the T'ai-yuan Wang. Each family was defined by specifying its focal ancestor, generally two or three centuries earlier, and included several hundred geographically scattered households.

3. There are also indications that in the T'ang betrothal gifts could be substantial even when both families had eminent pedigrees. In a short story by Chiang Fang (early ninth century), a Lung-hsi Li who had recently passed the *chin-shih* examination found that his mother had engaged him to a cousin, a Lu of a top-rank family (*chia-tsu*). The Lu family expected a betrothal gift of one million cash, even though the groom's family was a relative and social equal. As his family was not rich, Li had to borrow from friends and relatives to collect it all (*TPKC* 487:4008). If indeed this sum would be returned as dowry, then Li was collecting money for his own wife and children, and the bride's family, by insisting on the sum, was stipulating the money that was to be earmarked for their daughter's conjugal unit.

4. In fact, when his first wife died, Feng Ching married another of Fu Pi's daughters (*STPC* 6:90). Feng Ching may even have lived with Fu Pi, as *SSWCL* 9:94 says Fu's two daughters and their husbands and children all lived in his house.

5. The contrast between these two approaches is reminiscent of differences between England and continental Europe in early modern times as described by Macfarlane (1986:251–62). In Europe marriages were much more strictly confined to status equals. In England, there was a more flexible process of negotiation in which yeomen's daughters might marry younger sons of gentry, with wealth as much a factor in decisions as "blood."

6. Some forms for T'ang marriage letters (*hun-shu*) survive in Tun-huang. See Ebrey 1985.

7. Such engagement letters are often found in Sung literati's collected works (e.g., *CLC* 18:247; *KKC* 68:916–19; *LTLWC* 2:38–40; *PCWC* 64:8b–15b).

8. A distinction between land accompanying a bride in marriage and trousseau items was also made by Huang Kan (1152–1221), who argued that land became the property of the husband's family, while a widow could take her trousseau with her on remarriage (*MCC* 33:31a–b). Other writers, however, seem to have been quite willing to lump together land and hairpins.

9. I have not seen the term *ti-yin* elsewhere. Perhaps the eleven thousand is money or goods that will remain under the control of the wife and the five thousand money or goods that will go to the husband or to his larger family. The Sung imperial family similarly seems to have divided marriage payments into two categories, though the terms used are not the same (*SS* 115:2732).

10. This legal protection did not last into the Ch'ing period and thus contrasts with the situation described in Ocko's chapter here. Some of the forces leading toward weakening of women's property rights after the Sung are discussed at the end of this chapter.

11. This change had already taken place by the time the *Sung hsing t'ung* was issued in 963. See *SHT* 12:14a–b.

12. This generalization is based on reading forty-two epitaphs by nine authors in the *CTW*, an exercise that did not uncover any references to their dowries.

13. This is based on a study of 161 Sung epitaphs for women, of which 23 (about 15 percent) referred to their dowries.

14. I do not have space here to analyze the legal status of married women's control over their dowry. Suffice it to say that many Confucians—particularly those I have identified as holding a "descent line" (*tsung*) orientation (Ebrey 1984a)—seem to have opposed women's treating their dowries as their private property, though their arguments reveal that such an attitude was common.

15. One story even suggests that the bride's dowry should correspond to her husband's family property, not to the betrothal gifts he sent. In "The Honest Clerk," an official confides to a matchmaker: "My family has property worth 100,000 strings of cash. For a mate I need someone who will bring a dowry of 100,000 strings" (*CPTSHS* 13:44; cf. Yang and Yang 1957:29). This story is set in the Sung, but its exact date is unknown and may be early Ming.

16. A few other items of evidence are worth mentioning. Po Chü-i (772–846) wrote some model legal decisions for marriage disputes. Several make mention of the return of betrothal gifts when an engagement was broken (e.g., *CTW* 672:14b; 673:1b–2a, 18b–19a), but none refers to return of dowry or disputes over dowry, even in cases of divorce (e.g., *CTW* 672:17a; 673:6a–b, 11a–b). A T'ang guide to marriage ceremonies preserved in Tun-huang gives elaborate details for the ceremony of delivering the betrothal gifts, but no ceremony is outlined for delivering the dowry (Chao 1963:185–86). Yet in Sung times delivering the dowry was seen as an occasion for colorful display (*SMSSI* 3:33). Moreover, three studies of marriage in the T'ang (Chang 1976; Wong 1979; and Niu 1987) uncovered no evidence that provision of dowry was a major expense for girls' families.

17. There recently has been considerable debate on how "open" the Sung elite was (Hartwell 1982; Chaffee 1985; Lee 1985; Davis 1986; Hymes 1986). My own understanding of the situation is shaped especially by Chaffee's statistics on the rapid

growth in the educated class (as measured by participation in the examination system); by Hymes's demonstration (from a study of one prefecture) that those who entered the national elite were usually already members of the local elite, and his evidence that the local elite of this particular prefecture was almost entirely new in the Sung, having virtually no descent ties to T'ang officials; and by Davis's demonstration of how a relatively minor family, once it gained prominence in the national government, could smooth the way for dozens of descendants. See also Ebrey 1988.

18. Sung writers did not necessarily indicate whether someone of nonofficial background was of merchant background because merchants did not share the esteem of officials or educated landlords. But some references to marriages between families otherwise quite unequal raise one's suspicions. For instance, the epitaph for a woman, née Ch'en, whose father and grandfather had not been officials remarks that her father was too fond of her to marry her to someone in his own town, so he moved to the capital to choose a husband for her (*WLCC* 99:629–30). The one he chose was Ch'eng Lin (988–1056), whose father, brothers, uncles, great-uncles, and so on had all been officials (*OYHCC* 21:151–54). One can well imagine that the Ch'ens were merchants and offered a handsome dowry to facilitate this marriage into an official family.

19. For instance, Chao Li, a rich magistrate, in about 1030 met a young man who had passed the examinations three years earlier at age seventeen. This man's family seems to have been undistinguished: it had moved to its current location about a century earlier during the Five Dynasties and none of his three direct ancestors had been officials. Chao Li gave him his daughter as well as a handsome dowry (*KSC* 53:64b; *PCC* 37:489).

20. No Sung source I know makes this argument in full, but there are anecdotes of people thinking along these lines. For instance, the epitaph for a woman from the Li family in P'u-yang descended from the aristocratic Chao-chün Li family of the T'ang described her natal family as one that had produced officials for generations and had accumulated a great fortune. While she and her sisters were young, their dowries were prepared and set aside. When the woman in question reached marriageable age, the estate had declined somewhat because her brother Li Ti (971–1047) had repeatedly failed the *chin-shih* examination. At this point the girl emptied out her dowry chests to give everything to her brother. The brother accepted the property, then out of a sense of obligation to her secretly selected "a scholar of integrity" to be her husband, presumably because she could no longer marry someone rich. Li Ti made a good choice, however, for his sister's husband also passed the examination the same year he did (*HNHS* 4:3b–4a). In this case, then, property set aside for dowry was diverted to educational expenses, but the great success of the brother in his career made this in retrospect a wise choice and one that they could plausibly claim did not hurt the sister.

21. The lingering interests of a natal family in the disposition of dowry can be seen in legal cases in which the woman died without heirs. A woman's family was explicitly excluded as heirs to her dowry in the Sung code (*SHT* 12:12b). If an heir was posthumously set up for the woman and her husband, he would be the appropriate recipient of the dowry, but the wife's family could object if the husband's family tried to keep the dowry without establishing an heir. In a case recorded in *Ch'ing-ming chi*, a woman, née Ch'en, had brought a dowry of land worth 120 chung when she married

into the Yü family. She and her husband both died without children. Her husband's father, an official, did not want to set up an heir (apparently wanting to keep all the property for a young son he had had by a concubine). Ch'en's father, also an official, sued, and Yü was forced to select an heir who would inherit the dowry fields and continue the sacrifices for the couple (*CMC* 8:248–49). There are also several other cases in which the existence of dowry property underlies the continuing involvement of a woman's natal family in the affairs of her husband's family (e.g., *CMC* 6:191–92).

GLOSSARY

Chang Yao-tso　張堯佐
Chao-chün Li　趙郡李
Ch'en　陳
Cheng　鄭
Ch'eng Lin　程琳
chia-chuang　嫁妝
chia-shih　家世
chia-tsu　甲族
Chiang Pao　江裒
ch'in-ch'i　親戚
Ch'ing-ho Ts'ui　清和崔
Chu Yü　朱彧
chüan　絹
chuang-lien　妝(or 粧)奩
chung　種
Fan-yang Lu　范陽陸
Feng Ching　馮京
Fu Pi　富弼
han-ku　寒孤
Hou K'o　侯可
hsi-t'ieh　細帖
hu　斛
hu-chueh　戶絕
Hu Ying　胡穎
hun-shu　婚書
Kao-tsung　高宗
Li　李
Li Hua　李華
Li Ti　李廸
lien　奩
lien-chü　奩具
lien-chü chuang　奩具狀
Liu K'o-chuang　劉克莊
Liu Tsai　劉宰
Lung-hsi Li　隴西李
men-hu　門戶
men-ti　門第

na-cheng　納徵
na-pi　納幣
p'in-li　聘禮
p'in-ts'ai　聘財
Po Chü-i　白居易
Po-ling Ts'ui　博陵崔
Shen Yueh　沈約
Shih Chieh　石介
shih-ta-fu　士大夫
so　碩
Ssu-ma Kuang　司馬光
ssu-ts'ai　私財
Sun Chueh　孫覺
Sun Mien　孫沔
ta-fu　大夫
T'ai-tsung　太宗
T'ai-yuan Wang　太原王
ti-yin　締姻
Ting Chih　丁隲
ting-t'ieh　定帖
ts'ai-ch'an　財產
Ts'ai Hsiang　蔡襄
ts'ao-t'ieh　草帖
Tseng Pu　曾布
tsu-tsung　祖宗
Ts'ui　崔
Ts'ui Piao　崔儦
tsung　宗
tzu-chuang　資裝(or 粧 or 妝)
tzu-sung　資送
Wang T'ung　王通
Wang Yuan　王源
Weng Fu　翁甫
Yang Su　楊素
Yen Chih-t'ui　顏之推
Ying-yang Cheng　滎陽鄭
Yuan Ts'ai　袁采

REFERENCES

Primary Sources

CCC　　　*Chieh-chai chi* 絜齋集, by Yuan Hsieh 袁燮. Ts'ung-shu chi-ch'eng edition.

CCCC　　*Hsin-pien shih-wen lei-yao ch'i-cha ch'ing-ch'ien* 新編事文類要啓劄青錢. Photo reprint of 1324 edition.

CKCY　　*Chen-kuan cheng-yao* 貞觀政要, by Wu Ching 吳兢. Shanghai: Ku-chi ch'u-pan-she, 1978.

CL　　　　*Chu-tzu chia li* 朱子家禮, by Chu Hsi 朱熹. Ssu-k'u ch'üan-shu edition.

CLC　　　*Ch'en Liang chi* 陳亮集, by Ch'en Liang 陳亮. Taipei: Ho-lo t'u-shu ch'u-pan-she, 1976.

CLP　　　*Chi-le pien* 雞肋編, by Chuang Ch'o 莊綽. Ts'ung-shu chi-ch'eng edition.

CMC　　　*Ming-kung shu-p'an ch'ing-ming chi* 名公書判清明集. Peking: Chung-hua shu-chü, 1987.

CP　　　　*Hsu tzu-chih t'ung-chien ch'ang-pien* 續資治通鑑長編, Li T'ao 李燾. Reprint. Taipei: Shih-chieh shu-chü.

CPTSHS　*Ching-pen t'ung-su hsiao-shuo* 京本通俗小說. Shanghai: Chung-kuo ku-tien wen-hsueh ch'u-pan-she, 1954.

CS　　　　*Chung-shuo* 中說, by Wang T'ung 王通. Ts'ung-shu chi-ch'eng edition.

CTW　　　*Ch'üan T'ang wen* 全唐文, ed. Tung Kao 董誥 et al. Taipei: Ching-wei reprint of 1814 edition.

CWKWC　*Chu Wen-kung wen-chi* 朱文公文集, by Chu Hsi 朱熹. Taipei: Han-ching reprint of Po-na edition.

CWTS　　*Chiu Wu-tai shih* 舊五代史, by Hsueh Chü-cheng 薛居正 and Hsu Wu-tang 徐無黨. Peking: Chung-hua shu-chü, 1976.

CYIL　　　*Chien-yen i-lai hsi-nien yao lu* 建炎以來繫年要錄, by Li Hsin-ch'uan 李心傳. Ts'ung-shu chi-ch'eng edition.

CYTFSL　*Ch'ing-yuan t'iao-fa shih-lei* 慶元條法事類, by Hsieh Shen-fu 謝深甫. Tokyo: Koten kenkyūkai reprint of Sung edition.

ECC　　　*Erh-Ch'eng chi* 二程集, by Ch'eng Hao 程顥 and Ch'eng I 程頤. Peking: Chung-hua shu-chü, 1981.

HLPY　　*Hsin-pien hun-li pei-yung yueh-lao hsin-shu* 新編婚禮備用月老新書. National Central Library. Microfilm, Sung edition.

HMTC　　*Shih-wen lei-chü han-mo ta-ch'üan* 事文類聚翰墨大全, by Liu Ying-li 劉應李. 1307 edition.

HNHS　　*Ho-nan hsien-sheng wen-chi* 河南先生文集, by Yin Chu 尹洙. Ssu-pu ts'ung-k'an edition.

HTHS　　*Hou-ts'un hsien-sheng ta ch'üan chi* 後村先生大全集, by Liu K'o-chuang 劉克莊. Ssu-pu ts'ung-k'an edition.

HTS　　　*Hsin T'ang shu* 新唐書, by Ou-yang Hsiu 歐陽修 and Sung Ch'i 宋祁. Peking: Chung-hua shu-chü, 1975.

ICC　　　*I-chien chih* 夷堅志, by Hung Mai 洪邁. Peking: Chung-hua shu-chü, 1981.

KKC　　　*Kung-k'uei chi* 攻媿集, by Lou Yueh 樓鑰. Ts'ung-shu chi-ch'eng edition.

KSC　　　*Kung-shih chi* 公是集, by Liu Ch'ang 劉敞. Ts'ung-shu chi-ch'eng edition.

LCC　　　*Le-ching chi* 樂靜集, by Li Chao-ch'i 李昭玘. Ssu-k'u ch'üan-shu edition.

LTLWC   *Lü Tung-lai wen-chi* 呂東萊文集, by Lü Tsu-ch'ien 呂祖謙. Ts'ung-shu chi-ch'eng edition.

MCC   *Mien-chai chi* 勉齋集, by Huang Kan 黃幹. Ssu-k'u ch'üan-shu edition.

MLL   *Meng liang lu* 夢粱錄, by Wu Tzu-mu 吳自牧. In *Tung-ching meng-hua lu wai ssu-chung.*

MTC   *Man-t'ang chi* 漫塘集, by Liu Tsai 劉宰. Chia-yeh t'ang ts'ung-shu edition.

NCCIK   *Nan-chien chia-i kao* 南澗甲乙稿, by Han Yuan-chi 韓元吉. Ts'ung-shu chi-ch'eng edition.

OYHCC   *Ou-yang Hsiu ch'üan-chi* 歐陽修全集, by Ou-yang Hsiu 歐陽修. Taipei: Chung-kuo wen-hsueh ming-chu chi edition, Shih-chieh shu-chü, 1971.

PCC   *P'eng-ch'eng chi* 彭城集, by Liu Pin 劉攽. Ts'ung-shu chi-ch'eng edition.

PCKT   *P'ing-chou k'o-t'an* 萍州可談, by Chu Yü 朱彧. Ts'ung-shu chi-ch'eng edition.

PCS   *Pei Ch'i shu* 北齊書, by Li Te-lin 李德林 and Li Po-yao 李百藥. Peking: Chung-hua shu-chü, 1972.

PCTCC   *Pei-ch'i ta ch'üan chi* 北溪大全集, by Ch'en Ch'un 陳淳. Ssu-k'u ch'üan-shu edition.

PCWC   *P'an-chou wen-chi* 盤洲文集, by Hung Kua 洪适. Ssu-pu ts'ung-k'an edition.

PSHC   *Pei-shan hsiao-chi* 北山小集, by Ch'eng Chü 程俱. Ssu-pu ts'ung-k'an edition.

SHT   *Sung hsing t'ung* 宋刑統, by Tou I 竇儀. 1918; reprint, Taipei: Wen-hai, 1974.

SHY   *Sung hui-yao chi-pen* 宋會要輯本, ed. Hsu Sung 徐松 et al. Reprint. Taipei: Shih-chieh shu-chü, 1964.

SLKC   *(Hsin-pien tsuan t'u tseng-lei ch'ün-shu lei-yao) shih-lin kuang-chi* 新編纂圖增類羣書類要事林廣記, by Ch'en Yuan-ching 陳元靚. Naikaku bunko Yuan edition.

SMSSI   *Ssu-ma shih shu-i* 司馬氏書儀, by Ssu-ma Kuang 司馬光. Ts'ung-shu chi-ch'eng edition.

SS   *Sung shih* 宋史, ed. T'o T'o 脫脫 et al. Peking: Chung-hua shu-chü, 1977.

SSWCL   *Shao-shih wen-chien lu* 邵氏聞見錄, by Shao Po-wen 邵伯溫. Peking: Chung-hua shu-chü, 1983.

STPC   *Su Tung-p'o chi* 蘇東坡集, by Su Shih 蘇軾. Kuo-hsueh chi-pen ts'ung-shu edition.

STJC   *Shui-tung jih-chi* 水東日記, by Yeh Sheng 葉盛. Pai-pu ts'ung-shu chi-ch'eng edition.

SuiS   *Sui shu* 隋書, by Wei Cheng 魏徵 et al. Peking: Chung-hua shu-chü, 1973.

SWC   *Sung wen chien* 宋文鑑, by Lü Tsu-ch'ien 呂祖謙. Kuo-hsueh chi-pen ts'ung-shu edition.

TCMHL   *Tung-ching meng-hua lu (wai ssu-chung)* 東京夢華錄(外四種), by Meng Yuan-lao 孟元老. Shanghai: Chung-hua shu-chü, 1962.

THY   *T'ang hui-yao* 唐會要, by Wang P'u 王溥. Taipei: Shih-chieh shu-chü edition.

TLSHS   *Ts'u-lai Shih hsien-sheng wen-chi* 徂徠石先生文集, by Shih Chieh 石介.

Peking: Chung-hua shu-chü, 1984.

TLSI *T'ang lü shu-i* 唐律疏議, by Ch'ang-sun Wu-chi 長孫無忌 et al. Kuo-hsueh chi-pen ts'ung-shu edition.

TPKC *T'ai-p'ing kuang-chi* 太平廣記, ed. Li Fang 李昉 et al. Peking: Chung-hua shu-chü, 1961.

TYL *T'ang yü lin* 唐語林, by Wang Tang 王讜. Taipei: Shih-chieh shu-chü, 1967.

WH *Wen-hsuan* 文選, ed. Hsiao T'ung 蕭統. Kuo-hsueh chi-pen ts'ung-shu edition.

WLCC *Wang Lin-ch'uan ch'üan chi* 王臨川全集, by Wang An-shih 王安石. Taipei: Shih-chieh shu-chü, 1966.

YLMC *Yun-lu man-ch'ao* 雲麓漫鈔, by Chao Yen-wei 趙彥衛. Ts'ung-shu chi-ch'eng edition.

YSC *Yeh Shih chi* 葉適集, by Yeh Shih 葉適. Peking: Chung-hua shu-chü, 1961.

YSCH *Yen-shih chia-hsun chi-chieh* 顏氏家訓集解, by Yen Chih-t'ui 顏之推. Taipei: Wen-ming shu-chü, 1982.

YTC *Ta Yuan sheng-cheng kuo-ch'ao tien-chang* 大元聖政國朝典章. Facsimile reprint of Yuan edition.

Secondary Works

Ahern, Emily M. 1974. "Affines and the Rituals of Kinship." In *Religion and Ritual in Chinese Society,* ed. Arthur P. Wolf. Stanford: Stanford University Press.

Burns, Ian Robert. 1973. "Private Law in Traditional China (Sung Dynasty)." Ph.D. diss., Oxford University.

Chaffee, John W. 1985. *The Thorny Gates of Learning: A Social History of Examinations.* Cambridge: Cambridge University Press.

Chang Hsiu-jung 張修蓉. 1976. *T'ang-tai wen-hsueh so piao-hsien chih hun-su yen-chiu* 唐代文學所表現之婚俗研究 (A study of marriage customs revealed in T'ang literature). M.A. thesis, National Cheng-chi University, Taipei.

Chang Pang-wei 張邦煒. 1986. "Sung-tai pi-ch'in pi-chi chih-tu shu-p'ing" 宋代避親避籍制度述評 (An account of the Sung system of avoiding relatives). *Ssu-ch'uan Shih-ta hsueh-pao* 1:16–23.

Chao Shou-yen 趙守儼. 1963. "T'ang-tai hun-yin li-su k'ao-lueh" 唐代婚姻禮俗考略 (A brief study of wedding customs in the T'ang period). *Wen-shih* 3:185–95.

Chen, Chung-min. 1985. "Dowry and Inheritance." In *The Chinese Family and Its Ritual Behavior,* ed. Hsieh Jih-chang and Chuang Ying-chang. Taipei: Academia Sinica, Institute of Ethnology.

Ch'en Ku-yuan 陳顧遠. 1936; reprint, 1978. *Chung-kuo hun-yin shih* 中國婚姻史 (A history of marriage in China). Taipei: Commercial Press.

Cohen, Myron L. 1976. *House United, House Divided: The Chinese Family in Taiwan.* New York: Columbia University Press.

Ch'ü, T'ung-tsu. 1965. *Law and Society in Traditional China.* Paris: Mouton.

Comaroff, J. L. 1980. "Introduction." In *The Meaning of Marriage Payments,* ed. J. L. Comaroff. New York: Academic Press.

Davis, Richard L. 1986. *Court and Family in Sung China, 960–1279: Bureaucratic Success and Kinship Fortunes for the Shih of Ming-chou.* Durham: Duke University Press.

Dixon, Suzanne. 1985. "The Marriage Alliance in the Roman Elite." *Journal of Family History* 10.4:353–78.

Dull, Jack L. 1978. "Marriage and Divorce in Han China: A Glimpse at 'Pre-Confucian' Society." In *Chinese Family Law and Social Change in Historical and Comparative Perspective*, ed. David C. Buxbaum. Seattle: University of Washington Press.

Ebrey, Patricia Buckley. 1978. *The Aristocratic Families of Early Imperial China: A Case Study of the Po-ling Ts'ui Family*. Cambridge: Cambridge University Press.

————. 1981. "Women in the Kinship System of the Southern Song Upper Class." *Historical Reflections* 8:113–28.

————. 1984a. "Conceptions of the Family in the Sung Dynasty." *Journal of Asian Studies* 43.2:219–45.

————. 1984b. *Family and Property in Sung China: Yüan Ts'ai's Precepts for Social Life*. Princeton: Princeton University Press.

————. 1985. "T'ang Guides to Verbal Etiquette." *Harvard Journal of Asiatic Studies* 45:581–613.

————. 1986a. "Concubines in Sung China." *Journal of Family History* 11:1–24.

————. 1986b. "Early Stages in the Development of Descent Groups." In *Kinship Organization in Late Imperial China, 1000–1940*, ed. Patricia Buckley Ebrey and James L. Watson. Berkeley and Los Angeles: University of California Press.

————. 1988. "The Dynamics of Elite Domination in Sung China." *Harvard Journal of Asiatic Studies* 48:493–519.

Fang Chien-hsin 方建新. 1986. "Sung-tai hun-yin lun-ts'ai" 宋代婚姻論財 (Discussing wealth in Sung period marriages). *Li-shih yen-chiu* 歷史研究, no. 3:178–90.

Freedman, Maurice. 1979. "Rites and Duties, or Chinese Marriage." In *The Study of Chinese Society*, ed. G. William Skinner. Stanford: Stanford University Press.

Gallin, Bernard, and Rita S. Gallin. 1985. "Matrilateral and Affinal Relationships in Changing Chinese Society." In *The Chinese Family and Its Ritual Behavior*, ed. Hsieh Jih-chang and Chuang Ying-chang. Taipei: Academia Sinica, Institute of Ethnology.

Goody, Jack. 1973. "Bridewealth and Dowry in Africa and Eurasia." In *Bridewealth and Dowry*, by Jack Goody and S. J. Tambiah. Cambridge: Cambridge University Press.

————. 1976. *Production and Reproduction: A Comparative Study of the Domestic Domain*. Cambridge: Cambridge University Press.

————. 1983. *The Development of the Family and Marriage in Europe*. Cambridge: Cambridge University Press.

Harrell, Stevan. 1987. "Marriage, Mortality, and the Developmental Cycle in Chinese Lineages." Paper presented at the Conference on Chinese Lineage Demography.

Harrell, Stevan, and Sara A. Dickey. 1985. "Dowry Systems in Complex Societies." *Ethnology* 24.2:105–20.

Hartwell, Robert M. 1982. "Demographic, Political, and Social Transformation of China, 750–1550." *Harvard Journal of Asiatic Studies* 42:365–442.

Herlihy, David. 1985. *Medieval Households*. Cambridge: Harvard University Press.

Holmgren, Jennifer. 1985. "The Economic Foundations of Virtue: Widow-Remarriage in Early and Modern China." *Australian Journal of Chinese Affairs* 13:1–27.

————. 1986. "Observations on Marriage and Inheritance Practices in Early Mongol and Yüan Society, with Particular Reference to the Levirate." *Journal of Asian History* 20:127–92.

Hughes, Diane Owen. 1978. "From Brideprice to Dowry in Mediterranean Europe." *Journal of Family History* 3.3:262–96.

Hymes, Robert P. 1986. *Statesmen and Gentlemen: The Elite of Fu-chou, Chiang-hsi, in Northern and Southern Sung.* Cambridge: Cambridge University Press.

Johnson, David G. 1977a. "The Last Years of a Great Clan: The Li Family of Chao Chün in Late T'ang and Early Sung." *Harvard Journal of Asiatic Studies* 37:5–102.

————. 1977b. *The Medieval Chinese Oligarchy.* Boulder: Westview Press.

Lee, Thomas H. C. 1985. *Government Education and Examinations in Sung China.* Hong Kong: Chinese University Press.

Legge, James, trans. 1885; reprint, 1967. *Li Chi, Book of Rites.* New York: University Books.

Lü Ch'eng-chih 呂誠之. 1935. *Chung-kuo hun-yin chih-tu hsiao-shih* 中國婚姻制度小史 (A short history of marriage institutions in China). Rev. ed. Shanghai: Lung-hu shu-chü.

Ma Chih-su 馬之驌. 1981. *Chung-kuo ti hun-su* 中國的婚俗 (Chinese marriage customs). Taipei: Ching-shih shu-chü.

McCreery, John L. 1976. "Women's Property Rights and Dowry in China and South Asia." *Ethnology* 15:163–74.

Macfarlane, Alan. 1986. *Marriage and Love in England: Modes of Reproduction 1300–1840.* Oxford: Basil Blackwell.

Matsui Shūichi 松井秀一. 1968. "Hoku Sô shoki kanryô no ichi tenkei—Seki Kai to sono keifu o chûshin ni" 北宋初期官僚の一典型—石介とその系譜を中心に (A model of the early Northern Sung official, concentrating on Shih Chieh and his ancestry). *Tōyō gakuhō* 51.1:44–92.

Mauss, Marcel. 1925; reprint, 1966. *The Gift: Forms and Functions of Exchange in Archaic Societies.* New York: W. W. Norton.

Niida Noboru 仁井田陞. 1942. *Shina mibunhôshi* 支那身分法史 (A history of status law in China). Tokyo: Zayūhō kankōkai.

Niu Chih-p'ing 牛志平. 1987. "T'ang-tai hun-yin ti k'ai-fang feng-ch'i" 唐代婚姻的開放風氣 (The liberated style of marriage in the T'ang period). *Li-shih yen-chiu*, no. 4:80–88.

Saller, Richard P. 1984. "Roman Dowry and the Devolution of Property in the Principate." *Classical Quarterly* 34:195–205.

Steele, John, trans. 1917. *The I-li of Book of Etiquette and Ceremonial.* 2 vols. London: Probsthain.

Tai, Yen-hui. 1978. "Divorce in Traditional Chinese Law." In *Chinese Family Law and Social Change in Historical and Comparative Perspective*, ed. David C. Buxbaum. Seattle: University of Washington Press.

T'ao, Hsi-sheng 陶希聖. 1966. *Hun-yin yü chia-tsu* 婚姻與家族 (Marriage and family). Taipei: Jen-jen wen-k'u edition.

Twitchett, Denis. 1960. "Documents on Clan Administration I: The Rules of Administration of the Charitable Estate of the Fan Clan." *Asia Major*, ser. 3, 8:1–35.

————. 1973. "The Composition of the T'ang Ruling Class: New Evidence from Tunhuang." *Perspectives on the T'ang*, ed. Arthur F. Wright and Denis Twitchett.

New Haven: Yale University Press.

Umehara Kaoru 梅原郁. 1985. *Sōdai kanryō seido kenkyū* 宋代官僚制度研究(Studies of the Sung bureaucratic system). Kyoto: Dōhō.

Watson, Rubie S. 1981. "Class Differences and Affinal Relations in South China." *Man* 16:593–615.

———. 1984. "Women's Property in Republican China: Rights and Practice." *Republican China* 10.1a:1–12.

Wong, Sun-ming. 1979. "Confucian Ideal and Reality: Transformation of the Institution of Marriage in T'ang China (A.D. 618–907)." Ph.D. diss., University of Washington.

Yang, Hsien-yi, and Gladys Yang, trans. 1957. *The Courtesan's Jewel Box: Chinese Stories of the Xth-XVIIth Centuries*. Peking: Foreign Languages Press.

Yang Shu-ta 楊樹達. 1933; reprint, 1976. *Han-tai hun-sang li-su k'ao* 漢代婚喪禮俗考 (An investigation of marriage and funerary customs in the Han period). Taipei: Hua-shih ch'u-pan-she.

FOUR

The Marriage of
Sung Imperial Clanswomen

John W. Chaffee

The marriage connections of the Sung imperial clan might seem at first glance to be of questionable significance to the issue of marriage and inequality in China. Marriage of imperial clansmen and clanswomen did not affect succession to the throne or the creation of powerful consort families, like the imperial marriages studied by Jennifer Holmgren and Evelyn Rawski elsewhere in this volume. The imperial clan, in the Sung and other dynasties, was the closest the Chinese imperial system came to an hereditary aristocracy. Yet the clan might also be seen as a parasitic appendage of emperorship, an aristocracy without power because, in Northern Sung times at least, its members were barred from substantive, high-ranking political posts. Why, then, study the marriage relations of a group that was so obviously unique in Sung elite culture as the Chao clan?

The first and most obvious reason is that, like the medieval French royalty so brilliantly evoked by Georges Duby (1978), the Chaos were exemplary. Marriages of Chao princes and princesses were lavish affairs witnessed by the multitudes of the court and capital and enacted in accordance with detailed ritual codes (see also Rawski, in this volume). Even the weddings of distant kinsmen were public events given the prestige and the exchange of assets that accompanied them. Even if, as Holmgren argues in her chapter, imperial marriages reflected imperial needs more than the social practices of the elite, these marriages had great symbolic importance in the society at large. The second reason is that the Chaos were socially, politically, and economically powerful, though that power changed over time. Through most of the Northern Sung, they were excluded from political office and socially segregated within their palaces; but they were often influential with their kinsman, the emperor. In the Southern Sung, by contrast, the personal influence of the Chaos declined even as they came to fill local government posts in great numbers and produced two chief councillors.

The third reason is that marriage wove the Chaos into the fabric of Sung upper-class society. This paper will examine who, how, and where they married, but its particular focus will be the marriage of women out of the imperial clan. Because such marriages were a priori downward, or hypogamous (clanswomen were "sent down" [*chiang*] out of the clan in contrast to women being "selected" [*hsuan*] into the clan as wives), a built-in tension existed between an imperial clanswoman's status superiority and her gender inferiority. The problem of the highborn wife was common throughout Chinese history; what is of interest here is that it was commonly acknowledged and discussed for Sung clanswomen.

Finally, the Chao clan's marriage relations are of interest because of the abundant sources on them. Because the clan was an imperial, and not simply a private, concern, its marriage policy was the subject of a wealth of memorials, essays, edicts, and regulations. Most important are the seven *chüan* devoted to clan affairs and institutions in the *Sung hui-yao*.[1] The dynastic *Sung History*, Sung encyclopedias, memorial collections, and collected writings contain pertinent information too. The dynastic records of imperial princesses—daughters of emperors—together with the fourteen funerary inscriptions that I found for clanswomen (plus two other cases in which ample evidence of the marriage partners is available from other sources) do not begin to compare with those for clansmen.[2] The records are useful, however, as a biographical base for characterizing their marriages.

Using these sources in this essay, I shall attempt to piece together a picture of clanswomen's marriages, and changes in them, during the Sung. In doing so, I address three related questions. First, what kinds of exchanges were involved in the women's marriages and, more specifically, what were the purposes behind the government's clan marriage regulations? We shall see that an imposing array of goods and recruitment privileges constituted the official dowry of the clanswoman. Indeed, the inability of the groom's family to reciprocate in kind raises questions about the meaning of such marriage exchanges. Second, whom did the clanswomen marry? Drawing from both the imperial marriage regulations and inscription evidence, I shall show that the social and geographic backgrounds of the marriage partners varied both over time and according to the position of the woman within the clan. Third, how did these marriages deal with issues of inequality in light of the innate tension between the subordinate role clanswomen were supposed to assume in their husbands' families on the one hand, and the superior connections, resources, and power that they brought into their marriages on the other? Perhaps most important, we shall see how the same regulations and practices assumed very different meanings as the clan itself underwent radical changes. For that reason, we must first consider, if only briefly, the history, structure, and character of the imperial clan itself.

THE IMPERIAL CLAN

To begin on a semantic note, I am using the term "imperial clan" for the Chinese *tsung-shih* because by the Southern Sung it did in fact approximate the anthropologist's "clan"—that is, "a unilineal descent group of widest extent, in which the most inclusive relationships are not reckoned through a genealogy" (Goody 1983: 295).[3] A caveat is necessary because the clan had what it called the Office of the Jade Register (*Yü-tieh-so*), which maintained a comprehensive genealogy (*SS* 117:3890). By the thirteenth century, however, when thousands of clansmen were scattered around the empire and frequently related to each other only to the twelfth or thirteenth degree, the House of Chao acted far more like a clan than a lineage. This was especially true because the dynastic flight south at the end of the Northern Sung resulted in a loss of genealogical records that exhaustive efforts at reconstruction could not fully remedy.

At the beginning of the Sung, the House of Chao consisted of the Chao brothers K'uang-yin (929–76), Chiung (939–97), and T'ing–mei (respectively the emperors T'ai-tsu [r. 960–76] and T'ai-tsung [r. 976–97] and the prince of Wei) and their families,[4] and it seems to have functioned with a minimum of organization. By the middle of the eleventh century, however, the Chaos' numbers and residences had proliferated, and they had their own bureaucracy, staffed at first by clansmen, which issued increasingly detailed regulations for the clan.[5] This organization was necessary because of the clan's spectacular growth during the Northern Sung. A twelfth-century enumeration, by generation and branch, of the clan's genealogy is shown in table 4.1. There are problems with interpreting the figures for the later generations on the list, for they were still being produced at the time of its compilation. Record keeping was also disrupted by the Jurchens' capture of much of the clan during the 1126 invasion. For the earlier generations, however, we can see a truly remarkable record of growth. The twenty-three clansmen (clanswomen were not included) of the first generation grew to almost six thousand by the seventh. This fecundity, which I believe reflects the ready supply of concubines available to the Chao clansmen more than any unusual fertility on the part of Chao wives, presented the government with two problems.

First, the clan was becoming expensive. In 1067 the monthly support (in cash and grain) for the clan exceeded 70,000 strings, and this did not include expenses for birthdays, marriages, and funerals or the seasonal clothing allowances. This sum compared with 40,000 for the entire capital

TABLE 4.1   The Sung Imperial Clan: Generation Names and Membership

Generation No.	T'ai-tsu Generation Name	No.	T'ai-tsung Generation Name	No.	Wei-wang Generation Name	No.	Total
1.	Te 德	4	Yüan 元	9	Te 德	10	23
2.	Wei 惟	8	Yün 允	19	Ch'eng 承	32	59
3.	Ts'ung 從 and Shou 守	24	Tsung 宗	75	K'o 克	127	226
4.	Shih 世	129	Chung 仲	388	Shu 叔	561	1,078
5.	Ling 令	564	Shih 士	1,499	Chih 之	1,425	3,488
6.	Tzu 子	1,251[a]	Pu 不	2,130	Kung 公	1,774	5,155
7.	Po 伯	1,645	Shan 善	2,431	Yen 彦	1,824	5,900
8.	Shih 師	1,490	Ju 汝	1,022	Fu 夫	1,666	4,178
9.	Hsi 希	1,140	Ch'ung 崇	413	Shih 時	253	1,806
10.	Yü 與	110	Pi 必	19	Jo 若	24	153
Total		6,365		8,005		7,696[b]	22,066[b]

SOURCE: CYTC 1.1:24. This information, which CYTC gives in this form though without the totals at the right, is also found in WHTK 259:2056–7, but CYTC is earlier (1203) and the probable source for the WHTK. (The CYTC's source was the Hsien-yüan lei-p'u, the official imperial genealogy.) The table does not include those in the eleventh and twelfth generations, which had been named, nor does it include the direct descendants of Ying-tsung or Hui-tsung or the Nan-pan-kuan clansmen.

[a] WHTK gives 1,221, but that is an error, for it does not tally with the T'ai-tsu ten-generation total.

[b] CYTC gives 7,296 and 21,666 respectively, but the Wei-wang total is in fact 7,696 and the grand total 22,066.

bureaucracy and 110,000 for the capital armies (*SHY:TH* 4:31b). Second, the clan in the mid-eleventh century had begun producing children who were not mourning kin of the emperor—that is, beyond the already marginal fifth degree of kinship (*t'an-mien*). According to Han and T'ang precedents, they should have been sent out of the capital, given land, and then severed forever from imperial support. This would have solved the problem of the escalating costs of the clan. Yet, in two stages, the late Northern Sung emperors and their reform-minded chief councillors chose to break with tradition and support the nonmourning kin, albeit at reduced levels.

In 1069 the emperor Shen-tsung (r. 1068–85) ordered that kin of the sixth generation and below no longer be given names and official rank by the throne. Records of their births and deaths, however, were still to be maintained, and the men were to be permitted to take special examinations for entry into officialdom (*SHY:CK* 20:5b–6a). The following year sixth-generation kin were also ordered out of clan housing, a move prompted by severe overcrowding (*SHY:CK* 20:6a; *SHY:TH* 4:20b). One noteworthy change that eventually followed from the 1070 order occurred in 1082 when clansmen of the fifth degree and below were permitted, after the death of their parents, to form separate households and divide the family property (except for "fields held in perpetuity" [*yung-yeh t'ien*] and sacrificial objects). This practice, standard among commoner families, was said to have "never occurred" in the clan; hitherto, all of their support had come from the government (*SHY:TH* 5:8a–b). These distant clansmen and women now found themselves in a limbo of partial recognition and limited privilege, which as we shall see below informed their marriage relations as well.

Then, in 1102, chief councillor Ts'ai Ching (1046–1126) proposed an ambitious plan for two large residential complexes called the Halls of Extended Clanship (*Tun-tsung yuan*). Supported by charitable estates (*i-chuang*) endowed out of local governmental resources, the residences were to be established at the Western and Southern capitals, that is, Lo-yang and Ying-t'ien fu (*SHY:CK* 20:34a–b). This proposal, which was accepted by the emperor Hui-tsung (r. 1101–25), entailed two new bureaucracies known jointly as the Two Capitals Offices of Imperial Clan Affairs (*Liang-ching tsung-cheng-ssu*), which provided housing and support (in the form of cash and grain allowances, wedding and funeral expenses) for these clansmen and women. Their scale was impressive: in 1120 the southern Hall of Extended Clanship reported holdings of 44,000 *ch'ing* of fields (roughly 660,000 acres) and more than 23,600 rooms (*chien*) of buildings (*fang-lang*); even then there were complaints about insufficient resources and space (*SHY:CK* 20:36b–37a).

The decision of Shen-tsung and, then, Hui-tsung to support the nonmourning kin is an interesting issue that can only be touched upon here. Moroto Tatsuo has linked this decision to the Sung policy of elevating the civil over the military and suggests further that it was part of a general Sung ideology of benevolence (*onkeishugi*) (1958:628), though he does not say why that benevolence was applied at this time and to the imperial clan. One plausible explanation is that they were influenced by the renewed interest in the *tsung* (extended kinship group, or clan) voiced by such men as Ou-yang Hsiu (1007–72), Su Hsun (1009–66), and Ch'eng I (1033–1107) (Ebrey 1984a: 229–32). At a time when the scholar-officials were advocating stronger *tsung*, it would have looked amiss for the emperor to cut off most of the imperial clan, which was the quintessential *tsung*. This hypothesis, however, will have to await further consideration elsewhere.

The Extended Clanship Halls as well as the clan's entire K'ai-feng establishment came to an abrupt end with the loss of northern China to the Jurchen in 1126, though this was far from the end of the clan. Those who escaped fled pell-mell to the south. By the time a measure of stability and order were restored, the clan had two offices in Fu-chien—at Fu-chou and Ch'üan-chou (continuing the old Western and Southern Capital administrations)—and in Shao-hsing fu (Liang-che-tung) and Lin-an, the capital (*CYTC* 1.1:25–26). But few Southern Sung clansmen lived at the capital, partly because the government, citing high housing and living costs, early on discouraged them from settling there (*SHY:TH* 6:12b–13a). The general infertility of the Southern Sung emperors also meant that the clan had few close imperial kin. Thus Fu-chou, Ch'üan-chou, and Shao-hsing prefectures became the main centers of clan resettlement, with Ch'üan-chou claiming some 2,244 clansmen in the early thirteenth century (*CWCKCC* 15:11a); clansmen could be found in every part of the empire, often supervised only loosely by local officials and clan elders.

The dispersed and diminished circumstances of the imperial clan, however, were paralleled by a growth in the political power of many clan families. Although they had first been permitted to hold local offices (*wai-kuan*) in the 1070s, the disordered conditions of the early Southern Sung saw them employed in large numbers to fill vacancies in the bureaucracy and even the army. So widespread were they that quotas were established limiting the numbers of clansmen who could serve in a given county or prefecture (*SHY: TH* 5:32b–33a). Thereafter, though producing two chief councillors and a number of high-ranking officials in the court, they were most prominent in local government. The Chaos also became a major presence in the examinations, in which they were given preferred treatment (see Chaffee 1985: 106–8). There was a paradox here. The growing numbers and increasing genealogical distance of most Chaos from the emperor led to general reduction in status and affluence, but their humbler, less-threatening position undoubtedly facilitated their assumption of real, if limited, power. Thus they became more like the *shih-ta-fu* elite even while maintaining their imperial clan status, with its attendant privileges and regulations.

The Sung imperial clan thus underwent radical changes over the course of the dynasty. The wealthy, centralized, though politically powerless clan of the mid-eleventh century bore little resemblance to the Southern Sung clan, which was much humbler and more dispersed, yet contained many individually consequential members. Likewise, there were vast differences between the immediate imperial families, the holders of hereditary noble titles, and the distant kin who were, at times, reduced to poverty.[6] Yet all of them branched from the Son of Heaven in the eyes of the emperor and his officials and were governed by the same sets of concerns and regulations. As we turn to the clanswomen and their marriages, we must therefore keep in mind both the clan's diversity and hierarchy and also its unity, when viewed from the outside.

THE REGULATION OF MARRIAGE

The earliest Sung record of imperial clan marriage regulations dates from 1029, some seventy years into the dynasty, when the proliferation of clansmen was already rendering the less formal nuptial procedures obsolete. Emperor Jen-tsung ordered each clan palace—of which there were ten—to submit a list of clansmen aged eighteen and clanswomen aged fifteen (Chinese style) to be considered for marriages. While specifying administrative procedures including the appointment of eunuch investigators and the emperor's personal approval, the edict goes on to specify that marriage partners "whose talent and age are suitable" should be sought from among "the elite families of examination graduates" (*i-kuan shih-tsu*), families without artisans, merchants, or "miscellaneous elements" (*tsa-lei*), and with no history of treasonous activities (*SHY:CK* 20:4b).

Several aspects of this edict deserve comment. First, there was no question that all clan members should marry, and marry young. In contrast to Europe, where a variety of factors combined to limit marriage and therefore fertility, in China fertility was maximized in every way possible, and nowhere was that truer than for the imperial clan. There were, to be sure, clanswomen who became Buddhist or Taoist nuns,[7] but they were exceedingly rare. Second, clan marriages were considered state business in which the young clan member's immediate family had no formal role. The provision requiring the approval of the emperor himself was a mark of the importance accorded them, and as we shall see below the emperor himself at times initiated marriages. There was, finally, a great concern that the marriage partners come from proper families. The proscribed categories of artisan, merchant, and "miscellaneous elements" were the same as those for examination candidates, but the requirement that they come from elite families—which meant families with a history of government service—was not. The government wanted to ensure that its marriage ties were with families from the ruling elite.

TABLE 4.2   Imperial Clan Marriage Partners: Proscribed Groups

Year	Imperial Kin Affected (if specified)	Proscribed Marriage Partners
1029	—	offspring of artisans, merchants, or "miscellaneous elements" or from families with a history of treasonous activities
1077	5th degree	from families of "miscellaneous elements": where males had been slaves or females prostitutes or where parents or grandparents had lived on the border and served two regimes
1077	4th degree and above	offspring of clerks, officials via purchase or special skills, artisans, merchants, "miscellaneous elements," and those with a history of treasonous activities
1088	5th degree and above	same as 4th degree in 1077
1088	—	relatives of eunuchs
1213	6th degree and above	families of clerks

SOURCES: *SHY:CK* 20:4b; *SS* 115:2739; *HCP* 409:4b; *SHY:TH* 5:7b, 7:30a–b.

Over the succeeding half-century, this question of the social background of affinal relatives gave rise to a great deal of legislation (table 4.2). In 1058 it was decreed that commoners (*pai-shen-jen*) who married clanswomen needed either a three-generation record of office holding or one direct ancestor with at least capital rank, and moreover had to be recommended by a court or capital-rank official (*SHY:CK* 20:5a; *HCP* 187:10a). Six years later this was decreased to a flat requirement of two ancestors who had been officials (*SS* 115:2739), and in 1088 was further reduced, for clan members of the fifth degree, to one official (*HCP* 409:4b). The proscribed categories also underwent change. In 1077 families of "miscellaneous elements" were defined as those with slaves among the males or prostitutes among the females, and also as those with parents or grandparents who had lived along a border and had served two regimes. Clansmen and women within the fourth degree were barred from marrying the sons or grandsons of clerks, officials who had gained rank via purchase or special skills, in addition to the aforementioned artisans, merchants, and "miscellaneous elements."[8] It was further specified that the required paperwork was the responsibility of the groom's family, though the guarantors, the Office of Imperial Clan Affairs and the Palace Domestic Service, were all legally responsible for the information contained therein (*SS* 115:2739). Finally, in 1088 the proscriptions for the fourth-degree kin from 1077 were extended to fifth-degree kin (*HCP* 409:4b), and later that year a further category was added, marriage with the families of eunuchs (*nei-ch'en*), on the grounds that because they had access to the palace living quarters, marriage connections with them would be inappropriate (*SHY:TH* 5:7b).

These provisions dealt only with clan members within the fifth degree of mourning and initially, at least, nonmourning kin were not included. A lengthy memorial from 1069 proposing to restructure the rights and privileges of clan members specified that "nonmourning clanswomen" follow the marriage laws for commoner families, but then added that they "should not marry into nonelite (*fei shih-tsu*) families" (ibid., *TH* 4.33b). This qualification apparently was not included when the restructuring was enacted later that year, for the 1077 and 1088 edicts cited above mention only the use of the laws for commoner families. But by the thirteenth century if not before, restrictions were being applied to the nonmourning kin as well. A memorial by the Great Office of Imperial Clan Affairs in 1213 stated: "Although by law, legitimate imperial clansmen and women of the sixth degree and below are to marry according to the laws for commoner families, the commentaries [*chu-wen*] should be cited: that the sons and grandsons from families with miscellaneous elements or with a history of criminals or traitors are unacceptable as [marriage] relations." Further quoting the commentaries on the definition of "miscellaneous elements" (the exact language of the 1077 edict is used), the memorial stated that powerful and wealthy local families were conspiring with "unregistered clansmen" to obtain clan status for the latter and were then marrying them in order to gain official status for themselves. As a consequence, clerical families were thereafter barred from marrying with clansmen (*SHY:TH* 7:30a–b). I shall return to the issue of official rank as a reward for marriage and the problems associated with it; here it is enough to note that, having accepted the responsibility for continuing to support the nonmourning imperial kin, the government eventually found itself forced to police their marriages as well.

The government's active role in clan marriages was paralleled in other aspects of clanswomen's lives as well. For example, a fairly liberal attitude was taken toward divorce by clansmen and women. It was permitted if there were grounds for separation as spelled out in the law code or even evidence of incompatibility (*pu hsiang-an*), but, first, an investigation was required by the Office of Imperial Clan Affairs (*SS* 115:2739–40; *SHY:TH* 5:1a).[9] Also, in the philanthropic atmosphere of Hui-tsung's reign, special provisions were made for orphaned clanswomen and childless widows without close relatives to enter the Halls of Extended Clanship and receive an allowance of grain and cash. In addition, remarriage allowances were authorized for clanswomen who were nonmourning kin (*SHY:CK* 20:36a). The following year living quarters at the halls were authorized for orphaned clanswomen and for both legally divorced and widowed clanswomen who had returned to the clan, though if they had living parents, uncles, or brothers, they were required to live with them (*SHY:CK* 20:36a).

In the Southern Sung these precedents led to an acknowledged responsibility for the care of clan orphans and single women, though often that care took the form of the individuals having the right to draw their allowances from the local government coffers. These allowances were not large—in 1158 they were set at a string of cash and a *shih* of grain per month for those fifteen *sui* or over, half that for those younger (*SHY:TH* 6:30a)—but it was a significant commitment given the large numbers of kin potentially involved. A desire to contain costs could also lead to further regulation of the clanswomen's lives; in a memorial from 1162 we find an "unmarried clanswoman who has exceeded her time limit [for marriage]" (*wei-hsien wei-chia tsung-nü*) by a year, asking for an additional year to give her relatives time to arrange a marriage. If after that time she were still unmarried, she would receive the lesser allowance of a returned clanswoman (*SHY:CK* 20:40a). The proposal, which was accepted, is the only reference I have found to such a time limit, but it suggests the degree of involvement in the personal lives of these women that these regulations entailed.

OFFICIAL DOWRIES AND MARRIAGE EXCHANGES

One of the underlying reasons for the government's careful regulation of clan marriages was that marriage to a clanswoman brought a family not merely prestige but significant benefits as well. These benefits, or "official dowries" as I shall call them, took a variety of forms, most of them set according to the rank or relationship of the clanswoman to the emperors, past or present.

There was, first, the formal dowry, or *lien-chü*, the money and goods that the government provided at the woman's marriage. For an imperial princess (*kung-chu*), these could be considerable, as the following enumeration from the *Sung History*'s section on wedding ritual suggests: a jade belt with an outer coat, a silver saddle and bridle, and four hundred rolls of fine silk were the gifts stipulated for "joining relatives" (*hsi-ch'in*); ten thousand ounces (*liang*) of silver formed the "expenses for separating from the imperial household" (*pien-ts'ai*—twice the amount set aside for princes' betrothal gifts); and following the wedding, the princess was given a mansion (*chia-ti*), four fans, ten flower screens, and ten candlestick holders (*SS* 115:2732). There seems to have been considerable variation in what was actually given, especially in the Northern Sung when emperors were exceptionally generous to their daughters. In 1067 Shen-tsung remarked that the cost of marrying one princess could run to 700,000 strings of cash (*JCSP* 14:4a–b), while the marriage of Jen-tsung's daughter, the Yen-kuo princess (see Appendix, no. 4), in 1057 involved a dowry of twenty horses, twenty cows, two camels, two hundred sheep, fifty *ch'ing* of land (about eight hundred acres), three estates, ten slaves, two house officials, and four cooks (*SHY:TH* 8:11a).[10] Lesser but still sumptuous gifts are also detailed for commandary princesses (*chün-chu*, the daughters of the heir-apparent) and county princesses (*hsien-chu*, the daughters of princes, or *wang*): a gold belt for *hsi-ch'in*, five thousand ounces of silver for the *pan-ts'ai*, with other gifts valued at one-third those of emperors' daughters (*SS* 115:2732).

All clanswomen were supposed to receive at least some dowry. A dowry scale set during the Hsi-ning period (1068–77) specified five hundred strings for great-great-granddaughters of emperors (*yuan-sun-nü*), three hundred and fifty for clanswomen in the fifth generation, three hundred for those in the sixth, two hundred and fifty for those in the seventh, and one hundred and fifty for those in the eighth (*CYTC* 1.1:25).[11] The dowry amounts specified for the last three of these are of special interest because they were for women who are beyond the mourning circle, thus indicating the government's continuing support of their marriages. In 1137 these dowries were cut by two-fifths for the great-granddaughters, one-third for the sixth- and eighth-generation women, and two-sevenths for those in the fifth and seventh generations. But even so, financially pressed local governments (to which this responsibility had fallen) at times refused to pay. In one instance in 1162 funds for dowry payments had to be specially sent from the court to Ch'üan-chou. As one of the largest clan centers in the empire and the seat of a clan office, Ch'üan-chou had a particularly heavy burden (*CYTC* 1.1:25). Whether even these reduced dowries continued to be paid through the Southern Sung (especially as increasingly distant generations were produced) is hard to say, but one essay from the mid-thirteenth century suggests that some payments were maintained, though only in a form inadequate to help some unfortunate clanswomen. Fang Ta-ts'ung (1183–1247), himself the brother-in-law of a clanswoman (no. 15, Appendix), wrote in the course of an essay on the fiscal problems of the imperial clan, that,

According to precedent, when clanswomen get married they are to have a cash dowry (*tzu-chi*). Now there are those [in families] living outside [the clan residences] who are forced to marry when they have just come of age (at the hairpin ceremony) because [their families are] worried about the money and food they are wasting. Why is it that the prefectural officials do not want to relieve their grievous condition and give them the affection due the Heavenly lake [of imperial kin]? (*TAC* 26:7a)

Significant as the clanswomen's cash dowries were (and in the 1162 Ch'üan-chou case cited above it was claimed that many poor clanswomen were unwilling to marry without it), even more important were recruitment privileges conferred on the husband and his family, a practice established during the T'ang dynasty (*JCSP* 16:5b). The basic privilege, as enunciated in 1070, provided the husband with the low military service rank of attendant of the three ranks (*San-pan feng-chih*—rank 9B). If he were already an official, he was entitled to a promotion of one rank (*kuan*) (*SHY:TH* 4:23b–24a). The promotion privilege had previously been limited to husbands of clanswomen of the fourth-degree kin or above who were already capital-rank officials, but the 1070 edict extended it to all fifth-degree clanswomen's husbands, regardless of their rank or post. For the husbands of commandary and county princesses, a slightly higher initial rank of duty attendant (*Tien-chih*) was given, while the husbands of princesses were made commandant-escort (*Fu-ma tu-wei*) (*SS* 115:2732; *SMCTI* 33:11b–12a). In addition, beginning in 1064 the husbands of clanswomen were permitted to sit for the examinations in the Locked Hall Examination (*so-t'ing-shih*), a special preliminary examination for officials). They had previously been excluded from these examinations (*SHY:TH* 4:15a; *HCP* 202:1b–2a).

Although the evidence on recruitment privileges in the Southern Sung is scanty, it would seem that the examinations came to play an important role. According to Hung Mai, writing in the mid–Southern Sung, a commoner marrying a clanswoman of the fifth degree could receive the prestige title of "court gentleman for ceremonial service" (*Chiang-shih-lang*) if he were a *chü-jen* (that is, had passed the preliminary examinations); if not, he received the honorary military title of "gentleman for fostering temperance" (*Ch'eng-chieh-lang*) or "gentleman of trust" (*Ch'eng-hsin-lang*), both titles being equivalent to the Northern Sung "attendant of the three ranks." Although nominally higher than the civil rank, these designations were nevertheless less desirable because they were military (*JCSP* 16:5b). Whether these privileges were restricted to the marriages of mourning kin, however, is not entirely clear. If so, the vast majority of Southern Sung clanswomen would have been excluded. Li Hsin-ch'uan, a contemporary of Hung's, wrote that "those who have passed the preliminary examinations who marry clanswomen may enter the civil service" (*CYTC* 2.14:534). In a number of the cases discussed below, the husbands of Southern Sung clanswomen made use of their recruitment privileges. This evidence, together with Hung's assertion, suggests that the privileges were broadly applied.

Finally, the Southern Sung husbands of clanswomen were given the additional privilege of naming one son to office through protection, or *yin* (*CYTC* 1.6:86). Introduced in 1166, this privilege was separate from other protection privileges the husband might gain through his own or his family's accomplishments and further supports the notion of a liberal dispensation of recruitment privileges for clanswomen (or their husbands) in the Southern Sung. Indeed, it may be that as the state's ability to support lavish dowries declined, the government compensated in part with a lenient policy toward recruitment privileges, however shortsighted that would have been in the long run.

This legislated combination of dowry and privileges raises the question of the exchanges involved in clanswomen's marriages. These exchanges were like the royal dowries common to most European monarchial systems in that they drew on the resources of the state. But where royal marriages, in Europe at least, were made with other royalty as well as the nobility, in China there was no other royalty. Although it is true that in certain periods (such as the non-Han dynasties discussed by Holmgren and Rawski elsewhere in this volume) imperial clan marriages were used as an instrument of foreign policy, this seems not to have been the case during the Sung; indeed, imperial princesses without exception married Han Chinese. Whereas the largest royal dowries, like that of the Yen-kuo princess cited above, were personally tailored to women of the immediate royal family, the official marriage benefits for all other brides were impersonal, bureaucratic, and employed on a vast scale.

This evidence admittedly comes from the realm of political legislation rather than anthropological description. Still, assuming that the dowry legislation was largely adhered to (and for the Northern Sung at least that would seem reasonable), we can still ask after clan marriage exchanges. The state's role on behalf of the clan created such an asymmetry in the marriages as to render inapplicable much of the anthropological literature on dowry, such as Spiro's notion of economic exchange or Goody's of diverging devolution (Comaroff 1980: 3–8). Levi-Strauss's structural notion of marriage as a system of women for women exchanges (ibid., 26) is more useful, with the emperor, through the imperial clan, providing the ruling elite with women, dowries, and privileges, while the ruling elite reciprocated with women, loyalty, and service. Unlike the cultural structures that Levi-Strauss has so remarkably articulated, however, this structure was the invention of politics and was one of the building blocks of the Sung political order.

In their attempt to consolidate power and create a stable order, the early Sung emperors worked systematically to limit the power of all potential rivals, be they the military, families of empresses, great families with long traditions of office holding, or, as we have seen, the imperial clan. Their chief partner in this was the civil elite, which owed its position largely to land, wealth, the examinations, and bureaucratic achievement and was more broadly based than ever before. I would suggest that imperial marriages formed a part of that partnership, for they demonstrated imperial beneficence. The blessings of such marriages were admittedly mixed, for hypogamous unions put a strain on the grooms' families, as will be seen below; but the wealth, office, and potential influence still made such marriages attractive.

During the Southern Sung the government's role in deciding marriage matches seems to have ceased. The clanswomen's inscriptions speak in places of individual go-betweens and, once, of the need for official approval for the woman's husband to receive official rank but not at all of the government or clan organizations initiating and arranging marriages. Thus, if there had been broad political goals behind clan marriages in the Northern Sung, they must have disappeared, or at least have been greatly diluted, during the Southern Sung.

Another factor was at work apart from politics: that of honor. Honor, of course, was one of the assets the imperial clan had to offer. To quote Wang Meng-lung, who married Chao Ju-i (Appendix, no. 13; 1183–1221), "The honor of his wife is what a husband relies upon; the wealth of a husband is what contents his wife. This is certainly the rule when common families marry with the imperial clan" (*SHWC* 25:11a–12a). There was a concomitant fear of dishonor. The recruitment privileges, in one respect a measure of imperial grace, thus increasingly served to maintain the clan's respectability because they made even humble clanswomen attractive to elite families. In 1070 Wang An-shih argued in favor of a proposal to extend promotion privileges to officials marrying fifth-degree clanswomen: "This is a way of encouraging those who are officials to marry clanswomen and also [provides] a shortcut for entering officialdom" (*SHY:TH* 4:23b–24a; *HCP* 213:7a–b).

Wang was concerned not so much with making useful political connections for the emperor as ensuring that clanswomen and the clan itself be spared from improper marriages. In this he was not alone, for a recurring theme in writings on clanswomen's marriages was that they should not dishonor or sully the imperial clan. People did not always agree upon what constituted dishonor, however. In 1051 the head of the Bureau of Policy Criticism, Pao Cheng (998–1061), vehemently protested the pending marriage of a clanswoman to the son of one Li Shou, the former owner of an alum shop who had become an official via purchase. This match had been investigated and approved by censors and the Office of Imperial Clan Affairs, who declared that "this is not a family of skilled artisans or itinerant merchants." In other words, the regulations were designed to ensure an elite life-style and status (even if purchased) rather than ancestral background. Pao did not agree, arguing that suitable matches could be made only with families of renown and that "ritual teachings" (*li-chiao*) must be followed strictly (*SMCTI* 33:10b–11a).

The sources do not reveal the outcome of Pao Cheng's objections, but his suggestion that clanswomen's marriages into "upstart" families violated the natural order was echoed by others. In 1068 the censor Liu Shu (1034 *chin-shih*), in arguing unsuccessfully that clanswomen's marriages be restricted to currently serving civil and military officials, asserted that wealthy villagers falsely used the official genealogies of others to marry clanswomen. "For entangling the rules of the country," he wrote, "and dirtying that which is under Heaven, there is nothing worse than this" (*SMCTI* 33:11b–12a).

Even more remarkable, metaphorically and substantively, is a 1088 memorial by the drafting official P'eng Ju-li (1041–94) asking for a clarification of the marriage regulations for fifth-degree (*t'an-mien*) clansmen and women. Noting that fifth-degree kin are barred from marrying into "nonelite families" (*fei shih-tsu chih chia*), he said he did not know what constitutes "elite families" because the specific occupational prohibitions applied only to fourth-degree kin, thus opening the way to marriages with officials via purchase and even those with treasonous backgrounds. He then continued:

> In my opinion, that which accumulates greatly will flow lengthily and when far from the source will form a great lake. That is the nature of things. Now among the Son of Heaven's kin, if the ancestors reaching to the seventh generation are not forgotten, then their descendants stretching into the distance also cannot but be acclaimed. Even though the fifth-degree kin have all issued from the imperial ancestors and are identically connected to the body of the state (*kuo-t'i*), they are made dirty, rustic and remote, and all can be taken [in marriage] as commodities. This does not honor the imperial ancestors. (*SMCTI* 33:12b–13a)

The consequences of this he then paints in vivid if melodramatic colors:

> Powerful merchants and great traders, using wealth to dominate their communities, now pay from three to five thousand strings of cash to enter [officialdom] as instructors and registrars, and so steal the name of "elite family" (*shih-tsu*). By further payment of several thousand strings, they can seek to become palace kin [i.e., marry with the imperial clan] and thus gain the status of "official household" (*kuan-hu*). Stealing favor, robbing the state, relying on force, and humiliating the weak, how can this not be a disgrace to the state? (*SMCTI* 33:13a)

With this last assertion, P'eng adds a dimension to our notions of clan marriage exchanges, for here we see a different, sub-rosa, exchange of money for marriage and its attendant office, or at least allegations of it. The 1213 memorial mentioned above, which alleged conspiracies between powerful, wealthy families and unregistered clansmen, suggests his accusation had some basis in fact. We cannot say whether such exchanges were common, but given the clan's reduced circumstances in the Southern Sung it would not be surprising if they were.[12]

Even more interesting are the images the memorial uses and the attitudes they reveal. Although the common Sung metaphor for the imperial clan was "branches of Heaven" (*T'ien chih*), P'eng talks of the "body of the state," which can be sullied (thus echoing Liu Shu), but even more about a stream that flows to make a lake (recalling Fang Ta-ts'ung's earlier quoted reference to the "Heavenly lake of imperial kin"). His concern is with the purity of the imperial kin, and that was most threatened by the marriage of women. Because clanswomen had issued from the Son of Heaven, their husbands could pollute the ever-widening Heavenly lake.[13]

THE AFFINES

Whom did the clanswomen marry and where did they come from? Our biographical evidence for married princesses and clanswomen is limited, but taken together with other kinds of information, two hypotheses may be ventured. First, we know from the regulations described above that they were required to draw from the pool of bureaucratic families. And despite the complaints just discussed about merchants marrying into the clan, it is probable that until the late eleventh century at least, this requirement was largely fulfilled, for the clan was sufficiently small and concentrated. It would also make sense that the Northern Sung clanswomen generally married men whose families were either native to K'ai-feng or had settled there by virtue of official service. Because the imperial clan resided exclusively in K'ai-feng until the 1070s and did not move elsewhere in appreciable numbers until after 1102, K'ai-feng society would have been the natural focus of their marriage ties. K'ai-feng families so dominated the Northern Sung examinations (see Chaffee 1985:61–66) that the capital had plenty of bureaucratic families to supply spouses.

The available evidence supports the first hypothesis and is ambiguous about the second. The wives of Northern Sung clansmen came overwhelmingly from K'ai-feng families; of the fifty-seven wives of clansmen in Aoyama Sadao's guide to biographies, forty-eight (84 percent) of the fifty-seven clansmen's wives for whom family residence is known came from Kai-feng.[14] Of the other nine, six came from the north China plain and two others came from long-established and successful bureaucratic families in Lang-chou (Ssu-ch'uan) and Hang-chou (Liang-che-hsi).[15] In striking contrast to the marriages of clansmen, the husbands of Northern Sung princesses and clanswomen came predominantly from non-K'ai-feng families; of twenty-two for whom information about residency is available (Appendix, nos. 3–7, 20, 23–25, 27–28, 30–32, 36–37, 40–43, 45–46), nineteen came from provincial, predominantly northern families.[16] This does not mean that the husbands themselves were provincials; because most came from long-established families with records of high military or civil office, they had probably spent much or all of their youths in the capital. Still, such wide-ranging family origins suggest an attention to provincial alliances on the part of the Sung emperors.

Priscilla Ching Chung, in her study of Northern Sung palace women, found that the dynasty drew heavily from military families and very little from scholarly families. She points to T'ai-tsu's famous drinking speech to his generals, in which he offers to intermarry his family with theirs, as evidence of a kind of military alliance marriage strategy (1981: 24–35). Jennifer Holmgren, while agreeing with Chung, has argued further that a key element of such a marriage policy was that the military elite was declining and therefore did not pose a threat to the bureaucratic elite (see her chapter in this volume). The princesses' marriages generally support that finding, for nine husbands were from prominent military families (nos. 23, 25, 30–32, 36, 40–41, 44), compared to five from high-ranking civil families (5, 20, 27, 43,

37) and two from scholarly families (nos. 28, 42).[17] But these figures obscure an important change in the husbands over time. In the early Sung princesses married military men almost exclusively. By the late Northern Sung not only were husbands chosen more frequently from scholarly and high civil families, but husbands from military families appear to have turned civil. Ch'ien Ching-chen (husband of no. 23), the scion of the royal Ch'iens of Wu-yüeh and subsequently of early Sung generals, was known for his learning and activities as a local official in the south (Ch'ang et al. 1974–76 5:4085), and Wang Shih-yueh (1044–1102; husband of no. 40), offspring of the early Sung general Wang Shen-ch'i, was the son of a *chin-shih* and classically educated (ibid., 1:335). Moreover, being related to empresses could also be important, as was the case with nos. 3, 4, and 27. Thus, by the late Northern Sung, family and personal ties with the palace or ministerial service had largely replaced military considerations in determining clanswomen's marriages.

One other intriguing piece of evidence suggests that by the late Northern Sung, the clanswomen's recruitment privileges were already proving potent attractions for wealthy but undistinguished families. With echoes of P'eng Ju-li, Chu Yü wrote in 1119:

> In recent generations since clanswomen have become numerous, the [Office of] Clan Affairs has established several score official matchmakers to handle marriage discussions. Initially there were no limitations [with regard to] influential and wealthy families, and many gave gifts to the clan in their quest for matches, illicitly seeking an office so as to protect their households. Thereafter [these families and the clan] have sought each other out as kin. Rich people of the capital like the Ta-t'ung Chang family have married with as many as thirty or more county princesses. (*PCKT* 1:3–4)

The Southern Sung spouses exhibit quite different characteristics from their Northern Sung predecessors. First, they were truly dispersed geographically; none of them appears to have lived at the capital: four spouses came from the Chiang-nan circuits (no. 8 from Jao-chou, no. 9 from Fu-chou, no. 10 from Chi-chou, and no. 18 from Hung-chou), four from Liang-che-tung (nos. 12 and 14 from Ming-chou, no. 11 from Wu-chou and no. 13 from T'ai-chou), and three from Fu-chien (nos. 14 and 16 from Hsing-hua and no. 17 from Ch'üan-chou). This distribution was generally matched by the families of the clanswomen, but with a number of interesting differences. There are no indications that the families of nos. 8–12 and 17–18 lived in different prefectures from those of their husbands (although most of the inscriptions do not assert that their prefecture was the same), but the cousins Chao Ju-chieh (no. 15) and Pi-shan (no. 16) both moved from Ch'üan-chou, the seat of the Southern Imperial Clan Office, up the coast to Hsing-hua chun, and Chao Hsi-i (no. 14) moved from T'ai-chou north to Yin County of Ming-chou. Most remarkably, the family of Chao Ju-i (no. 13) was from Ch'ih-chou in Chiang-nan-tung, but she married Yuan Fu of Ming-chou, hundreds of miles to the east. These findings are interesting in the light of recent studies of Sung marriage patterns that have argued that the Southern Sung elites, in contrast to their Northern Sung counterparts, married predominantly with families from their own prefectures (see Hartwell 1982 and especially Hymes 1986). The Chaos, it would appear, were atypical and married more widely, though the precise social mechanisms for their doing so are still unclear.[18]

The social backgrounds of the Southern Sung husbands also differ from those in the Northern Sung. With the possible exception of the interregional bride Chao Ju-i, whose three-generation genealogy is not given, the clans-women's forebears were almost all officials, less exalted in rank but including many who had been active officials, which agrees with what we know about the clan in the Southern Sung.[19] Like their fathers and fathers-in-law, the Southern Sung husbands with just one exception (Lo Chin, the husband of no. 18) were or became officials. Two received *chin-shih* degrees (the husbands of nos. 13–14), in both cases after their marriages, and their wives are praised for their support. One husband, as we note above, entered via protection. We do not know how another four qualified for office (the husbands of nos. 8–9 and 12–13). Four husbands, however, either used their wives' privileges or explicitly chose not to do so. They thus merit further attention because their cases reveal a good deal about the use of this privilege and attitudes toward it.

For Lady Chao (no. 11), marriage to Hsu Shih came at the relatively late age of twenty-seven *sui*. Because the groom reportedly made the match "in the hopes of obtaining office and establishing his family," Lady Chao's privileges probably saved her from a life of spinsterhood. In writing about this, the philosopher Ch'en Liang (1143–94), who had been a friend of Hsu Shih's late father, Chieh-ch'ing, was initially dismayed: "I strongly regretted this [as it was] contrary to Chieh-ch'ing's intentions." He changed his mind, however, for he found that Shih "has increasingly worked at his studies and lately I have seen that his writings have daily improved." Moreover, upon meeting her, Ch'en found that she was "really unlike the daughter of a noble family" and had delighted even her mother-in-law. But then she died after just 130 days of marriage, much to everyone's distress (*CLC* 29:431).

In the case of Lady Chao of Lu-ling (no. 10), it was the husband who shared Ch'en's dislike of clanswomen's recruitment privileges, lacking as they did the prestige of more regular avenues. For years after their marriage, he disdained using his wife's privileges and lived the life of a poor aspiring scholar, studying, instructing his sons, and entertaining his fellow literati. Even after his younger brothers, a nephew, and many of his friends all became officials and he became an embittered recluse, he did not waver in this. At her suggestion, however, he sent some of his writings to the chief councillor

Chou Pi-ta (1126–1204), who upon reading them recommended him for office (*CCC* 129:10b–12a). Not all spurned the clanswomen's privileges, however. Fang Ta-yü (1181–1234), the husband of Chao Pi-shan (no. 16), passed the Hsing-hua prefectural examination in 1204 and availed himself of his wife's privilege immediately after failing the metropolitan examination the next year (*HTHSTCC* 151:11a–12a; *TAC* 34:2a–b, 35:3b). Ch'iu Shuang, the husband of Pi-shan's cousin, Shan-i (no. 17), also used his wife's privileges, but the matter was complicated and thus instructive. Ch'iu had agreed to marry Shan-i, an orphan, on the recommendation of her cousin and guardian, who had praised her highly and also undoubtedly pointed out the advantages in it for Ch'iu, for according to the inscription,

> Mr. Ch'iu had once been recommended in the local [examinations], so since he had married [a clanswoman], by the regulations of the Prince of P'u's House, he was supposed to receive office. But because there were those obstructing it, it seemed that it would have to be settled at the capital. Ju-jen [i.e., his wife Shan-i] said, "My oldest sister is married in Liang-che. We have long been separated and I have wanted to see her once [again]. Why don't we go together?" When Ch'iu finally received entry rank she was delighted but also encouraged him saying, "Scholars are supposed to achieve [success] on their own and not simply wait for imperial grace." Then suddenly, he was recommended for a post in [Liang-]che. She was very happy that he had gained a position of respect and established his name. (*HTHSTCC* 150:18a–b)

This passage is frustrating in its omissions—did they ever visit her sister?—but still instructive. The use of privilege we see, not as an automatic matter, but as a bureaucratic affair subject to delays and influence. The reference to the prince of P'u—the father of Emperor Ying-tsung (r. 1064–67)—is also interesting because all four of these clanswomen whose recruitment privilege was used or discussed were from that branch. Is this a coincidence or were they particularly favored? (Certainly they were all of humbler birth than the county princesses alluded to by Chu Yü earlier.) Because I know of no regulations according them special treatment, it must be left an open question. Perhaps most interesting is Shan-i herself. Although willing to use family connections to help her husband gain office, she appears to share the general disdain for relying exclusively on privilege. In fact, at the time of her premature death at twenty-eight *sui*, her husband was away sitting for the examinations, seeking the prestige and career advantages that accompanied the *chin-shih* degree.

THE ISSUE OF INEQUALITY

Imperial clanswomen entered marriage with considerable resources of their own. Apart from their official dowries and such gifts that their families and friends (or the emperor) might have bestowed on them personally, the most noteworthy were noble titles. These ranged in rank order from the exalted commandery princess (*chün-chu*) and county princess (*hsien-chu*) mentioned above, through lady of virtue (*shu-jen*), lady of eminence (*shih-jen*), lady of excellence (*ling-jen*), respectful lady (*kung-jen*), lady of suitability (*i-jen*), lady of peace (*an-jen*) to the humblest title, child nurturess (*ju-jen*).[20] In our group of fourteen (not counting the princesses), one was named consort of state (*kuo-fu-jen*, no. 7), one was a commandery lady (no. 3), two were ladies of suitability (nos. 9 and 14), two ladies of peace (nos. 12 and 15), and four were child nurturesses (nos. 13 and 16–18). In four cases no titles were mentioned (nos. 6, 8, and 10–11).

Commandery and county princesses received biannual clothing allowances plus monthly cash and grain stipends. From Hung Mai's example of a county lady receiving a stipend of almost one hundred strings of cash, it is clear that allowances could be substantial (*JCSP* 3.14:4a–b). Although no stipends are mentioned for the lesser-ranked ladies, all titled clanswomen were granted recruitment privileges for their sons, which apparently were different from the earlier-mentioned privileges for their husbands: all could have one son or grandson named to receive official rank upon their deaths, and commandery and county princesses could also name offspring after they had attended two suburban sacrifices—the former could name four, the latter one (*CYTC* 2.14:531).

Titles as such were not unique to clanswomen; wives of clansmen and important officials were also titled. But few other wives from nonclan families could begin to match the influence that was the clanswomen's by virtue of their imperial connections, influence that some put to use. The emperor Kao-tsung (r. 1126–62) rebuked one princess for repeatedly asking him to promote her husband and on another occasion gently chastised an elderly princess for favoring her own son over her stepsons, although this did not stop him from meeting either of their demands (*SS* 248:8782, 8775).

In addition, the rights and privileges of early Sung princesses were at odds with some of the basic patriarchal principles of Chinese society. They lived, not with their in-laws, but in the mansions provided upon marriage. In the late 1060s the Wei-kuo great senior princess (no. 42) brought her mother-in-law, who had been living alone since her son's marriage, to live in a guest-house and plied her with delicacies (*SS* 248:8779). Half a century earlier the Yang-kuo great senior princess (no. 43) had been ordered by her brother, Chen-tsung (r. 997–1022), to use female ritual forms (*fu-li*) when visiting her father-in-law's mansion (*SS* 248:8773). That she was commanded to do what other women did as a matter of course is explained in the biography of the Ching-kuo great senior princess (no. 30):

> In the old system, the imperial son-in-law reduced his father to the genealogical level of sibling. At the time [the princess's husband, Li] Tsun-hsu's father,

Chi-ch'ang, was deathly ill, and on Chi-ch'ang's birthday the princess visited
him using a daughter-in-law's rituals (*chiu-li*). The emperor [Chen-tsung] on
hearing of this, secretly sent various clothes, a precious belt and utensils to
help him live long. (*SS* 248:8774)

The Sung had inherited a system that claimed imperial prerogatives overrode considerations of generation and gender. But this did not sit well with
the dynasty's Confucian principles, so the emperors themselves led the
change. Indeed, as early as 1064 the imperial clan's etiquette regulations
stated that "imperial clanswomen shall all serve their parents-in-law and
their husband's relatives as if they were from the families of subjects" (*SS*
115:2739).

Such a rule only highlighted, however, the dilemma of reconciling the
clanswomen's status as offspring of the Son of Heaven with their roles as
wives and daughters-in-law. In the eyes of their (male) critics and biographers, there were two related problems. One was a belief that the clanswomen, by virtue of their luxurious and sheltered upbringing, tended to be
arrogant and spoiled. Although there was undoubtedly some truth to this
perception, it should be noted that scholar-officials of the eleventh century
had little sympathy for aristocratic life-styles. But even when the clanswoman was a model wife, the power and privilege of her imperial connection
could be problematical for her husband's family. The tension between the
competing inequalities of gender subordination and political hierarchy was
hardly unique to imperial clanswomen, but it was acute for them and thus
central to our understanding of their marriage relationships. In the remaining pages of this chapter I examine several specific cases stemming from
these problems and consider the responses to them.

Both arrogance and imperial influence were evident in the case of the
Yen-kuo princess. A favorite daughter of the emperor Jen-tsung, she had
received a lavish dowry in 1057, described above, when she married Li Wei,
the nephew of Jen-tsung's late mother the Chang-i empress (and therefore
her cousin). She was given the unprecedented Yen-kuo title in 1061 despite
protests that the designation was not mentioned in the ritual writings
(*SMCTI* 33:2b–4a). Despite this special attention—or possibly because of
it—an air of notoriety surrounded her. In 1060 she was criticized for using
her influence to obtain a promotion for her wet nurse's (*ju-mu*) nephew (*SHY:
TH* 8:11b). The following year a controversy erupted between the princess
and her husband's family that greatly upset the aged emperor and ended the
marriage.

The trouble began when the princess was drinking one day with a eunuch,
Liang Huai-chi, who served as her house manager, and saw her mother-in-
law, Lady Yang, watching her. Infuriated, she beat Lady Yang, who then
reported the matter to the emperor. Jen-tsung found his daughter and Liang

to blame and apparently ordered him and another eunuch removed from her household.[21] But when the princess then became hysterical and suicidal and tried to set her palace on fire, the emperor relented, although over the protests of Ssu-ma Kuang and other officials. The princess's palace supporters, after spying on Li Wei and trying unsuccessfully to gather incriminating evidence on him, nevertheless approached the emperor with unspecified accusations against Li. Jen-tsung's first response to this was silence, but after appeals by the empress and an attendant to the memory of his mother, he finally acted (this was in the first month of 1162) by confining the princess to the palace, sending Li Wei out as prefect of Wei-chou (in Ho-pei-hsi), sending Lady Yang to live with another son, exiling Liang Huai-chi, and dismissing various eunuchs who had been involved (*HCP* 196:4b–5b). This did not end matters, however. Once in Wei-chou, Li was apparently framed on charges of embezzling grain from the public granaries and exiled, while Liang Huai-chi's exile was canceled (*SMCTI* 33:6b–7b). In response to Li Wei's disgrace, his brother submitted a petition for him requesting a divorce, stating that "Wei is ignorant and stupid, inadequate to receive Heavenly grace, and so asks to be given a divorce." Before the emperor concurred, however, Ssu-ma Kuang delivered a passionate defense of Li. Reminding the emperor that the original intention behind the marriage had been to honor them, Ssu-ma stated: "Now Wei has been separated from his mother, their family has become outcast in its affairs, great and small are grieving [for them], and it may even [reach the point that they will be] unable to make a living " (*HCP* 196:6a; *SMCTI* 33:8a). Appealing once again to the memory of the Chang-i empress, whose death anniversary had just past, Ssu-ma asked for Li's return and greater acknowledgment of the princess's guilt. His appeal succeeded. The emperor demoted the princess to the lesser title of I-kuo princess (the only such demotion to occur in the Sung), citing her ill manners, troublesomeness, and disobedience (*STCLC* 40:215). He also granted the divorce but gave Li Wei two hundred *liang* of gold as a sign of his esteem (*HCP* 196:6a–b), saying, "Men of wealth and nobility need not all be imperial sons-in-law" (*HCP* 196:6a–b). He might have added that those who were need take great care.

Thirty-two years later another princess's marriage relations became a point of controversy, though in a different way. The Ts'ao-kuo princess,[22] one of the emperor Shen-tsung's three surviving daughters, was married in 1090 to Han Chia-yen, the son of the late chief councillor Han Ch'i (1008–75) and brother of Han Chung-yen (1038–1109), who headed the Bureau of Military Affairs from 1092 to 1096. The marriage, which was imperially ordered to honor the memory of Han Ch'i (*SS* 248:8780), was not a great success. Han was reportedly "lacking in decorum and disrespectful" toward his wife and would spend the night away from their residence without warning. As a punishment, he was censured and exiled to Ch'i-chou in Huai-nan-hsi (*HCPSP* 9:6b).

Then in a remarkable memorial, the outspoken P'eng Ju-li came to the defense of Han Chia-yen (*SMCTI* 33:8b–10b). P'eng begins with the familiar argument that the governance of the state, the family, and the husband-wife relationship are interrelated, stating: "If the distinctions between husband and wife are not proper, then when [the ruler] desires that his family affairs be ordered, the family's governance will fail, and as for desiring that the state be ordered, such a thing has never happened" (ibid., 9a). The ideal relationship, he suggests, is epitomized by the king's daughter in the *Book of Odes*, of whose wedding carriage it was said: "Are they not expressive of reverence and harmony,—The carriages of the king's daughters?" (Legge 1960:35). This may seem obscure, but P'eng explains that, "While the magnificence of the king's daughter's carriage and clothes are fitting for one who is noble and proud, she still upholds the way of the wife, and that is what makes her beautiful. Serving [her husband] she is subordinate, though originally she was above him" (*SMCTI* 33:9a). P'eng then turns to the case at hand, observing: "Now, because Chia-yen has been unable to subordinate the imperial princess, he has been discarded. This is a case of the wife gaining victory over her husband. If wives are able to gain victory over their husbands, then sons will defeat their fathers and subjects will defeat their ruler. If this source is once loosed, the stream will grow until it cannot be stopped" (ibid., 9a–b). Again, slightly later, he cautions: "Now if you cause wives to deceive their husbands, then in human relations [people will] revolt against their superiors, and customs will decay among those below" (ibid., 10a). Arguing that "small disputes" of a day and night should not be allowed to harm the "great love of a lifetime," P'eng ends by urging the emperor not to oppose his married relatives, so that his great ministers would then not dare to oppose him; thus might the stability of the state be ensured (ibid., 10a–b).

P'eng clearly thought that Han's shortcomings did not merit his punishment and thus shifted the blame to the princess, presumably for going to her brother the emperor rather than submitting quietly as a good wife should. We do not know whether his memorial, with its veiled threat to the young Che-tsung (r. 1086–1100) (a telling indication of the power and assurance of great families like the Hans) had any effect. What is interesting is his categorical insistence on the authority of the husband and the subordination of the wife, however exalted her family. This subordination, inconceivable for a princess in the early Sung, was largely unquestioned in our cases here of Southern Sung clanswomen. But before turning to them, let us digress briefly to consider one clanswoman whose assertiveness appears not to have interfered with her marriage.

From the time her mother was pregnant and her grandmother dreamed that a beautiful and brilliantly dressed young girl had descended from space (*HCCSC* 41:2b), Chao Tzu-chen (1097–1140), as seen in Sun Ti's lengthy inscription for her, had a dreamlike, larger than life character. Although she was apparently raised outside of K'ai-feng as a seventh-generation descendent of T'ai-tsung, not an imperial mourning kin, her family seems to have commanded considerable respect. At her birth she was given presents by five families, and she married Yang Ts'un-chung (1102–66) from a prominent Tai-chou family of generals. At the time of the Jurchen invasion, with her husband away in the wars, Tzu-chen was instrumental in aiding local defense forces in Liang-che (after the family moved south, which is not mentioned), providing shelter for loyal soldiers, feeding the hungry, as well as directing the education of her children inasmuch as she was well educated in poetry and writing (ibid., 2a–3b). When the court was established in Lin-an, she became friendly with the imperial children, was given twice-monthly visiting privileges at the imperial palaces and five "national lady" titles. During the illness that led to her premature death, the emperor ordered her treated by imperial doctors (*kuo-i*) (ibid., 1b).

Most interesting, however, were Tzu-chen's private activities. Through her stress on her children's education, Tzu-chen is credited with the civilianizing of the family, for her two sons both received *chin-shih* degrees and had successful civil careers (ibid., 4b, 5b). She was a devout Taoist "whose only delight lay in the study of the Yellow Emperor and Lao-tzu" (ibid., 4a). With a monthly stipend from her titles, which at one point accumulated to ninety thousand cash, she was also a noted philanthropist, providing relief to the hungry during a famine, supporting more than one hundred poor families on land she owned, and, most remarkably, providing the dowries of eighty-three orphaned young women (ibid., 4a–b).

With her many activities and accomplishments, Chao Tzu-chen was hardly typical of even privileged clanswomen or wives of high officials. Assisted by her clan status, she was able to use the opportunities created by the war and resettlement of the court and, through her ability and the force of her character, to make a mark for herself in Lin-an society of the 1130s. Still, one might ask how it was that she avoided the kinds of marital problems that we have seen above. That her husband was away at war (in all he fought in more than one hundred engagements and eventually rose to command the capital army) and was thus seldom at home undoubtedly helped (Ch'ang et al. 4:3163–64). But even more important is that her successes did not interfere with her acting as a model wife and mother, at least in the eyes of her biographer. Tzu-chen is praised for her humble life—eating simple food and doing laundry—in the years before the war when her husband, though talented, was ill-humored and without official rank (*HCCSC* 41:2b). As we noted earlier, she is credited with directing her sons' education and commended for running a serious and proper household establishment (3a). Together with service to one's in-laws (which is not mentioned, perhaps because her father-in-law and his father both died early in the Jurchen war), these were the essential tasks of the Sung literati wife. As we shall now see, it was mainly for these activities that Southern Sung clanswomen were praised.

If Chao Tzu-chen could be said to represent the imperial clanswomen at their social and political apex, Lady Chao (no. 6; 1121–58) in an equally remarkable way might be said to represent them at their humblest. A sixth-generation descendent of T'ai-tsung and thus not a mourning kin, she became at the age of eighteen *sui* the second wife (*chi-shih*) of Hung Shou-ch'ing, an official from a large and prominent Jao-chou family.

In any event, once with the Hungs, Lady Chao's good breeding, obedi-ence, and equable behavior made her very popular in the large household, which had some thirty brothers and cousins in her husband's generation, and in time she became renowned in the community at large. Her biographer, Hung Kua (himself a cousin of Shou-ch'ing's), relates that for some thirteen years (until she was thirty) the Hungs feared she would be taken back by her family to be married to someone else. Then, when she was thirty-three, her father, who had just become magistrate of Lin-ch'uan county in Fu-chou, sent his younger brother with a beautiful carriage to fetch her from the Hungs, with the apparent intention of making a better match for her else-where. But Lady Chao angrily refused to go, saying, "With my mother-in-law elderly and two sons young and foolish, I dare not trouble my seniors. My parents with various schemes cannot suddenly take me away" (PCWC 75: 6b). Asking his leave, she went back into the house and thereafter devoted herself to Hung family affairs, passing on to others gifts sent by her clan relatives, keeping peace in the women's quarters, and, in particular, nursing her mother-in-law. After she collapsed while dining with her mother-in-law and died at the age of just thirty-eight, she was mourned by one and all. The next year, however, she was posthumously titled and buried in imperial clan tombs (ibid., 7b).

The Hungs' just fears of losing Lady Chao, whose marriage was perfectly valid and legal, points to the high-handedness of clan families and makes Lady Chao's passionate commitment to the Hungs, particularly to her mother-in-law, all the more striking. Indeed, in Hung Kua's eyes she assumes heroic proportions. Having praised her for sticking to her principles when her family tried to reclaim her (ibid., 6b), Hung closes the inscription by comparing her with Po Chi from the state of Sung in the Spring and Autumn period, who, as Sung was being conquered and the palace destroyed, refused to leave the palace without her governess (*fu-mu*) and thus perished in the flames (ibid., 7b).[23] Just as Po Chi was able to act morally despite living in a dissolute age, so Hung marvels that this imperial clanswoman was able to maintain her integrity at a time when arrogance and licentiousness were common in renowned and exalted families.

This theme of virtue in spite of high birth runs like a refrain through many of the inscriptions:

> Although born noble and proud, she was frugal not wasteful, respectful not reckless, living in a poor and simple manner. (no. 6; *MLCM* 6: 47a)

> She was totally unlike the children of noble families. (no. 11; *CLC* 29: 431)

> At the time of her marriage, the literati all said, "The wife is of a noble type; they will not necessarily be happy together." However, she was reverent in her wifely rituals; her in-laws praised her filiality; [in acting by] the code of feminine conduct she was serious; towards her [husband's] kinsmen she was respectful. (no. 16; *HTHSTCC* 158:13b)

> She served her in-laws from dawn to dusk. . . . People did not know [from her actions] that she had the nobility of a Heavenly clan. (no. 10; *CCC* 129:10b)

> She was by nature noble and pure, without the bad habits of clanswomen. (no. 14; *MCC* 18:256)

We must take care to avoid assuming that all or even most clanswomen were like those described above. We are after all dealing with the inscriptions of the few clanswomen who for one reason or other had impressed their contemporaries. Besides, phrases such as "the bad habits of clanswomen" could have arisen either from problems families had had with clanswomen as marriage partners or from anticlan bias among the elite. Whichever the case, this evidence is revealing of contemporary attitudes about how married clanswomen should behave. They should not be spoiled, they should cheerfully fulfill their roles as wives and daughters-in-law, and they should devote themselves frugally and ascetically to promoting the fortunes of their new families, even when their husbands were leading cultured and leisured lives as private scholars (see, for example, *CCC* 129:10b–12a). To cite one last example, Chao Ju-i's (no. 13) husband, Wang Meng-lung, described their life while he was a struggling examination candidate (he received his *chin-shih* in 1208) in these terms:

> I went through the successes and failures of the examinations no less than ten times, and each time was away from her for a year. [I would return] to find my sons named, my daughters nurtured and suddenly grown up, and I did not yet even know them. But this is just the norm for the wives of literati. Lady Chao forgot that she was a noble imperial clanswoman and delighted in being the wife of a poor literatus. (*SHWC* 25:11a)

Chao Ju-i's life was a far cry from that of the great ladies of the Northern Sung or of Chao Tzu-chen. It probably reflects the humble circumstances of her own family as much as her husband's, but that is just the point. In the Southern Sung most clan families had declined to modest, though still elite, status and had privileges, but generally not the influence, that followed from close ties to the emperor and court. For clanswomen to prosper in these changed circumstances, they would have to adopt the attitudes and life-styles of the literati culture, which was coming into its own during the Sung. Although many, perhaps most, of the clanswomen and men may have persisted in their anachronistically aristocratic ways—thus their bad reputation—these women and their biographers pointed the way to the future and in so doing provided a resolution for the tension between the inequalities of rank and gender mentioned above. That the resolution unequivocally affirmed the subordination of women was perhaps only to be expected in a culture in which male achievement was at once essential, yet also in doubt, for their families' fortunes.

CONCLUSION

In her essay for this volume, Jennifer Holmgren has characterized the Sung as having achieved "a stable and equitable balance of power between the major parties," a balance that contrasts with both the imposing power of the emperor's affinal kin from the Han through T'ang and their powerlessness in the Ming. This finding accords well with the imperial clanswomen considered in these pages. We see on the one hand great dynastic concern for clan marriage relations and a willingness to support the status and honor of the clanswomen through dowries and official titles, even when their relationship to the throne was no longer a mourning one. On the other hand, we see an insistence that they conform to the Confucian norms of filial obedience to their husbands and in-laws, despite their high status.

The most remarkable feature of the Sung clanswomen, however, is to be found, not in balance, but in change. The imperial princesses of the eleventh century were a world apart from the literati-wife clanswomen of the thirteenth. The reasons for this change were numerous. The maturation and social leveling of the imperial clan over time meant that clan members were increasingly likely to be related to the emperor only distantly. This trend was accentuated by the relative infertility of the Southern Sung emperors, which reduced the numbers of close kin. The fall of the Northern Sung gave those clansmen who managed to survive the turmoils of the Jurchen invasion and escape to the south an unprecedented access to government posts. Their families thus had an entrée into local elite society that would otherwise have been unthinkable. Moreover, the shift in the imperial marriage pool from the military elite to the scholar-official bureaucratic elite further decreased the social distance between the imperial clan and local, predominantly literati, elite society.

This essay has not addressed the issue of the declining status of women during the Sung (see, for example, Yao 1983:75–104) and whether it was responsible for the subservience that characterized the exemplary clanswomen treated here. One reason for this omission is that there is considerable debate over just how much of a decline actually occurred during the Sung. A great deal of evidence suggests they were much better off than they were to be in the Ming and Ch'ing dynasties in their legal status, marriage practices, and the popularity of widow remarriage and foot binding (see Ebrey 1981, 1984b, and her essay in this volume). The most compelling argument for the decline thesis is that, with the fall of the aristocratic social order of the Six Dynasties–T'ang period and the rise of an examination-centered elite society during the Sung, in which male achievement was considered as essential to the maintenance of the patrilineal kinship group, the woman's roles of servant, nurturer, and loyal supporter of the patriline, even in widowhood, received renewed emphasis, especially by the neo-Confucian thinkers.

The general decline in status for women is not necessarily connected to the roles of the married imperial clanswomen. Ellen Soullière has shown for the Ming, when the subordination of women was certainly more marked than in the Sung, that the husbands of imperial princesses were deliberately drawn from inconsequential families and that they were expected to be ritually and behaviorally subordinate to the wives. Gender, however important, clearly took second place to the dynasty's determination to minimize the potential power of the affinal kin.

Because elite families commonly provided husbands for both princesses and clanswomen, the question of hypogamy vs. gender was a live issue during the Sung, particularly for the clanswomen for whom the hypogamy was not so marked. That their circumstances were necessarily more humble than those of their Northern Sung predecessors was a result of changes in the imperial clan; that their new ideal was that of the uncomplaining, self-sacrificing literati wife can be seen to reflect changes in the gender roles of elite society at large.

APPENDIX: PRINCESSES AND CLANSWOMEN CITED

1. An-k'ang commandery lady 安康郡主 (1168–1205), married Lo Liang-ch'en 羅良臣. (*SS* 248:8789)
2. An-te imperial lady 安德帝姬, daughter of Hui-tsung, married Sung Pang-kuang 宋邦光. (*SS* 248:8783)
3. Lady Chao (1009–68), commandery lady, married Hsiang Ch'uan-fan 向傳範 (1010–74) of K'ai-feng. (*YCC* 21:16a–18a)
4. Lady Chao (fl. 1060), titled Yen-kuo great senior princess 兗國大長公主 and later Ch'en-kuo great senior princess 陳國大長公主, daughter of Jen-tsung, married Li Wei 李瑋 of K'ai-feng. (*SMCTI* 33:2b–8a; *SS* 248:8776–77)
5. Lady Chao (fl. 1094), titled T'ang-kuo senior imperial princess 唐國大長公主, married Han Chia-yen 韓嘉彥 of An-yang hsien

安陽縣，Hsiang-chou 相州 (Ho-pei-hsi). (*SMCTI* 33:8b–10b; *SS* 248:8780)

6. Lady Chao (1091–1116) of Ju-chou 汝州 (Ching-hsi-pei), married Hao Chen 郝珵 of Lo-yang 洛陽. (Wu Su, "Tsu-ch'i Chao-shih mu-chih," in *MLCM* 6:47a)

7. Chao Tzu-chen 趙紫真 (1097–1140), titled Yang-kuo fu-jen 楊國夫人, married Yang Ts'un-chung 楊存中 (1102–22) of T'ai-chou 代州 (Ho-tung-lu). (*HCCSC* 41:1a–6b).

8. Lady Chao (1121–58), second wife of Hung Shou-ch'ing 洪壽卿 of Jao-chou 饒州 (Chiang-nan-hsi). (*PCWC* 75:5b–6b)

9. Lady Chao (d. 1170), titled proper lady, married Kuan Chien 管鑑 of Fu-chou 撫州 (Chiang-nan-hsi). (*ECHC* 4:5b–6b)

10. Lady Chao (1153–90), married Wang Fu 王孚 of Chi-chou 吉州 (Chiang-nan-hsi). (*CCC* 129:10b–12a)

11. Lady Chao (twelfth century), married Hsu Shih 徐碩 of Wu-chou 婺州 (Liang-che-tung). (*CLC* 29:431)

12. Lady Chao (1158–1213), titled peaceful lady, married Yuan Jen 袁任 of Ming-chou 明州 (Liang-che-tung). (*HCC* 21:17a)

13. Chao Ju-i 趙汝議 (1183–1221) of Ch'ih-chou 池州 (Chiang-nan-tung), titled child nurturess, married Wang Meng-lung 王夢龍 (1208 *chin-shih*) of T'ai-chou 台州 (Liang-che-tung). (*SHWC* 25:11a–12a)

14. Chao Hsi-i 趙希怡 (1177–1235) of T'ai-chou 台州 (Liang-che-tung), titled proper lady, married Yuan Fu 袁甫 of Ming-chou 明州 (Liang-che-tung). (*MCC* 18:256–57)

15. Chao Ju-chieh 趙汝偕 (1199–1249) of Ch'üan-chou 泉州 (Fu-chien), titled peaceful lady, married Ch'en Tseng 陳增 (1200–1266) of Hsing-hua chün 興化軍 (Fu-chien). (*HTHSTCC* 154:4b–5b)

16. Chao Pi-shan 趙必善 (1188–1260) of Ch'üan-chou 泉州 (Fu-chien), titled child nurturess, married Fang Ta-yü 方大與 (1181–1234) of Hsing-hua chün 興化軍 (Fu-chien). (*HTHSTCC* 158:13b–15a)

17. Chao Shan-i 趙善意 (1216–43) of Ch'üan-chou 泉州 (Fu-chien), titled child nurturess, married Ch'iu Shuang 邱雙 of Ch'üan-chou. (*HTHSTCC* 150:17b–19a)

18. Chao Ch'ung-yü 趙崇玉 (1206–58), titled child nurturess, married Lo Chin 羅晉 (1196–1266) of Hung-chou 洪州 (Chiang-nan-hsi). (*HTHSTCC* 158:9a–10b)

19. Ch'en-kuo princess 陳國公主 (d. 1117), Che-tsung's daughter, married Shih Tuan-li. (*SS* 248:8781)

20. Ch'en-kuo great senior princess 陳國大長公主 (d. 999), T'ai-tsu's daughter, married Wei Hsien-hsin 魏咸信 (946–1014) of Wei-chou 衛州 (Ho-pei-hsi). (*SS* 248:8772–73)

21. Ch'eng-te imperial lady 成德帝姬, Hui-tsung's daughter, married Hsiang Tzu-fang 向子房. (*SS* 248:8785)

22. Chia-te imperial lady 嘉德帝姬, Hui-tsung's daughter, married Tseng Yin 曾夤. (*SS* 248:8783)

23. Ch'in Lu-kuo Hsien-mu Ming-i great senior princess 秦魯國賢穆明懿大長公主 (1048–1133), Jen-tsung's daughter, married Ch'ien Ching-chen 錢景臻 of Hang-chou 杭州 (Liang-che-hsi). (*SS* 248:8777)

24. Ch'in-kuo K'ang-i senior princess 秦國康懿長公主 (d. 1164), Che-tsung's daughter, married P'an Cheng-fu 潘正夫 of Ho-nan. (*SS* 248:8782)

25. Ch'in-kuo great senior princess 秦國大長公主 (d. 973), T'ai-tsu's younger sister, married first Mi Fu-te 米福德, then Kao Huai-te 高懷德 (926–82) of Chen-ting fu 真定府 (Ho-pei-hsi). (*SS* 248:8771–72)

26. Ching-kuo great senior princess 荊國大長公主 (d. 1051), T'ai-tsung's daughter, married Li Tsun-hsü 李遵勗 (988–1038) of Lu-chou 潞州 (Ho-tung). (*SS* 248:8774–75)

27. Chou-han princess 周漢公主 (1240–61), Li-tsung's daughter, married Yang Chen 楊鎮 of Yen-ling 嚴陵. (*SS* 248:8789–90)

28. Ch'ung-te 崇德帝姬 imperial lady (d. 1120), Hui-tsung's daughter, married Ts'ao Shih 曹湜 of Chen-ting fu 真定府 (Ho-pei-hsi). (*SS* 248:8784)

29. Han Wei-kuo great senior princess 韓魏國大長公主, Ying-tsung's daughter, married Chang Tun-li 張敦禮 of K'ai-feng. (*SS* 248:8780)

30. Hsien-te 顯德帝姬 imperial lady, Hui-tsung's daughter, married Liu Wen-yen 劉文彥. (*SS* 248:8785)

31. Hsu-kuo senior princess 徐國長公主 (d. 1122), Shen-tsung's daughter, married P'an I 潘意 of Ta-ming fu 大名府 (Ho-pei-tung). (*SS* 248:8781)

32. Hsu-kuo great senior princess 徐國大長公主 (d. 990), T'ai-tsung's daughter, married Wu Yuan-i 吳元扆 (962–1011) of T'ai-yuan fu 太原府 (Ho-tung). (*SS* 248:8773)

33. Hsün-te imperial lady 洵德帝姬, Hui-tsung's daughter, married T'ien P'i 田丕. (*SS* 248:8785)

34. Ju-fu imperial lady 柔福帝姬 (d. 1141), Hui-tsung's daughter, married Hsu Huan 徐還. (*SS* 248:8785)

35. Jung-te imperial lady 榮德帝姬, Hui-tsung's daughter, married Ts'ao Sheng 曹晟. (*SS* 248:8783)

36. Lu-kuo great senior princess 魯國大長公主 (d. 1009), T'ai-tsu's daughter, married Shih Pao-chi 石保吉 (954–1010) of K'ai-feng. (*SS* 248:8772)

37. Mao-te imperial lady 茂德帝姬, Hui-tsung's daughter, married Ts'ai T'iao 蔡絛 of Hsing-hua chün 興化軍 (Fu-chien). (*SS* 248:8783)

38. Shun-te imperial lady 順德帝姬, Hui-tsung's daughter, married Hsiang Tzu-i 向子扆. (*SS* 248:8785)

39. T'an-kuo Hsien-hsiao senior princess 潭國賢孝長公主 (d. 1108), Shen-tsung's daughter, married Wang Yü 王遇. (*SS* 248:8781)

40. Wei Ch'u-kuo 魏楚國大長公主 great senior princess (d. 1085), Ying-tsung's daughter, married Wang Shih-yueh 王師約 (1044–1102) of Lo-yang 洛陽 (Ho-nan). (*SS* 8779)

41. Wei-kuo great senior princess 魏國大長公主 (d. 1008), T'ai-tsu's daughter, married Wang Ch'eng-yen 王承衍 of Liao-hsi 遼西, then Lo-yang 洛陽. (*SS* 248:8772)

42. Wei-kuo great senior princess 魏國大長公主 (d. 1080), Ying-tsung's daughter, married Wang Shen 王詵 of T'ai-yuan fu 太原府 (Ho-tung). (*SS* 248:8779–80)

43. Yang-kuo 楊國大長公主 great senior princess (d. 1033), T'ai-tsung's daughter, married Ch'ai Tsung-ch'ing 柴宗慶 of Ta-ming fu 大名府 (Ho-pei-tung). (*SS* 248:8773–74)

44. Yen Shu-kuo great senior princess 燕舒國大長公主 (d. 1112), Jen-tsung's daughter, married Kuo Hsien-ch'ing 郭獻卿. (*SS* 248:8778)

45. Yen-kuo great senior princess 兗國大長公主 (d. 1083), Jen-tsung's daughter, married Ts'ao Shih 曹詩 of Chen-ting fu 真定府 (Ho-pei-hsi). (*SS* 248:8778)

46. Yung-kuo great senior princess 雍國大長公主, T'ai-tsung's daughter, married Wang I-yung 王貽永 of T'ai-yuan fu 太原府 (Ho-tung). (*SS* 248:8774)

NOTES

1. These are *Ti-hsi* 4–7 (the clan annals) and 8 (imperial princesses and clans-women); *Chih-kuan* 20 (clan institutions); and *Ch'ung-ju* 1 (clan schools).

2. To locate inscriptions, I used Aoyama Sadao's (1968) index, eliminating those Chao women who either were not from the clan or who died without marrying. With a few exceptions, most of the rest of the information for princesses came from *SS* 248.

3. For similar definitions by anthropologists of China, see Freedman 1966 and, more recently, Ebrey and Watson 1986.

4. Two other brothers died without offspring.

5. The two major institutions were the Office of Imperial Clan Affairs (*Tsung-cheng-ssu*), established c. 1015 with responsibility for the clan sacrifices and the maintenance of genealogical records, and the Great Office of Imperial Clan Affairs (*Ta-tsung-cheng-ssu*), with responsibility for the education and governance of clansmen and women (see *SS* 117:3887–90; *SHY:CK* 20:1a–b, 17a–b). Individual clan palaces (*kung*) also had their own officials and administration.

6. One of the recurring topics running through the records of clan-related legislation was support for orphaned, widowed, and otherwise impoverished clansmen and women.

7. Three of the eighty-four imperial princesses mentioned in the *SS* biographical chapter on princesses were nuns (*SS* 248:8771–91). See also *SHY:TH* 4:29b for an amnesty decree allowing a clanswoman nun to return to her former lay status.

8. Later "the sons and grandsons of criminals" (*hsing-t'u-jen*) was also added (*SS* 115: 2739).

9. These provisions, dated 1077 (for the *SS*) and 1078 (for the *SHY*), also specified that all wedding gifts had to be returned. Thereafter, although remarriage was permitted, no gifts were to be involved and, in the case of clanswomen, the husband could receive no recruitment privileges. Finally, clanswomen were barred from marrying divorced men, unless they themselves had already been divorced.

10. In the Southern Sung on the few occasions when princesses (or those whom the emperor chose to treat as princesses) were married, the dowries were worth a mere 200,000 strings, according to Li Hsin-ch'uan (*CYTC* 1.1:22).

11. Another provision from about the same time (1070) provided clanswomen within the fifth degree a one-time allowance of three strings (*SHY:TH* 4:20a).

12. Given that the *SMCTI* was compiled by Chao Ju-yü (1140–96), who, as the first clansman to place first in the examinations and the first of two clansmen to serve as chief councillor, was the most famous clansman of his day, one is tempted to see contemporary significance in his choice of these last three memorials, which he used to close out his chapter on imperial clanswomen.

13. Jennifer Holmgren and Susan Mann both argue in their essays in this volume that the marriages of women were considered more important socially than those of men, so this may be viewed as another case in point. What is striking here, however, is that the importance of their marriages is phrased in terms of the honor of the imperial clan.

14. I am indebted to Bettine Birge, who generously made available her cards on all of the Chao wives cited in Aoyama.

15. See *OYWCKWC* 20:3b–9a, 37:10b–17a, for the biographies of the two, respectively Lady Ch'en of Lang-chou and Lady Ch'ien of Hang-chou.

16. Five each were from Ho-nan and Ho-tung, four from Ho-pei-hsi, two each from Ho-pei-tung and Liang-che, and one from Fu-chien. K'ai-feng accounted for three.

17. Information on the husbands is from Ch'ang et al. 1974–76 passim.

18. In Chao Ju-i's case, however, there is a suggestion that her match resulted from the enviable reputation developed by clanswomen of her branch. Her biographer, Yeh Shih (1150–1223), himself a native of Wu-chou and thus not a local man, wrote: "I have observed that in the present generation, only the clanswomen of the Western Bridge have the behavior of worthies and can pick from among the many literati" (*SHWC* 25:11b).

19. Yuan Fu, the husband of Chao Hsi-i (no. 14), was the son of Yuan Hsieh (1144–1224), who was a vice-minister of the Board of Rites (rank 3B), and Ch'en Tseng, the husband of Chao Ju-chieh (no. 15), was the grandson of Ch'en Chun-ch'ing (1113–86), who had served as administrator of the Bureau of Military Affairs (and whose protection privileges Tseng used to gain his initial entry to officialdom). Of the others, I have found references to ancestors who were officials of the husbands of nos. 6, 9, 16, and 18, but not for nos. 10–13 and 17, though in each of those cases there were brothers who had first become officials or very prominent family friends, which would indicate that they were indeed from established elite families.

20. I am following *CYTC* 2.14:531, except that it does not mention the "young lady" title. For that I am following the biography of Lady Chao (no. 10), where Yuan

Hsieh states that she was first ennobled (*feng*) as young lady, then later as peaceful lady (21:17b).

21. Although this is not mentioned in the *HCP* account, it is implied in a memorial dated the eleventh month of 1061 in which Ssu-ma Kuang protests the emperor's allowing the eunuchs to return (*SMCTI* 33:4a–b).

22. Her posthumous title and name were the T'ang-kuo princess Hsien-mu. Ts'ao-kuo was the title given to her at marriage (*SHY:TH* 8:30a–b).

23. This occurred in the thirtieth year of Duke Hsiang. See Hung 1937:329–30.

GLOSSARY

an-jen 安人
Chang-i huang-hou (Chang-i empress) 章懿皇后
Chao 趙
Chao Chiung 趙炅
Chao K'uang-yin 趙匡胤
Chao Shen 趙昚
Chao shih (Lady Chao) 趙氏
Chao T'ing-mei 趙廷美
Che-tsung 哲宗
Ch'en Chün-ch'ing 陳俊卿
Ch'en shih (Lady Ch'en) 陳氏
Ch'eng I 程頤
Ch'eng-chieh-lang 承節郎
Ch'eng-hsin-lang 承信郎
chi-shih 繼室
Ch'i-chou 蘄州
chia-ti 甲第
chiang 降
Chiang-nan 江南
Chiang-nan-tung 江南東
Chiang-shih-lang 將仕郎
chien 間
Ch'ien shih (Lady Ch'ien) 錢氏
chin-shih 進士
ch'ing 頃
chiu-li 舅禮
Chou Pi-ta 周必大
chu-wen 注文
chü-jen 舉人
chüan 卷
Ch'üan-chou 泉州
chün-chu 郡主
fang-lang 房廊
Fang Ta-ts'ung 方大琮

fei shih-tsu chih chia 非士族之家
fei t'an-mien nü i shu-hsing chih fa 非袒免女依庶姓之法
feng 封
Fu-chien 福建
Fu-chou (Fu-chien) 福州
fu-ma tu-wei 駙馬都尉
fu-mu 傅母
Han Ch'i 韓琦
Han Chung-yen 韓忠彥
Han Wei-kuo ta-chang kung-chu (Han Wei-kuo great senior princess) 韓魏國大長公主
Hang-chou 杭州
Hao Chen 郝肂
Ho-nan 河南
Ho-pei-hsi 河北西
Ho-pei-tung 河北東
Ho-tung 河東
hsi-ch'in 繫親
Hsiang Min-chung 向敏中
Hsiao-tsung 孝宗
hsien-chu 縣主
Hsien-yüan lei-p'u 仙源類譜
hsing-t'u-jen 刑徒人
Hsu Chieh-ch'ing 徐介卿
Hsu Huan 徐還
hsuan 選
Hsun-te ti-i (Hsun-te imperial lady) 洵德帝姬
Huai-nan-hsi 淮南西
Hui-tsung 徽宗
Hung-chou 洪州
i-chuang 義莊
i-jen 宜人

i-kuan shih-tsu 衣冠士族

I-kuo kung-chu (I-kuo princess) 沂國公主

Jen-tsung 仁宗

ju-jen 孺人

ju-mu 孺母

K'ai-feng 開封

Kao-tsung 高宗

kuan 官

kuan-hu 官戶

kung-chu 公主

kung-jen 恭人

kuo-fu-jen 國夫人

kuo-i 國醫

kuo-t'i 國體

Lang-chou 閬州

Lao-tzu 老子

li-chiao 禮教

Li Shou 李綬

Li-tsung 理宗

liang 兩

Liang-che-hsi 兩浙西

Liang-che-tung 兩浙東

Liang-ching Tsung-cheng-ssu 兩京宗正司

Liang Huai-chi 梁懷吉

Liao-hsi 遼西

lien-chü 奩具

Lin-an 臨安

Lin-ch'uan 臨川

ling-jen 令人

Liu Ch'iang-fu 劉强甫

Liu Shu 劉述

Lo-yang 洛陽

Lu-kuo ta-chang kung-chu (Lu-kuo great senior princess) 魯國大長公主

Lu-ling 廬陵

Nan-pan-kuan 南班官

nei-ch'en 內臣

onkeishugi 恩惠主義

pai-shen-jen 白身人

Pan I 潘意

Pao Cheng 包拯

P'eng Ju-li 彭汝礪

pan-ts'ai 辦財

Po Chi 伯姬

pu hsiang-an 不相安

P'u-t'ien 莆田

P'u-wang (prince of P'u) 濮王

san-pan feng-chih 三班奉職

Shao-hsing fu 紹興府

Shen-tsung 神宗

shih 石

shih-jen 碩人

shih-tsu 士族

shih-ta-fu 士大夫

Shih Tuan-li 石端禮

shu-jen 淑人

so-t'ing-shih 鎖廳試

Ssu-ch'uan 四川

Ssu-ma Kuang 司馬光

Su Hsun 蘇洵

sui 歲

Sun Ti 孫覿

ta-erh 大兒

Ta-tsung-cheng-ssu 大宗正司

Ta-t'ung 大桶

Ta-t'ung Chang 大桶張

T'ai-tsu 太祖

T'ai-tsung 太宗

t'an-mien 祖免

Tien-chih 殿直

T'ien-chih 天枝

T'ien-sheng 天聖

Ts'ai Ching 蔡京

Ts'ao-kuo kung-chu (Ts'ao-kuo princess) 曹國公主

Ts'ao Shih 曹詩

tsung 宗

Tsung-cheng-ssu 宗正司

tsung-shih 宗室

Tun-tsung yuan 敦宗院

tzu-chi 資給

wai-kuan 外官

Wang An-shih 王安石

Wang Shen-ch'i 王審琦

Wang Yü 王遇

wei-hsien wei-chia tsung-nü 違限未嫁宗女

Wei-wang (prince of Wei) 魏王

wu te yü fei shih-tsu chih chia wei hun-yin 無得與非士族之家為婚姻

Wu-yueh 吳越

Yang-kuo ta-chang kung-chu (Yang-kuo great senior princess) 揚國大長公主

Yang shih (Lady Yang) 楊氏

yin 蔭

Yin-hsien 鄞縣

Ying-tsung 英宗

Ying-t'ien fu 應天府

Yü-tieh-so 玉牒所

Yuan Hsieh 袁燮

yuan-sun-nü 元孫女

yung-yeh t'ien 永業田

REFERENCES

Primary Sources

CCC — *Ch'eng-chai chi* 誠齋集, by Yang Wan-li 楊萬里. Ssu-pu ts'ung-k'an edition.

CLC — *Ch'en Liang chi* 陳亮集, by Ch'en Liang 陳亮. Peking: Chung-hua shu-chü, n.d.

CWCKCC — *Chen Wen-chung kung ch'üan-chi* 真文忠公全集, by Chen Te-hsiu 真德秀. Ssu-pu ts'ung-k'an edition.

CYTC — *Chien-yen i-lai ch'ao-yeh tsa-chi* 建炎以來朝野雜記, 2 parts, by Li Hsin-ch'uan 李心傳. Ts'ung-shu chi-ch'eng edition.

ECHC — *E-chou hsiao-chi* 鄂州小集, by Lo Yuan 羅願. Ssu-k'u ch'uan-shu edition.

HCC — *Hsieh-chai chi* 絜齋集, by Yuan Hsieh 袁燮. Ts'ung-shu chi-ch'eng edition.

HCCSC — *Hung-ch'ing chü-shih chi* 鴻慶居士集, by Sun Ti 孫覿. Ssu-k'u ch'uan-shu edition.

HCP — *Hsu Tzu-chih t'ung-chien ch'ang-pien* 續資治通鑑長編, by Li T'ao 李燾. Taipei: Shih-chieh shu-chü, 1967.

HCPSP — *Hsu Tzu-chih t'ung-chien ch'ang-pien shih-pu* 續資治通鑑長編拾補, ed. Ch'in Hsiang-yeh 秦湘業. Taipei: Shih-chieh shu-chü, 1967.

HTHSTCC — *Hou-ts'un hsien-sheng ta ch'üan chi* 後村先生大全集, by Liu K'o-chuang 劉克莊. Ssu-pu ts'ung-k'an edition.

JCSP — *Jung-chai san-pi* 容齋三筆, by Hung Mai 洪邁. Pi-chi hsiao-shuo edition.

MCC — *Meng-chai chi* 蒙齋集, by Yuan Fu 袁甫. Ts'ung-shu chi-ch'eng edition.

MLCM — *Mang-lo chung-mu i-wen ssu-pien* 芒洛冢墓遺文四編, by Lo Chen-yü 羅振玉. *Shih-k'o shih-liao hsin-pien* 石刻史料新編, no. 19; published by Hsin-wen feng ch'u-pan-she.

OYWCKWC — *Ou-yang Wen-chung kung wen-chi* 歐陽文忠公文集, by Ou-yang Hsiu 歐陽修. Ssu-pu ts'ung-k'an edition.

PCKT — *P'ing-chou k'o-t'an* 萍洲可談, by Chu Yü 朱彧. Ts'ung-shu chi-ch'eng edition.

PCWC — *P'an-chou wen-chi* 盤洲文集, by Hung Kua 洪适. Ssu-pu ts'ung-k'an edition.

SHWC — *Shui-hsin wen-chi* 水心文集, by Yeh Shih 葉適. Ssu-pu ts'ung-k'an edition.

SHY:CK   *Sung hui-yao chi-kao* 宋會要輯稿, *Chih-kuan* 職官 section. Taipei: Shih-chieh shu-chü, 1964.

SHY:TH   *Sung hui-yao chi-kao, Ti-hsi* 帝系 section.

SMCTI   *Sung ming-ch'en tsou-i* 宋名臣奏議, by Chao Ju-yü 趙汝愚. Ssu-pu ts'ung-k'an edition. (This work was originally titled *Kuo-ch'ao chu-ch'en tsou-i* 國朝諸臣奏議 and was compiled in 1186.)

SS   *Sung shih* 宋史, ed. T'o T'o 脫脫 et al. Peking: Chung-hua shu-chü, 1977.

STCLC   *Sung ta-chao ling-chi* 宋大詔令集. Peking: Chung-hua shu-chü, 1962.

TAC   *T'ieh-an chi* 鐵菴集, by Fang Ta-ts'ung 方大琮. Ssu-k'u ch'üan-shu edition.

WHTK   *Wen-hsien t'ung-k'ao* 文獻通考, by Ma Tuan-lin 馬端臨. Taipei: Hsin-hsing shu-chü, 1964.

YCC   *Yun-ch'i chi* 鄖溪集, by Cheng Hsieh 鄭獬. Ssu-k'u ch'üan-shu edition.

Secondary Works

Aoyama Sadao 青山定雄. 1968. *Sōjin denki sakuin* 宋人傳記索引 (Sung biographical index). Tokyo: Toyo Bunko.

Chaffee, John W. 1985. *The Thorny Gates of Learning in Sung China: A Social History of Examinations*. Cambridge: Cambridge University Press.

Ch'ang Pi-te 昌彼得, Wang Te-i 王德毅, Ch'eng Yuan-min 程元敏, and Hou Chün-te 侯俊德. 1974–76. *Sung-jen chuan-chi tzu-liao so-yin* 宋人傳記資料索引 (Index to biographical sources for Sung figures). Taipei: Ting-wen shu-chü.

Chung, Priscilla Ching. 1981. *Palace Women in the Northern Sung, 960–1126*. Leiden: E. J. Brill.

Comaroff, J. L. 1980. "Introduction." In *The Meaning of Marriage Payments*, ed. J. L. Comaroff. London: Academic Press.

Duby, Georges. 1978. *Medieval Marriage: Two Models from Twelfth-Century France*. Baltimore: Johns Hopkins University Press.

Ebrey, Patricia. 1978. *The Aristocratic Families of Early Imperial China: A Case Study of the Po-ling Ts'ui Family*. Cambridge: Cambridge University Press.

———. 1981. "Women in the Kinship System of the Southern Song Upper Class." *Historical Reflections* 8:113–28.

———. 1984a. "Conceptions of the Family in the Sung Dynasty." *Journal of Asian Studies* 43:219–45.

———. 1984b. *Family and Property in Sung China: Yüan Ts'ai's Precepts for Social Life*. Princeton: Princeton University Press.

Hartwell, Robert M. 1982. "Demographic, Political, Social Transformations of China, 750–1550." *Harvard Journal of Asiatic Studies* 42:365–442.

Hung Yeh 洪業, ed. 1937. *Ch'un-ch'iu ching-chuan yin-te* 春秋經傳引得 (Combined concordance to the *Spring and Autumn Annals* and commentaries), vol. 1. Peking: Yenching University Library.

Hymes, Robert P. 1986. "Marriage, Descent Groups and the Localist Strategy in Sung and Yuan Fu-chou." In *Kinship Organization in Late Imperial China*, ed. Patricia Buckley Ebrey and James L. Watson. Berkeley and Los Angeles: University of California Press.

Johnson, David. 1977. *The Medieval Chinese Oligarchy*. Boulder: Westview Press.

Legge, James, trans. Reprint 1960. *The She King*. In *The Chinese Classics*, vol. 4. Hong Kong: Hong Kong University Press.

Moroto Tatsuo 諸戸立雄. "Sōdai no tai sōshitsu-saku ni tsuite" 宋代の対宗室策について (Policies toward the Sung imperial clan). *Bungaku* 22:623–40.

Soullière, Ellen F. 1988. "The Imperial Marriages of the Ming Dynasty." *Papers in Far Eastern History* 37:15–42.

Yao, Esther S. Lee. 1983. *Chinese Women: Past and Present*. Mesquite, Tx.: Ide House.

FIVE

Ch'ing Imperial Marriage and Problems of Rulership

Evelyn S. Rawski

The marriage patterns of the Ch'ing emperors who ruled China from 1644 to 1911 were fundamentally shaped by rulership strategies that influenced the stratification system in several distinctive ways. By limiting marital alliances to the elite of the Manchu, Mongol, and Chinese banner forces, the Ch'ing created a form of political endogamy that excluded ties between the ruling house and the Han Chinese bureaucrats. Imperial marriage patterns were closely tied to Ch'ing succession practices, which rejected eldest-son succession and delayed designation of the heir-apparent until the death of the emperor. This policy stimulated competition among the emperor's sons, weakened the position of the empress, who was not necessarily the most powerful of the emperor's consorts,[1] and minimized status differences between the wife (empress) and concubines. The fluidity of the actual power hierarchy among an emperor's consorts was reflected in the ritual and other privileges held by imperial concubines and in their social origins, which were frequently as elevated as those of empresses. The Ch'ing succession policy helped to support a marriage model that deviated significantly from the one found among commoners.

The Manchus who conquered China in the seventeenth century were descended from the Jurchen, a tribal people living in northeast Asia.[2] In the late fifteenth and early sixteenth centuries, Nurgaci (1559–1626), a petty chieftain, and his son Hung Taiji (1592–1643) united the loosely organized Jurchen tribes to create the Manchu confederation. They formed alliances with Mongol tribes and Chinese transfrontiersmen and organized their Manchu, Mongol, and Han allies into disciplined units, called "banners," to fight against the Ming state. These multiethnic banner forces were the key to the Manchu conquest of China and the establishment of the Ch'ing dynasty.

A conquest dynasty, the Ch'ing confronted major problems in controlling a Chinese population that outnumbered them forty-nine to one. While maintaining military primacy, the first rulers won over the Chinese literati by adopting the Confucian framework for government. Ch'ing emperors learned Chinese, patronized Chinese art and scholarship, issued hortatory edicts supporting Confucian values, continued the sacrifices in the state religion, and performed Chinese rituals at marriage and death. But, like the other non-Han dynasties analyzed by Jennifer Holmgren in this volume, the Manchus did not adopt the entire Chinese model. Their marriage system was substantially influenced by the political conditions they faced.

Like earlier non-Han dynasties, the Ch'ing used marriage exchange as an important tool for foreign alliances, both during and after the crucial conquest period. The stable circle of marriage partners for the Ch'ing ruling family was confined to the conquest elite and their peers in the steppe society. The multiethnic makeup of the victorious banner forces and the imperative need to maintain military supremacy shaped the policy allowing Manchus to marry Manchu, Mongol, or Chinese bannermen, but not Chinese in the civilian population.

One of the key problems of rulership—succession—heavily influenced Ch'ing marriage. Although the Manchus gradually shifted from their tribal custom of rule by council to one-man rule and father-son succession during the late seventeenth and early eighteenth centuries,[3] they did not adopt the succession customs of the Ming dynasty (1368–1644). The Ming, a Han Chinese ruling house, publicly installed the empress's first son as heir-apparent while he was still a child; if the empress were barren, the eldest son inherited the throne. In eleven of the fifteen cases of imperial succession in the Ming, a first son inherited the throne from his father. By contrast, there was only one instance, in the nineteenth century, of an empress's son actually mounting the Ch'ing throne, and two other instances, that same century, of the throne passing to the eldest son (table 5.1).[4]

The Ch'ing rejection of eldest-son succession was initially dictated by political struggles accompanying the emergence of one-man rule. The group leadership that seems to have been intended by Nurgaci broke down when his eighth son, Hung Taiji, became the undisputed supreme leader after his father's death. When Hung Taiji died in 1643, his brother Dorgon dominated the government as regent by selecting Hung Taiji's ninth son, an infant, to succeed over his older brothers. The next heir, chosen in 1661 as the emperor lay dying of smallpox, was preferred over an older brother partly because he had already had the disease.[5] The K'ang-hsi emperor did install his first son by the empress as heir, but found his heir-apparent grievously unfit for office and demoted him. By the early eighteenth century the Ch'ing rulers had substituted a system of secret succession in place of the Ming custom. The emperor would seal the name of his choice in a coffer to be opened only upon his death (Huang 1974:95–96).

TABLE 5.1   The Manchu Imperial Succession

Emperor	Reign Period	Birth Order[a]	Eldest Son	Mother's Rank[b]
Shun-chih	1644–61	9		C4
K'ang-hsi	1661–1722	3		C4
Yung-cheng	1722–35	4		C4
Ch'ien-lung	1735–95	5		C3
Chia-ch'ing	1796–1820	15		C2
Tao-kuang	1820–50	2	x	C1
Hsien-feng	1850–61	4	x	C1[c]
T'ung-chih	1861–74	1	x	C2
Kuang-hsu	1874–1908	—[d]		?
Hsuan-t'ung	1908–11	—[e]		?

[a] Among sons only.
[b] Highest rank attained during her husband's lifetime: C1 = empress, C2 = *huang-kuei-fei*, C3 = *kuei-fei*, C4 = *fei*.
[c] Entered as fourth-ranking concubine; promoted once son became emperor.
[d] The son of T'ung-chih's father's younger brother, or T'ung-chih's cousin.
[e] The son of Kuang-hsu's younger brother, or Kuang-hsu's nephew.

The Ch'ing rejection of the eldest-son succession principle, coupled with the secret and delayed designation of the heir, produced intense succession struggles. The contest for succession—which one scholar (Fletcher 1979) has likened to the "bloody tanistry" of successions in the Ottoman Empire—divided brother from brother, with the victor exterminating his rivals. To this day scholars write about the "usurpation" of the Yung-cheng emperor, who is said to have forged his father's will. It is perhaps no accident that this emperor was one of the most ruthless rulers in the history of the dynasty.

The Ch'ing abandonment of eldest-son succession was a destabilizing force on the imperial family. With succession a wide-open competition whose outcome was determined only on an emperor's deathbed, there could be no spatial and social separation of the heir from his siblings, as occurred in the Ming (for discussion of different succession regimes in Chinese history see Holmgren's chapter in this volume). There could be no discrimination in the education or marriage of one son as opposed to another, and sons were not barred from political participation. Unlike the Ming, which sought to exclude imperial agnates from governance, the Ch'ing emperor's sons, grandsons, and other agnates were assigned to carry out ritual, military, and diplomatic tasks, with their fitness for the throne evaluated by their performance.

The commoner norm dictating that sons of concubines ritually and legally regard the first wife (here the empress) as mother was not fully followed in the Ch'ing palace. Although an emperor had only one empress at a time, he could be survived by several empresses dowager because the first act of most

Ch'ing emperors was to promote their natural mothers to this status. As the mother of the emperor, such a woman could wield enormous power at court, greater than that of the empress: the most notorious example is Empress Dowager Tz'u-hsi, who easily manipulated her nominal superior Empress Tz'u-an to dominate Ch'ing politics from the 1860s until her death in 1908. Although the Ch'ing did not have a truly polygynous system of marriage, we shall argue that the system of imperial concubinage was distinctive, being neither strictly monogamous nor polygamous. In the Ch'ing imperial system, concubines enjoyed access to the ritual, legal, and social privileges accorded to the first wife or empress. Status differences among the consorts of an emperor were differences of degree, not of kind.

The sources for studying Ch'ing imperial marriage patterns are exceptionally rich. The ritual procedures are described in detail in the *Ta Ch'ing hui-tien* (Administrative Regulations of the Ch'ing Dynasty); the *Ch'in-ting ta-Ch'ing t'ung-li* (Comprehensive Rituals of the Ch'ing), produced in the eighteenth century; and in archival documents held by the Number One Historical Archives in Peking. These archival materials indicate that those planning the weddings of the T'ung-chih and Kuang-hsu emperors in the nineteenth century relied heavily on the *hui-tien* (KCTC no. 2379; P. Li 1983:80). The marriage partners (including concubines) of the imperial line are recorded in the genealogy of the Ch'ing imperial house, printed in the twentieth century, which is supplemented by the more comprehensive manuscript copy (*Ta Ch'ing yü-tieh*). The Number One Historical Archives also has abundant supplementary documentation on the personnel of the Inner Quarters in the records of the Imperial Household Department.

The emperor was the head of the Aisin Gioro lineage,[6] which was regulated by the Imperial Clan Court (*tsung-jen fu*). All marriages (along with births and deaths) were recorded in the imperial genealogy (*Ta Ch'ing yü-tieh*), which was periodically revised (*TJFTL*, 1.10a). Moreover, the marriages of all members of the main line (*tsung-shih*, consisting of the descendants of Taksi, the great-grandfather of the first Ch'ing emperor, Shun-chih), initially required the emperor's approval (*TCHTSL*, c. 1; *TJFTL*, 2.1a–9b). In the course of the dynasty, the growth of the lineage forced emperors to narrow the circle of kin whose marriages they arranged.[7] But even in the late nineteenth century the emperor retained the right to select brides for the sons of princes in his father's and his own generation, and grooms for the daughters of princes of the first six ranks (for the Sung, see Chaffee's chapter in this volume). In this paper, however, I focus on a much smaller subgroup; namely, the sons and daughters of emperors, and emperors themselves.

THE INFLUENCE OF MANCHU CUSTOMS

Like the Mongols (Holmgren 1986:144–45), the Jurchens seem to have had a tradition of marriage by seizure (S. Yang 1984; Shirokogoroff 1973) and to have practiced clan exogamy,[8] but they placed no restrictions on cross-generational marriage. Hung Taiji's empress, Hsiao-tuan, was joined in the emperor's harem by her two nieces. Shun-chih's (1638–61) second empress was a first collateral niece of his first empress, whom he had deposed in 1653. Imperial unions continued to disregard the generational principle into the nineteenth century, when one of the T'ung-chih (1856–75) emperor's concubines was the paternal aunt of his empress.

Worse (from the Chinese perspective), Manchu society originally practiced the levirate; that is, men were encouraged to marry their brothers' widows, sons to marry their father's widows (but never their birth mothers), and nephews the widows of their paternal uncles (Tao 1976:12; H. Li 1985). One assumes they practiced the levirate for the same reasons Mongols did: to maintain "the viability of the family patrimony" by keeping widows from leaving and taking their property with them (Holmgren 1986:153). Among Han Chinese, the senior levirate (marriage with an older brother's wife) was treated as incest. Some poor Chinese practiced the junior levirate, but from T'ang times at least such marriages were legally prohibited, punishable by strangulation, and according to Feng, "even in the few places where it is practiced, it is not considered respectable" (1967:51).

In 1631 and 1636 Hung Taiji publicly banned the senior levirate, along with marrying a father's widow and the widows of a father's brothers, as part of the Manchu adoption of Han Chinese customs. The new marriage rules were not always obeyed. Princess Mukushih, fourth daughter of Nurgaci, was divorced from her first husband, then married to Eidu, the famous hero of the Niohuru clan.[9] After Eidu's death, Mukushih married Turgei, his son by another woman (Li Feng-min 1984; Huang 1986:638). Although one scholar (Li Feng-min 1984) asserts that the couple was punished for this transgression, we should note that Mukushih lived to the ripe age of sixty-five, and Turgei, "highly regarded" by Hung Taiji (Hummel 1943 1:222), was rewarded for his military prowess after his marriage to Mukushih.

The Manchu rulers continued to observe Han Chinese generational rules with laxity, but in other respects their marriages came to comply with Chinese taboos. The marriage of a widow to her former husband's son or to her husband's brother is not found after 1648 in the imperial genealogy. Marriage to sisters, which was consonant with Chinese and Mongol traditions, was practiced by Manchu rulers (Feng 1967:46–48; Holmgren 1986:142–43). Hung Taiji, K'ang-hsi (1654–1722), and Hsien-feng (1831–61) all had sisters in their harems (K'ang-hsi had four sororal pairs), and the Kuang-hsu emperor (1871–1908) took two sisters as concubines when he married his empress in 1888.

Matrilateral cross-cousin marriages (marrying the mother's brother's daughter), practiced in some parts of China (Gallin 1963), was also favored by the Mongols (Krader 1963:24) and practiced by the Manchu rulers.

K'ang-hsi and Kuang-hsu both had concubines who were related to them in this way, and Nurgaci married at least two of his daughters to his sisters' sons.[10]

As in other non-Han dynasties (see Holmgren's chapter in this volume), after 1655 all Manchus were forbidden to marry Han Chinese who were not enrolled in the Eight Banners (Wang Tao-ch'eng 1985a:305–6; P'u 1982: 124). This prohibition was spelled out in the regulations of the Imperial Clan Court (*TJFTL* 31.19ab); those who disobeyed were punished, and any offspring expelled from the lineage. As we shall see, this rule, which permitted marriage within a group of long-term political followers, constituted a form of political endogamy.

MARRIAGE AND POLITICS

In the critical years before 1683, when the Manchu rulers were creating their empire, marriage exchanges functioned as an important means of winning new allies and stabilizing military coalitions. Rival Manchu tribal leaders, Mongol princes, Chinese frontiersmen, and Chinese generals were rewarded for their support with Aisin Gioro wives and enrolled in the Manchu, Mongol, and Chinese banners created during the early seventeenth century.

The banners were large civil-military units created in the early seventeenth century that replaced the small hunting groups of Nurgaci's early campaigns. Composed of companies, each with three hundred households of warriors and headed by a hereditary leader (Wakeman 1985:54–55), the banners became administrative units for registration, conscription, taxation, and mobilization of the tribes and peoples who joined the Manchu cause before 1644. To the eight Manchu banners were added, by 1635, eight Mongol (Ch'en 1984:114) and by 1642 eight Chinese banners (Wakeman 1985: 200–201). The conquest of China was achieved by these combined banner forces, in which less than 16 percent of the soldiers by 1648 were actually of Manchu origin (An 1983).

Table 5.2 summarizes the ethnic origins of the principal spouses of emperors, princes, and princesses. For the moment, we will focus only on the first wives of emperors and princes and the marriages of princesses, who were all first wives. Because later marriages followed the patterns begun by Nurgaci and his successor, Hung Taiji, they are included in the table, which ends with the children of the Hsien-feng emperor (1831–61).[11]

Empresses, *ti fujin* (wives of princes), and *efu* (husbands of princesses) came from a relatively small number of favored houses (see table 5.2). Of the 641 Manchu clans listed in the *Pa-ch'i Man-chou shih-tsu t'ung-p'u* compiled in 1745, only 31 were favored by the Aisin Gioro lineage with marriage. Among the Manchu clans, the Niohuru descended from Eidu supplied almost half of the empresses for the entire dynasty. Their bonds with the Aisin Gioro were

TABLE 5.2   Preferred Affines of Emperors, Princes, and Princesses

	Empress[a]	Princes' Wives[b]	Princesses' Husbands[c]	Total No. of Women
Ethnicity				
Chinese	0	4	4	8
Manchu	15	47	24	86
Mongol	5	10	35	50
Total no. of women	20	61	63	144
Manchu affines				
Donggo	0	3	1	4
Fuca	1	5	3	9
Guololo	0	2	1	3
Gūwalgiya	0	5	4	9
Irgen Gioro	0	3	2	5
Nara	0	7	4	11
Niohuru	5	4	4	13
Sirin Gioro	0	2	0	2
Tatara	0	2	0	2
Ula Nara	3	0	0	3
Yehe Nara	2	1	0	3
Other clans	4	13	5	22
Total no. of clans	8	23	12	

SOURCE: *TCYT.*

[a] Only empresses given that title during the emperor's lifetime are included. The table begins with Nurgaci and his offspring.
[b] The "first wife" of a prince.
[c] The husband of a princess; here only princesses born or adopted by emperors are counted.

exceptionally close. The Niohuru genealogy analyzed by Huang P'ei records seventy-seven of Eidu's male descendants and seventy-two Niohuru daughters marrying into the Aisin Gioro main line (Huang 1986:638). The Manchus also displayed a strong preference for Mongol spouses: 25 percent of empresses, 16 percent of princes' wives, and 55 percent of princesses' husbands were Mongol. The Khorchins, who were the earliest Mongol allies of the Manchus, were especially favored: twelve sons-in-law, an empress, and one prince's wife were Khorchin. There were no Han Chinese empresses, and the Chinese princely wives and husbands either date from the period of conquest or belonged to the Chinese banners.

Manchu Affines

The favored marriage partners among the Manchu clans were those who had allied themselves with the Aisin Gioro lineage. The exchange of wives had long been an accepted mode of cementing tribal alliances. The Manchus interspersed such alliances with the use of force to unify the Jurchen tribes. Of the Gūwalgiya, Niohuru, Sumuru, Nara, Donggo, Hoifa, Ula, Irgen Gioro, and Magiya clans that formed the so-called Eight Great Houses,[12] only the Hoifa is missing from the list of imperial affines presented in table 5.2. "Heroes" of the conquest period were often rewarded with Aisin Gioro brides. Hohori (1561–1624), of the Donggo clan (Hummel 1943 1:291), wed Nurgaci's eldest daughter. Fiongdon (1564–1620), of the Suwan Gūwalgiya clan (ibid., 247), distinguished himself in Nurgaci's military campaigns and obtained noble titles and wives for his sons.

Mongol Affines

Manchu marriages with Mongol nobles also increased as the Ch'ing armies expanded into central Asia in the late seventeenth and early eighteenth centuries. Earlier Chinese dynasties had given princesses to Mongol princes and other "barbarian" tribal leaders, but the Manchus conducted a bilateral exchange of wives on an unprecedented scale. The frequency of Manchu marriage exchanges with Mongol princes underlines the crucial importance of the Mongols in the Manchu conquest of Ming China.

From 1612 the Manchus wooed the Khorchin Mongols of western Manchuria and Inner Mongolia away from adherence to the Ming. Mongols who "came over" were showered with gifts and presented with Aisin Gioro wives. They in turn wed their daughters to the Manchu rulers. Nurgaci is said to have proclaimed: "The Manchus and Mongols have different speech [languages] but their clothing comes from the same origin, and they are brother states" (Lü 1985:18). Resisting the Chahar Mongol leader Ligdan Khan's attempts (supported by the Ming) to unify the Mongol tribes, the Khorchin allied with the Manchus to defeat Ligdan Khan in 1634. Once defeated, the Chahar Mongols were also wooed by the Manchus, who presented a Manchu princess to Ligdan Khan's heir in 1635. The Qalqa Mongols, who lived further west in what is now Outer Mongolia, were also courted: in 1617, for example, Nurgaci gave one of his nieces to Enggeder, son of a Qalqa khan who came over to the Manchu cause, and accepted another Qalqa prince's daughter as a daughter-in-law. By 1691 the Qalqa Mongols were absorbed into the Manchu state and reorganized into Mongol banners (Bawden 1968; Lattimore 1934).

Ch'ing marriage networks grew with the Manchu penetration of central and north Asia. The Tüshiyetü Khan exercised sovereignty over the Mongol tribes in east-central Outer Mongolia; their primary regional center, Urga (modern-day Ulan Bator), had been captured by Galdan, leader of the Zunghars, in 1688. In 1697, a year after the Ch'ing troops had defeated Galdan, a grandson of the Tüshiyetü Khan married K'ang-hsi's sixth daughter; several years later (1702) an alliance with the Jasaghtu Khan, who ruled over the Mongol tribes further west, was cemented by his marriage to the daughter of

a Manchu prince. In 1706 a descendant of the Sayin Noyan Khan, who held
the territory between the Jasaghtu and Tüshiyetü Khans, was married to
K'ang-hsi's tenth daughter (Bawden 1968).

The Ch'ing subjugation of the Western Mongols was achieved with the
aid of their Mongol allies; as Lattimore (1934:60) notes, "Manchu sovereignty was not achieved by outright conquest but was always based on alliance
with some one group of Mongols against another group and the status of Mongols within the empire was different from, and higher than, the Chinese."
By the nineteenth century the previously mighty Mongol domains were
supervised by Ch'ing appointees, the Mongol nobility held Ch'ing titles,
the once powerful tribes had been reorganized into banners, and the khans
"were little more than distinguished banner princes" (Fletcher 1978:51).

From 1636 onward Mongols were given Manchu titles of nobility. Mongol
nobles from 1614 on exchanged daughters and sisters with the Manchu
rulers, and were tied to the Aisin Gioro lineage by a complex network of
affinal exchanges. Manjusri (1599–1649), a Khorchin Mongol noble, was the
nephew of Empress Hsiao-tuan, Hung Taiji's wife. Two of Manjusri's
daughters married two of Hung Taiji's sons; in 1636 he was given the title
"Baturu chün-wang," designating leadership of one of the six political units
into which the Manchus divided the Khorchins. Empress Hsiao-tuan was
herself related to four of the six princes who ruled the Khorchins under the
Ch'ing (Hummel 1943 1:304). Moreover, her three daughters, and those of
her niece, Empress Hsiao-chuang (mother of the Shun-chih emperor), half-
Khorchin in descent, were all married to Mongol nobles. Other Mongols also
participated in these sustained marriage exchanges. For example, marriage
ties between the Aisin Gioro and the descendants of Bandi, son-in-law of
Hung Taiji and leader of the Aokhan Mongols, lasted for five generations
(Hua 1983:52).

The cultivation of ties extended beyond marriage. From 1659 onward,
sons of Manchu princesses could be reared in Peking at court (Chao 1984),
and from K'ang-hsi's reign, some Mongol boys of noble descent were invited
to Peking, where they were raised in the palace and attended school with the
Manchu princes (Hua 1983). The Shang-shu-fang, founded by the Yung-
cheng emperor (1678–1735) to educate imperial sons, grandsons, and other
princes (including sons-in-law), taught Mongol as well as Manchu and
Chinese (Kahn 1971:117–20). When they came of age, these Mongols were
married to princesses and frequently served the Ch'ing. Tsereng, the Qalqa
noble (Hummel 1944 2:756–57) who married K'ang-hsi's fourth daughter
(1706), performed exceptional military service in the Ch'ing campaigns
against Galdan and won commemoration in the Ch'ing imperial ancestral
temple in Peking. Septen Baljur, a Khorchin noble who married Ch'ien-
lung's third daughter, had a similar background (Hua 1983). Many Mongols

became an integral part of Ch'ing society: Ch'ung Ch'i, father of T'ung-chih's empress and a member of the Mongol Plain Blue Banner, was the son of a grand councillor and grand secretary, a *chuang-yuan* in the 1865 *chin-shih* examinations, and a Ch'ing official (Hummel 1944 1:208–9).

Marriages with Mongols did not end with the stabilization of China's Inner Asian frontiers in the mid-eighteenth century. By this period, the Ch'ien-lung emperor (1711–99) called the pattern of marrying Ch'ing princesses to Mongols a tradition that should be maintained (*TCHTSL* c. 1), although he also permitted (in 1751) princesses to marry into distinguished banner families (*TJFTL* 2.6a). Through the nineteenth century, successive emperors tried to preserve this marriage pattern by reiterating that the names of eligible young Mongols (and information on three generations of their forebears) must be sent to the Li fan yuan (Court of Colonial Affairs) for selection as sons-in-law (*TCHTSL* c.1; *TJFTL* 2.1a; Chao 1984; Hua 1983). The marriages between the Aisin Gioro lineage and the Mongol aristocracy continued into the nineteenth century; by the 1820s–1840s more than three thousand such marriages were recorded (Hua 1983:52). If we ignore the tribal designations, Mongol nobles were the single largest group with whom the imperial house exchanged marriage partners.

Chinese Bannermen

Chinese who came over to the Manchu cause in the years before 1644 were also showered with rank, honors, and Aisin Gioro wives. This policy was clearly expressed in a letter sent by Nurgaci to the commander of the Fu-shun garrison, Li Yung-fang, in 1618 during his first major campaign against the Ming (Wakeman 1985 1:60): "If you submit without fighting . . . I will let you live just as you did before. I will promote . . . the people with great knowledge and foresight . . . give them daughters in marriage and care for them. I will give you a higher position than you have and treat you like one of my officials of the first degree." Li Yung-fang surrendered the city and was treated "as a Chinese frontiersman admitted into the ranks of the Jin aristocracy" (ibid., 61); he married one of Nurgaci's granddaughters, fought alongside Nurgaci, and died a viscount. His nine sons continued to serve the Manchus and were enrolled in the Chinese Plain Blue Banner after 1642. At least one of them—the second son, Shuai-t'ai—also married into the Aisin Gioro lineage (Hummel 1943 1:499).

Sun Ssu-k'o, the son of a Ming officer who surrendered to Nurgaci in 1622, was enrolled in the Chinese Plain White Banner and helped to lead the Manchu troops in defeating the Eleuths at the battle of Jao Modo (1695); he was rewarded with a title, and his son was married to K'ang-hsi's fourth daughter (ibid. 2:682). Wu San-kuei, Shang K'o-hsi, and Keng Chi-mao, the three Han Chinese generals who were instrumental in the Manchu conquest of south China, were each granted princely titles otherwise reserved only for Manchus and Mongols, and were linked by marriage with the imperial house (*TCYT*; Hummel 1943 1:415–16; T'ang 1923:192–93).[13]

These Chinese bannermen—the term derives from the designation (*Han-chün*) used in 1642 when the Chinese banners were organized—served the Manchu rulers as advisers, generals, and officials in the crucial conquest period. Especially in the seventeenth century, their language and cultural knowledge made them favored appointees for local government posts in China. Chinese bannermen dominated the posts of governor and governor-general during the late seventeenth century (Wakeman 1985 2:1021–23, 1024, 1029, 1031–33). Wakeman concludes that the Shun-chih reign "saw the transformation of Han bannermen into a new supra-elite, acting almost like provincial janissaries for the throne," and even replacing Chinese degree holders in posts (ibid., 1020). Like other Manchu adherents, their loyalty and service to the throne frequently continued over many generations (ibid., 1018–20). The T'ungs of Fu-shun, sinicized Jurchen who joined the Manchu cause from 1618 to 1645, are an outstanding example of the rewards, which included promotion into a Manchu banner, heaped upon loyal Chinese bannermen (Crossley 1983; Hou 1982).

Chinese bannermen were sharply distinguished from Chinese captured in the early phases of the Manchu conquest, who became bondservants, a hereditary servile status. Mongol, Korean, and Chinese bondservants were used to till the estates created in north China for imperial kinsmen, banner officials, and bannermen (Wei, Wu, and Lu 1982). Organized according to the Eight Banner system, bondservants in the upper three banners (the Bordered Yellow, the Plain Yellow, and the Plain White) came under the direct personal control of the emperor in the late seventeenth and early eighteenth centuries and were appointed to positions within the Imperial Household Department (Torbert 1977). Their servile status did not prevent some bondservants from becoming rich and powerful; they were used for delicate and confidential tasks by the emperors, and some attained provincial and even central government posts (Spence 1966:13–15). And, as we shall see, daughters of Chinese bondservants could also enter the imperial harem.

The differentiation between Chinese bannermen and Chinese civilians was primarily a political one, but there is also evidence that "culturally the important distinctions of the early Qing period lay not between the Manchus and the Chinese-martial Bannermen but between the Bannermen of all origins and the conquered Chinese" (Crossley 1987:779). In the early stages the designation of Chinese bannermen had been applied to persons who were not necessarily racially Chinese, but who had been subjects of the Ming (ibid.). Many were in fact northeast Asians who had settled in Liaotung: sinicized Jurchens, Mongols, Koreans were thus called *nikan*, the Manchu word for persons who lived in the manner of Chinese. In fact, the early Mongol and the Chinese banners both enrolled descendants of Jurchen (ibid.). By the 1660s many Chinese bannermen were second- and third-generation descendants of officers who had joined the Manchu cause and were "barely distinguishable from the Manchu nobility" (Wakeman 1985 2:1017). Many had been "transfrontiersmen" who through long residence in Liaoning had become accustomed to Manchu ways and took on Manchu identity with Nurgaci's acquiescence (ibid., 1:45). Nurgaci classified "individuals on the basis of their culture primarily"; the K'ang-hsi emperor displayed his relaxed attitude toward ethnicity in his willingness to transfer whole Mongol tribes and Chinese lineages from the Mongol and Chinese banners to the Manchu banners (Crossley 1987:779). Indeed, K'ang-hsi's willingness to incorporate other ethnic groups into the banner system extended even to Russian prisoners of war, who were enrolled as a company in the Bordered Yellow Banner in 1685 (Wu 1987).

Support for the argument that the Manchus emphasized political rather than ethnic boundaries in their marriage patterns can be found in analysis of the circumstances surrounding the 1648 decision of the "Imperial Father Regent," Dorgon, to permit Manchu-Han marriages. In 1648 the Manchu conquest of China was far from assured, and Dorgon used various measures to try to obtain the voluntary compliance of Chinese to Manchu rule. Bannermen were prohibited (after 1644) from plundering civilians; from 1647 onward imperial pronouncements repeated the theme that "Manchu and Han are one family." The subject set for the palace examinations in 1649 was how Manchus and Han could be brought to live together (Kessler 1976:15–17; Chou and Chao 1986:408–9). In reality, this policy could not be implemented. Ethnic strife in Peking forced Dorgon to rule (October 5, 1648) that the two races should be separated so that each could "live in peace." The bannermen were eventually housed in separate walled garrison quarters in thirty-four cities across north China (Wakeman 1985 1:480).

The edict ordering the removal of all Chinese from the northern imperial city to the southern city in Peking was followed a day later by an edict permitting intermarriage to promote friendship between Manchus and Han. Details implementing this policy were announced on October 14 (*TCSL* 40.9ab, 11a, 14ab). In what can be interpreted as an effort to win over the Han populace, the edict specified that Manchus marrying Han women were required to take them as wives and not concubines.

We do not know how many individuals availed themselves of the opportunity offered by the 1648 edict;[14] what we do know is that the policy permitting intermarriage ended abruptly in 1655. Dorgon was dead; the young emperor responded angrily to a memorial from a Chinese official who criticized an expedition to Yangchow to buy Chinese women for the palace. The memorialist, Li K'ai-sheng, touched on the delicate ethnic situation, reminded the emperor that Yangchow had the "bandit spirit" (it had forcibly resisted the Ch'ing armies), and warned of the adverse public reaction to such activities. The emperor, who punished Li for his memorial, indignantly denied the truth of the charges and reiterated the Manchu tradition that excluded Chinese women from the imperial harem (*TCSL* 92.13b–15b, 20b).

The 1648 edict removing Chinese from the imperial city in Peking specifically exempted Chinese bannermen. Nor were the Manchus alone in thus separating Chinese bannermen from the rest of the Chinese population. Contemporary Han Chinese looked down on them as "racial renegades and no better than Manchus" (Kessler 1976:18) because they had betrayed the Ming cause. The distinction between Chinese bannermen and Han Chinese is clear in a 1651 complaint by a Han Chinese censor, who urged the emperor to stop relying so heavily on bannermen in top provincial posts (ibid., 17–18)—as we have already noted, Chinese bannermen dominated provincial posts during this period.

The early Manchu laxity toward "ethnic purity" was replaced in the mid-eighteenth century by a heightened concern with the maintenance of Manchu separateness. The empire was secured, the frontiers stabilized. The Ch'ien-lung emperor, who saw himself as the ruler of a multicultural empire, desired that "there should be orderly congruence of race to custom"; during his reign, oral genealogies were written down, every Manchu was fixed within a clan, and the major clans were traced back to the Chin dynasty that had ruled north China during the twelfth century. Concern for the preservation of Manchu identity was expressed in strictures on the maintenance of Manchu dress and the perpetuation of shamanism, the traditional Manchu religion. The prohibition against intermarriage with Han Chinese was no doubt strengthened by these new attitudes, and prevailed until the end of the dynasty.

In its emphasis on the military segment of society, Ch'ing imperial marriages greatly resembled those of the Northern Sung (Chung 1981), when virtually none of the imperial concubines came from the prominent scholar-official families. In the Ming, as in the Northern Sung, imperial marriage partners tended to be drawn from hereditary military families (Soullière 1988). Scholar-officials might consider themselves the sine qua non of the dynasty; that the imperial perception differed is suggested by the consistent priority given to *wu* (the military) over *wen* (the civilian officials) in imperial marriage.

THE RECRUITMENT OF WOMEN FOR EMPERORS AND PRINCES

The number of acknowledged empresses and concubines varied greatly by emperor, ranging from K'ang-hsi with 40 to Kuang-hsu with only 3. With 9 emperors (excluding the last emperor, P'u-i) claiming a total of 155 wives and concubines, the Ch'ing harems were relatively large.[15] Unlike the T'ang dynasty, with its elaborate structure for the imperial harem (Chung 1981:18–20), the Ch'ing hierarchy, defined in 1636, was relatively simple. Concubines were differentiated into seven ranks: the highest was *huang-kuei-fei*, then, in descending order, *kuei-fei, fei, pin, kuei-jen, ch'ang-tsai*, and *ta-ying*.[16] Rank determined the allotments of food, clothing, jewelry, etc., as well as cash stipends and maids, that a woman received (*KCTL* c. 3). The highest rank (empress dowager) received 300,000 taels a year (Lu 1982).[17]

The Ch'ing procedure for the selection of imperial and princely consorts was narrower than those of earlier dynasties.[18] The Ch'ing modified the Ming and Northern Sung practice of drafting women from the civilian population for palace service and selecting consorts from the palace maids (Chung 1981:9–11; Shan 1960). Beginning with Shun-chih's second empress in 1653 (Wei 1984:20), brides for the Aisin Gioro line were selected from the triennial draft of *hsiu-nü* (beautiful women) who were daughters of officials in the banners (*TCHTSL* c. 1114; *HPTL* 1.14a–23a). With the exception of specified individuals who became exempt in the course of the dynasty, the emperors enforced the requirement that every eligible girl had to appear in Peking in the draft before her betrothal, beginning from the age of thirteen to fourteen *sui*.

The *hsiu-nü* inspection was held in the capital. In Peking, the girls entered the Inner Quarters of the palace grouped by banner (Manchu, Mongol, and Chinese) and within each by age. The emperor and empress who personally inspected the girls to select brides for their sons and imperial agnates were furnished with the particulars of their family backgrounds and birthdates (the latter were used to compare the "eight characters" of the prospective couple); those passing the first draft were inspected by the senior empress dowager, who was provided with the ranks and names of the girl's maternal grandfather and her paternal forebears for three generations. Choices could thus be based not only on a girl's personal appearance but also on her family's status. The Yung-cheng emperor emphasized the latter: he ruled that the selection of empresses and concubines of ranks one through five should be made only from the families of hereditary banner officials above a certain rank (Wang Tao-ch'eng 1985a:306). The notion that father's rank determined that of his daughter in the imperial harem is supported by a blank form from the mid-nineteenth century, which equates a hereditary duke to a *fei*, a prefect to a *pin*, and so on (ibid., 311).

Some *hsiu-nü* were immediately selected as wives or concubines for princes, or for the emperor himself. The empresses of the K'ang-hsi, T'ung-chih, and Kuang-hsu emperors were selected from the *hsiu-nü* draft (*CTKTSH* illus. 225, 226, p. 165; Sun 1985:52). Empress Dowager Tz'u-hsi was chosen in the *hsiu-nü* draft of March 28, 1852, designated a sixth-rank concubine, and introduced into the palace on June 26, 1852 (Yü 1985a:130).

Hsiu-nü who did not enter the imperial or princely harems probably became ladies-in-waiting, serving for a five-year term and provided with stipends according to their rank. At the end of five years they were permitted to leave with a grant of twenty taels of silver. These *hsiu-nü* who caught the emperor's eye could still be promoted into the harem. This seems to have been the way Te fei, one of K'ang-hsi's favorite concubines, entered the palace. Te fei, who produced six children, was "originally a lady-in-waiting from the Uya clan" whose father was an officer in the banners (S. Wu 1979:36).

The other way to enter a princely or imperial household was through the draft for palace maids (*kung-nü*), who were selected from the daughters of bondservant officials in the upper three banners who were serving in the Imperial Household Department (Shan 1960; *TCHTSL* c. 1,218). Palace serving women were occasionally plucked out of the ranks; a not inconsiderable 16 percent of concubines entered the harem through this means.[19] Many were probably from humble backgrounds: in 1700 the emperor ordered that, "since the girls coming to the palace for . . . selection as palace maids were mainly from poor families, they be taken to warm quarters and fed with hot soup and rice when the weather was cold" (Torbert 1977:75).

Unlike the triennial *hsiu-nü* draft, the recruitment of palace maids took place once a year and was managed by the Imperial Household Department. Girls aged thirteen *sui* were brought to the palace for inspection and selection by the emperor. Most were assigned to the different palaces to fill the quota of maids assigned to the emperor, empress dowager, empress, and ranked concubines. Four hundred to five hundred palace maids and eunuchs were said to have staffed the palace during the K'ang-hsi reign; by Tz'u-hsi's time, there were eleven hundred maids alone (Shan 1960:97). Each maid was allocated a daily food ration, and received bolts of silk and cotton. Some received up to six taels of silver a year for their service (Lu 1982). Palace maids could be married off with dowries at age twenty-five if in general service, and at age thirty-five if they served imperial persons (*KTCL* 3.2a–3a).

In contrast to the lax policies concerning intermarriage with bondservants in the early Ch'ing, regulations preventing their selection as concubines or wives of males in the main line were put in place by the late nineteenth century. The Yung-cheng emperor himself noted in 1727 that the Manchus (unlike the Chinese) observed "strict separation and distinction between master and bondservant" (Torbert 1977:56–57). Intermarriage of regular bannermen and bondservants was forbidden (ibid., 68), and there were stringent rules against Aisin Gioro marrying bondservants from the lower five banners, that is, those banners not directly controlled by the emperor (*TJFTL* 31.20a–21a).

Imperial consorts of bondservant background, who had probably begun as palace maids, included Ch'ien-lung's third empress, the daughter of a palace overseer, and Chia-ch'ing's (1760–1820) first empress, the daughter of an Imperial Household Department manager (Torbert 1977:76). Two of Ch'ien-lung's concubines probably also came from bondservant families; the father of another was a Korean bondservant (ibid.). Two of Chia-ch'ing's concubines were initially palace maids (ibid., 75). One of K'ang-hsi's favorites was in fact of still lower status: her father was a state slave (*sin jeku jetere aha*) (ibid., 75; Yeh 1984:45). Information in the imperial genealogy on the fathers of two other imperial concubines—K'ang-hsi's Cheng fei and Chia-ch'ing's Shun-pin—suggests that they too may have come from bondservant backgrounds.

The *hsiu-nü* and palace maid drafts enabled the emperors to exercise the right of first choice over the daughters of officials in the regular Manchu, Mongol, and Han banners as well as in the upper three bondservant banners linked to the Imperial Household Department. The social status of the emperor's affines was mixed; it included aristocrats and slaves (the bondservants). The inclusion of the latter, in direct contravention of rules forbidding intermarriage between bannermen and bondservants (*HPTL* 1.29a–30a), is a most striking aspect of the Ch'ing marriage system.

Unlike the native Chinese dynasties studied by Holmgren, the Ch'ing tried to regulate the access of both affinal/maternal and sororal kin. By the early eighteenth century girls closely related to the empress or descended through their mothers from the Aisin Gioro line had to be explicitly identified as such in the *hsiu-nü* inspections. From 1800 the throne began issuing exemptions from the *hsiu-nü* draft to daughters of imperial princesses married to Mongols, sisters of the empress, empress dowager, and concubines of the first through fourth ranks. These regulations did not bar girls born to brothers of the empress and concubines of the first four ranks from the draft, and, as we have seen, imperial consorts were frequently related to one another. In the final analysis, it was not the policy governing selection of wives but the rejection of eldest-son (or empress's son) succession and the inclusion of low-status bondservant daughters in the harem that served as a check on the emergence of powerful affinal or sororal relatives.

THE STATUS OF WIVES AND CONCUBINES

Ebrey (1986) and Rubie Watson (see her chapter in this volume) have argued that commoners in Sung and contemporary China have not had polygynous unions because stringent ritual, legal, and social distinctions separated the wife ("first wife" in this chapter) from all other sexual partners. Holmgren (in this volume) has called the Chinese system "serial monogamy." According to Watson, concubines were sharply differentiated from wives in three critical aspects: their mode of entry into the household, their ritual obligations and privileges, and their social status. Wives entered their husbands' households with dowries; concubines did not. Concubines were purchased. The marriage rite was performed only for the wife; there could be serial marriages, but a man could have only one wife at a time. All children called the first wife "mother," and their filial obligations were directed to her and not to their natural mothers. Concubines were usually not commemorated after death, unlike wives. Wives came from respectable families with standing in their community, and marriage created a sustained relationship between the wife-givers and wife-takers, as contrasted to the complete absence of such relationships with a concubine's natal family, which was by definition of low status.

The Ch'ing imperial marriage system was not fully polygamous. As we have noted earlier, the concubines in the imperial harem were graded into a seven-rank hierarchy differentiated with respect to privilege and living allowances. Nowhere in the Ch'ing annals do we have true polygamy as described by Holmgren in her characterization of non-Han regimes in this volume, where all wives, or a group of senior wives, enjoyed equal status.

In other important respects, however, the Ch'ing system did not conform to the Chinese imperial system, described by Holmgren. Unlike the sons of Han Chinese rulers, the sons of the empress and of concubines were not clearly distinguished. And we shall see that the Ch'ing system also differed significantly from the system of monogamy practiced in Western Europe in permitting concubines' sons to be legitimate heirs to the throne. Furthermore, in contrast to the marriage system of native Chinese states (see Holmgren's essay in this volume), the Ch'ing allowed concubines to be promoted to empress.

Unlike the marriage system of Chinese commoners cited by Watson, the imperial system failed to sharply distinguish between the mode of entry, social status, and ritual obligations and privileges of the wife and concubines. Many empresses (seven of the eighteen women who held the status of empress during the dynasty, either during their lives or posthumously) entered the imperial harem as concubines, yet they (as empresses) received the same ritual investiture, emoluments, and privileges granted to the women who had entered as wives. This was also true for the six other concubines who were promoted to empress dowager only after the death of their spouse.

We have earlier noted that the Ch'ing rejection of the principle of eldest-son succession and the refusal to announce the heir until the emperor lay dying produced bitter succession struggles. The Ch'ing did not honor the principle, found in both the Ming and the Mongol dynasties, of favoring the sons of the first wife as heir. Did the status of the mother affect the choice of the heir? Historians cite the case of Yin-ssu, the K'ang-hsi emperor's eighth son by a woman of slave background (Liang fei). When Yin-jeng, K'ang-hsi's son by his empress, proved to be unfit for the throne, factions began to form around other potential contenders for the succession. Silas Wu notes that Yin-ssu's mother's low birth counted against him (1979:163), but apparently not sufficiently to disqualify him from consideration.

The Yung-cheng emperor was himself the son of a Manchu "maidservant in the palace" (Hummel 1944 2:916). Despite producing six children for the emperor, Yung-cheng's mother was ranked by K'ang-hsi only as a *fei*; her promotion to empress dowager came at her son's hands. Ch'ien-lung's mother, a Niohuru, was nonetheless the daughter of a middle-level servant (assistant majordomo) in Yung-cheng's princely household; she entered his establishment in 1704, gave birth to the future emperor in 1711, but was not promoted to the third rank (*fei*) until 1723–24, about the time her son was secretly designated heir-apparent (Kahn 1971:88). A *kuei-fei* when Yung-cheng died, she was named empress dowager by her son. The mother of the Chia-ch'ing emperor was from a bondservant family who entered the Ch'ien-lung emperor's harem as a concubine of the fourth rank. In the course of producing six children, she was gradually promoted to concubine of the first rank before her death in 1775 and was posthumously elevated to empress in 1795 when her son was designated heir-apparent. In fact, of the ten emperors who reigned in the Ch'ing dynasty, only one (Tao-kuang) was the son of a first wife or empress. In short, contrary to the Yin-ssu example, the imperial succession did not exclude sons of concubines; it did not prohibit the succession of sons from low-status mothers.

Mode of Entry and Social Status

No imperial concubines were purchased. In contrast to the customary Han Chinese practice, many imperial concubines entered the harem through the same *hsiu-nü* draft that selected empresses (see table 5.3 for ranks of entering consorts). As noted earlier, empresses and concubines of the first five ranks (C1–C6 in the table) were most likely selected through the *hsiu-nü* draft, while the lower-ranking concubines tended to have entered the palace as maidservants through the *kung-nü* recruitment process discussed earlier. Of the 155 women in the harems of the ten Ch'ing emperors, 76 percent entered as concubines through the *hsiu-nü* draft; i.e., they were chosen in the same way as were empresses (see table 5.3).

Many concubines came from the Manchu aristocratic lines that also provided empresses. When Shun-chih's second empress was installed in 1654, her younger sister also entered his harem as a concubine of the third rank. The younger sister of K'ang-hsi's empress entered K'ang-hsi's harem some decades later, gave him a son (1691), and was posthumously made a consort of the third rank after she died in 1696. K'ang-hsi's second empress was a daughter of Ebilun, a major personage of his day and son of Eidu, founder of the Niohuru clan; yet she entered the harem as a concubine of the third rank and was not made empress until 1677, less than a year before her death. The daughter of T'ung Kuo-wei, a major military leader, entered K'ang-hsi's

TABLE 5.3   Mode of Entry of Empress and Concubines

Emperor	Entered as								
	C1	C2	C3	C4	C5	C6	C7	C8	C9
Shun-chih	2	0	0	3	1	0	10	3	0
K'ang-hsi	1	0	4	3	2	7	19	4	0
Yung-cheng	1	2	0	1	0	2	0	0	3
Ch'ien-lung	1	2	0	0	1	17	0	7	1
Chia-ch'ing	1	1	2	0	0	6	0	4	0
Tao-kuang	2	1	0	0	1	9	0	7	0
Hsien-feng	1	0	0	0	2	10	2	1	0
T'ung-chih	1	0	0	1	2	1	0	0	0
Kuang-hsu	1	0	0	2	0	0	0	0	0
Hsuan-t'ung	—	—	—	—	—	—	—	—	—
Totals	11	6	6	10	9	52	31	26	4

SOURCES: *TCYT*, supplemented with information from *AHCL*, T'ang 1923, and Yü 1985b:57 on the Hsien-feng Emperor.

NOTE: C1 = empress;   C2 = *huang-kuei-fei*;   C3 = *kuei-fei*;   C4 = *fei*;   C5 = *pin*;   C6 = *kuei-jen*;
C7 = *shu-fei, ch'ang-tsai,* or *ta-ying*; C8 = palace service; C9 = other.

harem as a concubine of the second rank and was made empress in 1689, only one day before her death. The Kuang-hsu emperor's Tatara concubines were the granddaughters of a prominent provincial official, Yü-t'ai (*TCYT*; Hummel 1943 1:158–59).

Our discussion of the social backgrounds of concubines' families can be expanded. Table 5.4, which presents the clan affiliations of all imperial and princely consorts, includes 465 women, more than five times the number of imperial and princely first wives (cf. table 5.2). Again, the clustering of affines indicates that emperors and princes took their wives from a common pool (cf. table 5.2). This must of course be the case when the heir-apparent is not announced at an early age. Many of the bondservant women were concubines of low rank: among imperial concubines, for example, four of the seven Ch'en women never rose above the fifth rank, and only one, who had begun as a household servant, rose to the first rank. Miss Chang, who remained a lowly *shu-fei* despite giving birth to two daughters, and one each of the Lius and Wangs also entered as palace maids. Most had low rank; only two attained the title of concubine of the first rank.

What is equally striking, however, is the dominance of Manchu aristocratic clans like the Nara, the Niohuru, the Fuca, and the Gūwalgiya in this larger group of concubines. A finding that indirectly supports our argument that imperial concubines were not sharply differentiated from first wives lies in the varied ranks achieved by the women given by the Niohuru to the

TABLE 5.4 Leading Affines of Emperors and Princes

Affines	Imperial	Princely	Total
Number of consorts[a]	173	294	467
From families with one marriage	41	61	102
From families with two marriages	20	24	44
Mongol affines	25	25	50
Leading affines			
Chang	1	8	9
Ch'en	7	7	14
Fuca	5	12	17
Gūwalgiya	2[b]	18[b]	20
Heseri	6	1	7
Irgen Gioro	5	10	15
Li	3	17	20
Liu	4	13	17
Nara	7	18	25
Niohuru	15	8	23
Wang	3	13	16
Yehe Nara	9	4	13
Other surnames	20	55	75

SOURCE: *TCYT*, T'ang 1923.
[a] Excludes twelve imperial and two princely consorts whose surnames are unknown.
[b] Includes Suwan Gūwalgiya.

imperial house: they ranged from empress (seven) down to *shu-fei* (two). The Fuca daughters in the imperial harems included one empress and four concubines, none of whom was below the fourth rank. In contrast, the ranks achieved by the Nara women did not rise above the third-ranking *fei* and included some with the rank of *shu-fei*.

Entry into the imperial harem marked the onset of sustained relations between the concubine's family and the emperor, just as in the case of families providing a wife. It was the immediate gains, not the long-term rewards, of being related to a future emperor that induced respectable, even powerful families to give their daughters as concubines or ladies-in-waiting to princes and emperors. If the girl won the emperor's favor, her father's and brothers' careers would be transformed. Osi, father of the Shun-chih emperor's favorite concubine, was promoted from viscount to third-class earl "as a favor to his daughter" (Hummel 1943 1:301). Fiyanggu, the father of Yung-cheng's empress, was posthumously made a first-rank duke (*PCTC* 151.106). Chin Chien, the brother of Shu chia huang-kuei-fei, rose to become president of the Board of Works and the Board of Civil Appointments after his sister became Ch'ien-lung's favorite. Imperial favor raised A-pu-nai, the father of

K'ang-hsi's Liang fei, from slave to bondservant; it freed Kao Pin, the father of Ch'ien-lung's Hui-hsien huang-kuei-fei, from bondservitude, and Kao eventually became a grand secretary (Torbert 1977:75–76).

Imperial favor could transfer bannermen to the prestigious upper three banners—the Bordered Yellow, Plain Yellow, and Plain White—which had come under the emperor's control in the late seventeenth and early eighteenth centuries. In addition to T'ung Kuo-kang and T'ung Kuo-wei—who with their descendants were moved from the Chinese Plain Blue Banner to the Manchu Bordered Yellow Banner in 1688 (their sister was the K'ang-hsi emperor's mother)—we have the example of Ch'ung Ch'i, father of T'ung-chih's empress, who was shifted with his descendants from the Mongol Plain Blue Banner to the Manchu Bordered Yellow Banner after his daughter's marriage. Ch'ung Ch'i was also promoted to third-class duke as a sign of favor (Hummel 1943 1:208–9). Tz'u-hsi's branch of the Yehe Nara was also shifted from the Bordered Blue to the Bordered Yellow Banner after she became empress dowager in 1862 (Yü 1985b:127). Best of all, the imperial favor could wipe out career failure. Tz'u-hsi's father, Hui-cheng, died in official disgrace during the Taiping rebellion (1853); when Tz'u-hsi became empress dowager, she posthumously made him a third-grade duke (ibid., 133).

Ritual Incorporation

Whereas concubines in Han Chinese commoner households were purchased and entered without dowries or the wedding ritual, upper-ranking imperial concubines entered with dowries through the same process that selected empresses. Following precedents set by earlier dynasties (Soullière 1987: 179–85), the rituals of investiture for concubines of the upper four ranks were graded variations of the rituals that accompanied the taking of an empress. Although we shall focus on these rites of incorporation, we should note that postmortem commemoration in the Temple of the Ancestors and empirewide observance of their death days (Rawski 1988:236, 247) were accorded to all empresses and empress dowagers, regardless of their original status.

The model for all ranks was the "great wedding" (*ta-hun*), carried out when a reigning monarch took an empress, which followed the Chinese imperial tradition concerning wedding rituals. During the entire dynasty, this ritual was carried out only five times. Marriage, the event that marked the coming of age, was a necessary prelude to the end of a regency for a child emperor. The Shun-chih emperor, six *sui* when he was put on the throne in 1643, was married with the full rites in 1651 at the age of fourteen *sui*; K'ang-hsi, who ascended the throne at eight *sui*, was married at the age of twelve *sui* in 1665; T'ung-chih, who became emperor at six *sui*, was married at seventeen *sui*; and Kuang-hsü, who was four *sui* when he ascended the throne, was married at age nineteen (*TCYT*; also Hsin 1985).

The celebration of the imperial nuptials was an empirewide event that involved every citizen. During a "great wedding" (in 1888 lasting a total of twenty days) no punishments could be meted out. Officials wore special robes to mark the auspicious event; on the actual wedding day, everyone in the empire was required to wear red and green, the streets through which the wedding procession passed were cleaned, and the palace was decorated and refurbished. Of course, the state altars of Heaven and Earth as well as the ancestors were notified (with sacrifices) of the event, which was thus part of state as well as family ritual.

The sequence of events that comprised an imperial wedding began when the empress dowager, in consultation with the imperial princes, chose a bride (Wang Shu-ch'ing 1980; *TCHTSL* c. 324) and "ordered" the emperor to marry. To fix the betrothal (*na-ts'ai li*), two emissaries went with gifts (prescribed in the regulations)[20] and the imperial edict announced the betrothal to the mansion of the bride's father. Here the chief emissary read the edict aloud before the bride's father, who performed the full ritual obeisance (three prostrations, nine kowtows) in acknowledgment of the imperial grace. This betrothal ceremony was followed by a second, the *ta-cheng li*, when items to be used in the wedding itself were delivered to the bride's house by the emissaries, who announced the wedding date selected by the Board of Astronomy.

The dowry, normally given by the bride's family, was in this case prepared by the Imperial Household Department. Large quantities of court clothing, jewelry, gold and silver utensils, and furniture were presented to the bride several days before the wedding day, then ceremonially carried back to the palace.[21] The core of the wedding ceremony was the conferral of the title of empress on the bride (*ts'e-li*). The "gold seal" and "gold tablets" conferring the title of empress were presented to the bride at her father's house; the bride, dressed in the robes and accessories of an empress, was then carried to the palace in a sedan chair with the empress's regalia: she was the only female who (unescorted by the emperor) was permitted to enter through the Wu-men, the main gate to the palace (Shan 1960:100). The traditional nuptial chambers, in the east wing of the K'un-ning palace, were decorated with "double happiness" and other auspicious symbols (Yen Min 1980:13). The wedding ceremony was completed in the nuptial chambers, where the bride and groom sipped from the nuptial wine cup. On the next day the emperor and his bride paid their respects to the gods, immediate ancestors, and to his mother (the empress dowager). Several days later the couple received the congratulations of the court and officials; the empress dowager received congratulations; and the emperor and the empress dowager hosted banquets for the parents and relatives of the bride and bridegroom and for officials.

The "great wedding" parallels the ritual sequence found among Han

Chinese families. The betrothal, formalized with the presentation of gifts from the groom's family, is followed by the public transfer of the bride from her natal home to the palace, her appearance before her mother-in-law, and by banquets held to celebrate the event. But at critical points the ceremony modifies commoner practice to indicate the preeminent status of the groom. The bride's family members are his subjects; the bride's father must acknowledge the unequal relationship between wife-giver and emperor through obeisances; the rituals do not include the visit home by the bride, which was customary after a commoner wedding.

Gift exchanges also reflect the inequality of status between bride and groom. Here, as in the marriages of princes and princesses, the betrothal ceremony and the *ta-cheng li* are marked by presentations of gold, silver, livestock, furs, textiles, court clothing, and court accessories (including jewels) from the emperor to the bride, her mother, her father, her grandfather, and even her brothers. The banquet, held at the bride's father's house after the *na-ts'ai* rite, is provided by the Imperial Household Department and not by the bride's father. The Imperial Household Department provides all of the "dowry" as well as the bridewealth (Li P'eng-nien 1983) in a deliberate inversion of the commoner custom, which had the bride's family providing a dowry.

Archival documents concerning the "great weddings" of the T'ung-chih and Kuang-hsu emperors and information on the wedding of P'u-i, which was closely modeled on these historical precedents, provide evidence that imperial concubines entered the harem with rituals that resembled the taking of an empress. In the two "great weddings" of the nineteenth century, the empress's entry into the palace was preceded by the entry of concubines from highly ranked families. Four concubines, one of whom was the paternal aunt of the empress, entered the palace during the T'ung-chih emperor's "great wedding"; two sisters became the Kuang-hsu emperor's concubines during his "great wedding." And we know that the runner-up among the girls considered for empress was selected as his concubine during P'u-i's "great wedding" (P'u 1982).

A concubine also entered the palace with a "dowry" provided by the Imperial Household Department (KCTC nos. 2381, 2385; PAPS no. 2102). Unlike commoner women, whose namelessness reflected their subordinate status in Chinese society (R. Watson 1986), concubines of the upper four ranks, like empresses, were granted individual titles in life, and occasionally in death. The ritual for installation of concubines in the first three ranks, like the ceremonies for the installation of the empress, was also held in the T'ai-ho tien, the hall that was the center for court and state ritual (*KCTL* c. 2; *TCHTSL* c. 306). The patents of rank (a seal and tablets inscribed with the concubine's rank and name similar to those made for empresses and empresses dowager) were created whenever a woman was named to the first three ranks of concubines; concubines of the fourth rank were installed with a gold tablet but no seal. The investiture of concubines of the first three ranks was marked by sacrifices at the Temple of the Ancestors and the Feng-hsien-tien on the day preceding the ceremony to notify the ancestors about the event; this was omitted for the investiture of a fourth-ranking concubine.

Concubines selected for a "great wedding" received these symbols of rank in their father's house before they were conveyed to the palace (P'u 1982: 129). In 1872 the two fourth-ranking and one fifth-ranking concubines entered the palace two days before the empress. The third-ranking concubine joined them the next day. After entering the palace, all concubines worshiped before the ancestral portraits, paid their respects to the empresses dowager, and lit incense before the Buddhist altar in the palace in which they were to reside in a ritual that the new empress would herself perform the day after the nuptials (KCTC nos. 2379, 2381, 2383; P'u 1982:129).

The archival materials indicate that the ritual distinctions between the wife and concubines found in commoner households were not present in the Ch'ing system of imperial marriage. The rituals accompanying installation of imperial concubines of the first through fourth ranks resembled those for the installation of an empress: patents of ranks were conferred with prior no-tification of the ancestors, and the newcomer performed domestic rituals be-fore the palace equivalent of the domestic altar. The only ritual distinction enjoyed solely by the empress in a "great wedding" was her entry through the main gate;[22] concubines entered the palace through the Shen-wu, or back door. In a "great wedding," the newly installed concubines served as ladies-in-waiting for the empress on her wedding day and participated in the rites that took place on that occasion. They were also included in the major domestic court rituals that involved the empress during the course of the year (KTCL c. 2).

Not all concubines were so thoroughly integrated into the imperial family, however. The rituals show a clear distinction between the four highest ranks and lower-ranking concubines, who received no patents and who entered the palace without prior sacrifice at the ancestral altars (TCHTSL:306). These lower-ranking concubines were also the women most vulnerable to omission from the imperial genealogy.[23] At the same time, as we have already observed, it was entirely possible for even these low-ranking concubines to be promoted and even to attain the rank of empress.

CONCLUSION

The marriage patterns of the Ch'ing imperial house had a direct effect on the structure of power within Ch'ing society. Marriage exchange with banner allies was a vital element in the supraethnic policies of the early Manchu rulers during the conquest period. Later emperors confronted a different issue: how to prevent the Manchus from being completely assimilated into the Han Chinese population that they ruled. Although banner troops were stationed in separate garrisoned quarters in major cities in China, there were clear signs in the mid-eighteenth century of the loss of Manchu language skills among bannermen and indications that Manchu dress and other customs were being supplanted by Chinese norms. It is no accident that this was precisely the period that Manchu tradition and social structure were "fixed" by being written down; the concern with preservation of Manchu ethnicity voiced by the Ch'ien-lung emperor and his successors undoubtedly helped to perpetuate the prohibition against intermarriage with Han Chinese.

As Jennifer Holmgren points out in her chapter in this volume, the relation between marriage and politics is highly complex and variable. The Ch'ing system of political endogamy reinforced the historical master-servant tie of the Aisin Gioro with bannermen. The Ch'ing prohibition on marriage with Han Chinese outside the banner system removed Chinese officials from using this avenue to heighten their power: in contrast to the Chinese traditional historiography, which placed Chinese at the heart of the Ch'ing political system, our study suggests that they were only peripheral players in marriage politics.

The Ch'ing pattern of intermarriage with bannermen can be contrasted with the Northern Sung imperial house studied by Chaffee in this volume. Northern Sung emperors forged marriage alliances with the civil elite—or, more precisely, the civil elite residing in or near the Northern Sung capital— as a means of winning over potential rivals. The Ch'ing, like the Ming rulers (Soullière 1988), deliberately avoided marriages with the civil elite in an effort to prevent imperial consorts and their relatives from obtaining access to political power. At the same time, as we noted earlier, the Northern Sung, Ming, and Ch'ing rulers all used marriage as a means of reinforcing their bonds with the military elite.

The Ch'ing succession system also altered the structure of power within the harem. By rejecting the Ming principle of eldest-son succession, the Ch'ing made the sons of all consorts eligible to become emperor. As we have seen, the Ch'ing (like the Ming) took consorts from both the very top and the very bottom of the banner hierarchy: daughters of noble households mingled and competed for the emperor's favor with maids from bondservant families. Recruitment policies allowed distant sororal and maternal relations to enter the harem, where each served as a check on the others. The deliberate social fluidity among consorts and the possibility of having an "upstart" triumph over her social betters served as an institutionalized check on the political ambitions of any particular group among the banner elite.

The Ch'ing tried to make usurpation more difficult by widening the circle of potential competitors for imperial favor. We have been at some pains to demonstrate that on critical questions like succession, the sons of lower-ranking concubines could and frequently did win out over rivals with mothers of higher rank. The fluidity of succession subverted the hierarchical order of the harem and served to check the emergence of powerful imperial affines. When we survey the history of the dynasty, the problem of powerful affines is conspicuously absent.

In this chapter we have argued that the criteria used to determine the absence of polygyny among Chinese commoner families reveal that Ch'ing imperial marriage practices differ so markedly as to constitute a separate marriage model—one that is neither monogamy nor polygyny. Why then did the Ch'ing so emphasize hierarchy and gradations of rank in the ritual installation and living allowances of concubines?

Maurice Bloch has noted that rituals are not necessarily faithful reflections of social reality; rather, "the roles that people act in rituals do not reflect or define social status. . . . These roles are part of a drama that creates an image . . . that needs to be created because in many ways it contradicts what everybody knows" (1986:45). Chinese commoner families emphasize the primacy of the first wife precisely because in many cases it is not the first wife but a younger concubine who wins the master's affections and threatens to disrupt family harmony by her power to obtain an unfair share of the family's resources. The institutionalized emphasis on the primacy of the first wife aims to keep family tensions under control so that the patriline can be perpetuated. The vulnerability of the Ch'ing empress, who was frequently chosen without regard for the emperor's personal wishes, is compounded by her rivals' powerful relatives and elite social backgrounds. Nor, as the case of Tz'u-hsi demonstrates, did the empress installed during her husband's lifetime have more power because of her ritual superiority than the mother promoted to empress dowager by her son. The ritual acknowledgment of the empress as the head of the harem preserved the illusion of order in a situation that was in reality extremely fluid and dependent on the whims of the ruler.

If empresses were frequently only nominal heads of imperial harems, there could be no doubt that in the Ch'ing, as in virtually every dynasty, the emperor's mother, the empress dowager, did exercise real authority and power. Her legitimacy was firmly grounded in Confucian teachings: the highly publicized exercises in filial piety of the K'ang-hsi and Ch'ien-lung emperors may have been politically manipulative (S. Wu 1979; Kahn 1971), but the affection these rulers bore their grandmothers and mothers was no less real for all that.

Empresses dowager were frequently joined in the inner court councils by imperial princes, the agnates of the collateral branches of the ruling house. The Ch'ing succession system permitted younger sons to participate in government and to vie for the ultimate prize, the throne. The Ch'ing thus differs from native Chinese regimes, which barred nonheirs from politics and power. Throughout the dynasty, we find both imperial agnates and emperors' sons being appointed to carry out substantive tasks. These assignments continued even after the emperors had successfully overcome the collegial traditions of rule that had characterized most of the seventeenth century. The K'ang-hsi emperor tested his eldest son by making him regent while he himself led troops against the Western Mongols; he sent another son to command the Ch'ing banners in another campaign (S. Wu 1979). Imperial princes took civil service positions in the ministries; they also served as administrators in the banners and the Imperial Clan Court.

In the late seventeenth and eighteenth centuries, the political activities of imperial agnates were never a threat to the throne because of the strong leadership provided by the emperors. During the late nineteenth century, however, with a succession of infant-emperors, imperial agnates played leading roles in national politics. Prince Kung, son of the Tao-kuang emperor, was designated to handle negotiations with the foreign powers in 1860 when his half brother the Hsien-feng emperor fled Peking; of the four adjutants-general who were in charge in the capital in the last months of the Hsien-feng reign, three were imperial agnates and one was an imperial affine (Hummel 1944 2:666, 668, 924).

In the period from 1862 to 1897 China's government was dominated by the empress dowager Tz'u-hsi, who ruled not so much with the help of her natal kin as with the support of her husband's half brothers. The struggle for power that followed the Hsien-feng emperor's death was between two factions dominated by imperial agnates: the empress dowagers Tz'u-an and Tz'u-hsi (the biological mother of the T'ung-chih emperor) won this contest with the help of their brother-in-law, Prince Kung (Wright 1966:16–17). This alliance of imperial princes and the empresses dowager continued in the subsequent Kuang-hsu reign (Kwong 1984; Hummel 1943:384–86), when Prince Ch'un, father of the emperor and Tz'u-hsi's brother-in-law, enjoyed great influence at court. The marriage and succession practices of the Ch'ing had succeeded in preventing substantive political challenges to the throne from affines, but could not guard against challenges from agnates. The Manchu traditions of collegial rule by imperial agnates reemerged during the last decades of Ch'ing governance.

NOTES

1. Here and throughout this chapter, "consorts" refers to the empress and concubines of an emperor.

2. I am grateful to Pamela Kyle Crossley, who generously read an earlier draft of this paper and corrected my references to Manchu names and institutions, and to James L. Watson, who lent me books on Mongol society. I should also record my gratitude to the staff of the Number One Historical Archives in Peking for their help on my research in 1987 and 1988.

3. On Nurgaci's competition with his brother and his eldest son, see Yen Ch'ung-nien 1983:281, 283; on sibling rivalry in Hung Taiji's generation, see Sun and Li 1982:416–17.

4. But in the case of the T'ung-chih emperor, there was no choice because he was an only son. Ch'ing empresses, like their counterparts in earlier dynasties studied by Holmgren, were relatively infertile. Low fertility and high infant mortality meant that frequently there was no empress's son living at an emperor's death, so the deliberate rejection of such a candidate occurred only once in the whole dynasty.

5. For information on these Manchu rulers and emperors, see their individual biographies in Hummel, ed., 1943–44.

6. On the foundation myths, see Crossley 1987. The Aisin Gioro lineage conforms to the definitions proposed in J. Watson 1982; by contrast, the other Manchu descent groups that evolved out of the *mukun* of the pre-1644 era are called "clans" throughout this paper. See n. 8 below.

7. The 378 members of the main line (1660) are estimated to have increased to more than 29,292 persons by 1915 (Harrell et al. 1985:38).

8. The term "clan" is deliberately used in preference to "lineage" in an effort to differentiate the Manchu *mukūn* from the Chinese lineage, which it eventually came to resemble. The Manchu *mukūn* was a loosely organized kinship group based on the pastoral economy that could fission or combine according to economic circumstances. As Crossley (1987) notes, the production of written genealogies in the eighteenth century artificially fixed the clan as the historical center of Manchu culture and systematized clan identities for the first time in Manchu history.

9. This event is omitted from the *TCYT*, but appears in the Niohuru genealogy (Huang 1986:636) and has been "filled in" from the *shih-lu* account by Li Feng-min 1984.

10. According to Shirokogoroff (1973:70), the marriage of a male with father's sister's daughter was rare among Manchus in the twentieth century; this was the "disapproved" form of cross-cousin marriage among Han Chinese (Gallin 1963:108).

11. T'ung-chih and Kuang-hsu were childless; P'u-i, the last emperor, abdicated as a child. Here and elsewhere in this paper, the ranks given to Nurgaci's consorts are anachronistic; the first Manchu ruler to adopt the Chinese ranks was Hung Taiji. See Wang Shu-ch'ing 1986:57–61.

12. Not to be confused with the "T'ieh-mao-tzu wang" (princes of the iron cap), also known as the Eight Great Houses, who were all Aisin Gioro. For sketches of the founders of the Manchu aristocracy, see Yang and Chou 1986:46–63.

13. The marital relationships did not preclude execution of these imperial affines at the time of the San-fan uprisings: see Kessler 1976, chap. 4.

14. The imperial genealogy indicates that the daughter of a Chinese senior vice-president of the Ministry of Personnel, Shih Shen, joined the Shun-chih emperor's harem.

15. This was certainly the case when the Ch'ing is compared to the Northern Sung; Chung 1981:18–20 states that the largest number of consorts recorded in the Northern Sung was for the Hui-tsung emperor, who had nineteen; the average for the nine Sung emperors was ten, as compared with the Ch'ing average of seventeen.

16. During the reigns of the Shun-chih and K'ang-hsi emperors, the lowest rank was the *shu-fei* (ordinary consort).

17. Princes were in theory allowed to have a wife (*ti fujin*) and four concubines (*ts'e fujin*), but the genealogies also list lower-ranking concubines, called *shu fujin*, and, lower still, *ying-ch'ieh*. When a prince became emperor, the titles of his concubines were changed to accord with the imperial ranks.

18. That the Manchus closely studied the late Ming precedents in preparation for the selection of an empress for the first Ch'ing emperor is clear from a Grand Secretariat memorial dated November 25, 1653, in which Jirgalang, Prince Cheng, reported on the procedures used in 1577 to select the Wan-li emperor's empress: see LYYS. My thanks to Susan Naquin for this reference.

19. Wang Tao-ch'eng 1985a:306 argues that the distinction between the *hsiu-nü* and *kung-nü* draft came about after the Yung-cheng reign.

20. The horses and saddles that were included were not a Manchu addition: see Soullière 1987:194–95 for the comparable Ming gift exchanges. Horses, sheep, camels, and weapons were also part of the gift exchanges for the marriages of princes and princesses.

21. In the *ta-hun* section of the *TCHTSL*, c. 324, the term for dowry (*chuang-lien*) is used to describe items sent by the court to the bride. The illustration of the Kuang-hsu emperor's *ta-hun* (*CTKTSH*:256, illus. 399), which depicts the delivery of the empress's dowry to the palace, is erroneous in its assumption that the *chuang-lien* being delivered to the palace was provided by the bride's family: archival documents in Beijing include the *chuang-lien* lists for the T'ung-chih and Kuang-hsu *ta-hun* (KCTC), with notes on the subagencies within the Nei-wu-fu responsible for supplying each item.

22. This ritual distinction was thus granted only five times in the course of the dynasty.

23. Analysis of the entries in the various sources that supplement the imperial genealogy (*AHCL*; T'ang 1923) shows that there are eight imperial concubines (from the Shun-chih emperor on) whose surnames are unrecorded in the *TCYT*; all were childless. Three additional concubines of the Hsien-feng emperor whose surnames are unrecorded have been identified from archival sources as Yehe Nara women (Wang Tao-ch'eng 1985b:53), and they are not included in the figure cited. There are twenty-seven other concubines whose clan names are known, but whose father's names are unrecorded: of these eleven had children and are recorded in the *TCYT*, which also records only three of the remaining sixteen childless concubines. All of these twenty-seven concubines occupied the rank of *shu-fei* or *kuei-jen*. Imperial Household Department materials held in the Number One Historical Archives suggest that there were even greater omissions of concubines from the *TCYT*. Comparisons of the *TCYT* with lists of recipients of the annual palace distribution of gifts, held at the New Year, show that childless *kuei-jen*, *ch'ang-tsai*, and *ta-ying* were most likely to be dropped from the records because of their infertility and low status (Yü 1985b:57 for 1853–54 lists; PAPS nos. 1251, 1254, 642, for palace lists of 1751, 1756, and 1767; PAPS no. 1246, for palace lists of 1830, 1832, 1833, 1846; all included names of ranked concubines who were not listed in the *TCYT* or *AHCL*. Another indication of the extent of underreporting is provided by comparison of the numbers of empresses and concubines recorded in the *TCYT* for the Ch'ien-lung emperor (twenty-nine) with the forty-one women buried with him: Wang Lai-yin 1983:25.

GLOSSARY

ch'ang-tsai 常在
chi-fu 吉服
chin-pao 金寶
chin-shih 進士
chin-ts'e 金冊
ch'u-ting 初定
chuang-lien 粧奩
chuang-yuan 狀元
efu 額駙
fei 妃
feng-ying 奉迎
ho-ch'in 合卺
hsiu-nü 秀女
huang-kuei-fei 皇貴妃
ko-ko 格格
kuei-fei 貴妃
kuei-jen 貴人
Ku-lun kung-chu   固倫公主
kung-nü 宮女
Li fan yuan 理藩院

na-ts'ai li 納采禮
pin 嬪
Shang-shu-fang   上書房
shih-nü 使女
shu-fei 庶妃
shu fujin 庶福晉
sui 歲
ta-cheng li 大徵禮
ta-hun 大婚
ta-ying 答應
ti fujin 嫡福晉
ts'e-feng 冊奉
ts'e fujin 側福晉
ts'e-li 冊立
tsung-jen fu 宗人府
tsung-shih 宗室
wen 文
wu 武
ying-ch'ieh 媵妾

REFERENCES

Primary Sources

AHCL   *Ai-hsin chueh-lo tsung-p'u* 愛新覺羅宗譜. 1937–38 edition.

Ch'in-ting ta-Ch'ing t'ung-li 欽定大清通禮.

CTKTSH   *Ch'ing-tai kung-t'ing sheng-huo* 清代宮廷生活. 1985; reprint, Taipei: Nan-t'ien shu-chü, 1986.

HPTL   *Ch'in-ting hu-pu tse-li* 欽定戶部則例. 1865 edition.

KCTL   *Ch'in-ting kung-chung hsien-hsing tse-li* 欽定宮中現行則例. 1865 edition.

KCTC   Palace affairs (kung-chung tsa-chien), Rituals (li-i) section, Number One Historical Archives, Peking.

LYYS   Taken from the Grand Secretariat (Nei-ko) memorials deposited in the Institute of History and Philology, Academia Sinica, Taipei. Only one document, dated Shun-chih 10, tenth month, sixth day–1 (A17–166), was used in this paper.

NWFTL   *Tsung-kuan Nei-wu-fu hsien-hsing tse-li* 總管內務府現行則例. 1937 edition.

PAPS   Palace affairs, personnel section, Number One Historical Archives, Peking.

PCTC   *Ch'in-ting pa-ch'i t'ung-chih* 欽定八旗通志. 1739 edition.

T'ang Pang-chih 唐邦治. 1923. *Ch'ing huang-shih ssu-p'u* 清皇室四譜. Reprint, Taipei: Wen-hai, 1966.

TCHTSL   *Ch'in-ting ta-Ch'ing hui-tien shih-li* 欽定大清會典事例. 1899 edition.

TCSL   *Ta Ch'ing Shih-tsu Chang-huang-ti shih-lu* 大清世祖章皇帝實錄. 1937–38;
               reprint, Taipei: Taiwan Hua-wen shu-chü, 1964.
TCYT   *Ta Ch'ing yü-tieh* 大清玉牒. Number One Historical Archives, Peking.
               MS. Utah Genealogical Society, Salt Lake City, Utah, microfilm.
TJFTL   *Ch'in-ting tsung-jen-fu tse-li* 欽定宗人府則例. 1908 edition.

Secondary Sources

An Shuang-ch'eng 安双成. 1983. "Shun, K'ang, Yung san-ch'ao pa-ch'i ting-e
    ch'ien-hsi" 順康雍三朝八旗定額浅析 (Analysis of Eight Banner strengths in the
    first three Ch'ing reigns). *Li-shih tang-an*, no. 2:100–103.
Bawden, C. R. 1968. *The Modern History of Mongolia*. New York: Praeger.
Bloch, Maurice. 1986. *From Blessing to Violence: History and Ideology in the Circumcision
    Ritual of the Merina of Madagascar*. Cambridge: Cambridge University Press.
Brunnert, H. S., and V. V. Hagelstrom. 1911. *Present Day Political Organization of
    China*. Rev. N. T. Kolessoff, trans. A. Beltchenko and E. E. Moran. Peking.
Chao, Yun-t'ien 趙云田. 1984. "Ch'ing-tai ti 'pei-chih e-fu' chih-tu" 清代的
    '备指額駙'制度(The institution for picking imperial sons-in-law in the Ch'ing).
    Ku-kung po-wu-yuan yuan-k'an, no. 4:28–37.
Ch'en, Chia-hua 陳佳华. 1984. "Pa-ch'i chih-tu yen-chiu shu-lueh" 八旗制度
    研究述略 (Survey of research on the Eight Banner system). *She-hui k'o-hsueh
    chi-k'an*, nos. 5:109–16, 6:113–20.
Chou Yuan-lien 周远廉 and Chao Shih-yü 趙世瑜. 1986. *Huang fu she cheng wang
    To-erh-kun ch'üan chuan* 皇父攝政王多尔衮全傳 (The complete biography of Im-
    perial Father Regent Dorgon). Ch'angch'un: Kirin Memoirs Press.
Chung, Priscilla Ching. 1981. *Palace Women in the Northern Sung, 960–1126*. Leiden: E. J.
    Brill.
Crossley, Pamela. 1983. "The Tong in Two Worlds: Cultural Identities in Liaodong
    and Nurgan during the 13th–17th Centuries." *Ch'ing-shih wen-t'i* 4.9:21–46.
———. 1987. "*Manzhou yuanliu kao* and the Formalization of the Manchu Heritage."
    Journal of Asian Studies 46.4:761–90.
———. 1989. "The Qianlong Retrospect on the Chinese-Martial (Hanjun) Ban-
    ners." *Late Imperial China* 10.1:63–107.
Ebrey, Patricia. 1986. "Concubines in Sung China." *Journal of Family History* 11.1:1–
    24.
Feng, Han-yi. 1967. *The Chinese Kinship System*. Harvard-Yenching Institute Studies
    22. Cambridge: Harvard University Press.
Fletcher, Joseph. 1978. "Ch'ing Inner Asia c. 1800." In *The Cambridge History of China*,
    vol. 10, ed. John K. Fairbank. Cambridge: Cambridge University Press, pp. 35–
    106.
———. 1979. "Turco-Mongolian Monarchic Tradition in the Ottoman Empire." In
    Eucharisterion, ed. Ihor Sevcenko and Frank E. Sysyn, pt. 1, pp. 236–51. Cam-
    bridge, Mass.: Ukrainian Research Institute.
Gallin, Bernard. 1963. "Cousin Marriage in China." *Ethnology* 2.1:104–08.
Harrell, Stevan, Susan Naquin, and Deyuan Ju. 1985. "Lineage Genealogy: The
    Genealogical Records of the Qing Imperial Lineage." *Late Imperial China* 6.2:37–
    47.
Holmgren, Jennifer. 1986. "Observations on Marriage and Inheritance Practices in

Early Mongol and Yuan Society, with Particular Reference to the Levirate." *Journal of Asian History* 20:127–92.

Hou Shou-ch'ang 侯壽昌. 1982. "K'ang-hsi mu-hsi k'ao" 康熙母系考 (On the maternal ancestors of the K'ang-hsi emperor). *Li-shih tang-an*, no. 4:100–105.

Hsin Hao 心昊. 1985. "Kuang-hsu ta-hun tien-li tang-an" 光緒大婚典禮档案 (Records relating to the Kuang-hsu emperor's wedding rite). *Li-shih tang-an*, no. 2:132–34.

Hsu, Francis L. K. 1967. *Under the Ancestors' Shadow: Kinship, Personality and Social Mobility in China*. Stanford: Stanford University Press. Reissue, 1971.

Hua Li 华立. 1983. "Ch'ing-tai ti Man-Meng lien-yin" 清代的滿蒙联姻 (Marriage alliances of Manchus and Mongols in the Ch'ing). *Min-tsu yen-chiu*, no. 2:45–54, 79.

Huang, Pei. 1974. *Autocracy at Work: A Study of the Yung-cheng Period, 1723–1735*. Bloomington: Indiana University Press.

———. 黃培. 1986. "Ch'ing-ch'u ti Man-chou kuei-tsu (1583–1795)—Niu-hu-lu tsu" 清初的滿洲貴族 (1583–1795)—鈕祜祿族 (The early Manchu aristocracy: the Niohuru clan, 1583–1795). In *Lao Chen-i hsien-sheng pa-chih jung-ch'ing lun-wen chi* 勞貞一先生八秩榮慶論文集 (Festschrift for Professor Lao Chen-i), comp. Lao Chen-i hsien-sheng pa-chih jung-ch'ing lun-wen chi pien-chi wei-yuan-hui 勞貞一先生八秩榮慶論文集編輯委員會, pp. 629–64. Taipei: Commercial Press.

Hummel, Arthur W., ed. 1943–44. *Eminent Chinese of the Ch'ing Period*. 2 vols. Washington, D.C.: Government Printing Office.

Kahn, Harold L. 1971. *Monarchy in the Emperor's Eyes: Image and Reality in the Ch'ien-lung Reign*. Cambridge: Harvard University Press.

Kessler, Lawrence D. 1976. *K'ang-hsi and the Consolidation of Ch'ing Rule, 1661–1684*. Chicago: University of Chicago Press.

Krader, Lawrence. 1963. *Social Organization of the Mongol-Turkic Pastoral Nomads*. The Hague: Mouton.

Kwong, Luke S. K. 1984. *A Mosaic of the Hundred Days: Personalities, Politics, and Ideas of 1898*. Cambridge: Council on East Asian Studies, Harvard University.

Lattimore, Owen. 1934. *The Mongols of Manchuria: Their Tribal Divisions, Geographical Distribution, Historical Relations with Manchus and Chinese and Present Political Problems*. New York: John Day.

Li Feng-min 李風民. 1984. "Ho-shih kung-chu Mu-k'u-shih ti hun-p'ei wen-t'i" 和碩公主穆庫什的婚配問題 (The marriage problem of Princess Mukushih). *Ku-kung po-wu-yuan yuan-k'an*, no. 2:26.

Li Hsueh-chih 李学智. 1985. "Man-chou min-tsu ch'u-hsing ch'i chih hun-yin hsi-su" 滿洲民族初興期之婚姻習俗 (Marriage customs of the Manchus in the early period). *Pien-cheng yen-chiu-so nien-pao* (Kuo-li cheng-chih ta-hsueh) 16:45–65.

Li P'eng-nien 李鵬年. 1983. "Kuang-hsu-ti ta-hun pei-pan hao-yung kai-shu" 光緒帝大婚備辦耗用概述 (A general study of the expenditures for the Kuang-hsu emperor's wedding). *Ku-kung po-wu-yuan yuan-k'an*, no. 2:80–86.

Lu Kung 路工. 1982. "Huang-t'ai-hou ho kung-nü ti sheng-huo tai-yü" 皇太后和宮女的生活待遇 (The life conditions of the empress dowager and the palace maidens). In *Yen-ching ch'un-ch'iu* 燕京春秋 (History of the capital), comp. Pei-ching shih yen-chiu hui 北京史研究會. Peking: Pei-ching ch'u-pan-she.

Lü Ming-hui 盧明輝. 1985. "Shih-lun Ch'ing-ch'u Man-tsu t'ung-chih che tui Meng,

Han ti cheng-ts'e" 試論清初滿族統治者對蒙漢的政策 (Early Ch'ing policy toward the Mongols and Han Chinese). *Min-tsu yen-chiu*, no. 3:17–22.

Macfarlane, Alan. 1986. *Marriage and Love in England: Modes of Reproduction, 1300–1840*. Oxford: Basil Blackwell.

P'u Chia 溥佳. 1982. "P'u-i ta-hun chi-shih" 溥儀大婚紀實 (P'u-i's wedding). In *Wan Ch'ing kung-t'ing sheng-huo chien-wen* 晚清宮廷生活見聞 (Life in the palace in late Ch'ing), comp. Chung-kuo jen-min cheng-chih hsieh-shang hui-yi ch'üan-kuo wei-yuan-hui 中国人民政治協商會議全国委員會. Peking: Wen-shih tzu-liao ch'u-pan-she.

Rawski, Evelyn S. 1988. "The Imperial Way of Death." In *Death Ritual in Late Imperial and Modern China*, ed. James L. Watson and Evelyn S. Rawski, pp. 228–53. Berkeley and Los Angeles: University of California Press.

Shan Shih-yuan 單士元. 1960. "Kuan-yü Ch'ing kung ti hsiu-nü ho kung-nü" 関于清宮的秀女和宮女 (On the Ch'ing palace women). *Ku-kung po-wu-yuan yuan-k'an*, no. 2:97–103.

Shirokogoroff, S. M. 1924; reprint, 1973. *Social Organization of the Manchus*. New York: AMS Press.

Soullière, Ellen. 1988. "The Imperial Marriages of the Ming Dynasty." *Papers on Far Eastern History* 37:1–30.

Spence, Jonathan. 1966. *Ts'ao Yin and the K'ang-hsi Emperor, Bondservant and Master*. New Haven: Yale University Press.

Sun Hsiao-en 孫孝恩. 1985. *Kuang-hsu p'ing-chuan* 光緒評傳 (Biography of the Kuang-hsu emperor). Shenyang: Liao-ning chiao-yü ch'u-pan-she.

Sun Wen-liang 孫文良 and Li Chih-t'ing 李治亭. 1982. *Ch'ing T'ai-tsung ch'üan chuan* 清太宗全傳 (Biography of Hung Taiji). Kirin: Jen-min ch'u-pan-she.

Tao, Jing-shen. 1976. *The Jurchen in Twelfth-Century China*. Seattle: University of Washington Press.

Torbert, Preston M. 1977. *The Ch'ing Imperial Household Department: A Study of Its Organization and Principal Functions, 1661–1796*. Cambridge: Council on East Asian Studies, Harvard University.

Wakeman, Frederic. 1985. *The Great Enterprise: The Manchu Reconstruction of Imperial Order in Seventeenth-Century China*. 2 vols. Berkeley and Los Angeles: University of California Press.

Wang Lai-yin 汪萊茵. 1983. "Ho-hsiao kung-chu—Ch'ien-lung ti ti chang-shang ming-chu" 和孝公主—乾隆帝的掌上明珠 (Princess Ho-hsiao—the Ch'ien-lung emperor's jewel). *Tzu-chin ch'eng*, no. 2:25–26.

Wang Shu-ch'ing 王樹卿. 1980. "Ch'ing-tai huang-ti ti ta-hun" 清代皇帝的大婚 (The marriages of Ch'ing emperors). *Tzu-chin ch'eng*, no. 2:11–12.

———. 1986. "Ch'ing-tai hou-fei" 清代后妃 (Ch'ing empresses and concubines). In *Ch'ing kung shih-shih* 清宮史事 (Ch'ing palace affairs), ed. Wang Shu-ch'ing and Li P'eng-nien 李鵬年. Peking: Tzu-chin ch'eng.

Wang Tao-ch'eng 王道成. 1985a. "Ts'ung Hsueh P'an sung mei tai-hsuan t'an ch'i—kuan yü Ch'ing-tai ti hsiu-nü chih-tu" 從薛蟠送妹待選談起—関于清代的秀女制度 (From Hsüeh P'an's sending his sister to await selection—on the Ch'ing *hsiu-nü* system). In *Pei-ching shih-yuan* 北京史苑 (Historical reminiscences of Peking), comp. Pei-ching shih she-hui k'o-hsueh yen-chiu so, Pei-ching shih-yuan pien-chi pu 北京市社會科學研究所, 北京史苑編輯部. Peking: Beijing Press.

————. 1985b. "Yeh-ho-na-la yü Ai-hsin chueh-lo chia-tsu" 叶赫那拉與愛新覺羅家族 (The Yehonala and the Aisin Gioro descent groups). In *Hsi t'ai-hou* 西太后 (The empress dowager of the western palace), ed. Yü Ping-k'un 俞炳坤 et al. Peking: Tzu-chin ch'eng.

Watson, James L. 1982. "Chinese Kinship Reconsidered: Anthropological Perspectives on Historical Research." *China Quarterly* 92:589–622.

Watson, Rubie S. 1986. "The Named and the Nameless: Gender and Person in Chinese Society." *American Ethnologist* 13.4:619–31.

Wei Ch'i 未齊. 1984. "Ch'ing-tai ti-i-ts'u hsuan hsiu-nü" 清代第一次選秀女 (The first *hsiu-nü* selection in the Ch'ing). *Tzu-chin ch'eng* 26:20.

Wei Ch'ing-yuan 韦庆远, Wu Ch'i-yen 吳奇衍, and Lu Su 魯素. 1982. *Ch'ing-tai nü-pi chih-tu* 清代奴婢制度 (The Ch'ing bondservant system). Peking: Chung-kuo jen-min ta-hsueh.

Wright, Mary. 1966. *The Last Stand of Chinese Conservatism: The T'ung-chih Restoration, 1862–1874*. Stanford: Stanford University Press.

Wu, Silas. 1979. *Passage to Power: K'ang-hsi and His Heir Apparent, 1661–1722*. Cambridge: Harvard University Press.

Wu Yang 吳洋. 1987. "Ch'ing-tai 'E-lo-ssu tso-ling' k'ao-lueh" 清代'俄羅斯佐領'考略 (The Russian company in the Ch'ing). *Li-shih yen-chiu*, no. 5:83–84.

Yang Hsueh-ch'en 楊学琛 and Chou Yuan-lien 周远廉. 1986. *Ch'ing-tai pa-ch'i wang-kung kuei-tsu hsing-shuai shih* 清代八旗王公貴族興衰史 (The rise and fall of the Eight Banner aristocracy during the Ch'ing). Shenyang: Liao-ning jen-min ch'u-pan-she.

Yang Shao-hsien 楊紹猷. 1984. "Ming-tai Meng-ku tsu hun-yin ho chia-t'ing ti t'e-tien" 明代蒙古族婚姻和家庭的特点 (Special characteristics of Mongol family and marriage in the Ming). *Min-tsu yen-chiu*, no. 4:30–38, 15.

Yeh Chih-ju 叶志如. 1984. "K'ang, Yung, Ch'ien shih-ch'i hsin-che-k'u jen ti ch'eng-fen chi jen-shen kuan-hsi" 康雍乾時期辛者庫人的成分及人身関係 (The status and personal relations of *hsin-che-k'u* in the K'ang-hsi, Yung-cheng, and Ch'ien-lung eras). *Min-tsu yen-chiu*, no. 1:37–45, 36.

Yen Ch'ung-nien 閻崇年. 1983. *Nu-erh-ha-ch'ih chuan* 努尔哈赤傳 (Biography of Nurgaci). Peking: Jen-min ch'u-pan-she.

Yen Min 燕民. 1980. "Ti hou chieh-hun ti tung-fang" 帝后結婚的洞房 (The imperial nuptial chamber). *Tzu-chin ch'eng*, no. 2:13.

Yü Ping-k'un 俞炳坤. 1985a. "Tz'u-hsi chia shih k'ao" 慈禧家世考 (Tz'u-hsi's family background). *Ku-kung po-wu-yuan yuan-k'an*, nos. 3:127–33, 111; 4:9–17.

————. 1985b. "Tz'u-hsi ju-kung shih-chien, shen-fen, ho feng-hao" 慈禧入宮時間, 身份和封号 (The date of Tz'u-hsi's entry into the palace, her status and title). In *Hsi-t'ai-hou* 西太后 (Empress Dowager Tz'u-hsi), by Yü Ping-k'un et al. Peking: Tzu-chin ch'eng.

SIX

Grooming a Daughter for Marriage

Brides and Wives in the Mid-Ch'ing Period

Susan Mann

莫看十八姑娘粧
要觀八十婆婆喪
The bride's dowry at eighteen means nothing;
The grandmother's funeral at eighty tells all.
—NINGPO SAYING (HO CHU 1973:227)

Marriage was the ladder of success for women in late imperial China. Even the bride who began with a modest wedding ("three cups of weak tea and a bow at the family shrine") could end her life in bounty ("mouth full of sweetcakes, playing with grandsons"). A lavish dowry nonetheless meant something: it testified to the bride's family's status (Harrell and Dickey 1985), and it was likely to complement generous betrothal gifts, one gauge of the groom's ability to provide for a daughter's long-term security (Parish and Whyte 1978:180–83). In a society that frowned upon remarriage, an extravagant dowry marked a family's confidence that their daughter would marry only once. In addition, dowry provided an awesome public display, enabling the dowered bride to enter her new home with style and dignity. Perhaps most important of all, dowry that clearly matched or exceeded the likely betrothal gifts and wedding costs shouldered by the groom's family meant that the bride was not being sold. The pervasive traffic in women is described elsewhere in this volume by Rubie Watson and Gail Hershatter. The dowered bride belonged to that select category of women who were "espoused by betrothal" (*p'in tse wei ch'i*), chosen for their virtue to become wives, distinguished forever from concubines or courtesans.[1]

During the mid-Ch'ing period, dowry was the hallmark of a respectable wedding. Commoners went into debt and postponed marriages in order to dower their daughters in style. Whereas during the Sung period, as discussed in Ebrey's chapter here, the dowry was above all an upper-class

concern—families complained about expensive dowries because they dissi-
pated corporate estates—in Ch'ing times dowry givers quite clearly included families of more modest means. Such households might exhaust
their resources to marry off a daughter, a practice that also caused upper-
class writers to complain, as we see in the following remarks written by
Ch'en Hung-mou in the middle of the eighteenth century:

> When it comes to marriage, people care only about keeping up with the
> times. They spend extravagantly on material things. When they present be-
> trothal gifts (*p'in*) or make up a dowry (*lien-tseng*), the embroidered silks and
> satins and the gold and pearls are matched one for one. Utensils and articles
> for the home and business are the finest and the most expensive, and they
> must be beautifully made as well. The decorated pavilion to welcome the
> bride and her elegant sedan chair, the banquet where the two families meet
> and exchange gifts, all require the most fantastic outlays of cash. One sees
> the worst of this among poorer people, who will borrow heavily to give the
> appearance of having property, all for the sake of a single public display,
> ignoring the needs of the "eight mouths" at home. Families with daughters
> are the most burdened; the families with sons can procrastinate and put off
> [marriage plans].

Ch'en thought it would be a good idea if everyone limited dowry proces-
sions to six chests, an unlikely proposition in an area where twenty chests
was apparently de rigueur.[2]

Concern about dowry was only one aspect of the bitter competition for
status that pervaded eighteenth-century life. This competition produced an
unusual series of conversations about wives and brides in the writings of
mid-Ch'ing intellectuals. Their conversations, which appear in a variety of
texts (didactic, political, and scholarly), are reminiscent of Victorian writings on the subject of women. Like the Victorians, mid-Ch'ing writers valorized the woman's role as wife, manager, and guardian of the "inner apartments." In fixing the place of wives in the domestic sphere, they also sought
to fix the fluidity of social change that threatened to erode the boundaries
defining their own respectability. In questioning classical conventions governing women's behavior, they simultaneously reasserted those same conventions. In this essay I shall argue that their conversations about women
and marriage were a metonymic comment on larger social issues of mobility
and class during the eighteenth century.

The conversations—which I shall call a "new discourse on marriage"—
were part of the Confucian revival of the mid-Ch'ing period, a revival that
reached down through the ranks of the commoner classes and focused on the
family. Among the scholar-elite, "textual research" or "Han Learning" called
attention to the original language of ancient canonical works, including
marriage rituals and kinship terminology. Even commoners who could bare-

ly read were caught up in the revival because of state propaganda campaigns promoting a common ideal of domestic life that emphasized wifely fidelity and service. The state campaigns contributed in turn to a growing interest in compiling genealogies and family instruction books for upper-class households and those newly arrived at respectable status. As a result of these conditions—which affected scholarship, official duties, and personal writing—the elite men who presided over large families were led to ponder and comment anew on the ambiguous position of women in the Chinese family system.[3]

At the heart of the concern about family was the remarkable social mobility, both upward and downward, that marked the mid-Ch'ing era. Evidence for mobility comes from the revival of commerce and the flourishing of trade guilds; from the growth of new literati occupations outside formal government office; from an apparent rise in literacy rates among women as well as men; and from complaints about affluence, conspicuous consumption, and "petty" competition in the literary arts (Ho 1962; Naquin and Rawski 1987:58–59, 114–33). Surely the most striking development with respect to mobility in the mid-Ch'ing era was the series of imperial edicts eradicating the final remaining hereditary class barrier in Chinese society. Beginning in 1723, members of certain occupational and regional groups listed in the household registers as *chien*, or "debased," were declared eligible for commoner status once they had "purified" their family lines by abstention from polluting work for three generations (Terada 1959). Though the edicts did not eliminate "debased" status groups, I believe the promised emancipation of the lowborn and the intense scrutiny of "pure" blood lines that attended their proposed assimilation into the commoner classes were crucial elements in the changing consciousness this essay examines.

In sum, anxiety about blurred boundaries of all kinds—including the boundaries between "respectable" (*liang*) and "polluted" (*chien*) women—informed the conversations we are about to explore and gave them special urgency. At stake was not only the purity of marriage markets but also the reproduction of status in a competitive society. Classical revival, moral rebirth, and the unprecedented mobility of women throughout the stratification system prompted enormous concern about how to keep women in their place. Yet these conversations were only partly about women's roles within the family. They were also about marriage and the market: about reaffirming the endogamous marriage markets of the scholar-elite to exclude interlopers, and to distinguish educated women of the upper class from their cultivated sisters in the courtesans' salons. The literati writers of this era identified wives and daughters alike as women who carried forward the status of their families and the honor of their class in the face of threats from all sides.

HAN LEARNING AND THE RECOVERY OF
CLASSICAL MARRIAGE NORMS

The scholars of the Han Learning movement looked to pre-Sung texts for guidance as they sought the "original" pure meaning of Confucian norms and language. Among their rediscoveries was abundant material on the meaning of marriage. The *Li chi*, the *I li*, and the *Po-hu t'ung*, all important Han texts widely cited and read by these scholars, emphasized marriage as a rite of adulthood and stressed the proper preparation and education of women for marriage. A review of these texts will indicate the scope of their appeal in the mid-Ch'ing period.

Han texts describe marriage as a ritual that simultaneously marked the individual's entry into a world of adult responsibility and reconstituted the conjugal fulcrum of family life. As the next generation entered adulthood, moreover, the elder generation prepared to step aside. Even though mourning and burial were ranked higher in the ritual order, and even though a funeral usually cost more than a wedding, marriage was recognized as the "root," or foundation, of all ritual.[4] According to the *Li chi* (Book of Rites), marriage marked the second of the series of crucial ceremonies in the individual life cycle, following the ritual capping (for boys) and the ceremonial hairpinning (for girls). The "Ch'ü li" (Summary of Rules of Propriety) chapter says: "When one is ten years old, we call him a boy; he goes [out] to school. When he is twenty, we call him a youth; he is capped. When he is thirty, we say, 'He is at his maturity'; he has a wife" (Legge 1967 1:65; *LC* 1:4b).[5] A later passage, in the "Nei tse" (Pattern of the Family) chapter, elaborates on the significance of this transition to "maturity" at marriage: "At thirty, he had a wife, and began to attend to the business proper to a man. He extended his learning without confining it to particular subjects. He was deferential to his friends, having regard to the aims (which they displayed)"(Legge 1967 1:478–79; *LC* 12:15b).

The early years of marriage, then, for men marked the expansion of social networks and broad programs of study that prepared them for an official post (the next transition, conventionally said to begin at age forty). Marriage for the elite male was a significant public step toward a career in the larger society. For the upper-class woman, by contrast, the path leading to marriage steadily contracted her sphere of activities, confining her ever more strictly to the domestic realm. At the age of ten, just as her brothers were leaving the home to attend school, a young girl was cut off from all access to the world outside the home: she "ceased to go out from the women's apartments" and began instructions with a governess who taught her

pleasing speech and manners, to be docile and obedient, to handle the hempen fibres, to deal with the cocoons, to weave silks and shape waistbands, to learn woman's work in order to supply necessary clothing; to be present at the sacrifices, supplying the liquors and sauces, filling the various stands and dishes with pickles and brine, and assisting in setting out the appurtenances for the ceremonies. (Based on Legge 1967 1:479; *LC* 12:15b)

For the young lady, the counterpart of her brother's capping ceremony was the hair-pinning ritual, which took place at the age of fifteen, to be followed by marriage at the age of twenty to twenty-three years (Legge 1967 1:479; *LC* 12:16a). At that point, a portentous choice was made: she became a bride if she went through the rites of betrothal, a concubine if she did not (ibid.). Following the elaborate rituals signifying her transfer into the household of another family, the young woman centered her activities in the home of her husband's parents, concentrating her energies on the needs of that household.

We are accustomed to viewing this transition in a young woman's life as the nadir of her life cycle, the point at which she became least powerful, most vulnerable, most isolated, most alienated (Wolf 1972:128–41). Like all aspects of Confucian thought, however, norms governing marriage embodied what Benjamin Schwartz (1959) has called "polarities," and mid-Ch'ing writers were looking to dignify, not degrade, their women. They therefore focused on passages that both sanctioned wifely obedience and subservience and also stressed the dignity and authority of the wife in her new husband's family. A close reading of the Han ritual texts revealed that from the time of her entry into the home of her husband, the bride was ritually marked as his mother's successor. The *Po-hu t'ung* made this clear in a poignant passage: "The wedding is not [a case] for congratulations; it is [a case of] generations succeeding each other" (Tjan 1952 1:249; *PHT* 4 *shang*:255–56). In the *Po-hu t'ung*, as the groom goes out to meet the bride, his father reflects that the son is soon to replace him at the ancestral sacrifices: "Go and meet thy helpmeet, that [with her] thou mayst succeed me in the sacrifices to the ancestral temple. With diligence lead her, [but also] with respect, [for she is] the successor of thy mother after her death"(ibid.).[6]

Thus, although it is true that a young bride's sphere of activity remained confined to the "inner" domestic realm after her marriage, certain ritual texts nevertheless emphasize the power she acquired, barring misfortune, in her new sphere. It was these texts that caught the eye of status-conscious bride-givers in the mid-Ch'ing era, particularly the chapter on marriage in the *Li chi*.

The *Li chi* stresses wifely deference and submission, remarking frequently on the importance of "obedience," "duty," and "service." At the same time, it offers a view of the marital relationship that emphasizes affection, partnership, and shared responsibility. Affirming the overwhelming importance of finding a suitable wife, the *Li chi* elaborates on the wife's central role in her marital family. Noting that "the ceremony of marriage provides for the propitious union between two [families of different] surnames" (*LC* 44:1a), the text explains that the purposes of the bond were, first, to ensure the continuation of sacrifices in the ancestral temple, and, second, to secure the continuity of the family line. The *Li chi* emphasizes the seriousness and profundity of the rituals surrounding the exchange of information and gifts leading up to the engagement and the ceremonies marking the wedding itself. Part of the ceremony included the ritual eating of the same animal and sipping from cups made from halves of the same melon; this showed, according to the text, "that they now formed one body, were of equal rank, and pledged to mutual affection" (Legge 1967 2:429–30; *LC* 44:1b).

On careful reading, then, the *Li chi* could be interpreted to emphasize *distinctions* and *difference* more than hierarchy, dominance, or submission. A proper marriage was arranged and celebrated to underscore gender differences and to emphasize the complementary and separate responsibilities of man and woman in the conjugal relationship. Marriage was the primary human social bond demonstrating the "righteousness," or "propriety" (*i*), of each distinctive human role. Like all primary relationships, marriage required deference and submission (wives are to husbands as sons are to fathers and subjects to rulers). But the *Li chi* stressed that husband and wife interact to demonstrate harmony, and it implied that a filial son would learn how to establish a warm and responsible relationship with his father, not by observing his mother's deference, but by watching his parents' loving interaction. A father who abused his wife would invite only his son's resentment and rejection, and a resentful and rebellious son, as everyone knows, makes an unreliable subject. Thus the *Li chi* revealed how a wife mediates the critical filial bond tying father to son. She was the pivot around which loyal and compliant subjects were socialized (*LC* 44:1b).

The complementary responsibilities of husband and wife were also summarized in a concluding passage of the "Hun i" ("The Meaning of Marriage") chapter, which explains how, in ancient times, the Son of Heaven took charge of instructions pertaining to the "public and external government of the kingdom," while his wife instructed the palace women "in the domestic and private rule which should prevail throughout the kingdom" (Legge 1967 2:432–33; *LC* 44:3a). Thus, the regulation and harmony of families was the responsibility of women, just as the regulation and harmony of government was that of men.

The natural basis of this gender division of labor in the governance of public and private spheres was proved by its correlations with the natural world: when the public sphere was in disorder, an eclipse of the sun occurred; when the private realm was in disarray, the moon was eclipsed. The

Son of Heaven, or the queen, as appropriate, had to respond to these portents with purification rituals. Parents of the people, the emperor and empress, were like father and mother, each attending to his or her appropriate concerns (*LC* 44:3b).

In general, the language of classical texts masked hierarchy in this way, stressing not subordination but complementary spheres and "natural" sequential transformations. A discussion of the relationships among the five elements in the *Po-hu t'ung*, for example, offered a cosmological explanation for patrilocal marriage. Referring to the relationships among the five elements, the text says: "The son not leaving his parents models himself on what? He models himself on fire which does not depart from wood. The daughter leaving her parents models herself on what? She models herself on water which by flowing departs from metal" (Tjan 1952 2:442; *PHT* 2 *shang*:95). The principle of complementarity between husband and wife was apparent in other sections of the classics. Both the *Li chi* and the *I li* describe a particular ritual to be performed on the day after the wedding, dramatizing the importance of the entering bride. The ceremony required the parents of the groom first to toast the new bride. She then toasted them in turn, after which the parents were to leave the room by a door facing west, while the bride departed from the east. Commentators explain that these directions signify that the bride will ultimately take her mother-in-law's place in the family, becoming the woman responsible for carrying on the family line.[7] As a ritual statement, this ceremony followed by one day the rites in which the new bride served her parents-in-law a dressed pig, signifying her obedience.

For the bride, then, rituals expressing obedience were coupled with those emphasizing responsibility and authority. Obedience was critical not only because it upheld the authority of elders but also because it was essential to the harmony of the household; one day the bride herself would have to command obedience from younger women. The text repeatedly notes that the perpetuation of the family line depends on domestic harmony, for which the women who presided over the household were responsible. It is worth noting here that all power consigned to wives in the domestic realm was constrained on every side by fine distinctions of age and status. Teaching women how to use this power became an obsession of mid-Ch'ing scholars, who were drawn to these ritual texts, as we shall see, for reasons of their own.

Constrained or no, the idea of complementarity between spouses so evident in Han texts formed an important theme in mid-Ch'ing scholarly writing on women and the family. It appears prominently in the writings of Yü Cheng-hsieh (1775–1840), well known as a critic of foot binding, widow chastity, and the double standard (Ropp 1981:144–46).[8] A skilled philologist, Yü researched the history of language, which clearly influenced his views on women. In a short note on the historical meaning of the word *ch'i* (wife), Yü examined in some detail the "egalitarian" interpretation of marriage in

Han texts, explaining why the classics could not be invoked to support the subordination of women in marriage and the family (*KSTK* 4:105–6):

> The *Discourses in the White Tiger Hall* [*PHT* 4 *shang*:268] states that *ch'i* ('wife') means *ch'i* ('equal'), that is to say, she is equal to her husband. The "Chiao t'e sheng" chapter of the *Book of Rites* says: "Your husband is the person with whom you stand as an equal [*ch'i*] on the platform [of marriage]; you are never to leave him as long as you live." It is from this phrase that the word [wife] derived its meaning.
>
> Now the term *fu* ('husband') means *fu* ('to support, to steady, to prop up'). This term originally was a *yang* [masculine, strong, active] word. The word *ch'i* ('wife') derived from the word *ch'i* ('to perch, to settle, to rest for the night'), which is most assuredly a *yin* [feminine, weak, passive] term.
>
> The "Hun i" chapter of the *Book of Rites* says: "In ancient times, the emperor had one empress (*hou*), three consorts (*fu-jen*), nine concubines (*p'in*), twenty-seven mistresses (*shih-fu*), and eighty-one paramours (*yü-ch'i*)." The "Ch'ü li" chapter says: "The emperor has an empress (*hou*), consorts (*fu-jen*), concubines (*p'in*), mistresses (*shih-fu*), paramours (*ch'i*), and lovers (*ch'ieh*)."[9] It also states that the feudal lords have consorts (*fu-jen*), mistresses (*shih-fu*), paramours (*ch'i*), and lovers (*ch'ieh*). In this case, clearly, the term *ch'i* does not mean "equal."
>
> Confucians have a saying that an imperial paramour (*ch'i*) is the same as an imperial lover (*ch'ieh*), which they explain is because the term *ch'i* means "equal." And what are we to make of the "Ch'ü li" passage that mentions paramours and lovers in the same breath?
>
> The term *ch'i* must be understood in its specific context. It is used by everyone from the emperor to the common people.

In textual research, notes such as these offered no larger analytical or moral message. They nonetheless show us how scholars of the mid-Ch'ing era attempted to recover the consciousness and the values of the past and gave them new life in their writing and thought.

Understanding language in historical context made it possible, for instance, to distinguish the past practices of the imperial household and the ancient aristocracy from the standards that guided the scholar class in the present. Yü's short research note titled "Appellations" ("Ch'eng-ming") (*KSTK* 4:125) analyzed the classical terms used for affines, notably ego's wife's brothers and ego's sisters' spouses and their sons. The note specifically compared past practice with present custom, indicating that regular social intercourse between intermarrying families, including the brothers of wives and the spouses of sisters, was an important feature of mid-Ch'ing family life. We shall refer again to Yü Cheng-hsieh's textual research and to the complementarity of conjugal bonds when we examine the common interests of intermarrying families in the eighteenth century.

Probably the aspect of Yü Cheng-hsieh's thought that has received the most attention (where it pertains to the status of women) is his critique of the double standard implicit in the ban on widow remarriage—a prohibition that was widely observed among the upper classes of the Ch'ing period (Elvin 1984; Mann 1987). Yü's point of departure for his argument, in the essay "On Chaste Widows" ("Chieh-fu shuo"), was his research on the notion of *ch'i* (equality, matching) between husband and wife at marriage. He quotes from the "Chiao t'e sheng" chapter in the *Li chi*: "A match once made should never be broken" (*LC* 11:13b). This means, he says, that when one's spouse dies, one does not remarry. He concedes that Pan Chao in the Han, so widely cited as the model for young widows of later times, did in fact write that "a husband has a duty (*i*) to remarry; for a wife, there is no written prescription for entering a second marital relationship. Therefore, for a woman, her husband is like Heaven [and she can never replace him with someone else]." But confronting this passage, Yü comments:

> Although it is absolutely true that no written permission is given for women to remarry, there is at the same time an unwritten assumption that men should not take a second wife. The reason why the sages did not make this standard of conduct explicit in their teachings is the same as the reasoning that underlies the following passage: "The rites do not descend to the common people, nor do punishments reach up to gentlemen." When we make this statement, of course, we do not mean that commoners cannot follow the rites, or that gentlemen will never be punished. By the same token, men who wantonly seek wives just because the meaning of the *Book of Rites* was not explicitly spelled out are ignoring their true duty. According to the ancient rites, husband and wife were to be honored or despised together, as a single body. But a man sets his wife apart in a lower position when he invokes the ancient phrase "never be broken." He should realize that the "never" refers to both men and women alike. "Casting out a wife for the seven reasons" in fact describes seven ways to break a match; "if his wife dies, a man should remarry" is the eighth way. When the principles and duties of men are so broadly defined and unspecific, it is truly shameful to read so much into a few words and then use them to establish limits on wives alone. (*KSLK* 13:493)

Classical revival, then, in calling attention to the double standard, emphasized the privileged role of wives. The *Po-hu t'ung* took great pains to distinguish principal wives from concubines: "The rites forbid the betrothal of a woman as concubine. This means that she cannot be raised [to the position of principal wife]" (Tjan 1949 1:258; *PHT* 4 *shang*:264).[10]

There were good practical, as well as moral, reasons why mid-Ch'ing writers were concerned about widower remarriage, and these shall be examined below. The point here, however, is to stress again the impact of classical revival on the views of mid-Ch'ing literati. At every turn, it appears, they were discovering ways to valorize the status of brides and wives in their class and to emphasize the differences that separated marriageable women from concubines and women of lower rank.

FEMALE LITERACY AND WOMEN'S EDUCATION

The Han Learning movement coincided with a proliferation of guidebooks for educated women, including reprints of the *Instructions for Women (Nü chieh)* by Pan Chao, the illustrious female scholar (*nü-shih*) of the Han period. (Yü Cheng-hsieh's essay criticizing widow chastity begins by quoting from this important text, underscoring its high visibility in the mid-Ch'ing period.) Interest in women's education followed naturally from classical injunctions requiring special preparation and training for aristocratic young ladies, preferably in the ancestral hall of their descent groups. Women were educated for marriage, and the best education for marriage was training in the Four Attributes (*ssu te*) appropriate to wives: proper virtue, speech, carriage, and work (Legge 1967 2:431–32; *LC* 44:2b).

The connection between moral education and marriage was made explicit by Pan Chao, who used the idea of the Four Attributes to organize her own instruction book. Her text, a training book for wifehood, invoked concepts of complementarity in marriage found in the *Li chi*. She understood the *tao* of conjugal relationships to be metaphorically like the "natural" relationships of yin and yang, Earth and Heaven. She valorized marriage by calling attention to the honor accorded it in the *Li chi* and by emphasizing that it is celebrated by the first ode in the *Shih ching*. She also criticized views of marriage that stressed only the control of husbands over their wives, noting that though all classical texts portrayed marriage as a reciprocal relationship that depended on the wife's ability to "serve" her husband as well as on his ability to "control" her, both service and control depended on the "worthiness" (*hsien*) of each partner. Men, she noted, were educated so that they could understand the foundations of their authority and wield it effectively; women too required education if they were to serve properly in the domestic realm:

> Only to teach men and not to teach women—is that not ignoring the essential relation between them? According to the "Rites," it is the rule to begin to teach children to read at the age of eight years, and by the age of fifteen years they ought then to be ready for cultural training. Only why should it not be (that girls' education as well as boys' be) according to this principle? (Swann 1932:84–85; *NC shang*:4b–5a)

These views on women's education, and Pan Chao's own eminence as a scholar and intellectual, were taken seriously by scholars of Han Learning during the eighteenth century. Until that time, from the Six Dynasties period through most of the Ming, Pan Chao was probably best remembered as a celibate widow (Swann 1932:51). In the late Ming period, however, interest in female instruction took a new turn. Lü K'un anticipated the concerns of some mid-Ch'ing intellectuals: he was interested in the complementarity of the husband-wife relationship and concerned about educating women as fu-

ture mothers and heads of the domestic realm (Handlin 1975:36–38). Handlin, in her analysis of Lü K'un's own instruction book for women, the *Kuei fan*
(Regulations for the Women's Quarters), emphasizes that he was addressing
a "new audience" of commoners (*min-chien fu-nü*) who "suddenly have three
or five volumes in their chests" (ibid., 17).

During the eighteenth century, accessible schooling and rising standards
of living expanded the market for books. Commoners attuned to concerns
about proper marriage and behavior were avid consumers of works on managing the household. Women were part of this consumer market: literate
women were prominent in Buddhist sutra-reading societies and in poetry
classes, studying with Yuan Mei and other leading scholars (Ch'en 1928:
257–74).[11]

Concern about female education was mounting, as evidenced by the market for women's instruction books.[12] A compact new edition of basic books,
self-consciously styled *The Four Books for Women* (*Nü ssu-shu*), was bound and
printed before the middle of the nineteenth century under the editorship of
Wang Hsiang, who contributed one of the four works—a collection of his
own mother's instructions, the *Nü-fan chieh-lu* (A Brief Outline of Rules for
Women).[13] The other three books were Pan Chao's *Nü chieh*; a T'ang text
entitled *Nü Lun-yü* (Analects for Women), written by Sung Jo-hua; and the
Nei hsun (Instructions for the Inner Apartments), composed early in the
fifteenth century by the empress Hsu (Jen Hsiao-wen).

Education for women was the subject of a much-reprinted collection of
moral instructions by Ch'en Hung-mou. In the preface to his *Repository of
Rules for Education of Women* (*Chiao-nü i-kuei*), Ch'en explained the significance
of female education:

> The girl who begins as a daughter in your family marries out and becomes a
> wife; she bears a child and becomes a mother. A wise daughter (*hsien nü*) will
> make a wise wife and mother. And wise mothers rear wise sons and grandsons.
> The process of kingly transformation [literally, *wang-hua*, the transformative
> influence of the ruler on his subjects] therefore begins in the women's apart-
> ments, and a family's future advantage is tied to the purity and the education of
> its women. Hence education is of the utmost importance. (*CNIK* Preface: 2a)

Clearly, education was for Ch'en the mark that set apart the women of his
class—those given and those taken as brides—from everyone else. But what
sort of education should women receive? In Ch'ing times, upper-class women
were trained in the arts of needlework, poetry, painting, calligraphy, and
music-making.[14] Mastery of these arts alone, however, did not mark status,
for they were also claimed by professional female entertainers and courtesans. What set apart the marriageable women of Ch'en's class from the rest
was moral instruction: education in the *ta i*, or "ultimate significance," of
classical texts.

In an essay addressing this subject—significantly, the first of his works to command widespread attention—Chang Hsueh-ch'eng sketched the history of "women's learning," or "women's studies," since ancient times. The earliest women's studies, he argued, were in fact professional curricula that trained women for specific occupations. Thus, female historians studied one body of texts, female soothsayers another, female shamans still another—just as men would select one of the arts for specialized training for a particular office. Later, however, more general studies for women as a gender category developed, and a body of learning proper to females (as opposed to males) emerged. This "women's studies" literature emphasized womanly virtue, speech, appearance, and conduct and linked these to the example and scholarship of Pan Chao.[15]

In Chang's mind, moral education of the sort espoused by Pan Chao contrasted explicitly with training in the arts for professional female entertainers. Chang praised the Manchu government for taking a strong stand on this issue by banning female courtesans from the palace Office of Musicians (Chiao fang ssu) and distancing itself from the patronage and training of female entertainers. To teach women music and poetry without requiring prior rigorous training in the rites—especially the rites of family relationships—was to invite loose morals.

The removal of courtesans from the Office of Musicians, which Chang called "the most illustrious act of our august ruling dynasty" to date, loomed large in the minds of mid-Ch'ing intellectuals for another reason: it was the prelude to the general emancipation of debased peoples. The Office of Musicians was originally staffed by a hereditary class of professional entertainers called "music makers" (*yueh-hu*), some of whose descendants were already living in isolated communities in north China after being expelled from the palace in a political dispute early in the fifteenth century. The *yueh-hu* were the first of the major pariah groups named in the emancipation edicts, and scholars specifically linked the abolition of the hereditary court musicians' offices to the end of pariah status for the *yueh-hu*. Writing more than fifty years later, Yü Cheng-hsieh took the history of the Office of Musicians as his own point of departure for a long essay on the emancipation proclamations (*KSLK* 12:474–87).[16]

The end of debased-status groups, especially hereditary groups of female entertainers, threatened the integrity of endogamous marriage markets, and with it the very foundation of hierarchy among women.[17] As bearers of the honor and status of their class, marriageable female commoners had to be kept separate from those who were bought and sold.[18] Thus, debates about women's education simultaneously explicated and clarified anew the critical class barriers in this mobile society. One result was the essay by Chang Hsueh-ch'eng that attempted to draw more firmly the lines around the cloistered women's domain by scorning the attempts of some women to join male-

dominated poetry and writing groups. The ending of legal restrictions on
debased groups must be seen in the context of a more commercialized society
in which status barriers of all kinds were becoming less salient.

RULES FOR FAMILY LIVING: WOMEN IN THE DOMESTIC GROUP

To serve the new market, in addition to books on women's instruction,
guides to family living that addressed wifely roles were printed in affordable
new editions or privately circulated among friends. The classic family instruction books composed by Yen Chih-t'ui in the Six Dynasties period (*Yen-
shih chia-hsun*) and by Yuan Ts'ai in the Sung (*Yuan-shih shih-fan*) were
rescued from the rare book market and reprinted in the *Compendium from
the Never-Enough-Knowledge Studio* (Chih-pu-tsu-chai ts'ung-shu), bringing their
cost within the means of most scholarly families.[19] Reading and rereading
these old texts, a few scholars were inspired to compile their own books for
the education of their offspring and family members. (We shall examine one
such contribution, by Wang Hui-tsu, below.) Interest in advice books went
hand in hand with another new fashion: publishing "clan rules" to accompany the genealogies that were at the peak of their popularity during this
period (Hui-chen Wang Liu 1959a:71).

Even the so-called statecraft writers of the mid-Ch'ing era tried their hand
at essays on family matters. Wei Yuan's classic *Collected Writings on Statecraft
of Our August Dynasty* (Huang-ch'ao ching-shih wen-pien), compiled in 1824–
25, devoted an entire chapter (*chüan* 60) to essays on family instructions (*chia
chiao*), including the excerpt from Chang Hsueh-ch'eng's "Women's Studies"
(Fu hsueh) discussed above.[20] Essays in the section on ritual examine the
position of women in the patrilineal family system, especially the problematic
ritual place of concubines and successor wives.[21] Domestic relations, particularly the conjugal bond, were not irrelevant to statecraft, if we may judge by
Wei Yuan's selections.[22] Finally, the chapter on marriage rites in Wei Yuan's
collection begins with an essay on women's education: it was "the foundation
of a proper family, the beginning of kingly transformation" (*HCCSWP* 61:1–
2).

Wang Hui-tsu (1731–1807), himself a writer of the statecraft school who
published a famous guidebook for administrative aides, wrote his own guide
for the domestic realm: a set of family instructions dedicated to his children
and titled *Simple Precepts from the Hall Enshrining a Pair of Chaste Widows*
(Shuang-chieh-t'ang yung-hsun). (The title commemorates the two women
who were most responsible for shaping his views on such matters: his late
father's second wife and his own mother, who was a concubine.)[23] The work
is addressed to his sons and grandsons:

> Once while I was home nursing an illness, I began reading the *Yen-shih chia-
> hsun* and the *Yuan-shih shih-fan* every day, and I would expound on these texts to

my assembled family, to provide them with models for "maintaining their integrity while remaining involved with worldly affairs" [ch'ih-shen she-shih]. Sometimes I would expound upon the general principles; at other times I would give concrete examples as illustrations. Felicitous words, elegant deeds, and the foundations of day-to-day relationships between teachers and pupils—on each of these subjects, from time to time, I was pleased to offer formal teachings in the Way of proper conduct, which they in turn were to record by hand. Gradually my notes filled a satchel with jottings. I organized the notes that amplified the sentiments in the Yen and Yuan texts into six broad categories, encompassing 219 small items. These I arranged in six chapters.

The first is called "A Record of Those Who Went Before." It commemorates the wisdom of our ancestors, beginning with the events in the life of my late mother and her actual deeds, without repeating anything that has already been written down. The next chapter is called "Regulating the Self." This means, as Confucius once said, being able to follow your natural desires without transgressing what is right. The third chapter is called "Managing the Family." This chapter is limited to the discussion of a fundamental principle: continuing the ancestral line requires the guidance of mothers. Therefore the chapter deals in some detail with women's behavior. The fourth chapter, entitled "Responding to the Times," shows how if one has few occasions for blame, and few for regret, one will be able to rejoice many times over. The fifth chapter is called "Plan for the Future." It shows how to provide security for future generations, and how to sow the seeds of great things to come. The final chapter is entitled "Teachers and Friends," and includes a discussion of relationships in school. (SCTYH Preface:1a–b)

Picking up a theme from both the Yen-shih chia-hsun and the Yuan-shih shih-fan, Wang Hui-tsu examined the intricacies of remarriage and widowhood in a large Chinese family.[24] He lavished special attention on the plight of the widower who must find another mother for his children, a situation well understood in his own household, as his father took a second wife after the first died, though his own mother, a concubine, was still living. What kinds of problems confronted the widower? How irreplaceable was his first wife? And what pitfalls awaited the man who took a second wife instead of contenting himself with a concubine lacking the ritually high status accorded a spouse?

The first answer to these questions appears in a section entitled "Taking a second wife makes it hard to be a father":

Your first wife may not necessarily be wise, but the children she bears will not resent her on that account. In the unlucky event that she dies, however, you may have no choice but to take a successor wife. And if she happens to be unwise, and insists on making narrow distinctions [presumably between her children and others, or between her conjugal interests and those of the larger household], patching up the quarrels that result will be a source of grief for you.

If conditions are optimal and your new wife understands the larger moral principles of family relationships, she will always be unfailingly kind. But even in

those circumstances the children of your first wife will look on her as an outsider. And so if you give them instructions or assign them tasks, they will blame
all their failure to carry out your orders on their stepmother.

For you, the father, this means that reproof and admonitions to your children
will always provoke resentment and jealousy from them; even if you do nothing, you will invite slander from them. Who can be blamed for this situation?
(*SCTYH* 3:2a)

Clearly, the person to blame is the father, for making the mistake of remarrying. Elevating a second woman to the formal status of mother to all
one's children is a step to be taken only at the risk of alienating offspring and
losing one's authority over the coming generation.

Wang Hui-tsu commented further on the relationship between stepmothers and their stepchildren in a note entitled "Serving a stepmother":

Even if a stepmother is hard to please, she must be attended to according to the
rules of propriety. How much more true this is if your stepmother is easy to
please! Even so, we often find that a mother who is easy to please gets a reputation for being hard to please, even to the point where she is being called
"narrow-hearted" (*pu-i*) and the father is being called "unkind." Now what
kind of an attitude is that?

There are exceptions to this pattern. For instance, no one could have been
wiser than my [step]mother Lady Wang. Thus, when I was thirteen years of
age, she restrained me with orders that were strict and spartan. An agnatic
kinsman of my father's generation said to me privately: "Your mother treats
your younger sister far more kindly than she treats you." I denied this pas-
sionately, and thereafter I listened to her instructions more diligently than ever.
Within four years, my kinsman's son was dead, and a little over ten years later,
he himself died. Now his descendants are also dead, and this causes me to
wonder whether his words may not still be having an effect today. (*SCTYH*
3:2a–b)

A stepmother, we see here, easily became the object of gossip and slander
among kinsmen. Her commitment to her stepchildren was ambivalent, and
that ambivalence could readily be turned against her by gossip that alienated
her spouse's offspring. Few stepsons, we may imagine, were as loyal to their
stepmothers as the young Wang Hui-tsu.[25]

If the hapless widower chose not to remarry to avoid these problems, he
only faced new ones. The plight of one unfortunate soul, in a large household
full of conjugal units devoted to serving their own needs, is outlined in a
section titled "In serving a widowed father or mother, one must be even more
attentive than ever":

A widowed mother has her sons' wives to rely on and daughters to wait on
her—although the sons' wives will have their own children, and the daughters
their husbands and in-laws as well, so a widow cannot depend exclusively on

her own children; if she is ill, or in pain, or hungry, or thirsty, she may have no one to complain to.

But how truly desolate is the father who is old and living alone! Recently I visited an elderly kinsman who had lost his wife in middle age, and who had been sleeping and eating alone well past his eightieth year. He said to me: "My handkerchief has been ruined for a long time, and I've been trying to get another one, but I can't." And so saying, he began to weep. I was greatly distressed by this, and I went to report it to his sons. They paid no attention. Not long after, his sons too went the same route, poorer than he. The mirror of Heaven is close at hand—isn't it fearsome! (*SCTYH* 3:2b–3a)

Each of Wang's homilies makes clear the intractable complications stemming from the death of a first wife in households that observed Confucian family norms. The father who remarried to ensure care and companionship in his old age risked rebellion or alienation from his children; fathers shielded their children from the wiles of a stepmother at the price of a solitary and lonely retirement. Clearly, however, in mid-Ch'ing times this was the price they were expected to pay.

Further discussion of the problems involving first and successor wives, from a slightly different perspective, appeared in Ch'en Hung-mou's *Repository*. Though the classics taught women that "one's husband is one's Heaven," in reality a wife had to serve three heavens: her father-in-law, her mother-in-law, and her spouse (*CNIK hsia*:22b). Her primary duty there was to encourage him to be completely filial to his parents: "the full realization of filiality begins with the wife." But remarriage complicated the relationship between mother-in-law and daughter-in-law. For example, remarriage posed the possibility that a daughter-in-law might "distinguish between the first and the second." A "successor wife," that is, a woman who took the ritual place of a deceased first wife, might not command the respect of her status-conscious daughter-in-law. On this account, successor wives were warned to take care to be "polite" to their stepsons' wives, and daughters-in-law were enjoined never to make any distinction between the "first" and the "second" by such nasty little signs as passing through doorways first. Families were cautioned to watch for telltale signs of insubordination and correct the wayward daughter-in-law's thinking immediately (ibid., 24a).

These "petty distinctions" among women (widely decried as the source of all discord in Confucian families) could be drawn still more finely in cases where the daughter-in-law, as a ritually sanctioned first wife (*shih-hsi*), served a mother-in-law who was herself a concubine (*shu-ku*). In such cases, the advice to the daughter-in-law was clear: "You may not presume upon your status as first wife to slight a concubine" (*pu-k'o shih shih man shu*) (*CNIK hsia*:24b).

Ch'en's *Repository* therefore recognized that status-conscious (i.e., well-

educated) brides could not be counted on to abandon their class consciousness within the confines of the domestic sphere. And if they were hard on
mothers-in-law, they were even worse when it came to servants. Wives took
out their frustration, their boredom, and their jealousies on their servants
because propriety forbade striking relatives or even children. In fact, physical abuse of servants was so common among women of the upper classes that
one text in the *Repository* supplies detailed descriptions of types of abuse as a
warning to readers. Servants, by their conduct and appearance, offered a
living testimony to the faults of an abusive mistress: "One may enter her
home, observe her servants, and know whether she is a good wife or not"
(*CNIK hsia:*la–5a.) The *Repository* admonished its female audience that servants were not "a different order of being, like dogs or horses," but human. It
stressed that scholars and commoners could not own slaves, though slaves
were still employed in government service. Instead, male servants in commoner households were called "adopted sons" (*i-nan*) and female servants
"adopted daughters" (*i-hsi*, or *i-nü*), to signify that they were "just like family
members." They were to be so treated: well clothed, well fed, never abused
(ibid., 1a–5b).

If young women with servants could be abusive, they could also be lazy.
Sloth was a blot on the character of any bride, an all-too-common sign that
she had abandoned one of the four cardinal womanly attributes. Young ladies
who grew up waited on hand and foot never learned how to manage properly
their role as mistress of the family servants and keeper of the household
account books. Unlike wives in poor families—"busy all day, reeling thread,
cooking food, drawing water, pounding rice, minding the farm, serving
their mothers-in-law, suckling babies, generally working to exhaustion"
(*CNIK hsia:*14b)—the women who circulated through the marriage markets
of the rich were spoiled, above all, by servants. Nursemaids took care of their
children; maids and concubines even did their needlework! "All they have
to think about is making themselves beautiful. Everything is done for them,
so they don't know that rice comes from a stalk and silk is unreeled from
cocoons. They treat money like dirt, and living creatures like bits of straw"
(ibid., 15a).

Problems with household servants could be mitigated through fictive kin
ties and prolonged association. But relations with women of low status outside the household were always dangerous. Every instruction book contained
warnings about the "hags" whose marginal occupations gave them access to
the cloistered inner apartments—female physicians, religious adepts, go-
betweens, peddlers, nuns.[26] Wives had to be taught to "maintain strictly the
separation of the inner domain from the outside world," lest they become the
victims of gossip and manipulation by threatening females from outside who
would "turn their hearts astray" (*CNIK chung:*4a).

Repeated admonitions about the "six hags" reveal anxiety about female mobility and about defining boundaries around women. Women's religious practice, and the corrupting influence of the religious—not only nuns but also monks and priests—worried Ch'en Hung-mou, who wrote about the need to cloister women in an essay reprinted in the *Collected Writings on Statecraft* (*HCCSWP* 68:5b):

> A woman's proper ritual place is sequestered in the inner apartments. When at rest, she should lower the screen [in front of her]; when abroad, she must cover her face in order to remove herself from any suspicion or doubt, and prevent herself from coming under observation.[27] But instead we find young women accustomed to wandering about, all made up, heads bare and faces exposed, and feeling no shame whatsoever! Some climb into their sedan chairs and go traveling in the mountains. . . . We even find them parading around visiting temples and monasteries, burning incense and holding services, kneeling to listen to the chanting of the sutras. In the temple courtyards and in the precincts of the monasteries, they chat and laugh freely. The worst times are in the last ten days of the third lunar month, when they form sisterhoods and spend the night in local temples; and on the sixth day of the sixth month, when they believe that if they turn over the pages of the sutras ten times, they will be transformed into men in the next life.

The text goes on to condemn the monks and priests who seduce these mobile women in much the same tone reserved for the nuns and other "hags" who serve as liaisons between cloistered females and the outside world.

Again, concerns about women traveling abroad to monasteries were not new in the eighteenth century. But in the larger context of a mobile society, where competition for status was being promoted on many levels by action of the state, an obsession with boundaries in the writings of mid-Ch'ing scholars assumes a heightened significance. Concern about boundary crossing in the domestic realm, I would suggest, was a metaphor for concern about boundaries in the society as a whole. Within the scholar class, female literacy was breaking down the walls that separated the sexes and kept women pure from the contaminating influences of the outside world. In the society at large, mobility was eroding occupational and class barriers that had once served to segregate marriage markets. Though women were the focus of much of the anxiety that attended these changes, in the discourse we have examined, women became a vehicle for expressing concerns about status shared by all men of the scholar class.

CONCLUSION

That wives and marriage were a focal point in a discourse about class and mobility is hardly surprising. As in Renaissance Venice, nineteenth-century France, and colonial Mexico, marriage in mid-Ch'ing China was a contract that aimed above all at reproducing class structures.[28] State law, and the system of moral beliefs we call Confucianism, sanctioned norms governing marriage, and thereby protected the existing class hierarchy. However, those sanctions cut two ways: they could protect class-endogamous marriage markets, or they could undermine them. The discourse on marriage that emerged during the mid-Ch'ing period points to the ways in which the boundaries around sacrosanct marriage markets were being challenged. As the state moved to loosen status distinctions, Confucian morality was invoked to shore them up. Writers of the period show us, in their extended conversations about women and class, how the combined effects of affluence, literacy, and mobility threatened to destroy the conventions that lent stability and order to social life. Their conversations also remind us that codes lodging the honor of class and family in pure women were not confined to the shores of the Mediterranean. During periods of rapid social change, in China as elsewhere, women were named the guardians of morality and stability, charged with protecting the sanctuary of the family.

At the same time, as we have seen, women themselves posed part of the challenge to social order. Their literacy, their religiosity, and their own strivings for comfort and security helped to provoke the mid-Ch'ing discourse on marriage. What we know now about this discourse is based on what men said and wrote. But the time will come when we will be able to see beyond men's interests and show how women construed their own roles in the dramatic changes of the mid-Ch'ing era.[29]

NOTES

The author gratefully acknowledges research support from the Academic Senate Faculty Research Committee at the University of California, Santa Cruz. Fu Poshek and Yue Zumou provided invaluable research assistance. For critical readings of early drafts, I wish to thank Stevan Harrell, Robert Moeller, G. William Skinner, and participants in the conference, especially the editors and Diane Owen Hughes, Gail Hershatter, and Susan Naquin.

1. For a keen appraisal of these sentiments, see Kulp 1925:166–77, esp. 174–75.

2. Ch'en Hung-mou, "Feng-su t'iao-yueh" (Several short points on local customs), *HCCSWP* 68:4. Chen's comments on dowry reflect an apparent rise in women's status in marriage dating from about the tenth or eleventh century. Elsewhere in this volume, Patricia Ebrey shows that between the Han and the T'ang periods, dowry increasingly replaced betrothal gifts as the focus of concern of families seeking to marry off their children. She has also argued (1981) that by the Sung, China had shifted from a brideprice to a dowry system. So concerns about expensive dowries were hardly new in the eighteenth century. What was new about them was the greater participation of commoner households in the dowry system. Larger patterns of social and economic change from Sung to Ch'ing times, especially the elimination of fixed status barriers discussed later in this chapter, help to explain the increase in size and universality of dowry in China. See Harrell and Dickey 1985.

3. On the Han Learning movement, see Liang 1955; Elman 1984; Yü 1975; and Jones and Kuhn 1978. On the Ch'ing propaganda campaigns, see Mann 1985, 1986, 1987. On the blooming interest in genealogies, see Liu 1959a, 1959b.

4. All the ceremonies were to be performed with utmost care in order to underscore "the distinction to be observed between man and woman, and the righteousness to be maintained between husband and wife." That distinction and the ensuing righteousness produced in turn the "affection" that bound father and son; and the affection binding father and son supplied the foundation for the "rectitude" between a ruler and his minister: "Whence it is said, 'The ceremony of marriage is the root of the other ceremonial observances'" (Legge 1967 2:430). Mourning and sacrifice, as rituals, ranked higher in importance than marriage, according to the *Li chi*, but marriage was the "root" of all ceremony.

5. Legge notes in a footnote to this passage that age thirty should not be taken literally as the prescribed age for men to marry (Confucius, after all, was wed at twenty). Rather, he says, the passage means that no young man should reach the age of thirty still unmarried. The proper timing of marriage ceremonies is the subject of a review of classical injunctions printed in the *Collected Writings on Statecraft*; see Ting Chieh's essay "Marriage" ("Chia-ch'ü"), *HCCSWP* 61:17–18.

6. For more on classical views of marriage, see Tjan 1952 1:244–63.

7. See Steele 1917:30–31, which explains that after the parents-in-law have given a feast for the bride, at the conclusion of the toasts: "The father- and mother-in-law then descend before the bride by the western steps to indicate their demission of their position in the house, and the bride thereafter descends by the eastern steps, assuming the position they have demitted."

8. Ropp (1981) and Ch'en (1928:246–57) single out Yü Cheng-hsieh and Li Juchen, author of the *Ching-hua yuan*, as the main dissenters in an era of repressive sexual norms for women. My analysis takes a different view, placing Yü firmly within the mid-Ch'ing discourse on women and class. His critique of the chaste widow paradigm does not challenge the fundamental place of wives in the home; like the others, Yü celebrated women by valorizing the conjugal bond.

9. For a discussion of the evolution of this "empress-consort" system from classical ideals to the Northern Sung period, see Chung 1981:18–19. I am indebted to her translations of most of these elusive terms.

10. In fact the text here is ambiguous because the discussion about remarriage follows references to the "twelve wives" of the Son of Heaven. Clearly, it was not precisely known how to ensure that the ruler would produce a sufficient number of legitimate heirs. The text is also slightly ambiguous when discussing a case in which a principal wife predeceases her husband, citing precedents for promoting a concubine to the position of principal wife, and precedents that required a concubine simply to substitute for the deceased principal wife in the ancestral sacrifices. Motives for remaining faithful to a deceased spouse are suggested ("Why must he only marry once? It is to avoid debauchery and to prevent him casting away virtue and indulging in passion. Therefore he only marries once; the Lord of men has no right to marry twice" [Tjan 1949 1:252; *PHT* 4 *shang*:258]), but again they do not seem convincing where taking a concubine remained an option.

It is possible that the idea of faithful husbandhood (the paradigm of the *i-fu*, or faithful widower) was achieving new prestige in Ch'ing times. Elvin (1984:126) has observed that the definition of *i-fu* (righteous subject) was changed in the early Ch'ing period to refer strictly to husbands who refused to take a second wife after the death of a spouse. Such individuals would have been eligible, under the Ch'ing government's programs to enshrine local saints and worthies, for special recognition in shrines and on memorial arches in their home communities. However, a systematic search of local gazetteers has yielded no evidence that men were honored for being faithful husbands during the mid-Ch'ing period. Communities honoring so-called *i-fu* continued to celebrate the deeds of philanthropists and brave community defenders, following the historical meaning of the term.

11. A comprehensive survey of Ch'ing literary collections has identified works by 3,557 female authors (Hu 1985). The affluent Lower Yangtze region, economic heartland of the realm, was especially famous as the home of educated women: more than two-thirds of the eighty-five female poets whose works appeared in Ts'ai Tien-ch'i's mid-nineteenth-century anthology of works by female writers listed Kiangsu, Chekiang, Anhwei, or Kiangsi as their native place (Rankin 1975:41n).

12. The eighteenth century was the apogee of instruction books for women, beginning with Lan Ting-yuan's *Nü hsueh* (Studies for women), prefaces dated 1712, 1717, and 1718, and continuing through works collected by Ch'en Hung-mou, discussed below. See Ch'en 1928:275–82.

13. The title aptly likens these texts to the Four Books studied by men preparing for the civil service examinations. The exact date of publication of the *Nü ssu shu* is unclear (Liu Chi-hua 1934:30). According to Morohashi (3:6036.353), the first Japanese edition of the work appeared during the Kaei reign period (1848–54). I have seen an edition published in Yangchow in 1838, which is held at the East Asian Library, University of California, Berkeley. A widely available reprint (cited in the bibliography under *NC*) is dated 1893–94.

14. Dance appears to have remained the exclusive domain of courtesans and other professional entertainers, though further research may prove me wrong.

15. The rediscovery of Pan Chao and the reappearance of the motif of the female instructress in late imperial times has not yet been fully explored. See for example two seventeenth-century works by Ch'en Hung-shou, reproduced in Cahill 1967:33–34. Other painters of the Ming-Ch'ing period found educated women an appealing subject. See, for instance, a painting attributed to Tu Chin portraying the famous scene in which the aged scholar Fu Sheng recites the *Book of History* from memory to a scribe, assisted by his daughter. The daughter translates her father's words, spoken in an ancient dialect incomprehensible to courtiers, and thus becomes the critical intermediary in the transmission of the orthodox canon (Hyland 1987:31, citing unpublished papers by Stephen Little).

16. "Singing girls" in the Office of Musicians were permanently replaced by eunuchs as a result of an imperial decree issued in 1659 (Shun-chih 16), following a temporary reversal of a similar decree issued in 1651 (Shun-chih 8). In 1652 a separate edict forbade commoners from becoming prostitutes. These state policies are linked to a growing commercial market for female prostitutes and entertainers during the eighteenth century by Wang Shu-nu (1988:261–84).

17. Under Ch'ing law, no commoner female could legally marry a pariah male. Punishment for a violation of this law was one hundred strokes for both the would-be

husband and the head of the family of the bride (if he had knowingly betrothed his daughter to a man of debased status). By contrast, a commoner "who married a prostitute or singing girl went unpunished, but an official who married such a woman was considered dishonorable and given sixty strokes. The marriage was annulled and the woman was sent back to her . . . [natal] family" (Ch'ü 1961:161). Thus the marriage market drew clear lines between those families who held or stood to hold official rank, and those who did not. Contamination by intermarriage with a pariah female was risked only by families who did not aspire to the examination degrees. Note also that women were the bearers of their class's honor; pariah females could move up, commoner females could never move down, in this patriarchal family system.

18. Rules protecting class endogamy were part of China's earliest political culture. Bans on intermarriage (reinforced by bans on foot binding for pariah women) hark back to ancient class barriers (Ch'ü 1961:155–58). According to Ch'ü T'ung-tsu, the gap between the *shih* class (scholars) and the *shu* (commoners) in medieval times was so wide that the latter were regarded as "untouchables." Intermarriage between *shih* and *shu* was forbidden by law under some dynasties. In fact, according to Ch'ü, "class endogamy prevailed among the *shih* until the last days of the Five Dynasties (907–960)" (1961:158). This traditional endogamy within the *shih* class, lasting from the third through the ninth centuries, was paralleled by endogamy within the *shu*, or commoner, classes, which took great care in turn to distinguish themselves from both mean people and slaves.

19. The two works appear in volumes 11 and 14, respectively. On various Ch'ing editions of Yuan Ts'ai's work, see Ebrey 1984:324–27. The *Compendium* itself, compiled by the bibliophile Pao T'ing-po (1728–1814), was named for Pao's library in Hang-chou, where he kept an especially outstanding collection of rare Sung and Yuan books. He was one of the four most generous contributors to the Four Treasuries (Ssu-k'u) imperial compilation project in 1773. The Ch'ien-lung emperor is said to have named one of his own studios after Pao's (Hummel 1943 2:612–13). On the Never-Enough-Knowledge compendium, see Elman 1984:151–52. Elman explains that the inflated price of rare books in the eighteenth century increased the demand for collectanea that made expensive classical literature available at an affordable price.

20. Nivison (1966:274) comments that this essay was the first of Chang's writings to find a wide audience, appearing in anthologies and collectanea well in advance of his major historical and philological works. The *HCCSWP* reprints only a portion of the complete essay, under the title "Fu hsueh san tse" (Three precepts for women's studies). The point of the essay, which was in part a thinly veiled attack on Yuan Mei, is that women's education should be grounded in classical works and moral instruction, not poetry, and that men and women each have their own proper body of learning:

> In ancient times, studies for women began with the rites, and through them progressed to an understanding of poetry and the six arts; or women might achieve mastery of all these fields simultaneously. But later these studies for women were no longer transmitted, and those women who were accomplished and literate proclaimed themselves professional scholars alongside men, and flaunted their achievements. They did not realize that women originally had

their own studies, and that those studies always had their foundation in the rites. (*HCCSWP* 60:12a)
Ch'en Tung-yuan (1928:267) takes a conventionally uncritical view of Yuan Mei as patron of women's letters, and does not address Chang's critique.

21. See "A concubine who is a mother is not sacrificed to for more than one generation" (Ch'ieh-mu pu shih chi shuo), by Shao Ch'ang-heng (*HCCSWP* 67:19a–b), and two other essays arguing about the ritual place of wives and concubines in the ancestral shrine (ibid., 16a–17a, 18a–b). These writers too cited the *Li chi*, particularly the chapter titled "Record of Smaller Matters in Mourning Dress" ("Sang fu hsiao chi"), where the placement of concubines' tablets is discussed. See *Li chi* 15 (Legge 1967 2:450–59).

22. See, for example, the essay on domestic relations ("Nei lun") by T'ang Chen (*HCCSWP* 60:8a–9), and Liu Shao-pan's "Letter to my younger brother on the subject 'family division always starts with women'" (ibid., 10a–b).

23. Wang Hui-tsu's father, K'ai-mu, was first married to a woman surnamed Fang, and later took a concubine née Hsu. After his first wife died, he took a second wife, née Wang. When K'ai-mu died, neither the second wife nor the concubine remarried; both were honored with imperial rescripts of merit and a memorial arch in recognition of their chastity. See *SCTYH* 1:3a.

24. Both of the early texts contain warnings about taking a successor wife, though the *Yuan-shih shih-fan* is more optimistic than the *Yen-shih chia-hsun*: Yuan Ts'ai was certain that a "wise woman" could be found to meet the challenges of the role. See *YSCH* 1:7b–9b and *YSSF* 1:23b (Ebrey 1984:219).

25. Wang Hui-tsu's relationship with the "pair of chaste widows" has provoked comment. Patricia Ebrey points out that his widowed stepmother had only one stepson and no sons of her own, which may account for his close ties to her. Diane Hughes observes that the most ardent advocates of ideal family types may be those who were deprived of the ideal in their own experience.

26. This warning was sounded by Yuan Ts'ai (*YSSF* 3:17b; Ebrey 1984:304) and elsewhere throughout the lexicon of Ch'ing writings on the domestic realm (H. Liu 1959b:94). Wang Hui-tsu warned about the "three old women and the six hags," especially nuns (*SCTYH* 3:26a). The conventional list names Buddhist nuns, Taoist nuns, diviners, procuresses, go-betweens, instructresses, peddlers, herbalists, and midwives. Accepted translations of the Chinese terms vary widely. For the list, see Chao I 1957:832. One standard translation appears in Ayscough 1937:87.

27. The phrase *k'uei-ssu* here conventionally means to keep a household under surveillance with the intention of robbing it: to "case," in other words.

28. On marriage and the reproduction of class and status, see the following representatives of an extensive literature: Chojnacki 1975; Bourdieu 1976; and Arrom 1985:145–51. Stolcke (1981:39–40) offers a stimulating theoretical statement of this relationship. Maintaining the honor and purity of women, expressing status through dowry giving, and invoking the protection of state or church in the pursuit of class endogamy are cross-cultural patterns that appear in all complex societies.

29. See Dorothy Yin-yee Ko, "Toward a Social History of Women in Seventeenth-Century China." Ph.D. diss., Stanford University, 1989.

GLOSSARY

Chang Hsueh-ch'eng　章學誠

Ch'en Hung-mou　陳宏謀

ch'eng-ming　稱名

ch'i (equal)　齊

ch'i (paramour)　妻

ch'i (to perch)　棲

ch'i (wife)　妻

chia chiao　家教

Chiao fang ssu　教坊司

Chiao-nü i-kuei　教女遺規

"Chiao t'e sheng"　交特牲

"Chieh-fu shuo"　節婦說

ch'ieh (concubine)　妾

ch'ieh (lover)　妾

chien　賤

Chih-pu-tsu-chai ts'ung-shu　知不足齋叢書

ch'ih-shen she-shih　持身涉世

"Ch'ü li"　曲禮

fu (husband)　夫

fu (to support)　扶

Fu hsueh　婦學

Fu hsueh san tse　婦學三則

fu-jen　夫人

hou　后

hsien　賢

hsien nü　賢女

Hsu (Jen Hsiao-wen)　徐(仁孝文)

Huang-ch'ao ching-shih wen-pien
　皇朝經世文編

"Hun i"　昏義

i　義

i-fu　義夫

i-hsi　義媳

I li　儀禮

i-nan　義男

i-nü　義女

Kuei fan　閨範

k'uei-ssu　窺伺

Li chi　禮記

liang　良

lien-tseng　奩贈

Lü K'un　呂坤

min-chien fu-nü　民間婦女

Nei hsun　內訓

"Nei tse"　內則

Nü chieh　女誡

Nü-fan chieh-lu　女範捷錄

Nü lun-yü　女論語

nü-shih　女士

Nü ssu-shu　女四書

Pan Chao　班昭

p'in tse wei ch'i　聘則為妻

p'in (betrothal gifts)　聘

p'in (concubine)　嬪

Po-hu t'ung　白虎通

pu-i　不義

pu-k'o shih shih man shu　不可恃嫡慢庶

Shih ching　詩經

shih-fu　世婦

Shih hou-mu　事後母

shih-hsi　嫡媳

shu-ku　庶姑

Shuang-chieh-t'ang yung-hsun　雙節堂庸訓

ssu te　四德

Sung Juo-hua　宋若華

ta i　大義

tao　道

tso-hui　做會

Wang Hsiang　王相

wang hua　王化

Wang Hui-tsu　汪輝祖

Wei Yuan　魏源

yang　陽

Yen Chih-t'ui　顏之推

Yen-shih chia-hsun　顏氏家訓

yin　陰

Yü Cheng-hsieh　俞正燮

yü-ch'i　御妻

Yuan-shih shih-fan　袁氏世範

Yuan Ts'ai　袁采

yueh-hu　樂戶

yung-mien　擁面

REFERENCES

Primary Sources

Chao I 趙翼. *Kai-yü ts'ung-k'ao* 陔餘叢考. c. 1775; reprint, Shanghai: Commercial Press, 1957.

CNIK   *Ch'ung-k'an chiao-nü i-kuei* 重刊教女遺規, comp. Ch'en Hung-mou 陳宏謀. 1895 edition.

CPTC   *Chih-pu-tsu-chai ts'ung-shu* 知不足齋叢書, comp. Pao T'ing-po 鮑廷博. 1823; reprint, Shanghai: Ku-shu liu-t'ung-ch'u, 1921.

HCCSWP   *Huang-ch'ao ching-shih wen-pien* 皇朝經世文編, comp. Wei Yuan 魏源. Preface dated 1826; reprint, Taipei: Kuo-feng ch'u-pan-she, 1963.

Ho Chu 賀鑄. 1973. "Yung-su sang-li so-chi" 甬俗喪禮瑣記. In *Ning-po hsi-su ts'ung-t'an* 寧波習俗叢談, ed. Chang Hsing-chou 張行周. Taipei: Min-chu ch'u-pan-she.

IL   *I li* 儀禮. Ssu-pu pei-yao edition.

KSLK   *Kuei-ssu lei-kao* 癸巳類稿, by Yü Cheng-hsieh 俞正燮. 1833; reprint, Shanghai: Commercial Press, 1957.

KSTK   *Kuei-ssu ts'un-kao* 癸巳存稿, by Yü Cheng-hsieh 俞正燮. 1833; reprint, Shanghai: Commercial Press, 1957.

LC   *Li chi* 禮記. Ssu-pu pei-yao edition.

NC   *Nü chieh* 女誡, by Pan Chao 班昭. Reprinted in *Nü ssu-shu* 女四書. Shanghai, 1893–94 edition.

PHT   *Po-hu t'ung* 白虎通. Ts'ung-shu chi-ch'eng edition, vols. 238–39.

SCTYH   *Shuang-chieh-t'ang yung-hsun* 雙節堂庸訓, by Wang Hui-tsu 汪輝祖. Preface dated 1794; reprint, Taipei: Hua-wen shu-chü, 1970.

YSCH   *Yen-shih chia-hsun* 顏氏家訓. n.d.; reprint, *CPTC*, vol. 11.

YSSF   *Yuan-shih shih-fan* 袁氏世範. Preface dated 1788; reprint, *CPTC*, vol. 14.

Secondary Sources

Arrom, Silvia Marina. 1985. *The Women of Mexico City, 1790–1857*. Stanford: Stanford University Press.

Ayscough, Florence. 1937. *Chinese Women: Yesterday and Today*. Boston: Houghton-Mifflin.

Bourdieu, Pierre. 1976. "Marriage Strategies as Strategies of Social Reproduction." In *Family and Society: Selections from the Annales, Economies, Sociétiés, Civilisations*, ed. Robert Forster and Orest Ranum. Baltimore: Johns Hopkins University Press.

Cahill, James. 1967. *Fantastics and Eccentrics in Chinese Painting*. New York: The Asia Society.

Ch'en Tung-yuan 陳東原. 1928. *Chung-kuo fu-nü sheng-huo shih* 中國婦女生活史 (A history of the lives of Chinese women). Shanghai: Commercial Press.

Chojnacki, Stanley. 1975. "Dowries and Kinsmen in Early Renaissance Venice." *Journal of Interdisciplinary History* 5.4:571–600.

Ch'ü, T'ung-tsu. 1961. *Law and Society in Traditional China*. Paris: Mouton.

Chung, Priscilla Ching. 1981. *Palace Women in the Northern Sung, 960–1126*. Leiden: E. J. Brill.

Ebrey, Patricia. 1981. "Women in the Kinship System of the Southern Song Upper

Class." In *Women in China*, ed. Richard Guisso and Stanley Johannesen. Youngstown, N.Y.: Philo Press.

———. 1984. *Family and Property in Sung China: Yüan Ts'ai's Precepts for Social Life*. Princeton: Princeton University Press.

———. 1986. "Concubines in Sung China." *Journal of Family History* 11.1:1–24.

Elman, Benjamin. 1984. *From Philosophy to Philology: Intellectual and Social Aspects of Change in Later Imperial China*. Cambridge: Harvard University Press.

Elvin, Mark. 1984. "Female Virtue and the State in China." *Past and Present* 104: 111–52.

Handlin, Joanna F. 1975. "Lü K'un's New Audience: The Influence of Women's Literacy on Sixteenth-Century Thought." In *Women in Chinese Society*, ed. Margery Wolf and Roxane Witke. Stanford: Stanford University Press.

Harrell, Stevan, and Sara A. Dickey. 1985. "Dowry Systems in Complex Societies." *Ethnology* 24.2:105–20.

Ho Ping-ti. 1962. *The Ladder of Success in Imperial China: Aspects of Social Mobility, 1368–1911*. New York: Columbia University Press.

Hu Wen-k'ai 胡文楷 1956. *Li-tai fu-nü chu-tso k'ao* 歷代婦女著作考 (A review of women's writings throughout history). Rev. ed., Shanghai: Commercial Press, 1985.

Hummel, Arthur W., ed. 1943–44. *Eminent Chinese of the Ch'ing Period*. 2 vols. Washington, D.C.: U.S. Government Printing Office.

Hyland, Alice R. M. 1987. *Deities, Emperors, Ladies and Literati: Figure Painting of the Ming and Qing Dynasties*. Birmingham, Ala.: Birmingham Museum of Art.

Jones, Susan Mann, and Philip A. Kuhn. 1978. "Dynastic Decline and the Roots of Rebellion." In *The Cambridge History of China: Late Ch'ing, 1800–1911*, ed. John K. Fairbank. Vol. 10, p. 1. New York: Cambridge University Press.

Ko, Dorothy Yin-yee. 1989. "Toward a Social History of Women in Seventeenth-Century China." Ph.D. diss., Stanford University.

Kulp, Daniel Harrison. 1925. *Country Life in South China: The Sociology of Familism*. New York: Columbia University Teacher's College.

Legge, James, trans. 1967. *Li Chi: Book of Rites*. 2 vols. New Hyde Park, N.Y.: University Books.

Liang Ch'i-ch'ao 梁啟超. 1955. *Chung-kuo chin-san-pai-nien hsueh-shu-shih* 中國近三百年學術史 (Intellectual history of China during the last 300 years). Taipei: Chung-hua shu-chü.

Liu Chi-hua 劉紀華. 1934. "Chung-kuo chen-chieh kuan-nien ti li-shih yen-pien" 中國貞節觀念的歷史演變 (The historical transformation of the concept of chastity in China). *She-hui hsueh-chieh* 8:19–35.

Liu, Hui-chen Wang. 1959a. "An Analysis of Chinese Clan Rules: Confucian Theories in Action." In *Confucianism in Action*, ed. David S. Nivison and Arthur F. Wright. Stanford: Stanford University Press.

———. 1959b. *The Traditional Chinese Clan Rules*. Locust Valley, N.Y.: J. J. Augustin.

Mann, Susan (see also Jones, Susan Mann). 1985. "Historical Change in Female Biography from Song to Qing Times." *Transactions of the International Conference of Orientalists in Japan* 30:65–77.

———. 1986. "Shapers of a Common Culture: Moral Education under Qing Rule." Paper presented at the University of California, San Diego. October.

————. 1987. "Widows in the Kinship, Class, and Community Structures of Qing Dynasty China." *Journal of Asian Studies* 46.1:37–56.

Morohashi Tetsuji 諸橋轍次. 1957–60. *Daikanwa jiten* 大漢和辭典 (Great Chinese-Japanese dictionary). 12 vols. Tokyo: Taishūkan shoten.

Naquin, Susan, and Evelyn S. Rawski. 1987. *Chinese Society in the Eighteenth Century.* New Haven: Yale University Press.

Nivison, David S. 1966. *The Life and Thought of Chang Hsüeh-ch'eng (1738–1801).* Stanford: Stanford University Press.

Parish, William L., and Martin King Whyte. 1978. *Village and Family in Contemporary China.* Chicago: University of Chicago Press.

Rankin, Mary Backus. 1975. "The Emergence of Women at the End of the Ch'ing: The Case of Ch'iu Chin." In *Women in Chinese Society*, ed. Margery Wolf and Roxane Witke. Stanford: Stanford University Press.

Ropp, Paul. 1981. *Dissent in Early Modern China: Ju-lin Wai-shih and Ch'ing Social Criticism.* Ann Arbor: University of Michigan Press.

Schneider, Jane. 1971. "Of Vigilance and Virgins: Honor, Shame and Access to Resources in Mediterranean Society." *Ethnology* 10:1–23.

Schwartz, Benjamin. 1959. "Some Polarities in Confucian Thought." In *Confucianism in Action*, ed. David S. Nivison and Arthur F. Wright. Stanford: Stanford University Press.

Steele, John, trans. 1917; reprint, 1966. *The I-li, or Book of Etiquette and Ceremonial.* Taipei: Ch'eng-wen.

Stolcke, Verena. 1981. "Women's Labours: The Naturalisation of Social Inequality and Women's Subordination." In *Of Marriage and the Market*, ed. Kate Young, Carol Wolkowitz, and Roslyn McCullagh. London: CSE Books.

Swann, Nancy Lee. 1932. *Pan Chao: Foremost Woman Scholar of China.* New York: Century.

Terada Takanobu 寺田隆信. 1959. "Yōseitei no semmin kaihōrei ni tsuite" 雍正帝 の賤民開放令につで (The emancipation of the debased people during the Yung-cheng reign period). *Tōyōshi kenkyū* 18.3:124–41.

Tjan, Tjoe Som. 1949, 1952; reprint, 1973. *Po Hu T'ung: The Comprehensive Discussions in the White Tiger Hall.* 2 vols. Westport, Conn.: Hyperion Press.

Wang Shu-nu 王书奴. 1933; reprint, 1988. *Chung-kuo ch'ang-chi shih* 中国娼妓史 (A history of prostitution in China). Shanghai: Shang-hai san-lien shu-tien.

Wolf, Margery. 1972. *Women and the Family in Rural Taiwan.* Stanford: Stanford University Press.

Yü Ying-shih. 1975. "Some Preliminary Observations on the Rise of Confucian Intellectualism." *Tsing Hua Journal of Chinese Studies* 11:105–46.

SEVEN

Wives, Concubines, and Maids

Servitude and Kinship in the Hong Kong Region, 1900–1940

Rubie S. Watson

Anthropologists and historians have often written about the household as if it were a social actor with its own set of unquestioned goals, interests, and survival strategies. In study after study scholars have granted the household a single, unified voice; a voice, it should be noted, that is nearly always male. In recent years, this approach has come under increasing criticism (see, e.g., Dwyer and Bruce 1988; Hartman 1981; Rapp 1978; Thorne and Yalom 1982; Yanagisako 1984). In the China field Margery Wolf's work on the uterine family (1972) and Myron Cohen's discussion of women's private property (1976:164–91) clearly demonstrate that their informants' households were made up of different constituencies whose goals and ambitions were often at odds. The interests of women and men did not always coincide, nor, they argue, did all household women share the same agenda.

In the following pages I discuss the ways in which servile status and gender inequality interact to create conditions of subordination and hierarchy within the household itself. I argue that the inequality among household men differs from that among household women and that these differences are related to the overall structure of gender and class inequality. In what ways, I ask, are wives, concubines, and maids affected by gender and class stratification, and how do their ties to the household and family differ from one another and from coresident males? The reference point for this study is, as Robertson and Klein point out in their discussion of slavery and gender in Africa, at the "intersection of intra- and extrafamilial stratification" (1983:18).

In this paper I examine the status of wives, concubines, and "little maids" in the Hong Kong region from 1900 to 1940. The households discussed in this paper tended to be large, including concubines, slaves, indentured menials, and servants as well as three or four generations of family members. Some entered the household through birth or marriage while others arrived via a more circuitous route involving China's enormous market in people. Within a single household, attachments might involve relations between employer and employee, master and servant, owner and owned, debtor and lender.

In the households described in this paper, membership was highly fluid; there was, in fact, considerable turnover in both family members and their retainers. Furthermore, clear distinctions among people living in the same household were not always easy to make; servants, including servile menials, were often spoken of as kin, and kin were sometimes treated as servants. Within the households of the wealthy there was, however, one group who maintained a clearly demarcated and unambiguous position. These were men who through birth or adoption had shareholding rights in the family estate and, like their fathers and grandfathers before them, expected someday to assume the role of household head (*chia-chang*). Bound by ties of agnation, these men and boys had claims and attachments to the household and family that their sisters, who were destined to leave the communities of their birth, did not. Rights to residence, property, and placement in the ancestral cult clearly distinguished the household's male servants and slaves from the *chia chang* and his agnates.

If unambiguous boundaries could be drawn between groups of household men, what distinguished household women? In a recent article Patricia Ebrey has argued that in Sung China clear distinctions can be made between women related to the household head through ties of kinship and marriage and those "menial women" who entered the household through purchase, debt, or wage employment (1986:2, 6).[1] If "family women" were indeed different from coresident, menial women, in the period under discussion here, how did they differ? Can the same variables we use to distinguish household men be used to classify household women? In Chinese society, women as a category had a dependent status. In a recent article, Hill Gates argues that Chinese women suffered from a kind of sociocultural invisibility (1989:813). Before marriage they were under the control of their fathers; after marriage they were dependent on their husbands, and if they outlived their spouses, they fell under the jural authority of their sons. Their kinship status was ambiguous. Women, Margery Wolf points out, are only temporary sojourners in their father's households, and even at marriage their integration into their husband's family is only partial (1972:32–37; see also R. Watson 1981:610–611; 1986). Writing of the patrilineal family in rural Taiwan, Wolf comments that the bride is an outsider who serves the family of her husband but remains beyond its formal boundaries (1972:35). Chinese women could not inherit in their own right the family estate of their father or their husband; nor did they have shares in ancestral or lineage property (see Shiga 1978:110, 120). When considered against the standards of their brothers and husbands, it is clear that women were not equal partners in what Gates labels the "patricorporations" of late imperial China (1989:805) or, for that matter, in the wider society of which they were a part. If women did indeed stand outside the formal property-holding family, it would appear that economic criteria are not sufficient to distinguish among household women. Categories of men can be demarcated according to whether they had rights to material assets; with women the situation is more complicated.

Among household women there are two groups in particular—concubines (*ch'ieh*)[2] and "little maids" (in Cantonese, *mui jai*)—that defy easy categorization. Among a household's "unfree population,"[3] they came closest to assuming a kin role. There were, of course, important differences between the two; maids fell more easily within the servant category than did concubines, who participated more fully in the life of the family. Both groups of women, however, shared a marginal status that makes them difficult to classify.

If concubines and *mui jai* present problems of classification, how do they compare to the wives and daughters of the families they served? I have already noted that wives and daughters were not full shareholders in the family estate, nor did they wield the kind of authority and power that was the prerogative of the household head. Neither, it should be noted, could they aspire, like their brothers and husbands, to the status of *chia chang*. In the realm of family authority and property, therefore, it appears that categories of women are not as easily distinguished as are those of men. The situation is different, however, if we look to other factors.

Wives and daughters were responsible for the daily care of the household's ancestors and gods; concubines and maids had no such responsibility. Daughters left the household and wives entered it with considerable ceremony; the entries and departures of concubines, maids, and other menials were perfunctory, involving little or no ritualization. Wives had a claim on descendants' attention in the afterlife; menial women had none. These are important differences, but further distinctions can be made.

In order to understand how gender inequality affected household relations, we need to know more about the lives of the women. How did wives, concubines, and maids enter the household? Did they retain ties to their natal families and did their entry create new kin ties for their husbands, brothers, and future offspring? Are we right in assuming that all women were equally alienated from the family estate? The answers to these questions will help us to better appreciate the complex links between gender inequality and other forms of subordination.

Concubines and little maids were found throughout China but this discussion focuses on a Cantonese-speaking area of southeastern China.[4] Because British colonials took a keen interest in the *mui jai* population and conducted a number of investigations into their status, there exists a substantial literature on the *mui jai* problem in Hong Kong.[5] I rely in particular on one report published in 1937 by a specially constituted colonial commission (hereafter referred to as Report 1937); this publication, it should be noted, summarizes earlier investigations and recommendations. In 1977–78 and again in the summers of 1985 and 1988 I conducted fieldwork in the single-lineage village of Ha Tsuen in Hong Kong's New Territories. The material I collected there, both interviews and documentary data, have also been utilized in this analysis. During my fieldwork I was able to interview women who either had been served by *mui jai* or had themselves been *mui jai* or concubines.

While I was writing this chapter, Maria Jaschok's book, *Concubines and Bondservants: The Social History of a Chinese Custom*, was published. In a series of life histories, Jaschok concentrates on the experience of specific concubines and maids, providing rich detail on their personal backgrounds and the effect those had on their roles within the households they joined. Jaschok's book and this chapter, which seeks to examine concubines and maids in relation to the wives and daughters among whom they lived, provide each in its own way evidence of the class, status, and gender divisions that permeated the inner courts of many Chinese households.

MARKETS IN PEOPLE AND SERVICES

In the late imperial and Republican periods it was not uncommon for domestic servants and even industrial workers to have their labor coerced by ties of debt bondage or involuntary indenture (see, e.g., Honig 1986; Hershatter 1986; J. Watson 1980b). It is important to see *mui jai* and concubines within the context of this market in people. According to James Watson, until 1949 "China had one of the largest and most comprehensive markets for the exchange of human beings in the world" (ibid., 223). The forms of bonded and slave labor were highly variable. Joseph McDermott's discussion (1981) of bondservants highlights the complicated array of servile labor forms during the Ming period (1368–1644). Unfortunately, we have as yet no comprehensive studies that plot the trajectory of slavery and bondage during the late imperial and Republican periods. There are enormous gaps in our knowledge of the changing patterns of bondage in China. To what extent did the history of male and female bondage differ or converge? Were the bonds that held women different from those that enslaved or indentured men? Were females more likely to be pawned or sold than males?

In Hong Kong's New Territories during the Ch'ing, male slaves (*hsi min*), whose status was inherited through the male line, were attached to many wealthy households. With their emancipation at the time of the Republican Revolution in 1911, however, male slavery ceased to exist as a viable institution in this area (see J. Watson 1980b:245). Pawning and indenture, nevertheless, continued to be part of the labor scene until World War II, and women, it would appear, were well represented, perhaps overrepresented, among Hong Kong's unfree population.

In recent years scholars have argued (see, e.g., Robertson and Klein 1983; Clinton 1982) that in Africa and the southern United States the prevailing systems of gender inequality and of servitude interacted in complex ways to affect the lives of the free and unfree of both sexes. In the view of some students of sub-Saharan Africa, slavery itself was subsumed by the sexual division of labor and gender subordination. Many scholars of the antebellum South believe slavery perpetuated and strengthened gender discrimination and an ideology of female dependence (for a critical discussion of this view see Lebsock 1984). In China we have yet to appreciate the interaction between inequalities based on gender and those based on servitude. Detailed studies of slavery and indenture, domestic service, and labor contracts in late imperial China are necessary if we are to adequately address this interactive process.

In an 1879 sentencing of five people accused of kidnapping and selling children in Hong Kong, Sir John Smale, a Supreme Court justice, noted that two forms of "slavery" continued to be well represented in the colony. One was domestic servitude (presumably referring to *mui jai*) and the other was the acquisition of women for purposes of prostitution (Report 1937:123). Smale estimated Hong Kong's "slave population" in the 1870s to be 10,000 (out of a total population of 150,000). If I am correct in assuming that Smale's category of domestic slavery refers to *mui jai*, it seems likely that the vast majority of Hong Kong's servile population were girls and women. Andrea Sankar, an anthropologist who studied domestic servants in Hong Kong, points out that in the early 1900s *mui jai* constituted the majority of nonfamily labor in local households (1978:53). Evidence will be presented in this paper that suggests *mui jai* were present in substantial numbers until World War II.

A little maid (or *mui jai*, literally "little younger sister") is defined in the Hong Kong Commission Report of 1937 as "a girl who has been transferred from her own family, either directly or through a third party, to another family with the intention that she . . . be used as a domestic servant, not in receipt of regular wages and [not] at liberty to leave her employer's family of her own free will or at the will of her parent" (Report 1937:22). The definition concludes by noting that there was usually a document giving the details of the transfer and the "consideration passing" between parents (or *mui jai* dealer) and master.[6] The term of service was seldom specified, but it was expected that the master or mistress would marry off the *mui jai* when she was eighteen or so. It should be noted that little maids entered their master's household at the age of eight or nine years. At marriage the servant's obligation to her master ended and she was said to become a free person. Some households apparently failed to free their *mui jai*, keeping them indefinitely in their servile status. There are also indications that at least some masters resold their *mui jai* (see, e.g., Jaschok 1988:8, 45, 70, 72).[7]

In a 1922 report prepared by relief societies, the number of *mui jai* in Hong Kong was estimated at 10,000 (Report 1937:157; see also Jaschok 1988:87, 106). Whether this figure simply repeats Sir John Smale's estimate for 1879 or is in fact an accurate reflection of *mui jai* numbers in 1922 is difficult to determine at this point. Although the acquisition of new *mui jai* was prohibited by Hong Kong law in 1923 (Report 1937:159, 126), many local Chinese continued to incorporate little maids into their households, insisting these girls were really adopted daughters. In 1929 a formal register of *mui jai* was established and left open for six months; anyone possessing an unregistered *mui jai* after the closing date was considered to be in violation of the ordinance (ibid., 216). By June 1, 1930, when the register was sealed 4,252 *mui jai* had been recorded. The governor of Hong Kong hailed the registration a success and maintained that the previous figure of 10,000 *mui jai* had only been a guess. This was not the end of the debate, however. The Hong Kong Census of 1921 listed 8,653 *mui jai*, and many believed that the number of maids could not have declined so precipitately in the nine years after the census—a period, it should be noted, during which the general population was steadily increasing. Many knowledgeable sources claimed that many more *mui jai* (10,000–12,000) were living in the colony and chided the authorities for their weak enforcement of the registration provision (ibid., 216–17). In fact, the Chinese press during this period declared that the proportion of *mui jai* was increasing rather than decreasing (ibid., 216).

Although *mui jai* were most often found in the households of the urban middle and upper classes, they were by no means restricted to the cities. Rural shopkeepers and rich peasants could and did avail themselves of *mui jai* labor. In Hong Kong's hinterland (which includes the village of Ha Tsuen where I conducted research in 1977–78) I was told that *mui jai* were to be found in a number of village households prior to World War II. Unfortunately, there are no published estimates of the number of *mui jai* living in Hong Kong villages, but they were considered to be a normal part of the households of the rich (see J. Watson 1980b; R. Watson 1985:104). According to Ha Tsuen residents, *mui jai* worked as household servants in their village until 1951 when the last "little maid" left her master's house to become a concubine of a childless peasant.

Like *mui jai*, concubines (*ch'ieh*) were to be found in the households of the well-off, but their functions were, of course, different. Chinese concubines were recognized sexual partners who lived in their mate's household and whose offspring were legitimate. Legally a Chinese man could have only one wife (*ch'i*), and a concubine therefore had a lower social status than the wife (Shiga 1967; for Sung period see Ebrey 1986). In contrast to wives, concubines were not endowed with property when they moved to their consort's household; their families received no betrothal gifts and the concubines themselves received no dowries. Perpetuating the male line was the only respectable reason for taking a concubine, although this stricture was often ignored among the wealthy (for a general description of concubinage see Goody 1976:91; 1983:76). Concubines continued to have a legal status well into the Republican period on the Chinese mainland (see Lang 1946:118), and in Hong Kong they enjoyed legal protection until 1971, when laws were written forbidding unions with concubines (Evans 1973:22).

Surveys on the incidence of concubines in early twentieth-century China present conflicting results. According to Buck's 1930s survey data, concubines made up only 0.2 percent of family members in all of China (1937:367; for figures on Taiwan see Pasternak 1983:56–57). Other scholars working on specific populations, however, report significantly higher rates. According to Olga Lang, who conducted a survey of 1,700 high school and college students in the 1930s, 11.4 percent of the students reported that a concubine lived in their family (1946:220–21). This survey covered ten cities in north, south, and central China and apparently focused on middle- and upper-middle-class families (1946:x). Lang's material supports the commonly accepted view that concubines were most likely to be found among the wealthy (on this point see also C. K. Yang 1959:84; Eberhard 1962:130, 188; Lang 1946:39, 220). Sidney Gamble's work in a rural county near Peking and Martin Yang's research in Shantung also confirm the association with wealth. In a survey conducted during the 1920s, Gamble found that the rates of concubinage were "one in 18 for the families with over 100 *mu* [of land], but only one in 183 for the families with less than 50 *mu*" (1954:38). Yang reports that the Shantung villagers he studied in north China during the 1930s objected to concubinage even if a wife proved barren, and accordingly he found no concubines in the farming community of Taitou. Yang believes that both poverty and "social tradition" explain the lack of concubinage (1945:114).

My own research in Ha Tsuen and Baker's work in the New Territories community of Sheung Shui (1968:141) underline the link between wealth and political influence on the one hand and concubinage on the other. In the hamlet where I resided, there were three concubines still living in three separate households (out of a total of twenty-three households, 1977–78 data).[8] Two of these women were the concubines of important village leaders, and one belonged to a local businessman. Although Baker provides no overall figure for Sheung Shui as a whole, he found that twelve of the village's thirty-one elected representatives maintained a concubine in the early 1960s (1968:141).

Data from Hakka villages in rural Hong Kong and from the sericulture areas of the Pearl River Delta suggest that although economic status was an important factor in concubinage, wealth is not sufficient to explain it in every case. Both Elizabeth Johnson (1976:175) and Jean Pratt (1960:155) found concubines living in the poor Hakka communities they studied. And in Shun-

te County, northwest of Hong Kong, Marjorie Topley found that "concubinage appears to have been widespread among tenant farmers as well as
wealthier landowners" (1975:77).

Janice Stockard, in her recent book on marriage patterns in the Pearl
River Delta, describes an extremely interesting form of concubinage and
marriage in which wage-earning brides (often workers in the local silk industry) married, but chose not to live with, their "husbands." Such a woman,
who was recognized as *ch'i* (in Cantonese as *daaih pouh*), paid a lump sum of
money to her husband's family, which was used to purchase a concubine
(Stockard refers to such women as "secondary wives"), who then took up
residence with the husband. Children born of such unions accepted their
father's wife, not their concubine mother, as their *daaih ma*, or "great
mother." According to Stockard, such an arrangement had the advantage of
securing the appropriate status of wife and mother to the *ch'i*, without the
usual loss of economic independence. Such unions were especially important
in safeguarding a woman's position in the afterlife; the husband's family incorporated the tablet of the wife (*ch'i*) into their domestic ancestral cult at her
death (1989:48–69). Stockard points out that many "secondary wives" were
former *mui jai* (1989:29, 66).

The communities studied by Johnson, Pratt, Topley, and Stockard share
a pattern of male outmigration and reliance on women's labor (both in agriculture and in wage work). Whether these two factors alone or in combination with other forces produced the forms of concubinage we find in this area
remains to be seen. At this point it seems unlikely that concubinage can be
explained by a single set of economic or social factors. What is clear is that
concubines were a feature of many Chinese households, and that in such
households women from vastly different backgrounds and often with very
different goals were forced to interact.

Unfortunately, detailed studies of the "women's quarters" in elite households are rare in the China field.[9] Jaschok is one of the few historians to pay
attention to the inner household world of women. Her work dramatically
points up the conflicts that emerge when women from different backgrounds
are thrown together by decisions made by others. It has often been overlooked that clashes between the values and attitudes of, for example, an ex-
prostitute concubine and an upper-class wife were likely, and perhaps even
inevitable. Jaschok captures the cultural divide between these women when
she writes of the concubine Xiao-li: "Unhindered by female models of passive acquiescence, toughened by material deprivation in her childhood and
the need for survival against all odds, trained by a shrewd and worldly
woman, Xiao-li was no 'frog in the well'. . . but a calculating strategist who
quickly realized where her source of power and strength would lie and how to
utilize it" (1988:25; see also 27–28, 32). Jaschok argues that within the
household, women faced women as rivals "for emotional hold over 'key'
males" (ibid., 24).

MODE OF ACQUISITION: WIVES, CONCUBINES, AND MAIDS

The entry of wives, concubines, and maids into a household was marked by a transfer of money. The way people thought about and discussed these transfers, however, differed significantly. The language of gifts and reciprocity was used for wives; the idiom of the marketplace was used for concubines and maids.

The wife (or *ch'i*) went through a complicated set of rites before entering her husband's family (for detailed descriptions of these rites see Freedman 1967; R. Watson 1981). First, a formal betrothal took place, after which the bride's family was presented with money and food gifts. On the wedding day the bride was carried with great fanfare from her parents' house to the groom's village in a red sedan chair; in present-day Hong Kong a decorated Mercedes-Benz is used. Upon arriving at her new home, the bride worshiped her husband's ancestors. A marriage feast was held on the evening of the wedding day, and that night the marriage was consummated. On the final day of the marriage festivities food gifts (in Hong Kong a roast pig, sugar, and tea) were presented to the bride's family, signifying, my informants told me, the full acceptance of the bride as wife and daughter-in-law.

In marrying a wife, the transfer of gifts and money was sometimes one-sided—from groom's family to bride's. But the bride's family always made some return to the groom's side. Rich families gave substantial dowries to brides (see Dennerline 1986; Ebrey 1981; R. Watson 1981), but even among the poor the bride did not enter her husband's house empty-handed. At the very least, she would be accompanied by a few small pieces of jewelry, clothes, a chest, and some household articles. During my fieldwork in Ha Tsuen, village women stressed that a bride must bring something into the marriage lest she be labeled a concubine.

A concubine entered her master's household quietly, without any fanfare or ceremony. In fact, she was positively enjoined from traveling to her new household via the red sedan chair, which only the *ch'i* could use (see, e.g., Jamieson 1970:45–46; M. Yang 1945:113; Stockard 1989:30; Report 1937:13). Writing of the Hong Kong village of Sheung Shui in the early 1960s, Baker notes: "Concubines are frequently taken with no ceremony at all" (1968:50). The term *mai* (to buy) was used to describe the acquisition of a concubine; in most cases she was purchased outright for life (see J. Watson 1980b:232; for discussion of this point in earlier periods of Chinese history see Ebrey 1981:125; 1984:136; 1986:7). Concubines may have been purchased from a brothel (e.g., C. K. Yang 1959:84; Jaschok 1988:14), from dealers in concubines and maids, or from her parents (e.g., Freedman 1979:99). As already noted, Stockard points out that concubines in the Pearl River Delta were often ex–*mui jai* (1989:29; see also Topley 1975:77; Meskill 1979:226). Ideally concubines, like wives and unlike maids, were acquired for purposes of reproduction, although as I have already noted many men took concubines for their own pleasure or perhaps (as among the nouveau riche) to enhance their status.

In most cases, the only ceremony that a concubine performed on entering her master's household was the formal serving of tea to the principal wife. The concubine then assumed a recognized place in her new environment, and, significantly, children born to her while she resided in her master's house were deemed legitimate. According to the Ch'ing legal code, and later during much of the Republican period, the children of concubines had the same rights as those of the principal wife (van der Sprenkel 1962:15; Lang 1946:118; for Hong Kong see Evans 1973:22). Although it is true that the offspring of concubines were the legal heirs of their fathers, the mothers themselves usually were women from poor families or servile background. Their status, as I note above, was therefore well below that of the households they entered. In social reckoning they were clearly inferior to their consorts, their consorts' families, and even their own children, although as I have already noted such women were not necessarily powerless (see, e.g., Jaschok 1988:49, 59).

Maids, like concubines, were purchased. Unlike concubines who served for life, however, maids (at least in the Hong Kong region) were expected to serve only a limited period, usually until age eighteen or so. Once they were married, they ceased being servants—their part of the "bargain" having been fulfilled. Because their time of service was limited by the obligation of the master to marry them off, *mui jai* were more like indentured servants than slaves (see Report 1937:22). But for all practical purposes the *mui jai* was treated as if she "belonged" to her master. She generally had no contact with her parents and was usually married with the master, not her parents, acting as guardian. In fact, according to Ch'ing law a master was legally responsible for finding husbands for his female servants; failure to fulfill this obligation carried a punishment of "eighty blows" or a fine (Jamieson 1970:43). Like a daughter, the *mui jai*'s procreative life was supposed to start only when she left her master's house.

In Hong Kong a 1923 ordinance stipulated that if *mui jai* or their parents wished to be reunited and the secretary for Chinese affairs made no objection, the *mui jai* could be restored without a payment to the master (Report 1937:159). But such cases were rare. In the period of the 1930s, when information about reinstatement was most highly publicized, only fifty-two cases of restoration were recorded. According to the report, these involved, in almost equal proportions, instances in which the master, the *mui jai* herself, or her parents requested the change (Report 1937:168). When we consider that the *mui jai* population was more than four thousand (by some estimates ten thousand) during this period, and further that no restitution need be paid to the master, the small number of restorations suggests that in most cases the link between *mui jai* and their parents was not strong.

The evidence suggests that many parents severed their ties to or lost contact with their *mui jai* daughter once she was handed over to her master.[10] This was not inevitably the case, however. Jaschok describes cases of ex–*mui jai* who did search out and reestablish links to their natal families. The fact that these examples involved particularly forceful concubines who had effectively usurped the position of the wife or had been the recipient of their consort's largess may well be significant. These restorations were not always smooth, however; Jaschok describes one case in which a concubine was forced to pay off members of her family in order to keep them from creating a public nuisance outside her consort's stately mansion (1988:28–30).

The obligation to marry off the *mui jai* was often used as a rationale for arguing that these servants were really adopted daughters. But the villagers of Ha Tsuen claimed there was a clear difference between the bridewealth or dowry due a daughter and a *mui jai*. The latter, I was told, received only token marriage payments (see also Stockard 1989:29). In fact, village women still denigrate those they dislike by saying that their enemies' dowries were "as small as a *mui jai*'s." People in rural Hong Kong also use the phrase "married like a *mui jai*" to warn their children of the disgrace they would invite by failing to perform the basic set of marriage rites. Stockard's informants recalled cases in which even *mui jai* who married as principal wives were forced to use plain, wooden sedan chairs rather than the usual red ones (1989:30). Clearly, the stigma of being a *mui jai* did not disappear with marriage.

RELATIONS TO HUSBANDS, CONSORTS, AND MASTERS

Both wives and concubines were brought into the household as sexual partners and producers of heirs, but wives were expected to manage domestic tasks, while concubines were themselves managed. Although legally, at least, a concubine's offspring had the same status as the children of the principal wife, it was not unknown for a concubine's children to suffer discrimination and banishment either at the hands of their father or, more often, at the instigation of their half brothers once their father was out of the way (see, e.g., Meskill 1979:221; Johnson 1976:175; Jaschok 1988:38). In the village of Sheung Shui, Baker notes that in contrast to the sons of wives, adopted sons and concubines' sons required special validation rites (1968:49).

Maids were clearly servants. There is considerable evidence, however, that masters sometimes had sexual relations with *mui jai*. If children were born of such unions, it was left to the father to accept or reject paternity. Unlike the European pattern where legitimacy was defined by marriage sanctioned by the church, in China a father could legitimate his children simply by recognizing them publicly at naming rituals (*man yueh*) or at lineage/community rituals (*k'ai teng*) celebrating the birth of sons (see R.

Watson 1985:106–16; Freedman 1979:118). A maid, it should be noted, did not become a concubine or wife simply by bearing her master's children (see, e.g., Meskill 1979:230; Jaschok 1988:70).

Whereas the concubine and wife were linked to their consort by a recognized sexual tie, the *mui jai* might have had little to do with males in the household. As domestic servants, they fell under the effective control of the household's senior women. In fact, *mui jai* benefited women far more directly than men, for *mui jai* took over many of the chores that otherwise would have fallen to daughters and wives. Thus, although men may have been the "owners" of *mui jai*, women were their effective masters.

The literature suggests that a man could "sell" both his wife and his concubines (see, e.g., McGough 1976:126–27; J. Watson 1980b:231–32; for earlier periods see Ebrey 1986:11, 12). For example, he could pawn his wife or give her away in payment of a debt (for examples see Hershatter and Ocko in this volume). It appears that among the Chinese in British Malaya, *mui jai* were safeguarded against such transfers, but in Hong Kong they seem not to have enjoyed this protection. It is ironic indeed that wives and concubines may have been more vulnerable to pawning and resale than indentured servants.

FAMILY TIES: WIVES, CONCUBINES, AND *MUI JAI*

Quite by accident, when I was conducting fieldwork in 1977 I met the son of an ex–*mui jai* who had served one of Ha Tsuen's wealthiest families. This former *mui jai*, now a middle-aged woman living in a public housing estate in urban Hong Kong, continued to make formal New Year visits to her master's family in Ha Tsuen. In this regard she was unusual. To my knowledge she was the only *mui jai* among the six or more who had served this family to return for yearly visits. There was nothing unusual, however, about her marriage. In dramatic contrast to the daughters of the family she served, she had been married to an extremely poor man and her living circumstances were far from comfortable.

The kin status of concubines is perhaps more complex than that of wives or maids. Obviously, they were members of their consort's household, but to what extent were they incorporated into his family? As noted earlier, a concubine's first act upon moving into her master's house was to make a formal offering of tea to the principal wife. This rite of deference appears to have established the concubine in her master's household, marking the union as something more than a fleeting liaison. In Chinese society, it should be noted, concubines had a recognized status, whereas a mistress had none (see Report 1937:16; R. Watson 1985:111–12). Compared to the public and often elaborate marriage rites that marked the incorporation of a wife, the recognition of the concubine was basically a private, household affair involving only the principal wife and the concubine.

Upon entering a household, concubines were often renamed by their consort or perhaps by his wife (see, e.g., Jaschok 1988:148; for a Sung example see Ebrey 1986:17). Sometimes the concubine was addressed by her name or by a kin term with the diminutive prefix *sai* (a Cantonese term meaning "small" or "little"). In Hong Kong the son of a concubine often addressed his mother as "little mother" (*sai ma* in Cantonese) and the son of a principal wife might address his father's concubine as *sai jieh* (literally "little elder sister"). As anyone who is familiar with Chinese society knows, however, the use of a kin term does not necessarily imply kinship. Those who use such terms confer respect, claim intimacy, or mark the superiority/inferiority of the speaker. The term for younger sister (*mui*), which clearly alerts the listener to the fact that a superior is addressing an inferior, is made positively demeaning by the addition of *jai*, which translates as "little" or "diminutive." The same holds true, although perhaps less dramatically, for "little mother" or even "little elder sister."

Among Cantonese the rules governing the extent to which individuals are obliged to mourn various kin are taken very seriously. If a concubine has a son, he is obligated to mourn his biological mother for a requisite three years after death; however, no one else in the family is expected to mourn her. If at the time of her death the concubine has not produced heirs, no one is obliged to mourn (see, e.g., Shiga 1967:552–53). As for members of the concubine's natal family, there is no indication that they have any mourning responsibilities at all. Thus, the treatment of the concubine after death suggests that the biological tie between mother and son is upheld, but her status within her consort's and her natal family is in fact negated.

A concubine was not supposed to be directly involved with her consort's parents, nor was she allowed to worship his ancestors (Ch'ü 1961:125); these privileges were reserved for the wife. Furthermore, many lineages had regulations against listing concubines in written genealogies (see, e.g., Eberhard 1962:47; Meskill 1979:327 n. 20; Hui-chen Wang Liu 1959:90). In Ha Tsuen concubines' names were added to genealogies only if they produced male heirs (cf. Harrell 1985:83; Tsui-jung Liu 1975:16, 20). Baker reports a similar situation for Sheung Shui (1968:50).

Concubines who failed to produce sons could find themselves in a precarious position. The two New Territories families from whom I rented houses in 1969–70 and 1977–78 both had a history of serial concubinage. Neither of these families aspired to literati status, but in both cases the father of the present household head had taken in four or five concubines over a period of about thirty years. When they failed to produce sons, I was told by neighbors, the concubines were forced to leave or ran away. Whether they were "resold," no one knew or would tell me. In each case one concubine, the last of the series, remained permanently in the family. One of these women raised an adopted son and the other eventually gave birth to a son.

When a woman became a concubine she entered a private, domestic sphere. She was cut off from the outside world and became enmeshed in the private domain of her consort and his household. Her situation was similar to that of a wife, albeit more circumscribed. A wife had links to kin outside her husband's family; these relations gave her a recognized position among her husband's kin and in the wider community. Her father and brothers safe-guarded her position, and the status of her natal family helped to determine her own status as she entered her husband's household. Older women in Ha Tsuen put great store in the dowry they received and the manner in which their parents celebrated their betrothals. A concubine did not enjoy these associations and the protection they afforded.

Writing of concubines in Japanese-occupied Taiwan (1895–1945), James McGough quotes an adage that leaves little doubt about how local peasants viewed the disposition of a daughter who had been sold to others: "After you've sold a [daughter], you can't even call out [her] name. After you've sold a field, you can't even have access to its frontage" (1976:30). McGough argues that the sale of a daughter as a concubine implies the severing of her kin ties to her natal family (1976:29). Although, as Jaschok points out, some concubines did reestablish ties to their natal kin (see above), the evidence suggests that in most cases concubines tended to exist at the periphery of the world of family and kinship (cf. 1988:31–32, 76). Without kin, with little or no public (extradomestic) recognition of her role, with no dowry or bridal gifts to secure her status, the concubine bordered on being a nonperson.

Although concubines were not themselves kin, their children were accepted as members of their consorts' families. The offspring of concubines had social fathers, but did they have social mothers? Principal wives created matrilateral kinship for their offspring, concubines did not. A concubine's offspring were born into a recognized kin status within their father's family, but their father's wife, not the concubine, was seen as their formal mother. It seems likely that a concubine's sons, except in special circumstances, were denied the advantages and protections that matrilateral kin might provide. Writing of concubines' offspring in Africa, Meillassoux points out that they "were legally 'sons' and 'daughters,' whose social condition was weak be-cause they lacked a maternal lineage" (1983:57).

In China the children of concubines may have suffered from a "weak so-cial condition" not only because they lacked matrilateral kin but also be-cause their biological mothers had no dowry, nor were they likely to have private funds (*ssu-fang ch'ien*) to bestow upon them.[11] In Ha Tsuen a mother's dowry and private fund may have been used to help educate a son or marry off a daughter; business ventures and extras such as tutors, schoolbooks, uniforms, special trips, and special foods might also be funded by a mother's *ssu-fang ch'ien*. In a study of lineage development in Wu-hsi, Jerry Dennerline shows that a mother's dowry might be instrumental in preserving the economic interests of a son after the death of his father (1986:190–93). There is no doubt that a woman's dowry could create decided advantages for her children. To be without such maternal beneficence was no small matter. The children of a concubine, therefore, partook to a certain degree of their biological mother's marginality. Concubinage, it would appear, created differences not only among the women of a household but also among its children.

Because maids, like concubines, were bought, was their kin status likely to resemble a concubine's? Many Chinese justified their purchase of *mui jai* as charity, arguing that it was better for these girls to become "little younger sisters" than to run the risk of starving or being sold into brothels. In some cases affection developed between the *mui jai* and her master's family, but there was no disguising her servitude. The *mui jai* received no wages. She was housed, fed, and clothed by her master, who was not supposed to mistreat her or kill her, but other than that he appears to have had full control over her.

Whether most parents signed contracts that turned over full rights to their daughter once they accepted the master's payment is unclear at this point. A thorough search of available contracts is necessary before this issue can be settled with any certainty. We do know that many contracts specified that the fate of the *mui jai* was "the will of Heaven," which suggests that her parents retained no rights to her and could not serve as her protectors once the contract went into effect (for contract language see Jaschok 1988:146–49). It should be noted, however, that some contracts specified a conditional transfer. A girl's parents "might transfer her as a pledge for a loan, the girl's services being regarded as interest on the loan, on repayment of which the girl would be restored to the parents" (Report 1937:22; see also Stockard 1989:28–29). In these cases the arrangement resembled pawning more than indenture or slavery.[12]

Colonial authorities were under considerable pressure from the antislavery forces both in Hong Kong and abroad to do something about the *mui jai* problem (see, e.g., Report 1937:151–55, 161; Smith 1982). But local officials clearly felt they were dealing with a deeply entrenched customary practice (Report 1937:162); a simple outlawing of the practice, they argued, was futile. In any event, it is also clear that they were unwilling to take the necessary and, one might add, costly steps that would have eradicated the practice. For example, they balked at establishing agencies to house and find alternative employment for the girls who would have been thrown on the streets had the provisions against the *mui jai* system been enforced. They also hesitated to require proper wages for girls who would have been converted from *mui jai* into paid domestic servants had the system been banned. In 1929 a regulation went into effect stipulating that *mui jai* from ten to fourteen years of age were to be paid $1 per month and those over fourteen years were to receive $1.50 (Report 1937:167; see also Jaschok 1988:103–4). There was no effective oversight machinery, however, to see that even these small sums were in fact paid.

In dealing with the maidservant question colonial authorities were at pains to understand, some might say explain away, the payment made to the *mui jai*'s parents by her master. In 1923 it was decreed that the payment did not confer any rights of property over the *mui jai* (Report 1937:159). It was further stated that this payment was similar to a loan that the *mui jai*'s parents could repay whenever they wanted and thus regain control over their daughter. But the formal declaration had little effect on actual practice in Hong Kong. According to a minority report of the 1937 Commission (published as an appendix) these provisions were laws in name only.

To this point I have concentrated on the *mui jai* during her years as a servant, but what of her status once she married and escaped her master's house? I have already noted that *mui jai* tended to marry (with only token marriage payments) poor men or widowers or become concubines.[13] Like concubines, *mui jai* tended to be estranged from their natal kin, which in later life often meant they were unable to create affinal ties for their husbands or matrilateral ties for their children. Their small dowries may have also put their children at an economic disadvantage. It should be noted, however, that unlike concubines, ex–*mui jai* wives did have some dowry and could (if they had the resources) maintain their own *ssu-fang ch'ien*. If a *mui jai* was fortunate enough to be taken as a principal wife, she enjoyed some advantages over a concubine. As wives (*ch'i*), they could become the domestic managers of their husband's household, and, perhaps most important, they were formally recognized as the mother (both social and biological) of their children. Nevertheless, owing to their lack of natal kin, they must have found it difficult to attain the same status as wives who had never been *mui jai*. Thus, even in adulthood a *mui jai* could not escape her servant past.

CONCLUSION

In this paper I argue that wives, concubines, and maids are differentiated by the mode of their incorporation into the household of their husband or master. Concubines and maids were sold and were thus incorporated into their master's household with few or no links to the outside world. We have seen that while concubines and *mui jai* share a number of characteristics, their situations differed markedly in some important respects. Because concubines served for life, they tended to be less capable than *mui jai* of ever attaining any real independence. *Mui jai* could, after all, expect to achieve emancipation through a proper marriage, although many simply exchanged one servile situation for another as they moved from servitude to concubinage.

Taken on a case-by-case basis, some concubines undoubtedly enjoyed decidedly better living conditions than *mui jai*. Through force of personality or favoritism a concubine might become a powerful household figure effectively usurping the position of the wife herself. Jaschok provides some dramatic examples of such strong-willed and powerful women (see, e.g., 1988:31–32, 48–50). However, the institutional impediments that limited the concubine's freedom of action were indeed great. Among these impediments, perhaps the greatest was the concubines' inability to produce kinship. Writing of a successful concubine, Jaschok observes that her master gave her money and gifts but withheld "the protection and support needed to build up a position of dignity and recognition." Seen from the outside, Jaschok continues, the concubine "had acquired membership of a respected and wealthy family, but from the inside, she remained an outcast on the domestic periphery" (1988:31–32). The cruel and unscrupulous concubine is part of Chinese folklore, but the mirror image of the concubine as victim is also a familiar tale. It is perhaps this latter representation that comes nearer to capturing the experience of many women.

As both Jaschok and Stockard show, a concubine could become a mere extension of the wife. As her reproductive capacities were appropriated by the "great mother" and the patriline she served, the concubine lost her own identity in that of her mistress and rival (see Jaschok 1988:76; Stockard 1989:48–69). This point was most vividly expressed to me by one of my Ha Tsuen informants as she proudly showed me her "son's" wedding picture. My informant (a *daaih ma* whose husband had fathered five children by his concubine), the bridal couple and the groom's father had pride of place in the photograph. After a careful inspection of the photo, I found the concubine mother standing to one side and behind the crush of bride's parents, siblings, and their children. For me the photo revealed the bitter irony of the wife-concubine dilemma; neither my informant nor her husband's concubine could achieve the only meaningful role available to a village woman—that of wife *and* mother. Neither was complete according to local notions. The wife came closest to unifying the two feminine functions, but she did this at the expense of the self-effacing, nameless concubine. For the proud *daaih ma* this must have been indeed galling, but for the concubine it spelled a lifetime of humiliation, dependence, and marginality.

Social identity and social personhood, we are told, depend on one's kin status. Most definitions of slavery stress that a slave could not marry, was not allowed to have a normal family life, and in effect lacked the endowment of kinship (for a discussion of this point see J. Watson 1980a). If slavery is an inherited status, Chinese concubines and maids were not slaves, but shared with them a marginal kin status and were in this sense less than full persons.

In Chinese society kinship has economic, political, social, cultural, and personal significance. To be without kin in a society absorbed by kinship was no small matter. Kin ties define, integrate, locate, and socialize the unformed, undefined, and unregulated. Because of their ambiguous kin status, *mui jai* and especially concubines lived at the edge of the social world. Once they were transferred to their master, *mui jai* appear to have existed without parents or siblings (without kin in fact). If she were fortunate enough to be taken on as a *ch'i*, however, the former *mui jai* gained the right to be both a recognized wife and mother. The concubine was denied even this—once she entered her consort's household she appears never to have regained her kin status.

Although *mui jai* and concubines did not pass on their status to their children, their offspring were liable to suffer social handicaps not imposed on the children of a wife (that is, a *ch'i* who had never served as a *mui jai*). Their lack of matrilateral kin and of a mother's dowry may have created disadvantages for offspring, especially those born into elite families. In households where the children of concubines were competing for favor and resources with the children of wives, it would hardly be surprising to find nuanced but nevertheless important differences in their education or marriage opportunities. If we consider concubinage from this point of view, it would seem that the conditions creating a second-class status for the concubine may also have affected her offspring.

Chinese society may provide an exception to the commonly held view that to be a social person, one must be legitimately mothered as well as fathered (see, e.g., Fortes 1969:261). Jack Goody has argued, for example, that "kinship is everywhere bilateral" (1983:16). There is some question, I believe, as to whether the sons and daughters of *mui jai* and concubines are legitimately mothered. This is especially true of concubines whose children are full heirs yet lack a social mother who can produce or provide matrilateral kin.[14] It may be argued that the children of concubines achieve their personhood solely through their fathers. The extent to which they suffer any personal disadvantage owing to the circumstances of their birth remains an intriguing question.

It seems hardly worth noting that concubines were unmarried. However, this easily overlooked fact is an important element in their ambiguous kin status and in the social marginality they, as a group, were forced to endure. In Chinese society marriage marked the most important transition in a woman's life. Marriage, Stockard writes, was the path to spiritual security for Chinese women (1989:49). As Ha Tsuen villagers say, "a daughter is just passing through," waiting, presumably, to assume her true and proper role as wife and mother. Until she married, a Chinese woman had no resting place either in this life or the next. If she failed to marry, her natal family was often loath to support her, preferring to send her to a nunnery, a brothel, or into

domestic service. If she died before she became a wife, her spirit was transformed into a dangerous and unsettled ghost. A Chinese concubine suffered
the stigma that attached to all adult women who had no recognized place in
society. She belonged neither to the family of her parents nor to that of her
consort. She bore, in fact, the double burden of being a woman who was both
unmarried and sexually active.

As I note in the introduction of this chapter, Ebrey (1986) has argued that
concubines are best understood when they are categorized not as a kind of
wife but as a menial. It may be useful to push this argument further by
placing the discussion of concubinage (and *mui jai* status) in the context of
gender inequality and servitude. In late imperial and Republican China
there were many forms of servitude, and it is likely that further analysis will
show that these differences are often related to gender. There is already evidence that in the nineteenth and twentieth centuries girls and women who
served as domestic servants were more likely to be involuntarily tied to their
work than were male servants, at least in some areas of China. Sankar, for
example, points out that most domestic servants in Hong Kong were *mui jai*
or indentured laborers (1978). In a discussion of Taiwanese servants, the
historian Johanna Meskill found substantial differences between male and
female domestics during the late nineteenth century. Male servants, she
writes, "had contracts that stipulated pay and customary bonuses." She
adds that "the bulk of the maid servants were indentured, entering the Lin
household around the age of eight and serving, without pay, for about ten
years" (1979:230). Further investigations may show that in the early twentieth century the system of gender and class inequalities created a situation in
which girls from poor families were more vulnerable to pawning, sale, and
involuntary indenture than were males of similar socioeconomic status.

We already know that in China, as in many other peasant societies, servile
women often ranked below servile men. McDermott shows that during the
Ming, male bondservants could join free men in exchanging women. Referring to a sixteenth-century contract, McDermott describes the case of a
penniless man who was promised his subsistence and a wife (a maid in the
master's household) in return for twenty-two years of indentured labor.
Offspring from this marriage were "contracted, before birth, to serve their
father's master, and a *daughter* would have to stay 'as compensation' on the
termination of the father's contract" (1981:681, emphasis added). Here we
have a case of master and male bondservant deciding the fate of women who
were obviously their dependents. "The women in these male transactions,"
McDermott writes, "amounted to little more than objects of sale" (ibid.,
681). There is some justification for thinking that no matter what the status
group, Chinese women ranked below and were in some way dependent on
men.

The two categories of servile women discussed here had an ambiguous

relation to the families they served. Concubines and *mui jai* are said to have
been like family members, yet their status was not clearly defined. One suspects that such ambiguity would not have been tolerated for an enslaved or
indentured male servant. The ideology of patriliny is particularly strong in
the Pearl River Delta, where there are clear and rigid boundaries between
agnates and nonagnates. These boundaries restricted access to crucial resources, reserving them for a defined group of agnates; membership in the
patrilineal kin group determined rights to landed estates, political brokers,
and protection in an often violent environment. In a society where women
did not inherit family property and were considered to be of little political
consequence, there was no pressing need to clarify the kin status of a maid or
concubine. Thus, the boundaries that separated servile men from free men
were likely to prove far more rigid than those that delineated servile women
from free women (see also Robertson and Klein 1983; Meillassoux 1983:56;
J. Watson 1980b:249; Wright 1983:249). Whether this made male servitude
harsher than female servitude requires further analysis. What is clear is that
late imperial and Republican China were societies in which gender inequality significantly affected patterns of servitude.

Although I argue that the boundary between free (but dependent) women
and servile women was less clear than the boundary between free and unfree
men, it is important to note that in Chinese society the position of wife could
be clearly distinguished from that of concubine or *mui jai*.[15] Wives and
daughters played a role in household and family rituals denied to concubines
and *mui jai*. Wives had a publicly recognized role both inside and outside
the family. They had the status of legitimate kin and could provide their
offspring with matrilateral ties. They were also property holders, although
their relation to property lacked clear legal sanctions (see Ocko in this
volume).

Although a wife might not have enjoyed the legal protections granted her
brothers or husband, the possession of a dowry was an important economic
expression of the differences that set her apart from concubines and maids.
Although women may have been categorically alienated from full membership in the family estate and although their legal rights to dowry were ill
defined (see the chapters by Ebrey and Ocko and afterword in this volume),
ch'i were not without property altogether. In fact, one might say that the
dowry, and the property-holding status it legitimated, was a defining characteristic of wifely rank. It is perhaps ironically fitting that in late imperial and
Republican China the status of wife was contingent on such a tenuous hold
over what were often minuscule amounts of property. Compared with men,
all women were less than full members of their families, but wives occupied a
privileged position denied to concubines and maids. Thus, the capacity to
produce kinship and the ability to command dowry set "free women" apart
from the *mui jai* and the concubines who served them.

NOTES

Versions of this paper were presented at the American Anthropological Association Annual Meeting, Washington D.C. (1985), the Department of History Colloquium Series, University of Pittsburgh (1986), and at the Working Class History Group, University of Pittsburgh (1988). I am grateful for the comments I received on those occasions. I am especially indebted to Patricia Ebrey, Stevan Harrell, and James Watson for their assistance in revising this paper.

1. It should be noted that some scholars working in societies other than China (particularly in Africa) have found few significant differences between what are sometimes termed "free" and "unfree" women (for discussion see, e.g., Miers and Kopytoff 1977:28–29; Wright 1983:249).

2. In the villages of Hong Kong's New Territories, the terms *ch'i* and *ch'ieh* are not commonly used for wife and concubine. Rather villagers refer to a wife (*ch'i*) as a *daaih pouh* (or great, big woman) and a concubine as a *sai pouh* (or small, secondary woman).

3. Here I refer to people who entered a household through ties of slavery, pawning, or indenture. Usually they are said to have been purchased (*mai*).

4. For discussions of *mui jai* in Taiwan see Arthur Wolf 1974:147; McGough 1976:128–29, 198–99; Meskill 1979:230.

5. For a review of some of this material see Smith 1982.

6. There were in fact different kinds of *mui jai* contracts. For a discussion of contracts and examples of these documents see Jaschok 1988:93–94, 146–49.

7. In Taiwan this form of servitude (in Hokkien, *cha-bo-kan*) may have been harsher than the *mui jai* system in Hong Kong. In Taiwan it appears that "little maids" were more likely to be kept for life. Apparently masters in Taiwan did not feel it necessary to marry off these young servants (see Wolf, A. 1974:147; McGough 1976:128–29).

8. Figures for 1977–78 should not be taken as representative of rates of concubinage in the prewar period. Concubinage has been illegal in Hong Kong since 1971 and has very likely been declining since World War II.

9. For two studies that focus on the internal dynamics of women within wealthy households see Pruitt (1979) and Jaschok (1988).

10. As for the contracts themselves, deeds of sale suggest a complete break of kin ties (see, e.g., Jaschok 1988:146–47). Notes of presentation (see, e.g., ibid., 148–49) imply, however, some interest on the part of parents after the *mui jai*'s marriage. The actual practice must, at this point, remain an open question.

11. Myron Cohen defines *ssu-fang ch'ien* this way:

> Although wedding allocations create a new sphere of property rights involving both husband and wife, there are also the cash gifts given to the bride alone; these differentiate her as an independent property-holder with her own rights of disposal, and within the *fo* [*fang*, or household] these rights are not fully shared with her husband. Her money is known as "*se-koi*" ("private money"). . . . "*Se-koi*" is not liable to the financial manager's control in the bride's new family, nor to her husband's. (1976:178)

On *ssu-fang ch'ien* see also Gallin and Gallin 1982; R. Gallin 1984; R. Watson 1984. Of course, concubines may have acquired a private fund (although it was not called a *ssu fang ch'ien*) through presents given her by her consort. But the concubine had no customary right to property as did the wife.

12. In practice, there may be little difference in pawning, indenture, or slavery. Of the relation between pawning and slavery Nieboer writes: "The main fact is that the pawn is in 'bondage,' however temporarily, that he 'has to serve his master.' Therefore as long as the debt remains unpaid the pawn is in the same condition as a slave" (1971:40).

13. Both Topley (1975) and Stockard (1989) emphasize the point that *mui jai* were especially likely to be sold as concubines. In discussions with Ha Tsuen villagers I was aware that many assumed a close association between *mui jai* status and concubinage.

14. The contribution of the *ch'i* (or *daaih ma*) to the social persona of her husband's children by a concubine would appear to be minimal, although further research on this question is necessary.

15. The existence in Chinese society of private property, of a complex system of social ranking, and of a less "open" kin system appears to have created greater differences between servile and nonservile women than in the African societies described by Miers and Kopytoff (1977:28–29) and Wright (1983:249).

GLOSSARY

Terms marked (C) are in Cantonese and those marked (H) are in Hokkien; all other terms are in Mandarin.

ca-bo-kan (H) 媚媒嫺	*mu* 畝
ch'i 妻	*mui* (C) 妹
chia-chang 家長	*mui jai* (C) 妹仔
ch'ieh 妾	*sai* (C) 細
daaih ma (C) 大媽	*sai je* (C) 細姐
daaih pouh (C) 大婆	*sai ma* (C) 細媽
jai (C) 仔	*sai pou* (C) 細婆
mai 買	*ssu-fang ch'ien* 私房錢
man yueh 滿月	

REFERENCES

Baker, Hugh. 1968. *A Chinese Lineage Village, Sheung Shiu.* Stanford: Stanford University Press.

Buck, John Lossing. 1937. *Land Utilization in China.* Nanking: University of Nanking Press.

Ch'ü, T'ung-tsu. 1961. *Law and Society in Traditional China.* Paris: Mouton.

Clinton, Catherine. 1982. *The Plantation Mistress: Woman's World in the Old South.* New York: Pantheon.

Cohen, Myron. 1976. *House United, House Divided: The Chinese Family in Taiwan.* New York: Columbia University Press.

Dennerline, Jerry. 1986. "Marriage, Adoption, and Charity in the Development of Lineages in Wu-hsi from Sung to Ch'ing." In *Kinship Organization in Late Imperial China, 1000–1940*, ed. Patricia Buckley Ebrey and James L. Watson. Berkeley and Los Angeles: University of California Press.

Dwyer, Daisy, and J. Bruce, eds. 1988. *A Home Divided: Women and Income in the Third World*. Stanford: Stanford University Press.

Eberhard, Wolfram. 1962. *Social Mobility in Traditional China*. Leiden: E. G. Brill.

Ebrey, Patricia. 1981. "Women in the Kinship System in the Southern Song Upper Class." In *Women in China*, ed. Richard Guisso and Stanley Johannesen. Youngstown, N.Y.: Philo Press.

————. 1984. *Family and Property in Sung China: Yüan Ts'ai's Precepts for Social Life*. Princeton: Princeton University Press.

————. 1986. "Concubines in Sung China." *Journal of Family History* 11:1–24.

Evans, D. M. Emrys. 1973. "The New Law of Succession in Hong Kong." *Hong Kong Law Review* 3:7–50.

Fortes, Meyer. 1969. *Kinship and the Social Order: The Legacy of Lewis Henry Morgan*. London: Routledge & Kegan Paul.

Freedman, Maurice. 1967. *Rites and Duties, or Chinese Marriage*. London: G. Bell & Sons.

————. 1979. "Colonial Law and Chinese Society." In *The Study of Chinese Society: Essays by Maurice Freedman*, ed. G. William Skinner. Stanford: Stanford University Press.

Gallin, Rita. 1984. "Rural Industrialization and Chinese Women: A Case Study from Taiwan." *Journal of Peasant Studies* 12.1:76–92.

Gallin, Bernard, and Rita Gallin. 1982. "The Chinese Joint Family in Changing Rural Taiwan." In *Social Interaction in Chinese Society*, ed. S. L. Greenblatt, R. W. Wilson, and A. A. Wilson. New York: Pergamon Press.

Gamble, Sidney. 1954. *Ting Hsien: A North China Rural Community*. Stanford: Stanford University Press.

Gates, Hill. 1989. "The Commoditization of Chinese Women." *Signs* 14.4:799–832.

Goody, Jack. 1976. *Production and Reproduction: A Comparative Study of the Domestic Domain*. Cambridge: Cambridge University Press.

————. 1983. *The Development of the Family and Marriage in Europe*. Cambridge: Cambridge University Press.

Gronewold, Susan. 1982. "Beautiful Merchandise: Prostitution in China, 1860–1936." *Women and History* (Special Issue) 1:1–114.

Harrell, Stevan. 1985. "The Rich Get Children: Segmentation, Stratification, and Population in Three Chekiang Lineages, 1550–1850." In *Family and Population in East Asian History*, ed. Susan Hanley and Arthur Wolf. Stanford: Stanford University Press.

Hartman, Heidi. 1981. "The Family as the Locus of Gender, Class, and Political Struggle: The Example of Housework." *Signs* 6.3:366–94.

Hershatter, Gail. 1986. *The Workers of Tianjin, 1900–1949*. Stanford: Stanford University Press.

Honig, Emily. 1986. *Sisters and Strangers: Women in Shanghai Cotton Mills, 1919–1949*. Stanford: Stanford University Press.

Jamieson, G. 1921; reprint, 1970. *Chinese Family and Commercial Law*. Hong Kong: Vetch & Lee.

Jaschok, Maria. 1988. *Concubines and Bondservants: The Social History of a Chinese Custom*. London: Zed Press.

Johnson, Elizabeth. 1976. *Households and Lineages in a Chinese Urban Village*. No. 77–18, 170. Ann Arbor: University Microfilms.

Lang, Olga. 1946. *Chinese Family and Society*. New Haven: Yale University Press.

Lebsock, Suzanne. 1984. *The Free Women of Petersburg: Status and Culture in a Southern Town, 1784–1860*. New York: W. W. Norton.

Liu, Hui-chen Wang. 1959. *The Traditional Chinese Clan Rules*. Locust Valley, N.Y.: J. J. Augustin.

Liu, Tsui-jung. 1985. "The Demography of Two Chinese Clans in Hsiao-shan, Chekiang, 1650–1850." In *Family and Population in East Asian History*, ed. Susan Hanley and Arthur Wolf. Stanford: Stanford University Press.

McDermott, Joseph. 1981. "Bondservants in the T'ai-hu Basin during the Late Ming: A Case of Mistaken Identities." *Journal of Asian Studies* 40:675–701.

McGough, James. 1976. *Marriage and Adoption in Chinese Society with Special Reference to Customary Law*. No. 77–5852. Ann Arbor: University Microfilms.

Meillassoux, Claude. 1983. "Female Slavery." In *Women and Slavery in Africa*, ed. Claire Robertson and Martin Klein. Madison: University of Wisconsin Press.

Meskill, Johanna. 1979. *A Chinese Pioneer Family: The Lins of Wu-feng, Taiwan, 1729–1895*. Princeton: Princeton University Press.

Miers, Suzanne, and Igor Kopytoff. 1977. "African 'Slavery' as an Institution of Marginality." In *Slavery in Africa: Historical and Anthropological Perspectives*, ed. Suzanne Miers and Igor Kopytoff. Madison: University of Wisconsin Press.

Nieboer, H. J. 1910; reprint, 1971. *Slavery as an Industrial System: Ethnological Researches*. 2d rev. ed. New York: Burt Franklin.

Pasternak, Burton. 1983. *Guests of the Dragon: Social Demography of a Chinese District, 1895–1946*. New York: Columbia University Press.

Pratt, Jean. 1960. "Emigration and Unilineal Descent Groups: A Study of Marriage in a Hakka Village in the New Territories, Hong Kong." *Eastern Anthropologist* 13: 147–58.

Pruitt, Ida. 1979. *Old Madam Yin: A Memoir of Peking Life*. Stanford: Stanford University Press.

Rapp, Rayna. 1978. "Family and Class in Contemporary America: Notes Towards an Understanding of Ideology." *Science and Society* 42:278–300.

Report. (*Mui Tsai in Hong Kong and Malaya: Report of Commission*). 1937. Issued by Colonial Office, Colonial no. 125. London: His Majesty's Stationery Office.

Robertson, Claire. 1983. "Post-Proclamation Slavery in Accra: A Female Affair." In *Women and Slavery in Africa*, ed. Claire Robertson and Martin Klein. Madison: University of Wisconsin Press.

Robertson, Claire, and Martin Klein. 1983. "Women's Importance in African Slave Systems." In *Women and Slavery in Africa*, ed. Claire Robertson and Martin Klein. Madison: University of Wisconsin Press.

Sankar, Andrea. 1978. "Female Domestic Service in Hong Kong." In *Female Servants and Economic Development*, ed. Louise Tilly et al. Ann Arbor: Michigan Occasional Papers in Women's Studies, no. 1.

Shiga, Shūzō 滋賀秀三. 1967. *Chūgoku kazoku hō no genri* 中國家族法の原理 (Basic principles underlying Chinese family law). Tokyo: Sobunsha.

———. 1978. "Family Property and the Law of Inheritance in Traditional China." In *Chinese Family Law and Social Change in Historical and Comparative Perspective*, ed. David C. Buxbaum. Seattle: University of Washington Press.

Smith, Carl T. 1982. "The Chinese Church, Labour and Elites and the Mui Tsai

Question in the 1920's." *Journal of the Hong Kong Branch of the Royal Asiatic Society* 21: 91–113.

Stockard, Janice. 1989. *Daughters of the Canton Delta: Marriage Patterns and Economic Strategies in South China, 1860–1930.* Stanford: Stanford University Press.

Thorne, Barrie, with Marilyn Yalom, ed. 1982. *Rethinking the Family: Some Feminist Questions.* New York: Longman.

Topley, Marjorie. 1975. "Marriage Resistance in Kwangtung." In *Women in Chinese Society,* ed. Margery Wolf and Roxane Witke. Stanford: Stanford University Press.

van der Sprenkel, Sybille. 1962. *Legal Institutions in Manchu China.* London: Athone.

Watson, James L. 1976. "Chattel Slavery in Chinese Peasant Society: A Comparative Analysis." *Ethnology* 15:361–75.

———. 1980a. "Slavery as an Institution, Open and Closed Systems." In *Asian and African Systems of Slavery,* ed. James L. Watson. Oxford: Basil Blackwell.

———. 1980b. "Transactions in People: The Chinese Market in Slaves, Servants, and Heirs." In *Asian and African Systems of Slavery,* ed. James L. Watson. Oxford: Basil Blackwell.

Watson, Rubie S. 1981. "Class Differences and Affinal Relations in South China." *Man* 16:593–615.

———. 1984. "Women's Property in Republican China: Rights and Practice." *Republican China* 10.1a:1–12.

———. 1985. *Inequality among Brothers: Class and Kinship in South China.* Cambridge: Cambridge University Press.

———. 1986. "The Named and the Nameless: Gender and Person in Chinese Society." *American Ethnologist* 13:619–31.

Wolf, Arthur. 1974. "Marriage and Adoption in Northern Taiwan." In *Social Organization and the Applications of Anthropology: Essays in Honor of Lauriston Sharp,* ed. Robert J. Smith. Ithaca: Cornell University Press.

Wolf, Margery. 1972. *Women and the Family in Rural Taiwan.* Stanford: Stanford University Press.

Wright, Marcia. 1983. "Bwanikwa: Consciousness and Protest among Slave Women in Central Africa, 1886–1911." In *Women and Slavery in Africa,* ed. Claire Robertson and Martin Klein. Madison: University of Wisconsin Press.

Yanagisako, Sylvia. 1979. "Variance in American Kinship: Implications for Cultural Analysis." *American Ethnologist* 5:15–29.

———. 1984. "Explicating Residence: A Cultural Analysis of Changing Households among Japanese-Americans." In *Households: Comparative and Historical Studies of the Domestic Group,* ed. Robert McC. Netting, Richard Wilk, and Eric Arnould. Berkeley and Los Angeles: University of California Press.

Yang, C. K. 1959. *A Chinese Village in Early Communist Transition.* Cambridge: MIT Press.

Yang, Martin. 1945. *A Chinese Village, Taitou, Shantung Province.* New York: Columbia University Press.

EIGHT

Prostitution and the Market in Women in Early Twentieth-Century Shanghai

Gail Hershatter

In 1917 a man named Huang brought an eleven-year-old girl named Hsueh Feng to Shanghai. There he took her to the House of Pearls (Han-chu chia), an elegant brothel run by Old Three Wang, a madam who was "unsurpassed in rounding up talent for her house." Huang pawned Hsueh Feng to the brothel for 350 yuan, the pawn period being set at eight years. It is not clear whether Huang was a relative of the girl, a professional trafficker in women, or both. But apparently the girl's family knew where she was, for soon afterward some relatives appeared at the brothel and asked to see the madam. Explaining that Hsueh's parents had died and there was no money to bury them properly, the relatives asked Old Three Wang to increase the pawn price and buy Hsueh Feng outright. The madam agreed; henceforth Hsueh Feng became the permanent property of the brothel.

Eleven years passed, during which Hsueh, as a beautiful adolescent, served as a prostitute-in-training (*ch'u-chi*). The details of her duties in the brothel in those years are not recorded, but she was not yet expected to have sexual relations with the customers or to entertain them alone. In 1928 she began to entertain guests, taking the professional name of Old Seven, since she was the seventh prostitute in the House of Pearls. Even then her work appears to have consisted of singing for rich men at parties; she was referred to as a "small teacher" (*hsiao hsien-sheng*), a term that in the trade meant "virgin prostitute."

At one of these parties, Old Seven caught the eye of a wealthy young man named Lu Min-kang, who was a partner in an export firm with offices on the Shanghai docks. Lu, age twenty-three, was from Ch'ung-ming, north of Shanghai. Though he showed up at work only occasionally, his position in the firm was secure because his father owned substantial amounts of stock. Lu paid several formal calls on Old Seven, observing the elaborate courtesies required of patrons in upper-class brothels. But the madam, Old Three Wang, looked on him with disfavor because she felt he did not give generous-enough tips when Old Seven sang. Protecting her investment, perhaps hoping to sell Old Seven's first night to someone who was freer with his money, the madam kept a close eye on Old Seven and refused to let her out alone.

Nevertheless, Lu found an opportunity to meet Old Seven secretly one night, and during their encounter Old Seven "broke with the behavior of a virgin prostitute." The two decided they wanted to spend their lives together, but Lu did not follow the usual procedure of offering to buy Old Seven from the madam. Instead, the couple fled the brothel one day in 1929, taking with them several suitcases of clothing and gold jewelry. The madam looked for them in vain. The next day she received a letter from a lawyer. The letter said that Old Seven had been pawned as a prostitute, but that her pawn period had long ago expired. She had been young, ignorant, and trampled underfoot, the letter continued, and now that she was grown she wanted to regain her freedom and break relations with the brothel. The lawyer gave Old Three Wang two days to produce the "illegal" contract that bound Old Seven to the brothel so that it could be invalidated. If she did not meet the deadline, the letter warned, she would be dealt with according to law.

Undaunted, Old Three Wang retained a lawyer of her own. She also located Lu and Old Seven in their hiding place in the southern part of the city and sent someone there to talk to (and perhaps threaten) them. When he saw the visitor, Lu "raged and roared," and the encounter concluded on worse terms than it had begun. Shortly thereafter the courts undertook an investigation of the case (*SP* July 10, 1929:7).

The legal disposition of this case was not reported in the press, and it is not clear what became of Old Seven. But her story contains many elements common to the lives of prostitutes in Republican-era Shanghai: the poverty and crisis in Hsueh Feng's family, the pawning or sale of daughters into prostitution, the long training period and close guarding of prostitutes in the more exclusive brothels, and the elaborate rituals of entertainment and nego-tiation that preceded any sexual encounter with an upper-class prostitute. In finding a young patron who was willing to free her from the life, Hsueh was fulfilling the dream of many young women who hoped to leave the brothels on the arm of a rich man. The resort to litigation was characteristic of both madams and prostitutes. And the use of violence and intimidation, though only hinted at in this particular case, was an integral part of work relations in the trade.

Recent scholars and activists writing on prostitution have renamed it "sex work" (Delacoste and Alexander 1987), reminding us that it must be under-stood in the context of other forms of paid labor available to women. In Shanghai prostitution was indeed one of just a few situations in which women could earn an income. But the Shanghai market in female labor was not a free one, in two senses. First, women had little choice about where they worked because the female labor market was structured by regional and family connections. Second, women themselves often were not free workers; that is, they were frequently kidnapped or purchased by contractors who then sold their labor to factories or sold them outright as maids, concubines, and prostitutes. An even more common arrangement for prostitutes was to be pawned to a brothel by their families or by traffickers for a specified period of time. Whether sold or pawned, a woman had limited or no control over her income and working conditions, nor did she have the right to leave a brothel unless she redeemed the pawn pledge. In placing Shanghai prostitution on the continuum of work, we must be mindful that the women themselves were treated primarily as commodities rather than producers of commodities.

Prostitution must be placed on another continuum as well: one of claims on women's sexual services. This continuum included concubinage and marriage as well as prostitution because all of these were means by which others acquired claims on a woman's person.[1] All women in late imperial and Republican China, Sue Gronewold writes in her study of prostitution, were "regarded fundamentally as disposable merchandise, as commodities. The prostitute's singularity lay in being a strictly sexual commodity" (1982:50). Prostitution and marriage thus become merely different forms of transaction in the same market. Although this formulation calls attention to an important similarity between married women and prostitutes, it diverts attention from the struggle that prostitutes in particular waged, sometimes successfully, to gain a modicum of control over the disposition of their sexual services.

In China, decisions about entry into marriage or prostitution were usually made for the woman by others, most frequently family members. Among the poor, prostitution and marriage drew from the same pool of women; families who could afford to do so were at great pains to keep their daughters eligible for marriage and off the prostitution market. Sometimes poor married women found it necessary to work as prostitutes; sometimes prostitutes left the brothels to become concubines or wives. Both prostitution and marriage exhibited an elaborate hierarchy of different statuses and degrees of permanence; arrangements in both varied by class. Both were vehicles for mobility up and down. Prostitution even mimicked certain of the rituals of marriage and family life.

Yet prostitution and marriage exhibited important differences as well. A prostitute was dependent upon her madam, who controlled her contact with both her natal family and her customers. (Pimps played a less important role, helping some brothels to solicit customers but apparently having little direct control over the prostitutes.) The madam had long-term claims on the body of the prostitute, while the claims of the client were short term. After a pawned prostitute served out her allotted time, her natal or marital family might reassert their claims on her. In short, demands on a prostitute's person were divided among a number of parties, whereas in marriage short- and long-term claims were not separated in this way. Prostitution, unlike marriage, was not for the purpose of reproduction, although both married women and prostitutes attempted to use pregnancy as a strategy to enhance their own positions. Prostitution was regarded as a temporary stage in a society in which all women were expected to marry. This chapter examines similarities between prostitution and marriage in Shanghai, as well as movements of individual women from one institution to the other.

The changing Shanghai market in women must be understood in the context of the city's rapid growth in the first half of the twentieth century.[2] The population of Shanghai, including the International Settlement and the French Concession, almost tripled between 1910 and 1930 from about a million to more than three million. At the conclusion of World War II its population was roughly the same as in 1930, but by 1947 it had grown again by one-third.[3] Immigrants from other parts of China made up more than 82 percent of this population in 1910, more than 90 percent in 1930 (Lo Chih-ju 1932:27, table 43). Women migrants to Shanghai found work in manufacturing, particularly cotton textiles; as household servants or wet nurses; as itinerant peddlers; and as entertainers or prostitutes.[4]

But far more men than women immigrated to Shanghai. In the Chinese-governed sector of the city in the early 1930s, there were typically 135 men to every 100 women, dropping to an average of 124 to 100 in the three years after World War II (SCA 1933, Population, 2, table 3; SSWH 1948: 14, 16, 18). The ratio was even more skewed among Chinese adults in the International Settlement (156:100 in 1930) and the French Concession (164:100 in 1930) (Lo Chih-ju 1932:30). Republican period social reformers were fond of pointing out that the predominance of unattached men in the urban population increased the demand for commercial sexual services.

To reconstruct the living and working conditions of prostitutes in early twentieth-century Shanghai, this paper begins with a description of the complex class structure of prostitution and a rough estimate of the numbers of women involved. Then it explores common elements in the family background and personal history of prostitutes in addition to the financial arrangements by which a woman entered a brothel. It examines the brothel as a social world with its own rules, codes, and risks and also asks how a prostitute's working life mimicked the rituals of courtship and marriage (with respect to customers) and family life (with respect to madams). Finally, the essay considers the "career path" of prostitutes, particularly the exit into marriage or concubinage. How permeable was the boundary around prostitution, by whom could it be crossed, and under what circumstances? The paper concludes with some observations about the Shanghai market in women.

HIERARCHIES OF PROSTITUTION

One way to untangle the complex structure of prostitution in Shanghai is to look at the types of prostitutes that provided sexual services to different classes of men, from the well-educated scion of the elite to the transient foreign sailor. At the beginning of the twentieth century, the prostitutes most often written about were those who entertained the local literati. Famed as singers and storytellers, they were commonly addressed with the respectful term *hsien-sheng*, most frequently translated into English as "sing-song girl." The public spaces where they performed were known as storytelling houses, their private dwellings as storytellers' residences (*shu-yu*). The term *shu-yu* was also used to refer to them as a group ("Demi-monde" 1923:783; T'u 1948:*hsia*, 76; Lemière 1923:127–28; Wang Ting-chiu 1932:"P'iao," 1–2).

Storytelling-house prostitutes traced their entertainer pedigree back a thousand years. Famed for their beauty, their extravagant dress, and their elaborate opium and tobacco pipes, they were equally renowned for their ability to sing and accompany themselves on stringed instruments, skill at composing poetry, refined artistic sensibilities, and conversational skill. Their professional names (chosen upon their entry into the house) were meant to invoke both sensual pleasure and literary associations. Some took studio names (*chai*) such as "Fragrant Nest" or "Drunken Flowers Retreat." Others chose names like those used by the male literati, such as "the master of the lodge wherein verses are hummed." One famous nineteenth-century sing-song girl took the name Lin Tai-yü, after the heroine of *Dream of the Red Chamber* (Lemière 1923:127–28, 130; Arlington 1923:317; "Demi-monde" 1923:783).

Members of the storytelling-house class regarded themselves as skilled entertainers rather than providers of sexual services; they prided themselves on "selling their voices rather than their bodies." One Republican-era description of them, colored perhaps by nostalgia, reported that these women had such high moral principles that if one was discovered having secret relations with a sweetheart, then her bedding was burned and she was driven out. Other accounts say they did "sell their beauty" in their residences, but kept this practice secret and made their reputations as singers (Lemière 1923:127–28; Wang Ting-chiu 1932:"P'iao," 1–2; Liu 1936:136; "Demi-monde" 1923:783; T'u 1948:*hsia*, 76). In the early decades of the twentieth century the popularity of this geisha-style service declined; at least one source hints that the cause of its downfall was the unwillingness of the women to have sexual relations with their customers. By the 1920s the storytelling-house class had been absorbed into the next lower class of prostitutes, though the term *shu-yu* was used intermittently as late as 1948 ("Demi-monde" 1923:783; Lemière 1923:127–28; T'u 1948:*hsia*, 76; Wang Ting-chiu 1932: "P'iao," 1–2; Yü 1948:11).

The next lower class, called "long three" (*ch'ang-san*), was named after a domino with two groups of three dots each. Traditionally, "long-three" prostitutes charged three yuan for drinking with guests and three more for spending the night with them; the name remained long after the fee structure changed. Like the storytelling-house women, the "long-three" prostitutes performed classical songs and scenes from opera, dressed in elaborate costumes, and specialized in hosting banquets and gambling parties for merchants and well-placed officials. In the era before taxis became common, women rode to these parties in horse-drawn carriages or were carried on the shoulders of male brothel servants "like a Buddhist pagoda," providing live advertisement for the services of their house (T'u 1948:*hsia*, 76). The "long-three" brothels in Hui-le Li, a lane off Fu-chou Road, were the most famous. Sometimes wealthy customers would request that a woman accompany them to a dramatic performance or other place of entertainment (Henderson 1871:14; T'u 1948:*hsia*, 76). The woman's brothel charged a set fee for all such services. Though they were less sexually available than lower-class prostitutes, a patron who went through a long "courtship" process and paid elaborate fees to the woman and her madam could hope for sexual favors ("Demi-monde" 1923:783–85; T'u 1948:*hsia*, 76; Wang Ting-chiu 1932: "P'iao," 1–2; Yü 1948:11; Liu 1936:136; Yi 1933:39).

Next in the hierarchy were the "one-two" prostitutes, also named for dominos. In the 1940s their fees were quoted as one yuan for providing melon seeds and fruit (called a "dry and wet basin") and two yuan for drinking companionship, though an evening in their company could cost considerably more. Sources agree that the singing of "one-two" prostitutes was not as good, nor their sexual services as expensive, as the "long three." "One-two" houses were most numerous along Peking Road and in the French Concession (Yü 1948:11; T'u 1948:*hsia*, 76–77; "Demi-monde" 1923:785; Wiley 1929:65; Yi 1933:39).

The largest group of brothels in the next grade down were called "salt-pork shops" (*hsien-rou chuang*). Unlike all the grades above them, they were devoted exclusively to the on-demand satisfaction of male copulative desires, with little attention to singing, banqueting, or other ancillary forms of entertainment. Women were the "salt pork"; as a 1932 guidebook put it, "the price in the shop depends on the taste of the meat. Everyone knows that a slice costs three yuan, and an entire night five to eight yuan." In these houses customers were said to divide up the women as though cutting salt pork (Wang Ting-chiu 1932:"P'iao," 27–28). Another 1930s guide reminded its readers that salt pork was no longer fresh meat and that it might in fact be rotten (Wang Chung-hsien 1935:23–24). In the late 1940s laborers were the main clientele of the salt-pork shops. Many of these brothels were located near the French Concession's Bridge of the Eight Immortals (*Pa-hsien ch'iao*) (T'u 1948:*hsia*, 77; Wang 1932:"P'iao," 25; Yü 1948:11).

By far the largest group of prostitutes in Republican Shanghai were the "pheasants" (*yeh-chi* or *chih-chi*), streetwalkers whose name suggests both their gaudy dress and their habit of "go[ing] about from place to place like wild birds" ("Demi-monde" 1923:785–86). Every evening groups of them could be seen on both sides of the main streets aggressively seeking customers. Guidebooks of the period repeatedly warned Shanghai visitors to beware of the pheasants, whose eager assaults on passersby could shade over into pickpocketing. Mixing his ornithological metaphors, one author warned that pheasants fastened onto their prey "like an eagle seizing a chick" (T'ang 1931:152–53). Their prices as reported in 1932 ranged from one yuan for what was euphemistically called "one cannon blast-ism" (*yi-p'ao chu-yi*) to seven yuan for a night (Wang Ting-chiu 1932:"P'iao," 49).

Although pheasants worked the streets, they were by no means independent of the brothel system. Most operated under the control of madams, often under more restrictive conditions than their higher-status sisters. Brothel attendants supervised them as they went about finding customers, who were then brought back to the brothel (T'u 1948:*hsia*, 77). "No matter the weather, hot or cold, rain, frost, or snow, when evening came they must stand in groups and call out to men and on the least response they must take hold of them and cajole them to respond," commented a 1923 article. "If not successful, the girls were beaten" ("Demi-monde" 1923:786). In at least one respect they were certainly worse off than other prostitutes: because they did not remain in brothels, they frequently came into conflict with the local police, who enforced the municipal ordinance against street soliciting (see, for example, *SP* July 22, 1929:7). One guide advised Shanghai visitors that the only way to shake off a determined pheasant was to drag her into the street, because then she would become fearful of police intervention and desist in her efforts (T'ang 1931:152–53).

Lowest of all in the hierarchy of prostitution were the employees of brothels called "flower-smoke rooms" (*hua-yen chien*) and "nailsheds" (*ting-p'eng*). Flower-smoke rooms were places where a customer could smoke opium and visit prostitutes ("flowers") simultaneously. After 1933, when opium was banned, they reportedly disappeared. Nailsheds, scattered throughout the city, were rudimentary brothels that catered to rickshaw pullers and other laborers; the prices ranged from two chiao for quick sex to one yuan for the night (1932 figures) (T'ang 1931:154; Yi 1933:39; T'u 1948:*hsia*, 77; Wang Ting-chiu 1932:"P'iao," 50–51).

Like workers in other sectors of the Shanghai economy, most prostitutes were not of local origin. Outsiders were in the majority in part because Republican-period Shanghai was an expanding city that attracted peasants with the hope of work while rural crisis and war were pushing them out of the countryside. They also reflected the presence in Shanghai of powerful merchant and official cliques who hailed from Canton, Ningpo, and the cities of the lower Yangtze; men from all these regions apparently preferred prostitutes from their own native places. Finally, those who trafficked in sexual services preferred to resell women far enough from home that their families would not clamor for the return of the goods or a share of the profits (Wiley 1929:52–53). Brothel owners who bought women from other regions increased their ability to control them because "if the prostitute [was] removed from her home community she [was] absolutely at the mercy of her keepers" (ibid., 66–67). For the same reason, "Shanghai girls, as a rule, when sold or mortgaged, are shipped off to some far away place," as one contemporary account noted (Lemière 1923:133).

As with most occupations in Shanghai, regionalism played an important role in the hierarchy of prostitution. Women in the top two classes came mainly from cities in the Kiangnan, notably Suchou (famed for its beauties), Wuhsi, Nanking, Hangchou, and Ch'angchou (Lemière 1923:133; Yi 1933: 39–40; Wiley 1929:53, citing Morris 1916). Even those in the top classes who came from Shanghai proper did their best to affect a Suchou accent and claim Suchou as their native place (T'u 1948:*hsia*, 76–77; Yü 1948:11). Prostitutes of the grade of "one-two" and below came largely from Yangchou and other parts of Supei, like the laborers who patronized their brothels. Supei prostitutes also carved out special niches for themselves in the sexual service market; for example, some specialized in rowing out to the junks moored on the Huang-p'u River to sell themselves to the Chinese sailors (Yi 1933:39–40; *SP*, April 6, 1929:7). This intersection of class and regional divisions, with Supei people at the bottom, mirrored the larger occupational structure of Shanghai (Honig 1987).

Regional divisions shaped prostitution in other ways as well. Distinct groups of prostitutes from Canton and Ningpo serviced the merchant and official groups from those cities who were resident in Shanghai. In the 1920s warlord conflicts drove many wealthy Cantonese to migrate to Shanghai, where they opened large businesses like Sincere and Wing On; the ranks of Cantonese long-three prostitutes increased accordingly. Ningpo prostitutes, supervised by madams, lived in and worked out of hotels in the Wu Ma Lu and Da Hsin Chieh area, receiving guests with Ningpo-style snacks of salted fish and crabs. The high-status Cantonese and Ningpo prostitutes kept to their own communities and generally did not welcome guests who were not from their native places (Wiley 1929:52; Yi 1933:39–40; Lemière 1923:133; Wang Ting-chiu 1932:"P'iao," 34–35).

Another group of Cantonese women, who traced their presence in Shanghai to the early nineteenth century, specialized in entertaining foreign sailors. They were known as "saltwater sisters" (*hsien-shui mei*), which may have been a reference to their maritime patrons; but one source explains that their name was a transliteration of "handsome maid" into Cantonese (*hansui mui*) (T'u 1948:*hsia*, 77). They were reputed to be "more hygienic than some

others, partly because of the Cantonese love of cleanliness, and partly because they wish to attract foreigners" ("Demi-monde" 1923:787–88). (This
emphasis on cleanliness was far more pronounced in guides to Shanghai
written by foreigners than in the Chinese literature, though the latter also
featured occasional warnings about venereal disease.) Nevertheless, their
solicitation of foreign sailors, and the resultant spread of venereal disease,
attracted the attention of the British admiral who in 1877 requested that
Shanghai open a lock hospital (a hospital devoted to the treatment of venereal
disease) to examine and register Cantonese prostitutes. Undaunted, the
women proceeded to use their hospital registration cards, each with a photo
identification, as advertisements for their services. Examinations continued
until 1920, when prostitution was officially (though ineffectively) phased out
in the International Settlement (SVC 1920:83–84).

Foreign prostitutes came to Shanghai from all over the world, recruited by
the shadowy traffickers that reformers called "white slavers." Among them
were many Russians, whose numbers grew larger after the Russian Revolution; in the 1930s one observer noted that eight thousand Russian prostitutes resided in Shanghai. Many were brought in from the northern city of
Harbin and either worked openly as prostitutes in "Russian houses" (*Lo-sung
t'ang-tzu*) in the French Concession and the Hung-k'ou area or became taxi
dancers who sold sexual services for an extra fee. Japanese prostitutes also
worked in the Hung-k'ou area, sometimes doubling as maidservants or waitresses. Foreign prostitutes apparently drew most of their clientele from
among the foreign community and transient sailors, but some of them entertained Chinese customers as well (O'Callaghan 1968:11–12; Champly
1934:188; Hauser 1940:267; T'ang 1931:153–54; T'u 1948:*hsia*, 77; Yi
1933:41).[5]

In addition to native place, beauty also determined a woman's place in
the hierarchy of prostitution. A Suchou woman, no matter how well her relatives or fellow villagers were known to the owner of a long-three brothel,
could not hope to become a prostitute there unless she was beautiful. Less
attractive women could work only as servants in these houses. At the same
time, particularly beautiful women from other regions sometimes entered
high-class houses without the benefit of connections. One small but prosperous brothel, a former resident of the neighborhood recounted, had two
prostitutes, one from Suchou and one from Shantung, but "the second one
was so beautiful you couldn't tell she was from Shantung." As one moved
down the hierarchy, the prostitutes reportedly became less beautiful (Sun et
al. 1986).

A third factor determining a woman's place in the hierarchy was age.
Many prostitutes in *ch'ang-san* houses first entered the brothels as children,
purchased by the madams as "foster daughters" (*yang-nü*). If a woman had
already passed adolescence, then no upper-class house would want her;

madams reasoned that she was already untrainable or that she would not be able to work enough years to pay back the investment. Pheasants and other low-class prostitutes were frequently in their twenties or even older (Yü 1948:11; Wiley 1929:66–67). Of five hundred prostitutes surveyed in 1948, almost half had begun work between the ages of fifteen and nineteen; the largest group was between the ages of twenty and twenty-four at the time of the interviews (Yü 1948:11). Women who began work at the top of the hierarchy might descend to less prestigious establishments as they aged if they were unable to devise a successful exit strategy.

NUMBERS ✗

It is impossible to say how many women worked as prostitutes in Shanghai. The inconsistent attitude of multiple municipal governments meant that no systematic statistics were collected. Even more unlucky for the researcher, brothel owners often had an interest in concealing their business from the authorities, if only to avoid paying bribes. Virtually every observer of the Shanghai scene commented that licensed brothels were outnumbered by unlicensed ones and by disguised forms of prostitution. Taxi dancers in the dance halls, masseuses in the massage parlors, waitresses in the vaudeville houses, guides in the tourist agencies, female vendors of newspapers, cigarettes, and fruit, and itinerant menders of sailors' clothing all engaged in prostitution, either because their jobs required it or because their precarious incomes needed augmenting (T'ang 1931:154; Yü 1948:11). Though they were seldom counted among the ranks of prostitutes in contemporary surveys, these part-time, or "disguised," prostitutes must be considered in estimating the size of the sexual-service sector and understanding the employment alternatives for women.

The fragmentary statistics available indicate the steady growth of prostitution. A 1920 report of the Special Vice Commission (SVC) counted 4,522 Chinese prostitutes in the International Settlement alone, or 1 out of every 147 Chinese residents, male and female, of the settlement. If the greater population of Shanghai was taken as 1.5 million, the report added, and if prostitutes in the French Concession were figured in, then 1 in 300 Chinese residents of Shanghai sold sexual services for a living (SVC 1920:84). These figures did not include what the report referred to as "sly" prostitutes, and in fact another set of statistics collected at around the same time found more than 60,000 prostitutes at work in the two foreign areas, most of them of pheasant rank or below (Wiley 1929:45; Yi 1933:39). By 1935 combined estimates of licensed and unlicensed prostitutes ran to 100,000, with much of the increase attributed to rural disaster and Depression-related factory closings (Lo Ch'iung 1935:37). A postwar study put the number of full-time prostitutes at 50,000 but suggested that the figure should be doubled to take account of women "whose activities approach those of prostitutes" (Yü 1948:10). If the Shanghai population at that time is taken as 4.2 million, then 1 in every 42 city residents was directly involved in prostitution. There may even have been more prostitutes than cotton spinners. Shanghai, China's largest industrial city, had about 84,000 cotton spinners out of a total of 173,432 women working in industry (Honig 1986:24–25).[6] But prostitution played a part in the Shanghai economy far beyond its direct significance as an employer of women. Many a small shop survived on the sale of goods and services to the upper-class brothels. "In the vicinity of her residence," a writer observed in 1929, "are numerous tailoring shops, hair dressers, makers of silk and satin shoes, embroidery shops, whose trade is enriched by her patronage" (Wiley 1929:74). Brothels also provided a venue for the meeting of the Shanghai powerful; merchants concluded deals and officials made alliances in upper-class brothels (T'u 1948:*hsia*, 76). For all of these reasons, prostitution touched virtually every sphere of Shanghai life.

⊀ ENTRY

Poverty led most women into prostitution, poverty that either drove their families to sell them, caused them to choose prostitution themselves, or made them vulnerable to the wiles of traffickers. Of twenty news stories about prostitutes reported in the Shanghai newspaper *Shih-pao* between March and November 1929, half explicitly mentioned family poverty as the cause of entry into prostitution. Five of the stories mentioned that the women were fatherless (three were orphans). Eight women had been sold or pawned by relatives (including parents, spouses, and others) and ten by traffickers; one had agreed to enter prostitution herself to pay off family debts. In the remaining case, two women were approached by traffickers but escaped (*SP* March 2; April 6, 8, 12, 19; May 23, 29; June 10, 17; July 6, 10, 15, 18, 19; August 21; September 20; October 14, 20; November 16, 25, 1929:7).[7]

Little is known about how poor families decided whether to sell their daughters as brides, maidservants, or prostitutes, though it is generally assumed that they attempted to emulate richer families in keeping their daughters on the marriage market and out of the brothels. But for a poor woman marriage was not a lifetime guarantee of respectability.[8] In the twenty cases just mentioned, eight of the prostitutes were married; most of them had been kidnapped, but one had been pawned by her husband, and another was tricked into prostitution when she left her husband to look for work because he refused to support her. Of the five hundred prostitutes surveyed in 1948, two-thirds were unmarried, a fifth were widows, and more than 9 percent had living spouses (Yü 1948:11; Yü and Wong 1949:236, table V). The percentage of married women and widows was higher among lower-class prostitutes (*SP* August 26, 1929:7; Yü and Wong 1949:236, table V). Though the data are not conclusive, they suggest that disintegration of family networks through death or poverty, or detachment from family networks in order to find work in Shanghai, greatly increased a woman's chances of ending up in a brothel.

Women entered brothels of all classes in Shanghai under one of three arrangements. A small number (estimated by one investigator at less than 5 percent) entered as employees, or "free persons" (*tzu-chi shen-t'i* or *tzu-chia shen-t'i*), paid all expenses themselves, and controlled their own work. A free prostitute in theory controlled her own earnings, but in practice she had to give half or more of her income to the madam in return for use of the brothel facilities. Often the madam kept complete control of the finances and paid each prostitute a fixed salary per season ("Demi-monde" 1923:784–85; Lemière 1923:131; Yi 1933:40–41; Lo Ch'iung 1935:35).

The majority of prostitutes were mortgaged (*ya-chang* or *pao-chang*) by relatives, traffickers, or themselves for a fixed term, much like pawned goods ("Demi-monde" 1923:784–85; Lemière 1923:131; Yi 1933:40–41). In six cases of pawning reported in the Shanghai press in 1929, the price ranged from seventy to four hundred yuan.[9] Women in the upper price range were virgins who could be expected to command a high defloration fee (*SP* April 8, 19; May 29; July 10; August 21; October 20, 1929:7).

The remaining women, known as "completely uprooted" (*tu-chueh*, or *t'ao-jen*), were sold outright to the brothel by relatives or traffickers ("Demi-monde" 1923:784–85; Lemière 1923:131; Yi 1933:40–41; Zhang and Sang 1987:32–33). Prostitutes who had been sold, rather than pawned, were regarded by the madams as their private property. They could be released from service only if someone paid what the brothel owner regarded as "a fair market price" (O'Callaghan 1968:13–14). In seven cases reported in the press where women were sold outright, the price ranged from 140 to 600 yuan (*SP* April 6; June 10; July 15; October 14; November 16, 25, 1929:7).

Trafficking in women was big business in Shanghai. Traffickers, both men and women, would go to rural districts that suffered from flood or famine and purchase girls and young women "for a couple of dollars apiece," reported a foreign observer in 1940, "and if they were lucky, they could resell the choice ones for a thousand dollars in Shanghai" (Hauser 1940:268). Equally common, and featured more prominently in the cautionary tales of the Shanghai press, were urban traffickers who preyed upon recent migrants to the city and sold them into brothels by trickery or force. "The methods of the procurers and procuresses are so subtle and ingenious that no one— unless associated with the traffic—knows exactly how they do their work," warned one foreign writer in 1927:

> Their favorite recruiting grounds are the theaters, tea houses, amusement parks, and other public places. . . . Many of the hotel boys, the theater ushers, the waiters in the restaurants, the flower girls, newspaper sellers, Mafoos (carriage men), maid servants, and even ricksha coolies are aiding and abetting in this traffic. The most dangerous of all perhaps are the women hair dressers, and

the sellers of jewelry, because they have easy access to the household and can exercise their influence freely. (McCartney 1927, cited in Wiley 1929:56)

Some professional traffickers pretended to be labor recruiters, promising to introduce women into legitimate jobs as servants or factory workers in Shanghai (*SP* March 2, 1929:7; Zhang and Sang 1987:31). They played on native-place ties to win the confidence of the women and their families. A woman from Suchou named Yang A-p'o, for instance, became acquainted with a man named Feng San-chuan who also resided in Shanghai. When Feng had to go to Hangchou on business, Yang offered to find his wife a maidservant's job so that she could remain in Shanghai. Several months later Feng returned from Hangchou looking for his wife, only to find that Yang had sold her into a brothel. Yang offered him two hundred yuan to acquire another wife, but he declined and sued her in court (*SP* April 12, 1929:7).

Other traffickers made no attempt to entice women, but instead kidnapped them by force. One such case involved a married woman named Hsiao (née Wang) who was grabbed by three men as she washed clothes on a riverbank in Supei. Gagged and restrained, she was taken to Shanghai. Her case came to public attention when, after several months of streetwalking, she spotted her kidnapper on the street and alerted the police (*SP* April 6, 1929:7). Another woman, new to the city, was forcibly pawned by the owner of the rickshaw her husband pulled (*SP* August 21, 1929:7). A third sought lodging in a local monastery while looking for work in the city, only to be mortgaged into prostitution by the monks (*SP* October 20, 1929:7). It was not uncommon for male traffickers to rape or seduce young women before selling them into prostitution, thus making their return to a spouse or the marriage market more difficult (T'ang 1931:481; *SP* October 14; November 25, 1929:7). A woman's entry into prostitution thus was sometimes accomplished by outright violence that removed her from whatever protection her family could offer.

BROTHEL LIFE

In Ta-ch'ing li, a lane off of Chiu-chiang Road, residents of every class crowded together in the 1940s. Doctors, fortune-tellers, owners of opium and gambling dens, businessmen and shop employees lived in close proximity. The monied classes resided in large apartments, while their poorer neighbors lived ten to a room. Of the four hundred residences in the lane, twenty-four were brothels. Though not of the highest grade, they nevertheless boasted many of the accoutrements of fancy establishments. In the late 1940s Ta-ch'ing li was home to 101 prostitutes, many recruited by the madams from their own native places.

To open a brothel in this lane or anywhere else in Shanghai, a madam (known as the *lao-pao*) needed not only money but also "background": marriage or a liaison with a local hoodlum, connections to the neighborhood police or to gang bosses. Local madam Ting Ts'ai-ch'un, for instance, was the lover of a police officer. Sometimes the madam's money and "background" had been acquired in a previous career as a prostitute. In other cases madams had begun their careers as brothel servants; this was the case with Big Pockmark and Small Pockmark, two madams in Ta-ch'ing li (Sun et al. 1986). Madams frequently owned as well as operated these establishments (Henderson 1871:12), though sometimes they shared ownership with a male boss. If a madam owned the establishment, she took charge of renting the house, meeting police regulations, and recruiting women (Wiley 1929: 59). After they opened their brothels, madams had to cultivate connections with the local police, usually through the payment of quasi-legal taxes like the "street-standing tax" (*chan-chieh chuan*) and the "friendliness tax" (*ho-ch'i chuan*). Prompt payment of these fees ensured that when the police came to inspect an establishment there would be no trouble, and if a madam became embroiled in a court case the local police would intercede. These police connections could be invoked by the madam in conflicts with the neighbors or used to bring an unruly prostitute into line (Lu 1938:14–15).

Once a woman was sold or pawned to a brothel, the madam had claims on her person that resembled those shopowners had on their apprentices or labor bosses on their contracted laborers. In the upper-class brothels, at least, the harshness of the madam/prostitute relationship was obscured by the language of kinship. Most prostitutes in Ta-ch'ing li, for instance, were addressed by terms used for adopted daughters and were taught to address the madams as "mama." The "family" consisted of a "father" (the owner or the madam's paramour), a "mother" (the madam), five or six adopted "daughters," and servants to do the housework. Larger brothels had a complete complement of cooks, bookkeepers, runners, and rickshaw pullers, but the Ta-ch'ing li establishments were more modest. The madams played cards or gambled with the neighbors, who were careful to avoid epithets like "madam" or "prostitute" when a conflict broke out because such an insult could not be easily repaired. In general, the madams treated these young women well, gave them enough to eat and wear, and made sure that they were strictly supervised by female servants. The more beautiful prostitutes-in-training were educated in chess, poetry, and music. During the day the "daughters" of the madams dressed like any other girl on the lane. Only their habit of sleeping until noon and their resplendent dress after five in the evening distinguished them from the neighbors (Sun et al. 1986; "Demimonde" 1923:785).

Relationships in the brothels mimicked familial relationships in less benign ways as well. Daughters in most Chinese families had little to say about the choice of their marriage partner or the timing of the match. At marriage,

they passed from the control of their natal families to that of their husbands, who had claims on their labor and their sexual and reproductive
services. Similarly, prostitutes exercised no autonomy over when and to
whom they would begin to sell their sexual services. A "daughter" in one of
these houses was carefully groomed for her first night with a customer, which
usually happened sometime after she turned fourteen. The privilege of
defloration (*k'ai-pao*) was expensive, and the madam would do her best to
locate a wealthy businessman or industrialist whose first-night fee would
repay the cost of raising the girl. The man who could afford such a fee was
permitted to take the young woman to a rented room for the night; the entire
defloration fee went to the madam. In top-class houses, first-night rituals were
especially elaborate. The occasion was marked by a solemn ceremony that
included lighting candles and bowing to images, much like a marriage rite.
The patron then hosted a banquet for his friends at the brothel, a procedure
known as "celebrating the flower" (*tso hua-t'ou*) (Sun et al. 1986).

Little is known about how young women were prepared for their first
sexual encounter. In some respects they appear to have been as sequestered,
and as ignorant, as their counterparts who were married to upper-class men.
Madams in the higher-grade brothels took care that their virgin "daughters"
did not go out unchaperoned; they worried about the girls, recalled a resident
of one brothel district, "just like parents worried about their children." They
did not want to risk a casual sexual encounter with a local hoodlum, or a love
affair, and the consequent loss of the lucrative first-night fee.

Even after a prostitute had spent her first night with a man, the madam
continued to exercise a great deal of control over the sale of her services
(what kind, when, how often, to whom, and for how much money). As mentioned earlier, providing sexual services was a minor part of an upper-class
prostitute's duties. She spent much of her time attending parties given by
powerful men, where she engaged in light conversation, drinking, and music
making (Wei 1930:13). In the 1920s she was paid one yuan for each call, even
if it was only several minutes in duration, and might make dozens of such
stops in the course of a working evening, either alone or accompanied by a
servant (Lemière 1923:131; Wiley 1929:72). Sometimes wealthy customers
would request that a prostitute accompany them to a dramatic performance
or other place of entertainment (Henderson 1871:14; T'u 1948:*hsia*, 76). The
woman's brothel charged a set fee for all such services.

An upper-class prostitute thus moved around more than the sheltered
daughters of respectable urban families. As one contemporary observer put
it, "She can visit the races, the theatre, make journeys unaccompanied by a
male member of the family, and engage in many other activities denied to her
sisters within the home" (Wiley 1929:74). It is not clear, however, that an
upper-class prostitute was able to control where she went, when, or with

whom; much of her social schedule was probably arranged by the madam. The ability to move around did not necessarily mean freedom of movement.

But there were exceptions to the ironclad control of the madams. Very famous or very beautiful prostitutes had some control over their own sexual services. And money was not the only variable; as one guidebook lamented, "Many are those who spend ten thousand pieces of gold, and never get to touch her" (T'u 1948:*hsia*, 76). A 1932 guide to Shanghai, in a section entitled "Key to Whoring" ("P'iao ti men-ching"), elaborated on this theme. It explained that some patrons could not "get into the water" even after hosting several expensive banquets, while others "tasted the flavor" without hosting even one. The key, explained the author, lay in the behavior of the patron. He should be careful to exhibit not only wealth but also good taste in dress and choice of male companions. If he was "foolish when appropriate and serious when appropriate," then even the most popular prostitute would eventually become a "prisoner of war at [his] feet" (Wang Ting-chiu 1932:"P'iao," 6). Accounts of this kind never mentioned the madam as arbiter of such encounters; the woman was portrayed as having a degree of autonomy in her choice of customers.

Although upper-class prostitutes often commanded high fees, they had little or no direct control over the income they earned. Direct fees for a woman's services were usually paid to the brothel staff, not to the prostitute. The more elegant brothels "had their shroffs and they sent their customers chits at the end of the month, like any other business establishment" (Hauser 1940:268). A house made money not only on its women but also on its banquet facilities and domino games; the madams, rather than the prostitutes, received this income (Wiley 1929:60). When a high-class prostitute went out on a social call, accompanied by her attendants, she was expected to divide the money she received with servants, musicians, and the brothel owner (Lemière 1923:131).

Three-quarters of the five hundred prostitutes questioned in 1948 said their income was average or above (*chung-teng yi-shang*), though their comparison group was not specified; the investigators commented that since the currency devaluation prostitutes were much better off than salaried urban workers. But the survey added that "after exploitation by the brothel owners and middlemen, and after waste and consumption, their life is by no means well-to-do" (Yü 1948:13). One of the few ways that an upper-class prostitute could amass wealth of her own was if a customer gave her money or presents in addition to paying the madam's fee. This private wealth was known as *ssu-fang ch'ien*, the same term used for a married woman's private savings (Sun et al. 1986; R. Watson 1984:4–9). But a woman did not always have clear title to these presents. In a 1929 case, for instance, a popular prostitute received some valuable jewelry from an admirer. Later she fell ill and pawned the jewelry to pay her medical bills. When one of the Shanghai tabloids published this information, her erstwhile patron was furious and demanded that she return the jewelry. Unable to comply, she tried to kill herself by jumping from a ferry sampan into the river (*SP* May 20, 1929:7).

As one moved down the hierarchy of prostitution, women apparently had even less control over the sale of their sexual services. In the "one-two" houses, customers were accepted readily whether they were regulars or strangers (T'u 1948:*hsia*, 77). Prostitutes in the salt-pork shops and even lower-grade establishments received customers in cubicles called "pigeon sheds" (*ko-tzu p'eng*), each one just big enough for a bed. The women spent a certain amount of time with each customer, depending on the size of the fee, then went on to the next one (Sun et al. 1986; Zhang and Sang 1987:32). The pheasants, too, remained under surveillance by brothel servants, even when soliciting on the streets. Neither their freedom from the physical confines of the brothel nor the fact that as a group they were somewhat older than upper-class prostitutes guaranteed them greater control over their working lives. In addition, women who had been sold outright to a brothel apparently had less freedom to refuse customers than "free prostitutes" (Zhang and Sang 1987:33).

In the 1948 survey of five hundred prostitutes, most women were found to have had ten to thirty sexual encounters per month, with some women reporting as many as sixty (Yü 1948:13). But even the high figure may not accurately reflect the experience of lower-class prostitutes. Madams reportedly forced these women to have sexual relations with anywhere from four to twenty men a night, while saltwater sisters sometimes serviced twenty to thirty customers a night (Lo Ch'iung 1935:36; Zhang and Sang 1987:32; T'ang 1931:153). Such accounts are indirectly supported by the complaint of reformers that lower-class prostitutes were the chief cause of venereal disease because they spread it more widely and quickly than others (Yü 1948:13; "Demi-monde" 1923:786).

In some brothels women were expected to continue work even if they were menstruating or in the second trimester of pregnancy; such practices are said to have led to disorders ranging from menorrhagia to frequent miscarriage. After a miscarriage, a prostitute was put back to work as quickly as possible (Zhang and Sang 1987:32; Lo Ch'iung 1935:36). To prevent pregnancy, madams gave their prostitutes live tadpoles to eat on the theory that the "cold element" in tadpoles would counteract the "heat" of pregnancy. The same remedy was applied as an abortifacient (Sun et al. 1986).[10] Venereal disease undoubtedly brought on infertility, stillbirth, and miscarriage. A 1948 survey found a very low rate of pregnancy among a sample of five hundred prostitutes (Yü 1948:13).

The actual incidence of venereal disease among prostitutes is impossible to determine. A 1931 guidebook, its author intent on advertising the pleasures of Shanghai's entertainment quarters, estimated that only 1 or 2 percent of all prostitutes were infected (T'ang 1931:154). But soon after the Japanese occupation, an investigative committee organized by women reformers under the auspices of the city government found that all of the pheasants rounded up in one relief effort (a total of thirty) had syphilis, and many suffered from gonorrhea as well (Ch'en Lu-wei 1938:21–22). A 1948 government report commented that most women contracted venereal disease within a year or two of beginning work as prostitutes. Of 1,420 working prostitutes examined by the municipal health authorities in 1946, 66 percent had venereal disease; the percentage was 62 percent for 3,550 women examined the following year. Most of these were cases of tertiary syphilis; the report noted that the numbers would have been still higher if a more reliable test for gonorrhea were included (Yü 1948:11, 13). Women who were examined and treated in government clinics represented only a tiny percentage of all prostitutes, most of whom had no contact with the medical system. Many who contracted syphilis were treated in the brothels with crude home remedies.

An examination of violence in the brothels makes clear the lack of control that prostitutes had over their working lives. Accounts of violence used by madams and brothel servants against prostitutes filled the Shanghai press during the Republican period. These reports usually concerned practices in lower-class brothels, where the madams beat their prostitutes for failing to bring customers home, for refusing to receive customers, for infractions of brothel rules, for stealing or being careless enough to let customers steal from them ("Demi-monde" 1923:786–87; *SP* April 8; May 29; June 10; July 6, 18; November 16, 1929:7; January 28, 1928:7). Some madams were sadistic as well as brutal; one put a cat inside the pants leg of a new prostitute who did not want to sleep with customers and whipped the cat until it lacerated the woman's leg (Ch'en Lu-wei 1938:22). When prostitutes fled to escape such abuse, they found scant refuge on the streets of Shanghai. The lucky ones were picked up by the police and remanded by the courts to the Door of Hope or another relief organization, with the ultimate expectation that they would find a spouse (*sung-t'ang tse-p'ei*) (*SP* February 23; July 6, July 15, 1929:7). The others got no help from local patrolmen, who were often receiving regular payoffs from the madam. If a prostitute complained directly to police headquarters, the brothel owner might be fined a few dollars. But with no other way to make a living, a woman usually had to return to work as a prostitute (Ch'en Lu-wei 1938:22).

Very little is known about how the prostitutes regarded their work or themselves. Undoubtedly their outlook varied depending on whether the madam was cruel or kind, whether or not they had to entertain many guests, whether or not they became ill or pregnant. Certainly beautiful prostitutes in prestigious houses led a comfortable life compared with what they might have expected in their families of origin. They ate well, dressed beautifully, and enjoyed the glamour surrounding their occupation. "Since seduction is her trade," commented a 1929 observer, "her dress sets her off from other women. Her rich apparel of brilliant silk makes her much better dressed than any class of women save the very rich. On the streets she is the object of attention for those who wish to see the new styles in feminine dress" (Wiley 1929:74). A 1920 newspaper article reported that upper-class prostitutes often wore jewels worth five or six thousand dollars (*NCH* June 26, 1920, cited in Wiley 1929:74). Of the five hundred prostitutes of all grades surveyed in 1948, 56 percent declared themselves satisfied with their occupation, mainly because it provided them with a relatively secure livelihood in a period of economic uncertainty. Less than a quarter were unhappy with their current circumstances (Yü 1948:12).

Nevertheless, social workers reported a variety of less sanguine attitudes on the part of prostitutes. Some, they found, articulated feelings of depression, inferiority, and suspicion (ibid., 12–13). Relief workers who interviewed such women reported that they were "as though anesthetized . . . numbed to the conditions of their existence." Unfortunately for the reformers, such emotional numbness did not translate into docility or willingness to reform. Given literacy training, the women in one program tore up their books and asked, "Why should we 'chew yellow beansprouts' here when in our 'own homes' servants will address us as 'Miss'?" In despair the social workers responsible for this program commented that "prostitutes are not ordinary women; they have deeply rooted vulgar practices, know no shame in their behavior, assume airs of importance, are lazy and full of ailments, like to sleep and cry, and are especially good at trickery" (Ch'en Lu-wei 1938:21–22). A former prostitute interviewed in the 1980s recalled the strategies women used to justify their existence to themselves:

> You've got to have some idea in your head to keep you going. Otherwise you just couldn't take it, going with all those men. At first I just felt it was my fate and nothing could be done about it. Later I believed some of the things the other girls said. The craziest idea was it wasn't men having fun with us, but us having fun with them and they still had to pay good money. (Zhang and Sang 1987:33)

For these women, as for the prostitutes rounded up by the municipal government in the 1950s campaign to eradicate prostitution, it was no longer possible to imagine life outside the brothel system. Women dragged from the brothels in police raids during the 1950s often clung to their madams, weeping piteously and shouting, "Don't take me away from my 'mama'" (Ts'ao 1986). Though the madams might be oppressive and the effects of venereal disease debilitating, the fictive kinship networks of the brothels represented the only stable family many of these women knew, and they were loathe to leave it for an uncertain future.

EXIT

When prostitutes imagined life outside the brothel system at all, they thought of becoming the wives or concubines of rich men. A quarter of the prostitutes surveyed in 1948 wanted to leave the life and marry a rich husband (Yu 1948:12) who was willing to pay off her "mortgage" or, if she had been sold outright, reimburse the madam for her purchase price plus interest and expenses. Some women, especially ones who were still young and attractive, left "the life" by this route (e.g., *SP* April 8, 1929:7), though such reports may have been exaggerated for their value in selling papers.[11]

For many women, an interim arrangement that might lead to a more permanent union was to be "rented" by a single patron. The man would pay a monthly fee to the madam and would either visit the woman regularly or take up residence in the brothel. Alternatively, he might install the woman in quarters of her own. Men who could not yet afford to redeem a prostitute's pawn pledge or buy her outright made use of this arrangement. In the late 1920s monthly rental fees could run as much as fifty yuan (Wei 1930:14; *SP* July 31, 1929:7).

In their search for a secure future, prostitutes used sexual strategies, particularly their capacity to bear children. Just as married women consolidated their positions in their husbands' families this way, so some prostitutes used pregnancy as a way out of prostitution and a ticket to marriage or at least concubinage. Ch'iao-nan, a young prostitute in Ta-ch'ing li, had a patron who was the scion of a wealthy family. Because she was beautiful, her madam treated her well and guarded her carefully and was reluctant to allow the young man to buy her out of the brothel. When Ch'iao-nan became pregnant, she and her lover agreed that she would not have an abortion. She refused the required doses of tadpoles, and when her pregnancy became so far advanced that there was no hope of her continuing to attract customers, the madam finally permitted her lover to purchase her (Sun et al. 1986). In cases like this, pregnancy was the occasion for struggles between prostitutes and owners over who controlled the disposition of sexual services and fertility decisions.

Women who were bought out of the brothels as concubines sometimes kept up contact with the madams who had raised them (Sun et al. 1986). Some reports indicate that women who had led active social lives as upper-class prostitutes found family life too sequestered and left their new husbands to seek a situation in which they enjoyed more autonomy (Lemière 1923:133). Others found that life as a concubine was in some respects less secure than life as a prostitute, depending as it did on the continuing favor of only one man. Women from lower-class brothels could seldom hope for a match with a rich man; some became wives of widowers and older men who could not afford a conventional match (Wiley 1929:76).

Many prostitutes did not cross over into marriage, but remained in the sexual service business. If their looks declined before they had accumulated private money or connections, they became servants in the brothels. The more fortunate ones opened their own establishments and became madams. In Hui-le li, the only madams who actually resided in the lane were those who had just crossed over from prostitution into sexual service management. After making some money as madams, they moved elsewhere, returning to the lane only during working hours (Sun et al. 1986). Life as a madam afforded a woman a rare degree of autonomy. Although a madam, as noted earlier, needed to cultivate protection from men who might also threaten her, she was able to operate as a petty entrepreneur with the opportunity to amass considerable personal wealth.

The type of crossover strategy most frequently reported in the press, however, involved neither marriage nor becoming a madam, but flight. Women who could no longer tolerate the conditions of their employment, particularly in lower-class brothels, simply slipped out of the houses and sought refuge on the streets. One story reported in detail in the press involved a seventeen-year-old woman whose professional name was Red Cloud. Her madam was exceptionally cruel; Red Cloud was compelled to solicit customers on the street until four in the morning. If she failed to bring in business she was forced to kneel on broken tiles with a pan of water on her head, and was forbidden to sleep. Driven beyond endurance, Red Cloud fled the brothel early one morning and leaped into a rickshaw parked at the end of the lane. Upset to the point of incoherence, she could not tell the puller where to go, so she directed him by means of hand motions. After nine hours of running through almost every district in Shanghai, the hapless puller lost patience and asked her where she wanted to go. At this point she realized that she had no money to pay him, so she offered to marry him instead. Delighted, the puller told her that he might be too old for her (he was thirty-six), but that he had three younger brothers at home, all unmarried. He took her to his house in the Cha-pei district, whereupon his brothers immediately began to argue over who should have her as a wife. The tumult alerted some inquisitive neighbors, who suspected that the woman had been kidnapped and turned her and all the brothers in to the police (*SP* May 29, 1929:7).

It was not easy for prostitutes to free themselves from the control of the brothel system. Brothel owners employed both legal and illegal forms of coercion to keep women in their employ, particularly if the women had been mortgaged to them and the term had not yet expired. The power of such coercion can be seen in the case of Ma Jui-chen, a prostitute who briefly passed through a reform organization in the late 1930s. Ma was released from the reform school on court order and remanded to the custody of her mother. But as they left the courtroom, her mother told her that the madam had threatened the mother's life if she did not get the daughter released immediately. On the street they found the madam and several of her "friends" (*hsiang-hao*) waiting to escort them back to the brothel. The madam wanted to beat Ma and demanded immediate compensation for the two months' income she had lost while Ma was incarcerated. If Ma did not pay her immediately, she threatened to turn her over to the "boss" (*lao-pan*), whom Ma referred to as "the highest penal official in the brothel," a man who might well kill her or sell her into another city. Then some of the madam's "friends" mediated. They convinced Ma and her mother to kneel in front of the madam and beg that Ma be allowed to continue to work in order to pay off the debt. Ma was sent back onto the street to solicit customers under the watchful eyes of the brothel servants.

For two days Ma deliberately failed to bring in customers. The madam cut off her food and threatened to have her hung up and beaten if she did not bring in some business before midnight. Ma fled to the local police station, which took her into protective custody. But when the police went to arrest the madam, they found that she had disappeared, warned by local detectives with whom she had a well-developed financial relationship. The police could only hold Ma in protective custody for twenty-four hours, and when they let her out one of the madam's "friends" took her to the madam, who had already seized her mother. Both mother and daughter were severely beaten. Only then did a bystander intervene and help Ma drag the madam and her accomplices to the police. But when the case went to court, the judge agreed that Ma and her mother were contractually bound to work for the madam; he ordered the mother to work as a maidservant in the brothel, while Ma was permitted to work outside as a maid. In this way she could pay off her debt while avoiding work as a prostitute. Only after the debt was cleared could she and her mother hope to return to the countryside district where Ma had grown up. State power thus intervened to legitimize and perpetuate the conditions of servitude in the brothels (Lu 1938:14–15).

Even when her pawn period was up, a prostitute often found it difficult to leave the brothel. Often she had nowhere to go. Moreover, madams, reluctant to lose a lucrative property, often tricked ignorant and illiterate women into agreeing to extensions on their contracts (*SP* April 8, 1929:7). When a woman did leave the brothel, it was invariably with financial help from a patron or someone else; in this arena women had little autonomy.

Only a woman who could prove that she had been forced into prostitution could hope to get legal help in fleeing the brothel system. Many cases that came before the courts in the Republican period thus centered around the contention, made by a prostitute or her relatives, that she had not voluntarily entered the brothel and they had not voluntarily sold her there. Madams routinely contested these assertions, saying that women had been sold to them as foster daughters or pawned as prostitutes. Because pawning or sale was a contractual transaction, madams frequently produced the signed contracts in court as proof that all parties had agreed to the arrangement.

Brothel owners who had acquired women by irregular means were not above forging such contracts or tricking women into signing them after the fact. The prostitutes, in turn, often contended that such documents had been signed under duress (*SP* April 8, 12; July 15; November 16, 1929:7).

The many efforts made by parents and other relatives of prostitutes to find and free them testify to the continuing ties between prostitutes and their kin, particularly in cases where the women had been kidnapped or tricked rather than sold. One peasant man brought a complaint against a madam after he came to Shanghai on business and saw his daughter soliciting customers at an amusement hall (*SP* June 10, 1929:7). Another peasant told the court that his your~er brother's wife had been kidnapped and sold by her own relatives; the wife corroborated his testimony and asked to be released to his custody. Interestingly, the madam argued that the woman had been sold by her own father and that she could produce a contract to that effect, implying that this would make the sale legal and irrevocable (*SP* June 17, 1929:7). In a third case, a man from the rural hinterland of Shanghai discovered his fiancée working in a brothel four years after she had disappeared from their home county. He bought her from the madam (negotiating the asking price of a thousand yuan down to eight hundred) and married her (*SP* November 25, 1929:7).

But if a woman testified that she had become a prostitute of her own free will, then not even the protests of her relatives could free her. In a 1929 case, for instance, the mother of Sun Feng-ying petitioned the municipal court, saying her married daughter had been kidnapped and pawned into a French Concession brothel. But Sun herself testified that she had volunteered to become a prostitute to help pay the debts incurred by her husband's family when her sister-in-law became ill. The court dismissed the mother's complaint (*SP* April 19, 1929:7). Conversely, a woman who did not wish to become a prostitute but was forced into it by relatives did have legal recourse. One woman retained a lawyer to petition the court to enjoin her mother from harassing her; the mother had forced her to engage in prostitution from age fourteen to twenty-nine (*SP* May 23, 1929:7). Both types of cases were exceedingly rare; usually the interests of the woman and her family were arrayed together against those of the brothel owners. In fact, it would appear that it was virtually impossible for a woman to leave the brothel system for a secure future unless she had either a rich patron or a loyal family (natal or marital) that was willing to testify for her in court.

Some prostitutes who grew old in the system without finding a rich patron or accumulating enough money to open their own establishment would adopt a daughter who could care for them in their old age or at least could yield a hefty brideprice when married off. However, for those prostitutes who had neither the means nor the foresight to invest in this arrangement, age brought a descent into less prestigious brothels, then into the ranks of

Shanghai beggars and itinerant entertainers (*SP* September 4, 1929:7; Wiley 1929:51–52).

CONCLUSION

How should we classify the market in prostitutes? In many ways, Shanghai prostitutes fit James Watson's definitions of slaves—they were acquired by purchase, their labor was secured by coercion (though the degree of actual physical force employed varied enormously), and they did not have, and could not attain, kinship status with their owners (1980a:8). They had a price on their heads, one that apparently correlated to market considerations of supply and demand as well as individual attributes of beauty, age, and virginity. Furthermore, they could be and often were resold. In short, it is tempting to regard these women as market commodities.

But portraying Shanghai prostitutes as slaves—that is, as fully detachable commodities that could be owned, bought, and sold—presents several problems. First, they were not fully detachable. Many prostitutes remained legally, emotionally, or financially attached to their natal or marital families. Using the language of slavery obscures the temporary nature of servitude for the majority of women who were pawned into prostitution. It also ignores the degree to which a fictive kinship structure was necessary in legitimating and maintaining the coercive relationship between madam and prostitute. Finally, the scattered evidence we have on struggles between prostitutes and their employers over claims on the woman's person indicates that both parties thought of the relationship as contractual rather than rooted in slave status and that the contracts were contestable in court. At a minimum, if these women were commodities, at least some of them put up an extraordinary struggle against such a status. To emphasize unduly the market transaction surrounding their entry into prostitution directs attention precisely away from the complex and variegated struggle of these women to assert some control over their working lives. It is more accurate, if less analytically tidy, to emphasize the ambiguity in their status, to say that they were treated as both persons and things by their families and by the madams who purchased long-term claims on them.

Conversely, if Shanghai prostitutes were not simply commodities themselves, neither had they "progressed" to the stage of selling their labor as a commodity for wages. Many of them received no regular wages, and even those who were in theory paid for their labor seldom saw or controlled the income. They were less than fully "free" to sell their labor to the highest bidder, or even to move from one workplace to another. Of course, in this lack of freedom they had much in common with other laborers; contract workers in the cotton mills and apprentices in small workshops had limited control over their own wages or mobility. Although less is known about domestic servants, it seems probable that their employers regulated their living arrangements and leisure time in addition to their work. But the degree of control asserted over prostitutes by their employer/owners was extreme even by these standards. Prostitution in China involved more than wages for sex work; it included control by madams over a woman's fertility, sexual access, mobility, and life-style, as well as her labor. Rather than regarding the labor of prostitutes as fully commodified, it seems more accurate to say that what was being purchased were claims on a woman's attributes and services, rather than her actual labor, and that these claims were contestable in the courts and through flight from the brothel system.

The language of commodification causes another problem when applied to women up and down the hierarchy of Shanghai prostitution: it obscures status differences among the women themselves and imposes a false uniformity on their experience. The status of all prostitutes derived from the class background of their customers rather than their own family backgrounds. However derivative, a woman's status translated into real differences in daily working conditions, personal control over income, and possibilities for negotiating an advantageous exit from prostitution into concubinage or madamhood. The experience of a storytelling-house courtesan was radically different from that of a saltwater sister, and the two might well have had difficulty viewing themselves as members of a single profession. Noting the structural similarities of commodification should not blind us to the inequality among prostitutes, an inequality that mirrored the complex class structure of Shanghai society.

The language of commodification, then, cannot be applied neatly either to the women themselves or to their labor. Nevertheless, it must be said that in early twentieth-century Shanghai there was a growing market in which claims on women's bodies were exchanged: that is, that the commodification of women's bodies outside the marriage market was becoming more common. Perhaps the most important thing we can say about the Shanghai market in prostitutes is that it appears to have grown and changed during the first half of the twentieth century. During that period what had essentially been a luxury market in top-class courtesans became a market primarily geared to supplying sexual services for the growing numbers of unattached (though not necessarily unmarried) commercial and working-class men of the city. The increase in demand was apparently accompanied by a boom in supply, fed by a burgeoning population of refugees and peasants in distress with daughters they could not support. We cannot yet trace the fluctuating value of women on this larger market as brides, maid-servants, concubines, or prostitutes. But it certainly looks as though the "popularization" of prostitution was accompanied by degenerating conditions of work for the individual prostitutes, or at least that more and more women participated in the less privileged and more vulnerable sectors of the trade. This trend, combined with the growth of various distinct reform currents among foreigners and Chinese in Shanghai, led to a series of loud, though largely ineffective, calls for the regulation or abolition of prostitution. Not until the early 1950s did the municipal government succeed in abolishing this particular market in women.

NOTES

I wish to acknowledge helpful comments from the participants in the Conference on Marriage and Inequality in China, particularly Susan Mann, Susan Naquin, Rubie Watson, and Arthur Wolf. In addition, various drafts of this chapter were given critical readings by Wendy Brown, Christina Gilmartin, Emily Honig, Lisa Rofel, Margery Wolf, Christine Wong, and Marilyn Young. All interpretations and errors are my responsibility.

1. For a theory of female subordination linked to the exchange of rights in women, particularly through marriage, see Rubin 1975.

2. For a brief overview of changes in the city, see Honig 1986:9–40. Pan 1983 provides a useful synthesis of Shanghai guidebooks dealing primarily with the Republican period.

3. The population of greater Shanghai (including foreign settlements) was 1,185,859 in 1910; 3,112,250 in 1930; 3,370,230 in 1945; 3,830,039 in 1946; and 4,494,390 in 1947 (sources for 1910 and 1930: Lo Chih-ju 1932:21, table 29; for 1945–47: SSWH 1948:14, 16, 18).

4. Available statistics on the occupational structure of Shanghai do not permit a complete portrait of the sexual division of labor. According to statistics collected by the municipal government of Greater Shanghai (that is, excluding the foreign settlements), Shanghai's population went from 1.7 million in 1930 to 1.8 million in 1931, then declined to slightly less than 1.6 million in 1932. Of these residents, about one-fifth were classified as industrial workers, and another one-fifth were in household service. See SCA 1933: 5, table 6, for details on occupation.

Only in industry do we have comprehensive information on the position of women. Most women industrial workers were employed in the textile industry. In 1928, for example, women made up 57 percent of total industrial workforce and women working in the textile industry constituted 90 percent of female factory labor force (for details see SCA 1933: Labor, 1, table 1. For 1929, also see Shanghai Bureau of Social Affairs 1929).

5. Foreign prostitutes in Shanghai are the subject of a vast literature, including a 1932 League of Nations *Report on Traffic in Women and Children in the Far East* and an array of accounts by travelers and reformers. See, for instance, Champly 1934; De Leeuw 1933:114–45; Crad 1940:134–45 (an account cribbed from De Leeuw); and, for a modern summary, Chou 1971:104–5, 112–13. Although these women were an important part of the sexual service market in Shanghai, their experience is beyond the scope of this essay.

6. Honig 1986:24–25, gives the total number of female industrial workers in Shanghai as 173,432 in 1929. Of these, the largest number (84,270) were employed in cotton spinning. Of 54,508 women workers counted in 1946, 35,306 were cotton spinners.

7. Family structure must have influenced a woman's entry into prostitution as

well, though it has not been possible to obtain demographic data on this. Families without sons, for instance, may have been more inclined to pawn a daughter into prostitution as a means of securing a continuing income from her. Families with sons may have been more willing to sell daughters outright, or they might have found themselves more able to raise a daughter, marry her, and use the brideprice to get a wife for the son.

8. The language of respectability is used with caution here. Virtually nothing is known about twentieth-century peasant attitudes toward selling female family members into prostitution. Was it regarded as shameful? If the women, or their families, felt shame, was it because selling a daughter to a brothel was a sign of poverty, or because moral considerations intervened? This question prompts others: did peasant communities regard such a sale as a practical decision made under economic duress with no stigma attached? Did the selling of one daughter into prostitution prejudice the marriage prospects of other children? If morality figured into the decision, then what sort of moral discourse was created? How did it differ from elite moral discourse and from the discourse of social purity being generated by Western reformers in the treaty ports? Though these questions are currently unanswerable, Susan Mann's research on pariah communities in Qing society reminds us that the descendants of debased (*jian*) people, including prostitutes, were legally discriminated against as late as 1821 (1988). How these legal proscriptions affected poor peasant life and thought remains to be investigated.

9. A one-year study of 305 working-class Shanghai families in 1929–30 found that their average annual income was 417 yuan and their average annual expenditure was 454 yuan, giving rise to an average annual deficit of 38 yuan. These figures indicate both the precariousness of working-class life (a problem magnified in the countryside) and the considerable significance to family welfare of pawning a daughter or wife as a prostitute. The survey was conducted by the Bureau of Social Affairs of the municipal government of Greater Shanghai; the figures are cited by Hinder 1942:23–24.

10. Research on the effectiveness of tadpoles as an oral contraceptive was conducted in China in 1957. In one Chekiang study, women swallowed twenty-four and twenty live tadpoles on two successive days shortly after their periods. The experiment was not a success; within four months 43 percent of the women became pregnant, while the consumption of tadpoles may have exposed them to parasitic diseases. In 1958 tadpoles were "officially declared to have no contraceptive value" (Tien 1973:249–51).

11. As one former prostitute mused bitterly, "No, there was never one who wanted to buy me out and marry me. That only happened in novels . . . I was riddled with disease. I had syphilis and I was a heroin addict. No one would have wanted me for a wife" (Zhang and Sang 1987:32).

GLOSSARY

chan-chieh chuan	站街捐	*ch'u-chi*	雛妓
ch'ang-san	長三	*chung-teng yi-shang*	中等以上
chih-chi	雉鸡	*erh-san*	二三

Han-chu chia   含珠家
ho-ch'i chuan   和氣捐
hsiang-hao   相好
hsiao hsien-sheng   小先生
hsien-jou chuang   咸肉庄
hsien-shui mei   咸水妹
hsien-sheng   先生
hua-yen chien   花烟间
k'ai-pao   开苞
ko-tzu p'eng   鴿子棚
lao-pan   老闆
lao-pao   老鸨
Lo-sung t'ang-tzu   羅宋堂子
pao-chang   包账
P'iao-ti men-ching   嫖的門徑

shu-lou   书楼
shu-yu   书寓
ssu-fang ch'ien   私房錢
sung-t'ang tse-p'ei   送堂擇配
t'ao-jen   讨人
ting-p'eng   钉棚
tu-chueh   杜绝
tzu-chi shen-t'i   自己身体
tzu-chia shen-t'i   自家身体
tso hua-t'ou   做花头
ya-chang   押账
yang-nü   养女
yao-erh   么二
yeh-chi   野鸡
yi-p'ao chu-yi   一砲主義

REFERENCES

Arlington, L. C. 1923. "The Chinese Female Names." *China Journal of Science and Arts* 1.4:316–25.

Champly, Henry. 1934. *The Road to Shanghai: White Slave Traffic in Asia.* Trans. Warre B. Wells. London: John Long.

Chang Hsin-hsin 張辛欣 and Sang Yeh 桑曄 (see also Zhang Xinxin and Sang Ye). 1985. "Chiu-yü hsin-chih" 舊雨新知 (Clients old and new). *Tso-chia* 1. Reprinted in *Pei-ching jen* 52. Shanghai, 1986.

Ch'en Jen-ping 陳仁炳. 1948. *Yu-kuan Shang-hai erh-t'ung fu-li ti she-hui tiao-ch'a* 有關上海兒童福利的社會調查 (A social investigation concerning the welfare of Shanghai children). Shanghai: Shang-hai erh-t'ung fu-li tsu-chin hui.

Ch'en Lu-wei 陳露薇. 1938. "Shou-jung chi-nü ti ching-kuo" 收容妓女的經過 (The process of taking in prostitutes). *Shang-hai fu-nü* 1.1:21–22.

Chou, Eric. 1971. *The Dragon and the Phoenix: Love, Sex, and the Chinese.* London: Michael Joseph.

Courbin, Alain. 1986. "Commercial Sexuality in Nineteenth-Century France: A System of Images and Regulations." *Representations* 14 (Spring): 209–19.

Crad, Joseph. 1940. *Traders in Women: A Comprehensive Survey of "White Slavery."* London: John Long.

De Leeuw, Hendrik. 1933. *Cities of Sin.* New York: Harrison Smith & Robert Haas.

Delacoste, Frederique, and Priscilla Alexander, eds. 1987. *Sex Work: Writings by Women in the Sex Industry.* Pittsburgh: Cleis Press.

"The Demi-monde of Shanghai." 1923. *China Medical Journal* 37:782–88.

Gronewold, Sue. 1982. *Beautiful Merchandise: Prostitution in China 1860–1936.* New York: Institute for Research in History and the Haworth Press.

Hauser, Ernest O. 1940. *Shanghai: City for Sale.* New York: Harcourt, Brace.

Henderson, Edward. 1871. *A Report on Prostitution in Shanghai.* Shanghai: North-China Herald Office.

Hinder, Eleanor M. 1942. *Social and Industrial Problems of Shanghai.* New York: Institute of Pacific Relations.

Honig, Emily. 1986. *Sisters and Strangers: Women in the Shanghai Cotton Mills, 1919–1949.* Stanford: Stanford University Press.

———. 1987. "The Making of an Underclass: Subei People in Shanghai." Paper prepared for the Social Science Research Council Conference on Economics and Chinese History, Oracle, Arizona, January 1988.

Lemière, J. Em. 1923. "The Sing-song Girl: From a Throne of Glory to a Seat of Ignominy." *China Journal of Science and Arts* 1.2:126–34.

Liu P'ei-ch'ien 柳培潛. 1936. *Ta Shang-hai chih-nan* 大上海指南 (A guide to greater Shanghai). Shanghai: Chung-hua shu-chü.

Lo Chih-ju 羅志如. 1932. *T'ung-chi piao chung chih Shang-hai* 統計表中之上海 (Shanghai in statistical charts). Nanking: Kuo-li chung-yang yen-chiu yuan.

Lo Ch'iung 羅瓊. 1935. "Ch'ang-chi tsai Chung-kuo" 娼妓在中國 (Prostitution in China). *Fu-nü sheng-huo* 1.6:34–40.

Lu Wei 露薇. [Chen Lu-wei 陳露薇]. 1938. "T'iao-ch'u huo-k'eng yi-hou: chi-nü Ma Jui-chen tzu-shu" 跳出火坑以后：妓女馬瑞珍自述 (After jumping out of the fiery pit: an account in her own words by prostitute Ma Jui-chen). *Shang-hai fu-nü* 1.12:14–15.

McCartney, J. L. 1927. "Chinese Military Medicine." *U.S. Naval Medical Bulletin* (October).

Mann, Susan. 1988. "Pariah Communities in Qing Society." Paper prepared for the Annual Meeting of the Association for Asian Studies, San Francisco.

———. 1983. "What Can Feminist Theory Do for the Study of Chinese History?" Paper presented at the California Regional Seminar in Chinese Studies, Berkeley.

Miers, Suzanne, and Igor Kopytoff, eds. 1977. *Slavery in Africa: Historical and Anthropological Perspectives.* Madison: University of Wisconsin Press.

Morris, M. C. 1916. "Chinese Daughters of the Night." *Missionary Review* (October).

NCH. North-China Herald. Shanghai.

O'Callaghan, Sean. 1968. *The Yellow Slave Trade: A Survey of the Traffic in Women and Children in the East.* London: Anthony Blond.

Pan Ling. 1983. *In Search of Old Shanghai.* Hong Kong: Joint Publishing Co.

Robertson, Claire C., and Martin A. Klein, eds. 1983. *Women and Slavery in Africa.* Madison: University of Wisconsin Press.

Rubin, Gayle. 1975. "The Traffic in Women: Notes on the 'Political Economy' of Sex." In *Toward an Anthropology of Women*, ed. Rayna Reiter. New York and London: Monthly Review Press.

Shanghai Bureau of Social Affairs. 1929. *Wages and Hours of Labor, Greater Shanghai, 1929.* Shanghai.

SCA. Shanghai Civic Association/Shang-hai shih ti-fang hsieh-hui pien-chi 上海市地方協會編輯. 1933. Shanghai Statistics/*Shang-hai shih t'ung-chi* 上海市統計. Shanghai.

SSWH. Shang-hai shih wen-hsien wei-yuan-hui 上海市文獻委員會. 1948. *Shang-hai jen-k'ou chih-lueh* 上海人口志略 (Brief record of the Shanghai population).

SP. Shih-pao 時報. Shanghai.

SVC. Special Vice Committee. March 19, 1920. "Vice Conditions in Shanghai." *Municipal Gazette* 13.681:83–86.

Sun Li-ch'i, Yu Hui-ch'ing, Yuan Hsiang-mei, Chang P'ei-hua, and Ts'ao Chu-hsien (former residents of Shanghai's brothel districts). 1986. Group interview with author. Shanghai, November 15.

T'ang Yu-feng 唐幼峯. 1931. *Hsin Shang-hai* 新上海 (New Shanghai). Shanghai: Shang-hai yin-shu-kuan.

Tien, H. Yuan. 1973. *China's Population Struggle*. Columbus: Ohio State University Press.

Ts'ao Man-chih. 1986. Interview with author. Shanghai, November 10.

T'u Shih-p'in 屠詩聘, ed. 1948; reprint, 1968. *Shang-hai ch'un-ch'iu* 上海春秋 (Shanghai annals). Hong Kong: Chung-kuo t'u-shu pien-yi-kuan.

Wang Chung-hsien 王仲賢. 1935. *Shang-hai su-yü t'u-shuo* 上海俗語圖說 (An illustrated primer of Shanghai proverbs). Shanghai: Shang-hai she-hui ch'u-pan-she. Reprint. Hong Kong: Shen-chou t'u-shu kung-she.

Wang Ting-chiu 王定九. 1932. *Shang-hai ti men-ching* 上海的門徑 (Key to Shanghai). N.p.: Chung-yang shu-tien.

Watson, James L. 1980a. "Introduction." In *Asian and African Systems of Slavery*, ed. James L. Watson. Berkeley and Los Angeles: University of California Press.

————. 1980b. "Transactions in People: The Chinese Market in Slaves, Servants, and Heirs." In *Asian and African Systems of Slavery*, ed. James L. Watson. Berkeley and Los Angeles: University of California Press.

Watson, Rubie. 1984. "Women's Property in Republican China: Rights and Practice." *Republican China* 10.1a:1–12.

Wei, W. Lock. July 1930. "Sing-song Girls." *Mentor* 18:12–15, 50.

Wiley, James Hundley. 1929. "A Study of Chinese Prostitution." M.A. thesis, University of Chicago.

Wolfe, Barnard. 1980. *The Daily Life of a Chinese Courtesan Climbing Up a Tricky Ladder*. Hong Kong: Learner's Bookstore.

Yi Feng 乙楓. 1933. "Ch'ang-chi wen-t'i yen-chiu" 娼妓問題研究 (Research on the problem of prostitution). *Fu-nü kung-ming yueh-k'an* (February): 31–44.

Yü Wei 郁維. 1948. "Shang-hai ch'ang-chi wu-pai ke-an tiao-ch'a" 上海娼妓五百個案調查 (An investigation of 500 cases of prostitution in Shanghai). *Shih-cheng p'ing-lun* 10:9–10 (October 15, 1948), 10–14.

Yü Wei and Amos Wong. 1949. "A Study of 500 Prostitutes in Shanghai." *International Journal of Sexology* 2.4:234–38.

Zhang Xinxin and Sang Ye (see also Chang Hsin-hsin and Sang Yeh). 1987. *Chinese Lives: An Oral History of Contemporary China*. Ed. W. J. F. Jenner and Delia Davin. New York: Pantheon.

NINE

Marriage and Mobility under Rural Collectivism

William Lavely

The structure of economic inequality was radically altered in China by the Communist party when it took power in 1949. In a series of land reallocation measures—beginning with land reform in the early 1950s and leading to full collectivization and the establishment of communes in 1958—the party created a rural environment in which people were no longer divided into classes of tenants, wage laborers, smallholders, and landlords. Although some of the most radical features of the commune system were later revised, it was not until the 1980s and the introduction of the new "responsibility system" that the machinery of collectivization was dismantled. This chapter will investigate how rural collectivism affected marriage.

As stated in the Introduction, every marriage changes the standing of the relevant parties in a variety of ways, major and minor. In this chapter I focus on one of the most concrete and observable of these changes: the physical movement of a woman at marriage from one locality to another. In China, as elsewhere, some localities are better than others. The implied "spatial hierarchy" thus becomes a factor in the mate-selection process.

The linking of spatial and social stratification is not new. It is implicit in G. William Skinner's conception of social structures patterned by spatial hierarchies of economic exchange (1977). But in rural China after 1949 spatial inequalities were thrown into very sharp relief. As economic inequalities within villages declined and migration was curtailed, place of residence became a crucial indicator of living standards; and as location emerged as a mark of social status, mate selection was increasingly molded by the spatial hierarchy.

If any theory guides this study, it is that the mate-selection process is analogous to that of commodity exchange. The essential idea is common to that of demography's "marriage market," sociology's theory of exchange

(Homans 1958; Blau 1964; Nye 1979; Shornack 1986), anthropology's reciprocity (Sahlins 1972; Lévi-Strauss 1976; Arhem 1981), and to explicitly
economic approaches to mate selection (Becker 1976; England and Farkas
1986). Whether the marriage bargain is struck by parents, the principals
themselves, or jointly, each side will act rationally to maximize its position.
Because residence is a crucial determinant of economic success in contemporary rural China, females (or those acting for them) seek through marriage
to move to a higher level in the spatial hierarchy. For males (or their agents),
place of residence is a resource that, along with other attributes, will influence their degree of success in the marriage market.

Survey and register data from a rural commune in Szechwan (some data
cover the period 1978–80; other data cover 1950–80) are consistent with
these propositions. Women have shown a strong tendency to move up
through the spatial hierarchy via marriage. Moreover, the mate-selection
process sorts women into upwardly or downwardly mobile streams that tend
to reinforce the relationship between location and status. The phenomenon is
significant because marriage migrations account for a major part of physical
mobility in rural China.

MARRIAGE AND STRATIFICATION AFTER 1949

Rural marriage has changed since 1949, but it remains strongly patrilocal:
that is, women change residence at marriage, but men rarely do.[1] A woman
moves to where her husband lives, which is generally in his parents' household or next door to it. Although the taboo against same-village and same-
surname marriages has broken down, most marriages take a woman to a
different village.[2]

If anything, the economic arrangements of the collective encouraged patrilocal marriages and have generally discouraged neolocal or uxorilocal
unions. In the past, patrilineal solidarity tended to keep outsider males
from moving into the community; still, outsiders could sometimes gain a foothold by purchase of land or entering into tenancy. Men could also enter the
community by assuming the status of *chui-hsu* (uxorilocal son-in-law), a status
that caused no economic loss to the community. But the economy of the
collective inherently proscribed an open community membership. That is,
males and their progeny were in effect given a share in perpetuity of the
collective property. As a result, outside males were virtually never permitted
to take up residence in the collective, and recent government efforts to promote a modern version of uxorilocal marriage have met with failure. It should
be noted that outside women are viewed quite differently, perhaps because
women are subsumed under existing patrilineages and, unlike alien males,
do not establish new or competing groups.

Although the institution of arranged marriage has undergone change since 1949, mate-selection criteria remain highly objective, with personal attraction remaining a relatively minor factor. Marriages are still arranged by parents, but it is now generally with the advice and consent of the principals. In one survey of women aged twenty to twenty-nine in 1981, 55 percent of women reported that their parents had chosen their husband and another 17 percent said it was a joint decision (M. Wolf 1985:171). Mate selection involves a go-between. Engagement often occurs after a single meeting of the couple, if neither party raises any objections to the match. Because parents are generally able to screen the field of potential spouses, and the prospective couple has little opportunity to get acquainted before a decision is made, subjective or personalistic criteria are rarely taken into account.

In any case, it is not clear that reduced parental control over mate selection has necessarily led to vastly different outcomes. "Arranged marriage" often conjures up the image of families crassly vying for advantage, fathers scheming for brideprices or political connections, and the private hopes of daughters trampled in the scramble for money and status. Families, it is true, sometimes put their own economic interests before concern for a daughter's welfare, selling or pawning her as a prostitute, concubine, or "little daughter-in-law," well aware that her life would be hard (see the chapters by Hershatter and Watson here and Wolf and Huang 1980). But the assumption that the goals of the parents are inevitably at odds with those of their daughter is doubtful. On the parents' side, we have Margery Wolf's nuanced account of women in rural Taiwan, in which the mother's sentimental attachment to her daughter is a powerful motive to secure for her a satisfactory match (1972:109–10). On the daughter's side, we have numerous accounts of what rural women themselves desire in a marriage partner: political clout, good class origins, wealth, and a "future" (Croll 1981:86–97).

In China, homogamous pairings are perhaps typical, but hypergamy is not unusual. The expression *men-tang hu-tui* (to match gates) is probably the ideal for families seeking a daughter-in-law, but for those in need of a son-in-law, "matching gates" would constitute the bare minimum. Hypergamy springs in part from an asymmetry of interests between the two families—an asymmetry inherent in patrilocality. For a rural Chinese woman, the social and economic status of the family she joins will largely determine her own status for the rest of her life. A mate of superior standing is thus always in her best interests, and those of her parents as well, because they will accrue status from their affines. By contrast, a bride's social status has little influence on a groom's living standards, and the groom's family, although concerned with the social standing of their affines, must also consider the bride's reproductive potential, her potential contribution to household production, and other personal qualities. Above all, a bride must be able to fit into the family, and a bride from a high-status family might not adapt well to humble surroundings, a fact long recognized, and even rued, by imperial families, as Chaffee shows in his chapter here.[3]

A revolution in stratification and mobility, wrought by the radical changes of the 1950s, altered mate-selection criteria. Land reform and collectivization reduced status differentials within communities, and class labels and the new political hierarchy created a new rural elite. At the same time, no institution effectively redressed regional differences. Household registration regulations and the structure of the collective itself effectively halted migration. Residence thus emerged as a crucial index of economic status in rural China, and hypergamy increasingly became defined spatially.

A restructuring of the rural economic and class hierarchy was one of the first, and most successful, projects of the Communist party. It involved (1) economic leveling through land reform and collectivization; (2) inverting the traditional status hierarchy via assignment of class labels and the persecution of "bad" classes; and (3) establishing a new political order in which the Communist party and its local deputies monopolized political power.

The post-Mao reforms of the 1980s, it should be noted, have begun to alter the picture described here and below. Class labels have been officially lifted, and decollectivization and the rise of peasant entrepreneurship have reduced cadre power and are creating a new rural elite. These changes are outside the scope of this chapter.

The new class and political hierarchy established in the 1950s strongly influenced mate selection. Parish and Whyte found evidence of class endogamy: lower- or lower-middle-class peasant males tended to marry females with the same status, as did those with "landlord" and "rich peasant" labels. "Bad class" males had difficulty finding brides (1978:179). Croll (1981:86–92) has described how party membership and cadre status became sought-after qualities in a prospective spouse.

The egalitarian economic regime also influenced marriage. Land reform led to a significant redistribution of income to the rural poor; the subsequent pooling of land and labor under the collectives further leveled household incomes within "teams," the unit of collective accounting. But income levels were highly dependent on the team's natural endowment, and there was no effective mechanism (for example, graduated taxation) to redistribute income among teams or across local regions. The attempt in the Great Leap Forward (1958–60) to raise the level of accounting to the brigade or commune ended in failure (Lardy 1978:180–81).

Migration was one other mechanism that could have redressed regional inequalities, but it was regulated by the household registration directives instituted in 1955. This and related regulations were designed to prevent an influx of peasants into cities and towns, but they also effectively prevented intrarural movements.[4] Economic migrants needed permission from their

TABLE 9.1   Eastern Szechwan Counties by
Per Capita Income of Agricultural
Population, 1980

Income (in yuan)	No. of Counties	Percentage of Counties
250+	4	3
200–249	6	4
150–199	22	17
100–149	76	58
<100	23	18
Total	131	100

SOURCE: *CKNYCCTTC.*
NOTE: Cities are omitted from this table, as are the three
autonomous *chou* (Liang-shan Yi, Kan-tzu Tsang, and
A-pa Tsang).

home unit as well as receiving unit, but for reasons recounted above that permission was usually impossible to obtain. Opportunities for mobility— higher education, the army, advancement through the party, or temporary work in state units—were extremely rare in rural areas (Potter 1983).

Spatial inequalities in rural China are significant, both at the local and the regional levels. In Nan-ch'üan (a relatively homogeneous commune on the Ch'eng-tu Plain that will be discussed in some detail below) per capita team income in 1980 varied by a factor of 2.5 to 1. Elsewhere, team incomes in the same commune have been observed to vary by as much as 7 to 1 (Parish and Whyte 1978:54). In eastern Szechwan in 1980 per capita distributed collective income of entire counties ranged from a low of 40–60 yuan to a high of 150–200 yuan (*CKNYCCTTC*:37–38). The range of total incomes was similar (table 9.1). Between local units of far-flung areas, the range of incomes must be very much larger.

This is not to argue that spatial inequality was a creation of the rural revolution, but rather to point out that economic leveling made it more important. Variations among communities began to overshadow those within them. Increasingly, the economic lot of families was defined by their location in the spatial hierarchy.

The effects of this on mate selection can be illustrated by the experience of Chen village in Kwangtung (Chan, Madsen, and Unger 1984). Chen village had historically been poor relative to its neighbors, although this had never prevented it from acquiring brides from richer villages because even they contained poor tenant households willing to match gates with the Chens. But land reform and collectivization leveled such social distinctions, and

Chen village males found themselves at a uniform disadvantage in the marriage market. A shortage of brides emerged. In response, the Chen families adopted a strategy of village endogamy (ibid., 188–89).

Economic reforms and migration controls suddenly rendered the spatial hierarchy a salient indicator of social status, a development not lost on those who select grooms. The result, noted with consternation in China (see Ji, Zhang, and Liu 1986), has been a wave of women using marriage to move to more prosperous areas—spatial hypergamy.

RESEARCH SETTING AND SOURCES OF DATA

Data for this study were gathered in Nan-ch'üan Commune, Shih-fang hsien (county), in 1980–81. Shih-fang is located in the Ch'eng-tu Plain, seventy kilometers north of Ch'eng-tu, Szechwan's capital. Data are drawn from two sources: three annual migration registers for Nan-ch'üan Commune for the years 1978–80, and a sample survey of 527 ever-married women conducted in Nan-ch'üan in the spring of 1981 by this writer and associates from Szechwan University. Both the registers and the survey have been described elsewhere (Lavely 1982; 1984).

Sloping gently from the foot of the Tibetan Plateau, the Ch'eng-tu Plain contains the richest agricultural land in the Szechwan basin. An intricate system of waterworks and canals distributes mountain waters to the far reaches of the plain. Most Szechwan counties have effective irrigation covering less than 40 percent of their area; all counties in the plain have irrigation over 60 percent of their areas, and most have more than 80 percent. Agricultural incomes in the Ch'eng-tu Plain are also higher. The agricultural population in the plain's median county had a per capita income of 150–200 yuan in 1980, compared with a median of 100–150 for all Szechwan counties (*CKNYCCTTC*).

Shih-fang has an elite position among the counties of the Ch'eng-tu Plain. Its main crops are rice, rape seed, and winter wheat, but a large part of its income comes from a profitable cash crop, tobacco. Shih-fang was one of two counties in Szechwan to cultivate more than 100,000 *mu* of tobacco in 1980, which made Shih-fang one of five counties in the plain that year with a per capita income of more than 250 yuan; this put Shih-fang's income in the top 3 percent of counties in eastern Szechwan (see table 9.1).[5]

Shih-fang is a slender, north-pointing rectangle of a county divided sharply between mountains and plain. The southern tier lies in the plain and contains sixteen of Shih-fang's nineteen communes (reorganized after 1981 as townships). The northern tier is mountainous, containing three communes in addition to state-run mines and lumber camps. On the extreme north Shih-fang borders the Mao-wen Ch'iang Tsu Autonomous County, but there is no apparent interaction between the mountain Ch'iang and the lowland Han Chinese of Shih-fang. The county seat of Shih-fang, Fang-t'ing *chen*, lies in the south of the county and is served by a railroad.

Nan-ch'üan Commune (formerly Ho-hsing) is located seven kilometers west of the county seat. According to commune records, Nan-ch'üan's population was 17,298 at the end of 1979, of which 98 percent were classified as in the agricultural sector. Agricultural density was 1,184 per square kilometer, and per capita income in 1979 was 256 yuan. Data on income for neighboring communes are unavailable, but there were no apparent differences between Nan-ch'üan and neighboring communes in standard of living. However, Nan-ch'üan's propinquity to the county seat offers clear social and economic benefits. Market days in Fang-t'ing are festive events, well-attended by sellers and buyers from Nan-ch'üan. Fang-t'ing has a cinema, an opera house, restaurants, and other amenities and diversions that are unavailable in commune markets.

Nan-ch'üan was organized into thirteen brigades, each averaging about three hundred households. Brigades were in turn divided into teams which averaged about forty households. Elsewhere in China, brigades generally correspond to the natural village, and teams to hamlets. In the Ch'eng-tu Plain such divisions are less clear because the population is settled in dispersed clusters (*yuan-tzu*), each containing about ten households.

According to the retrospective data of the commune survey, 94 percent of marriages since 1950 have been "major," that is, the virilocal union of Chinese tradition. A maximum of 6 percent of the marriages have been uxorilocal, although most of these are not so in the classical sense but instead result from unions between Nan-ch'üan women and men with an urban registration, often the employees of state mines or residents of the county seat. It is extremely difficult for a rural resident to transfer legally to an urban residence, and marriage across the rural-urban divide thus usually produces split households. In the commune, women in such marriages usually maintain residence with their parents and the spouses commute between their two households.

Migration registers include only marriage moves that involve a change of brigade. Marriages within a brigade do not involve a change of registration and thus are not counted as a migration. Since 1950 about 20 percent of Nan-ch'üan marriages have occurred within the brigade. Altogether, 42 percent of Nan-ch'üan brides come from within the commune; 36 percent come from other communes of the county; and 21 percent come from beyond the county, of which about half are from beyond the Ch'eng-tu Plain. The commune survey data reveal that although brides from neighboring counties were not uncommon in the 1940s—about 15 percent of brides came from outside Shih-fang—it is only since the mid-1960s that substantial numbers have come from distant counties.

TABLE 9.2   Migration to and from Nan-ch'üan Commune, 1978–80, and
Annual Migration Rates

	To		From		Gross		Net
Reason	N	%	N	%	N	%	N
Marriage	350	61	266	48	616	55	84
Other	221	39	283	51	504	45	−62
Total	571	100	549	100	1,120	100	22
Annual Migration per 1,000	10.9		−10.4		21.3		.4

SOURCE: Commune migration registers.
NOTE: Omits returning educated youth ($N = 123$) and within-commune migrations (seventy-two in marriage and sixty-nine for other reasons).

Migration registers do not record short-term visits or illegal migrants, but it is fair to say that they capture a large part of long-term population movement. Temporary sojourns, such as stints in state factories, the army, or jail, are all recorded there, along with more permanent relocations. It is remarkable, then, that the movement of women in marriage accounts for about half of all the recorded migrations and thus a large portion of all relocation in rural China. Nan-ch'üan's registers (table 9.2) are apparently not atypical in this regard; a study of Ta-hsing County, Peking, found a similar percentage.[6] Nan-ch'üan migration in 1978–80 was low by the standards of a market economy,[7] although there is reason to believe the commune was experiencing unusual mobility in the period under the new economic policies then being introduced.[8] Unusual numbers of women were probably marrying into Nan-ch'üan in the period because the ratio of in-marriages to out-marriages (350 to 256) could not have remained at such high levels for long.

COUNTIES OF CHOICE

Because Shih-fang County is near the pinnacle of Szechwan's rural economic hierarchy, women would do well to marry into Shih-fang, or, if they are Shih-fang residents, to avoid marrying out. This is, of course, exactly what they do (table 9.3). As table 9.3 shows, the inflow of women (fifty-four from other counties) exceeds the outflow (eighteen departing). Observe also that in-marrying women are from low-income counties—a median of 100–150 yuan—while out-marrying women are generally heading for counties with incomes of 200–250 yuan or above.

It is natural for a daughter to wish to marry close to home—unless, of course, home is a hardscrabble county in the Szechwan basin. Some brides

TABLE 9.3   Nan-ch'üan Marriage Migrations, by Income of
County of Origin or Destination

Origin or destination	In-marrying (by origin)	Out-marrying (by destination)
Migrations to or from Shih-fang County[a]		
<100	1	0
100–149	40	1
150–199	5	0
200–249	6	12
250–299	2	0
300–349	0	5
Migrations within Shih-fang County		
Nan-ch'üan Commune	72	72
Other Shih-fang Communes	223	241
Unknown	73	10
Total	422	341

SOURCE: *CKNYCCTTC* in commune migration registers, 1978–80.
[a] Per capita income of the county agricultural population in yuan, 1980.
Statistical test: Collapsed to a 2 by 2 table dividing counties at 200 yuan income,
chi-squared = 45.6 (1 df), p < .001.

TABLE 9.4   Nan-ch'üan Marriage Migrations, by Distance from
Shih-fang County

| Distance (in km) | Origin | | Destination |
	1950–77[a]	1978–80[b]	1978–80[b]
< 30	18	11	15
30–119	9	17	3
≥ 120	22	24	0
Total *N*	49	52	18
Mean	92	116	26.4
SD	73	98	17.8

[a] From women's responses to survey.
[b] From commune migration registers.
Statistical tests: Contrasting mean distance of 1950–77 origins with mean for
1978–80 destinations, t = 5.7 (df = 65), p < .001. Contrasting mean distance of
1978–80 origins with mean for 1978–80 destinations, t = 6.2 (df = 68), p < .001.

come to Shih-fang from remarkable distances (table 9.4). More than a third of in-marrying women come from counties that are over 120 kilometers away. Once a tie to a distant county is established, more matches are made as women introduce their sisters and cousins to men in Shih-fang. Many of the long-distance introductions, however, may be the work of professional matchmakers.[9]

In-marrying women often come from great distances, but out-marrying women tend to stay in the immediate area. Of eighteen women leaving the county, fourteen married men from adjacent counties—P'eng, Kuang-han, and Mien-chu. Two married Ch'eng-tu residents—perhaps men on its rural fringe—and only one woman married a man from a county outside the Ch'eng-tu Plain, San-t'ai (table 9.5).

Women migrating to Shih-fang generally come from poorer counties in the Szechwan basin but not from the remote periphery of the Upper Yangtze macroregion as delineated by G. William Skinner (1977). Shih-fang is adjacent to —indeed, contains part of—a large economic and social "periphery," but it is apparently beyond the connubium. Although marriages between Han men and aboriginal women were a typical frontier phenomenon historically, no cases of marriage in Nan-ch'üan involved any minority nationalities, including the neighboring Ch'iang. Under collective socialism, commerce with minority areas mainly took place under the aegis of government agencies. Controlled economic relations between mountains and plains (and, possibly, unpublished regulations governing relations between Hans and certain nationalities) have probably confined the marriage area mainly to counties of the Szechwan basin (see table 9.5).

COMMUNES OF CHOICE

The principles that influence the movement of women across great distances also govern the marriage choices of short-distance movers. More than 80 percent of marriages are contracted within county boundaries, but even these movements reveal a geographic hierarchy. The relative attractiveness of a place should be directly measurable from the movement of women. A net flow of women from Nan-ch'üan to another commune indicates that the other commune is a relatively more desirable place; conversely, a net flow away indicates the opposite (table 9.6; cf. map 9.1).

Communes adjacent to Nan-ch'üan—namely, Liang-lu-k'ou, Yun-hsi, Min-chu, Ssu-p'ing, and Yuan-shih—have the highest frequency of nuptial exchange with Nan-ch'üan and, along with Nan-ch'üan itself, constitute the core of the commune's connubium. But the balance of entering and exiting brides varies among these six communes. While forty-four women married from Liang-lu-k'ou to Nan-ch'üan, only thirty-six went in the opposite direc-

TABLE 9.5   Nan-ch'üan Marriage Migrations, by County of Origin or
Destination, Ranked by Distance from Shih-fang, 1950–77 and 1978–80

County	Distance (in km)	Origin 1950–77[a]	Origin 1978–80[b]	Destination 1978–80[b]
Kuang-han (c)	15	11	1	3
P'eng (a)	20	5	9	11
Mien-chu (a)	20	1	1	1
Te-yang (c)	20	1	0	0
Hsin-tu (c)	30	1	0	0
Chin-t'ang (c)	50	1	6	0
Kuan (a)	50	1	0	0
Ch'eng-tu (c)	55	0	1	2
Wen-chiang (c)	60	1	0	0
Chung-chiang (c)	60	1	3	0
An (p)	65	0	1	0
San-t'ai (c)	80	0	3	1
Chien-yang (c)	80	4	3	0
Chiang-yu (a)	120	0	1	0
Le-chih (c)	120	2	1	0
Ch'iung-lai (c)	120	1	0	0
She-hung (c)	125	0	1	0
Yen-t'ing (c)	130	0	4	0
P'eng-hsi (c)	140	2	1	0
Sui-ning (c)	150	5	0	0
Tzu-chung (c)	170	0	6	0
An-yueh (c)	180	2	0	0
Pao-hsing (p)	180	0	1	0
Nan-pu (a)	180	7	0	0
Ya-an (p)	180	1	0	0
Sung-p'an (p)	200	1	0	0
T'ien-ch'üan (p)	200	0	2	0
Lung-ch'ang (c)	220	0	1	0
P'eng-an (c)	220	0	2	0
Kuang-an (a)	270	0	1	0
Mian-yang (a)	270	1	0	0
Feng-tu (p)	400	0	2	0
Chiang-pei (c)	400	0	1	0

NOTE: Counties designated in Skinner n.d. as core, periphery, or divided between core and periphery, are respectively designated c, p, and a.
[a] From women's responses to survey.
[b] From commune migration registers.

TABLE 9.6   Nan-ch'üan Marriage Migrations, 1978–80,
by Commune of Origin or Destination

Commune	Origin	Destination	Net	Gross
Pa-chiao	2	1	−1	3
Fang-t'ing	1	5	+4	6
Ho-feng	1	2	+1	3
Hung-pai	0	2	+2	2
Hui-lan	4	3	−1	7
Liang-lu-k'ou	44	36	−8	80
Ling-chieh	4	1	−3	5
Lung-chu	8	4	−4	12
Ma-ching	5	5	0	10
Min-chu	30	32	+2	62
Nan-ch'üan[a]	72	72	0	144
Ch'ien-ti	7	4	−3	11
Ssu-p'ing	21	46	+25	67
Shuang-sheng	11	12	+1	23
Yin-feng	17	18	+1	35
Yung-hsing	2	0	−2	2
Yuan-shih	13	22	+9	35
Yun-hsi	42	33	−9	75
Tsao-chiao	10	15	+5	25
Other Shih-fang	1	0		
Total	294	313		

NOTE: Migrations accounted for in this table are recorded in commune migration
registers, 1978–80.
[a] Marriages contracted within a team involve no change in registration and are
not recorded in the registers.

tion; twenty-one women came to Nan-ch'üan from Ssu-p'ing, but forty-four
Nan-ch'üan women married into Ssu-p'ing.

The net movements reveal a clear pattern. On map 9.1, showing Shih-
fang county, communes with net gains of women are shaded; communes with
net losses are unshaded. Across the southern flank of the county, along the
east–west road linking the county seats of Shih-fang, P'eng, and Te-yang
counties, lies a clear band of "preferred" communes. The ratio of net to total
moves rises in the environs of the county seat and decreases markedly in the
northern tier of communes. It would appear that Nan-ch'üan women have a
penchant for husbands residing near the county seat or close to Nan-ch'üan,
in that order.

The foregoing has demonstrated how spatial stratification affects marriage
migrations. In the next section we shall see how individual characteristics
determine selection into upwardly or downwardly mobile streams.

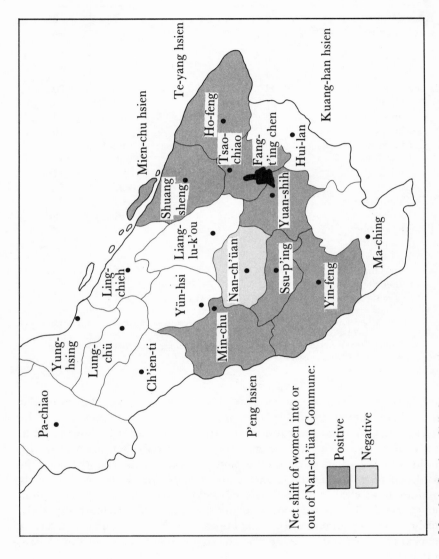

Map 9.1. Southern Shih-fang county

Te-yang hsien

Kuang-han hsien

Mien-chu hsien

Ho-feng

Tsao-chiao

Fang-t'ing chen

Hui-lan

Shuang-sheng

Yuan-shih

Liang-lu-k'ou

Ma-ching

Ling-chieh

Yün-hsi

Nan-ch'üan

Ssu-p'ing

Yin-feng

Yung-hsing

Min-chu

Lung-chü

Ch'ien-ti

Pa-chiao

P'eng hsien

Net shift of women into or
out of Nan-ch'üan Commune:

Positive

Negative

BRIDES' EDUCATION AND MOBILITY

If women hope to improve their lot through marriage, not all of them succeed. The reasons for such failures are complex, but it is still possible to explain the process in a general way. I shall take the simple approach of describing one measurable characteristic—education—of women who marry up or down the "spatial hierarchy."

First, the counties of Szechwan and communes of Shih-fang must be classified according to their "desirability" relative to Nan-ch'üan. Communes of Shih-fang that enjoyed a net positive movement of Nan-ch'üan women (the shaded communes on map 9.1) were classified as "Shih-fang—desirable." All others in Shih-fang were classified "undesirable." Counties that had per capita incomes in excess of 200 yuan in 1980 and received brides from Nan-ch'üan were classified as "desirable." All others had incomes under 200 yuan and were thus classified as undesirable. This scheme should not be treated as an ordinal scale because it is unclear whether "undesirable" communes of Shih-fang are more or less desirable than "desirable" counties.

Movements to more desirable areas correlate with a woman's educational level. In table 9.7 mean years of education are tabulated by the desirability of place of origin or destination for in- and out-migrants; women who marry within Nan-ch'üan Commune have 3.1 years of education on average.[10] Women who marry into the more desirable communes of Shih-fang have 3.5 years, while those who move to the undesirable communes of Shih-fang have 3.0 years on average. Those who move to desirable counties have 3.1 years. This pattern repeats itself in reverse for in-marriers to Nan-ch'üan. Women coming to Nan-ch'üan from the communes of Shih-fang have 3.0 years; those coming from desirable counties outside of Shih-fang have 4.4 years; and those coming from the poor counties of the Szechwan basin have 4.2 years.

Simply stated, better-educated women are moving up the spatial hierarchy; the lesser educated are moving down. It is certainly not the case that the average education of in-migrants reflects the average education in the region of their birth. The residents in poorer counties of the Szechwan basin, for example, have educational attainments well below that of the Ch'eng-tu Plain,[11] yet they are sending more highly educated women. It would appear on the one hand, then, that when Nan-ch'üan men import brides from low-income counties, they are getting women with higher-than-average levels of education. On the other hand, Nan-ch'üan's exchange of brides with the better-endowed communes of Shih-fang is decidedly unequal. Not only does Nan-ch'üan send more women to Ssu-p'ing and Yuan-shih than it receives, but it sends better-educated brides only to receive women with lower education in return.

TABLE 9.7   Average Years of Education of In- and Out-marrying Women, 1978–80, by Origin or Destination

Origin or Destination[a]	Out-marrying (by destination)		In-marrying (by origin)	
	Education	N	Education	N
Nan-ch'üan	3.1	61	3.1	61
Shih-fang (d)	3.5	130	3.0	84
Shih-fang (u)	3.1	82	3.0	96
Counties (d)	4.0	13	4.4	5
Counties (u)	—	0	4.2	43
Total (nonmissing)	3.2	286	3.4	289
Missing		52		133

SOURCE: Commune migration registers, 1978–80.

NOTE: Education was recorded in the registers as illiterate, lower elementary, upper elementary, lower middle, upper middle, and college. It is likely that this classification represents any exposure at these levels rather than graduate status. The levels were translated into years of education as follows: illiterate = 0; lower elementary = 3; upper elementary = 5; lower middle = 7; upper middle = 9; college = 11.

[a] Classification of communes and counties as desirable (d) or undesirable (u) was on the basis of the net flow of women from Nan-ch'üan. Communes in southern Shih-fang County that received a positive net gain of women from Nan-ch'üan (i.e., Fang-t'ing Chen, Ho-feng, Min-chu, Shuang-sheng, Ssu-p'ing, Yin-feng, Yuan-shih, and Tsao-chiao) were classified as desirable. Neighboring counties that received a net gain of Nan-ch'üan women (Ch'eng-tu, Kuan, Kuang-han, P'eng, and Mien-chu) were also classified as desirable. These counties had annual per capita incomes for the agricultural population of over 200 yuan. All undesirable counties had incomes of under 200 yuan.

Statistical tests: *Out-marrying.* Contrasting mean education of women marrying within Nan-ch'üan with women marrying to desirable communes of Shih-fang, t = 1.48 (df = 189), p < .20 (2-tailed). *In-marrying.* Contrasting mean education of women marrying within Nan-ch'üan with women marrying from undesirable counties, t = 2.56 (df = 102), p < .02.

A SEGMENTED MARKET

By focusing on the spatial hierarchy and a single attribute, education, the discussion thus far has greatly simplified the operation of the marriage market. We shall investigate other characteristics below, suggesting in the process that the market is segmented into economic and social groupings with particular interests, and that marriage movements within these market segments have characteristic spatial patterns.

Who marries women from the relatively poor, undesirable areas? The answer—relatively poor men—can be deduced from the marriages of women from undesirable communes and counties into teams whose income is low in relation to the commune as a whole.

It should be added that this is a relatively demanding test of the proposition that spatial inequalities influence marriage movements because

TABLE 9.8   Mean Per Capita Team Income in
1980, by Origin of Respondent: Nan-ch'üan
First Marriages, 1966–81

Origin[a]	N	Team Income[b]
Nan-ch'üan	108	396
Shih-fang (d)	37	413
Shih-fang (u)	37	372
Counties (d)	19	401
Counties (u)	38	366
Total	240	390

SOURCE: Commune survey.
[a] See n. a in table 9.7.
[b] The total of collective income and private-plot income of the team in 1980, divided by the population of the team. Stratum means are computed by giving equal weighting to women.

such variations within Nan-ch'üan Commune are minimal. A casual inspection of Nan-ch'üan in 1980 revealed less economic variation than one can observe by rounding a block in a tract-house subdivision in the United States. The commune is situated on a featureless plain with unlimited access to water; houses were invariably constructed of rammed earth and straw thatch. Survey data revealed, however, some variation in living standards across brigades and subbrigade units (teams) of the commune. Team income per capita in 1980 (including all private plot and sideline income) had a mean of 390 yuan, a standard deviation of 87, and ranged from 290 up to 700. Below-average teams tended to be concentrated in the northwest quarter of the commune, farthest from Fang-t'ing *chen*.

Data from the commune survey show that women migrating to Nan-ch'üan are also sorted by the economy of teams within the commune (table 9.8). The data refer to respondents of the survey whose first marriage occurred in the period 1966–81. The index of team per capita income was produced by attributing the total per capita income of the team to each respondent, and then taking an average of that income for respondents of each origin. The index thus represents the average value of the team joined by women of a given origin.

The differences shown are small but consistent: women from low-income counties move to teams with the lowest per capita incomes. For other origins the income means are consistent with the proposition that women marrying "down" to Nan-ch'üan are marrying into better teams of the commune, while women marrying "up" to the commune are marrying into teams that are less well-off.

TABLE 9.9   Mean Brideprice and Dowry, by Origin of Respondent: Nan-ch'üan First Marriages, 1966–81

Origin[a]	N	Brideprice (in yuan)	Dowry (in yuan)	BP/Dowry[b]
Nan-ch'üan	108	123	143	.86
Shih-fang (d)	37	113	110	1.02
Shih-fang (u)	38	100	121	.82
Counties (d)	19	120	169	.71
Counties (u)	38	66	82	.80
Total	240	109	127	.86

SOURCE: Commune survey.
[a] See n. a in table 9.7.
[b] The brideprice:dowry ratio is here calculated in the aggregate from the data in this table.
Statistical tests: *Brideprice.* Contrasting brideprice of brides originating in Nan-ch'üan with that of brides originating in undesirable counties, t = 3.48 (df = 144), p < .001. *Dowry.* Contrasting dowry of brides originating in Nan-ch'üan with that of brides originating in undesirable counties, t = 3.53 (df = 144), p < .001.

It would appear then that Nan-ch'üan has a segmented market. Men (or teams) of average or superior means generally contract marriages in the local area; those with lesser means are more likely to go afield of the traditional market area. They are more likely to do so because of the financial advantages afforded by such matches (table 9.9). The commune survey asked each woman three questions: (1) the value of the goods in her dowry, (2) the value of gifts sent by her husband's family, and (3) the value of cash sent by her husband's family. In addition, probes were in some cases used to elicit a list of goods received; this was then translated into cash values. No attempt was made to adjust for change over time in the value of goods or money. The brideprice figure given in table 9.9 is the sum of goods and cash received from the groom's family.

I hasten to add that I believe these values are far from the real absolute value of goods exchanged in the typical Nan-ch'üan marriage. Evidence from all other sources suggests that typical exchanges involve sums of a magnitude greater than those listed here. "Marriage by purchase" has been officially stigmatized and austerity in nuptial matters repeatedly glorified. Respondents in our survey answered questions under the gaze of local officials, and it is likely that many downplayed the truth or discounted the actual amounts by a large factor.

These deficiencies notwithstanding, I believe the data are useful in ratio form or in comparing stratum means. Previous work with these data has revealed consistent and interpretable patterns (Lavely 1983). The data in table 9.9 should nevertheless be treated with caution, and the reader may judge whether the patterns are the product of chance.

Nan-ch'üan men who marry women from low-income counties pay only about 60 percent as much in brideprice as do men who marry women from the local area—doubtless an attractive feature of such matches for men in this market segment (see table 9.9). Women from the low-income counties bring far less valuable dowries than do local women, but the amount probably does not seem so little to their fathers, given the standards of their home counties. But launching one's daughter into a marriage in the Ch'eng-tu Plain is probably worth the extra expense. Parents may feel that a daughter will be happier there and may perhaps some day send some money home.

The highest brideprice is paid for women from Nan-ch'üan, but an even larger amount comes back in the form of a dowry. Again, a family may be willing to put more into a dowry so that a daughter can stay closer to home. But for both families, a match made close at hand will involve real affinal ties, and traditional matters of face will enter in. It would not do for either party to skimp, but (particularly because Nan-ch'üan is near the top of the spatial hierarchy) the groom's family is in a stronger position. After all, they can find less-expensive brides all over Szechwan. Given these conditions, we might expect the dowry to exceed the brideprice.

Brides coming from the desirable communes of Shih-fang are the only group who are unambiguously moving down the spatial hierarchy. It also happens that the brideprice-dowry ratio of this group is the highest of all. Because Nan-ch'üan is probably not the commune of first choice for most of these women, and Nan-ch'üan affines are not their family's first preference either, excessive dowries are unnecessary. At the same time, the groom's parents may see value in having affines in the prosperous communes ringing the county seat, and a bride from there may thus be seen as a "catch" warranting a substantial brideprice.

Of course, the same logic applies at lower levels of the spatial hierarchy. On the one hand, Nan-ch'üan parents put a lower value on affinal ties with Shih-fang's less prosperous and more distant communes, and brideprices reflect this. On the other, parents—and daughters—from those communes are eager to make the tie, so the dowry rises accordingly.

The high dowries of and brideprices for women from desirable counties. are less easy to understand. Permit me to speculate that matches in this category represent grooms in yet another market segment. Skinner (1964:36) has suggested that local marketing systems are united at higher levels by elites who exchange, among other things, brides. It is possible that brides from neighboring P'eng, Kuang-han, and Mien-chu counties represent a version of this. If these matches are indeed quasi-political or mercantile alliances contracted by local notables on both sides, then the considerations of face

TABLE 9.10   In- and Out-marrying Women of Poor Peasant Status,
1978–80, by Origin or Destination

	Out-marrying		In-marrying	
Origin or Destination[a]	% Poor	N	% Poor	N
Nan-ch'üan	45	47	45	47
Shih-fang (d)	54	96	61	57
Shih-fang (u)	65	66	62	90
Counties (d)	89	9	54	11
Counties (u)	—	0	70	37
Total	59	218	60	242

SOURCE: Commune migration registers, 1978–80.
NOTE: The following statuses were recorded in the registers under class status: poor, middle, and rich peasant; landlord; educated youth; and cadre. (Neither of the latter two types appears in this table.) The year 1980 was officially the last time class status was recorded in population registers.
[a] See n. a in table 9.7.

and the high expectations for affinal ties would explain the costly marriage payments. I have no data on the parents of brides and grooms, but perhaps the husbands of respondents provide some clue. Taking the same base of 240 women by origin as in tables 9.8 and 9.9, the following percentages have husbands who are cadres: Nan-ch'üan, 14; Shih-fang—D, 24; Shih-fang—U, 10; Counties—D, 21; Counties—U, 13. Brides from nearby desirable counties, like those from the prosperous communes of Shih-fang, are more likely to be married to men of high status. It seems plausible that these grooms come from families with political connections—families that by dint of their prestige or wealth could bring a bride from a more desirable area. The very high dowries (and low brideprice-dowry ratio) are consistent with the notion that these are matches between families of wealth and status. But this is merely speculation.

Under rural collectivism class origins were a consideration in mate choice.[12] The best class background was that of poor peasant; middle peasant, rich peasant, and landlord backgrounds were below the ideal. Class origin had more important implications for males than females because, unlike residency status, class origin was passed through the male line. An undesirable class background was thus less of a stigma for women than for men. It is remarkable, then, that poor peasant women are more mobile than those of other designations. This is revealed in table 9.10, which shows the percentage of women with poor peasant backgrounds, tabulated by their place of origin or destination.

Poor peasants form a majority of the rural population, and their distribution on the landscape should be fairly even. At least there is no reason to believe that Nan-ch'üan should have a deficit of poor peasants relative to surrounding areas. Yet only 45 percent of marriages within the commune involve women from poor peasant families. From this we can deduce that middle and rich peasants tend to marry within the commune.

The less desirable classes may incline toward commune endogamy in order to build affinal ties because the stigma of their class status may make such families more dependent on their affines for social and economic support. (Classes are also likely to be endogamous, as Parish and Whyte found [1978:179], but this is a separate issue.) Another reason for local endogamy may be that neighborhood matches depend less on objective criteria and are influenced more by personal characteristics. When a matchmaker carries a brief resumé from a distant place, an inferior class label may tip the scales against the match; but when it involves a neighbor family, affect and other considerations may overshadow class origin.

Women of inferior class status, whether through defensive affinal strategy or their lower valuation on the wider market, are inclined to marry within their own commune.

IMPLICATIONS

To summarize, this discussion of mate selection in Shih-fang permits us to draw the following conclusions. First, women generally move up by engaging in spatial hypergamy. Second, women are sorted into distinct migrant streams according to their personal attributes; for example, better-educated women are more likely to move up. Third, the mate-selection process is differentiated by social domains or market segments that themselves have implications for marriage migrations: the poor generally draw brides from further down the spatial hierarchy, while those with inferior class designations tend toward local endogamy. Finally, the overarching assumption for the entire discussion is that the mating selection operates like a market, in which the bride's side seeks to maximize her position in the spatial hierarchy. Measurable characteristics, such as education, brideprice, and class, all seem to bear out the market analogy.

All of this raises questions. Here I would like to address briefly the generalizability of these findings and their demographic and social structural implications.

Our vantage on marriage migrations has been from the top of the rural economic hierarchy. From below, they are likely to look quite different. The poorest locales should experience a net loss of women in marriage, and men in those places would face a severe marriage squeeze. Women with better qualifications would be the first to be recruited as brides by wealthier areas, while men with poorer qualifications would be the last to find brides. Beyond this, however, it is difficult to predict the possible responses to this geographically structured marriage squeeze. Chen village, finding it difficult to attract brides, broke sharply with the tradition of village exogamy, and same-village matches became the norm. In his chapter in this volume, Jonathan Ocko discusses "exchange of relatives" as an alternative when brides are difficult to secure. Many other responses are possible.

Another question concerns the extent to which the marriage market is influenced by other global factors affecting the economy, demography, and social structure. I have described the peculiar spatial aspects of rural marriage as a product of the socialist collective, but did this phenomenon predate the collective period, and will it persist under the post-Mao economic reforms?

As I have argued above, the economic reforms of the 1950s cast the spatial hierarchy into sharp relief. Although the spatial hierarchy was not an innovation of the Socialist revolution, its rigidification and insitutionalization were. Other factors may have broadened the marriage area. Improvements in long-distance transport and communications opened a wider market for brides. At the same time, collective organization may have eroded affinal ties, thereby reducing the utility of local matches.

Still, the process described here was probably a feature of traditional rural Chinese marriage, although perhaps hidden amid local social variations and unrelated population movements. The traditional market for female servants, concubines, and prostitutes in cities and towns, along with higher female mortality, created a shortage of marriageable women that would have intensified competition for brides and put poorer locales at a disadvantage.

As for the current reforms, they are undoing the rigid world of the collectives, but not completely and not immediately. Status differentials within communities are on the rise; economic diversification and greater labor mobility are reshuffling the spatial hierarchy. A man's fortune now depends less on his residence, and his residence has lost some of its permanence. Still, for farmers and the new proletarians alike, economic opportunities will remain tied to access to markets. Although the correspondence between marriage migrations and the spatial hierarchy will wane, it is not likely to disappear.

Finally, the operation of the marriage market offers insights into China's demography and social structure. The underlying spatial structure of the marriage market implies that males at the top of the spatial hierarchy occupy a favorable position. Other things being equal, the ratio of brideprice to dowry should be lower, male marriage ages should be lower relative to females, and males should marry and remarry with greater frequency than males lower in the hierarchy. Females at the top of the hierarchy should experience a marriage squeeze.

The upwardly mobile stream of women would also affect females' spatial distribution, depending on the demography of the underlying populations.

TABLE 9.11   Distribution of Szechwan Counties by Percentage Female, 1982, and by Agricultural Income Per Capita, 1980

Females	Income Per Capita (yuan)[a]					
	< 100	100–149	150–199	200–249	250+	Total
< 34	5	18	3	—	—	26
34	15	33	5	—	—	53
35	3	19	12	2	1	37
36	—	5	1	2	1	9
≥ 37	—	1	1	2	2	6
Total	23	76	22	6	4	131
Mean %[b]	34.5	34.6	35.1	36.7	37.0	34.8

SOURCES: Income data from *CKNYCCTTC*. Population data from *Population Atlas of China* (State Council Population Census Office, 1987).
NOTE: Females here are aged fifteen to forty-nine as a percentage of the population fifteen and over. This table accounts for 131 eastern Szechwan counties.
[a] Cities are omitted from this table, as are the three autonomous *chou* (Liang-shan Yi, Kan-tzu Tsang, and A-pa Tsang).
[b] Equal weighting for counties.

Assuming that each male is permitted to marry one female, the number of women who could migrate to a favored region before the market reached saturation is limited to the number of eligible males in the population. But the effect on the sending populations will vary with the overall number of eligible females. If there is a preexisting deficit of females in the total population or in the sending population—as there is likely to be (see n. 13)—then the marriage migrations could have a substantial influence on the distribution of females, regardless of the limits imposed by the assumption of monogamy.

The distribution of reproductive-age females in Szechwan is in fact related to the spatial hierarchy. Table 9.11 shows the distribution of Szechwan counties by agricultural income per capita and by the proportion of reproductive-age women of the population, defined as females aged fifteen to forty-nine as a percentage of the total population fifteen years of age and over. There is a clear relationship between income and the proportion of females: in counties with incomes of less than 100 yuan per capita, reproductive-age women make up 34.5 percent of the population, compared with 37.0 percent for counties with incomes over 250 yuan.

That such percentages are mainly the result of marriage migrations is a plausible hypothesis, but it cannot be proved here. If the county populations were stable—that is, were closed to migration and had experienced constant birth and death rates over a long period—then we would expect the proportion of women aged fifteen to forty-nine to be roughly constant across counties. Rural women aged fifteen and over in 1982 were born in a period of uncontrolled "natural" fertility, a condition consistent with the asumption of stability. But many other factors, including the famine of 1959–62, could have produced distortions in county age-sex structures, which vary systematically with the economic hierarchy.[13]

Shortages of reproductive-age females obviously imply a marriage squeeze for men at the bottom of the hierarchy; they also imply lesser reproductivity in these populations. If there are 7 percent more women aged fifteen to forty-nine, and if all women bear children at the same rate, the population with more women will have crude rates 7 percent higher. The emigrant counties not only lose women who move away but also lose the children that the women would produce.

In theory, then, counties richer in resources have greater reproductive success. And because mate selection also sorts women by personal characteristics—promoting those with better education, for example—the result would be to improve the educational level of the receiving counties. To the extent that education is a proxy for health and other attributes, mate selection could affect other population characteristics as well.

The market analogy will raise questions in the minds of some; are we arguing, they may ask, that women are being bought and sold? Is there a continuum, as Gail Hershatter suggests in her chapter here, between the market in prostitutes and the market for brides? There are undeniable semblances between commodity markets and marriage markets, but the latter refers to a much broader and more complex set of transactions. In mate selection, something is being exchanged, and someone is doing the exchanging. There are sharp qualitative differences, however, between this kind of transaction and the sale of a good. The rights and claims transferred in marriage are not total or absolute, as in the sale of slaves, and they may be quite limited. In marriage the woman herself may have considerable control over the transaction. And husbands and their families may also give over certain rights to the bride (for example, in property). Within the realm of Chinese marriage, there is considerable variation in the kinds of rights that are transferred, the extent of control over the transaction exercised by the woman, and the degree to which the woman herself gains rights to property or power within her husband's family. In this sense, there is not just one continuum but many. No doubt in some times and places, marriage exchange leans to the commodity end of these continua.

The process of mate selection is sufficiently complex to tax the ingenuity of econometricians. Individuals can act rationally within this complex structure because for any particular family or daughter, choices are made from among a relatively simple set of alternatives. In the aggregate, these choices produce a market that is a clearinghouse for a special kind of spatial and social mobility. The process affects only women and it affects all who marry. It takes account of their economic standing, their education, and no doubt many other personal factors. It then relocates them permanently in space. One result is to alter marriage chances at the extremes of the spatial hierarchy. But the process works more subtle changes across every spatial stratum, continuously promoting women of higher status and demoting those of lower, thereby reinforcing the link between social and spatial stratification.

NOTES

Data for this study were collected under the auspices of the Committee on Scholarly Communication with the People's Republic of China. I am grateful for the assistance of the Institute of Population Research of Szechwan University, the Shih-fang County People's Government, and Nan-ch'üan Commune. The study was conceived during my tenure as American Council of Learned Societies/Mellon Fellow for Chinese Studies at the Population Studies Center, University of Michigan. G. William Skinner's generous comments on an earlier paper provided the inspiration for this one. Patricia Ebrey, Stevan Harrell, James McCann, Jonathan Ocko, Rubie Watson, and Martin Whyte offered valuable comments.

1. In certain regions, a substantial minority of marriages were uxorilocal. Wolf and Huang (1980) and Pasternak (1983) have described the incidence of this in Taiwan in the late Ch'ing and colonial periods.

2. In Nan-ch'üan Commune, Szechwan, to be introduced below, marriages within the village accounted for 20 percent of marriages in the 1950–81 period.

3. As Parish and Whyte put it: "Individual personality and health factors are critical in the choice of the bride, since she will have to leave her home and fit into her husband's family. In selecting the groom, on the other hand, it is not simply his individual characteristics that are important, but those of his entire family, since at least initially the couple's livelihood will depend on the health of this larger unit" (1978:178).

Margery Wolf notes: "The parents of a young man are less concerned about the girl's family than the girl's family is about them, but they do have some criteria. 'Matching doors' is important. Richer girls make poor wives for farmers" (1972:108).

4. The regulations are contained in the appendix to Tien 1973.

5. Three counties on the Tibetan Plateau in western Szechwan (formerly Hsik'ang Province) had 1980 per capita incomes of more than 250 yuan probably because of the high prices paid for livestock and other pastoral products.

6. Of migrants to Ta-hsing in 1980–82, 48 percent were the result of marriage. When demobilized soldiers returning home were deducted, marriage accounted for 80 percent of the population movement. See Ji, Zhang, and Liu 1986:162–63.

7. The gross and net migration rates observed in table 9.2 are only about a quarter the levels observed in contemporary rural Taiwan. (See the series of annual Taiwan-Fukien Demographic Factbooks, published by the Ministry of the Interior, Republic of China.)

8. Half of Nan-ch'üan's nonmarital migrants in 1978–80 transferred to Fang-t'ing chen, most of them in 1980. It is possible that they were the vanguard of the rapid expansion of town populations that followed soon after.

9. Professional matchmaking was apparently a sensitive subject in Nan-ch'üan.

Out of 527 surveyed women, only 10 reported that they had been introduced to their husband through a professional matchmaker, an incidence that seems extraordinarily low.

　10. Years of education were attributed to the actual educational categories listed in the register. See table 9.7, n. 1, for a fuller explanation.

　11. *The Population Atlas of China* shows rates of illiteracy and semiliteracy for the population aged twelve and over by county. Counties in the Ch'eng-tu Plain are in the range 15 to 24.9 percent, while the rest of the Szechwan basin is more than 25 percent. See State Council Population Census Office 1987:86–87.

　12. For anecdotal evidence on this, see Croll 1981:88–92.

　13. For example, sex-specific differentials in mortality, if varying across regions, could contribute to an imbalance of the sexes. Local-level mortality data are not available, but the sex ratio of births gives a clue about infant mortality rates. Abnormally low proportions of female births indicate underreporting of females, which is likely related to infant or early-childhood mortality. The following statistics from the Chinese National One-per-Thousand Fertility Survey refer to rural births in the counties of eastern Szechwan from 1952 to 1967:

County income	No. of births	Females as % of births
< 100 yuan	4,236	46.6
100–149	17,385	47.9
≥ 150	5,555	48.1
Total	27,176	47.7

Two aspects of these statistics relate to this discussion. The first is the apparent relationship between percentage of female births and county income, which would contribute to the relationship observed in table 9.11. The other is the low percentage of females overall. Over the entire period, the implied sex ratio of births is approximately 110 males to 100 females. If this ratio represents mortality rather than a simple undercount, then it implies a structural deficit of females that would aggravate the marriage squeeze for men.

GLOSSARY

A-pa Tsang　阿坝藏
An　安
An-yueh　安岳
chen　鎮
Ch'eng-tu　成都
Chiang-pei　江北
Chiang-yu　江油
Ch'iang　羌
Chien-yang　簡陽
Ch'ien-ti　前低
Chin-t'ang　金堂
Ch'iung-lai　邛峽
chou　州
chui-hsu　贅婿

Chung-chiang　中江
Fang-t'ing　方亭(鎮)
Ho-feng　禾豐
Ho-hsing　和興
Hsi-k'ang　西康
Hsin-tu　新都
Hui-lan　回瀾
Hung-pai　紅白
Kan-tzu Tsang　甘孜藏
Kuan　灌
Kuang-han　廣漢
Le-chih　樂至
Liang-lu-k'ou　兩路口
Liang-shan Yi　涼山彝

Ling-chieh 靈傑
Lung-chü 龍居
Ma-ching 馬井
Mao-wen Ch'iang-tsu
 茂汶羌族(自治縣)
men-tang hu-tui 門當戶對
Mien-chu 綿竹
Min-chu 民主
Nan-ch'üan 南泉
Nan-pu 南部
Pa-chiao 八角
Pao-hsing 寶興
P'eng 彭
P'eng-hsi 蓬溪
San-t'ai 三台
she-hung 射洪
shuang-sheng 雙盛

Shih-fang 什邡
Ssu-p'ing 四平
Sui-ning 遂寧
Sung-p'an 松潘
Ta-hsing 大興
Te-yang 德陽
T'ien-ch'üan 天全
Tsao-chiao 皂角
Tzu-chung 資中
Wen-chiang 溫江
Ya-an 雅安
Yen-t'ing 鹽亭
Yin-feng 隱豐
Yuan-shih 元石
yuan-tzu 院子
Yun-hsi 云西
Yung-hsing 永興

REFERENCES

Primary Sources

CKNYCCTTC. *Chung-kuo nung-yeh ching-chi ti-t'u-chi* 中國農業經濟地圖集. Chung-kuo nung-yeh k'o-hsueh-yuan nung-yeh tzu-jan tzu-yuan ho nung-yeh ch'ü-hua yen-chiu-so 中國農業科學院農業自然資源和農業區劃研究所, 1983.

State Council Population Census Office and Institute of Geography of the Chinese Academy of Sciences. 1987. *The Population Atlas of China.* Hong Kong: Oxford University Press.

Secondary Sources

Arhem, Kaj. 1981. "Bride Capture, Sister Exchange and Gift Marriage among the Makuna: A Model of Marriage Exchange." *Ethnos* 46.1–2:47–63.

Becker, Gary S. 1976. *The Economic Approach to Human Behavior.* Chicago: University of Chicago.

Blalock, Hubert M., Jr. 1972. *Social Statistics.* New York: McGraw-Hill.

Blau, Peter. 1964. *Exchange and Power in Social Life.* New York: John Wiley & Sons.

Chan, Anita, Richard Madsen, and Jonathan Unger. 1984. *Chen Village.* Berkeley and Los Angeles: University of California Press.

Croll, Elisabeth. 1981. *The Politics of Marriage in Contemporary China.* Cambridge: Cambridge University Press.

England, Paula, and George Farkas. 1986. *Households, Employment, and Gender: A Social, Economic, and Demographic View.* New York: Aldine.

Homans, George. 1958. "Social Behavior as Exchange." *American Journal of Sociology* 63.6:597–606.

Ji Ping, Zhang Kaiti, and Liu Dawei. 1986. "Marriage Motivated Population Movement in the Outskirts of Beijing." *Social Sciences in China* 7.1:161–80.

Lardy, Nicholas R. 1978. *Economic Growth and Distribution in China*. Cambridge: Cambridge University Press.

Lavely, William R. 1982. "China's Rural Population Statistics at the Local Level." *Population Index* 48.4:665–77.

————. 1983. "A Rural Chinese Marriage Market." Paper presented to the Morrison Seminar in Demography, Stanford University.

————. 1984. "The Rural Chinese Fertility Transition. A Report from Shifang Xian, Sichuan." *Population Studies* 38.3:365–84.

Lévi-Strauss, Claude. 1976. "The Principle of Reciprocity." In *Sociological Theory*, ed. Lewis A. Coser and Bernard Rosenberg. New York: Macmillan.

Nye, F. Ivan. 1979. "Choice, Exchange, and the Family." In *Contemporary Theories about the Family*, ed. Wesley R. Burr, Reuben Hill, F. Ivan Nye, and Ira L. Reiss. Vol. 2. New York: Free Press.

Parish, William L., and Martin King Whyte. 1978. *Village and Family in Contemporary China*. Chicago: University of Chicago Press.

Pasternak, Burton. 1983. *Guests in the Dragon: Social Demography of a Chinese District, 1895–1946*. New York: Columbia University Press.

Potter, Sulamith. 1983. "The Position of Peasants in Modern China's Social Order." *Modern China* 9.4:465–99.

Sahlins, Marshall. 1972. *Stone Age Economics*. Chicago: Aldine.

Shornack, Lawrence L. 1986. "Exchange Theory and the Family." *International Social Science Review* 61.2:51–60.

Skinner, G. William. 1964. "Marketing and Social Structure in Rural China." Pt. 1. *Journal of Asian Studies* 24.1:3–43.

————. 1977. "Cities and the Hierarchy of Regional Systems." In *The City in Late Imperial China*, ed. G. William Skinner. Stanford: Stanford University Press.

————. N.d. "China's Regional Systems: A Research Guide." Unpublished manuscript.

Sorokin, Pitirim A. 1927. *Social and Cultural Mobility*. New York: Harper & Brothers.

Tien, H. Yuan. 1973. *China's Population Struggle*. Columbus: Ohio State University Press.

Wolf, Arthur, and Chieh-shan Huang. 1980. *Marriage and Adoption in China, 1845–1945*. Stanford: Stanford University Press.

Wolf, Margery. 1972. *Women and the Family in Rural Taiwan*. Stanford: Stanford University Press.

————. 1985. *Revolution Postponed: Women in Contemporary China*. Stanford: Stanford University Press.

TEN

Women, Property, and
Law in the People's Republic of China

Jonathan K. Ocko

Other chapters in this volume have dealt with the relationship of women to property in social practice, Ebrey and Watson examining women as owners of dowry, Hershatter and Watson looking at women who could be bought and sold like property. In this chapter I focus on the connections between social practice and enacted law, particularly enacted laws in the People's Republic of China (PRC) designed to alter the relationship of women and property in an effort to decrease gender inequalities in Chinese society.

Although enough of traditional China's gender bias (*chung-nan ch'ing-nü*) survives for Margery Wolf (1985) to write of "revolution postponed" and Judith Stacey (1983) to deny one was ever intended, the law concerning the relation of women to property has undergone a substantial transformation since the Ch'ing. This paper examines the post-1950, and especially the post-1980, portion of that transition.

From the end of the Ch'ing dynasty until the promulgation of the Republic of China's Civil Code in 1930, the law underwent relatively little change, and traditional customs in the countryside experienced substantial continuity. Marriage was a contractual relationship between families. The marriage, and the bride, "belonged to" the groom's family. Women related to property through marriage. Sometimes they received landed dowry, but more often they were excluded from inheritance because they were marrying out of their natal families. Women assumed control of marital property only at the death of their husbands, and then only in a fiduciary capacity. The 1930 Civil Code expanded women's inheritance rights and construed marriage as the "personal property" of the couple, but real property was still essentially the husband's.

In the Communist base areas the effort to create a regime of separate property and freer divorce that benefited women gave way over time to a more conservative approach. The 1950 marriage law clearly established marriage as "personal property," but ideological and cultural attitudes meant that in practice marriage continued to be treated as "social property," much like land and other means of production. Collectivization rendered moot much of the concern about property, regardless of gender. In the waning years of the Cultural Revolution property consciousness recrudesced, but women did not benefit from it. With the advent of economic reforms in the late 1970s and early 1980s, however, new types of property rights proliferated. The marriage law of 1980 and the inheritance law of 1985 protected women's claims to both new and old forms of property and legally buttressed their status within their families. Although in practice many women remained subordinated and the concept of marriage as personal property met continued resistance, the changes of the last decade have meant that legally and increasingly in reality Chinese women need no longer relate to property only through marriage.

By drawing on legal cases to examine the interplay between law and practice, I seek to peek "behind the legal curtains, where real life is enacted" (Engels 1978:743). My PRC case materials come from casebooks prepared for use in Chinese university law departments, from handbooks designed to deal with common questions on family law, and from case summaries published in newspapers and journals. There is the possibility, of course, that evidence drawn from dispute cases before a formal adjudicating body present a skewed view of humanity. Certainly court cases are manifestations of failures—either to comport with the rules or to resolve the conflict informally—and one should not conclude from the myriad cases of wife beating in contemporary China that all Chinese men are so inclined. Yet just as Geertz's consideration of dispute resolution in the villages of South and Southeast Asia tells us something of the legal sensibilities of these groups, court cases can illustrate the boundaries of acceptable behavior and the role of the state in defining these boundaries. They also point to occasions when practice commonly diverges from the law and give important clues for establishing which transgressions are and are not punished.

Before the twentieth century women in Ch'ing China related to property above all through marriage. According to a common Chinese saying, daughters do not really belong to you; unlike sons, they are in an important sense lost to their natal families. In the Ch'ing they did not "belong in" their own families and were not entitled to a share of the family inheritance. To accord a daughter some measure of dowry upon her marriage was customary, and failure to do so might cause a family to lose face, but the award remained discretionary rather than mandatory and, as Rubie Watson reminds us (1984:8), may have been largely derived from the groom's betrothal gifts.[1] Patricia Ebrey notes elsewhere in this volume (chap. 3, n. 16) that in the T'ang dynasty, Po Chü-i's model legal decisions focused on betrothal gifts rather than dowry. Similarly, Ch'ing law gives scant attention to dowry and impinges not at all on dowry as a relationship between a daughter and her natal family. It simply states that a widow who remarries must relinquish to her husband's family all claim both to her husband's property and to her dowry (*TLTI* 247:087–02). By contrast, the Ch'ing code comprises several statutes concerned with betrothal gifts and payments associated with various forms of marriage. The basic thrust of these provisions condemns all transactions in women with the exception of ordinary betrothal.

From the perspective of the law, betrothal presents were an integral, appropriate part of marriage. Indeed, if a marriage agreement had not been signed, the woman's family's acceptance of the payment signified establishment of the betrothal (*TLTI* 291:101–000). The Ch'ing code distinguished betrothal gifts from rental, pawning, and sale of women because the purpose of these gifts was the establishment of a permanent marital relationship. A betrothal gift was distinct from a commercial transaction.

The code's implicit test of the legitimacy of an exchange was motive: family formation passed it; profit making did not.[2] Of course, as with any rule, there were exceptions. The poor's mortgaging and rental of their wives and daughters as servants violated no law. The code did address the pawning and rental of wives and daughters to be wives and concubines (*TLTI* 293–94: 102–00). However, just how offensive the state considered this behavior remains unclear. The editors of a private edition of the code labeled it "shameless" (*TCLL* 1021), but injuring one's husband while resisting being rented out for sex was not necessarily a mitigable offense (*HAHL* 1968:2528–30). The penalties (with the exception of ones for such fraudulent practices as misrepresenting a wife as a sister and then spiriting her back) did not exceed beatings, perhaps because the arrangement was temporary. Yet, however temporary the relationship, the woman was expected to consummate her "marriage" with the mortgagee/renter. This may explain why Ch'ien-lung decreed that subsequent to such a transaction, offenses between the woman and her first husband were to be treated as between ordinary people (*TCLL* 1023). For the duration of the hiatus, they were in effect divorced. Presumably, resumption of cohabitation reinstituted their marital and first-degree mourning relationship.[3]

Actual divorce was an entirely different matter that was controlled by the seven grounds for divorce and the three grounds for disallowing one (*TLTI* 311–12:116–00). In certain circumstances the code required divorce. For example, it prescribed dissolution of the marriage (*li-i*) when the husband coerced the wife into adultery or when the marriage violated the statutes (*TLTI* 1087:367–00; 314:117–04), and it permitted him to sell her as a wife (*mai-chia*) to someone other than her lover if she had committed adultery (*TLTI* 1079:366–00). But the code proscribed, albeit without significant effect, divorce by sale without due cause (*mai-hsiu*).[4] Like mortgage or rental, this act preceded the wife's illicit sexual relations (*chien*), but unlike them, it was irrevocable. The title of the statute under which sale without due cause was proscribed, "Toleration by a spouse of a wife's or concubine's infidelity" (*tsung-jung ch'i-ch'ieh fan-chien*), and comments by judicial officials underscore the authorities' view that the woman's loss of virtue was tantamount to adultery.[5] Nevertheless, the drafters recognized that the wife might be the subject rather than the object of the act, and they accordingly provided stricter measures for the wife who colluded with a prospective purchaser to induce her ingenuous husband to make the sale. Yet, whether she acceded to her husband's initiative in order to escape his poverty or engineered the divorce herself, the wife was not a truly free agent. She remained in some sense the "property" of her natal kin, who could object to the sale and demand instead a divorce that returned her to them (*TCLL* 3225–26; Kang-i 1887, 4:17–18).

However critical we may be of these various practices, we must understand that under Ch'ing law they did not constitute trafficking (*mai-pan*), that most notorious manifestation of women as property, discussed here in Hershatter's chapter. The code dealt with this phenomenon in statutes on forcibly seizing "good women" (*liang-nü*) to be wives or concubines (*TLTI* 305–11), on buying good women to serve as prostitutes (*TLTI* 1094–96), and on the kidnapping and selling of people (*TLTI* 726–35). The last provision punished a husband for selling his wife as a maidservant, but the others impinged on marriage only to the degree that they controlled the activities of the traffickers who preyed on women, especially single and widowed ones, and thereby affected the numbers and distribution of women available for either ordinary marriage or marriage by purchase (*TLTI* 727:275–00).

Until the 1930 Civil Code, Republican law on matters of marriage and divorce was essentially Ch'ing law.[6] Accepting betrothal gifts did not constitute sale of one's daughter, but coercing a daughter to marry or a daughter-in-law to remarry was forbidden. A husband could sell his wife if she had committed an "immoral act," but to sell her with or without her consent for any other reason, including poverty, was a crime (van der Valk 1968:328, 260, 332). Selling a wife specifically for profit, such as to a brothel, was an even greater offense, yet one that was not uncommon, as Gail Hershatter's essay demonstrates. In late imperial and Republican China there were also markets in categories of people other than married women. James Watson (1980:228–29) reminds us that markets existed for both male and female children (who could be legally sold on account of poverty) and for adult men, but women's vulnerability was greater because their position in the family was less secure than their male counterparts'. One way of expressing this is to say that women belonged to, rather than belonged in, their families.

Clearly, some women were treated more as things than persons. Yet, however betrothal gifts made it appear, families did not dispose of, or sell a daughter into, a first marriage as a wife. They "married her out." Husbands

divorced wives by selling them; families sold widows and daughters into concubinage or prostitution. Marrying a daughter established a set of relations
between families; selling a woman did not. (On this point see Watson's
paper in this volume.)

Having examined women as property, I shall now turn to women as
holders of property. Women's property rights in the Ch'ing were severely
restricted. Although they may well have brought to the marriage movable
property in the form of clothing and jewelry and intangible "property" in the
form of political connections, generally they would have come bereft of substantial real property, for that belonged to the patriline. In traditional China
property was theoretically a trust that provided for the maintenance of ancestral sacrifices, so heirs were attached to property rather than property being
attached to heirs. Because men were ultimately responsible for the ancestral
sacrifices and the ancestral cult itself, women were not entitled to receive
their father's property except when they had no brothers. Even in these
cases, adoption of a son was frequently preferred to uxorilocal marriage.
Otherwise, although custom allowed a father to apportion some property
(sometimes including even land) for daughters' dowries, daughters in the
Ch'ing were not legally *entitled* to anything.[7]

In the Ch'ing, a woman's marriage did not completely sunder her relations with her natal family (Ocko 1989), but it did alienate her from their
property regime and make her part of her husband's or his family's regime.
There, just as the husband's fractional claim on family property was not
recognized until a decision was made to divide the household or until his
father's death, the wife's assertion of control over that share was not recognized until her husband's death. If she had sons, the property could be kept
undivided under her management even after their maturity.[8] Indeed, in 1916
the Republican Supreme Court interpreted Ch'ing law to mean that even
after sons assumed management of their father's property, they could not
dispose of it without their mother's approval (van der Valk 1968:80).
Moreover, once the partition occurred, so long as the widow remained unmarried, she could retain for her support a portion of the estate.

The widow was a trustee, however, and not an owner. She may have been
more than a "passive reactor," but because she could not act independently,
she was not a fully empowered "transactor" (J. Watson 1980:282). If she did
not have a son of her own, she was expected to adopt a male heir under the
guidance of the lineage leaders or her husband's agnatic kin. Other relatives
might challenge her selection, and an heir to whom a widow entrusted her
support and management of the property might abuse her, but the widow
could seek protection in the courts. Essentially, if she had not remarried and
had adopted an heir by the rules, she was entitled by law to control her
husband's property (and her dowry if she had one) until her son or heir
assumed control at his maturity (Ocko 1989).[9] Widows without heirs were

prey to being forcibly remarried by their in-laws. The in-laws could obtain not only new betrothal gifts but also the widow's dowry and share of the patrimony, both of which she would be required to relinquish (Ocko 1989; Wolf and Huang 1980:227–28; Spence 1979:71–76; *TLTI* 247:078–02; 295:105-01).[10] Klapisch-Zuber's work (1985) demonstrates that this could never have happened in Renaissance Italy because widows who remarried took their dowry with them and left behind their children. The "good mother" who stayed to rear her children made it possible for her late husband's family to retain the use, if not the control, of her dowry. And Jerry Dennerline has shown that at least in some elite families in Wu-hsi, the managerial and intrafamily political skills of widows created charitable estates that ensured both their own and their children's positions (1986:191–93, 202, 204). Yet in other locales and other status groups, the Chinese "good mother" may have remained, not because she controlled property, but in spite of it.

Once the 1930 Civil Code affirmed women's right to inherit property even when they had brothers, a new matrimonial property regime had to be established that provided for both the real and personal property a woman might bring to a marriage.[11] Each of the three Peking drafts of the family law (1911, 1915, 1925) had grappled with the issue and produced conservative outcomes. Essentially, the established rule was that, unless otherwise agreed in a prenuptial contract, a wife's property at the time of marriage became the husband's. Although managed and used by the husband, the wife retained ownership of this property (van der Valk 1969:94–96). The trousseau, jewelry, and household utensils that she brought with her, gifts that she received, and income that she earned from her own labor were excepted and designated "separate property." "Separate property" does not appear to have included land. Whereas the 1930 Civil Code significantly expanded the scope of the wife's property rights, it failed to achieve sexual equality. It established a statutory property regime of union of property in which the wife kept exclusive management of her separate property but contributed all other property she owned at the time of the marriage, as well as any property inherited during the marriage, to the "union property." The husband made a similar contribution, and both maintained ownership of their respective shares. The right to manage both shares and the "fruits" from them belonged to the husband alone (Civil Code, articles 1013–20).[12]

Before achieving power in 1949, the Communists in their rural base areas initially dealt with property only in the context of divorce. Their regulations assumed that both husband and wife brought into the marriage property that they owned and were entitled to manage separately, and so stipulated that at divorce benefits gained from property jointly managed were to be divided equally (Meijer 1971:282 [art. 17], 284 [art. 13], 286 [art. 18]). Exclusive and common property were not defined, however, until the 1941 Chin-ch'a-chi draft marriage regulations. Property owned before marriage and each spouse's wages were exclusively owned and not to be managed by the other without express consent. Common property was only that acquired by the common management of the couple, and it was to be managed by mutual consent (Meijer 1971:293, arts. 15, 16, 17, 19). Three years later the party backed away from this system of separate property and in 1950 abandoned it completely in favor of a "community of property" regime in the marriage law. Community of property means that family property consists of property both owned before and acquired during marriage (Yang and Yang 1981:159). Community of property does not by definition specify that husband and wife have equal ownership and management rights, but article 10 of the 1950 marriage law required it.

The vicissitudes in the codification of women's relation to property were paralleled by changes in thinking about to whom the marriage itself belonged. During the Ch'ing, marriage was patriline property. Betrothal agreements were contractual arrangements between two family lines represented by the family heads. The "rights in person" of the wife, in particular the right over procreation, were conveyed from her natal family to her husband's upon payment of the betrothal gifts or, as Kopytoff and Miers suggest, childwealth (1977:8). The primary purpose of marriage was continuing the family line. In this sense, the marriage, like the property needed to maintain ancestral sacrifices, belonged to the family. Indeed, not only the husband but also any of his lineal descendants had legal standing to accuse his wife of adultery (Meijer 1976:89).

The concept of marriage as personal property first appeared, at least in law, in 1907 when Shen Chia-pen's revision of the Ch'ing Criminal Code eliminated the prerogative of the husband's family to control a daughter-in-law. Conservatives objected to these infringements of the old family system, and it seems unlikely the idea of marriage as personal property spread widely. By stipulating freedom of marriage and facilitating divorce, the Kuomintang's 1930 Civil Code appeared to lend support to the notion of marriage as personal property; but the husband retained a greater property right in it than the wife. He had the final say on matters concerning children, presumptive custody in the event of divorce, and more grounds for divorce. Such provisions, much like Pa Chin's *Family*, published in 1931, demonstrated how unduly optimistic Lu Hsun had been twelve years earlier to write that perhaps K'ung I-chi (i.e., Confucianism) was really dead.

In the 1930s and 1940s the family law policy of the Communist party— driven forward by urban radicals intent on guaranteeing women's rights and retarded by culturally conservative rural cadres—suffered from its own set of internal contradictions. Communist policy treated marriage as personal property both in the sense that it belonged to the couple and in the sense that it was an entitlement. Land reform in the base areas gave hope to the poor peasant and the landless hired laborer that they could finally afford a wife. Inevitably this promise to men of entitlement clashed with the promise of empowerment to women. Men had the wherewithal to make the betrothal gifts, but women did not necessarily want to be bound to marry by their parents' acceptance of the gifts, and once married they wanted to be able to divorce.[13] Yet the demands of the struggle for production and against the Nationalists and Japanese superseded the interests of women petitioning for divorce. Neither the peasant nor the soldier, it was believed, could fulfill his duty if he were distracted by family difficulties (Chao and Yü 1984:173–76). Marriage, then, was social as well as personal property.

The 1950 marriage law reflected this dichotomy. As a weapon of the "new democracy" against "feudal" practices, it incorporated principles of freedom of choice and gender equality; but as an instrument of socialist construction, it cast the family as a "cell of society" (Meijer 1971:77–78). A sharp increase in divorce and the shift of land ownership and production from household to collective soon prompted the party to emphasize that marriage as personal property was suitable only in capitalist societies. In China, marriage had to be considered social property for it was the precondition for the formation of families; and families promoted social cohesion and stability through their socialization of children. This theme endured for the next thirty years. In 1980, with feudal family relations putatively no longer the problem they had been in 1950 and household production reemerging, the State Council promulgated a new marriage law that took seriously the concept of marriage as personal property. Together with the inheritance law (1985), this new legislation created the framework for restructuring the relation of women to property and of women to marriage as both personal and social property.

PROPERTY AND MARRIAGE FORMATION IN CONTEMPORARY CHINA

The government of the PRC has consistently opposed "marriage by purchase." In the 1950 marriage law this was not interpreted to prohibit all betrothal exchanges but only "the *exaction* [emphasis added] of money or gifts in connection with marriage" (article 2). Its targets were those who fixed a price for a daughter or widow and those who set gifts as a condition for agreeing to the marriage of their daughter or widowed daugher-in-law (Meijer 1971:172).

As with much legislation concerning the family in China, the rules were widely ignored, especially in rural areas, unless a political campaign put muscle into enforcement. The cost of this disdain was not high because, although violating the rules was illegal and therefore subject to criticism, it was not criminal. "Buying" and "selling" wives continued.[14] Thus article 3 of the 1980 revised marriage law repeated the language of its predecessor, and legal scholars once again sought to define the terms of acceptable behavior. Marriage by sale (*mai-mai hun-yin*) involves a marriage arranged or coerced by a third party for the purpose of obtaining property. In the less-offensive marriage to exact property (*chieh hun-yin so-ch'u ts'ai-wu*), the couple marries voluntarily, but the bride's side demands substantial gifts, sometimes as a precondition for the marriage (*CFCP*, November 28, 1987, 2). Even though third parties, usually the bride's parents, receive something, so long as the bride is the chief beneficiary, such behavior does not constitute marriage by sale. Property and money given directly and without compulsion to the bride are simply gifts (Wang and Wu 1983:2; Sung 1984:11–12).

The nature of the betrothal gifts depends not only on whether the couple is rural or urban but also on city of residence. Although many urban residents claim not to take these matters too seriously (M. Wolf 1985:158–59; Honig and Hershatter 1988:141–42), the "marriage-related consumption" that comprises these gifts, together with the costs of a wedding and wedding travel, are substantial and are borne largely by the man and his family (Ch'ien et al. 1988:220–22). One recent newspaper article complained that a couple's every meeting, from their first to their wedding day, is marked by an exchange of gifts (*FCJP*, May 12, 1988, 3; M. Wolf 1985:175). In major urban centers, the watches, bicycles, and sewing-machine gifts of the 1970s have been replaced by color televisions, refrigerators, pianos, and furniture sets worth over one thousand yuan (Ch'ien et al. 1988:227, n. 5). Even soldiers stationed in rural areas are expected to give gold jewelry, double-tub washing machines, and double-door refrigerators (*FCJP*, May 12, 1988, 3), while rural families may give substantial quantities of foodstuffs in addition to cash amounts up to two thousand yuan (*HYAL* 3–4, 29, 31–32; *FHTC*, May 1986, 6). Because engagements and betrothal agreements no longer have legal effect, there is no formal framework to define respective rights in interests. Yet given the amounts of property involved, disputes about ownership are proliferating in mediation groups and the courts as agreements to marry or marriages themselves collapse.

In some areas, many of the betrothal gifts or much of their value accrue to the married couple themselves, as a form of dowry or indirect dowry (Whyte and Parish 1984:136). But even if there is no such reversion, a large brideprice without certainty of return through dowry or labor is an effective affirmation of the male's economic standing. Similarly, rather than have her family display its social standing through a dowry, a woman can define herself in comparison to her peers by the quality and size of her betrothal gifts and wedding festivities. In 1931 in the first marriage law of the Kiangsi Soviet, dowry as well as brideprice were forbidden as part of the attack on arranged and mercenary marriages. But by the 1934 revision, the prohibition on dowry had been excised. Other than this singular instance, the party has reserved its opprobrium for betrothal gifts and ignored dowry (Croll 1984:57).

The party's continuing lack of interest in dowry reflects the fact that it is passed from parents to daughter and thus lacks the commercial aura of betrothal gifts that move between families. For a daughter, though, a dowry is of some consequence, returning a measure of the income she has contributed to the family's community property and providing her a measure of marital financial independence. Family community property (*chia-t'ing kung-yu ts'ai-ch'an*) is composed of any property created by family members living together. It includes income from collective and individual labor, marital community property, and individual property. Except at partition, Chinese families traditionally do not distinguish among the various elements and will draw from the total pool to help children establish their own households (Yang and Yang 1985:208–9, 216). Croll (1984:58) notes that in the competition for resources between siblings, daughters will lose out to sons, who must disburse substantial betrothal gifts in order to bring in a wife. That few daughters object to this pervasive custom, a Chinese legal scholar argued, does not make it right for parents to give them less than their fair share of family property (Yang and Yang 1985:216). Nor does it mean that dowry is diminishing. My reading suggests that rises in dowry parallel those in brideprice.[15] Yet even when no part of a dowry is composed of recycled betrothal gifts, a woman and her family do not seem to be as oppressed by the task of gathering it as men are by the drive to acquire their share of wedding expenses. There are no tragic tales of young women driven to crime to pay for their marriages (Honig and Hershatter 1988:155–58; *HYAL* 29; Chung-kuo hun-yin 1983:38–39).

There is some indication that in well-to-do villages dowries are becoming more significant (*JMJP hai-wai-pan*, January 9, 1986, 2), but in economically backward areas, especially those in which the cost of marriage has remained high, "exchange of relatives" (*huan-ch'in*) has developed as an alternative to betrothal gifts. In one Shantung commune they constituted 15 percent of the 940 marriages surveyed (Wu 1985:28). This money-saving barter relationship consists at its simplest level of an exchange of daughters between two families, each with an unmarried son, but as many as eight transfers have been reported (*CFCP*, June 11, 1987, 3; Wang and Wu 1983:49). Like the other forms of arranged marriage, *huan-ch'in* victimizes women. It reminds them that in a still predominantly patrivirilocal society they are inferior to a brother. Their interests and needs can be sacrificed in order to meet his needs and those of the patriline. Parents and families vigorously oppress resistance to these arrangements not only on the principle of parental authority but also because one daughter's withdrawal can subvert the plans of several families. Although some of the pairings work out and couples are reluctant to separate when a multilateral agreement unravels, the intimidating beatings and threats that seem to be part of *huan-ch'in* arrangements would appear to produce more suicides and multiple family breakups than happy marriages (*HFAL* 1983:404; *CFCP*, June 11, 1987, 3; *HYAL* 1–3, 5–6, 44–48; Wang and Wu 1983:49).

The case of *Ting Feng-ch'in (F) v. Wu T'ien-chu (M)* is typical of cases that have reached the courts. In 1978 in order to get a bride for his son, Yung-ming, Ting's father got a matchmaker to work out a three-way exchange. His daughter Feng-ch'in would marry Wu T'ien-chu, whose younger sister would then marry Yu Ch'un-lin. Ch'un-lin's younger sister, Yu Hsiao-ying, would in turn marry Ting's older brother, Ting Yung-ming. Ting and Wu disliked each other at first sight, but Ting's father threatened to break his daughter's legs if she failed to go through with the wedding. The three couples registered their marriages in 1980, but Ting slept with her clothes on, and she and Wu never consummated their marriage. Within six months Ting had twice run back to her family, but her father had driven her off each time. She told him she could not stand the sight of Wu, to which he responded that he would solve that problem by tearing out her eyes. Saved by her mother, Ting resumed sporadic residence with Wu, but finally filed for divorce late that year. The court investigators ordered her to return to her own house, but when her father ejected her, Ting ran away. Without a plaintiff, the court dropped the charges. At this point, Wu decided that if he could not have a wife, no one could. He retrieved his sister from the Yus and sent her away. Yu in turn ordered his sister home from the Tings, even though she and her husband (Ting Feng-ch'in's brother) got along well and had a five-month-old child. Beaten when she refused to leave, Ms. Yu committed suicide. In 1981 Ting Feng-ch'in again filed for divorce, which she eventually obtained after mediation failed (*HYAL* 1984:1–3).

WHO OWNS WHAT?

In 1950 the party abandoned its support of a separate property system and adopted a community of property arrangement that merged the property each spouse had owned before marriage with what they either individually or collectively acquired during the marriage. Why this shift in matrimonial property regimes occurred is unclear. Meijer suggests that the move was made in anticipation of a socialist society where the abolition of private property would make questions of what belonged to whom and how to protect the rights of the wife largely irrelevant (1971:202). Another possible explanation is that, whatever fault scholars find in Engels's view that emancipation of women was rooted in economic change, male peasants readily accepted the proposition that a propertied woman was an independent one. Land reform's distribution of land to women unnerved them. As Parish and Whyte put it: "Poor peasants were less enthusiastic about marriage struggle than they were about class struggle" (1978:159). The drafters of the marriage law may have felt it necessary to placate rural males by designing a legal structure more conducive to their ideas of male control over property. Indeed, in practice male control of property was respected. Article 23 of the marriage law stated that in the event of divorce, a wife shall "retain such property as belonged to her prior to marriage," but distinguishing that pre-marital property from family property and protecting women's interests proved difficult for cadres and courts in the 1950s (Meijer 1971:233–38). Principles of equality in property may also have been subordinated to economic needs because the same article also provided that, in cases of disagreement over division of family property, the courts should apply "the principle of benefiting the development of production."

Concern about property was muted, but not eliminated, by collectivization and the disregard during the Great Leap and the Cultural Revolution for the 1954 Constitution's protection of "the right of citizens to own lawfully earned incomes, savings, houses and other means of life" (article 11). Outside the major cities, disputes over ownership of housing continued unabated through the Cultural Revolution. The introduction of economic reforms during the last decade brought with it a new range of property. Because the more complicated legal questions of ownership and inheritance were left for the 1985 inheritance law and the general principles of civil law articulated in 1986, the revised marriage law (1980) did not address the issue of property per se (Chu 1986:190–96). It did, nevertheless, restructure the marital property regime in a way that strengthened women's rights. Community property replaced community of property. This means that unless couples agree to designate certain income as belonging to only one of them, all property (including inheritance) and income acquired during the marriage are possessed and managed jointly (article 13). If a wife forgoes a salaried job to stay home to care for children she cannot be prevented from claiming an equal share (Yang and Yang 1981:158).

Two other important revisions in the 1980 law were (1) the introduction of special consideration for the rights and interests of the wife in case of disputed divorce settlements (article 31), and (2) the deletion of special consideration for the development of production in allocating property at divorce (1950 Law, article 23). The 1950 phrasing undermined women's rights in the period before collectivization because men were assumed to be capable of greater contributions toward production (viz., gender-based workpoint allocations in the communes) and thus deserving of greater shares (Meijer 1971:234–35). As private ownership even of some means of production has become possible over the last decade, the two revisions carve out a potential expansion of women's property rights. But I suspect that property settlements in the countryside will still be guided by a production presumption that favors males. Moreover, article 29 of the inheritance law incorporates the view that the needs of production outweigh the principle of equal distribution (Ch'en 1984:82).[16]

There is evidence that over the last seven years the higher incomes produced by economic reforms have meant that an increasingly large portion of mediation and judicial work consists of property-related divorce disputes (*JMJP*, June 27, 1983, 4; *China Daily*, April 7, 1987, 1). In 1986 the *China Daily* (July 10, 1986, 3) reported that among private entrepreneurs divorces had increased from 20 in 1983 to 144 in 1985 as a consequence of quarrels over money. In some instances the newfound wealth simply leads to male midlife crises. In Hunan a man and his wife each worked diligently on responsibility contracts, he in a factory, she on the land. Together they amassed 40,000 yuan, built a new two-story house, and filled it with all the modern conveniences. All he needed to make things perfect, the man decided, was a new good-looking wife, so he began an affair with a nineteen-year-old woman, beat his wife of sixteen years when she tried to persuade him to halt his affair, and even tried to bribe the judge in the divorce hearing. Mediation persuaded him of his error, and the couple reportedly built its assets up to 100,000 yuan (*CFCP* 6.11.1987:3). Another husband, clearly uncomfortable with the rule on community property, asked the lawyers at Peking's Number 10 Law Firm to write a nuptial agreement by which his wife would renounce her claim to the 400,000 yuan he had just received for licensing a patent. He assured the lawyers that despite his wife's absence, she concurred. Told that nothing could be done without her, he returned the following week, still without his wife, but with her alleged signature on an agreement. Instructed either to notarize the signature or to bring his wife with him, the man left and never returned (Liu, May 27, 1986).

Many cases are complicated because the 1980 marriage law contains no clear-cut provisions on premarital (*hun-ch'ien*) property. Whereas most commentators agree that in general such property remains the possession of each spouse, divorce cases from the 1980s suggest that making fast definitions of premarital income and maintaining impermeable barriers between spouses' premarital property are difficult (Yang and Yang 1981:157; Sung 1984:126–27, 131; Chung-kuo fa-hsueh hui: 1985:43; Wu 1985:142–46). To begin with, it is not clear when individual income ceases to be acquired and community property begins to be created. The law uses the phrase "during the lifetime of the marital relationship" (*hun-yin kuan-hsi ts'un-hsu ch'i-chien*). Because registration is the sine qua non for a legal relationship, this event should be definitive (T'ang 1988:46–47), but legal commentators suggest otherwise. One argues that community property is created when a couple begins its joint life (Yang Chen-shan 1985:208), while another describes a threshold lying between registration and connubial living. If one spouse could prove that he or she alone had acquired something during this time, it reverted to his or her ownership. Otherwise, everything else obtained during this time, including gifts, was presumptively community property (Wu 1985:145).[17]

Even before registration, the situation is not clear-cut. One would expect that wedding gifts exchanged by the couple and their families—clothes, watches, and money—and purchases the bride and groom both make out of their personal income in preparation for their married life—furniture and perhaps housing by the man, bedding and a trousseau (*chia-chuang*) by the woman—would be personal property because they all appear to fit the definition of premarital (Sung 1985:126). Yet this is not always the case. Before getting married in 1981, Mr. Liu gave Ms. Lin one thousand yuan to buy clothes and goods for the wedding. After two years they agreed to divorce on grounds of incompatibility but quarreled over the property settlement. From among the items she had purchased, he wanted about two hundred and fifty yuan of goods. Replying that the original one thousand yuan had been an unsolicited gift, she refused to relinquish anything. The court of first instance held for Ms. Lin, but on appeal Mr. Liu's claim was validated. As the authors of the casebook explained it, Liu gave her the gift to buy goods for the wedding, not for her personal use. It ought to be viewed as marital community property (Ch'ang 1987:398–99)!

How long the marital relationship lasts, as well as when it begins, shapes decisions about property settlements. Over the course of a long marriage, individual premarital property may be commingled with community property and thereafter identified as such. Conversely, as the case of Ms. Wu and Mr. Chang illustrates, a short marriage vitiates claims of community property interest. They met in March 1982, married in August 1982, and agreed to divorce in January 1983. Ms. Wu's divorce petition sought sixty yuan a month in support for the seven months until the birth of their child, child custody, half the "daily use articles (*sheng-huo yung-p'in*)," and half the capital and the goods Chang had in the dry-goods pushcart he operated as an individual business (*ko-t'i hu*). In response, Chang offered twenty yuan a month in support, asked for custody of their child, and flatly rejected Ms. Wu's claim to any property. The business was his alone, and he alone had paid for all the household goods. Mediation resulted in an equal division of the household goods but could not resolve the conflict over Chang's business, which was settled by the courts. Both the first and appellate courts affirmed Chang's assertion that because of the brevity of the marriage, his business could not be considered common property, but the appellate court awarded custody of the child to Wu along with a two-hundred-yuan lump sum payment for medical expenses (Ch'ang 1987:400).

For many questions in divorce settlements there is no legal answer. If one spouse has bought the furniture and the other has paid for the wedding banquet, should the furniture be equally divided? If one spouse has consumed all premarital property and the other has not, should an adjustment be made? As one commentator observed, premarital property could be moved about and transformed. If a woman bought a house with her dowry (*p'ei-chia*),[18] while her spouse expended property on their living expenses, only she has something tangible left. The house was presumptively hers, but socialist morality required that she offer him some compensation. And if the couple has been married for some time, has children, and has made repairs and improvements on the house, then the house should be treated as common property (Wu 1985:131). Socialist morality and customs are the basis of last resort for judicial decisions. Lacking law, judges are to rely on policy, and if that offers no solution, on socialist morality. Yet in protecting women's interests in divorce-related property disputes, judges need reach only to the broad language of article 31 (special consideration for the rights and interests of the wife in case of disputed divorce settlements) to find a firm hook on which to hang their decisions. Enforcing these decisions may be problematic if rural cadres and villagers are to be relied on for support, because many of them are not deeply imbued with the putative socialist morality.

The Chinese press has recently focused on the rapid increase in divorce, but the relative rate of divorce (Whyte and Parish 1984:188; Honig and Hershatter 1988:210) remains low, and women's associated property problems pale in comparison to those experienced by widows and daughters in matters of inheritance (CCAL 3–5, 7–8, 13–15, 19–23, 119–22). The marriage law of 1950 stated that spouses could inherit the property of each other and their children. Yet despite constant exhortative directives from higher authorities (Yu, Liu, and Li 1985:50, 53, 62–63, 65, 81, 88), widows and daughters, especially in rural areas, encountered opposition to the realization of their inheritance rights. Divorce meant that the wife would take half the community property; but when death terminated the marriage, the widow was entitled to her half of the community property as well as a share of her husband's half.[19] More to the point (although this right was not codified until 1985), she could take that property away, leaving her in-laws bereft not only of their son but also of much of his estate as well. According to Parish and Whyte, widows often remarried soon after their husbands' death (1978:194). The case evidence that I examined indicates that for both widows and daughters marriage invited disinheritance. Even in-laws who could accept a widow's right to her late husband's property balked at her carrying it off into a new marriage. "You can have either the property or a new husband but not both," they would tell her (Sung 1984:150).

The persistence of this sort of "feudal" thinking and the increase after 1978 in the numbers of inheritance cases as well as in the size and value of estates prompted the decision to issue the inheritance law in 1985 (*JMJP*, May 15, 1985, 4; Yu, Liu, and Li 1985:11; Chou 1985:34).[20] Like its 1950 predecessor, the 1980 marriage law simply provided for reciprocal inheritance between spouses and between parents and children. But experience had demonstrated that more substantive legislation was needed to implement the 1982 Constitution's guarantee of sexual equality (article 48). The provisions of the inheritance law deal specifically with the new forms of inheritable property that came into being with recent economic reforms and with many of the problems revealed in the cases discussed below. Housing and savings, woods, livestock, cultural and literary materials, means of production legally permitted to be privately owned (machinery, tractors, trucks), and property rights in copyrights and patents, in addition to income and personal property, may all be inherited (article 3). Male and female rights of inheritance are equal (article 9). Spouses and children are established as first-order statutory heirs (article 10). The allocation of one-half the joint property to the surviving spouse is specified (article 26). The rights of a surviving spouse to inherit from in-laws for whom they had cared (article 12; Ch'ang 1987:438–42) and to remarry without compromising the ability to manage inherited property are guaranteed (article 30).

For at least a decade before the inheritance law was promulgated, courts anticipated its principles in resolving inheritance disputes, many of which revolved initially around the death benefits a man's widow and parents received from his unit. Because the property right in them arises only after the man's death removes him from the common life of his family and marriage, the payments are not construed as part of either family or marital community property. They are intended for the support of the deceased's dependents—a retired or incapacitated parent, a pregnant wife, a young child. The issue should be one of who is most in need, but it appears that some parents simply seize the money or use the wife's remarriage as a pretext for denying her a share (*HYAL* 1984:416–17; CCAL 1980:7–8; *CFCP* 5.1.87:3; Min-chu yü fa-chih 10.87:46).

Ordinarily in China having personal connections (*kuan-hsi*) is advantageous, but as the widows Ting Hsiu-ying and Yü Chin-lien discovered, a locally influential brother-in-law, if inclined toward "feudal thinking," can quickly strip them of their late husbands' property. Married in 1958, Ting and Li Yung-pin lived with their adopted daughter in a rural area. Yung-pin's younger brother, Yung-nien, lived in town where he was in charge of propaganda work. In the late 1960s Yung-nien got Yung-pin to adopt his younger son, Shu-hua, and arranged the transfer of Shu-hua's household registration to Yung-pin's village. Yung-nien's purpose was twofold: to avoid Shu-hua's being "sent down" (*hsia-fang*) to the countryside during the 1960s and to position him to inherit his uncle's three-room tile-roofed house.

When Yung-pin died in 1974, his adopted daughter paid for the funeral. Shu-hua did nothing. Moreover, neither Shu-hua nor Yung-nien showed any concern about Ting's declining standard of living until she decided to pay off her debts by selling the house she and Yung-pin had built. Then, with the support of the patrilineal relatives, Shu-hua and Yung-nien accused her of attempting to steal their property and drove Ting from the house. On its wall, they hung a big-character poster: "Whatever dog's head dares to buy this house will have its head smashed." Obdurately resistant to mediation efforts, Shu-hua and his father continued to threaten Ting and the court and to argue that the courts had no business meddling in family affairs. On this point they had initial support from the masses, who reportedly argued: "Ting Hsiu-ying is a widow. Take the house and give it to Shu-hua. She can find someone and get remarried. That'll finish it. What inheritance right does she have to fight over?" Finally, after forty mediation sessions and a mass meeting, Ting recovered her property, but Yung-nien and Shu-hua appear to have suffered nothing more than criticism (CCAL 1980:4–5).

In another case, a widow's vulnerability was exacerbated by her political problems (ibid., 119–22). Yü Chin-lien's late husband Lo Han had been a construction worker and secretary of the party branch in his unit. In 1966, after he was falsely labeled a counterrevolutionary, Lo, his mother, and his wife were jailed. He obtained the women's release and committed suicide. Fired for being a counterrevolutionary's family member, Yü Chin-lien, who maintained contact and tried to help her mother-in-law financially, decided to change her political status by remarrying.[21] In 1971 the older woman was fatally injured, and within days after her unit buried her, one Teng Yung-chien locked up her house, built some years earlier by Yü and Lo, and refused to let Yü in. In the meantime, Teng carted away all the furniture and clothing Yü and Lo had owned and sold the house for six hundred yuan without giving a penny to Yü. Teng was the mother-in-law's son from a previous marriage and the half brother of Lo. Ashamed by his mother's remarriage to Lo's father in 1946, Teng had cut off all contact until her death, at which time he had his son put a spirit tablet at the head of her coffin to proclaim his status as heir.

Because Teng was a factory director and Yü a "black element," she had to wait until her husband's name was cleared in 1978 before suing to recover the property. At the trial, Teng's representative presented two pleadings: first, that although Yü had adopted a son, Teng had not been informed, and that in any case, because the adoptee's household registration was still in the countryside, he had no right to inherit.[22] Second, he argued that Teng should inherit because he was Lo's half brother by the same mother and their only surviving blood relative. Furthermore, it was contended that he had arranged the funeral and had his son set up the spirit tablet. According to the report of this case, those in attendance considered these dispositive arguments, but Yü's rebuttal persuaded the court. She had built the house with her own labor, and so it was already one-half hers. Where did it say, Yü asked, that a woman without children could be so cheated, or that a woman could not remarry, or that a widow could not inherit her husband's property?

Yü's claim about the house being half hers was a valid one that touched on a point often ignored, namely, the survival of the wife's interest. Even before the 1985 inheritance law explicitly restated it, the principle that one-half of a husband's estate belonged to the wife was embedded in the 1950 and 1980 marriage laws. When a husband died, only that half of the property that was his was at issue, and that portion was statutorily divided equally between the widow and her children.[23] It is important to distinguish, commentators note, between family property (*chia-t'ing ts'ai-ch'an*), which includes that of children under eighteen, and marital community property (*fu-ch'i kung-t'ung ts'ai-ch'an*), and also between a couple's community property and the husband's estate, which comprises only one-half the community property (Yu, Liu, and Li 1985:504; CCAL 1980:75; Ch'ang 1987:478–82). According to the editors of a collection of inheritance cases, the common mistake of treating the community property as the husband's is a "manifestation of feudal thinking" (CCAL 1980:75).

Just as there was opposition to widows' rights, so there was opposition to the legitimate inheritance rights of daughters, especially married ones (ibid., 13). Not fulfilling the obligation to care for one's parents could void the right to inherit, but even some courts improperly held that "marrying out" (*ch'u-chia*) should have the same effect (ibid., 27–29, 37–39; *CFCP*, August 3, 1987, 3).[24] In a case from the early 1980s, we find some important continuities with the two widows' cases just cited; namely, the persistence of patriarchal thinking, with lineage and even cadre support for it.

In East Taiping Village the Wangs were a large descent group and held many of the cadre positions in the brigade and team. Wang Yü-hua led a women's team in her production brigade. Her three older sisters had all married, so she lived alone in the three-room house her parents left her when they died in 1978. In 1979 when she announced her plans to marry, a distant paternal cousin with whom she ordinarily had no contact, Wang Tse-fa, and his wife Lin, suddenly made repeated visits to her. They kept pressing her to let them take charge of her wedding and provide her a dowry, but the startled Yü-hua graciously declined. While she was away getting married, the agnatic relatives (*tsu-ch'in*) attempted to force her second-eldest sister to sign an adoption agreement that designated Wang Tse-fa their father's heir (*ch'u-chi shu*). These relatives rebuked the sister for refusing to sign and simply prepared one on their own. Returning to find Tse-fa in possession of her property, Yü-hua quarreled with Lin. The tumult attracted all her relatives, who sided with Lin. Cursing and shouting insults, they threateningly surrounded Yü-hua and drove her from her own house.

In 1979 the commune, acting on Yü-hua's complaint, voided the adoption agreement and affirmed her inheritance rights; but Wang Tse-fa appealed to the district court, which reversed the commune. Yü-hua asked the higher court for still another hearing. The court found that Yü-hua's father had repeatedly refused to adopt Tse-fa as his heir. At the time their father died, the sisters handled his burial. His clansmen relatives, however, undeterred by the deceased's opposition to an adopted heir, proposed a leading role for Tse-fa at the funeral. They wanted him to smash an old plate to scare off the spirits, thus signifying his role as lead mourner.[25] The daughters refused to allow this arrangement. Noting that Yü-hua had never agreed to accept Tse-fa's offer of a dowry in exchange for the house and that the adoption agreement was nullified from the outset by its unilateral character, the court summoned the relatives, lectured them on the appropriate law, obtained an admission of error from Tse-fa, and returned the house to Yü-hua.

MARRIAGE AS PERSONAL AND SOCIAL PROPERTY IN THE PRC

As argued above, to think of marriage in the PRC as personal property is to think of it as an entitlement. Marriage is something that provides a measure of security by combining incomes and by providing children who will lend support in old age. Marriage limits independence by binding one person to another, but in the PRC it also fosters independence by providing an opportunity to live apart from parents. If remarriage is an unlikely prospect because divorced women are deprecated and considered less-attractive brides or because a second brideprice must be paid, then spouses will be loath to relinquish that entitlement, even if the relationship is not harmonious. Conversely, even a good marriage may be abandoned if it does not produce the expected return, e.g., better housing, higher status, or children, especially male children (*CFCP* 1.15.87:3; 3.7.87: 3; Honig and Hershatter 1988:215).

The behaviors associated with marriage as personal property may clash with the concerns embodied in the concept of marriage as social property. Marriage is a precondition for family. Much as it was in traditional China, Europe, and America, the private family in the PRC is very much a public institution (Flandrin 1979:1; Stone 1977:22; Grossberg 1985:1, 25). It may no longer promote social order by subordinating its members to the family head, but its socialization of children and care for the elderly continues to promote social cohesion and stability. It remains a matrix for social and political relations and a foundation for public morality. Indeed, to a surprising extent, in China the family rather than the individual is still the operative social unit. In fact, as a consequence of the rural and urban economic reforms of the 1980s, the family is an increasingly important unit of production. Marriage, as the root of families, is subjected to the control of society to an exceptional degree. The law does not merely bar certain marriages (e.g., underage brides or close kinship) but also requires the marrying parties to obtain permission to marry from their relevant units. Laws, as well as custom and policy, also determine in the PRC when marriage as personal property should be subordinated to marriage as social property. The difference between the two notions is most clearly seen through a discussion of divorce.

In a repeat of the experience in the 1950s, the promulgation of the 1980 marriage law stimulated a sharp increase in divorce cases: from 210,000 in 1979 to 340,000 in 1981, to around 400,000 in 1985 (Wu 1985:122–23). The actual number of divorces also increased from 3 percent of all marriages in 1979 to 5.5 percent in 1983 (*CFCP*, March 7, 1987, 2; Honig and Hershatter

1988:210). Given the onus customarily attached to initiating a divorce, it is also remarkable that 70 to 80 percent of the petitioners between 1980 and 1985 were women (*CFCP*, January 15, 1987, 3; March 7, 1987, 3).[26] The authors of a recent survey of 5,400 divorce cases in Taiyuan between 1981 and 1985 offer a number of explanations for this disparity (*CFCP*, January 15, 1987, 3). For the moment I would like to focus on two: that the new marriage law freed women from the feudal concept that they were bound in marriage because a good woman did not marry twice; and that with an independent source of income women were less reluctant to be on their own. No longer was it a case of "marrying a dog and having to be with it forever (*chia-kou sui-kou*)."

The tenacity with which some women in the late 1950s, 1960s, and 1970s held on to loveless marriages suggests that Johnson's conclusions that poor women identified security and well-being with traditional family ideals were not peculiar to just the early years of the PRC (1983:124–25). If they had fulfilled their duties as wives and daughters-in-law, their resistance to divorce would be supported by their in-laws and the community. In these instances, the wife's concept of marriage as personal property and the community's concept of marriage as social property coalesced and mutually reinforced each other (Chung-kuo hun-yin 1983:108–12).

The case of *Tseng (M) v. Ch'ien (F)* is illustrative (*HYAL* 1984:346–49). When Ch'ien came to Tseng's house, she was a mature, strong eighteen-year-old. Tseng was just sixteen, and everyone in the village remarked on how ill-suited they were. Within a year he asked for a divorce. His petition rejected, he left and obtained a position in a city. Ch'ien falsely accused him of improper relations with another woman in the hope that his unit would pressure him to return. Frustrated in her effort to bring her husband back, Ch'ien nonetheless refused to let him go, swearing she would rather die than allow a divorce. Finally, as in other cases (*HYAL* 1984:336–38), the 1980 law brought about the dissolution of their marriage.

Trying to forestall divorce judgments by such methods as intimidating (*wei-hsieh*) courts or by threatening suicide appears to be an increasingly common problem (Huang 1986:46; Ch'ang 1987:363–64). A divorce case that exemplifies this obdurate and often self-destructive resistance (associated more often than not with women) became the subject of national debate in late 1985 (*CFCP*, November 20, 1985, 3; January 1, 1986, 3). On November 6 Chung-kuo fa-chih-pao (p. 3) published a judge's account of a nettlesome case. Yang (M) and Chou (F) married in 1972 on the basis of political compatibility two months after they met. Their relations soured on their honeymoon when they visited his home in the countryside and further deteriorated when she suffered a gynecological disease that prevented their having sex and children. In 1976 they separated their finances and lived apart but then in

1980 adopted Yang's niece as their daughter. Instead of ameliorating tensions, the child exacerbated them, so in 1983 Yang, claiming that the marriage had no foundation and that affection was ruptured (*kan-ch'ing p'o-lieh*), filed for divorce. Chou opposed the petition on the grounds that as an orphan she could not be abandoned and that she still loved Yang. By the time they appeared in court for the hearing, both their faces were bruised from their brawls over custody of the child. Citing its belief that Chou wanted to build a good marriage, its concern that she was an orphan, and its finding that both parties were at fault, the court rejected Yang's petition for divorce.

Yang appealed. Chou reacted by flooding the Women's Federation with letters and mimeographed materials about her case, in which she blamed Yang for the collapse of their marriage and called on the federation to "rescue a woman, rescue me." She also told the appellate court that a divorce would kill her. Enraged by Chou's letter campaign and threats, Yang responded in kind by informing the court that he had a degenerative eye disease that would worsen if he were forced to continue living with a woman who slandered him. With this evidence before it, the appellate court concluded that there had never been much to this marriage, granted the divorce, and ordered Yang to pay Chou one thousand yuan. Chou responded to the decision first by threatening suicide and then by developing a case of hysterical paralysis. In an effort to speed her recovery, the appellate court vacated its judgment and announced it would reexamine the case. Having derailed the legal process, Chou had her lawyer tell Yang that he could have his divorce for thirty thousand yuan. However, a despairing Yang had written out his will and attempted suicide.

Over the next six weeks letters to the editor debated who was at fault and how the case should be resolved. The published letters overwhelmingly supported Yang and criticized Chou for trying to drag out a loveless marriage. A few suggested that women's rights were being overlooked. One such writer asserted that Chou's anguished threats to commit suicide had shown her love for Yang. But for our argument here, the most germane letters are from a woman who self-deprecatingly described herself as culturally backward, from a cadre from the Canton Women's Federation (*CFCP*, January 13, 1986, 3), and from an editor of the China Women's Federation magazine, *Chung-kuo fu-nü* (ibid., January 15, 1986, 3). The first wrote that Chou should no longer rely on a man to improve herself. She should get out on her own, and, if she wanted to, she should find herself another husband. The editor expanded this argument. For her, the tragedy of this case was the typical reluctance of the woman to be independent. She wrote that women become overly attached to their marriage and family because they have no alternatives. Once they marry, especially once they have children, they have little contact with old friends and find it hard to participate in social activities. In sum, they lose their independence. Clearly, even many women with separate incomes preferred to retain a marriage in which they were just "making do" (*ts'ou-he*) to being on their own.[27]

It may well be that reluctance to relinquish the personal property of marriage characterizes only women married before the late 1970s. Younger women appear to regard marriage as personal property as well, but in their view this means that they can acquire and dispose of it as they see fit. Two studies of divorce in the early 1980s (one from rural Shantung [Yü 1987–88], the other from Tientsin [Kao 1987–88]) show most divorces occurring within the first five years of marriage. The rural study confirms other reports that most petitions are filed by women and furthermore argues, in sharp contrast to Honig and Hershatter's findings from Shanghai (1988:225), that because they can remarry easily and obtain another set of betrothal gifts and cash, women are not hesitant to divorce (Yü 1987–88:98; *FCJP*, February 15, 1988, 3).

This attitude of younger women clashes directly with the thinking of men, many of whom regard marriage as personal property for much the same reason some regarded their wives as personal property—they had been "purchased." The T'ai-yuan survey supports the argument of many scholars who maintain that the payment of betrothal gifts inclined husbands to oppose divorce (Parish and Whyte 1978:194–97; Johnson 1983:212–14; Yü 1987–88:98). Men who have paid one thousand to ten thousand yuan in betrothal gifts are unlikely to desire divorces. Although they may demand and illegally seize compensation, PRC law does not support such claims. Thus, a divorce not only deprives them of the fruit of assiduous saving but also leaves them without the assets to marry again (*CFCP*, January 15, 1987, 3). Moreover, because husbands resent being denied what they view as an entitlement, their opposition sometimes becomes violent (*HFAL* 1983:403).

Indeed, many divorce petitions from women are precipitated by a husband's behavior. A particular issue, and a common source of wife abuse, is failure to conceive or to produce male children (ibid., 142–43; Criminal Code, art. 132; Wang and Wu 1983:5). The wife, it should be noted, is nearly always blamed. A particular concern to legal commentators is the number of party members and cadres who abuse their wives or daughters-in-law, sometimes driving them to suicide to avoid the court's reluctance to grant divorces on the basis of a wife's infertility or failure to bear male children (Wang and Wu 1983:5, 54–58; *HYAL* 1984:144–45; Criminal Code, art. 182.2; Honig and Hershatter 1988:291).[28] As Emily Honig and Gail Hershatter argue, this refusal hardly serves the best interests of women. It may offer a measure of economic protection, but it also condemns them to remain in a hostile relationship (1988:218). Yet if marriage is viewed as social property, this attitude makes some sense. Chinese legal experts begin with the assumption that despite the love and affection (*kan-ch'ing*) that still exists between the couple, men are influenced by feudal thinking to submit the petition. By holding the marriage together, these experts argue, society has a chance to preserve a marriage that still has a reasonable foundation and to reform the husband's feudal thinking by criticism (Wu 1985:127–28). Indeed, allowing a divorce without "educating" the husband would simply leave him free to repeat his behavior in another marriage (Ch'ang 1987:291–93)!

Some officials extend this same approach to cases of "disliking the old and loving the new" (*hsi-hsin yen-chiu*). These refer to instances when the husband or wife becomes involved with a third party, although the phrase almost always appears in connection with men's petitions for divorce. Labeled Ch'en Shih-meis, after a historical figure who abandoned his old wife, such husbands are often denied a divorce as punishment for violating socialist morality. Critics object that this punishes the other spouse just as much and fails to comport with the law (Wu 1985:129). But it is often the third party that becomes the authorities' focus. Various authors urge imposing administrative sanctions, party discipline, or even criminal punishment on the third party (Huang 1986:47; Yü 1987–88:102), and Shanghai has passed regulations making third-party intervention in a marriage illegal (Honig and Hershatter 1988:220). Having the state be a party to marital disputes exemplifies the view of marriage as social property. In the United States, action against a correspondent in a divorce suit is a civil matter between the parties. The state has no standing, and some family law experts in China think the PRC should follow this pattern. They regard the state's role as plaintiff against the third party as analogous to the standing traditionally allowed the husband's family as plaintiff against an adulterous daughter-in-law. In line with the 1986 Civil Law's emphasis on horizontal relations, they propose that a disgruntled spouse, alone, should have the standing to bring a complaint against and seek damages from a third party (Liu, May 27, 1986; Chang 1987:20–21).

The tensions between the concepts of marriage as social/personal property appear nowhere more clearly than in the issue of what actually constitutes destruction of connubial affection (*kan-ch'ing p'o-lieh*). The pivot around which all divorce decisions must now revolve, this provision was added to the 1980 marriage law because the 1950 law had stipulated only that divorce should be granted when mediation was fruitless. Without a standard for determining the futility of mediation, the granting of divorces could be avoided by interminable mediation. The drafters of the 1980 revision recognized that it was wrong "to employ the law as an instrument to enforce the maintenance of marital relations already broken up" not only because it prolonged the pain and suffering of the parties but also because it could precipitate violence (Chu 1986:193–94). They therefore wrote article 25 to read: "In dealing with a divorce case, the people's court should try to bring about a reconciliation of the parties. In cases where it is confirmed that connubial affection has been destroyed and where mediation has had no effect, the divorce should be granted." The intent was to facilitate dissolution of the dead marriage, not to encourage divorce per se.

If both parties desire a divorce and there are no disagreements over property or child custody, a simple visit to the marriage registration office can achieve a divorce. If only one party wants a divorce or there are conflicts over property or custody, then article 25 permits direct appeal to the courts. Yet a number of organizations and even courts wrongly insist that a plaintiff must first pass through the mediation organizations. Legal specialists see this as another symptom of hostility to divorce. They find no fault with mediation, for the courts themselves must first attempt it before passing judgment, but they consider it wrong to use mediation as an impediment to divorce (Yang and Yang 1981:180–81).

Failure of mediation does not mean that affection has been destroyed. If a court believes that there is still even an iota of affection left in the relationship, it may refuse to grant the divorce (ibid., 181). Yet for a court to determine when connubial affection has been destroyed is highly problematical because connubial affection itself is ill-defined. Is a voluntary marriage inherently based on love? Is there love if people have shared their lives for a number of years? Is love an intellectual and emotional bond (Honig and Hershatter 1988:215)? Given the paucity of true love matches in China, mediators and legal writers tend toward the second of the three views. They argue that even if a marriage were arranged and the foundation poor, love may grow through the years. Just because parents arranged a marriage is no reason to end it. Indeed, in mediating marriage disputes, the older women who are the mediators will often cite either Li Shuang-shuang's (the heroine of a mid-1960s film) or their own marriages as examples of initially loveless relations that eventually developed warmth and affection (Chung-kuo hun-yin 1983:102; Wilkinson 1973:88–134). The belief that marriages are an entitlement, but those based from the outset on love are a privilege, appears still to be pervasive.

An article that appeared in 1986 in China's most authoritative law journal, *Fa-hsueh yen-chiu* (Hao and Li 1986), embodies this view. The authors argue that two moralities inform the way divorce problems are treated: a morality of love (*ai-ch'ing tao-te*) and a morality of duty (*i-wu tao-te*). While granting that love-based marriages are ideal, they emphasize that only 15 to 20 percent of Chinese marriages are based purely on love (p. 34). Because the marital relationship forms families that in turn function as units of production, of support for the young, infirm, and aged, and of education for the young (p. 36), the morality of duty treats marriage, not as an individual activity, but as a complicated relationship of rights and duties. The dissolution of this relationship must therefore be considered on the basis of marital duty and social responsibility (p. 34). A marriage, the authors reminded their readers, is meant to serve and not harm the material and spiritual interests of the marital partners and family members. Divorce, though, is psychologically stressful and potentially materially damaging. For both partners, its unsettling affects militate against fully attentive work. For the wife, it can be financially debilitating because women's incomes are generally lower. Despite years of advocating sexual equality, the authors admit, China still suffers from significant gender discrimination in school promotions, hiring, job assignments, and income (p. 37). Beyond the couple, the effect is most pronounced on the children. Citing the high percentage of American and Russian juvenile offenders who come from "broken" homes, the authors leave no doubt that only a morality of duty that subordinates the interests of the individual to those of society can "save the children" (pp. 38, 44).

CONCLUSION

Traditional ideological constructs are very much alive today in the PRC, though, like Margery Wolf (1985:260), I do not think the party intended them to be. Judith Stacey argues that the gender-based social hierarchy of traditional China has been perpetuated by a new "socialist/public" patriarchy that displaced the old private one. The public patriarchy's extension of state supervision over all aspects of personal life affects everyone, but is particularly baneful for women (1983:227–35). The Chinese themselves admit that in urban as well as rural areas the reality of gender equality falls short of the rhetoric, that "the ideology of the men's family system" continues "to inhibit women's full participation in political as well as economic life" (M. Wolf 1985:189). "Otherwise," cadres in the Shanghai Women's Federation told me, "the federation would have no reason to stay in business."

There are still parents who attempt to determine (sometimes brutally) their daughters' marriage choices (*CFCP*, January 6, 1987, 4); husbands who, whether or not they have paid substantial betrothal gifts, continue to treat their wives as property over which authority has been conveyed to them by marriage, beating them and refusing to allow them intellectual or social lives outside the family (*HFAL* 1983:403, 417–18; *HYAL* 1984:117–18, 120; Wang and Wu 1983:3–4; Chu 1986:79–81); and even kidnappers of and traffickers in women who persist in seeing women as a valuable commodity from which a profit can be made (Chang, Ts'ao, and Tung 1988:21, 25; Honig and Hershatter 1988:290). The Chinese see no connection, however, between these excesses and the ethos of the present regime, which of course they would deny is patriarchal (unless privately complaining about the nongender-specific problem of patriarchal/authoritarian leadership styles). They blame them instead on remnants of "feudal thinking" that have not been completely expunged. As Honig and Hershatter observe, "Except in the case of infanticide, violence against women was usually not linked in a systematic way to the subordinate position of women in society" (1988:274).

This persistent legacy raises questions about the role of law and whether changes in enacted law influence changes in practice or merely reflect changes in social and economic organization. The answers are particularly important to women who have been told by the Chinese press to "depend on the law and the Party to chastise discriminators" (ibid., 338). Certainly, the changes in enacted law have been substantial since the revolution in 1949. The 1950 marriage law precipitated an upsurge in divorce and property claims by women. In the mid-1970s some courts had already begun to grant divorce more freely; but the 1980 marriage law accelerated that trend. Moreover, it added the provision that wives were entitled to their own lives outside the marriage. Indeed, one recent legal treatise argues that while economic independence is critically important for wives, the freedom to have social relationships outside the family and attain educational accomplishments may be an even more crucial safeguard to spousal equality in marriages (Jen 1988:210).

In 1985 the inheritance law, incorporating principles already employed by some courts, guaranteed the inheritance rights of daughters and widows and in particular confirmed the widow's right to take property away with her into a new marriage. The 1986 General Principles of Civil Law ratified many of the new economic forms that had grown up over the previous eight years and added new elements, in addition to promising greater economic latitude for individuals, especially women. The contract household, for example, need no longer be the "natural household," which was nearly always headed by a male, but only those members who actually participated in the business (articles 27, 28).

Two factors make assessing the influence of the law difficult. The first is what Vivienne Shue has called "the reach of the state." From the outset, the nascent "party/state center *did not, could not,* and *plainly did not wish to,* control everything" (Shue 1988:104). Particularly in the rural areas, the center's truncated reach meant that localities could deflect its "normative penetration" (p. 69) and maintain their own resilient set of social ideals alongside the somewhat attenuated central values (pp. 45, 69–70). Moreover, because "patriarchy is not only a domestic ideology but a social ideology as well" that permeates all of society (M. Wolf 1985:163), "feudal remnants" have also perdured in the thinking of urban residents, not to mention the cadres and party leaders who made the decisions on how aggressively and thoroughly to attack attitudes and policies that derogated women or discriminated against them.

Judgments about the efficacy of the law must also be made in light of the impermanence of legal institutions over the last thirty-eight years. The anti-rightist movement in 1956 and 1957 dismantled the legal profession, and the Cultural Revolution suspended the courts and the procuracy from 1966 to 1973. For nearly ten years, seeking to enforce rights, much less property rights, made little sense. In 1972 when the courts reopened, though, plaintiffs appeared with divorce petitions and suits over inheritance and property division. As in the Ch'ing, these reconstituted courts served as stages for didactic drama that instructed the community as well as the parties to the case on the normative values of the state. In the Ch'ing tax evasion was pervasive, but tax cheats found that courts would not hear their suits until taxes had been paid. Similarly, villagers (and urban residents) may pay little heed to the marriage or inheritance laws; but if a dispute cannot be resolved by informal mechanisms, it will have to come before the court, where the framework is legal rather than customary. As forms of property have grown in number and property relationships become more complicated in China of the 1980s, the courts have become a more frequent venue for conflict resolution, giving more opportunities to bring practice into line with law. Moreover, for the first time since the founding of the PRC, family law and economic policy are moving in tandem. The marriage law's support for a woman's life outside her marriage and the inheritance law's guarantee of a widow's removal of her late spouse's estate mirror the economic policies (embodied in the General Principles of Civil Law) that allow enterprises to do business with organizations outside their "system" and to lease collectively owned assets to outside contractors. As we remarked at the outset, property is a social relationship. As the economic reforms replace vertical, administrative control with horizontal, voluntary relations between equals, one may see a parallel reordering of women's relation to property. In any case, the PRC has to a large extent consolidated a major transformation it began in 1950. Women need no longer relate to property only through marriage. But China still has a considerable way to go before equality of property rights and spousal relations are the norm.

NOTES

The research for this paper was undertaken with support from the Faculty Research Funds of North Carolina State University and the Duke Law School. I would also like to thank the foreign affairs and law departments of People's and Fudan universities for their assistance.

1. Rubie Watson suggests avoiding the use of the phrase "indirect dowry" in the Chinese context, and I have followed her example (1981:605).

2. Betrothing the same woman simultaneously to two different men was illegal (*TLTI* 291:101–00; Parish and Whyte 1978:160). Also see Ebrey and Watson in this volume.

3. I have been unable to find any material that would answer the question of what

the woman's mourning relationship was to her new "husband" and to members of his family.

4. The concept of "without cause" is implicit in the legislation. See Bodde (1967:428–32).

5. *Chien* is a broad term that means rape and consenting pre- or extramarital sexual relations. For a discussion of rape, see Ng 1987.

6. The basically powerless Supreme Court in Peking tried throughout its decisions to establish the principle of free choice in marriage.

7. As with so much else in Chinese society, whether or not daughters received land as part of their dowries probably depended on local custom, regardless of what the code said. Rather than continue the endless debate about what practice was, it may be time to put a hold on drawing conclusions based on small regional samples and attempt collectively to produce a more comprehensive set of data.

8. A magistrate's remark that widows should not possess deeds before division of property leads us to infer that fears about a widow's alienation of patrimony may have led some to accept her right to a share of income but not to a share of management (*THTA* 22608).

9. On widows generally see Mann 1987; Dennerline 1986; Elvin 1984.

10. In light of Susan Mann's work (1987:48–52), it could be observed that some families faced a conflict between their desire to profit financially from the widow's landed property and their claim to derive prestige from sustaining a chaste widow.

11. See Ch'en (1984:81) and Chou (1985:35) for highly critical assessments of these provisions.

12. The couple could make alternative arrangements by contract, but in community of property the management right belonged to the husband (Civil Code, Art. 1032).

13. Chinese texts on family law fondly quote Lenin's dictum that "there is no freedom of marriage without freedom of divorce."

14. In one egregious case from 1975 a rural couple sold their daughter to four different men within a period of several months before she was returned to her first husband, and in another the woman sold herself (Ch'ang 1987:278, 493–94).

15. Margery Wolf (1985:178) found a similar pattern, whereas Croll (1984:57, 59) and Parish and Whyte (1978) reported decreasing dowry linked to increasing betrothal gifts. My own sense is that, given the singular local character of Chinese marriage customs, everyone is right.

16. A responsibility contract itself is not inheritable, but the proceeds of one are. In both testamentary and statutory inheritance, the division of that private property necessary for the fulfillment of a contract must be carried out with the demands of the contract in mind.

17. In one case, a mother tried to recover the property she had given as wedding presents to her deceased daughter. The mother appeared to regard these items as recoverable dowry, whereas the court seemed to consider them as part of an inheritance (*HYAL* 1984:417–18).

18. The text used this term for dowry in a gender-neutral way, but it normally refers to money a woman's parents give her to take into marriage and is distinct from her trousseau (*chia-chuang*), which she provides from her own income.

19. If the man died prior to the promulgation of the marriage law, his estate was to be held in common by the mother and son (Yu, Liu, and Li 1985:53).

20. For a translation of the inheritance law, see Schwartz 1987:457–64.

21. A child's class label was determined by his father's (Chan, Madsen, and Unger 1984:193), although a mother's standing could certainly impinge on it as well (Liang and Shapiro 1984). It would be intriguing to conduct a study that would examine Cultural Revolution marriages according to political hypergamy and hypogamy and then follow them up today to evaluate the effect the new status criteria have had on the marital relationship.

22. The question of whether an heir's household registration allows occupancy of disputed property appears to be a fairly common one in inheritance cases. (In re. *Yu Pao-hui v. Yu Yao-liang.* Peking Intermediate People's Court, May 1986.)

23. This was a major issue in re. *Yu Pao-hui v. Yu Yao-liang.* Peking Intermediate People's Court, May 1986.

24. Because a parent may now devise his property through a will, it is possible on the one hand for a parent to attempt to disinherit his daughter, even if she has fulfilled her responsibility to care for him. On the other hand, if a will fails to meet certain conditions, it has no legal effect, and the affected person may petition a court to so declare. One of the conditions a will must meet is to demonstrate that it is not based on "the feudal thinking of male superiority" (*chung-nan ch'ing-nü*) (Sung 1984:154).

25. Establishing oneself as a relative's posthumous adoptive son and heir by erecting spirit tablets, smashing plates (*shuai-p'en*), and waving the banner (*ta-fan*) at a funeral is apparently a fairly common practice. Female relatives will also assert their claims by trying to take charge of burial (CCAL 1980:24–25, 92, 119–22).

26. It is widely believed that whichever spouse first petitions for divorce should receive a smaller share of the common property (Sung 1984:130).

27. For an egregious instance of a loveless marriage fiercely retained by a woman for nearly thirty years, see *Min-chu yü fa-chih* 1986 (9):39–40.

28. Unlike the Ch'ing, the PRC does not ordinarily consider driving someone to suicide a crime. In this instance the man was convicted of abusing the woman. If an inevitable cause and effect between the defendant's actions and the victim's suicide can be shown, a defendant can be found guilty of causing injury or death, but even then only by analogy (*HFAL* 1983:404–5).

GLOSSARY

ai-ch'ing tao-te 愛情道德
chia-chuang 嫁妝
chia-kou sui-kou 嫁狗隨狗
chia-t'ing kung-yu ts'ai-ch'an 家庭共有財產
chia-t'ing ts'ai-ch'an 家庭財產
chieh hun-yin so-ch'ü ts'ai-wu 借婚姻索取財物
chien 姦
chung-nan ch'ing-nü 重男輕女

ch'u-chia 出嫁
fu-ch'i kung-t'ung ts'ai-ch'an 夫妻共同財產
hsi-hsin yen-chiu 喜新厭舊
hsia-fang 下放
huan-ch'in 換親
huan-ch'in hun-yin 換親婚姻
hun-yin kuan-hsi ts'un-hsu ch'i-chien 婚姻關係存續期間
i-wu tao-te 義務道德

kan-ch'ing p'o-lieh　感情破裂
kan-she　干涉
ko-t'i hu　個體戶
kung-i　公益
li-i　離異
liang-nü　良女
mai-chia　賣嫁
mai-hsiu　賣休
mai-mai hun-yin　買賣婚姻
mai-pan　買辦
pao-pan mai-mai　包辦買賣
p'ei-chia　陪嫁
p'in-chin　聘金

sheng-huo yung-p'in　生活用品
shuai-p'en　摔盆
ta-fan　打幡
ts'ai-li　彩禮
tso-chu　作主
ts'ou-ho　湊合
tsu-ch'in　族親
tsung-fa　宗法
tsung-jung ch'i-ch'ieh fan-chien
　縱容妻妾犯姦
t'ung-yang hsi　童養媳
wei-hsieh　威脅

REFERENCES

Primary Sources

CCAL　　Civil Law Teaching and Research Section, Peking Institute of Law and Politics, ed. *Chi-ch'eng an-li hui-pien* 繼承案例滙編 (Collected inheritance law cases). Peking: Pei-ching cheng-fa ta-hsueh min-fa chiao-yen-shih, 1980.

CFCP　　*Chung-kuo fa-chih pao* 中國法制報 (China Law News).

FCJP　　*Fa-chih jih pao* 法制日報 (Legal System Daily).

FHTC　　*Fa-hsueh tsa-chih* 法學雜誌 (Law Magazine).

HAHL　　*Hsing-an hui-lan* 刑案滙覽 (Conspectus of penal cases). 1834 preface; reprint, Taipei: Ch'eng-wen, 1968.

HFAL　　*Chung-hua jen-min kung-ho-kuo hsing-fa an-li hsuan-pien* 中華人民共和國刑法案例選編 (Selection of case materials on the criminal law), ed. Materials and Criminal Law Teaching and Research Sections, Law Department, China People's University. Peking: Chung-kuo jen-min ta-hsueh fa-lü hsi, 1983.

HYAL　　*Chung-hua jen-min kung-ho-kuo hun-yin fa an-li hsuan-pien* 中華人民共和國婚姻法案例選編 (A selection of marriage law cases), ed. Materials and Civil Law Teaching and Research Sections, Law Department, China People's University. Peking: Chung-kuo ren-min ta-hsueh fa-lü hsi, 1984.

JMJP　　*Jen-min jih-pao* 人民日報 (People's Daily).

STTA　　Shun-t'ien fu tang-an, fa-lü tz'u-sung 順天府檔案, 法律詞訟 (Shun-t'ien prefecture archives, law and litigation). Peking, First Historical Archives.

TCLL　　*Ta-Ch'ing lü-li hui-t'ung hsin-tsuan* 大清律例會通新纂. Reprint. Taipei: Wen-hai, 1964.

TLTI　　*Tu-li ts'un-i* 讀例存疑 (Doubts on reading the penal code), comp. Hsueh Yun-sheng 薛允升. Taipei: Chinese Materials and Research Aids Service Center, 1970.

THTA　　*Tan-Hsin tang-an* 淡新檔案 (The legal archives of Tan-shui Prefecture and Hsin-chu County, Taiwan). Microfilm.

Secondary Sources

Bodde, Derk, and Clarence Morris. 1967. *Law in Imperial China*. Cambridge: Harvard University Press.

Chan, Anita, Richard Madsen, and Jonathan Unger. 1984. *Chen Village: The Recent History of a Peasant Community in Mao's China*. Berkeley and Los Angeles: University of California Press.

Ch'ang Feng 常風. 1987. *Min-shih an-li hsuan-pien chi fen-hsi* 民事案例選編及分析 (Selection and analysis of civil cases). Peking: Nung-ts'un tu-wu ch'u-pan-she.

Chang P'an-shi, Ts'ao Chung-yu, and Tung Shih-chang. 1988. "Characteristics of Women Abduction-Traders." In "Chinese Women, vol. 3," ed. Stanley Rosen. *Chinese Anthropology and Sociology* 20.3.

Chang Yü-min 張玉敏. 1987. "Ch'ien-lun ti-shan-che ch'a-tsu ti min-shih tse-jen" 淺論第三者插足的民事責任 (A brief discussion of the civil liability for interference by the third party). *Fa-hsueh tsa-chih*, no. 1:20–21.

Chao K'un-p'o 趙崑坡 and Yü Chien-p'ing 俞建平. 1984. *Chung-kuo ke-ming ken-chü-ti an-li hsuan* 中國革命根據地案例選 (Selection of cases from Chinese revolutionary base areas). Taiyuan: Shan-hsi jen-min ch'u-pan-she.

Chao Zhongfu. 1985. "The PRC's Marriage Law." Paper presented at Duke University, Durham, North Carolina, April 1985.

Ch'en Yu-tsun 陳又遵. 1984. "Lun wo-kuo-ti i-ch'an fen-p'ei yuan-tse" 論我國的遺產分配原則 (China's principles for distributing inherited property). *Fa-hsueh yen-chiu*, no. 5:79–83.

Ch'ien Chiang-hung, Chang Chie, Yang Shanhua, and Chang Lun. 1988. "Marriage-related Consumption by Young People in China's Large and Medium Cities." *Social Sciences in China* 1:208–28.

Chojnacki, Stanley. 1975. "Dowries and Kinsmen in Early Renaissance Venice." *Journal of Interdisciplinary History* 5.4:571–600.

Chou Hsien-ch'i 周賢奇. 1985. "Shih-lun wo-kuo chi-ch'eng-fa ti hsing-chih ho t'e-tien" 試論我國繼承法的性質和特點(Discussion of the form and characteristics of Chinese inheritance law). *Fa-hsueh yen-chiu*, no. 5:32–36.

Chu, David K., ed. 1986. "One Hundred Court Cases on Marriage." *Chinese Sociology and Anthropology* 8:1–2.

Ch'üan-kuo fu-lien 全國婦聯 (China Women's Federation). 1984. *Pao-hu fu-nü erh-t'ung ho-fa ch'üan-i chiang-hua* 保護婦女兒童合法權益講話(A discussion of the protection of the legal rights of women and children). Peking: Fa-lü ch'u-pan-she.

Chung-hua jen-min kung-ho-kuo Kuo-wu-yuan kung-pao 中華人民共和國國務院公報(State Council Bulletin). n.d. Peking.

Chung-kuo fa-hsueh hui hun-yin fa-hsueh yen-chiu-hui中國法學會婚姻法學研究會 (Marriage Law Research Group of the China Law Society) and Chung-hua ch'üan-kuo fu-nü lien-ho hui 中華全國婦女聯合會(China Women's Federation), eds. 1985. *Hun-yin chia-t'ing chi-ch'eng chiu-shih wen* 婚姻家庭繼承九十問 (Ninety questions on marriage, family, and inheritance). Peking: Chung-kuo fu-nü ch'u-pan-she.

Chung-kuo hun-yin chia-t'ing yen-chiu-hui 中國家庭研究會 (Chinese Marriage and Family Research Society), ed. 1983. *Hun-yin chia-t'ing wen-chi* 婚姻家庭文集 (Selected writings on marriage and family). Peking: Fa-lü ch'u-pan-she.

Civil Code of the Republic of China. N.d. Trans. Hsia Ching-lin. N.p.

Dennerline, Jerry. 1986. "Marriage, Adoption, and Charity in the Development of Lineages in Wu-hsi from Sung to Ch'ing." In *Kinship Organization in Late Imperial China, 1000–1940*, ed. Patricia Buckley Ebrey and James L. Watson. Berkeley and Los Angeles: University of California Press.

Elvin, Mark. 1984. "Female Virtue and the State." *Past and Present* 104:111–52.

Engels, Friedrich. 1978. "Origin of the Family, Private Property and the State." In *The Marx and Engels Reader*, ed. Robert Tucker. New York: W. W. Norton.

Flandrin, Jean Louis. 1979. *Families in Former Times*. Cambridge: Cambridge University Press.

Goody, Jack. 1973. "Bridewealth and Dowry in Africa and Eurasia." In *Bridewealth and Dowry*, by Jack Goody and S. J. Tambiah. Cambridge: Cambridge University Press.

Grossberg, Michael. 1985. *Governing the Hearth: Law and the Family in Nineteenth-Century America*. Chapel Hill: University of North Carolina Press.

Hao Li-hui 郝力揮 and Liu Chieh 劉杰. 1986. "Li-hun wen-t'i-ti tao-te ch'ung-t'u yü fa-lü hsieh-t'iao" 離婚問題的道德衝突與法律協調 (Legal harmonization of moral conflicts in questions of divorce). *Fa-hsueh yen-chiu*, no. 6:34–44.

Harrell, Stevan, and Sara A. Dickey. 1985. "Dowry Systems in Complex Societies." *Ethnology* 24:2105–20.

Hirschon, Renée, ed. 1984. *Women and Property—Women as Property*. London: Croom Helm.

Honig, Emily, and Gail Hershatter. 1988. *Personal Voices: Chinese Women in the 1980s*. Stanford: Stanford University Press.

Huang Shuang-ch'üan 黃雙全. 1986. "Yao cheng-ch'ueh ling-hui kuan-yü li-hun wen-t'i-ti fa-lü kuei-ting" 要正確領會關於離婚問題的法律規定 (Having an accurate grasp of regulations concerning divorce). *Fa-hsueh yen-chiu*, no. 4:43–47.

Hughes, Diane Owen. 1978. "From Brideprice to Dowry in Mediterranean Europe." *Journal of Family History* 3:262–96.

Jen Kuo-tiao 任國釣. 1988. *Hun-yin-fa t'ung-lun* 婚姻法通論 (A general survey of the marriage law). Peking: Chung-kuo cheng-fa ta-hsueh ch'u-pan-she.

Johnson, Kay Ann. 1983. *Women, the Family and Peasant Revolution in China*. Chicago: University of Chicago Press.

Kang-i 剛毅. 1887. *Shen-k'an ni-shih* 審看擬式 (Model draft judgments). Peking.

Kao Lien. 1987–88. "Current Characteristics of Divorce among Young Couples." In "Chinese Women, vol. 2," ed. Stanley Rosen. *Chinese Anthropology and Sociology* 20.2.

Klapisch-Zuber, Christine. 1985. *Women, Family, and Ritual in Renaissance Italy*. Chicago: University of Chicago Press.

Kopytoff, Igor, and Suzanne Miers. 1977. "African 'Slavery' as an Institution of Marginality." In *Slavery in Africa: Historical and Anthropological Perspectives*, ed. Suzanne Miers and Igor Kopytoff. Madison: University of Wisconsin Press.

K'uai Te-mo 蒯德模. 1874. *Wu-chung p'an-tu* 吳中判牘 (Legal decisions from Soochow). Collected in *Hsiao-yuan ts'ung-shu*.

Liang Heng and Judith Shapiro. 1984. *Son of the Revolution*. New York: Vintage.

Liu Shu-p'ing. 1986. Interview with author. Law Department, China People's University, Peking, May 27.

McCreery, John L. 1976. "Women's Property Rights and Dowry in China and South Asia." *Ethnology* 15.2:163–74.

Mann, Susan. 1987. "Widows in the Kinship, Class, and Community Structures of Qing Dynasty China." *Journal of Asian Studies* 46.1:37–56.

Meijer, M. J. 1971. *Marriage Law and Policy in the People's Republic of China.* Hong Kong: Hong Kong University Press.

———. 1976. *The Introduction of Modern Criminal Law in China.* Arlington, Va.: University Publications of America.

Min-chu yü fa-chih 民主與法制 (Democracy and law). Monthly.

Ng, Vivienne W. 1987. "Ideology and Sexuality: Rape Laws in Qing China." *Journal of Asian Studies* 46.1:57–70.

Ocko, Jonathan. 1989. "Hierarchy and Harmony: Family Conflict as Seen in Ch'ing Legal Cases." In *Orthodoxy in Late Imperial China*, ed. Kwang-Ching Liu. Berkeley and Los Angeles: University of California Press.

P'an-yü lu-ts'un 判語錄存 (Record of judgments). 1883.

Parish, William L., and Martin King Whyte. 1978. *Village and Family in Contemporary China.* Chicago: University of Chicago Press.

Schwartz, Louis B. 1987. "The Inheritance Law of the People's Republic of China." *Harvard International Law Journal* 28.2:433–64.

Shiga, Shūzō. 1978. "Family Property and the Law of Inheritance." In *Chinese Family Law and Social Change in Historical and Comparative Perspective*, ed. David C. Buxbaum. Seattle: University of Washington Press.

Shue, Vivienne. 1988. *The Reach of the State: Sketches of the Chinese Body Politic.* Stanford: Stanford University Press.

Spence, Jonathan. 1979. *Death of Woman Wang.* New York: Penguin.

Stacey, Judith. 1983. *Patriarchy and Socialist Revolution in China.* Berkeley and Los Angeles: University of California Press.

Stone, Lawrence. 1977. *The Family, Sex, and Marriage in England, 1500–1800.* New York: Harper and Row.

Strathern, Marilyn. 1984. "Subject or Object? Women and the Circulation of Valuables in Highlands New Guinea." In *Women and Property—Women as Property*, ed. Renée Hirschon. London: Croom Helm.

Sung P'ei-ch'ing 宋培清, ed. 1984. *Hun-yin chia-t'ing fa-lü tzu-hsun* 婚姻家庭法律咨詢 (Legal advice on marriage and family). Chiang-su jen-min ch'u-pan-she.

T'ang Te-hua 唐德華, ed. 1988. *Chi-ch'eng chiu-fen pai-li chien-hsi* 繼承糾紛百例簡析 (Simplified analysis of 100 inheritance disputes). Peking: Pei-ching ch'u-pan-she.

van der Valk, M. H. 1968; reprint. *Interpretations of the Supreme Court at Peking, 1915–1916.* Taipei: Cheng-wen.

Wang Chen-shao 王貞韶 and Wu Hui 吳慧. 1983. *Hun-yin an-li fen-hsi* 婚姻案例分析 (Analysis of marriage cases). T'ai-yuan: Shan-hsi jen-min ch'u-pan-she.

Wang Ch'ung 王冲, Lin Hsin 林新, Chang Chung-fu 張忠福, Wu Tsung-li 吳宗理, Ning Tien-pi 宁殿弼, eds. 1986. *Hsin-hun shou-ts'e* 新婚手冊 (Handbook on the new marriage). Shenyang: Liao-ning k'o-hsueh chi-shu ch'u-pan-she.

Watson, James L. 1980. "Transactions in People: The Chinese Market in Slaves, Servants, and Heirs." In *Asian and African Systems of Slavery*, ed. James L. Watson. Berkeley and Los Angeles: University of California Press.

Watson, Rubie. 1981. "Class Differences and Affinal Relations in South China." *Man* 16:593–615.

———. 1984. "Women's Property in Republican China: Rights and Practice." *Republican China* 10.1a:1–12.

Whitehead, Ann. 1984. "Men and Women, Kinship and Property: Some General Issues." In *Women and Property—Women as Property*, ed. Renée Hirschon. London: Croom Helm.

Whyte, Martin King, and William L. Parish. 1984. *Urban Life in Contemporary China*. Chicago: University of Chicago Press.

Wilkinson, Endymion, trans. 1973. *People's Comic Book*. Garden City, N.Y.: Anchor Books.

Wolf, Arthur, and Huang Chieh-shan. 1980. *Marriage and Adoption in China, 1845–1945*. Stanford: Stanford University Press.

Wolf, Margery. 1985. *Revolution Postponed: Women in Contemporary China*. Stanford: Stanford University Press.

Wu Ch'ang-chen 巫昌禎, ed. 1985. *Hun-yin-fa chiao-ch'eng* 婚姻法教程 (A course in family law). Peking: Chung-kuo cheng-fa ta-hsueh ch'u-pan-she.

Ya Erh-t'u 雅爾圖. 1740. *Ya Kung-hsin cheng-lu* 雅公心政錄 (The political records of Ya Erh-t'u).

Yang Chen-shan 楊振山. 1985. "Shih-lun wo-kuo-ti chia-t'ing ts'ai-ch'an kung-yu ch'üan" 試論我國的家庭財產共有權 (Thoughts on community rights in family property in China). In *Min-fa wen-chi* 民法文集 (Writings on civil law), ed. T'ao Hsi-p'u 陶希晋. Taiyuan: Shan-hsi jen-min ch'u-pan-she.

Yang Ta-wen 楊大文, ed. 1981. *Hun-yin-fa chiao-ch'eng* 婚姻法教程 (A course in marriage law). Peking: Fa-lü ch'u-pan-she.

Yu Ssu-jung 尤斯榮, Liu Yü-ch'in 劉玉琴, and Li Ch'üan-i 李全義, eds. 1985. *Chi-ch'eng-fa shou-ts'e* 繼承法手冊 (Inheritance law handbook). Kirin: Chi-lin ta-hsueh fa-lü hsi.

Yü Hsiang-yang. 1987–88. "Why Rural Divorces Are on the Rise." In "Chinese Women, vol. 2," ed. Stanley Rosen. *Chinese Sociology and Anthropology* 20.2.

AFTERWORD

Marriage and Gender Inequality

Rubie S. Watson

"Marriage," Abner Cohen has written, "is everywhere intimately intercon-nected with social hierarchy" (1974:72). Anthropologists, historians, and sociologists have provided us with studies detailing the role that marriage plays in celebrating, maintaining, and changing caste hierarchies in South Asia (see, e.g., Tambiah 1973; Parry 1979), class structures in Europe (see, e.g., Bourdieu 1972; Duby 1978; Goody 1973, 1976, 1983; Hughes 1978; Chojnacki 1975), and gender inequality in Melanesia (see, e.g., Strathern 1972). Marriage may be an occasion for marking an already existing status hierarchy or confirming a group's elevation within that hierarchy. Marriage is nearly always concerned with the transfer of resources and so is closely bound up with the world of property relations and economic inequalities.

In this Afterword I am concerned specifically with the relation between marriage and gender inequality. Most of the contributors to this volume have either touched on, or directly considered, this theme. Here I attempt to inte-grate these contributions with earlier work and, in the process, suggest ques-tions for the further study of gender and marriage in Chinese society.

As a number of chapters in this volume show, studies of gender subor-dination ultimately involve discussions of other forms of inequality. Sherry Ortner has argued elsewhere that in hierarchical societies "certain nongender-based principles of social organization take precedence over gen-der"; "the logic of hierarchical systems," she continues, "inherently tends towards (even if it never reaches) gender equality" (1981:396–97). In such societies, men and women of the same status, rank, or class, Ortner argues, are "more similar" to one another than to individuals of their own sex but of different backgrounds. Although Ortner is certainly correct in arguing that women in status-conscious societies like China are never "just women,"[1] at this point I remain skeptical of any view that deemphasizes the importance of gender in Chinese society. The extent to which gender affects the lives of Chinese women, including their membership in classes and status groups, is far from a settled issue.

At one level the chapters in this volume can be read as commentaries on the complex relation between gender and other forms of inequality. This relationship is particularly well illustrated by the many ironies of the female predicament in China: women may be property holders but have few or no legal rights to property, they may be decision makers without the authority to make decisions, they may have physical mobility but are socially and economically constrained, they may exercise the power of an emperor but have no right to the imperial title.

The chapters on imperial marriage in this volume provide especially dramatic examples of the relationship between rank and status on the one hand and gender on the other. As Holmgren shows, each of China's imperial dynasties was faced with the same dilemma: how could the influence of the emperor's kin be minimized? Agnates could be exiled to the periphery, but the situation with affines and matrilateral kin was often more complicated. A Ming solution involved the strategic use of misalliance. Ming rulers, according to Soullière, "consciously and consistently [selected] marriage partners . . . from families of no social consequence" thus effectively limiting the influence of consorts and imperial affines (1988:1). Other ruling lines managed things differently. The T'o-pa Wei, like the Ming, opted for consorts of no social importance. But, as Holmgren points out in her chapter, they went further than the Ming when they sought "to separate the wife's biological function of producing an heir from her political role." Although the T'o-pa, a non-Han dynasty, accepted primogeniture, they rejected the principle of succession by the empress's son. In this way they sought to curtail the power of the emperor's wifely and maternal kin.

The Manchu provide yet another solution. As Rawski shows in this volume, Ch'ing emperors eschewed marital alliances with the Han elite, preferring instead to marry within a restricted circle of non-Han banner forces. Rejecting eldest-son succession, the Ch'ing delayed designation of the heir-apparent until the death of the emperor. Under this arrangement, any of the emperor's consorts, even palace maids, could produce the heir to the throne. "This policy" Rawski writes, "stimulated competition among the emperor's sons, weakened the position of the empress, . . . and minimized status differences between the wife (empress) and concubines." It also checked the power of the emperor's matrilateral-affinal kin.

Each of these solutions involved not only a radical reordering of the usual alignment between emperor and consort kin but also a significant change in the relationship between the ruler and the women of his harem.[2] The Ch'ing were perhaps the most extreme in this regard. In an important sense Ch'ing strategy involved denying, or at least underplaying, a consort's ability to claim rank and status in her own right. The cavalier promotion and demotion of Ch'ing imperial women suggests that they did not carry status in the same sense as men did. The power of Ch'ing consorts and their families was greatly decreased by treating the emperors' sexual partners primarily as women and only secondarily as members of classes, ranked hierarchies, and families.[3] They were, in a sense, interchangeable; a palace maid of slave background could produce an heir and might be promoted to empress or empress dowager as easily as could the refined daughter of a high-ranking banner official. The Ch'ing harem was socially fluid; in this world, Rawski writes, "daughters of noble households mingled and competed for the emperor's favor with maids from bondservant families."

Holmgren's discussion of marriage patterns in Han and non-Han ruling houses, Chaffee's chapter on the Sung imperial clan, and Rawski's on the Ch'ing imperial family reveal the oppositions that exist between a system of royal privilege and a relation of pronounced gender inequality. When an individual is both royal and female, does rank or gender take precedence? As Chaffee remarks in chapter 4: "The tension between gender subordination and political hierarchy was hardly unique to imperial clanswomen, but it was acute for them and thus central to our understanding of their marriage relationships." Imperial women were, of course, a highly atypical group. But when we turn to the more prosaic terrain of Chinese commoners, a similar pattern of conflicting yet interrelated hierarchies emerges.

In a recent article, Hill Gates argues that late imperial China was constructed around the illusion that "women were more like things than people" (1989:799). "By the economic manipulation of women's work, marriages, and persons," Gates writes, "women could be made to yield resources convertible into property belonging to men." Daughters and wives, she contends, were a kind of ballast, albeit a profitable one, that could be jettisoned when the survival of the patricorporation demanded (ibid., 814). As both Gates and Hershatter in this volume argue, Chinese women were indeed polyvalent—being both human and woman, kinfolk and stranger, person and commodity. In the following discussion, some of the forces that contributed to that polyvalence are examined.

MARRIAGE, GENDER INEQUALITY, AND PATRILOCAL RESIDENCE

Patriliny, patriarchy, and patrilocal residence have both structured and been structured by gender and class in Chinese society. Here I deal specifically with the relation between China's preferred form of postmarital residence and gender; questions of patriliny and patriarchy are discussed in a latter section. In China, most unions have involved the transfer of the bride to her husband's household, which, at least initially, has often been headed by her husband's father or a senior agnate. Although not all newly married couples have lived patrilocally, residence with the husband's family has remained both numerically and symbolically significant. This has been especially the case in rural areas where more than 80 percent of the population live and where village exogamy has remained the usual practice.[4] Among this population, parents must depend for support on their sons, not their daughters. The children that women raise, the fields they tend, and the elderly they support belong, not to their natal families, but to the families they join as brides. The preference for sons is expressed in many ways. In the past, boys were better educated than girls, and even today rural girls are less likely to receive as much schooling as boys. Sons often were given better food, clothing, and health care. The continuing practice of female infanticide and the markets in women that Hershatter describes for Republican China (see chapter 8) testify to the expendability of daughters.

The majority of Chinese brides enter their husbands' families and communities as strangers. At marriage a young woman must establish her credentials in circumstances that may be far from welcoming. In contrast, most grooms continue to live and work in the environment they have always known. Writing of the plight of the rural daughter-in-law, Judith Stacey succinctly summarizes the conventional wisdom on this point. Patrilocal residence and patrilineal inheritance, she argues, create an environment in which there is a "significant advantage for sons over daughters" (1983:219). Villagers recognize, Stacey continues, that "the skills of local daughters will be lost to [her natal] community when the daughters marry" (ibid., 220). The peasant view of daughters as "excess baggage" has lost, it would appear, little of its relevance in contemporary China.

One of the areas in which the clash between inequalities of gender and rank is particularly pronounced is the postmarital residence of imperial princesses. In chapter 4 Chaffee notes that, unlike the usual commoner practice, early Sung princesses lived, not with their husbands' families, but in the mansions provided for them by virtue of their connection to the emperor. In her original conference paper, Rawski notes that although Ch'ing princesses lived neolocally, the marriage rites themselves were conducted as if residence were patrilocal. That is, on the wedding day the bride was ushered into the groom's house, even though she would not live there and even if her family had provided the couple's actual residence. In the Ch'ing case it would appear that this conflict between rank and gender—between the status of princess and of wife—was symbolically overcome, even if only for the duration of the marriage rites themselves, by placing the imperial bride in her proper role as daughter-in-law within her husband's family.

My own observations of a very different population (Cantonese villagers in rural Hong Kong) suggest that here, too, propriety demands that the bride be established within the husband's household, no matter where the couple actually intend to live. In all the marriages I witnessed during fieldwork in 1969–70 and again in 1977–78, the bride ceremoniously entered her father-in-law's house and the "new room" (*hsin-fang*), which had been ritually treated to ensure the fertility of the new couple. This ritualization of patri-locality, I suggest, sends the message that women belong within the family —first their father's and then their father-in-law's; women, according to this reasoning, must be daughters-in-law before they can be wives. It is also tempting to conclude that underlying such ritualization is the belief that marital fertility can be endowed only within the properly constituted world of family, gender hierarchy, and control by elders.

In recent years patrilocal residence has been singled out as one of the major reasons for women's continuing oppression in postrevolution China (on this point see K. Johnson 1983:111–12, 128; Croll 1984:52–53; Stacey 1983:190, 218–19). In chapter 9 Lavely argues that collectivization, in fact, may have strengthened patrilocality. It had the effect, he writes, of closing communities to incoming males because the addition of an outside male amounted to a gift in perpetuity of a share in the collective property. Such thinking, of course, assumes that men, not women, have shareholding rights in collective property and therefore that incoming women are less threatening than incoming men. In this regard, the collective bears a striking resemblance to agnatic corporations of the pre-1949 period. Under these circumstances, Lavely concludes, it is hardly surprising that government efforts to promote a modern version of uxorilocal marriage have met with failure.

It is also clear that antagonism toward changes in women's property rights in post-1949 China, as outlined by Jonathan K. Ocko in chapter 10, are related in part to the continuing practice of patrilocal residence. In the People's Republic, Ocko argues, marriage continues to invite the disinheritance of women. Families have often been loath to endow a daughter or daughter-in-law with property or skills because of the possibility, near certainty in the case of a daughter, that these resources will be alienated from the family itself.

In China patrilocal residence means that women do not experience the residential, emotional, or economic continuity enjoyed by their brothers and husbands. For women, marriage nearly always implies a change of residence, but what is less well understood is the social mobility that this change may entail. At marriage a young woman may not only move from one family and community to another, she may also raise or lower her living standard. Lavely shows that during much of the postrevolution period women accounted for the bulk of rural population movements. In an effort to control migration and urban growth, the authorities who came to power in 1949 decided to restrict geographical mobility. This policy, in combination with a decline in intravillage inequality resulting from collectivization, led to an increasing convergence of geographic and economic hierarchies. Spatial inequality, Lavely writes, was not created by the revolution, but it was made more pronounced by the economic leveling of the post-1949 period. As variations between villages began to overshadow differences within a single community, Lavely notes that the economic lot of families increasingly came to be defined by their location in the spatial hierarchy. Upon marriage women could, however, leave their community of birth, and some (the better-educated, especially) did manage to move up the spatial hierarchy to areas better endowed than their own. Lavely is not specifically concerned with the extent to which women, as a group or as individuals, benefited from their ability to change residence. One suspects that although some women improved their lot by making a good marriage in a prosperous community, the disadvantages of patrilocality (outlined above) continued to affect most rural women. At this point it is too early to tell whether the economic reforms of the 1980s (and the consequent increase in male migration levels) make the relation between social and spatial hierarchies less salient. The extent to which the new economic reforms have provided women, as well as men, with opportunities for migration and economic advancement is an obvious topic for further study. Research into the effects of the reforms should also consider whether the rise in rural to urban migration has affected postmarital residence: are male and female migrants residing neolocally, or do wives tend to remain in rural villages under the watchful eyes of their affines?

WOMEN AND PROPERTY / WOMEN AS PROPERTY

Marriage in Chinese society is about the movement of things as well as persons. Betrothal gifts, dowry, and prestations made by wife-givers or wife-takers are all part of the complex calculus of family life in Chinese society. As the essays in this volume show, betrothal gifts and dowry have been basic features of Chinese marriage for many centuries. Women are not, however, coparceners in family or lineage property. How then do we understand China's version of the dowry complex? In Europe, where dowry has been particularly well studied, it has often been seen as a form of premortem inheritance. Jack Goody argues that dowry is associated with systems of "diverging devolution" in which both sons and daughters receive portions of the parental estate (1973, 1976, 1983). For some scholars, dowry is also linked to the strength of the conjugal unit and the status of women.

Although the view that dowry is a form of diverging devolution has been widely accepted, a number of scholars dispute the more specific claim that dowry is essentially a form of inheritance (for a general discussion of this point see, e.g., Harrell and Dickey 1985; Ortner 1981:398; Tambiah 1989). For them, dowry is primarily a defense mechanism that keeps daughters from making claims equal to those of their brothers. Stanley Chojnacki, writing about medieval Italy, argues that girls were excluded from a share in the *fraterna* (or enduring joint inheritance) and were therefore precluded from playing any role in the "paternal family's economic life" (1975:575). Diane Hughes points out that in the medieval Mediterranean world, dowry came to be seen as "a daughter's final claim on the estate" (1978:279) and "rose to prominence as a form of disinheritance within a social group whose organization had become significantly less bilateral" (ibid., 290). For Hughes, the increasing importance of dowry was associated with a strengthened patrilineal principle and a crisis in status created by demographic growth, land shortage, and commercialization (ibid., 287–88).

Many scholars have been concerned not only with questions of dowry and inheritance but also with the extent to which brides control their dowries. Using material from northwestern India, Ursula Sharma (1980) asks if it is the bride, her husband, the husband's family, or the new conjugal unit (the bride and groom together) who receives/controls the dowry. Substantial portions of the dowry, she argues, are given, not to the bride, but to the groom and his family. Sharma contends that the amount (small compared to a brother's inheritance portion), kind (movable as opposed to immovable property), and control an Indian woman exercises over her dowry suggest that premortem inheritance is not the most appropriate label for these "bridal gifts" (on this point see also Madan 1975:237; Parry 1979:239; Vatuk 1975).[5] There is justification for arguing that in India some forms of "dowry" would be described more appropriately as "groomprice" (see Caplan 1984). In such cases the cash given to the bridegroom is often the largest expenditure of the entire wedding (see, e.g., Rao 1970:136).

Earlier work on Chinese dowry, together with discussions in this volume, makes it possible to clarify a number of important issues. In chapters 1 and 3 Thatcher and Ebrey show that from early times Chinese brides have received at least some goods at the time of their marriage. My discussion in chapter 7 supports this finding and emphasizes the role that property plays in defining wifely status itself. Can Chinese dowry be considered a form of diverging devolution or premortem inheritance? Following the lead of our South Asianist colleagues, we must also ask whether women could, on their own account, control and manage their dowries.

Well into the twentieth century inheritance in Chinese society involved the equal division of the family estate among brothers. Household division might occur at the death of the household head or at a time agreed upon by the coparceners. A daughter, under limited circumstances, might be used to channel the property of her heirless father to his grandsons (her offspring) through the mechanism of uxorilocal marriage (see Wolf and Huang 1980:61, 98–99, 106; Pasternak 1983; cf. Tambiah 1973:77–85). But, as

Ocko points out in chapter 10, daughters had no legal right to receive an inheritance that equaled or even resembled their brothers' and, as already noted above, were not recognized shareholders in family property.

Nonetheless, Chinese brides did not begin their married life empty-handed. They may have brought only a few clothes, bedding, and a piece or two of jewelry, but the possession of these goods (whether funded by the groom's parents or the bride's) was, as Ebrey points out in chapter 3, a fundamental part of Chinese marriage exchange. In the visual arts and in oral folklore, marriage was as likely to be represented by the dowry procession as by the sedan chair that bore the bride to her new home.

In chapter 3 Ebrey shows that lavish betrothal gifts supplied by the groom's family were the hallmark of marriage exchanges among the T'ang elite. During Sung times, however, this pattern changed whereby daughters of the elite received substantial dowries from their natal families. The phenomenon of dowry was not new to the Sung, but the amount and source of these transfers constituted a decided departure from earlier practice. According to Ebrey, the Sung pattern signals a change from a system wherein families and patrilines endowed wife-givers with betrothal gifts that were returned as dowry (and so eventually were reabsorbed by the groom's family) to a system of diverging devolution in which members of the elite "began regularly transmitting a portion of their wealth outside the boundaries of their patrilineal descendants." Large dowries continued to be a part of elite marriage exchange throughout the late imperial period (see, for example, Mann's reference to dowry among the Ch'ing elite, chapter 6).

Discussions in this volume show that although dowry was a characteristic feature of Chinese marriage,[6] it never received the formal stamp of approval accorded betrothal gifts. In chapter 1, Thatcher provides a summary of the rites to be performed at betrothal and marriage in the Spring and Autumn period. Significantly, there is no mention of dowry, although Thatcher notes that betrothal gifts "had important symbolic functions." According to Ebrey, "one was not married ritually without some token transfer of objects from the groom's family to the bride's." Dowries, whether from the groom's family or the bride's, whether extravagant or paltry, were largely ignored by the state and, if considered at all, were derided in the moral teachings of the Confucian literati as mercenary social climbing (see Ebrey's chapter). "To accord a daughter some measure of dowry upon her marriage," Ocko writes in chapter 10, "was customary, and failure to do so might cause a family to lose face, but the award remained discretionary rather than mandatory" (see also Freedman 1966:55; McCreery 1976). In Ch'ing law, Ocko writes, "betrothal presents were an integral, appropriate part of marriage"; dowry was accorded no such recognition. This is indeed an interesting problem, and is one to which I shall return in a latter section of this essay.

If we accept that daughters had no clearly mandated right to property, that the goods they did receive were mediated through marriage, and further that dowry enjoyed little or no official recognition, it would appear that the relation between Chinese women and dowry differed markedly from that described for Europe. That is, throughout most of Chinese history women received dowry but in effect had no rights of inheritance (cf. Rheubottom 1980). China's particular mix of betrothal gifts and dowry also highlights the differences between European and Chinese patterns.

There is at present little detailed information on marriage exchange among ordinary Chinese prior to the nineteenth and twentieth centuries. What evidence we do have for this later period suggests, however, that most peasants used betrothal gifts to create dowry and that wife-giving families sometimes kept sizable portions of these gifts for themselves (for a review of this literature see Parish and Whyte 1978:182; K. Johnson 1983:11; Watson 1981, 1984). Class, status, and perhaps region were all factors in determining the amount each side contributed. The possibility, therefore, that many, perhaps most, ordinary Chinese women were endowed by their husbands' families with greater amounts of property than they received from their own natal families supports the view that dowry, at least as it concerns women's property rights and kinship affiliations, was constituted differently in China and in Europe.

Comparisons to India are also instructive. Patriliny, patrilocal residence, and male bias in property transmission are also present in India, but, unlike China, female property rights in Indian society appear to be better developed not only in customary law and practice but also at the ideological level. China has dowry, but it does not exhibit the cultural valuation of dowry so powerfully expressed in Indian society (see for discussion Tambiah 1973: 59–100; 1989).

Although marriage rites in China give no clue as to the source of the dowry, knowing exactly who provided which elements is important for understanding how women relate not only to property but also to their natal families and those of their husbands. Whether the bride's or groom's family contributed the bulk of the dowry also has implications for affinity. As Lavely suggests in this volume, large betrothal gifts and even larger dowries are likely, according to his Szechwan data, to involve "real affinal relations" and marriages in which the bride and groom reside in nearby communities. Ebrey argues forcefully that part of the appeal of dowry among the Sung elite related to its use in attracting the "best sort" of affines (see chapter 3). In the Chinese context a woman who entered her husband's family with goods provided nearly exclusively from the groom's betrothal gifts may have experienced, at least initially, a different relationship to and standing in her husband's family than those who received lavish gifts from their parents.

One also suspects that in such circumstances a woman's father, for example, might find himself in a less-than-secure position from which to make claims on his son-in-law and future descendants.

Compared with the situation Sharma describes for northwestern India, Chinese women seem to have had appreciably more influence over the goods they received at marriage. This control was never complete, however, and from Ming times at least, appears to have varied over the course of a woman's life. Writing about the Sung period, Ebrey argues that women had an important role in managing the land, which often formed a portion of the dowries of the elite (1981). Sung women, it should be noted, could take their dowries with them when a marriage ended (see chapter 3). In Ming and Ch'ing times, however, a widow who remarried or a divorced woman lost both her dowry *and* her children to her husband's family (see chapters 3 and 10; see also Holmgren 1985; Mann 1987). One wonders whether the idea of dowry was itself undergoing change during this period. Was dowry becoming a transfer of wealth from the wife-givers and wife-takers to the next generation of grandchildren rather than a direct endowment of the bride herself, as it presumably had been in the Sung? Considerable evidence suggests that during the late imperial period the daughters of the elite might more appropriately be considered the trustees rather than the masters of their dowries.

As we move from a focus on the elite to a discussion of ordinary, rural women in the twentieth century, we find both differences and continuities. One major difference was the makeup of the dowry itself; village women rarely received land as part of their endowment (for discussion of this point see Watson 1984). In chapter 10 Ocko refers to a category of women's property, which he translates as "separate property" (*ssu-fang ch'ien*, literally "private room money" or "private fund"). *Ssu-fang ch'ien* is married women's property and, according to Ocko, includes the trousseau (or jewelry and household goods brought by the bride at the time of the marriage), gifts she received before marriage (presumably from relatives and friends, not members of the immediate family), and income earned from her own labor. "'Separate property'" he states, "does not appear to have included land." Myron Cohen argues that the possession of *ssu-fang ch'ien* "differentiate[s] [the bride] as an independent property-holder with her own rights of disposal," which are not fully shared with her husband (1976:178; see also Gallin and Gallin 1982; R. Gallin 1984; Stockard 1989:21; Watson 1984; M. Wolf 1975:135). The size of this fund is a closely guarded secret, and even a father-in-law must pay interest if he is forced to borrow from his daughter-in-law.

But women do not remain in permanent control of their private fund, according to Cohen (cf. Tambiah 1989). Like the wives of the literati, their hold over dowry is tenuous. Cohen argues that *ssu-fang ch'ien* is really *fang* (branch) property in temporary disguise, by which he means that wives are the only members of joint families who can hold individual property. They retain this "private fund" until the joint family divides, at which time the private fund is merged with the new household's general fund. Margery Wolf has taken issue with this last point, arguing that a woman's private fund is not *fang* property at all, but the property of the uterine family (that is, a woman and her children, especially her sons) (1975:135). Wolf's argument suggests that *ssu-fang ch'ien* is not tied to the joint family or to a stage in a woman's life course or a family's domestic cycle but is, in fact, a form of women's property that wives reserve for their own use and that of their children. According to Ocko, the 1930 Civil Code, which in limited respects improved women's inheritance rights, stipulated that a woman could own property but that the right to manage these resources belonged to the husband alone. *Ssu-fang ch'ien*, it should be noted, was excepted from the husband's management (see chapter 10).

At this point a number of questions remain unanswered. Does a woman maintain her private fund only as long as she and her husband are part of the joint family? At the time of household division does she retain a portion of the fund for her own use, does she build a new fund, or does she forfeit her right to maintain private property? There is no doubt that the greater availability of wage labor for women and the increasingly commercialized environment of the late imperial period had an effect on *ssu-fang ch'ien*, but at this point we do not know if private funds are a recent innovation or have long historical roots. Ebrey refers to a category of property in Sung times called "wife's assets" (*ch'i ts'ai*; presumably these assets originated as dowry) that was not merged with the common household fund but was often managed by husbands (1984:117). The essence of *ssu-fang ch'ien* was that it not only belonged to women but was also managed by them. Whether the "private funds" of nineteenth- and twentieth-century village women were an outgrowth of "wife's assets" is at this point unclear. Did the form and/or source of a woman's property determine the control she exercised over it? Further investigations of this question need to be made. Should dowry and *ssu-fang ch'ien* be considered distinct categories of women's property? Should we distinguish the jewelry, clothes, and furniture (i.e., personal effects or trousseau) given to a woman from the land, shops, and businesses she receives, and should all of this in turn be separated from the cash the bride acquires from marriage gifts and her own personal earnings? It is also worth considering whether goods originating from the bride's family were treated differently from contributions made by the groom's family or by friends and more distant kin.

Since the marriage law of 1950 there have been significant legal changes in women's property rights. Legally and increasingly in reality, Ocko writes, "Chinese women need no longer relate to property through marriage." In practice, however, Ocko's discussion shows that there has been less than full compliance with either the spirit or letter of these laws. In chapter 10 he details the changing context of marriage from Ch'ing times to the reforms of the 1980s, arguing that marriage in China was primarily a form of family property well into the twentieth century. That is, marriage was a relation between families and was established for purposes of continuing the family line both as a biological and a socioeconomic entity. In such a system, Ocko argues, there is an important sense in which the "marriage, and the bride, 'belonged to' the groom's family." The concept of marriage as personal property first appeared in Chinese law when a 1907 revision of the Ch'ing code took away the right of the husband's family to control the daughter-in-law. The 1930 code enlarged the idea of marriage as personal property by stipulating freedom of marriage and facilitating divorce, although, as Ocko contends in chapter 10, "the husband retained a greater property right in [the marriage] than the wife."

In the Communist base areas of the 1930s and 1940s marriage was treated as personal property both in the sense that it belonged to the husband and wife and in the sense of entitlement. In order to gain recruits to their cause, the Communist guerrillas promised their male followers wives. This pledge of entitlement, Ocko argues, clashed with their promises to empower women. He documents the shift toward a new form of marriage as social property during the post-1949 era in which the state claimed a significant stake in marital unions.[7] This analysis is particularly useful because it exposes an important mechanism of gender subordination in the Maoist period. When issues of production, Socialist morality, government policies, or family concerns conflicted with women's rights, it was nearly always women who lost out. The tensions between marriage as social property and marriage as personal property and the clash between men's entitlement and women's empowerment are central to any analysis of gender inequality in the post-1949 period. These opposing principles are at the core of what Judith Stacey (1983) refers to as the substitution of one form of patriarchy for another during the Republican-Socialist transition of the mid-twentieth century.

The concept of marriage as a kind of property that belongs to families is also useful for understanding the process that turns women into something that husbands and households possess. Hershatter's chapter on Shanghai prostitutes forces us to recognize that in China women could be objects as well as subjects. Marriage, she points out, was not the only destiny for a Chinese woman. In early twentieth-century Shanghai, prostitutes outnumbered the largest category of female factory workers (i.e., cotton spinners); and in the late 1940s Hershatter estimates that one out of every forty-two Shanghai residents was directly involved in prostitution. Girls and women were sold into prostitution, concubinage, and slavery; they were pawned and indentured by their parents and sometimes even by their husbands (see for discussion chapters 7, 8, and 10). For some, servile status was not a permanent condition; as Hershatter notes there is evidence that Shanghai prostitutes occasionally married. It is also clear, however, that many women, once they were forced out of the family and into the marketplace, never regained the status of family member (on this point see also chapter 7).

China's market in girls and women must be seen in the context of a society that continued to treat women as less than the social equals of men. As Ebrey notes in her introduction to this volume, "throughout [Chinese] society, from the imperial court to the peasant household, men outranked women." If all women did indeed fall below the standards set by men and if men could be fathers as well as officials, literati, landlords, woodcarvers, and so forth, were women in some sense "just women"? Is it possible to distinguish wives from the concubines and maids with whom they shared their households and sometimes their husbands, or should wives be seen as part of the Chinese market in people? Did marriage stand at one end of a continuum that included indenture, pawning, and slavery?

Discussions in this volume make it clear that the Chinese themselves attached great importance to separating marriage from commercial transactions. The condemnation of any kind of marriage exchange that smacked of trafficking in women was a recurring theme. Ebrey quotes a Confucian scholar who, in the seventh century, wrote: "Discussing wealth in arranging a marriage is the way of the barbarians," and in Sung times, too, there were those who railed against the evils of mercenary marriages. The Ch'ing code, Ocko points out, paid considerable attention to distinguishing betrothal gifts from the rental, pawning, or sale of women. According to Ocko, the "test of the legitimacy of an exchange was motive: family formation passed it; profit making did not."

Although it is tempting to argue that this was predominately a literati issue, ethnographic evidence suggests otherwise. As I note in chapter 7, the Cantonese village women I interviewed were always careful to stress that they had come to their husbands with property, no matter how insignificant. The pride they took in their small dowries and in the red sedan chairs that transported them as brides to their husbands' households can be read, I suggest, as an attempt to distinguish themselves and their marriages from the transactions that made women into concubines and prostitutes. Village women may not have expressed themselves in the language of the elite, but their message was clear: Wives are married, not bought.

If, as the discussions in this volume suggest, property was central to the status of wife, the importance that women attached to their dowries is hardly surprising. The size of the dowry not only enhanced or diminished familial status but also in an important sense defined the woman as commodity or wife. As Mann points out in chapter 6, dowry "meant that the bride was not being sold."

In her chapter, Mann provides insights into the elite's preoccupation with separating marriage from commerce, in addition to exploring the whole issue of feminine honor in the androcentric world of Ch'ing China. The use of women to represent cultural values and tensions is a common phenomenon in many societies (see, e.g., Bloch 1982; Campbell 1964; Gold 1985; Papanek 1979; Peristiany 1966). Until recently, however, little attention has been paid to this aspect of gender inequality in Chinese society. In Ch'ing China and earlier, women's deportment and the marital union itself offered a language and set of symbols for talking about proper social relations. As Mann points out, according to the tenets of the Han Learning movement, the husband-wife relationship is at the core of all social relations in that it represents the very essence of hierarchical complementarity. Mann's chapter suggests to me that wifely deference and submission served as a model of what might be labeled "properly constituted inequality" in Chinese society. Mann has provided us with an intriguing analysis of the ways in which women, their bodies and behavior, became a metaphor, perhaps in the Chinese case a surrogate, for control over the social order itself. In this analysis one is reminded of Verena Stolcke's statement that "the subordination of women is one of the prerequisites for the maintenance of social relations of domination" (1981:34).

Mann's analysis links ideology to political economy by placing literati discourse in the context of an increasing level of commercialization and the emergence of a nouveaux riches who were challenging the economic and moral superiority of the traditional elite. "In fixing the place of wives in the domestic sphere," she writes, "[the literati] sought to fix the fluidity of social change that threatened to erode the boundaries defining their own respectability." It is indeed interesting to compare Mann's discussion of literati glorifications of refined femininity to Jaschok's descriptions of the households of Hong Kong's commercial elite where concubines, unencumbered by such refinements, could usurp the rightful role of wife and daughter-in-law. Here in this intensely commercialized and competitive environment, the literati nightmare of a "world turned upside down" seemed a reality. Colonial Hong Kong, Jaschok points out, did not provide the kind of moral community within which tradition-bound sanctioning agents could be effective (1988: 62). It was not only Hong Kong's nouveaux riches, we should note, who posed a threat to "properly constituted inequality"; the Manchu court itself provided the unsettling spectacle of bondservants who could become empresses and high-born ladies who could be brushed aside and ignored. The increasing vulnerability of the cherished hierarchies of the past no doubt was a major factor in converting many literati men into avid champions of a highly restrictive code of women's honor.

CHANGING RELATIONS: PATRILINY, MARRIAGE, AND GENDER

This volume and an earlier work on Chinese agnatic groups (Ebrey and Watson 1986) offer complementary discussions of how the post-T'ang movement away from an inherited system of status to a more open society affected kinship, family, and gender. The available evidence suggests that Chinese lineage building was in part a response to the less certain environment of the late imperial era (see, e.g., Twitchett 1959; Beattie 1979; Ebrey and Watson 1986). Lineages with their corporate property and written genealogies were, according to Twitchett, "to a very great extent the product of Sung times" (1959:97–98; see also Ebrey 1986b; D. Johnson 1983). Patrilineal descent groups were useful, Twitchett maintains, in building secure local institutions and served to consolidate the position of the literati elite who no longer could rely on hereditary privileges. In her introduction to this volume, Ebrey argues that lineage development was not the only response to China's changing political economy. The elaborate dowries of the Sung and post-Sung period can also be linked to the requirements of this new era. According to Ebrey, commercialization and the emergence of an elite that depended on wealth rather than inherited status were key factors in the development of the Chinese dowry complex.

Dowries were adopted by the elite, Ebrey argues, because they "made better bait than betrothal gifts." According to this reasoning, dowry, which consisted of property transferred outside the patriline, strengthened affinal ties and created the potential for more flexible family strategies. In the highly structured world of patrilineal descent and partible inheritance among brothers, a lavishly endowed bride might elevate one brother over another. In fact, it may be precisely this potential for fraternal inequality that accounts for the distaste that many neo-Confucian thinkers expressed for large dowries and ties through women.

At first glance lineages and dowry appear to have little to do with each other. But Ebrey shows in chapter 3 that these seemingly unrelated elements are in fact directly linked. As noted above, both lineage and dowry complexes were responses, albeit initially independent ones, to the same set of economic and political circumstances. They were also connected in another, perhaps more fundamental, sense. According to Ebrey, the strengthening of patrilineal principles had the effect of arresting the shift toward diverging devolution. The neo-Confucians' "call for a 'revival of the descent line system' (*tsung*)," she writes, "was motivated in part by their objection to the strength of affinal relations and their fears concerning the breakup of patrimonies." Tension between the need to build lineages and so strengthen local agnatic ties on the one hand and the need to provide dowries and so expand networks and claim status on the other characterized the post-T'ang period.[8] These tensions had obvious implications for the subordination of women. As Gates argues, the increasing commoditization of land, labor, and capital during the Sung "threatened the bureaucratizing state [and] the wealth-based ruling class that still depended heavily on unfree labor and household patriarchs" (1989:824).

There is increasing evidence that a number of factors, including the particular constellation of late imperial China's patrilineal/patriarchal regime, constituted an effective challenge not only to women's property claims but also to the expansion of women's rights in general. During this period lineage rules requiring the adoption of male heirs rather than succession by daughters and regulations reinforcing the negative image of uxorilocal marriage were common (see, e.g., Liu 1959:72–77). Legal restrictions on the property rights of widows (see chapters by Ebrey and Ocko) and Ch'ing statutes that made it difficult for women to prove rape (Ng 1987) testify to a hardening of attitudes. Hershatter's discussion of expanding markets in women during the nineteenth and twentieth centuries, the Ming-Ch'ing discourse on women's honor, and an increasing preoccupation with widow chastity coupled with outbreaks of widow suicide (see Mann's chapter; Elvin 1984; Holmgren 1985; Mann 1987; T'ien 1988) support the view that in many respects women as women did not fare well in late imperial China.[9]

Although there were certainly improvements in women's economic opportunities and in their legal rights during the twentieth century, members of agnatic groups, buttressed by a patrilineal dogma, continued to act against any principle that would grant real property rights to daughters. Even after forty years of collectivization and economic reform, such interests remain strong (see, e.g., Honig and Hershatter 1988; K. Johnson 1983; Parish and Whyte 1978:195–96; Stacey 1983). In chapter 10, Ocko describes a case from the 1970s in which an agnatic group fought (including the use of violence) against the rights of a uxorilocally married daughter who claimed her father's property after his death. There was still, it should be noted, no recognition of women's inheritance rights among Hong Kong villagers during the 1970s.

Agnation, affinity, lineage building, and lavish dowries may all have played a role in safeguarding the position of the elite and in providing avenues of mobility for those who wished to improve their lot. But, as Ebrey points out in the Introduction, the state apparatus and the official ideology of neo-Confucianism reserved its greatest support for only one of these principles: Patrilineal descent was promoted to the near exclusion of other ties, and this of course had a profound consequence not only on women's property rights but also on their ability to perform as the social equals of their brothers and husbands.

Why, given China's pronounced gender inequality, was property in the form of dowry transferred to women at all? Ortner argues that dowry as a form of property transfer tends to be found in those hierarchical societies where there is a recognition of women's membership in class and status groups but where internally stratified kin groups are patrilineal and exogamous (1981:396–98). She points to China and India as examples of such societies.[10] Ortner emphasizes the link between different women's property regimes and kinship forms; in this volume the approach has been less structural and more historical (see particularly Ebrey's chapter). In the case of China there is, I argue, a tension between the various positions that women hold as representatives of a subordinated gender and as members of class and status groups. This tension appears to have become particularly prominent in the post-T'ang era and has persisted into the twentieth century. The dowry complex that Ebrey describes in this volume developed in the context of a society where women were both bearers and markers of status; in other words, Chinese women were both persons and signs. In China the forces of patriarchy/patriliny, of commercialization, of state power, and of bureaucratization created a system within which gender subordination neither overcame nor was overcome by class or rank. Chinese women were, to be sure, united with men into important common interest groups, but they were also women, and their lives were powerfully affected by that fact.

Although China's economy and polity have undergone enormous changes, gender subordination continues to condition to a significant degree people's experience and life opportunities. This should not lead us, however, to the view that gender inequality is a sui generis structure or that women's subordination is derived from an unchanging kinship order, as some scholars have suggested (see, e.g., K. Johnson 1983:25). Gender subordination in China is fundamentally a historical problem. Throughout this volume the stress has fallen, not on the independence of gender subordination, but on the way that subordination interacts with other forms of inequality.

In a recent review article, Sacks argues for a construction of class that is both "gendered" and attentive to racial/ethnic diversity (1989). She calls for an analytical framework that would "comprehend class, race, and gender oppression as parts of a unitary system" (ibid., 545). Sacks's discussion focuses on American society, but many of the questions she poses are applicable to China, especially to the China of the late imperial period. We have yet to achieve an analytical approach that "genders" inequality in Chinese society. What is clear at this point is that our analyses of domination and stratification must take gender more into account and, further, that these discussions must be informed by historical analysis.

A great deal of research remains to be done on changing patterns of gender inequality in China. We have yet to fully understand how commercialization and the status insecurities of the late imperial period affected attitudes toward women. To what extent and in what sense did Ming-Ch'ing society become less accommodating to women? Just as the T'ang-Sung transition involved changes in gender and kin relations, so too did the Republican-Socialist transition of the twentieth century produce more than a repackaging of preexisiting arrangements. The radical agenda of the Maoists undoubtedly had a profound effect on family and gender relations. To argue that China's social engineers have fallen short of the stated goals of gender equality is not to suggest that no changes have occurred. Recent developments in the wake of economic reforms point toward further changes, but their significance remains unclear. The next generation of anthropologists and historians must confront these questions. For the present we can only speculate that China is yet again entering a period of transition in the domain of kinship, family organization, and women's roles in society.

NOTES

1. In her discussion, Ortner argues that in hierarchical societies (she is concerned specifically with Polynesia) women are never defined primarily by gender and age. Although she is essentially concerned with the shared interests that units like caste and ranked lineages create and the entitlements that membership in these groups make possible for women, Ortner by no means denies the presence of male bias in the societies she analyzes (1981:396–97).

2. See the chapters in this volume by Holmgren, Rawski, and Thatcher for discussions of the significance of the rule of succession in consort selection, in the role of consort kin, and in the influence of consorts themselves.

3. There was indeed a hierarchy among Ch'ing consorts, but Rawski argues that it was not rigid: "The ritual acknowledgment of the empress as the head of the harem preserved the illusion of order in a situation that was in reality extremely fluid and dependent on the whims of the ruler."

4. There are exceptions, however, to this pattern (see, e.g., Chan, Madsen, and Unger 1984:189–91). It also seems likely that the single-child family policy will eventually lead to a decrease in the rate of patrilocal residence among newly married couples.

5. In a recent restatement of his views on women and dowry in northern India, Tambiah writes: "I have indicated the need to revise Goody's and my inaccurate formulation in *Bridewealth and Dowry* of dowry as a woman's premortem inheritance which upon her marriage joins her husband's assets to form a conjugal fund" (1989:425). He goes on to argue that the goods that accompany the bride can be divided into three parts: "one part . . . that the bride may keep as her personal property, the second part, the most substantial, being controlled by the groom's joint family . . . and susceptible to use as 'circulating goods' in the marriage of its daughters, and the third part meant as gifts to the women of the groom's joint family and his married sisters and father's sisters" (1989:425–26). Tambiah concludes that the essential theses of *Bridewealth and Dowry* (i.e., "that in propertied India there is usually a diverging devolution or double transmission of property to and through both males and females and that this transmission emphasizes vertical bonds between parents and children at the cost of lateral lineage bonds") are sustained.

6. Here I refer to dowry in its broadest sense, including goods given to the bride but purchased or supplied out of the groom's betrothal gifts.

7. The family, of course, retained a substantial interest in marriage of the young in the post-1949 era; for discussion of this see, e.g., Croll 1981:142–43, 151–52.

8. See for discussion Hartwell 1982 and Hymes 1986.

9. Ebrey suggests that, legally, the status of concubines may have improved during the Ch'ing dynasty. By or during the Ch'ing, Ebrey notes, a concubine acquired

the right to become a wife under certain circumstances, the prohibition against forcing widows to remarry was extended to concubines, and their names could now be listed on ancestral tablets. According to Ebrey, changes in attitudes toward social ranking and in servitude arrangements, along with new employment opportunities for women, may have contributed to a rise in the status of concubines. Ebrey also makes the interesting and ironic point that as the relative status of concubines improved, the status of wives may well have declined (1986a:19–20). It is important to remember that Ebrey refers only to the formal (legal) status of concubines.

10. In contrast, Ortner associates women's inheritance rights with cognatic kinship systems (1981:398).

GLOSSARY

ch'i ts'ai 妻財

hsin-fang 新房

ssu-fang ch'ien 私房錢

tsung 宗

REFERENCES

Beattie, Hilary. 1979. *Land and Lineage in China: A Study of T'ung-ch'eng County, Anhwei, in the Ming and Ch'ing Dynasties.* Cambridge: Cambridge University Press.

Bloch, Maurice. 1982. "Death, Women and Power." In *Death and the Regeneration of Life,* ed. Maurice Bloch and Jonathan Parry. Cambridge: Cambridge University Press.

Bourdieu, Pierre. 1972. "Marriage Strategies as Strategies of Social Reproduction." In *Family and Society,* ed. Robert Forster and Orest Ranum. Baltimore: Johns Hopkins University Press.

Campbell, John. 1964. *Honour, Family and Patronage.* New York: Oxford University Press.

Caplan, Lionel. 1984. "Bridegroom Price in Urban India: Class, Caste and 'Dowry Evil' among Christians in Madras." *Man* (n.s.) 19:216–33.

Chan, Anita, Richard Madsen, and Jonathan Unger. 1984. *Chen Village: The Recent History of a Peasant Community in Mao's China.* Berkeley and Los Angeles: University of California Press.

Chojnacki, Stanley. 1975. "Dowries and Kinsmen in Early Renaissance Venice." *Journal of Interdisciplinary History* 4:571–600.

Cohen, Abner. 1974. *Two-Dimensional Man: An Essay on the Anthropology of Power and Symbolism in Complex Society.* London: Routledge & Kegan Paul.

Cohen, Myron. 1976. *House United, House Divided: The Chinese Family in Taiwan.* New York: Columbia University Press.

Croll, Elisabeth. 1981. *The Politics of Marriage in Contemporary China.* Cambridge: Cambridge University Press.

———. 1984. "The Exchange of Women and Property: Marriage in Post-Revolutionary China." In *Women and Property—Women as Property,* ed. Renée Hirschon. London: Croom Helm.

Duby, Georges. 1978. *Medieval Marriage: Two Models from Twelfth-Century France.* Baltimore: Johns Hopkins University Press.

Ebrey, Patricia. 1981. "Women in the Kinship System in the Southern Song Upper Class." In *Women in China*, ed. Richard Guisso and Stanley Johannesen. Youngstown, N.Y.: Philo Press.

———. 1984. *Family and Property in Sung China: Yüan Ts'ai's Precepts for Social Life.* Princeton: Princeton University Press.

———. 1986a. "Concubines in Sung China." *Journal of Family History* 11:1–24.

———. 1986b. "The Early Stages in the Development of Descent Group Organization." In *Kinship Organization in Late Imperial China, 1000–1940*, ed. Patricia Buckley Ebrey and James L. Watson. Berkeley and Los Angeles: University of California Press.

Ebrey, Patricia Buckley, and James L. Watson, eds. 1986. *Kinship Organization in Late Imperial China, 1000–1940.* Berkeley and Los Angeles: University of California Press.

Elvin, Mark. 1984. "Female Virtue and the State in China." *Past and Present* 104:111–52.

Freedman, Maurice. 1966. *Lineage Organization in Southeastern China.* London: Athlone.

Gallin, Rita. 1984. "Rural Industrialization and Chinese Women: A Case Study from Taiwan." *Journal of Peasant Studies* 12.1:76–92.

Gallin, Bernard, and Rita Gallin. 1982 . "The Chinese Joint Family in Changing Rural Taiwan." In *Social Interaction in Chinese Society*, ed S. L. Greenblatt, R. W. Wilson, and A. A. Wilson. New York: Pergamon Press.

Gates, Hill. 1989 . "The Commoditization of Chinese Women." *Signs* 14.4:799–832 .

Gold, Penny S. 1985. *The Lady and the Virgin: Image, Attitude, and Experience in Twelfth-Century France.* Chicago: University of Chicago Press.

Goody, Jack. 1973. "Bridewealth and Dowry in Africa and Eurasia." In *Bridewealth and Dowry*, by Jack Goody and S. J. Tambiah. Cambridge: Cambridge University Press.

———. 1976. *Production and Reproduction: A Comparative Study of the Domestic Domain.* Cambridge: Cambridge University Press.

———. 1983. *The Development of the Family and Marriage in Europe.* Cambridge: Cambridge University Press.

Harrell, Stevan, and Sara Dickey. 1985. "Dowry Systems in Complex Societies." *Ethnology* 24:105–20.

Hartwell, Robert. 1982. "Demographic, Political, and Social Trends of China, 750–1550." *Harvard Journal of Asiatic Studies* 42.2:365–442.

Holmgren, Jennifer. 1985. "The Economic Foundations of Virtue: Widow-Remarriage in Early and Modern China." *Australian Journal of Chinese Affairs* 13:1–27.

Honig, Emily, and Gail Hershatter. 1988. *Personal Voices: Chinese Women in the 1980's.* Stanford: Stanford University Press.

Hughes, D. O. 1978. "From Brideprice to Dowry in Mediterranean Europe." *Journal of Family History* 3:262–96.

Hymes, Robert P. 1986. *Statesmen and Gentlemen: The Elite of Fu-chou, Chiang-hsi, in Northern and Southern Sung.* Cambridge: Cambridge University Press.

Jaschok, Maria. 1988. *Concubines and Bondservants: The Social History of a Chinese Custom.* London: Zed Press.

Johnson, David. 1983. "Comment on J. L. Watson's 'Chinese Kinship Reconsidered.'" *China Quarterly* 94:362–65.

Johnson, Kay Ann. 1983. *Women, the Family, and Peasant Revolution in China*. Chicago: University of Chicago Press.

Liu, Hui-chen Wang. 1959. *The Traditional Chinese Clan Rules*. Locust Valley, N.Y.: J. J. Augustin.

McCreery, John. 1976. "Women's Property Rights in China and South Asia." *Ethnology* 15:163–74.

Madan, T. N. 1975. "Structural Implications of Marriage in North India: Wife-givers and Wife-takers among the Pandits of Kashmir." *Contributions to Indian Sociology* (n.s.) 9:217–43.

Mann, Susan. 1987. "Widows in the Kinship, Class, and Community Structures of Qing Dynasty China." *Journal of Asian Studies* 46:37–56.

Ng, Vivienne W. 1987. "Ideology and Sexuality: Rape Laws in Qing China." *Journal of Asian Studies* 46:57–70

Ortner, Sherry. 1981. "Gender and Sexuality in Hierarchical Societies: The Case of Polynesia and Some Comparative Implications." In *Sexual Meanings: The Cultural Construction of Gender and Sexuality*, ed. Sherry Ortner and Harriet Whitehead. Cambridge: Cambridge University Press.

Papanek, Hanna. 1979. "Family Status Production: The 'Work' and 'Non-Work' of Women." *Signs* 4.4:775–81.

Parish, William, and Martin Whyte. 1978. *Village and Family in Contemporary China*. Chicago: University of Chicago Press.

Parry, Jonathan. 1979. *Caste and Kinship in Kangra*. London: Routledge & Kegan Paul.

Pasternak, Burton. 1983. *Guests of the Dragon: Social Demography of a Chinese District, 1895–1946*. New York: Columbia University Press.

Peristiany, J. G. 1966. *Honour and Shame: The Values of Mediterranean Society*. Chicago: University of Chicago Press.

Rao, M. S. A. 1970. *Urbanization and Social Change: A Study of a Rural Community on a Metropolitan Fringe*. New Delhi: Orient Longmans.

Rheubottom, David. 1980. "Dowry and Wedding Celebrations in Yugoslav Macedonia." In *The Meaning of Marriage Payments*, ed. J. L. Comaroff. London: Academic Press.

Sacks, Karen. 1979. *Sisters and Wives: The Past and Future of Sexual Equality*. Urbana: University of Illinois Press.

———. 1989. "Toward a Unified Theory of Class, Race, and Gender." *American Ethnologist* 16.3:534–50.

Sharma, Ursula. 1980. *Women, Work, and Property in North-West India*. London: Tavistock.

Shiga, Shūzō. 1978. "Family Property and the Law of Inheritance in Traditional China." In *Chinese Family Law and Social Change in Historical and Comparative Perspective*, ed. David C. Buxbaum. Seattle: University of Washington Press.

Soullière, Ellen. 1988. "The Imperial Marriages of the Ming Dyasty." *Papers on Far Eastern History* 37:1–30.

Stacey, Judith. 1983. *Patriarchy and Socialist Revolution in China*. Berkeley and Los Angeles: University of California Press.

Stockard, Janice. 1989. *Daughters of the Canton Delta: Marriage Patterns and Economic Strategies in South China, 1860–1930*. Stanford: Stanford University Press.

Stolcke, Verena. 1981. "The Naturalization of Social Inequality and Women's Subordination." In *Of Marriage and the Market*, ed. Kate Young, Carol Wolkowitz, and

Roslyn McCullagh. London: CSE Books.

Strathern, Marilyn. 1972. *Women in Between: Female Roles in a Male World, Mount Hagen, New Guinea*. New York: Seminar Press.

Tambiah, S. J. 1973. "Dowry and Bridewealth and the Property Rights of Women in South Asia." In *Bridewealth and Dowry*, ed. Jack Goody and S. J. Tambiah. Cambridge: Cambridge University Press.

———. 1989. "Bridewealth and Dowry Revisited: The Position of Women in Sub-Saharan Africa and North India." *Current Anthropology* 30.4:413–35.

T'ien, Ju-kang. 1988. *Male Anxiety and Female Chastity: A Comparative Study of Chinese Ethical Values in Ming-Ch'ing Times*. Leiden: E. J. Brill.

Twitchett, Denis. 1959. "The Fan Clan's Charitable Estate, 1050–1760." In *Confucianism in Action*, ed. David Nivison and Arthur Wright. Stanford: Stanford University Press.

Vatuk, Sylvia. 1975. "Gifts and Affines in North India." *Contributions to Indian Sociology* 9:155–96.

Watson, Rubie S. 1981. "Class Differences and Affinal Relations in South China." *Man* 16:593–15.

———. 1984. "Women's Property in Republican China: Rights and Practice." *Republican China* 10.1a:1–12.

Wolf, Arthur P., and Huang Chieh-shan. 1980. *Marriage and Adoption in China, 1845–1945*. Stanford: Stanford University Press.

Wolf, Margery. 1972. *Women and the Family in Rural Taiwan*. Stanford: Stanford University Press.

———. 1975. "Women and Suicide in China." In *Women in Chinese Society*, ed. Margery Wolf and Roxane Witke. Stanford: Stanford University Press.

CONTRIBUTORS

John W. Chaffee is associate professor of history at the State University of New York—Binghamton. He is author of *The Thorny Gates of Learning in Sung China* (1985), coeditor with Wm T. de Bary of *Neo-Confucian Education: The Formative Period* (1989), and editor of the *Bulletin of Sung-Yuan Studies*. His current research is focused on the imperial clan in the Sung dynasty.

Patricia Buckley Ebrey is professor of East Asian studies and history at the University of Illinois at Urbana-Champaign. Her books include *The Aristocratic Families of Early Imperial China* (1978), *Family and Property in Sung China* (1984), and *Kinship Organization in Late Imperial China, 1000–1940*, coedited with James L. Watson (1986), and *Confucianism and Family Rituals in Imperial China* (forthcoming). She is currently working on a book on marriage in Sung China.

Gail Hershatter is associate professor of history at the University of California, Santa Cruz. She is the author of *The Workers of Tianjin, 1900–1949* (1986) and coauthor with Emily Honig of *Personal Voices: Chinese Women in the 1980's* (1988). She is currently working on a book on prostitution in early twentieth-century China.

Jennifer Holmgren is research fellow in the Department of Far Eastern History, Research School of Pacific Studies, at the Australian National University. Her books include the *Chinese Colonization of Northern Vietnam* (1980), the *Annals of Tai: Early T'o-pa History According to the First Chapter of the Wei-shu* (1982), *Marriage and Power in Imperial China* (forthcoming), and numerous articles on the non-Han dynasties and women in Chinese history.

William Lavely is assistant professor of international studies and sociology at the University of Washington and has written on a variety of topics on the demography of the Chinese population.

Susan Mann is professor of history at the University of California, Davis. She is the author of *Local Merchants and the Chinese Bureaucracy, 1750–1950* (1987) and several articles on women in the Ch'ing period. She is currently writing a cultural history of women in the Ch'ing period.

Jonathan K. Ocko is associate professor of history at North Carolina State University and adjunct associate professor of legal history at Duke University School of Law. He is the author of *Bureaucratic Reform in Provincial China* (1983) and has for the last several years concentrated his research on Chinese law.

Evelyn S. Rawski is professor of history at the University of Pittsburgh. She is author of *Agricultural Change and Peasant Economy in South China* (1972), *Education and Popular Literacy in Ch'ing China* (1979), coauthor with Susan Naquin of *Chinese Society in the Eighteenth Century* (1987), and coeditor of *Popular Culture in Late Imperial China* (1985) and *Death Ritual in Late Imperial and Modern China* (1988). She is currently writing a book on the Ch'ing imperial clan.

Melvin Thatcher is area manager of Asia/Pacific Acquisitions for the Genealogical Society of Utah and research associate at the Centre of Asian Studies, University of Hong Kong. A student of the Chou era, he has written several articles dealing with issues in the society, government, and historiography of the Eastern Chou period. He is currently studying the kinship and political systems of the Spring and Autumn state of Ch'u.

Rubie S. Watson is associate professor of anthropology at the University of Pittsburgh. Her research interests are in family, kinship, and gender. She is author of *Inequality among Brothers: Class and Kinship in South China* (1985) and has published articles on local elites and gender. She is currently writing a book entitled "Dutiful Daughters and Loyal Wives: Women and Community in Chinese Society."

INDEX

Compositor: Asco Trade Typesetting Ltd.
Text: 10/12 Baskerville
Display: Baskerville
Printer: Edwards Brothers, Inc.
Binder: Edwards Brothers, Inc.